Property of: Erin O'To... P9-CQX-955

This book is an excellent source of information needed to pass the MOUS (Certification) exams. Explanations are clear and thorough. These folks know the material and share it well.
Amazon reviewer

Great learning tool... I took the exam without knowing anything about this application. I learned all the how to's by doing the exercises. ... This book was easy to follow and a good reference point as well.
Amazon Reader Reviewer

I used this guide for my Word Expert exam and passed. It's comprehensive enough to double as an intermediate course in Word. Unlike other study guides, it will definitely increase your productivity in Word.
Amazon reviewer

We have used this book for over a year and have found it to be not only a study guide, but a good reference book. Our students have obtained results that we are proud of. I recommend this book if you are serious about taking your MOUS and Master certification.
Amazon reviewer

Most readable, understandable technical book I've found... This logically presented work took me quickly from (an) abject novice level to a comfortable intermediate-plus. Unlike most technical works, this one is both practical and readable. It prepared me efficiently and thoroughly for the MOUS exam.
Amazon Reader Review

Couldn't have passed the exam without it!... I've been a Word user for years but there were features I hadn't explored and needed to master for the MOUS exam. The material in the book is presented in a very straightforward manner—easy to understand—and easy to apply to any work situation.
Amazon Reader Review

I did each of the Hands On assignments, then went back and studied what I struggled with. I aced the test today. The book was structured well and was easy to understand. I will be using other books by these authors.
Amazon reviewer

This book is the most comprehensive book I found on the Office 2000 MOUS exams. Covers the most important topics and is easy to read. The authors really seem to know their stuff. I hope to take the Word exams soon and think that this book will help me pass.
Amazon Reader Review

MOUS: Office XP Study Guide

OBJECTIVE	CHAPTER NUMBER
Word 2002 Core	
Inserting and Modifying Text: Insert, modify, and move text and symbols; apply and modify text formats; correct spelling and grammar usage; apply font and text effects; enter and format Date and Time; apply character styles	1
Creating and Modifying Paragraphs: Modify paragraph formats; set and modify tabs; apply bullet, outline, and numbering format to paragraphs; apply paragraph styles	1
Formatting Documents: Create and modify a header and footer; apply and modify column settings; modify document layout and Page Setup options; create and modify tables; preview and print documents, envelopes, and labels	2
Managing Documents: Manage files and folders for documents; create documents using templates; save documents using different names and file formats	2
Working with Graphics: Insert images and graphics; create and modify diagrams and charts	3
Workgroup Collaboration: Compare and merge documents; insert, view and edit comments; convert documents into Web pages	4
Word 2002 Expert	
Customizing Paragraphs: Control pagination; sort paragraphs in lists and tables	5
Formatting Documents: Create and format document sections; create and apply character and paragraph styles; create and update document indexes and tables of contents, figures, and authorities; create cross-references; add and revise endnotes and footnotes; create and manage master documents and subdocuments; move within documents; create and modify forms using various form controls; create forms and prepare forms for distribution	5
Customizing Tables: Use Excel data in tables; perform calculations in Word tables	6
Creating and Modifying Graphics: Create, modify, and position graphics; create and modify charts using data from other applications; align text and graphics	6
Customizing Word: Create, edit, and run macros; customize menus and toolbars	7
Workgroup Collaboration: Track, accept, and reject changes to documents; merge input from several reviewers; insert and modify hyperlinks to other documents and Web pages; create and edit Web documents in Word; create document versions; protect documents; define and modify default file locations for workgroup templates; attach digital signatures to documents	8
Using Mail Merge: Merge letters with a Word, Excel, or Access data source; merge labels with a Word, Excel, or Access data source; use Outlook data as mail merge data source	9
Excel 2002 Core	
Working with Cells and Cell Data: Insert, delete and move cells; enter and edit cell data including text, numbers, and formulas; check spelling; find and replace cell data and formats; work with a subset of data by filtering lists	10
Managing Workbooks: Manage workbook files and folders; create workbooks using templates; save workbooks using different names and file formats	10
Formatting and Printing Worksheets: Apply and modify cell formats; modify row and column settings; modify row and column formats; apply styles; use automated tools to format worksheets; modify Page Setup options for worksheets; preview and print worksheets and workbooks	11
Modifying Workbooks: Insert and delete worksheets; modify worksheet names and positions; use 3-D references	12
Creating and Revising Formulas: Create and revise formulas; use statistical, date and time, financial, and logical functions in formulas	12
Creating and Modifying Graphics: Create, modify, position, and print charts; create, modify, and position graphics	13
Workgroup Collaboration: Convert worksheets into Web pages; create hyperlinks; view and edit comments	14
Excel 2002 Expert	
Importing and Exporting Data: Import data to Excel; export data from Excel; publish worksheets and workbooks to the Web	15
Managing Workbooks: Create, edit, and apply templates; create workspaces; use data consolidation	15
Formatting Numbers: Create and apply custom number formats; use conditional formats	17
Working with Ranges: Use named ranges in formulas; use Lookup and Reference functions	18

SYBEX

OBJECTIVE	CHAPTER NUMBER
Excel 2002 Expert *(Continued)*	
Customizing Excel: Customize toolbars and menus; create, edit, and run macros	17
Auditing Worksheets: Audit formulas; locate and resolve errors; identify dependencies in formulas	16
Summarizing Data: Use subtotals with lists and ranges; define and apply filters; add group and outline criteria to ranges; use data validation; retrieve external data and create queries; create Extensible Markup Language (XML) Web queries	19
Analyzing Data: Create a Microsoft PivotTable®, Microsoft PivotChart®, and PivotTable/PivotChart Reports; forecast values with what-if analysis; create and display scenarios	20
Workgroup Collaboration: Modify passwords, protections, and properties; create a shared workbook; track, accept and reject changes to workbooks; merge workbooks	21
PowerPoint 2002 Core	
Creating a Presentation: Create presentations (manually and using automated tools); add slides to and delete slides from presentations; modify headers and footers in the Slide Master	22
Inserting and Modifying Text: Import text from Word; insert, format, and modify text	22
Inserting and Modifying Visual Elements: Add tables, charts, clip art, and bitmap images to slides; customize slide backgrounds; add OfficeArt elements to slides; apply custom formats to tables	23
Modifying Presentation Formats: Apply formats to presentations; apply animation schemes; apply slide transitions; customize slide formats; customize slide templates; manage a Slide Master; rehearse timing; rearrange slides; modify slide layout; add links to a presentation	24
Printing Presentations: Preview and print slides, outlines, handouts, and speaker notes	25
Working with Data from Other Sources: Import Excel charts into slides; add sound and video to slides; insert Word tables on slides; export a presentation as an outline	25
Managing and Delivering Presentations: Set up slide shows; deliver presentations; manage files and folders for presentations; work with embedded fonts; publish presentations to the Web; use Pack and Go	25
Workgroup Collaboration: Set up a review cycle; review presentation comments; schedule and deliver presentation broadcasts	25
Access 2002 Core	
Creating and Using Databases: Create Access databases; open database objects in multiple views; move among records; format datasheets	26
Creating and Modifying Tables: Create and modify tables; add a predefined input mask to a field; create Lookup fields; modify field properties	27
Creating and Modifying Queries: Create and modify Select queries; add calculated fields to Select queries	27
Creating and Modifying Forms: Create and display forms; modify form properties	28
Viewing and Organizing Information: Enter, edit, and delete records; create queries; sort records; filter records	28
Defining Relationships: Create one-to-many relationships; enforce referential integrity	29
Producing Reports: Create and format reports; add calculated controls to reports; preview and print reports	30
Integrating with Other Applications: Import data to Access; export data from Access; create a simple data access page	30
Outlook 2002 Core	
Creating and Viewing Messages: Display and print messages; compose and send messages to corporate/workgroup and Internet addresses; insert signatures and attachments; customize views	31
Scheduling: Add appointments, meetings, and events to the Outlook calendar; apply conditional formats to the Outlook calendar; respond to meeting requests; use categories to manage appointments; print calendars	32
Managing Messages: Move messages between folders; search for messages; save messages in alternate file formats; use categories to manage messages; set message options	33
Creating and Managing Contacts: Create and edit contacts; organize and sort contacts; link contacts to activities and journal entries	33
Creating and Managing Tasks and Notes: Create and update tasks; modify task organization and Task view; accept, decline, or delegate tasks; create and modify notes; use categories to manage tasks and notes	34

Exam objectives are subject to change at any time without prior notice and at Microsoft's sole discretion. Please visit Microsoft's Training and Certification website (www.microsoft.com/traincert) for the most current listing of exam objectives.

SYBEX

MOUS:
Office XP

Study Guide

MOUS:
Office XP
Study Guide

Gini Courter
Annette Marquis

San Francisco • London

Associate Publisher: Neil Edde
Acquisitions and Developmental Editor: Jeff Kellum
Editor: Linda Recktenwald
Production Editor: Kelly Winquist
Technical Editors: Ashlee Wiebe, Craig Vazquez
Contributors: Karla Browning, Felicia Buckingham
Book Designer: Bill Gibson
Electronic Publishing Specialist: Rozi Harris, Interactive Composition Corporation
Proofreaders: Nancy Riddiough, Dave Nash, Laurie O'Connell, Emily Hsuan, Yariv Rabinovitch, Sarah Tannehill, Abigail Sawyer, Amey Garber
Indexer: Ted Laux
Cover Designer: Archer Design
Cover Photographer: Natural Selection

Copyright © 2002 SYBEX Inc., 1151 Marina Village Parkway, Alameda, CA 94501. World rights reserved. No part of this publication may be stored in a retrieval system, transmitted, or reproduced in any way, including but not limited to photocopy, photograph, magnetic, or other record, without the prior agreement and written permission of the publisher.

Library of Congress Card Number: 2002103163

ISBN: 0-7821-4113-7

SYBEX and the SYBEX logo are either registered trademarks or trademarks of SYBEX Inc. in the United States and/or other countries.

Screen reproductions produced with FullShot 99. FullShot 99 © 1991–1999 Inbit Incorporated. All rights reserved. FullShot is a trademark of Inbit Incorporated.

Internet screen shot(s) using Microsoft Internet Explorer 5.5 reprinted by permission from Microsoft Corporation.

Microsoft, the Microsoft Internet Explorer logo, Windows, Windows NT, and the Windows logo are either registered trademarks or trademarks of Microsoft Corporation in the United States and/or other countries.

SYBEX is an independent entity from Microsoft Corporation, and not affiliated with Microsoft Corporation in any manner. This publication may be used in assisting students to prepare for a Microsoft Certified Professional Exam. Neither Microsoft Corporation, its designated review company, nor SYBEX warrants that use of this publication will ensure passing the relevant exam. Microsoft is either a registered trademark or trademark of Microsoft Corporation in the United States and/or other countries.

TRADEMARKS: SYBEX has attempted throughout this book to distinguish proprietary trademarks from descriptive terms by following the capitalization style used by the manufacturer.

The author and publisher have made their best efforts to prepare this book, and the content is based upon final release software whenever possible. Portions of the manuscript may be based upon pre-release versions supplied by software manufacturer(s). The author and the publisher make no representation or warranties of any kind with regard to the completeness or accuracy of the contents herein and accept no liability of any kind including but not limited to performance, merchantability, fitness for any particular purpose, or any losses or damages of any kind caused or alleged to be caused directly or indirectly from this book.

Manufactured in the United States of America

10 9 8 7 6 5 4 3 2 1

SYBEX

To Our Valued Readers:

Since its inception, Microsoft's MOUS program has established itself as a highly respected certification for business desktop application users worldwide. By encouraging individuals to develop advanced skills with Microsoft Office, the MOUS program is helping to fill the demand for qualified, knowledgeable people in the workplace. And with the recent rollout of the MOUS XP track, business professionals can now certify themselves on the latest release of Microsoft Office. This latest update to the MOUS program has been met with considerable enthusiasm in the business world, from both certification candidates and corporations seeking individuals possessing the skills required for today's competitive job market.

Sybex is proud to have helped thousands of MOUS certification candidates prepare for their exams over the years, and we are excited about the opportunity to continue to provide office professionals with the skills they'll need to succeed in the highly competitive marketplace.

The authors and editors have worked hard to ensure that the Study Guide you hold in your hand is comprehensive, in-depth, and pedagogically sound. We're confident that this book will exceed the demanding standards of the certification marketplace and help you, the MOUS certification candidate, succeed in your endeavors.

As always, your feedback is important to us. Please send comments, questions, or suggestions to support@sybex.com. At Sybex we're continually striving to meet the needs of individuals preparing for certification exams.

Good luck in pursuit of your MOUS certification!

Neil Edde
Associate Publisher—Certification
Sybex, Inc.

Software License Agreement: Terms and Conditions

The media and/or any online materials accompanying this book that are available now or in the future contain programs and/or text files (the "Software") to be used in connection with the book. SYBEX hereby grants to you a license to use the Software, subject to the terms that follow. Your purchase, acceptance, or use of the Software will constitute your acceptance of such terms.

The Software compilation is the property of SYBEX unless otherwise indicated and is protected by copyright to SYBEX or other copyright owner(s) as indicated in the media files (the "Owner(s)"). You are hereby granted a single-user license to use the Software for your personal, noncommercial use only. You may not reproduce, sell, distribute, publish, circulate, or commercially exploit the Software, or any portion thereof, without the written consent of SYBEX and the specific copyright owner(s) of any component software included on this media.

In the event that the Software or components include specific license requirements or end-user agreements, statements of condition, disclaimers, limitations or warranties ("End-User License"), those End-User Licenses supersede the terms and conditions herein as to that particular Software component. Your purchase, acceptance, or use of the Software will constitute your acceptance of such End-User Licenses.

By purchase, use or acceptance of the Software you further agree to comply with all export laws and regulations of the United States as such laws and regulations may exist from time to time.

Software Support

Components of the supplemental Software and any offers associated with them may be supported by the specific Owner(s) of that material, but they are not supported by SYBEX. Information regarding any available support may be obtained from the Owner(s) using the information provided in the appropriate read.me files or listed elsewhere on the media.

Should the manufacturer(s) or other Owner(s) cease to offer support or decline to honor any offer, SYBEX bears no responsibility. This notice concerning support for the Software is provided for your information only. SYBEX is not the agent or principal of the Owner(s), and SYBEX is in no way responsible for providing any support for the Software, nor is it liable or responsible for any support provided, or not provided, by the Owner(s).

Warranty

SYBEX warrants the enclosed media to be free of physical defects for a period of ninety (90) days after purchase. The Software is not available from SYBEX in any other form or media than that enclosed herein or posted to www.sybex.com.

If you discover a defect in the media during this warranty period, you may obtain a replacement of identical format at no charge by sending the defective media, postage prepaid, with proof of purchase to:

SYBEX Inc.
Product Support Department
1151 Marina Village Parkway
Alameda, CA 94501
Web: http://www.sybex.com

After the 90-day period, you can obtain replacement media of identical format by sending us the defective disk, proof of purchase, and a check or money order for $10, payable to SYBEX.

Disclaimer

SYBEX makes no warranty or representation, either expressed or implied, with respect to the Software or its contents, quality, performance, merchantability, or fitness for a particular purpose. In no event will SYBEX, its distributors, or dealers be liable to you or any other party for direct, indirect, special, incidental, consequential, or other damages arising out of the use of or inability to use the Software or its contents even if advised of the possibility of such damage. In the event that the Software includes an online update feature, SYBEX further disclaims any obligation to provide this feature for any specific duration other than the initial posting.

The exclusion of implied warranties is not permitted by some states. Therefore, the above exclusion may not apply to you. This warranty provides you with specific legal rights; there may be other rights that you may have that vary from state to state. The pricing of the book with the Software by SYBEX reflects the allocation of risk and limitations on liability contained in this agreement of Terms and Conditions.

Shareware Distribution

This Software may contain various programs that are distributed as shareware. Copyright laws apply to both shareware and ordinary commercial software, and the copyright Owner(s) retains all rights. If you try a shareware program and continue using it, you are expected to register it. Individual programs differ on details of trial periods, registration, and payment. Please observe the requirements stated in appropriate files.

Copy Protection

The Software in whole or in part may or may not be copy-protected or encrypted. However, in all cases, reselling or redistributing these files without authorization is expressly forbidden except as specifically provided for by the Owner(s) therein.

To the members of the International Association of Administrative Professionals (IAAP), who are constantly striving to improve their skills to be the very best at what they do.

Acknowledgments

A project such as this requires so many people to make it work. The authors may be the most visible, but they are just the tip of the iceberg. At least five different editors have taken a stab at this book. Proofreaders, abstractors, layout and design people, and even marketing people are crucial in transforming this book from an idea to the finished product you are holding in your hands. And we can't forget the lawyers. We would especially like to thank Kristine O'Callaghan who has drafted our contracts since we began writing for Sybex in 1994. She has seen us through many contracts, contract extensions, and contract revisions over the years. We are going to miss her reliability and her thoroughness. We'd also like to welcome Monica Baum. Thanks for taking over to handle contract changes. And we can't forget our main gal, Senoria Bilbo-Brown, who has gone out of her way on numerous occasions to make sure our advances reached us in a timely way. Her initiative and thoughtfulness have saved us from the poorhouse on too many occasions to count. Thanks, Sen!

The day-to-day management of this book fell to Jeff Kellum, Developmental Editor, and Kelly Winquist, Production Editor. They were there for all the ups and downs, and we appreciate their fortitude in putting up with us—we may be a lot of fun but we are not always the easiest to handle. Somehow, though, we got through it together and we admire their stamina. We would also like to thank Linda Recktenwald, aka EditorIII. Her collaboration in the sometimes-perplexing times was reassuring. Making the writing understandable is an important task, but the book is worthless if it's not technically correct. This book had two technical editors, Ashlee Wiebe and Craig Vazquez, who checked and double-checked to make sure the information we presented was accurate. We are grateful for the thorough testing that these two gave our materials. If you run across any errors in this book, it is probably because we didn't listen.

We would also like to thank the layout and design team, Rozi Harris and the team at ICC. Not only did they create a great-looking book, they worked tirelessly to tighten up the design so we could include as much as possible in the pages available—no easy task when a book runs long. We appreciate their help in keeping the book length under control.

Finally, we want to thank Felicia Buckingham for her contributions to the Outlook sections of the book, and we especially want to thank Karla Browning for her work on PowerPoint. We can always count on Karla to submit her material on time and with a minimal amount of fuss. She is not only good at what she does, she is reliable and good-spirited about the whole adventure. It's always a pleasure to work with her on any project.

Contents at a Glance

Contents

Table of Exercises

Introduction

The *MOUS: Office XP Study Guide* is designed to prepare you for the Microsoft Office User Specialist exams and, in the process, make you a more knowledgeable Office user. Most Office users use less than 15 percent of the programs' features—they learn what they need to know to accomplish a particular task. Chances are, however, that the methods they use are neither the most efficient nor the most effective. Hidden in Office's menus and toolbars are an incredible array of tools designed to help you produce every type of document from a simple letter to a 500-page online manual, with charts, spreadsheets, graphics, and an accompanying presentation. Knowing how to delve more deeply into the applications' features is what sets a competent user apart from the rest. By the time you finish this book, you will be well equipped to impress your colleagues (and maybe even your employer) with your ability to tackle any project with confidence and skill.

About This Book

This book is a study guide organized around the MOUS objectives published by Microsoft. On the perforated card in the front of the book you'll find a comprehensive list of MOUS objectives (skill sets and activities) you need to know to pass the MOUS exams. It's a good idea to start by reviewing the objectives for both the Core and Expert exams so you know what you're aiming for. This book covers each of the activities listed in the guidelines.

Visit the Microsoft Certification site, http://www.microsoft.com/traincert/ mcp/mous/requirements.asp, to get the most current information about the MOUS exam guidelines.

Although you don't need to be an experienced Office user to use this book, we recommend that you have some experience with each of the applications. This book covers each objective, first for the Core exam and then, when appropriate, the Expert exam. The order of these objectives is not the order in which we would teach the skills to new users or the order in which most users learn them. If you've never used the applications before, you may find this challenging and perhaps even disconcerting. If you have used the applications before, then this book will guide you, step by step, through the MOUS exam objectives. By the time you finish the chapters relating to an exam, you'll be ready to pass the corresponding MOUS exam.

If you are new to Microsoft Office and would like to start at the beginning or would like to have a thorough mastery of all of the Microsoft Office applications, we recommend *Mastering Microsoft XP Premium Edition, Mastering Microsoft Excel 2002,* and *Mastering Microsoft Outlook 2002*—same authors, same publisher, but each of these books uses a more sequential and much more comprehensive approach to learning each application than you will find in this book.

To prepare for an exam, we recommend that you work through one chapter at a time in the relevant part of the book. At the beginning of each chapter, you'll find a list of the objectives covered in that chapter. Even if you are confident about a particular skill, we suggest that you review the section to make sure you've interpreted the objective the same way we do. Each section begins with an introduction to the topic, and then each objective is identified in the chapter this way:

Microsoft ✓ *Exam Objective*	**Use Excel data in tables**

After we present an overview of the topic, you'll find a practice exercise for each objective that you can walk through to learn how to accomplish the tasks identified in the objective. The exercises are the real meat of the chapter. The exercises are designed to give you real-life experience with the exam objectives. We've tried to make the exercises easy to follow using common examples. The exercises you have to complete on the exams are generally more simplistic and may include only a portion of the steps we've included. As there is no way to predict what you might actually be faced with, we've made the exercises as comprehensive as possible with the goal of giving you an in-depth understanding of each topic. If you can complete the exercises, you should have no trouble with the exam questions.

Using the Practice Files

To make the exercises easier to complete, most exercises have a corresponding file, which can be downloaded from the Sybex website. These documents are named for the chapter and exercise they are to be used in. So, for example, if you want to complete Exercise 5.5, you would find a document named *5-5.doc* in the files you downloaded for the chapter. Whenever it made sense, we've also included a copy of the document at the end of the exercise so you can see what it's supposed to look like when you have finished. These documents include the word *Post* in their names. So, for example, the document that shows the results of Exercise 5.5 would be named *5-5 Post.doc*. To download these documents, go to *www.sybex.com* and search for this book by title in the online catalog. When you find the book, open its page in the catalog and click the Downloads link. The practice files are grouped by chapter, so you can choose which ones you want to work with.

The practice files available on the Sybex website are compressed in a Zip file format. To use the files, you will first have to unzip them using WinZip or another unzipping utility. WinZip is available as shareware from *www.winzip.com*.

Notes, Tips, and Warnings

Throughout the book, you'll find additional comments about the material in the form of notes, tips, and warnings.

Notes provide additional information about a topic.

You'll also find notations in the exercises. These are preceded with the word *Note* so you can distinguish them from steps in the exercise.

Tips offer another way of doing something or a shortcut to completing a particular task.

Warnings suggest possible problems you may encounter when completing a task incorrectly or things to look out for along the way.

We hope you'll find that each of these extra comments helps you to understand Office more fully so you can apply your skills to even more complex Office applications.

A Word About the MOUS Exams

The MOUS exams are not, for the most part, question and answer (some of the Outlook questions may be multiple choice or True/False). They are designed so you can demonstrate the skills you have by responding to a specific scenario. For example, you may be presented with a document and asked to apply a Heading 1 style to some particular text. You aren't given multiple choices to pick from—you can either accomplish that task or not. Sometimes the instructions ask you to complete one task and sometimes they include several. You are given partial credit for completing part of a question, so you are better off doing what you can with each one. If you skip a question, there is no going back, so make sure you aren't able to complete the question before choosing to skip one. Each test is timed, so you must act pretty quickly to move through the questions in the time allotted, generally around 45 minutes. The best way to succeed on a MOUS exam is to be completely comfortable with how to accomplish each objective and then read each question carefully before proceeding. Pace yourself and you'll be fine.

A Final Check

When you complete an entire chapter, review the Summary at the end of the chapter to make sure you are comfortable with the items presented. Review the objectives once again and see if there are any topics that you are uncertain about. Go back and review those sections in the text and try the exercises a second time using your own documents. If you're still having difficulty, make a note of it and go on to the next topic. Working on related topics sometimes causes the topic with which you're struggling to fall into place.

When you've finished all the topics, you're ready to take the MOUS exam. Do the best you can—you can always take it again if you find out the first attempt was only a practice round.

We'd Love to Hear From You!

We've provided you with a variety of tools to help you on your path to certification. We hope that you'll find them useful, challenging, and fun as you improve your Microsoft Office skills. If you'd like to let us know about your experiences with this book and with taking the exams, we'd love to hear from you. Good luck!

Annette Marquis and Gini Courter
Sybex Inc.
1151 Marina Village Parkway
Alameda, CA 94501
E-mail: *authors@triadconsulting.com*

Microsoft Word 2002 Core Exam

Chapter

1

Creating Basic Documents

MOUS WORD 2002 CORE EXAM OBJECTIVES COVERED IN THIS CHAPTER:

- ✓ Insert, modify, and move text and symbols
- ✓ Apply and modify text formats
- ✓ Correct spelling and grammar usage
- ✓ Apply font and text effects
- ✓ Enter and format Date and Time
- ✓ Apply character styles
- ✓ Modify paragraph formats
- ✓ Set and modify tabs
- ✓ Apply bullet, outline, and numbering format to paragraphs
- ✓ Apply paragraph styles

Before the word processor there was the typewriter. The typewriter sure beat writing by hand or paying someone to print your work, but the typewriter was quite unforgiving. One mistake at the bottom of the page and the whole page had to be retyped. Electric typewriters introduced different typefaces and even on-the-fly correction, but both features were cumbersome and limited in their use. Word processors offered the promise of unlimited editing capability—the power to write, rewrite, and correct text easily and painlessly. As word processing programs caught on, an equally important set of tools became commonplace—tools that allowed users to move beyond basic text formats such as bold and italic and apply text effects such as shadows, superscripts, and subscripts to a huge selection of font types. With these developments, users were finally able to produce documents that rivaled professional printing.

This chapter familiarizes you with many of the skills you need to create attractive, well-written documents and to do so with a minimal amount of headache. We'll start with creating, editing, and formatting text and show you how to select just the text you want to work with. After it's selected, you can move words, sentences, and entire paragraphs around the document. We'll then show you how to change the way text appears on the page and on the screen by applying text formats, font and text effects, and character styles.

After you enter text, checking to see that it's correct is not a bad idea. If you are not the winner of the National Spelling Bee and grammar was the class you slept through right after lunch, then putting Word's Spelling and Grammar features to work could save you some embarrassing moments. This section illustrates what you can count on and what to watch out for in this sometimes-complicated arena.

Knowing how to work with text is not enough, however, to assemble impressive documents. You also need to know how to format paragraphs, pages, and entire documents. In this chapter, we'll also show you how to modify paragraph formats, work with tabs, apply bullets, use outline and numbering formats, and apply paragraph styles. Chapter 2, "Working with Documents," covers how to work with pages and documents.

By the time you have finished this chapter, you will have some additional tools in your toolbox that will speed up your work and give you better results. By learning more than one way to accomplish a task, you not only become more efficient but you might even be able to impress your coworkers at the same time.

Before you begin this chapter, you should go to the Sybex website and download the file 4113Ch01.zip. This package contains the files necessary to complete some of the exercises in this chapter. In addition, it contains files of what most of the documents should look like after you complete the exercises.

Inserting and Modifying Text

If you have any experience with Word, then you are already familiar with the basics of entering and editing text. When you start typing in an open Word document, the text you type appears on the screen. When Word reaches the end of a line, it automatically wraps to the next line, and that's about all there is to it. Or is it? Many users learn to use Word by trial and error. After all, it's just typing, right? If they find something that works, it seems easier, or at least safer, to keep doing it that way even if there might be an easier or more efficient way. In this section, we'll demonstrate how to make the most of the text you enter, from positioning it correctly to formatting it so that it drives your point home.

Entering and Editing Text and Symbols

Assuming that you have some familiarity with the keyboard, entering text is the easy part. After you enter it, things get a little tougher. You have to make sure that it says what you want it to say, it makes sense, and it has impact. Retyping a document to make corrections and changes is not the answer. With a few clicks of the mouse, you can whip any text into shape. The trick is knowing the most efficient ways to make the changes you want to make.

Microsoft Exam Objective	Insert, modify, and move text and symbols

Although it may not be obvious at first glance, this objective expects you to know how to do each of the following things:

- Enter and correct text
- Move text using cut and paste and drag and drop
- Insert, modify, and move symbols

However, before you can make changes to text, having a few tricks up your sleeve will make the whole process a lot less painful.

Throughout this book, we'll show screen pictures that display both the Standard and Formatting toolbars rather than the personalized toolbars that share one row. It's easier to find the toolbar buttons you are looking for if you change the default option to show both toolbars and full menus. You can do this by choosing View ➢ Toolbars ➢ Customize and checking the Standard And Formatting Toolbars On Two Rows and Always Show Full Menus check boxes on the Options tab.

Entering and Correcting Text

To enter text in Word, begin typing in the document window. Text you enter displays at the flashing insertion point (cursor). If you've left something out in the text you've typed, you can insert it by positioning the insertion point where you want the text to appear and typing; the existing text moves over to accommodate the new text. You can also overtype existing text by switching to Overtype mode (press the Insert key).

In Normal view, Word displays a black horizontal line at the left margin.

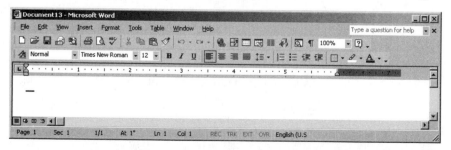

This line represents the end of your document. In Normal or Outline view, you cannot move the insertion point or insert text or objects below the End of Document marker.

To switch between views in Word, click the View buttons to the left of the horizontal scroll bar or select a view from the View menu.

Moving the Insertion Point Efficiently

You can use the arrow keys to move the insertion point up a line, down a line, and one character to the left or right, but using the special keys listed in Table 1.1 might get you there a whole lot faster.

TABLE 1.1 Navigation Keys

Key	Action
Home	Move to the beginning of the current line
End	Move to the end of the current line
Ctrl+Home	Move to the beginning of the document
Ctrl+End	Move to the end of the document
Page Up	Move up one screen
Page Down	Move down one screen
Left arrow	Move one character to the left
Right arrow	Move one character to the right
Ctrl+left arrow	Move one word to the left
Ctrl+right arrow	Move one word to the right

Correcting Text

To change small amounts of text that you've already typed, use the Backspace and Delete keys on the keyboard. Backspace deletes text to the left of the insertion point, and Delete deletes text to the right of the insertion point. Press either key multiple times to delete the desired text. To delete whole words at a time, press Ctrl+Backspace or Ctrl+Delete.

Click the Undo button on the Standard toolbar to delete text you have just typed.

If you want to replace larger amounts of text, it pays to select the text first. You can replace any text by selecting it and typing the new text. Selected text is automatically deleted when you press any key on the keyboard. Word has a number of methods you can use to select text. We describe many of them in the next section.

Selecting Text

You can spot Word power users because they use the minimum number of steps to complete a task. They're not just proficient; they're efficient, particularly with skills that are used frequently in Word. Knowing several ways to select text will let you streamline many of the other tasks you'll be doing with your documents.

Although you can always drag the mouse pointer over text to select it, Word offers you a number of other options. You can use any of these methods, but you'll find some methods are easier to use in certain situations. For example, if you've ever tried to drag to select text over multiple pages, you have already experienced the wonders of an out-of-control accelerated mouse pointer. But if you choose another method, such as Shift-select (see Table 1.2), you can select text smoothly without getting any new gray hairs.

TABLE 1.2 Selecting Text with the Mouse

To Select	Do This
A word	Double-click anywhere in the word.
A sentence	Hold Ctrl and click anywhere in the sentence.
A paragraph	Triple-click anywhere in the paragraph.

TABLE 1.2   Selecting Text with the Mouse *(continued)*

To Select	Do This
A single line	Move pointer into the left margin area known as the selection bar. When the pointer changes to a right-pointing arrow, point to the desired line and click.
The entire document	Choose Edit ≻ Select All from the menu bar, or hold Ctrl and click in the left margin or triple-click in the left margin.
Multiple lines	Move the pointer to the left margin into the selection bar area. With the right-pointing arrow, point to the first desired line, and then hold down the mouse button and drag to select additional lines.
Multiple words, lines, or sentences	Move the I-beam into the first word, hold the mouse button, drag to the last word, and release.
Multiple words, lines, or sentences using Shift-select	Click within the first word, move the I-beam to the last word, hold Shift, and click. Everything between the two clicks is selected.

Special tip for keyboarders: You can hold Shift and use any of the navigation keys to select text. For example, hold Shift and press Home to select from the current word to the beginning of the line. Hold Shift and press the down arrow to select from the current insertion point position to the line below.

In Word 2002, you can select multiple, noncontiguous sections of text (see Figure 1.1). Select the first section, and then hold Ctrl while dragging additional sections of text. Any formatting or other feature you use applies to all the selected text.

FIGURE 1.1 Word 2002 allows multiselection.

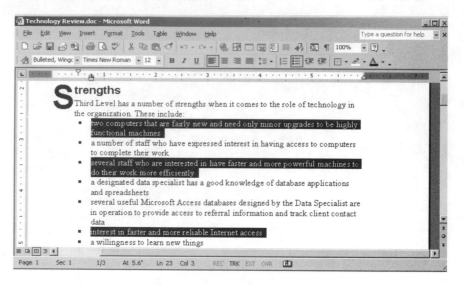

In Exercise 1.1, you will be focusing on inserting and correcting text.

Inserting and Modifying Text

1. Create a new, blank Word document by launching Word or by clicking the New button on the Standard toolbar if Word is already open.

2. Type the following paragraph. Do not press Enter when you reach the end of a line.
   This is the 4th sentence. This is the third sentence. This is the second sentence. This is the 1st sentence.

3. Move the mouse pointer after the first period, and click to reposition the insertion point. Press the spacebar to insert a space after the sentence.

4. Type **This is the sixth sentence.** Notice how the text moves over to accommodate the inserted text. This is an example of Insert mode.

5. Switch from Insert mode to Overtype mode by pressing the Insert key on the keyboard. You can tell you are in Overtype mode because OVR appears in black on Word's status bar.

EXERCISE 1.1 *(continued)*

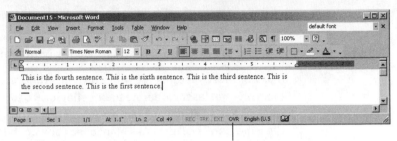

Overtype Mode indicator

6. Position the insertion point to the left of the "s" in "sixth" and type **fifth**. Word overtypes the new text over the existing text. This is an example of Overtype mode. Press Insert again to return to Insert mode.

7. Press the backspace key five times to delete "fifth" and type **last**.

8. Select "4th" and type **fourth**. Select "1st" and type **first**.

9. You'll be using this document in other exercises in this chapter, so let's save it now. Choose File ➢ Save or click the Save button on the Standard toolbar and save the document with the filename `Sentences Exercise.doc`.

To keep all the documents together that you create as part of the exercises in this book, you may want to create a folder in your My Documents folder or whatever your default save location is. With the Save As dialog box open, click the Create New Folder button on the toolbar and enter a name for the folder, such as `MOUS Practice`. When you click OK, the folder opens so you can save this and other documents to it.

When Word Misbehaves

Word 2002 tries to make your life easier right from the first letter you type by watching what you're doing and figuring out how it can be most helpful. As you enter text, Word takes several behind-the-scenes actions. These actions include the following:

- If the Office Assistant is active, the Office Assistant evaluates what you are doing to see if it has any suggestions to offer.

- The AutoCorrect feature automatically corrects misspelled words that are in its dictionary, such as "teh" and "adn."

- The Spelling and Grammar feature reviews your text to determine if there are other possible misspellings or grammatical errors.

If any of these features are more disconcerting than helpful, you can turn them off or at least moderate their behavior. To turn off the Office Assistant, right-click the Office Assistant and choose Options from the shortcut menu. Clear the Use The Office Assistant check box on the Options tab of the Office Assistant dialog box; to change AutoCorrect features, choose Tools ➢ Auto-Correct Options; and to change Spelling and Grammar options, choose Tools ➢ Options and click the Spelling And Grammar tab.

Moving and Copying Text

Word provides two methods for moving and copying text. Cut, copy, and paste works well just about anytime, while drag and drop is most efficient for short moves and copies. We will look at both these methods in the following sections.

Moving and Copying with the Cut, Copy, and Paste Buttons

The traditional method of moving and copying text is using the Cut, Copy, and Paste features on the toolbar and menu bar. You can move or copy anything easily and efficiently by following these four steps:

1. Select the text (or graphic, table, or whatever) using any of the selection methods described earlier in this chapter.

2. Click the Cut button if you want to move the selection or the Copy button if you want to copy the selection.

3. Move the insertion point where you want the selection to appear.

4. Click the Paste button.

Moving and Copying with Drag and Drop

You'll find it more efficient to move or copy text over short distances using a method called *drag and drop*. Drag and drop works best when you can see both the *source* (the location of original text) and the *destination* (the place that you want the moved or copied text to appear). Select the text you want to move or copy, hold down the right mouse button, and drag the insertion point to where you want to paste the text. Release the mouse button, and then select Move Here or Copy Here from the shortcut menu.

You can also use the left mouse button to drag and drop selected text, but when you do, Word won't open the shortcut menu. Instead, Word moves the selection to the new location with no questions asked. If you want to copy text with the left mouse button, hold down the Ctrl key before dropping the text.

The shortcut menu with commands to move or copy appears when you use the right mouse button to drag and drop a selection or object in many Windows applications, including Windows Explorer.

Inserting, Modifying, and Moving Symbols

Symbols are characters that are not part of the typical alphanumeric character set. Symbols include characters such as the copyright symbol ©, a smiley face ☺, and the division symbol ÷. Many fonts include additional symbol characters in the font set. In addition, several fonts that come with Windows and Word, such as Wingdings, Monotype Sorts, and Webdings, contain only symbols. Symbols behave exactly like other characters. You can select them, delete them, move them, and copy them just as you would the letter *a* or the number *1*. Symbols are available from the Symbol dialog box (Insert ➢ Symbol), as shown in Figure 1.2.

FIGURE 1.2   The Symbol dialog box gives you access to all the symbols available in Word.

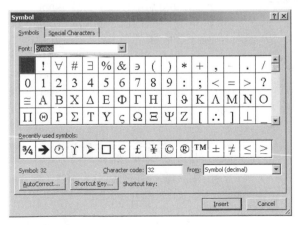

The Special Characters tab of the Symbol dialog box, shown in Figure 1.3, contains characters that you might use in writing, such as an em dash —, and en dash –, or a paragraph mark ¶.

FIGURE 1.3 A number of commonly used symbols are available from the Special Characters tab of the Symbol dialog box.

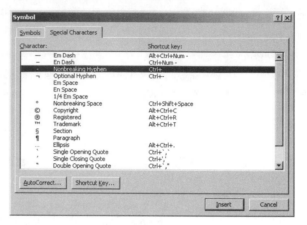

In addition, you can access some symbols, such as the copyright symbol, using AutoCorrect. For example, if you type an open parentheses (, the letter c, and a close parentheses), Word automatically converts it to the copyright symbol ©. You can see the symbols that are available through AutoCorrect by choosing Tools ➢ AutoCorrect Options.

When Word makes an autocorrection you do not want, you can click Undo to retain the text you typed. You can also point to the corrected text and then to the blue line that appears underneath it. Click the Smart Options button that appears, and choose the Change Back To option.

Exercise 1.2, in addition to giving you practice with selecting and moving text, demonstrates how to insert symbols into your documents. You'll also be using the Undo and Redo features of Word to undo changes that you make.

EXERCISE 1.2

Selecting and Moving Text and Working with Symbols

1. Open the document you created in Exercise 1.1 named Sentences Exercise.doc if it is not already open.

2. Select the sentence that reads "This is the first sentence." and use cut and paste to move it to the beginning of the paragraph. You may have to press the spacebar to insert a space after the sentence.

3. Use drag and drop to rearrange the other sentences so they are in the correct order.

4. Click the Undo button on the Standard toolbar several times to see the sentences revert to their original order. Click the Redo button on the Standard toolbar until the sentences are in their correct order again.

5. Move the insertion point to the beginning of the paragraph, and click the Save button to resave the document.

6. Choose Insert ➢ Symbol. Explore the fonts that include symbol characters by choosing a font from the Font drop-down list and scrolling through the available characters. Click the Special Characters tab and review the special characters available.

7. Click back on the Symbol tab and select a symbol. Click Insert to insert the symbol into the paragraph.

8. Click the Close button to see the symbol in the document.

9. Select the symbol you inserted and copy it so that it also appears at the end of the paragraph.

10. Press Enter twice and type **(c) 2002, Sybex, Inc.** AutoCorrect should automatically convert (c) to ©.

11. Click the Save button to resave the document.

Emphasizing Text with Text Formats

Word uses a generally accepted font, Times New Roman 10 pt Regular as its default font. However, if that is the only font you use, your documents will look pretty boring. By changing fonts, font sizes, and text formats, you can add aesthetic appeal to your documents, making them appear interesting to read even if what you have to say is a little lacking in content.

Microsoft ✓ *Exam* *Objective*   **Apply and modify text formats**

In Exercise 1.3, you will be changing fonts, font styles, sizes, underlines, and colors.

EXERCISE 1.3

Applying and Modifying Text Formats

1. Open Sentences Exercise.doc, which you modified in Exercise 1.2, or open the file 1-3.doc.

2. Position the insertion point at the beginning of the document, and press Enter twice to create space at the top of the document.

3. Move the insertion point to the top of the document and type **Sentences Exercise**.

4. Select the text you typed. Click the down arrow on the Font drop-down list on the Formatting toolbar and select Arial from the list of font choices.

5. Click the down arrow on the Font Size drop-down list and choose 14.

6. Click the Bold, Italic, and Underline buttons on the Formatting toolbar to apply each of these formats to the selected text.

If you are using Personalized toolbars that share one row, each of these buttons may not be visible on the Formatting toolbar. Click the Toolbar Options button on the right end of the Formatting toolbar and select the button you want to add from the list of available buttons.

7. Click the down arrow on the Font Color button and choose a color from the color palette.

EXERCISE 1.3 *(continued)*

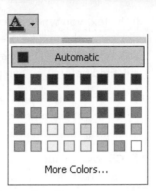

8. Click somewhere else in the document to deselect the text and see the results of the changes.

9. Select the title again and choose Format ➢ Font to open the Font dialog box. Choose a different font, font style, and size. Notice how the text changes in the Preview window at the bottom of the dialog box.

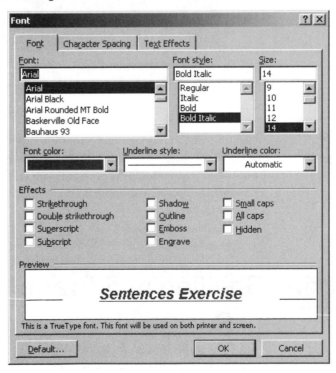

EXERCISE 1.3 *(continued)*

If the text you typed does not appear in the Preview window, you did not select the text before opening the Font dialog box. Click Cancel and select the text before reopening the Font dialog box. Text must be selected before you can make any font format changes.

10. Select a color from the Font Color drop-down list or choose More Colors at the bottom of the palette to select from a wider range of colors.

11. Choose an underline style from the Underline Style drop-down list. Use the Underline Color drop-down list to apply a color to the underline style you've chosen.

12. Click OK to accept the font format changes.

13. Select the symbols you inserted in the document (you can select them both by selecting the first one and holding Ctrl while you select the second one) and change their format.

14. Select other text in the document and change the format of the text until you are comfortable making text format changes.

15. Close the document and click No to discard the changes.

Use discretion when applying an underline to text. In the era of the World Wide Web, people have come to expect an underline to indicate a hyperlink to another document. This is especially true when viewing a document online. Use bold and italic to emphasize text rather than underlines, and you'll avoid a lot of frustration.

Checking Spelling and Grammar

Spelling and grammar may not have been your best subjects in school, but with some help from Word, you can avoid embarrassing mistakes that could cost you that perfect job or big promotion.

Microsoft
✓ ***Exam***
Objective

Correct spelling and grammar usage

With Word's Check Spelling As You Type and Check Grammar As You Type options, you can check spelling and grammar on the fly or can choose to wait and check an entire document at once. To check spelling as you go, right-click any word that Word has marked with a red wavy underline. To check grammar as you go, right-click any word with a green wavy underline.

If you'd rather wait until you have finished writing, click the Spelling And Grammar button on the Standard toolbar at that time.

Regardless of whether you are checking as you go along or at the end of the document, Word offers you a number of ways of dealing with a word that isn't in the spelling dictionary or a potential grammar error. These choices are available from the shortcut menu that opens when you right-click a word or from the Spelling And Grammar dialog box, shown in Figure 1.4.

FIGURE 1.4 Choose the correct spelling of a word from the list of suggestions offered in the Spelling And Grammar dialog box.

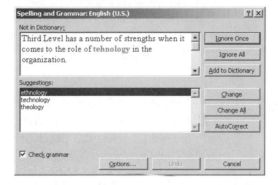

Ignore Once   This option ignores the selected occurrence of the word or this occurrence of a grammar error.

Ignore All or Ignore Rule   This option ignores all occurrences of the word in this document or all occurrences of the particular grammar rule in question.

Add To Dictionary (Spelling Only)   This option adds the word to the Custom dictionary so Office will recognize it in the future.

Change   This option changes the word after you choose one of the suggested corrections or edit the word manually.

Change All   This option changes all occurrences of the word or grammatical error in this document after you choose one of the suggested corrections or edit the word manually.

AutoCorrect (Spelling Only)   This option corrects the word (after you choose or enter a correction) and adds it to the AutoCorrect dictionary so it will be corrected automatically in the future.

Explain (Grammar Only)   This option opens Word Help to give you more information about the grammar rule at issue.

Delete (Grammar Only)   This option appears if you type the same word twice in a row.

By default, Word checks grammar along with spelling when you click the Spelling And Grammar button on the Standard toolbar. If you would prefer not to check the grammar, clear the Check Grammar check box in the Spelling And Grammar dialog box when it first opens.

When Word is checking spelling and grammar, watch the label on top of the text box in the Spelling And Grammar dialog box. It identifies the reason the text was flagged, such as Fragment, Use Of I, Contraction, etc., so you're not left trying to figure it out yourself.

If you would prefer to wait until you have finished entering and editing text to check the spelling and grammar, you can turn off the Automatic Spelling And Grammar option. Choose Tools ➢ Options ➢ Spelling And Grammar, and deselect the Check Spelling As You Type and Check Grammar As You Type check boxes.

Although Word 2002's Grammar Checker is a dramatic step forward in electronic proofreading, it regularly makes recommendations to fix text that is already correct or misses sentences that are obviously wrong. If you are uncertain, check another grammar reference.

In Exercise 1.4, you'll have a chance to practice checking spelling and grammar.

EXERCISE 1.4

Correcting Spelling and Grammar Usage

1. Open the file 1-4.doc.

2. Right-click Grammar and choose Grammar from the shortcut menu.

3. Right-click "check" and choose "checks."

4. Click the Spelling And Grammar button on the Standard toolbar, and respond to the additional spelling and grammar errors as they are identified.

   Because "As" is part of the name of a check box, we've chosen to ignore the suggested capitalization suggestion by choosing Ignore Once for each of the two occurrences.

5. Close the file and choose No to discard the changes.

Using Font and Text Effects to Enhance Text

Font effects available in Word provide additional tools for you to enhance text for a printed document. You can use font effects to create subscripts (H_2O), superscripts (x^2), and even hidden text in a document. Text effects, on the other hand, are designed to enhance documents that you are creating for online viewing. Text effects add an animated effect to the selected text. Font and text effects are both available from the Font dialog box (Format ➢ Font).

Microsoft ✓ *Exam* *Objective*	**Apply font and text effects**

In Exercise 1.5, you will apply font and text effects to existing text in a document.

EXERCISE 1.5

Applying Font and Text Effects

1. Open the file 1-5.doc.

2. Select 2 in H20 in the first line of text.

EXERCISE 1.5 *(continued)*

3. Choose Format ➤ Font to open the Font dialog box. Select Subscript from the Effects choices.

4. Click OK to apply the effect and close the dialog box.

5. Select the title Test Your H_2O and reopen the Font dialog box.

6. Apply Outline and All Caps to the selected text.

7. Click the Text Effects tab and select Sparkle Text from the list of Animation choices.

8. Click OK to close the Font dialog box.

9. Select other text in the document and apply text formats (see Exercise 1.3) and font and text effects. Note that although you can see text effects, you have to view the document onscreen to see the animations that accompany them.

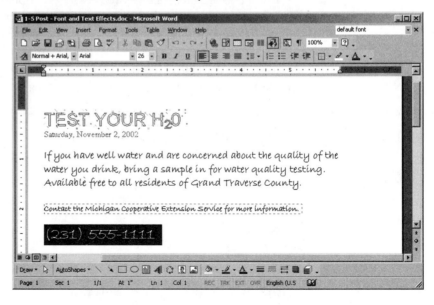

10. Close the document and discard the changes.

Inserting Dates and Times

Typing a date and time into a document is no different than entering any other text. However, if you use Word's Date and Time feature, you can easily insert today's date and the current time (based on the Windows system clock) in a variety of formats. And better yet, for documents that you want to always reflect the current date, Word can update the date automatically. Obviously, you would not want to use this feature on a document where tracking the original date is important. However, if it's a document you update on a regular basis, having Word update the date for you assures that you always date the document correctly

Microsoft
✓ ***Exam***
Objective

Enter and format Date and Time

In Exercise 1.6, you will learn to insert dates and times and also insert dates and times with a variety of formats that update automatically.

EXERCISE 1.6

Entering and Formatting Date and Time

1. Open a new blank document.

2. Choose Insert ➤ Date And Time to open the Date And Time dialog box.

3. Review the list of available date and time formats.

4. Select the option that shows *Month/Date/Year Hour:Minutes:Seconds AM/PM* (e.g., 1/15/2002 4:57:19 PM) and click OK to insert it into the document.

5. Press Enter twice, and open the Date And Time dialog box again (Insert ➤ Date And Time).

6. Select the same Date and Time format as in step 4.

EXERCISE 1.6 *(continued)*

7. Click the Update Automatically check box. This inserts a date and time field into the document rather than actual text. Word automatically updates the field to the current date and time each time you print the document.

8. Click OK to insert the date and time field. You can distinguish the date and time field from the actual text by clicking it. Notice that the field turns gray when it is selected.

9. Click the Print button to see the field update to the current date and time.

10. Close the document without saving.

Word's AutoText feature is a quick way to enter today's date. AutoText saves keystrokes by prompting you with the text it thinks you want to enter. For example, type the first four letters of the current month. When the full month appears above the text, press Enter. Press the spacebar, and the date and year should appear. Press Enter again to enter the entire date. You can also use this with other date formats. For example, if you type the number of the month and a slash and then the date and a slash, the date appears as M/D/YY. Press Enter to accept the suggested entry. If this feature is not working for you, check to see that Show AutoComplete Suggestions is checked in the AutoText dialog box (Insert ➢ AutoText ➢ AutoText).

Formatting Text Using Character Styles

Styles is a Word feature that streamlines formatting by saving commonly used formats so you can reapply them to selected text. In Word 2002, you can create and apply styles to characters, paragraph, tables, and lists. For the purposes of the MOUS exams, you need to learn only about character and paragraph styles.

Microsoft ✓ *Exam* *Objective* **Apply character styles**

Word has a number of built-in styles already created that you can apply to text. Many of the predefined character styles, such as Hyperlink and HTML Definition, are used in creating HTML documents for the Web. However, after you learn to create character styles, you can create them for other purposes. Character styles can include any of the font formats such as bold, italic, and underline and font effects such as shadow and superscript, which you learned about earlier in this chapter.

You'll learn how to apply character styles in Exercise 1.7 and paragraph styles later in this chapter in Exercise 1.18. Creating character and paragraph styles are MOUS Expert skills and are covered in Chapter 5, "Advanced Document Formatting."

EXERCISE 1.7

Applying Character Styles

1. Open a new blank document.

2. Enter the following text:
   Character Style
   a Word feature that streamlines formatting by saving commonly used formats so you can reapply them to selected text.

3. Select the words Character Style by dragging over the text.

4. Click the Styles And Formatting button on the Formatting toolbar.

5. When the task pane opens, click the down arrow on the Show drop-down list and choose All Styles from the list.

6. Scroll through the Pick Formatting To Apply list of predefined styles that appears in the Styles And Formatting task pane. You can identify the type of style by the icon on its right.

EXERCISE 1.7 *(continued)*

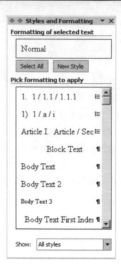

7. Find HTML Definition in the list of character styles, and click it to apply it to the selected text. The text appears in Times New Roman 12 pt Italic.

8. Select the word "selected" in the paragraph of text.

9. Find Strong in the list of styles and click it to apply it to the selected text. The text appears in Times New Roman 12 pt Bold.

10. Close the document and discard the changes.

Because both HTML Definition and Strong are HTML character styles, Word assigns HTML tags to text formatted using these styles that can be recognized by web browsers.

Creating and Modifying Paragraphs

Text entered into Word is formulated into paragraphs, paragraphs into pages, and pages into documents. As long as you never press Enter, your document consists of only one paragraph. However, as soon as you press Enter, even if it's to create a blank line, you have created a paragraph. A paragraph in Word can contain a blank line, a single character, a line of text, a few sentences, or multiple pages. Many of Word's formatting options, such as alignment and bullets, apply to paragraphs. Before you can successfully format a document, you must be able to format paragraphs as well as isolated text. In this section, we'll show you how to modify paragraph formats, use tabs, apply bullet, outline, and numbering formats, and apply paragraph styles.

Modifying Paragraph Formats

Paragraph formats include alignment, indentation, spacing between paragraphs, line spacing, and line and page breaks.

Microsoft ✓ *Exam* *Objective*   **Modify paragraph formats**

We will discuss each of these paragraph formats in the following sections.

Aligning Paragraphs

Paragraph alignment is probably the single-most-used paragraph format. Alignment determines how a paragraph lines up in relation to the margins. A paragraph can be left-aligned, centered, right-aligned, or justified. Figure 1.5 shows examples of each type of alignment.

FIGURE 1.5   Text can be aligned in four ways.

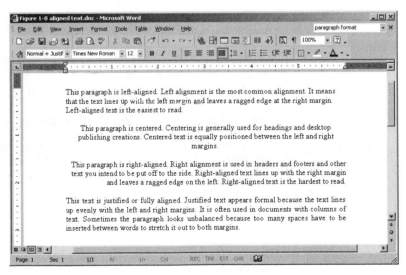

In Exercise 1.8, you will practice aligning paragraphs.

Aligning Paragraphs

1. Open the file 1-8.doc.

2. Click in the first paragraph and click the Align Left button.

3. Click in the second paragraph and click the Center button.

4. Click in the third paragraph and click the Align Right button.

5. Click in the fourth paragraph and click the Justify button.

6. Close the document and click No to discard the changes.

Paragraph formats are applied to entire paragraphs, so you do not have to select the paragraph first as long as the insertion point is somewhere within the paragraph. If you want to modify more than one paragraph at a time, you must select the desired paragraphs.

Indenting Paragraphs

Indenting refers to the distance a paragraph is from the left or right margin. Word offers three ways to access paragraph-indenting features: the Formatting toolbar, the ruler, and the Paragraph dialog box.

Indenting Paragraphs Using the Formatting Toolbar

Using the Formatting toolbar is a simple way to apply left indents to paragraphs by clicking the Decrease Indent and Increase Indent buttons.

Exercise 1.9 shows you how to use these buttons to indent paragraphs.

EXERCISE 1.9

Increasing and Decreasing Indents Using the Formatting Toolbar

1. Open the file 1-9.doc.

2. Position the insertion point somewhere in the paragraph you want to indent (or if you are working with a longer document, select multiple paragraphs); then click the Increase Indent button to increase the left indent by a half inch.

3. Click the Increase Indent button again to increase the left indent by another half inch.

4. Click the Decrease Indent button to decrease the indent.

5. Click the Decrease Indent button again to return the paragraph to the left margin.

6. Close the document and click No to discard the changes.

Creating Indents Using the Ruler

The second method of indenting paragraphs—using the ruler—can take a little work to master, but it's a visual way to set left, right, first line, hanging, and dual indents. You can use the ruler to set tabs, indents, and left and right margins in Page Layout view.

If you prefer to do most of your work without the ruler, hide the ruler by choosing View ➤ Ruler. To make the hidden ruler temporarily visible, point to the narrow gray line under the toolbars (at the top of the document) and the ruler will reappear. When you move the pointer away from the ruler area, the ruler will slide back under the toolbars.

There are four indent markers on the ruler, shown here:

- **First Line Indent** works the same as pressing Tab on the keyboard. The first line of text is indented from the left margin.

- **Hanging Indent** (sometimes called an *outdent*) "hangs" the remaining lines in a paragraph to the right of the first line when this marker is positioned to the right of the first line indent marker.

- **Left Indent** sets a paragraph off from the rest of the text by moving all lines in from the left margin.

- **Right Indent** moves text in from the right margin and is typically combined with a left indent to make a *dual indent*. Dual indents are used most commonly to set off block quotations.

First Line indent

Hanging indent

Left indent

Right indent

Exercise 1.10 walks you through how to use the ruler to apply and remove indents. Using the ruler takes a little practice, so you may want to repeat this exercise several times until you feel comfortable with each indent.

EXERCISE 1.10

Adjusting Indents Using the Ruler

1. Open the file 1–10.doc.

2. Click in the paragraph about first line indents and drag the first line indent marker to the right to indent the first line of the paragraph.

3. Click in the paragraph about hanging indents and drag the hanging indent marker to the right to outdent the first line of text.

4. Click in the paragraph about left indent markers. Drag the left indent marker on the ruler to the half-inch mark.

5. Click in the paragraph about right indents and drag both the left and right indent markers to indent all lines of each paragraph from the left and right margins to create a dual indent.

6. Close the document and click No to discard the changes.

You can use the ruler to set indents before entering text. Position the insertion point where you plan to enter the new text before dragging the indent marker to the new location. The indents will apply to all newly entered text until you change the indent settings. If you forget which marker is which, point to any marker for a moment and view the ScreenTip.

If you select paragraphs that do not share the same indent settings, one or all of the indent markers on the ruler are dimmed. Click the dimmed marker(s) to make the indent settings the same for all the selected paragraphs.

Indenting Using the Paragraph Dialog Box

The third way to set indents is by using the Paragraph dialog box, shown in Figure 1.6. To access the dialog box, choose Format ➢ Paragraph or right-click and choose Paragraph from the shortcut menu.

FIGURE 1.6 The Paragraph dialog box

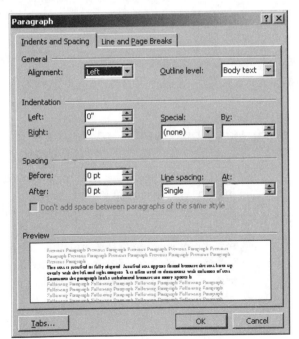

Although not as dynamic as using the ruler or as convenient as using the Formatting toolbar, the Paragraph dialog box offers a straightforward way to change indents. In Exercise 1.11, you'll use the Paragraph dialog box to set left and right indents.

EXERCISE 1.11

Indenting Using the Paragraph Dialog Box

1. Open the file 1-11.doc. Click in the paragraph of text and open the Paragraph dialog box (Format ➤ Paragraph or right-click and choose Paragraph).

2. Click the Indents And Spacing tab if it is not already selected.

3. Click the spin arrows next to the Left and Right text boxes, or enter decimal numbers directly in the text boxes.

4. Click the Special drop-down menu to select First Line or Hanging indent. If you want the indent to be more or less than 0.5 inches, enter the special indent value in the By control by either typing the amount or using the spin arrows to select a value.

5. Click OK to close the Paragraph dialog box and see your changes.

6. Close the document and click No to discard the changes.

Spacing between Paragraphs

Spacing between paragraphs can improve the appearance of a document by increasing or decreasing white space and by more closely associating headings to the subsequent paragraphs. Spacing, represented by point size, can be added before and after paragraphs. For example, rather than inserting an entire line between a heading and the paragraph that follows it, you can insert 6 pt spacing before and after the paragraph to fit more text on a page. Figure 1.7 shows a document before paragraph spacing has been applied to the headings, and Figure 1.8 shows the same document after spacing has been applied.

FIGURE 1.7   In this document, there is no space between headings and subsequent paragraphs.

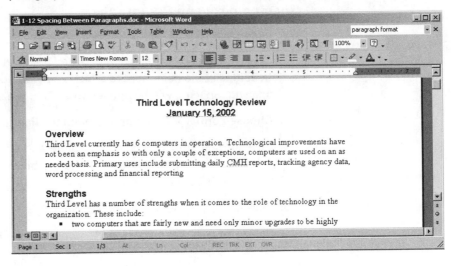

FIGURE 1.8   Paragraph spacing has been applied to the headings to allow 6 pt of space before and after the headings.

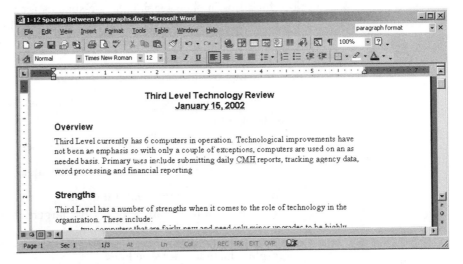

In Exercise 1.12, you'll use the Paragraph dialog box to apply spacing between paragraphs.

EXERCISE 1.12

Spacing between Paragraphs

1. Open the file 1-12.doc.

2. Select the first paragraph heading, and hold Ctrl to select the other headings in the document to which you want to apply the same spacing. Spacing will be applied to each of the selected headings.

3. Choose Format ≻ Paragraph to open the Paragraph dialog box.

4. Click the spin arrows next to the Before and After text boxes, or enter decimal numbers directly in the text boxes. In this case, enter **6 pt** in both Before and After.

5. Click OK to see the paragraph spacing.

6. Close the document and click No to discard the changes.

Adjusting Line Spacing

Line spacing is another type of paragraph format. Word offers a number of options for adjusting line spacing. Single-spacing is the default line spacing. You can apply line spacing based on the number of lines at the current font size, e.g., 1.5, 2, or 3 lines, or by the desired point size, 12 pt, 14 pt, and so on.

Line spacing options include the following:

- **Single** provides enough room to comfortably display the largest character on a line.

- **1.5 Lines** gives you one-and-a-half single lines.

- **Double** provides twice as much room as single spacing.

- **At Least** lets you enter a minimum line spacing for the selection. This line spacing adjusts automatically if a larger size font is used.

- **Exactly** evenly spaces all lines regardless of the size of the fonts or graphics included in those lines.

- **Multiple** is used to enter specific line spacing, such as 1.25 or 4 lines.

Exercise 1.13 shows you how to apply basic line spacing using the toolbar button and more advanced spacing using the Paragraph dialog box.

EXERCISE 1.13

Applying Line Spacing to Selected Paragraphs

1. Open the file 1-13.doc and move the insertion point to the second paragraph.

2. Click the drop-down menu arrow on the Line Spacing button on the Formatting toolbar to see the menu of line spacing choices. Select 1.5 from the list. Notice how the paragraph changes.

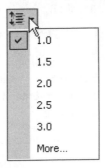

3. Click the Line Spacing drop-down arrow again and choose 2.0 from the menu of choices.

4. For greater than triple spacing, or to use the At Least, Exactly, and Multiple options described earlier, click the More choice on the drop-down menu to open the Paragraph dialog box.

5. Click the Line Spacing drop-down list on the Indents And Spacing tab of the Paragraph dialog box and choose At Least. Enter **15** in the At text box (you have to select the text in the text box to replace it). This number refers to point size, so 15 is equivalent to a 15 pt font. Click OK to see the results of the changes.

When you use the At Least setting, the line spacing adjusts appropriately if the font size is larger than the line spacing.

6. Select the paragraph and change the font size to **18** to see the adjustment in line spacing.

Use the Exactly setting if you do not want the line spacing to change regardless of the font size.

7. Repeat Step 4 and choose Exactly from the Line Spacing drop-down list. Enter **12** in the At text box. Click OK to see the results of the changes.

EXERCISE 1.13 *(continued)*

Because the line spacing setting is smaller than the font size, the lines appear on top of each other. Use the Exactly line spacing option when you want to designate line spacing at a larger point size than the font, as in the example in step 8.

8. Repeat step 4 and choose Exactly from the Line Spacing drop-down list. Enter **20** in the At text box. Click OK to see the results of the changes.

   Use the Multiple line spacing option to enter a specific number of lines rather than a point size.

9. Repeat Step 4 and choose Multiple from the Line Spacing drop-down list. Enter **4** in the At text box. Click OK to see the results of the changes.

10. Close the document and click No to discard the changes.

To see all the formatting that is applied to a paragraph, choose Help ➢ What's This?, and then click the paragraph. The Reveal Formatting task pane appears, displaying paragraph and font formatting related to the paragraph. Click the Close button on the task pane to turn it off.

Working with Tabs

One of the most common uses of a tab is to indent the first line of a paragraph. Tabs are also used to line up text in parallel columns. A tab stop works as a horizontal marker in a paragraph. Pressing the Tab key moves the cursor from one tab stop to the next.

Microsoft ✓ *Exam Objective*	**Set and modify tabs**

Tabs can be used to create parallel columns, vertically aligning text within a document. However, Word's Tables feature—presented in Chapter 2—provides a much better option for creating parallel columns.

A new document includes tab stops at half-inch intervals. The default tab stops are dark-gray tick marks that appear on the gray bar at the bottom of the ruler. You can change the default settings by using the ruler or the Tabs dialog box. You need to choose both the alignment type and the location for each tab stop you want to use. There are five basic types of tab stops, shown in Figure 1.9, as listed here:

- **Left:** The default type; text appears to the right of the tab stop.

- **Center:** Text is centered under the tab stop.

- **Right:** Text appears to the left of the tab stop.

- **Bar:** This type is used to create a vertical line between columns of tabbed data.

- **Decimal:** This type is used for numeric entries; text lines up with the decimal point.

FIGURE 1.9   The five types of tab stops are all used in this document.

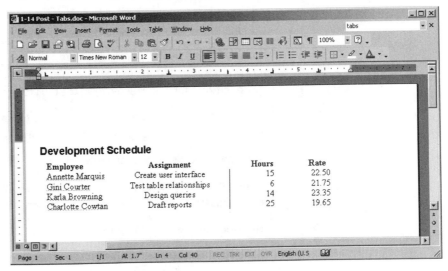

At the left end of the ruler is a Tab Selection button that allows you to select the type of tab you want to set (see Figure 1.10). By default, the button is set on Left Tab.

FIGURE 1.10 The ruler showing the Tab Selection button

Tab Selection button

Using tabs can be a challenging skill if you are not aware of how the Tabs feature works. Exercise 1.14 walks you through what you need to know to set tabs correctly using the ruler.

EXERCISE 1.14

Setting Tab Stops Using the Ruler

1. Open the file 1-14.doc.

2. Select the second line (the one containing the word Employee).

3. Click the Tab Selection button on the ruler to toggle through the different tab choices. Choose Center Tab and click 2.5 on the ruler.

4. Click the Tab Selection button again and choose Right Tab. Click 4 on the ruler.

5. Click 5 on the ruler. Because Right tab was still selected, a right tab is applied to the selected paragraph. If you choose the wrong tab type at any point, drag the tab stop off the ruler and apply the correct tab. If you position a tab incorrectly, drag the tab stop to the correct location.

6. In the first line under Employee, enter the following (pressing Tab after each entry and Enter after the final entry):

   Annette Marquis, Create user interface, 15, 22.50

7. In the next line under Annette, enter the following (pressing Tab after each entry and Enter after the final entry):

   Gini Courter, Test table relationships, 6, 21.75

8. In the next line under Gini, enter the following (pressing Tab after each entry and Enter after the final entry):

   Karla Browning, Design queries, 4, 23.35

9. In the next line under Karla, enter the following (pressing Tab after each entry and Enter after the final entry):

   Charlotte Cowtan, Draft reports, 25, 19.65

10. To insert a bar tab between the columns, select the four rows of data excluding the column headings. Click the Tab Selection button and choose Bar Tab. Click 3.5 on the ruler.

11. To adjust the distance between columns, select all five rows including the column headings, and drag the last tab to 5.5 and the tab that is at 4 to 4.5. To adjust the position of the bar tab, you must select only the rows that contain the bar or it will not be visible on the ruler.

12. To convert the final right tab to a decimal tab, select the four rows of data. Drag the right tab that is at 5.5 off of the ruler. Select Decimal Tab from the Tab Selection button. Click the ruler at 5.5. Because this lines up numbers at their decimal, you may prefer to drag the tab to the left a few spaces so they line up with the column heading.

13. Use File ➢ Save As to save this document as **Tab Stops**.

14. Close the document and click Yes to save the changes.

If you want the tab stops to apply to existing text, be sure to select the text first—before clicking the ruler. Unless you select the entire document or the last paragraph in the document, the tab stops apply only to the selected paragraph(s). You can, however, set the tab stops for a blank document before you start entering text, and then the tab stops can be used throughout the document. To clear a tab stop, simply drag it off the ruler.

You may notice two additional stops on the Tab Selection tool after the five tab choices. These are First Line Indent and Hanging Indent. Use them to make it easier to select the indent markers on the ruler. When either tool is selected, you can click anywhere on the ruler (avoid the top gray bar) to move the corresponding indent marker to that position.

Setting Tab Stops and Leaders Using the Tabs Dialog Box

You can also create tab stops using the Tabs dialog box. Make sure the insertion point is located where you want the new tab stops to begin. (If the text you want to format is already entered, select it.) Access the Tabs dialog box, shown in Figure 1.11, by choosing Format ➢ Tabs from the menu bar.

FIGURE 1.11   The Tabs dialog box

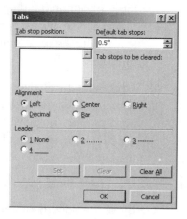

In the Tab Stop Position text box, type the location for the tab stop you want to create. In the Alignment section, choose how you want text to align at the tab stop. The Leader section lets you select a *leader* to lead the reader's eye across the text. Leaders are used most commonly in documents such as agendas, price lists, and schedules. The leader (see Figure 1.12) precedes the tabbed text.

FIGURE 1.12   Text with tab stops and leaders

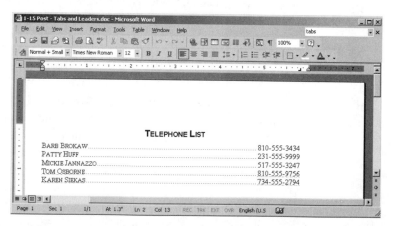

In Exercise 1.15, you'll use the Tabs dialog box to create tab stops with dot leaders.

Using the Tabs Dialog Box to Create Tab Stops with Leaders

1. Create a new document, type a title, **Telephone List, and press Enter**. Format the title anyway you want. The title in Figure 1.12 is Arial 14 pt Bold, All Caps, Centered, with 6 pt spacing before and after the paragraph.

2. Position the insertion point on the blank line below the title. Choose Format ➢ Tabs to open the Tabs dialog box. The insertion point appears in the Tab Stop Position field.

3. Enter **5.81** in the Tab Stop Position field.

4. Select Right as the Alignment Type and 2 as the Leader.

5. Press OK to save the new tab settings.

6. Type a person's name and press Tab. The insertion point should move to the right side of the page, and a dot leader should be visible. Enter a phone number. Because the tab is a Right tab, the phone number appears just to its left. Press Enter.

7. Repeat Step 6, adding four additional names and phone numbers.

8. Close the document without saving the changes.

To see where tabs have been typed in existing text, click the Show/Hide button on the Standard toolbar. You'll see a right-pointed arrow to indicate a tab.

To remove an existing tab stop, select it from the list and click the Clear button in the Tabs dialog box. Clicking Clear All removes all of the tab stops you added and reverts to the default tab settings. When you have finished setting tab stops, click OK to close the Tabs dialog box.

Creating Bulleted and Numbered Lists

Bulleted and numbered lists make a document easier to read because key points stand out on the page. Lists are easy to scan and easy to reference.

Microsoft ✓ Exam Objective

Apply bullet, outline, and numbering format to paragraphs

Word has three types of list formats: bulleted lists, numbered lists, and outline numbered lists (referred to as the outline format in the Microsoft exam objective). All three are simple to create whether or not you have already entered the text. Bulleted lists are identified by the graphic character that precedes the paragraphs of text. Numbered lists begin with numbers or letters. Outline format is used to create multiple-level lists using bullets, numbers, or letters. Figure 1.13 shows examples of each kind of list.

FIGURE 1.13 Bulleted, numbered, and outline numbered lists

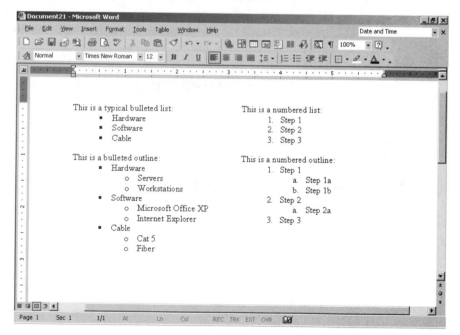

In Exercise 1.16, you'll learn how to create lists from scratch using Word's automatic bullets and numbering feature. In Exercise 1.17, you'll learn to apply bullets and numbering to an existing list.

EXERCISE 1.16

Applying Bullet, Outline, and Number Formats Automatically

1. Create a new blank document.

2. Type an asterisk (*), press Tab, and enter a favorite activity. Press Enter. When you do, Word automatically changes the asterisk to a bullet character, indents the list, tabs it appropriately, and adds a second bullet.

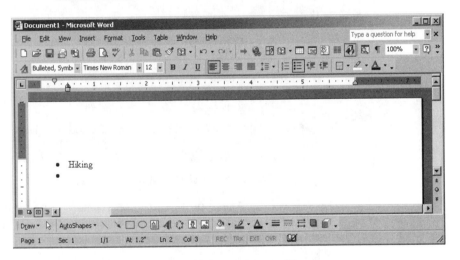

3. Type another favorite activity and press Enter.

4. Enter three more items in the list.

5. Position the insertion point to the right of the first activity in the bulleted list, and press Enter. This creates a new line. Press Tab to create a sub-bullet. List three tools or pieces of equipment you need for your first activity.

6. When you have finished with this list, click to the right of the second activity, press Enter and Tab, and list three things you need for this activity.

EXERCISE 1.16 *(continued)*

7. Skip to the last activity and enter three subpoints. When you press Enter after the last subpoint, hold Shift and press Tab to create another main bullet point. You can also use the Increase Indent and Decrease Indent buttons to create new bullets and sub-bullets.

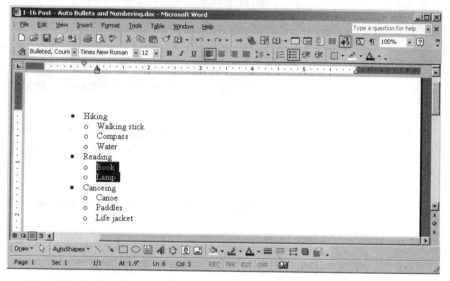

8. Press Enter twice to start a new list.

9. Type **1.** and press Tab. Type **Trees**. When you press Enter, Word automatically indents the list, adjusts the tabs, and adds a second number.

10. Press Tab and type **Oak**. Press Enter and type **Maple**, **Beech**, and **Aspen**, pressing Enter after each one.

11. Press Shift+Tab to create a new main bullet point, and then type **Birds** and press Enter.

12. Add three types of birds as subpoints under Birds.

13. Add **Flowers**, **Insects**, and **Animals** to the list as main bullet points. Press Enter twice at the end of the list to turn off automatic numbering.

14. Close the document without saving.

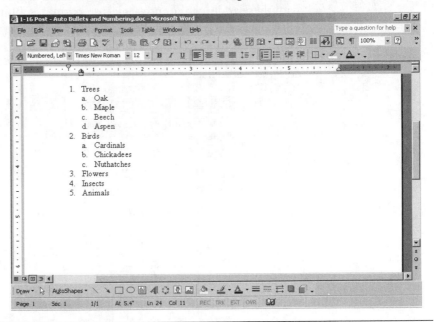

EXERCISE 1.17

Applying Bullets and Numbering to an Existing List

1. Open the file 1-17.doc.

2. Select the four cities, and click the Bullets button on the Formatting toolbar.

3. With the list still selected, press the Numbering button on the Formatting toolbar.

4. With the list still selected, click the Numbering button again to turn off Numbering.

5. Close the document without saving it.

Many more options are available to use with the bullets and numbering tools. For example, you can choose the numbering style you want to use, i.e., 1., 2., 3. or I, II, III, and the bullet character you want to use. To experiment with these additional options, choose Format ➢ Bullets And Numbering to open the Bullets And Numbering dialog box shown in Figure 1.14.

FIGURE 1.14   The Bullets And Numbering dialog box offers additional options for bulleted and numbered lists.

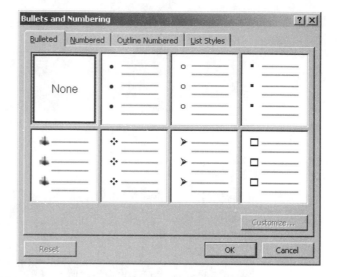

Applying Preformatted Styles to Paragraphs

Earlier in this chapter, you learned about applying character styles to text. Paragraph styles are actually a commonly used type of style. Paragraph styles can include all of the text formatting contained in character styles and all of the paragraph formatting features such as alignment, indentation, tabs, spacing, line spacing, and bullets and numbering.

Microsoft ✓ *Exam Objective*	**Apply paragraph styles**

Every new Word document is created with the Normal paragraph style. By default, this style is Times New Roman 10 pt Regular text, Left aligned, with no other formatting. Three additional paragraph styles are available in every document from the Style drop-down list on the Formatting toolbar. These are Heading 1, Heading 2, and Heading 3 styles. In addition, you can access All Styles by activating the Styles And Formatting task pane (click the Styles And Formatting button on the Formatting toolbar), and have a large number of paragraph styles to choose from. Figure 1.15 shows examples of several paragraph styles. What is not obvious in this figure is that all of the heading styles include paragraph spacing before and after the text.

FIGURE 1.15   Paragraph styles are available from the Style drop-down list and from the Styles And Formatting task pane.

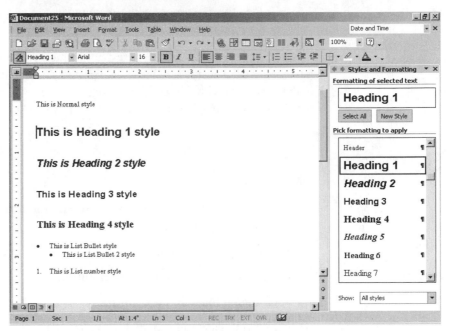

Exercise 1.18 introduces you to heading styles and shows how to apply them to your paragraphs.

EXERCISE 1.18

Applying Paragraph Styles

1. Open the file 1-18.doc.

2. Select the first heading and apply a Heading 1 style by clicking the Style drop-down list and choosing Heading 1 from the list.

EXERCISE 1.18 *(continued)*

3. Select the second heading and apply a Heading 2 style by clicking the Style drop-down list and choosing Heading 2 from the list.

4. Select the third heading and apply a Heading 3 style by clicking the Style drop-down list and choosing Heading 3 from the list.

5. Select the second and third headings again (hold Ctrl to select multiple paragraphs) and apply a Heading 1 style to both headings by clicking the Style drop-down list and choosing Heading 1 from the list.

6. Close this document without saving.

The biggest reason that styles are a huge time-saver is that after paragraphs have been assigned styles, you can change a style and have it affect all the text in the document with that style. You'll need to know about how to create and modify styles for the Word Expert exam. For more about styles, see Chapter 5.

Summary

This chapter focused on text and paragraph formatting in Word. We covered the following topics:

- Inserting text and making corrections to existing text
- Using spell check and grammar options
- Changing fonts and text formats
- Inserting date and time fields to automatically update the date and time in a document
- Applying character styles
- Applying paragraph formats such as alignment, indentation, spacing, and line spacing
- Using five types of tabs to create parallel columns of text and two methods for applying them
- Automatically creating numbered and bulleted lists and using outlining for multilevel lists
- Using preformatted styles and applying them to existing text

Chapter

2

Working with Documents

MOUS WORD 2002 CORE EXAM OBJECTIVES COVERED IN THIS CHAPTER:

- ✓ Create and modify a header and footer
- ✓ Apply and modify column settings
- ✓ Modify document layout and Page Setup options
- ✓ Create and modify tables
- ✓ Preview and Print documents, envelopes, and labels
- ✓ Manage files and folders for documents
- ✓ Create documents using templates
- ✓ Save documents using different names and file formats

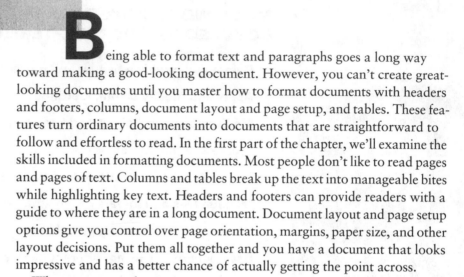

Being able to format text and paragraphs goes a long way toward making a good-looking document. However, you can't create great-looking documents until you master how to format documents with headers and footers, columns, document layout and page setup, and tables. These features turn ordinary documents into documents that are straightforward to follow and effortless to read. In the first part of the chapter, we'll examine the skills included in formatting documents. Most people don't like to read pages and pages of text. Columns and tables break up the text into manageable bites while highlighting key text. Headers and footers can provide readers with a guide to where they are in a long document. Document layout and page setup options give you control over page orientation, margins, paper size, and other layout decisions. Put them all together and you have a document that looks impressive and has a better chance of actually getting the point across.

When you are ready to print, you can preview the printed document before you send it off to the printer. If it's a letter you're printing, why handwrite the envelope or, worse yet, fire up the old electric typewriter, when you can print right on the envelope? We'll show you how to print a single envelope or even a single label if your printer doesn't handle envelopes quite so well.

Chapter 5, "Advanced Document Formatting," covers additional tools you can use to format documents, such as footnotes and tables of contents.

In the second part of the chapter, you'll learn the skills necessary to manage the documents you create. Office applications have many file-management tools incorporated into the Open and Save As dialog boxes. Learning to use these effectively can save you time and trouble. In this chapter, you'll learn to open and save files, create subfolders, and navigate the folder structure to find what you are looking for. You'll also learn to save documents using different names and convert documents to different file formats. Finally, you'll learn to create and save documents templates that you can use over and over again without risking the original document. Templates provide standardization and protection to document formats, such as a fax cover sheet, that you want to reuse.

Before you begin this chapter, you should go to the Sybex website and download the file 4113Ch02.zip. This package contains the files necessary to complete some of the exercises in this chapter. In addition, it contains files of what most of the documents should look like after you complete the exercise. These files are affixed with the word *Post*.

Formatting Documents

If you've ever been on the way to the copy machine and dropped a 20-page document that did not have page numbers, you have experienced the value of numbering firsthand. Page numbers generally appear in the header or footer of a document and are one of the more common uses of the half-inch or so at the top or bottom of the page. In this section, we'll show you how to create and modify headers and footers.

We'll then take you into the world of columns. In this content, we're referring to newspaper, or what are sometimes called serpentine, columns. Like a snake, text winds its way down one column and up the next. Here, you'll learn how to apply and modify column settings for that departmental newsletter you've been meaning to write.

Document layout and page setup options include, among other things, top, bottom, left, and right margins, portrait or landscape page orientation, the paper size you plan to use to print the document, header and footer margins, and vertical alignment of text on a page. These options give you control over how the document will look when it is finally printed.

Tables are another form of columns, called parallel columns. In a parallel column, text in the first column directly relates to text in the second column and so on. You might use tables, for example, to create a schedule of events where column 1 is the date, column 2 is the time, column 3 is the event description, and column 4 is the location. If you don't know how to use tables, you probably use tabs to put text in parallel columns. Tabs work fine, but with tables you have much more control over how the text flows in each column and many more formatting options available to you. In addition, it's much easier to add information to a table than to tabbed text, where you might need to reset the tab stops.

When you're finally ready to print, you can preview the document to see how it's going to look and give it a once-over before committing it to ink and paper. After it's printed, you can print the envelope or mailing label to go with it. With Word, you can print a single label from a typical sheet of thirty and use the same sheet over and over again until every label has been used. It's amazing how many people don't know this feature exists, so this is one of those skills that you can learn and then impress your coworkers with your technological savvy.

Working with Headers and Footers

A header appears in the half-inch or so at the top of the page, and a footer appears at the bottom. What makes headers and footers unique is that they appear on every page of the document unless you specify otherwise. A header or footer may contain information about the document such as the document's title, page numbering, the document's author, or a host of other things that you want repeated on every page.

Microsoft ✓ *Exam* *Objective*	**Create and modify a header and footer**

In Exercise 2.1, you'll learn how to create a header and footer. Exercise 2.2 shows you how to make changes to it.

EXERCISE 2.1

Creating Headers and Footers

1. Either open the file 2-1 or create it yourself by following these steps:

   a. Create a new blank document.

b. Type **Departmental Annual Report** and format it as a title; in other words, center it and change the font to 16 pt Arial Bold or something similar.

c. Press Enter twice after the title and then press Ctrl+Enter to create a new page. Press Ctrl+Enter a second time to create a third page. You can tell you have three pages in the document by looking at the left section of Word's Status bar at the bottom of the application window. It shows you what page you are currently on and then what page you are on out of how many total pages.

d. Move back to the first page by pressing Ctrl+Home.

e. If you created the document from scratch, click the Save button and save the document to your default folder location, entering the name **Headers and Footers Practice** in the File Name text box in the Save As dialog box. If you opened the file from the Sybex website, resave the document using this new name (File ➢ Save As).

2. Switch to Print Layout view if you are currently in another view. Choose View ➢ Print Layout or click the Print Layout View button on the horizontal scroll bar. You can create headers and footers in other views but you must be in Print Layout view or Print Preview to see them

3. Choose View ➢ Header And Footer to switch to the document's background. In the document's background, you can see text in the foreground but it appears gray. The Header And Footer toolbar also appears.

Note: The Header And Footer toolbar may float in the document or may appear with the Standard and Formatting toolbars.

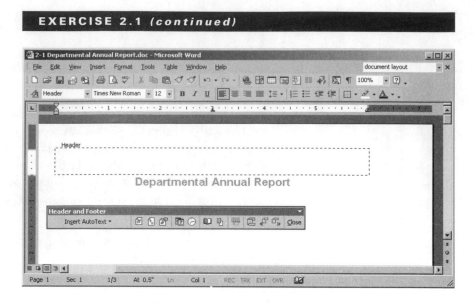

EXERCISE 2.1 *(continued)*

4. In the Header area of the document, type the report's title, in this case, **Departmental Annual Report**. Press Enter.

5. Click the Insert AutoText button on the Header And Footer toolbar and choose Page X Of Y from the list of AutoText entries. With this option, Word automatically inserts the current page number in place of the X and the total number of pages in place of the Y. The X and Y are field codes like the Date And Time field code you learned about in Chapter 1, "Creating Basic Documents."

6. Click the Switch Between Header And Footer button on the Header And Footer toolbar. This takes you to the Footer section of the document.

7. Click the Insert AutoText button on the Header And Footer toolbar and choose Author, Page #, Date from the list of choices. This inserts your name, the page number, and today's date.

EXERCISE 2.1 *(continued)*

Note: If your name does not appear in the Author field, it's because Word doesn't know who you are. To fix this, choose Tools ≻ Options and click the User Information tab. Enter your name in the Name box in the User Information section. You may also want to complete the Initials and Mailing Address fields because Word uses those in letters and to mark comments.

8. Click the Close button on the Header And Footer toolbar to switch out of Header And Footer view.

9. To see the header, scroll to the top of the document. The header appears gray because it is in the background now. Scroll to the page break between the first two pages to see the footer and the page 2 header.

10. Click the Close button to close the document, and click Yes to save the changes.

In the previous exercise, you created a header and footer for a document. However, the page number was repeated in both the header and the footer. In Exercise 2.2, you'll see how to delete the page number in the footer and move the page number from the header to the footer. If you don't like the format of the date that was inserted, you can change it to whatever format you prefer. We'll show you how to do this in this exercise. We'll also change a document layout option to eliminate the header and footer on the first page of the document. Although this is not a required part of the exam objective, it's standard for the first page of a document to not have a header or footer or to have a modified one from the rest of the document. This creates a cleaner first page and is especially important if you are including a title page as page 1 of the document. You'll learn more about how this option works in Chapter 5.

EXERCISE 2.2

Modifying Headers and Footers

1. Reopen Headers and Footers Practice, which you saved in Exercise 2.1, or open the file 2-2.

2. To get to the Header And Footer view, choose View ≻ Header And Footer or double-click the header or footer section of the document.

3. Select the header text "Departmental Annual Report" and reformat it as Arial 12 pt Bold.

4. Select "Page 1 of 3" and press Cut on the Formatting toolbar.

5. Move to the footer by either clicking the Switch Between Header And Footer button on the Header And Footer toolbar or scrolling down to the footer section of the document.

Note: If you are not on page 1 of the document, press Ctrl+Home to move to the top of the document.

6. Select "Page 1" in the footer text.

7. Press the Paste button on the Formatting toolbar to replace the existing page number style with the Page 1 Of 3 format.

Note: The Date field may wrap to the next line. If this happens, press the Backspace key to move it back into position.

8. Select the line of text in the footer by clicking the mouse pointer in the left margin outside the footer boundary in the area known as the selection bar.

9. Change the font to Arial 12 pt.

10. The date appears in the default date format set in the Date And Time dialog box (Insert ➢ Date And Time). To change the format of the date, click somewhere in the footer to deselect the footer text and then right-click the Date (field code).

11. Choose Edit Field from the shortcut menu to open the Field dialog box.

12. Select the date format you would prefer from the Field Properties Date Formats list. Click OK to accept the new date format.

13. Click the Page Setup button on the Header And Footer toolbar.

14. Select the Different First Page check box on the Layout tab of the Page Setup dialog box and click OK.

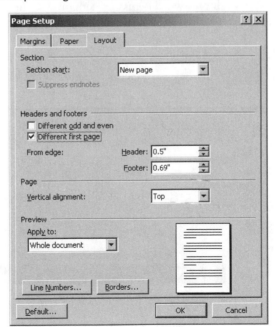

EXERCISE 2.2 *(continued)*

By choosing a different first page header and footer, Word eliminates the header on page 1 of the document. But notice that if you scroll to pages 2 and 3, the header and footer appear. You can use this feature when you don't want a header and footer on page 1, or you can use it to enter different text in the page 1 header and footer from the text in the subsequent pages.

15. Click the Close button on the Header And Footer toolbar to return to the document. The header and footer should appear only on pages 2 and 3.

16. Resave the document.

Creating and Modifying Columns

Columns offer an option for presenting text on a page. A long list of one- or two-word items can actually take up less space and may be easier to read if it appears in columns. You might also want to use columns if you are creating a newsletter or want to present information in a newsletter format. You may discover that people are more prone to read a document formatted like a newspaper than they are a lengthy single-column report because it looks more interesting.

Microsoft ✓ *Exam* *Objective*	**Apply and modify column settings**

In Exercise 2.3, you'll convert an example of single-column text to multiple columns and then modify column settings using the Columns dialog box.

EXERCISE 2.3

Applying and Modifying Column Settings

1. Open a document such as the one you created in Exercise 1.16 (1–16 Post) in the previous chapter or create one by entering a bulleted list of at least 10 or 12 items.

2. Select the text in the list. Click the Columns button on the Standard toolbar and drag to select 2 Columns. You can create up to six columns using the Columns toolbar button.

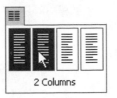

2 Columns

3. Release the mouse button to convert the list into two columns.

4. Add some additional items to the first column by clicking at the end of a line and pressing Enter to create new bullets. Notice how the items in the list shift to the second column to maintain relative balance between the columns. Word always tries to maintain this balance unless you tell it otherwise.

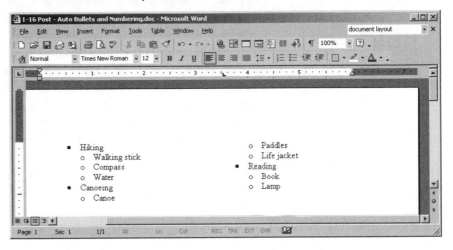

5. To designate where you would like the first column to break, position the insertion point in front of the item you want to move to the second column. Choose Insert ➢ Break and choose Column Break from the Break dialog box that opens.

6. To make additional modifications, select the list and choose Format ➤ Columns to open the Columns dialog box.

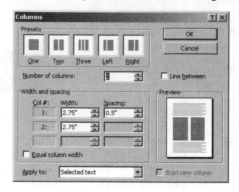

7. In the Columns dialog box, you can change the number of columns, the width of each column, and the distance between columns, and you can add a line between the columns. You can also choose from five preset columns layouts. Click each one to see the column width and spacing between columns. Notice that the Equal Column Width check box is checked on the first three options but not on the last two. With the last two preset column layouts, one column is wider than the other. If you want to change the column width or spacing of one of the first three presets, clear the Equal Column Width check box and then adjust the width and spacing using the up and down arrows next to each column setting. If you want to increase the number of columns, enter the preferred number, up to a maximum of 12, in the Number Of Columns text box. For this example, change the number of columns to **3** and leave them of equal width. Also, select the Line Between check box to insert a vertical line between the columns.

8. Click the OK button to close the Columns dialog box.

9. Save the document as **Columns Practice**. Choose File ➤ Close to close the document.

10. For further practice with columns, open a document with paragraphs of text and convert a couple of paragraph into columns by following the same steps above.

If nothing appears in the third column, it's because of the column break you inserted in step 5 of the exercise. When you insert a column break, Word no longer attempts to balance the columns. Nothing will move into the third column until column 2 reaches the end of the page. To force Word to balance the columns again, you can delete the column break. The easiest way to do this is to switch to Normal view (View ➢ Normal), click the Column Break divider, and press Delete. Switch back to Print Layout view; the list should now be balanced across all three columns.

Preparing a Document for Print with Page Setup Options

When you create a new blank document in Word, it has top and bottom margins of one inch and left and right margins of 1.25 inches. Its orientation is set to Portrait (vertical) as opposed to Landscape (horizontal) and to a letter-size page ($8^1/_2" \times 11"$). Any of these options can be changed in the Page Setup dialog box, shown in Figure 2.1.

FIGURE 2.1 The Page Setup dialog box contains options for changing margins, page orientation, and paper size.

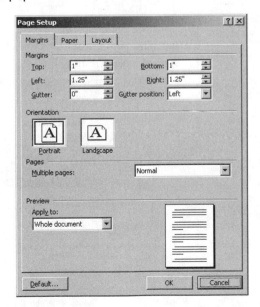

Microsoft
Exam
Objective

Modify document layout and Page Setup options

In Exercise 2.4, you'll change margins, page orientation, and paper size. You'll also change vertical alignment to position text between the top and bottom margins.

EXERCISE 2.4

Changing Document Layout and Page Setup Options

1. Click the New button to create a new blank document.

2. Choose File ➢ Page Setup to open the Page Setup dialog box shown earlier in Figure 2.1. Notice the default margin settings.

3. On the Margins tab, click the Landscape Orientation option and notice the change in margin settings.

4. Change the Top and Bottom Margins settings to 1" by clicking the down spin arrows three times.

5. Change the Left and Right Margins to 1.25". Because the spin arrows move the settings in increments of .1, you cannot use them to get to 1.25. Instead, type **1.25** in each text box.

6. Click the Paper tab, and select Legal from the Paper Size drop-down list. The width automatically changes from 8.5" to 14" and the height from 11" to 8.5".

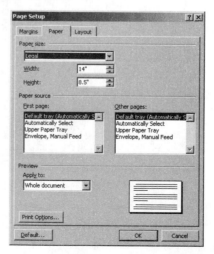

7. Click the Layout tab. You visited this tab earlier in the chapter (you came here from the Header And Footer toolbar), so it should look familiar.

8. Select Center from the Vertical Alignment drop-down list in the Page section of the Layout tab. With this setting, any text you type will be vertically centered between the top and bottom margins. It is most commonly used for the title page of a report or a letter that is less than one page long.

9. Click OK to save the Page Setup options. Because you chose vertical centering, the insertion point appears in the middle of the document at the left margin. To see how you might use this option, click the Center button on the Formatting toolbar, change the font to Arial, 36 pt Bold, and type **Word Formatting Secrets**.

10. Click the drop-down arrow on the Zoom button and change the zoom to 50% or lower to see the whole page and the effects of the changes you made. You can revisit Page Setup at any time to change the page setup and document layout options.

11. Close the document and save the changes.

Using Tables for Tabular Data

Tables are one of the most useful features available in Word. Using tables, you can present attractive tabular data with custom formatting, effortless editing, and considerable flexibility. Tables also play a significant role in web page design by forming the structure of a page to facilitate the placement of text and graphics. In this section, we'll show you how to create and modify tables, and in Chapter 6, "Customizing Tables and Graphics," we'll cover more of the advanced features.

A table is nothing more than a container for rows and columns of data. You can use a table to create a schedule, to represent numeric data, or to present a telephone list. Any time you find yourself pressing the Tab key more than once at the beginning of a paragraph, think about creating a table to hold the tabular text.

Create and modify tables

In Exercise 2.5, you'll create a table using the Insert Table button on the Standard toolbar and format it using AutoFormat.

EXERCISE 2.5

Creating and AutoFormatting Tables

1. Click the New button on the Standard toolbar to create a new blank document.

2. Click the Insert Table button on the Standard toolbar and drag to select four columns and two rows.

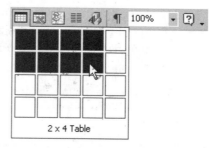

3. Release the mouse button to insert the table into the document.

4. In the first cell, type **First Name**. To move to the second column, press Tab.

5. Type **Last Name** in the second column and press Tab. Type **Work Phone** in the third column and **Home Phone** in the fourth column. Press Tab at the end of the row to move the insertion point to the first column, second row.

6. Enter the name and phone numbers of someone you know. When you press Tab at the end of this row, Word adds a new row to the table. Enter four more names and phone numbers into the table.

7. This is a good time to save the document, i.e., after you've entered data and before you start making modifications. Save the document as **Tables Practice**.

8. For quick and easy formatting, Word's AutoFormat feature can do the trick. AutoFormat automatically applies borders, border colors, font colors, font styles, shading, cell alignment, and table alignment to the table. Choose Table ➤ Table AutoFormat to open the Table AutoFormat dialog box.

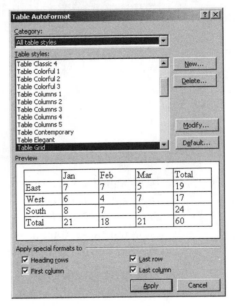

9. Scroll through the list of AutoFormat choices. Depending on the contents of the table you created, you can clear the check boxes at the bottom of the dialog box to remove special formatting from the Heading Rows, First Column, Last Row, and Last Column. Choose Table Colorful 2 AutoFormat with special formatting applied only to the heading row. Click Apply when you've found a format you like.

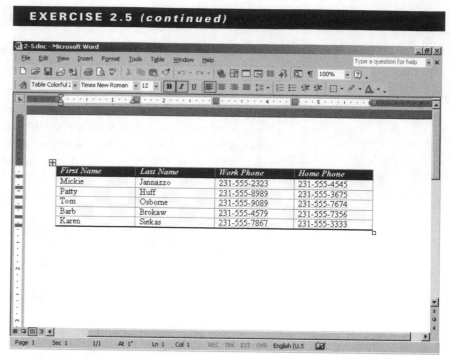

EXERCISE 2.5 *(continued)*

10. To change the AutoFormat, click in the table and choose Table ➢ Table AutoFormat again. To prepare this table for the next exercise, choose Table Normal from the AutoFormat Tables Styles list in the Table AutoFormat dialog box. Click Apply to apply the changes and close the dialog box.

11. Resave the document.

AutoFormatting a table is an efficient way to format a table, but you can also format a table manually. In Exercise 2.6, you'll learn to modify the table using the Tables And Borders toolbar and the Table Properties dialog box.

EXERCISE 2.6

Modifying a Table Manually

1. Reopen Tables Practice, the document you created in Exercise 2.5, if it is not already open, or open the file 2-6. To apply and modify

EXERCISE 2.6 (*continued*)

table formats, click the Tables And Borders button on the Standard toolbar. The pointer changes to a pencil shape. Turn off the Draw Table button by clicking the first button on the Tables And Borders toolbar—the arrow pointer reappears.

2. Using the Tables And Borders toolbar, you can apply borders, line styles, line widths, border colors, and shading. To apply any of these formatting options, you must first select a cell, multiple cells, or the entire table. To select

   a single cell, click the cell

   multiple cells, drag over the cells

   a column, move the mouse pointer to the top of the table and click when you see a downward-pointing black arrow

   a row, move the mouse pointer to the left of the row outside the table and click when you see a right-pointing arrow

   the entire table, move the mouse pointer to the top left of the table and click the four-headed arrow outside the table

   Practice selecting different parts of the table.

3. Select the first row of the table by dragging over the cells or by moving the mouse pointer outside the table to the left and clicking. Change the shading color by clicking the down arrow on the Shading Color button and choosing a color from the color palette that opens. While the row is still selected, change the font to Arial, 12 pt Bold. Click the table to deselect the row and see the results of the changes.

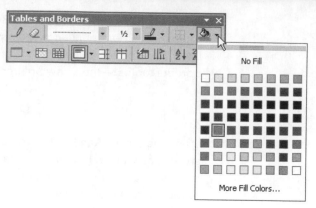

4. To add a column to the table, click a column and choose Table ≻ Insert ≻ Columns To The Right or Columns To The Left. For this exercise, click the third column and choose Columns To The Left. Type **Pager** in the first row of the new column.

5. To add a row to the table, click the row before or after the one you want to add and choose Table ≻ Insert ≻ Rows Above or Rows Below. For this exercise, click the top row and choose Rows Above.

6. Make this new row a title row by merging the cells to create a single column. Select the row and click the Merge Cells button on the Tables And Borders toolbar.

7. Type **Staff Telephone List** in the new row.

8. Widen the row by pointing to the bottom border of the first row, and when the pointer changes to a two-headed pointer, click and drag the border down about a half-inch.

9. Select the third row in the table and choose Table ≻ Delete Rows.

10. Center the title vertically and horizontally in the wider row by clicking the first row and clicking the down arrow on the Align button on the Tables And Borders toolbar. Select the Align Center button from the menu that opens.

EXERCISE 2.6 (*continued*)

11. Center the table between the left and right margins by clicking the table and choosing Table ➢ Table Properties to open the Table Properties dialog box.

12. Click the Center Alignment button.

13. Click OK to close the dialog box and apply the changes.

14. Select the second row to insert a bottom border below it. Click the Line Style button on the Tables And Borders toolbar and choose the first line style. Click the Line Weight button and choose $1^{1}/_{2}$" Line Weight. Click the Line Color button and choose a line color. Click the Border button and choose Bottom Border to apply the border.

15. Select the entire table. Click the Border button and choose Outside Border to apply a border to the table with the same line style, weight, and color as you applied in step 14.

16. Close the document and save the changes.

Previewing and Printing Documents, Envelopes, and Labels

When you are ready to print a document, you can preview it first to make sure it looks like you expect it to before sending it to the printer. You can also create and print envelopes and labels without dusting off that old typewriter.

Microsoft ✓ ***Exam Objective***   **Preview and print documents, envelopes, and labels**

In Exercise 2.7, you'll preview and print a letter.

EXERCISE 2.7

Previewing and Printing Documents, Envelopes, and Labels

1. Open the file 2–7.

2. Click the Print Preview button on the Standard toolbar to see what the letter will look like when it is printed.

3. In Print Preview, the mouse pointer changes to a magnifying glass. Click anywhere in the document to increase the zoom to see the document more clearly.

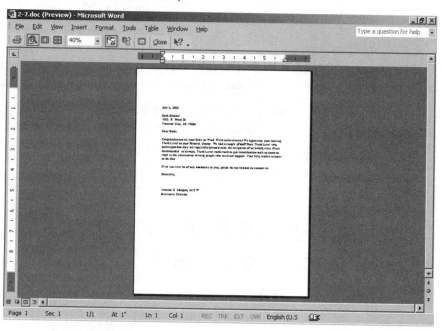

4. If you want to change something in the document, click the Magnifier button on the Print Preview toolbar. This turns the magnifier off so you can edit the document. Click the Magnifier button again to turn it back on.

EXERCISE 2.7 *(continued)*

5. When you are pleased with the way everything looks, click the Print button on the Print Preview toolbar to send the document directly to the default printer.

6. If you want to change print settings or make more substantive changes, click the Close button on the Print Preview toolbar to return to the Document window.

7. When you are ready to print again, click the Print button on the Standard toolbar or choose File ➢ Print to open the Print dialog box.

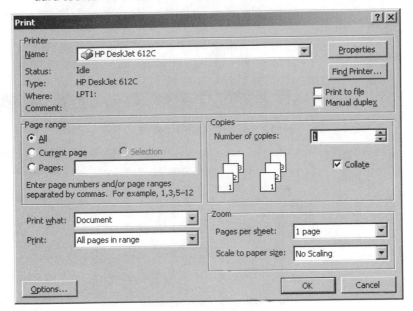

8. Select a printer from the Printer Name drop-down list in the Print dialog box.

9. Select the print range by choosing All, Current Page, or entering the pages you want to print in the Pages text box.

10. Enter how many copies you want to print in the Number Of Copies text box. If you want the pages collated, i.e., 1,2,3 as opposed to 1,1, 2,2,3,3, select the Collate check box.

EXERCISE 2.7 *(continued)*

11. When you are ready, click the OK button to send the document to the printer.

12. Save the document as **Letter to Barb**.

Now's it time to create an envelope to accompany the letter you created in Exercise 2.7. If your printer can't handle envelopes, you can create and print a single mailing label to put on the envelope instead.

If you want to create a form letter and then create labels to send to a number of people, you want to use Word's Mail Merge feature. You can learn about Mail Merge in Chapter 9, "Merging to Create Letters and Labels."

In Exercise 2.8, we'll walk you through the steps you need to know to create envelopes.

EXERCISE 2.8

Creating Envelopes

1. Open the Letter to Barb you created in Exercise 2.7, if necessary, or some other letter that contains an inside address (the recipient's address).

2. Choose Tools ➢ Letters And Mailings ➢ Envelopes And Labels to open the Envelopes And Labels dialog box.

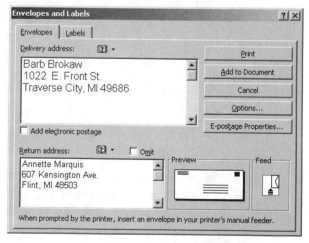

EXERCISE 2.8 *(continued)*

3. If your letter contains an inside address, the recipient's name and address appear automatically in the Delivery Address box on the Envelopes tab. If you previously entered your address information on the User Information tab of the Options dialog box (Tools ➤ Options ➤ User Information), then your information appears automatically in the Return Address box. You can edit the information in either box just as you would any other text.

4. If you are printing on an envelope that has a preprinted return address, click the Omit button above the Return Address box.

5. Click the Options button to change the default envelope options, including the envelope size, delivery point barcode, fonts, and address positions.

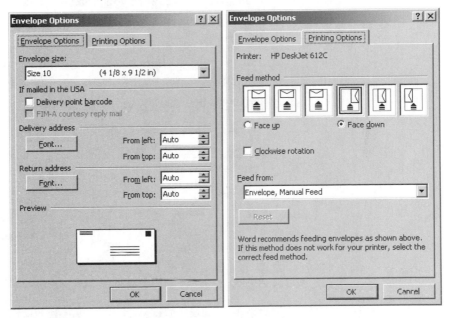

6. On the Printing Options tab, you can change the way the envelope feeds into the printer if Word has it wrong. Click OK to return to the Envelopes And Labels dialog box.

EXERCISE 2.8 *(continued)*

7. Put the envelope in the printer and click Print to print the envelope.

8. If you'd rather save the envelope with the letter to print later, click Add To Document on the Envelopes tab of the Envelopes And Labels dialog box. Word creates an envelope page and inserts it at the top of the document.

In Exercise 2.9, you'll learn how to create labels.

EXERCISE 2.9

Creating Labels

1. Open the Letter to Barb you created in Exercise 2.7, if necessary, or some other letter that contains an inside address (the recipient's address).

2. Choose Tools ➢ Letters And Mailings ➢ Envelopes And Labels, and click the Labels tab on the Envelopes And Labels dialog box.

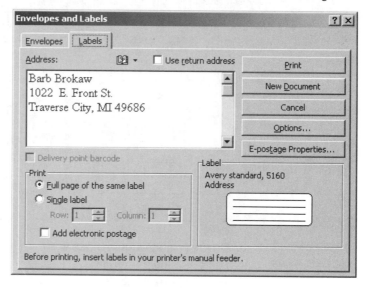

EXERCISE 2.9 *(continued)*

3. Verify the address that appears in the Address box or edit it as necessary. If you want to create a label for the return address instead, select the Use Return Address check box.

4. Word assumes that you plan to use standard address labels. A sheet of standard address labels includes thirty 1" × 2.63" labels on a page. If you want to use a different size label, click the Options button to select a different label from the Label Options dialog box.

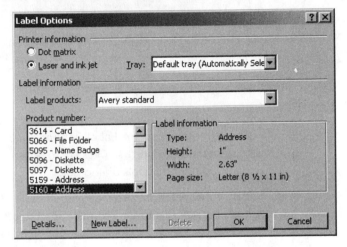

5. Choose the label maker from the Label Products list or, if you are using a generic equivalent, choose the name brand that is most similar.

6. Scroll through the list of product numbers to select the actual label you are using. If the label isn't there, we recommend going back to the store. However, if you really want to use the labels you have, choose the type of printer you plan to use from the Printer Information choices and click the New Label button to define the parameters of your labels. Click OK to save the new label.

EXERCISE 2.9 (continued)

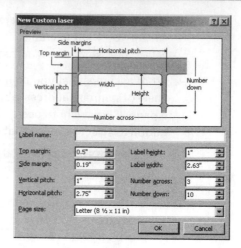

7. Select the new label from the list of available labels in the Product Number list in the Label Options dialog box. Custom labels appear at the top of the list. Click OK to return to the Labels tab of the Envelopes And Labels dialog box.

8. You can choose to create a full page of the same label or a single label. If this is a person you mail to often or if you are creating return address labels, choose Full Page Of The Same Label. If you want to create only one label, choose Single Label. Word automatically prints the label in the top-left corner of the label sheet using the label in the first row and first column. If you have already used that label, choose the first available label on the sheet by selecting the row and column.

9. To send the label or labels directly to the printer, click Print but be sure to insert the label sheet in the printer beforehand.

If you are creating return address labels or a sheet of the same label, you may want to save the labels in a new document so you can reuse them without going through the process of creating the labels again. Click the New Document button and then save the document before sending it to the printer. When you want to reprint the same labels, just open the saved document and send it to the printer.

10. Close the document.

Managing Documents

Knowing how to create documents is important, but if you don't know how to save them, organize them, and retrieve them, it's all pretty pointless. If you learn how to manage documents effectively, you never have to worry about remembering where you filed something or whether you can open a file someone sent you. If you already know how to manage files and folders using My Computer or Windows Explorer, you're a step ahead of the game. However, if you feel lucky whenever you find a document you saved to reopen it, this section is for you. Tools to find files, rename them, store them in folders, and convert files from different file formats are right at your fingertips in Word.

After you've successfully stored a document that you want to use as a model for other documents, you also never have to worry about accidentally overwriting it if you learn how to save the document as a template. As a template, you can reuse it, without worry, time and time again.

Managing Files and Folders in Word

Word's Open and Save As dialog boxes and New Document task pane include a number of tools to help you work with files. When you want to open a saved file, you can use the Open dialog box or the New Document task pane. You can also create a new document—one that has not already been saved—using the New Document task pane. When you want to save a document for the first time or resave a document with a different name, to a different location, or in a different format, you use the Save As dialog box. In this section, we'll focus on the Open dialog box and the New Document task pane—we'll cover the Save As dialog box a little later in this chapter.

Microsoft ✓ *Exam* *Objective*	**Manage files and folders for documents**

In Exercise 2.10, you'll explore the Open dialog box, shown in Figure 2.2, and learn how to find and open any available document. In addition, you'll learn how to create folders, move or copy files into folders, and rename and delete files and folders. You'll also see how to add a folder to the My Places bar for convenient access.

FIGURE 2.2 The Open dialog box is a great place to manage files and folders.

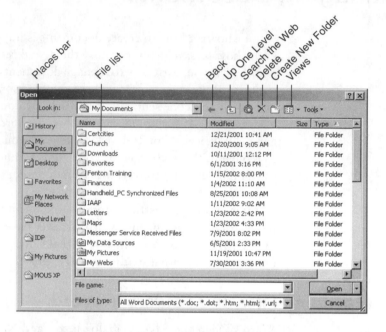

Opening Documents from the Open Dialog Box

1. Choose File ➢ Open to access the Open dialog box. The My Documents folder opens by default. To access a folder within the My Documents folder, for example, the My Pictures folder, double-click it in the file list. The folder name moves up to the Look In text box, and the files in the folder appear in the file list.

2. Click the Back button on the Open dialog box toolbar to return to the My Documents folder. The Back button takes you back to the last folder you were viewing. If you have accessed multiple folders, you can click the Back button multiple times to reverse your steps.

3. Click the Up One Level button to move up one level in the Folder structure. If you are viewing the My Documents folder, clicking Up One Level moves you to the Desktop, the top level in the structure. If you are in the My Pictures folder, clicking Up One Level takes you back to My Documents.

4. To search for files on the Internet, click the Search The Web button. This launches Internet Explorer. If you have always-on Internet access, this takes you immediately to a Microsoft search site, search.msn.com. If you have a dial-up connection or are not connected to the network, a connection dialog box opens. You can choose to connect or stay offline. If you click Stay Offline, you cannot do the search. Close Internet Explorer to return to the document, or choose File ➢ Open to go back to the Open dialog box.

5. To delete a file, select it and click the Delete button. If you want to delete more than one file, select them individually by holding Ctrl and clicking each one. To select contiguous files, select the first file you want in the list, hold Shift, and select the last file you want. Do not delete files unless you are 100% sure of what they are and 110% sure you want to delete them. Otherwise, it's better to leave them alone.

6. To create a folder to organize documents, click the Create New Folder button. Enter a name for the new folder and click OK.

7. To move files to the new folder, select the file or files you want to move (see step 5 to see how to select multiple files). You can use drag and drop if the new folder and the files you want to move are both visible—point to the selected files, drag them to the new folder, and drop them. If you can't see both the files you want to move and the new folder, select the files and press Ctrl+X to cut them. The files remain where they are but the file icons become transparent. Open the new folder by double-clicking it. The folder name appears in the Look In text box. Press Ctrl+V to paste the files into the folder. You can use the same technique to copy files, except you press Ctrl+C rather than Ctrl+X.

8. To change how you view the files in the Open dialog box, click the down arrow on the Views button. Views change how many files you can see at one time and how much information is available about each file. Select the view you prefer from the Views menu.

EXERCISE 2.10 *(continued)*

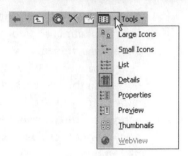

9. The Tools menu contains a number of file-management tools. You can search for files, rename files, delete files, print files, and add files to Favorites and folders to My Places. You can also view and edit a file's properties by selecting the file and choosing Tools ⮞ Properties.

   a. To add a folder to the Places bar, select the folder and choose Tools ⮞ Add To "My Places." An icon for the folder is added to the bottom of the Places bar. Right-click the Places bar to change the order of the items and to change the size of the icons so you can see more folders.

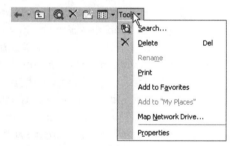

   b. To search for a file that you cannot find, choose Tools ⮞ Search. This opens the Search dialog box.

   c. Enter a word or phrase that appears in the file, the filename, or the file properties of the file you want to locate. This searches the entire contents of the file, the filename, and the file properties.

    d. Select the file locations you want to search from the Search In drop-down list.

    e. Select the file types you want to include in the search. If you know it's a Word document you are looking for, click the Results Should Be drop-down list, click the Office Files check box to deselect the entire list, and then click Word to include only Word documents in the search.

    f. Click the Search button to begin the search. Word returns the results in the Results text box. When you find the file you are looking for, double-click it to open it.

10. When you have finished working in the Open dialog box, you can open a file by double-clicking it or selecting it and clicking the Open button. You can also click the down arrow on the Open button to choose from several other options. Choose Open Read-Only or Open As Copy to preserve the original file and be forced to resave the file with a different name after you make changes to it. Choose Open In Browser if the file is a web page (*.htm, *.html) or other type of web page document. Choose Open And Repair if the file does not open normally. Open And Repair tries to repair a corrupted file.

The New Document task pane, new to Word 2002 and shown in Figure 2.3, is another way you can access files you want to work with. To open the task pane, choose File ➢ New.

FIGURE 2.3 The New Document task pane is a new way to create new files and access previously saved files.

The task pane, which appears on the right side of the Word application window, is divided into four sections:

- **Open A Document** lists the last four files you saved and has a More Documents link to open the Open dialog box described earlier.

- **New** includes Blank Document, Blank Web Page, and Blank E-mail Message.

- **New From Existing Document** is similar to Open As Copy. Click Choose Document to access the Open dialog box to select the file you want to use as the basis for a new document.

- **New From Template** lists recently used templates and links to access other templates. You'll learn more about templates in the next section.

At the bottom of the New Document task pane are three additional links:

- **Add Network Place** launches the Add Network Place Wizard, which you can use to create and use shared folders on your internal network and on external networks outside your organization.

- **Microsoft Word Help** launches Word's Help system.

- **Show At Startup** is an option that determines whether the New Document task pane opens automatically when you launch Word.

Using Pre-existing Templates and Creating Your Own

A template saves time by protecting documents that you need to reuse. Although Open Read-Only, Open As Copy, and Open As New, described earlier, provide some level of protection, it's too easy to forget to choose one of these options and overwrite your model document. By saving it as a template, you never have to worry about destroying the original. You can even place the template in a shared network folder so others can use it without concern that some other user will accidentally overwrite it, making it unusable for everyone else.

Word has a number of templates you can use for different types of documents, including letters, faxes, memos, reports, and even resumes. Some of these templates are installed as part of Word's typical installation and some are installed on demand. If you don't find the template you want or you want to customize one of the predefined templates, you can create your own templates and make them available from the Templates dialog box along with all the other templates.

Microsoft regularly makes additional templates available for free on the Microsoft.com website. You can access these templates if you have a web connection by choosing File ≻ New and clicking Templates On Microsoft.com.

| *Microsoft* ✓ *Exam* *Objective* | **Create documents using templates** |

In Exercise 2.11, you'll explore Word's predefined templates and learn how to create and save a custom template.

EXERCISE 2.11

Using, Creating, and Saving Templates

1. Choose File ➢ New to open the New Document task pane.

2. Click General Templates in the New From Template section to open the Templates dialog box.

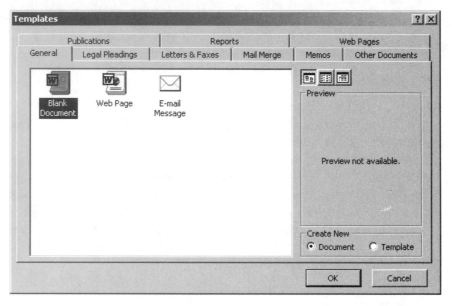

3. Click each tab to view all of the available predefined templates.

4. For this exercise, click the Memos tab and double-click Contemporary Memo to open a document based on the Contemporary Memo template.

You can use this document to create a memo or you can customize it and resave it as a personal memo template.

5. To create a memo, click in the memo fields To, From, and Re and enter replacement text. Select all of the memo text and replace it with the contents of your memo. Click File ➢ Save to open the Save As dialog box, and save the document as you would any other document.

6. To create a customized memo template that you can use again and again, enter the information you would use on every memo—your name, for example—and make other editing changes you want to the memo form.

    a. If you want to remove the circle graphic, click it so that handles appear around it and press the Delete key. The other graphic elements are in the background, so to delete them you have to switch to Header And Footer view (View ➢ Header And Footer). You can then select them and delete them.

    b. While in Header And Footer view, you may want to edit the footer or add something to the header. Remember to select Different First Page Header from the Page Setup dialog box if you don't want the header and footer to appear on the first page. See "Working with Headers and Footers" earlier in the chapter if you need to review the steps to do this.

7. When you've finished entering everything you want to appear on a standard memo form, you are ready to save the template. Choose File ➢ Save As to open the Save As dialog box.

8. From the Save As Type drop-down list, choose Document Template (*.dot). The Save In folder automatically changes to the Templates folder.

9. If you want to save the customized template to the General tab of the Templates dialog box, enter a name for the template in the File Name text box and click Save. If you want to create a templates subfolder for you to save your customized templates to, click the Create New Folder button and enter a name for the folder. This new folder becomes a tab in the Templates dialog box. When you click the tab, just the templates you save there appear. After you create the new folder, double-click it in the file list to open it (or single-click if your operating system is set to open folders with a single click), and the folder moves to the Save In text box. Enter a name for the template in the File Name text box and click Save.

EXERCISE 2.11 *(continued)*

10. To use the saved template, close the open document template, choose File ➢ New, and click General Templates from the New From Template section of the New Document task pane. If you save the template to the General tab, it is visible as soon as the dialog box opens. If you created a templates folder for it, click the tab you created and your template appears on the new tab. Double-click the template, and Word opens a document based on the template that you can use to write your first memo on the new form.

You can create a new template based on any other template by selecting the template in the Templates dialog box and choosing the Template option button on the bottom right of the dialog box.

In Exercise 2.11, you learned how to use the Contemporary Memo template and create a customized template based on it. Word includes a number of other templates, and each one works a little differently. To prepare for the exam, we recommend that you open several other templates, read the instructions included with each one, and practice working with them and customizing them as you did in the previous exercise.

Saving and Converting Documents

In our experience, the number one question asked by beginning Office users is "What is the difference between Save and Save As?" If you know the answer, go to the head of the class. If you are still not sure, here is your chance to clarify the difference once and for all. The first time you save a document, it doesn't matter which option you choose. Both Save and Save As take you to exactly the same place, the Save As dialog box, shown in Figure 2.4. This is because the first time you save a document, you have to tell Word what you want to name it and where you want to file it. After the first time, the only time you choose Save As is when you want to save a copy of the file or change the format of the file from a Word document to another type of document. If you are working with a document you've already saved, clicking the Save button or choosing File ➤ Save overwrites the original document. Choose Save As whenever you don't want to do this.

FIGURE 2.4 In the Save As dialog box, you can save documents, rename documents, create folders, and save copies of documents in Word and other document formats.

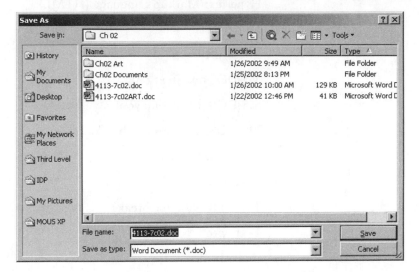

You can avoid the confusion by getting into the habit of choosing Save. When you need Save As, either it appears automatically (the first time you save a document) or you choose it because you want to save a copy of the document.

If you are sending a document to someone else who does not have Word or you are creating a document for use on a website, the Save As dialog box offers you the choice to save the file in a different file format. This is called converting a document. Following is a list of document types to and from which Word can convert documents. If the exact version of the software to which you want to convert the document isn't in the list, choose the more comparable earlier version; for example, for a WordPerfect 7 document, choose WordPerfect 5.*x* for Windows.

You can also use the Open dialog box to convert a non-Word document that someone sent you so you can work with it in Word. Choose the file type of the document from the Files Of Type drop-down list and open the file. If Word recognizes the format, it opens it directly. If it doesn't, Word opens the File Conversion dialog box to help you identify the encoding that makes the file readable.

Word is able to open documents in all of the formats listed below:

Document formats

Encoded plain text (auto-detected)

Hypertext Markup Language (HTML)

Lotus 1-2-3

Microsoft Excel

MS-DOS text (text only)

MS-DOS text with layout

MS-DOS text with line breaks

Rich Text Format

Text only

Text only with line breaks

Text with layout

Unicode files

Word 6.0 for Windows and Word 7.0 (Word 95) for Windows Export

Word 8.0 for Windows (Word 97)

Word version 2.*x* for Windows

Word version 3.*x*–5.*x* for MS-DOS

Word version 4–5.*x* for the Macintosh

Word version 6 for MS-DOS

Word version 6.*x* for Windows

WordPerfect 5.0 Secondary File

WordPerfect 5.1 for DOS

WordPerfect 5.1 or 5.2 Secondary File

WordPerfect 5.*x* for Windows

WordPerfect version 5.0

WordPerfect version 6.*x*

Works version 3.0 for Windows

Works version 4.0 for Windows

Microsoft ✓ *Exam* *Objective*	**Save documents using different names and file formats**

In Exercise 2.12, you will save a document to a new location using a different name and also convert it to a different file format.

EXERCISE 2.12

Saving Documents Using Different Names and File Formats

1. Open any Word document, such as Letter to Barb you created in Exercise 2.7.

2. Choose File ➢ Save As to open the Save As dialog box.

3. Create a new folder by clicking the Create New Folder button and entering a name. Double-click the new folder to open it.

4. Change the name of the document in the File Name text box. If you were to save the document now, you would be saving a copy of the original document under a new name and in a different folder location. If that is all you want to do, click Save to save the copy and close the dialog box.

5. To convert the document to a different format, such as Microsoft Works 2000, open the Save As Type drop-down list from the Save As dialog box, scroll down, and choose Works 2000 (*.wps) from the list. Word automatically changes the document extension to .wps. Click Save to convert the document.

Document extensions, the three characters after the filename, are not visible by default. If you want to make them visible, open My Computer from the Desktop and choose Tools ➢ Folder Options. Click the View tab and clear the Hide File Extensions For Known File Types check box. Click the Like Current Folder button, and then click Yes and OK to apply the change to all of the folders on your system.

6. Depending on the version of software to which you are converting, Word may present a warning message that you may lose some formatting during the conversion because the other software does not have the same formatting features as Word 2002. Click Yes to continue with the conversion—Word returns to the document when it is finished.

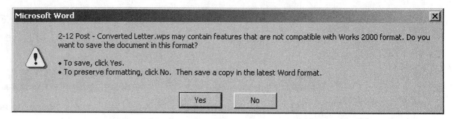

7. Choose File ➢ Open to see how Word saved the file. Change the document types you are viewing to All Files in the Files Of Type drop-down list. Open the folder you created to see the Works document—notice the different icon in front of the file to indicate what kind of file it is.

When you open a file in Word that was created in a different format and then resave it, Word warns you that it will resave it in Word format. If you want to retain the original format, choose Save As and resave the file in that format.

Summary

In this chapter, we reviewed the tools you can use to format and manage documents in Word. We covered these topics:

- Working with headers and footers, including creating a different first page header. We also discussed how to use AutoText entries to create headers and footers and how to edit them to meet your specifications.

- Working with newspaper columns and how to modify and balance columns.

- Using the Page Setup options to prepare a document for printing.

- Using tables to present parallel columns, including using AutoFormat and modifying tables manually.

- Previewing documents before printing, and creating and printing envelopes and labels.

- Using the file-management tools available in the Open dialog box. These included creating folders, renaming and deleting files, moving and copying files, and adding and customizing the Places bar. We also briefly covered using Search to find files that you cannot locate.

- Using predefined templates and creating custom templates that you can use over and over again.

- Saving documents and converting documents to different file formats.

Chapter

3

Creating and Using Graphics

MOUS WORD 2002 CORE EXAM OBJECTIVES COVERED IN THIS CHAPTER:

- ✓ Insert images and graphics
- ✓ Create and modify diagrams and charts

The old saying "A picture is worth a thousand words" is true—pictures, or graphics, can really enhance your message. Images add visual interest to a document and can enhance almost every document, making them more interesting and often more inviting. In some documents, such as newsletters, graphics have come to be an expected ingredient. Graphics can illustrate a concept, serve as a corporate logo, or simply make your document look better. Graphics can consist of charts, line art, text, clip art, or photos. You can either use existing images stored in a file or create your own graphic objects.

In this chapter, you'll learn how to insert graphics from a variety of sources into Word documents and how to create and modify diagrams and charts. If you'd like to learn more about modifying graphics after you insert them, refer to Chapter 6, "Customizing Tables and Graphics."

Before you begin this chapter, you should go to the Sybex website and download the file 4113Ch03.zip. This package contains the files necessary to complete some of the exercises in this chapter. In addition, it contains files of what most of the documents should look like after you complete the exercise. These files are affixed with the word *Post*.

Working with Graphics

Before you can begin to work with images and graphics, you need to know some things about how Office XP organizes images so you can find the art you are looking for. In addition to the art that comes with Office XP, you can organize you own images and access images from the Web using the Microsoft Clip Organizer.

Inserting Pictures into Documents

In Office XP, the task pane offers options for searching for or organizing clips. You can quickly access clips online or look at tips for finding the perfect clip. After you find the clip you want, you can insert it directly into your document.

Microsoft Exam Objective

Insert images and graphics

In Exercise 3.1, you'll use the task pane to search for clip art and then insert it into a document.

NOTE

The first time you open the Insert Clip Art task pane, you are prompted to catalog your media files. You'll have better luck searching for clips if you let Office do this, and it takes only a few minutes.

EXERCISE 3.1

Searching For and Inserting Clip Art

1. Create a new blank document by clicking the New button on the Standard toolbar.

2. To access the Microsoft Clip Organizer, click the Insert Clip Art button on the Drawing toolbar. If the Drawing toolbar is not visible, click the Drawing toolbar button on the Standard toolbar.

Or, you can choose Insert ➢ Picture ➢ Clip Art to display the task pane with Clip Art options.

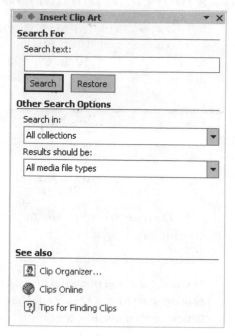

3. Enter a keyword or two in the Search Text box. (See Table 3.1 for tips on what to enter.) For this exercise, enter **business, computer**.

4. Choose which collection(s) you wish to search by selecting from the Search In drop-down list. Click the Everywhere check box to search All Collections.

5. Choose the type of file you're looking for—clip art, photographs, movies, or sound—from the Results Should Be drop-down list. Select All Media File Types.

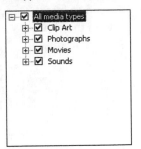

6. Click the Search button to display clips that meet your criteria.

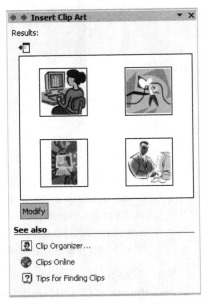

7. If you wish to search again using different terms, click the Modify button to return to the Search pane so you can modify the search criteria.

EXERCISE 3.1 *(continued)*

8. When you move the mouse pointer over a clip, a drop-down arrow indicator, called the Clip Options button, appears on its right border. Click the Clip Options button to see a shortcut menu with options, such as Insert, Copy, and Delete From Clip Organizer, for working with the clip.

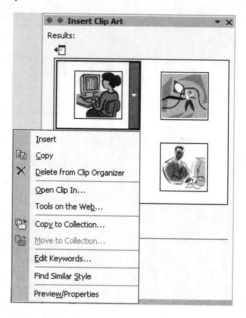

9. To insert a clip, choose Insert from the shortcut menu (or, if you have not opened the shortcut menu, you can click the clip to insert it). After the clip is placed in your document, chances are you will want to adjust its size, position, and text-wrapping properties. See "Positioning and Resizing Pictures" in Chapter 6.

10. Close the document without saving the changes. This also closes the Insert Clip Art task pane.

The Microsoft Clip Organizer, shared by all of the Office applications, has been dramatically revised in this version of Office. It contains an even broader selection of clips, including pictures, sounds, and motion clips. Although you can still browse the clips by category (referred to as *collections*), it is now much easier to search for the clips you want. The Microsoft Clip Organizer is a great place to catalog and manage all of the graphics, sound files, and animated graphics files you have stored anywhere on your system. The Microsoft Clip Organizer is a freestanding application you can also launch directly from the Programs menu— look for a folder called Microsoft Office Tools and launch it from there. You can organize your clips, import clips from other sources, search and browse the clips, and insert clips into applications that are not part of the Office suite.

You can have better luck searching for clips if you make use of the search tips listed in Table 3.1.

TABLE 3.1 Search Tips

Search For	Results to Expect
A particular word: **school**	Clips that are cataloged with **school** as a keyword
Multiple words separated by commas: **school, teacher**	Clips that have one or both of the keywords you typed
Words in quotes: **"school teacher"**	Clips that have **school teacher** as a keyword
Multiple words without quotes or commas: **school teacher**	Clips that have both keywords you typed
Filenames with wildcards: **sc*.jpg**	Media clips with filenames such as **school.jpg** and **scooter.jpg**

Not all of the clips visible in the Clip Organizer are installed in a typical Office installation. When you try to insert a clip that was not installed, you may be prompted to insert the Office XP CD-ROM that contains the clip.

Inserting Pictures from Other Sources

In addition to using the Clip Organizer as a source of art, you can insert pictures into your document from any file you can access, such as a CD or floppy disk. You can also format pictures inserted from a file by using the buttons on the Picture toolbar. In Exercise 3.2, you'll insert a picture that isn't in the Clip Organizer.

EXERCISE 3.2

Inserting a Picture from Another Source

1. Locate a clip art image or photograph. If you or a friend has a Sony Mavica camera, take a picture and save it on a floppy disk or CD. Or if you have film to develop, ask to also get the pictures put on a disk. You can also download a photo, 3.2 Puerto Rico.jpg from the Sybex website.

2. Open a document where you want the picture to appear.

3. Choose Insert ➢ Picture ➢ From File, or display the Picture toolbar and click the Insert Picture button to open the Insert Picture dialog box.

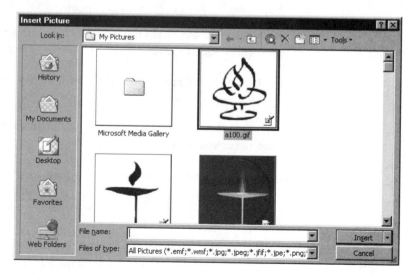

4. Locate the picture file.

5. Click the Insert button to insert the selected picture into your document.

6. Close the document and click Yes to save the changes.

Inserting Scanned Graphics and Digital Photos

With today's digital cameras, scanners, and endless CD-ROMs filled with photos and clip art, it's pretty easy to capture just the right images for your documents. This may take a little legwork, but if a picture is out there, there is a way to turn it into a digital image. Office has built-in tools to accept images directly from scanners and digital cameras.

To import images from a digital camera, scanner, or other TWAIN device, first make sure the device is connected to your computer and the software for the device is installed through Windows. Exercise 3.3 walks you through the steps of importing images.

Importing Images from a Scanner or Camera

For this exercise to work, you must have a scanner or digital camera connected to the computer.

1. Set up the picture in the scanning device.

2. Choose Insert ➤ Picture ➤ From Scanner Or Camera.

3. Select the device you want to use from the Device drop-down list in the Insert Picture From Scanner Or Camera dialog box.

4. Choose the resolution you want—Web Quality or Print Quality—depending on how you plan to use the picture.

5. Click Insert, or if you are using a scanner and want to change the image settings, choose Custom Insert. If the Insert button is unavailable because your scanner doesn't support automatic scanning, you must choose Custom Insert.

You can modify, reposition, and resize scanned images and digital photos just like any other images. See Chapter 6 for more information about working with graphic images.

Using Microsoft Drawing Tools

If you want to design your own graphic objects, Microsoft Draw has a bundle of tools for you to use. You can unleash your creativity or just have fun drawing your own graphics using the drawing tools on Office XP's Drawing toolbar. The Drawing toolbar is available in Word, Excel, and PowerPoint, and some drawing tools are available in the Access toolbox. You use the same methods to create a drawing with the drawing tools no matter which application you are using.

To display the drawing toolbar in Word, use either of these methods:

- Click the Drawing button on the Standard toolbar.

- Right-click any toolbar and choose Drawing, or choose View ➤ Toolbars and then select Drawing from the toolbar list.

 When you display the Drawing toolbar, your Word document automatically changes to Print Layout view if it is not already in that view.

The Drawing toolbar includes two broad categories of menus and buttons. The first set, beginning with the AutoShapes drop-down list button and ending with the Insert Picture button, is used to create drawing objects. The remaining buttons on either side of this set are used to format existing objects.

Working with the Drawing Canvas

When you create an object with the Drawing toolbar, Word inserts the objects into the drawing canvas. With the drawing canvas, you can create drawings in which multiple objects maintain their position in relation to one another. You can easily adjust the size of the drawing canvas to fit any size drawing you create. You can also format the drawing canvas itself by adding colors, lines, and fills, changing the size of the drawing area, and adjusting the layout in relation to text on the page.

To activate the drawing canvas and the Drawing Canvas toolbar, shown in Figure 3.1, just click any object tool on the Drawing toolbar.

FIGURE 3.1   You can adjust the drawing canvas to fit any size drawing and keep drawing objects together.

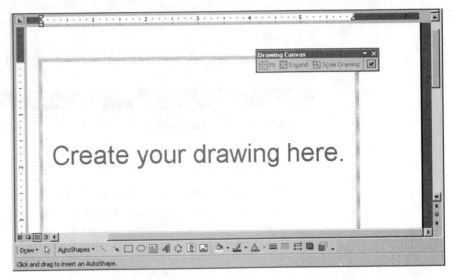

You can add any number of different objects, such as lines, ovals, rectangles, AutoShapes, and WordArt to the drawing canvas and then resize and reposition them in the canvas. (You'll learn more about resizing and repositioning graphics in Chapter 6.) When you click outside the drawing canvas, all of the objects contained within it move together as if they were a single object.

Circumventing the Drawing Canvas

If all you want is a simple line or other single object, using the drawing canvas may seem like overkill. To create an object without using the drawing canvas, click the object button you want on the Drawing toolbar, and when the drawing canvas appears in your document, press Esc to dispose of it. You can then drag to create the object without the added overhead the drawing canvas offers. You can also turn the drawing canvas off permanently by choosing Tools ➢ Options and on the General tab, clearing the Automatically Create Drawing Canvas When Inserting AutoShapes check box.

Inserting AutoShapes

AutoShapes is a collection of graphic objects such as lines; basic shapes such as triangles, cylinders, hearts, and braces; block arrows; and flowchart shapes you can insert into documents. Whether or not you plan to use the drawing canvas in Word, when you click the AutoShapes button in any application, a submenu appears with a list of AutoShape categories.

In Exercise 3.4, you'll insert an AutoShape into a document.

EXERCISE 3.4

Inserting AutoShapes

1. Create a new blank document. Click the Drawing button on the Standard toolbar to activate the Drawing toolbar, if it is not already visible.

2. Click the AutoShapes button on the Drawing toolbar to see the list of AutoShape categories. If you would like to keep the AutoShapes menu available, point to the title bar at the top of the menu and drag the toolbar onto the document window.

3. Click a category, such as Basic Shapes, and select a shape. When the menu closes, position the insertion point where you want to place the AutoShape, and then click in your document to insert it.

4. When you click to insert the selected AutoShape, it is created in its default size. If you want to create a custom size, position the insertion point in your document after selecting an AutoShape (notice that the mouse pointer appears as a crosshair). Drag diagonally (from the top left to the bottom right) to insert an AutoShape in a custom size.

5. If you've already inserted the AutoShape, click to select it, and then drag one of the AutoShape's corner selection handles, the small circles that surround a selected AutoShape, to increase or decrease its size. To ensure that you are resizing the shape proportionally, you may want to hold down the Shift key as you drag the corner selection handle.

6. To move the AutoShape, point to it and drag when the pointer changes to a four-headed arrow.

7. Close the document without saving the changes.

Working with Special AutoShapes

Callout AutoShapes are text boxes used for annotating other objects or elements. When you insert a callout in your document, the insertion point automatically appears inside the callout. To place text in any closed AutoShape except those created using the Lines category, right-click the AutoShape and choose Add Text from the shortcut menu. When you do, the insertion point appears in the object, and the Text Box toolbar appears.

Curve, Freeform, and Scribble objects in the Line menu are AutoShape line objects that can be used to create any type of shape. Each of these tools works somewhat differently, so you should play with them a little to see which works best for the drawing you want to create. To create a Curve, Freeform, or Scribble AutoShape, follow these steps:

1. Click the AutoShapes drop-down list button and highlight Lines to display its menu of AutoShapes.

2. In the menu, click the Curve, Freeform, or Scribble button.

   a. To create a curve, click the Curve button and then click in the document where you want to begin. Move the mouse pointer and click again to create the first line. Move the mouse pointer again to create a curve and click where you want to change direction. Double-click to form the end of the line, or rejoin the beginning point of the first line to close the shape.

   b. To create a freeform shape, click the Freeform button. Click and drag the mouse pointer to draw a line. Double-click to end the shape, or rejoin the beginning point of the first line to close the shape.

   c. To use the Scribble tool, click the Scribble button. Click and drag the mouse pointer to draw a line. Release the button to create the shape, or rejoin the beginning point of the first line to close the shape.

Creating Flowcharts

Almost anyone involved in business today has been asked at one time or another to create a flowchart. Even if you don't know what all the different shapes mean, a basic flowchart is a great way to analyze the steps of a process. AutoShapes provides all the tools you need to create professional-looking flowcharts with minimal effort.

   To create a flowchart you need two objects: shapes and lines to connect the shapes. With AutoShapes, you can create the flowchart shapes and then use connectors to connect the shapes. After the two shapes are connected, you can move one or the other of them and have it retain its connection. Figure 3.2 shows a simple flowchart using connectors.

FIGURE 3.2   To design a flowchart, create shapes using the Flowchart shapes and then use connectors to pull them all together.

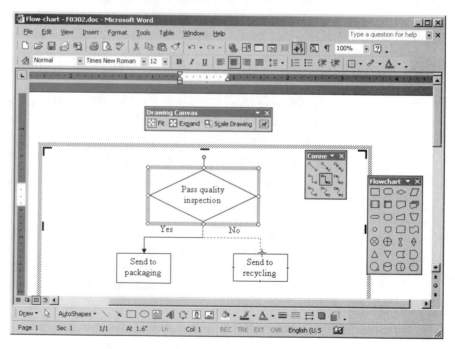

In Exercise 3.5, you'll create a flowchart using AutoShapes.

Creating a Flowchart

1. Create a new blank document.

2. Select the first Flowchart shape you want to use from the AutoShapes ➢ Flowchart menu. For this exercise, choose the Decision shape. Click in your document to create the shape within a drawing canvas.

   If you turn off the drawing canvas option as discussed earlier in the chapter, you cannot connect the flowchart objects. To turn the drawing canvas back on, choose Tools ➢ Options and select Automatically Create Drawing Canvas When Inserting AutoShapes on the General tab. You must then re-create the shape you created in step 1.

3. Right-click the object and choose Add Text to enter the text **Pass quality inspection** into the shape. Resize as necessary. To center text in the shape, click the Center button on the Formatting toolbar.

4. Create a Flowchart object using the Process shape, and position it underneath and to the left of the first object.

5. Right-click the object, choose Add Text, and enter **Send to packaging**. You may have to resize the shape by dragging the shape's handles to accommodate the text. You can also select the text and change the font size so it can fit in a smaller shape.

6. Select a connector from the Connectors submenu on the AutoShapes menu.

7. Move the pointer into the first Flowchart object; blue handles appear on the sides of the object.

8. Click the handle you want to connect and drag toward the second object. When blue handles appear on the second object, drag the line to connect to the side you want. Click to complete the connection.

9. Add a second Process shape to the right of the first one and enter the text **Send to recycling**.

10. Repeat Steps 6–8 to draw a connector to this shape.

EXERCISE 3.5 *(continued)*

11. Close and save the document.

To insert text on the lines, such as Yes and No, create a text box using the Text Box button on the Drawing toolbar. To remove the border from the text box, click the Line Style button on the Drawing toolbar. Choose More Lines, and on the Colors And Lines tab, change the Line Color to No Line.

The Drawing toolbar has a number of other tools to create lines, arrows, rectangles, ovals, text boxes, and WordArt and to format these objects with fill colors, line colors, and line styles.

Although you are not expected to know how to create all of these objects for the Word Core MOUS exam, you should take your time experimenting with the other drawing tools.

By adding a splash of color and design to your documents with these simple objects, you'll make your documents be noticed in ways that plain text just can't. One of these additional tools on the Drawing toolbar, Insert Diagram Or Organization Chart, is the focus of one of the MOUS objectives, so we'll show you how to use this feature in the next section.

Constructing Diagrams and Organizational Charts

Microsoft Organization Chart has been available as an add-in application for many versions of Office. For the first time, however, you can create organizational charts as a built-in feature of Office XP. In addition, you can create other types of diagrams such as Cycle and Venn diagrams.

Microsoft
✓ *Exam*
Objective

Create and modify diagrams and charts

To create a diagram, click the Insert Diagram Or Organization Chart button on the Drawing toolbar. This opens the Diagram Gallery dialog box, from which you can choose a diagram type.

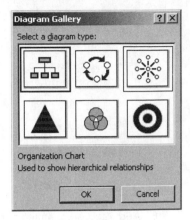

Creating an Organization Chart

When you select the Organization Chart from the Diagram Gallery dialog box, Office creates an Organization Chart object with four boxes: one manager and three subordinates. You can add additional boxes, delete boxes, and reposition boxes to fit your specific needs. In Exercise 3.6, we'll show you how.

EXERCISE 3.6

Creating an Organization Chart

1. Create a new blank document, and click the Insert Diagram Or Organization Chart button on the Drawing toolbar.

2. Click the first button on the Diagram Gallery dialog box to select an organization chart, and click OK.

3. Click the top box and enter your name, press Enter, and type **President**.

4. Click the left box and enter another person's name. Press Enter and type **Sales Director**. Enter additional names and titles in the remaining two boxes.

EXERCISE 3.6 *(continued)*

5. To add an additional box, click to select the box to which the new box is related, and choose Insert Shape from the Organization Chart toolbar. If you click the down arrow to the right of the Insert Shape button, you can choose to add a subordinate, coworker, or assistant. Select the Sales Director box, and choose Subordinate from the drop-down menu.

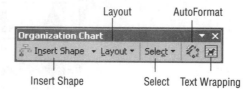

6. Add a coworker shape and an assistant shape to the other two boxes.

7. Delete the coworker shape you just created by selecting it and pressing Delete.

8. The Layout button on the Organization Chart toolbar gives you options to change the layout of your chart from the standard horizontal configuration to one that is more vertical. To change the layout, select the manager shape at the top of the section you want to alter and then select Both Hanging, Left Hanging, and Right Hanging from the Layout drop-down menu.

9. You can also change the size of the Organization Chart object by choosing Fit Organization Chart To Contents, Expand Organization Chart, or Scale Organization Chart from the Layout menu. To have Office automatically rearrange and resize the org chart to fit the object frame, choose AutoLayout from the Layout menu (this option may not do anything if you've already used one of the other sizing options).

10. As charts become more complex, it becomes harder to select individual sections that you want to move or alter in some way. You can use the Select button on the Organization Chart toolbar to do the selecting for you. Select the first box in a section you want to select, and then choose from the following:

   a. **Level** to select all the boxes on the same level

    b. Branch to select all subordinates

    c. All Assistants to select the assistants in the branch you select

    d. All Connecting Lines to select the lines connecting with the box you select

11. To make your org chart stand out, click the AutoFormat button on the Organization Chart toolbar. This opens the Organization Chart Style Gallery shown here.

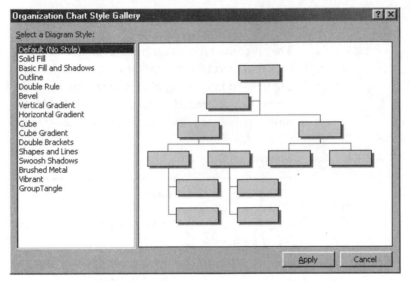

12. From here, you can choose a style for your chart that affects the box shape and style, colors, fills, and lines. With some of the Auto-Format styles, you have to change the size of the font you are using or increase the size of the boxes to accommodate the text.

13. After you complete an organizational chart and want to position it within a report or larger document, you may become concerned with how the text wraps around the object. You can change the text wrapping by clicking the Text Wrapping button on the Organization Chart toolbar.

14. Close and save the document.

If you work in company that has a nontraditional organizational structure, i.e., shared leadership, partnership, or other less-hierarchical structure, you have to be creative to represent your structure with this tool. You cannot position an additional box at the top level. In this case, you might want to use the top level to represent your overall company, board, or maybe even your customers. Another option is to create your organizational chart using AutoShapes and connectors (see "Inserting AutoShapes" and "Creating Flowcharts" earlier in the chapter).

Creating Conceptual Diagrams

The other five types of diagrams available from the Diagram Gallery when you click the Insert Diagram Or Organization Chart button on the Drawing toolbar can be used interchangeably to represent a process or related concepts. Select the type of diagram that most closely resembles the message you want to communicate. Table 3.2 shows the types of diagrams and how they can be used.

TABLE 3.2 Conceptual Diagrams

Diagram	Name	Use
	Cycle diagram	Represents a process that has a continuous cycle.
	Radial diagram	Shows relationships of multiple entities/concepts to a central point.
	Pyramid diagram	Illustrates entities or concepts that are based on a foundation.
	Venn diagram	Demonstrates entities that overlap.
	Target diagram	Identifies steps toward a central goal.

The Diagram toolbar, shown in Figure 3.3, is similar to the Organization Chart toolbar with only a couple of exceptions.

FIGURE 3.3   Use the Diagram toolbar to add elements and format the diagram.

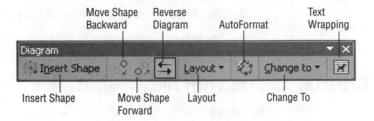

In addition to Insert Shape, Layout, AutoFormat, and Text Wrapping buttons, you also have the ability to change the level or position of a particular shape using the Move Shape Backward, Move Shape Forward, and Reverse Diagram buttons. You can also use the Change To button to convert a diagram from one type to another, for example, if you created a Pyramid diagram and now feel your message would be better communicated by a Venn diagram. In Exercise 3.7, you'll create a Cycle diagram.

EXERCISE 3.7

Creating a Cycle Diagram

1. Create a new, blank document.

2. Click the Insert Diagram Or Organization Chart button on the Drawing toolbar.

3. Select the Cycle diagram and click OK.

4. Click the text box on the right and type **Conduct customer satisfaction survey**.

5. Click the text box on the bottom and type **Review results in QI Committee**.

6. Enter **Develop recommendations for improvement** in the text box on the left.

7. While the third text box is still selected, click the Insert Shape button on the Diagram toolbar. If you have resized any text boxes or made any other design changes, you may be asked if you want to turn AutoLayout on to continue. Click Yes. The new shape and text box appear to the left of the selected text box.

EXERCISE 3.7 *(continued)*

8. Enter **Make necessary changes to improve service** in the new text box.

9. Click AutoFormat and choose an AutoFormat option.

10. Close the document and save the changes.

Creating Charts with Microsoft Graph

Microsoft Graph is Office XP's add-on charting tool that lets you create charts to represent numerical data. Although you can create more dynamic charts using Excel, Microsoft Graph is an easy-to-use tool that lets you create attractive charts right in your Word documents. In Exercise 3.8, you'll create a chart using Microsoft Graph.

EXERCISE 3.8

Creating a Chart with Microsoft Graph

1. Create a new blank document or open an existing document to which you'd like to add a chart.

2. Choose Insert ➤ Object from the Application menu to open the Object dialog box.

3. Select Microsoft Graph Chart from the Object Type list and click OK.

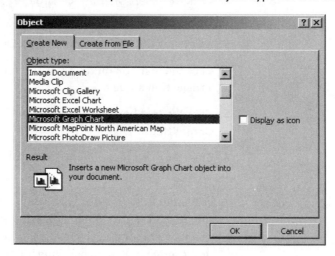

Alternatively, you can choose Insert ➤ Picture ➤ Chart to launch Microsoft Graph.

4. Graph contains two windows: a datasheet, which includes sample data, and a chart.

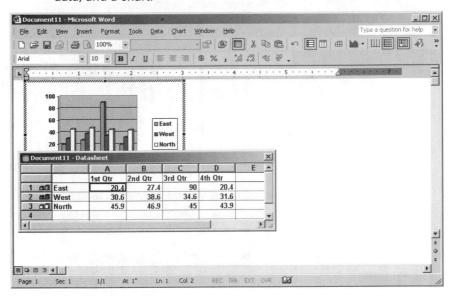

5. Replace the labels (text) in the top row and left column with your labels and the values in the remaining cells with your numbers, and you have a basic bar chart. Enter the data shown here in the datasheet. You may have to expand the Datasheet window to see all of the data. As you enter data, the chart changes to reflect the new data.

		A	B	C	D	E
		FG	3 - point	Blocks	Steals	
1	Player 1	14	6	2	1	
2	Player 2	19	9	2	1	
3	Player 3	6	3	4	3	
4	Player 4	23	2	1	0	
5	Player 5	15	2	0	0	
6						

Document12 - Datasheet

You can easily select all the data in the chart and delete it by clicking the gray button on the top left of the datasheet (above the row numbers and to the left of the columns) and then pressing the Delete key.

EXERCISE 3.8 *(continued)*

6. In this example, you may notice that not all of the data labels, which identify the columns of data, appear in the chart. This is because they are too wide. To change the alignment of the text, right-click the data labels and choose Format Axis from the shortcut menu.

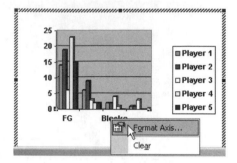

7. Click the Alignment tab, drag the Orientation arrow down to −45 degrees, and click OK (you'll do more formatting in Exercise 3.9).

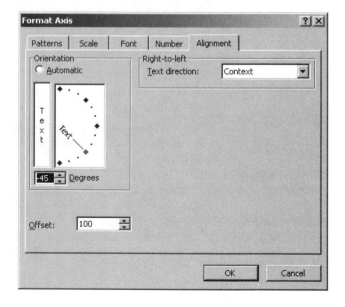

8. To delete a column or row you don't need, click the column or row header in the datasheet and press Delete.

9. Close the datasheet at any point to place the chart in your document.

10. Resize and reposition the chart object as you would any other object. To change the text wrapping on the chart, first activate the Picture toolbar (View ➤ Toolbars ➤ Picture). Select the chart and click the Text Wrapping button on the Picture toolbar as described earlier in this chapter.

11. To edit the contents of the chart, double-click the chart to open the Chart object so you can edit the individual objects inside it. To select the entire object again for moving or sizing, click outside the chart, and then click once on the Chart object.

12. Close the document and save the changes.

Formatting a Chart

Microsoft Graph is an OLE server, which means it creates objects that you can use in other applications. While your chart is active or whenever you double-click a chart in a document, the toolbars and menus change from the primary application's to Graph's. You have all the features you'll need to create a great looking representation of your numerical data.

In Exercise 3.9, you'll format a chart and objects within the chart.

EXERCISE 3.9

Formatting a Chart

1. Open 3-9.doc from the Sybex website. Double-click the chart to activate it. Right-click and choose Chart Options to open the Chart Options dialog box.

2. Enter **Basketball Individual Stats** in the Chart Title box on the Titles tab of the Chart Options dialog box and press Tab.

3. Enter **Stats** in the Category (X) Axis text box.

4. Enter **AVG PG** in the Value (Z) Axis text box.

5. Click the Gridlines tab and select the Major Gridlines check box in the Category (X) Axis section.

6. Click OK to close the Chart Options dialog box.

7. Right-click the Value Axis Title text (AVG PG), and choose Format Axis Title from the shortcut menu. Click the Alignment tab, and drag the Orientation arrow to 90 degrees. Click OK.

8. Point to the selection handle on the bottom-right corner of the chart object and drag to make the chart larger—you may have to move the datasheet out of the way by dragging its title bar.

9. Click the blank area of the document to insert the chart into the document.

10. Close and resave the document.

When the chart is active, you can also format individual elements of the chart. For example, you can select the Player 1 Data Series and change the color of the columns. To do this, it's easiest to use the Chart Objects drop-down list on the Chart toolbar to select the object and then click the Format [*Object Name*] button.

Summary

This chapter focused on using Word's graphics tools. Even though the Word Core exam has only two objectives related to graphics, we included more depth so you can feel comfortable working with graphics in your documents. Think how impressive your next proposal will be when you include a flowchart, an organization chart, and a diagram to illustrate your points.

In this chapter, we covered the following topics:

- Inserting pictures from the Microsoft Clip Organizer

- Locating and inserting pictures from sources other than the Microsoft Clip Organizer

- Using the Drawing toolbar and the drawing canvas, including eliminating the drawing canvas temporarily and permanently

- Inserting and modifying AutoShapes

- Creating a flowchart

- Using organization charts and conceptual diagrams

- Using Microsoft Graph to create charts based on numerical data

Chapter

4

Collaborating in a Workgroup

MOUS WORD 2002 CORE EXAM OBJECTIVES COVERED IN THIS CHAPTER:

✓ Compare and Merge documents

✓ Insert, view and edit comments

✓ Convert documents into Web pages

Workgroup collaboration is not a new concept. People collaborate every day with coworkers, with members of a project team, and with interdepartmental committees. What is often lacking from these teams, however, is an efficient and effective way to collectively develop the documents that report on the work of the group. Word offers a wide array of workgroup tools that help you manage all types of input from the various members of the team. The Word Core exam expects that you'll be familiar with three of these tools, Compare and Merge, comments, and converting documents into web pages. Compare and Merge is a new feature of Word 2002 that combines all of the changes in two versions of the same document. You can use the second tool, comments, to make notations throughout a document for other onscreen readers to view. You might comment on why you made a particular revision, the definition of a term, or additional information that needs to be inserted. Finally, by converting a document to a web page, you can make it accessible to all members of a team by posting it to your company's intranet or other web presence.

In this chapter, we'll show you how to use these workgroup collaboration features to thrust your team into high gear. In Chapter 8, "Taking Collaboration to Another Level," you'll learn about additional collaboration features, such as revision tracking and saving document versions, as you prepare for the Word Expert exam. So let's begin with comparing and merging documents.

NOTE Before you begin this chapter, you should go to the Sybex website and download the file 4113Ch04.zip. This package contains the files necessary to complete some of the exercises in this chapter. In addition, it contains files of what most of the documents should look like after you complete the exercise. These files are affixed with the word *Post*.

Comparing and Merging Documents

Although Word provides a number of features that could help you avoid having multiple copies of the same document, for example, revision tracking and saving versions (both discussed in Chapter 8), the fact is that no matter how experienced you are with these features, at some time or another you are going to end up with two versions of the same document. In a common example, maybe you took a copy home on a floppy to work on it and then forgot to copy the changes before doing additional editing at the office. Trying to incorporate the changes from both documents manually can create a significant headache. But with Word's Compare and Merge feature, you can merge the two documents into one and have Word point out the changes to you.

Microsoft ✓ *Exam* *Objective*	**Compare and Merge documents**

You can use Compare and Merge to merge changes from two copies of the same document, and you can also use Compare and Merge to append one document to the end of another document. In both cases, you can make the changes to one of the existing documents or you can create an entirely new document that contains the changes.

To use Compare and Merge extensively, you need to know how to use revision tracking and how to accept and reject revisions. This is covered in Chapter 8. Also, do not confuse Compare and Merge with the Mail Merge feature discussed in Chapter 9, "Merging to Create Letters and Labels."

In Exercise 4.1, we'll show you how to merge two copies of the same document to incorporate the changes of another person.

EXERCISE 4.1

Comparing and Merging Documents

For steps 1 and 2 of this exercise, you work in Human Resources and your supervisor has asked you to draft an employment philosophy for your organization.

EXERCISE 4.1 *(continued)*

1. Open the file 4-1.

2. Save the document as **Employment Philosophy**.

In steps 3 and 4, your supervisor is reviewing and editing the draft document you sent her.

3. Make the following changes to the document:

   a. Delete *"will"* in the first and second bullet points.

   b. Replace *"will be"* with **are** in the third and fourth points.

   c. Delete *"will"* in the last point and replace *"who they are accountable to"* with **to whom they are accountable**.

4. Save the document as **Compare and Merge Practice** and close it.

In steps 5–8, you use Compare and Merge to see the changes your supervisor made.

5. Open 4-1 and choose Tools ➤ Compare And Merge Documents. This opens a dialog box similar to the Open dialog box.

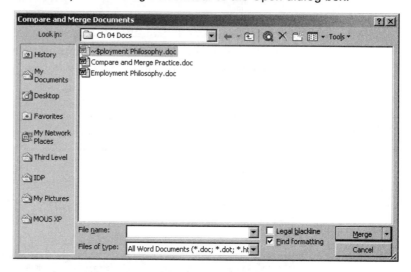

6. Select Compare and Merge Practice from the list of documents and click the Merge button.

Merge displays all changes in the target document (the one you just located in the Compare And Merge Documents dialog box.). Alternatively, you can click the down arrow on the Merge button to choose from these options:

- Merge Into Current Document displays all changes in the current document (the one you had open to begin with).

- Merge Into New Document displays results in a new, third document that you can choose to save if you wish.

If you click the Legal Blackline check box in the Compare And Merge Documents dialog box, Compare is the only choice available. The Legal Blackline option creates a new document that shows only the differences between the two documents without changing the original documents.

7. If you are in Print Layout view (View ➤ Print Layout), each change is identified by a dotted line leading to a descriptive balloon.

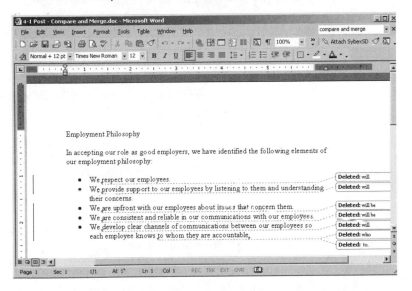

8. If you are in Normal view (View ➤ Normal), each deletion is identified by a strike through the word. Insertions are not identified by default except by the vertical line that appears in the left side of the document where changes have been made.

EXERCISE 4.1 *(continued)*

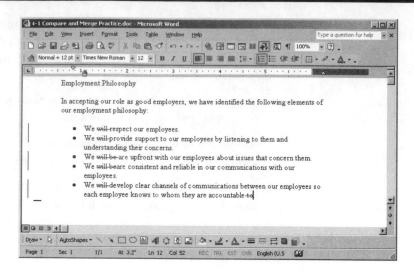

In Chapter 8, you'll learn about accepting and rejecting these revisions, but for now you can hide the changes in the document so you can print it without making a definite commitment to the changes.

9. To hide the changes in the document, click the Display For Review drop-down list on the Reviewing toolbar and choose Final. If the Reviewing toolbar is not visible, choose View ➢ Toolbars ➢ Reviewing to display it.

In Final view, everything appears as if you had accepted all the changes from your supervisor.

10. To see the changes again, select Final Showing Markup from the Display For Review drop-down list. Resave the document.

Occasionally, you may open a document and receive a message asking if you would like to merge this document into another document of the same or similar name. You may wonder how Word knows this is a copy of an existing document when you haven't told it so and you haven't asked it to combine them using Compare and Merge. Word assigns a random number to each document to assist in the merging process. This hidden number associates one document with another. If you have security concerns about Word tracking relationships between documents, you can turn this feature off by clearing the Store Random Number To Improve Merge Accuracy check box on the Security tab of the Options dialog box (Tools ➢ Options).

Compare and Merge is a valuable first step toward workgroup collaboration. But wouldn't it be nice to know why your supervisor made the changes she did? With comments, you can make notations, or even add sound recordings, throughout a document that show up only on screen and not in the printed document. In this next section, we'll show you how to create and edit comments.

Using Comments to Communicate with Team Members

The purpose of any document you create is to communicate your message. While you are creating a document and, in some cases, even after it is created, it's valuable to be able to communicate messages that are not part of the major document. Using comments, you can communicate with members of the team that is developing the document, you can document the sources of facts in the document, and you can make notes about revisions that still need to be made.

Microsoft
✔ *Exam*
Objective

Insert, view and edit comments

In Word 2002, comments come in two forms: text and audio. Text comments can be viewed on screen and they can be printed. Audio comments can be played back through your computer's sound system. In both cases, a single document can contain comments from multiple reviewers. In this next section, we'll explore how to insert text and audio comments into a document.

Inserting Comments

When you insert a text comment, Word places a comment indicator at the insertion point and displays the text of the comment in a balloon. If you are in Normal view, balloons are not visible, so the Reviewing pane opens instead.

In Exercise 4.2, you'll insert text comments into an existing document.

EXERCISE 4.2

Inserting Comments

1. Open Compare and Merge Practice, which you created in Exercise 4.1, or open the file 4-2. Switch to Print Layout view (View ➤ Print Layout, or click the Print Layout View button on the left end of the horizontal scroll bar).

2. Position the insertion point in the first bullet point before the "r" in "respect."

3. Click the New Comment button on the Reviewing toolbar, or choose Insert ➤ Comment. If the Reviewing toolbar is not visible, choose View ➤ Toolbars ➤ Reviewing.

4. Type your comment in the balloon that opens on the right of the document. In this case, type **Changed to present tense to indicate continuous commitment**.

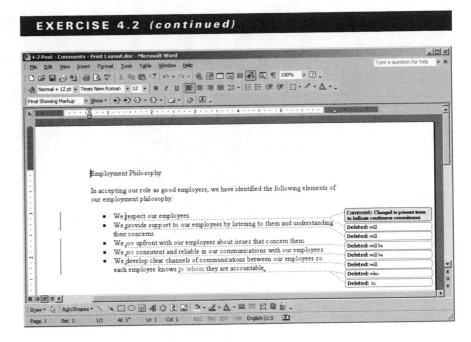

5. Click outside the balloon to insert the comment. The comment is indicated in the document by an I-beam.

6. Switch to Normal view (View ➤ Normal, or click the Normal View button to the left of the horizontal scroll bar). Position the insertion point at the end of the last bullet point.

7. Click the New Comment button on the Reviewing toolbar—a Reviewing pane opens at the bottom of the screen. Type the following comment at the insertion point in the Reviewing pane: **We need to include additional bullets regarding compensation and benefits.**

EXERCISE 4.2 *(continued)*

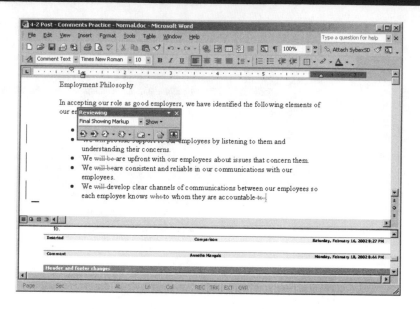

8. To insert the comment, click anywhere in the document. You can toggle between the document and the Reviewing pane by pressing F6.

9. Choose File ➢ Save As to save the document as **Comments Practice**.

You can also create voice comments using a microphone and recorder such as Microsoft Sound Recorder. To do this, click the drop-down arrow next to the New Comment button on the Reviewing toolbar and choose Voice Comment.

Computer microphones come in a number of styles and qualities. You can purchase a computer microphone of acceptable quality for less than $25 at your local computer or office supply store.

Viewing Comments

When you receive a document with text and voice comments or if you have made comments for your own reference, how you view them depends on the document view you choose. Text comments are visible in balloons by default in Print Layout view. To make them visible in Normal view, or if you've disabled balloons in the Track Changes options, you must display the Reviewing pane.

In Exercise 4.3, you'll practice viewing comments in Print Layout and in Normal view.

EXERCISE 4.3

Viewing Comments

1. Open Comments Practice or open the file 4–3.

2. In Print Layout view, you can view comments in the balloons on the right of the screen. If balloons are not visible, click the Show button on the Reviewing toolbar and choose Options. In the Track Changes dialog box, select the Use Balloons In Print And Web Layout check box.

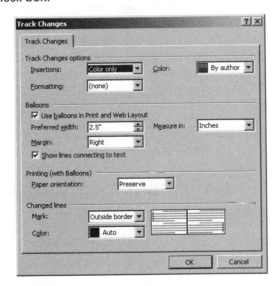

EXERCISE 4.3 *(continued)*

3. To see who created the comment, hover the pointer over the comment balloon. A screen tip opens with the author's name and the date and time the comment was inserted. You can also hover over the Speaker icon to see information about who created the voice comment and when it was created.

If you insert a comment and the author's name appears as Unknown, you need to enter your user information so Word knows how to identify you. To do this, choose Tools ➢ Options and enter your name on the User Information tab. The next comment you insert will contain the correct identifying information.

4. Switch to Normal view. Click the Reviewing Pane button on the Reviewing toolbar to activate the Reviewing pane at the bottom of the screen.

5. Use the vertical scroll bar on the Reviewing pane to view the comments and the author information.

6. To play the voice comment, double-click the Speaker icon. If you don't hear anything, be sure your speakers are turned on and the volume is at an adequate level. To see the identifying screen tip, point to the Speaker icon and hover for a second.

Editing Comments

You are free to edit the text in any comments that you create. However, if another user created the comments, you probably are not able to edit it. In Exercise 4.4, you'll edit comments.

EXERCISE 4.4

Editing Comments

In this exercise, you'll edit and delete comments in both Print Layout and Normal views. You'll also edit a sound comment.

1. Open the file 4-4. Switch to Print Layout view, if necessary. Click after "*indicate*" in the first Comment balloon and type **our**.

2. Click anywhere in the second comment. Click the drop-down arrow on the New Comment button on the Reviewing toolbar and choose Delete Comment.

3. Switch to Normal view. Click after "employees" in the last bullet point, click the New Comment button, and type **Should we say "employees and management" here?** Click in the document to insert the comment.

4. Click after "*here*" in the comment you just typed, and insert **or is this enough**.

5. To edit a voice comment, you have to re-record it. Click the Speaker icon and press the Delete key to delete it. Click the drop-down arrow on the New Comment button on the Reviewing toolbar and choose Voice Comment. You can then record a new voice comment.

6. To delete a voice comment, click the Speaker icon and press the Delete key on the keyboard.

7. Save and close the file.

Now you know how to insert, view, and edit comments. If you have a document with comments, you can hide the comments in Print Layout view by clicking the Show button on the Reviewing toolbar and clicking Comments to deselect it. Likewise, you can turn off other reviewing elements, such as Insertions and Deletions, to show only the comments by clicking each element in the list to deactivate it.

Although comments provide a valuable way to communicate about a document, if you want a number of people to read a document, there is no more powerful tool than the Web. In this next section, we'll show you how to convert any Word document to an HTML document so it can be published to a website.

Converting Documents to Post to a Website

The Web is a dynamic and exciting way to communicate information. If you are working on a team, you can post team schedules, project lists, reports, and other information to a team website. Because Word 2002's native format is HTML, the language of the Web, it is not difficult to convert Word documents into web pages.

Convert documents into Web pages

Converting documents into web pages is simply a matter of instructing Word to save the document as an HTML document (`.htm`) rather than a Word document (`.doc`). All of the text, formatting, and design elements you've included in your document should convert without problems. In Exercise 4.5, you'll convert a document to a web page. Although not called for in this exam objective, we'll first spruce it up a little by adding some formatting and a web theme to the page to make it look more like a web page. After you save the file, we'll preview it in Internet Explorer.

EXERCISE 4.5

Converting Documents into Web Pages

1. Open `Employment Philosophy`, which you created in Exercise 4.1, or open the file 4-5.

2. Click in the first line, "Employment Philosophy," and choose Heading 1 from the Style drop-down list on the Formatting toolbar.

3. Choose Format ➤ Theme, and select Capsules from the list of available themes. If Capsules is not available on your system, choose another theme of your choice.

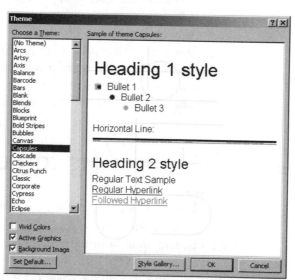

EXERCISE 4.5 *(continued)*

A theme changes the document's background and text and paragraph formatting so that it looks good on a website. By choosing the same theme for all the related pages of a web, you can create a consistent and attractive look for your site. Notice that after you apply a theme, Word automatically switches to Web Layout view. In this view, the document has no visible margins and no page breaks.

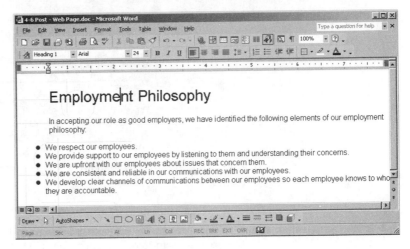

4. To save the document as a web page, choose File ➢ Save As Web Page. This opens the Save As dialog box with a couple of minor distinctions. The Save As Type option is automatically set to Web Page, and a Page Title section appears.

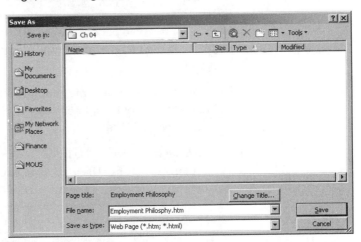

The title of a web page is the name that visitors see when they save the page in their Favorites folder. If you don't assign a title to the page, Word uses the filename or the first line of text in its place. Although this may be fine some of the time, it is generally not as friendly to outsiders. Always check to make sure the Page Title is descriptive of the page contents.

5. Click the Change Title button, enter **Our Employment Philosophy** in the Set Page Title dialog box, and click OK.

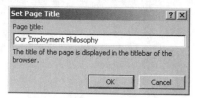

6. Enter `Employment Philosophy - First Draft` as the filename, and click OK.

7. To preview the file in Internet Explorer, choose File ➢ Web Page Preview. This launches Internet Explorer and displays the page in the browser window. The comments in the document appear in the web page with the initials of the creator. Point to a comment to see a screen tip with the comment contents.

Note that when you save a document as a web page, Word saves the document as an HTM file and also creates a folder called *[File Name]_ Files*. This folder contains any graphic files and other supporting files needed for the web page. Because we applied a theme to this web page, the folder contains the image files that compose the bullets and background.

8. Close the file and save the changes. You may also want to close Internet Explorer by right-clicking its icon on the Windows Taskbar and choosing Close.

The post file for this exercise is `Employment Philosophy - First Draft` rather than `4-5 - Post`. The web page support files are in the folder `Employment Philosophy - First Draft_files`.

Congratulations, you just created a web page! That wasn't so hard, was it? Although there is a lot more you can do to web pages to make them useful as collaborative tools, making the conversion from Word to the Web is as simple as that. In Chapter 8, you'll learn more about creating web pages in Word and about adding hyperlinks to connect pages together.

Summary

This chapter focused on basic collaboration tools. We covered the following topics:

- Using Compare and Merge to combine changes made to two copies of the same document or two different documents

- Inserting, editing, and viewing comments

- Converting documents to web pages

Microsoft Word 2002 Expert Exam

PART

II

Chapter

5

Advanced Document Formatting

MOUS WORD 2002 EXPERT EXAM OBJECTIVES COVERED IN THIS CHAPTER:

- ✓ Control pagination
- ✓ Sort paragraphs in lists and tables
- ✓ Create and format document sections
- ✓ Create and apply character and paragraph styles
- ✓ Create and update document indexes and tables of contents, figures, and authorities
- ✓ Create cross-references
- ✓ Add and revise endnotes and footnotes
- ✓ Create and manage master documents and subdocuments
- ✓ Move within documents
- ✓ Create and modify forms using various form controls
- ✓ Create forms and prepare forms for distribution

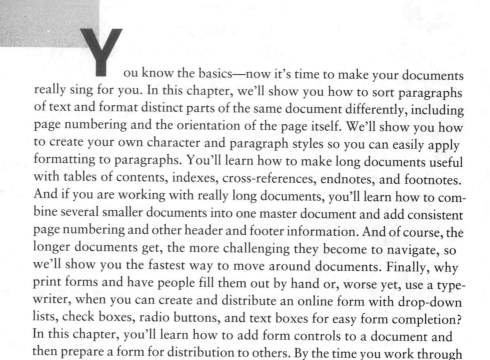

You know the basics—now it's time to make your documents really sing for you. In this chapter, we'll show you how to sort paragraphs of text and format distinct parts of the same document differently, including page numbering and the orientation of the page itself. We'll show you how to create your own character and paragraph styles so you can easily apply formatting to paragraphs. You'll learn how to make long documents useful with tables of contents, indexes, cross-references, endnotes, and footnotes. And if you are working with really long documents, you'll learn how to combine several smaller documents into one master document and add consistent page numbering and other header and footer information. And of course, the longer documents get, the more challenging they become to navigate, so we'll show you the fastest way to move around documents. Finally, why print forms and have people fill them out by hand or, worse yet, use a typewriter, when you can create and distribute an online form with drop-down lists, check boxes, radio buttons, and text boxes for easy form completion? In this chapter, you'll learn how to add form controls to a document and then prepare a form for distribution to others. By the time you work through this chapter, no document, regardless of length or complexity, will be able to slow you down.

Before you begin this chapter, you should go to the Sybex website and download the file 4113Ch05.zip. This package contains the files necessary to complete some of the exercises in this chapter. In addition, it contains files of what most of the documents should look like after you complete the exercises. These documents are affixed with the word *Post*.

Customizing Paragraphs

In Chapter 2, "Working with Documents," you learned how to create tables to present tabular data, and you may have already seen the sorting buttons on the Tables and Borders toolbar. But did you know that you can use the same sorting tools to sort entire paragraphs?

Sorting Paragraphs in Lists and Tables

If you input data into a table or paragraphs of text in a document, Word doesn't require you to manually move it around to put a list of names, for example, into alphabetical order. One click of a button and Word alphabetizes for you.

Microsoft
✓ *Exam*
Objective

Sort paragraphs in lists and tables

Sorting is simply defined as rearranging text or numbers into ascending (A–Z or 1–10) or descending (Z–A or 10–1) order. You can choose a single level of sort to alphabetize a glossary of key terms or a multiple level of sort to alphabetize a list in a table. For example, in a table, you could sort by Department, then by Last Name, and then by First Name. When you choose multiple levels of sort, you generally want to choose the broadest category first and then narrow it down with each subsequent choice. By choosing the department first, all the people in the same department are organized together and then they are sorted alphabetically by last name within each department. Only the people who share the same last name in a single department are then sorted by first name. In Exercise 5.1, you'll learn how to sort data in a table.

EXERCISE 5.1

Sorting in Tables

1. Open 5-1.doc from the downloaded files for this chapter.

2. Click in the table and choose Table ➤ Sort to open the Sort dialog box.

EXERCISE 5.1 *(continued)*

In the Sort dialog box, you can identify whether or not the table has a header row (row of column names) and, if it does, whether to use the header row to establish the sort order you want to apply. You can sort up to three levels deep.

3. Verify that Header Row is selected in the My List Has field at the bottom of the dialog box.

4. Select Department from the Sort By drop-down list.

5. Verify that Text is selected in the Type drop-down list. You can also sort by Number and by Date.

6. You would choose Ascending to sort alphabetically A–Z and Descending to sort Z–A. In this case, leave the default setting, Ascending.

7. Verify that Paragraphs is selected in the Using drop-down list. You can also sort by fields, if you are using field codes.

8. Choose Last Name in the first Then By drop-down list and First Name in the last Then By drop-down list. In both cases, the type is Text and the Using choice is Paragraphs.

9. Click OK to close the dialog box and sort the data. The data in the table should be sorted alphabetically by Department, then by Last Name, and then by First Name.

Note: You also could have chosen to sort by Dept Number rather than Department, but if you did, you would have to have chosen Number in the Type drop-down list for Dept Number.

10. Save and close the document.

You can also sort data in tables quickly by activating the Tables and Borders toolbar (click the Tables And Borders button on the Standard toolbar). Click the column you want to sort by and click the Sort Ascending or Sort Descending button on the Tables And Borders toolbar.

Sorting paragraphs of texts typically involves just one level of sort. Words sort paragraphs by the first word or field of a paragraph. If the first word is the same in two paragraphs, it moves on to the next word until it finds a difference to decide the sort order. In Exercise 5.2, you'll sort a list of references entered in paragraphs.

EXERCISE 5.2

Sorting Paragraphs

1. Open 5-2.doc from the files downloaded for this chapter.

2. Select the paragraphs of text you want to sort. In this example, select all of the paragraphs in the document except the heading, References.

3. Choose Table ➢ Sort to open the Sort dialog box.

4. Choose Paragraphs in the Sort By drop-down list and leave the default settings, Text and Ascending for the Type and Sort Order.

5. Verify that No Header Row is selected in the My List Has section.

6. Click OK to close the dialog box and reorder the paragraphs.

7. Save and close the document.

The process for sorting numbers and dates in tables or paragraphs is no different than sorting text except that you choose Number or Date in the Type drop-down list in the Sort dialog box. If you choose Number, Word ignores all characters except the numbers, and the numbers can be in any location in a paragraph. If you choose Date, Word recognizes hyphens, forward slashes (/), commas, and periods as valid date separators and colons (:) as valid time separators.

Working with Document Sections

Word uses sections to organize documents for formatting purposes. A *section* is a contiguous portion of a document that has a specified number of columns and uses a common set of margins, page orientation, header and footer, and sequence of page numbers.

Microsoft
✓ *Exam*
Objective

Create and format document sections

Word automatically inserts section breaks when you do the following:

- Format text as columns.
- Change Page Setup options and indicate that you want the changes to apply from This Point Forward.

You can manually insert a section break to apply a different page size or header and footer formatting within a document. For example, if you want a different header in each chapter in a document, put section breaks between the chapters before you create the headers.

In Exercise 5.3, you'll manually insert a section break and then change the page orientation in the second section.

EXERCISE 5.3

Inserting Section Breaks to Format Document Sections

1. Open 5-3.doc from the files downloaded for this chapter.

2. Position the insertion point where you want the break to begin, in this case, in the blank row at the end of the page, and choose Insert ➢ Break. The Break dialog box appears.

In the Section Break Types area, you can select one of the following options to specify where you want the new section to begin:

Next Page inserts a section break and starts the new section at the beginning of the next page. You might use this type of break when you want to change page orientation.

Continuous inserts a section break without inserting a page break. Any subsequent text you type directly follows the existing text. This break works well when you want to change the number of columns.

Even Page inserts a section break and starts the new section at the beginning of the next even-numbered page in the document. If the section break is inserted on an even-numbered page, Word leaves the intervening page (an odd-numbered page) blank.

Odd Page inserts a section break and starts the new section at the beginning of the next odd-numbered page in the document. If the section break is inserted on an odd-numbered page, Word leaves the intervening page (an even-numbered page) blank.

3. Choose Next Page.

4. Choose OK to insert the section break and create a new page.

5. Choose File ➢ Page Setup to open the Page Setup dialog box.

6. On the Margins tab, choose Landscape in the Orientation section and verify that This Section is selected in Apply To drop-down list in the Preview section.

7. Click OK to close Page Setup and apply the new page orientation to the second section.

8. To view the page orientations of the two sections, click the Print Preview button and choose 1 × 2 Pages from the Multiple Pages button.

9. Click Close to close Print Preview. Save and close the file.

Section break marks can be seen in both Normal and Outline views by default. You can also see section break marks in both Web Page and Print Layout views when you display nonprinting characters in your document. To do so, use either of the following procedures:

- Click the Show/Hide ¶ button on the Standard toolbar.

- Choose Tools ➢ Options ➢ View, check the All check box in the Formatting Marks area, and then choose OK.

Section break marks appear as double-dotted lines with the words *Section Break* and the type of break (*Continuous*, for example) in them.

To delete a section break, place the insertion point anywhere on the break and press Delete.

Controlling Pagination

If you are creating a document that is longer than one page, then you generally want to include page numbering. If the pages are numbered, you don't have to worry quite so much about distrusting a document that has been collated and stapled in the wrong order. Applying Word's page numbering feature to a document assures that even if you insert and delete text, the final document will have the correct page numbers.

Microsoft ✓ *Exam* *Objective*	**Control Pagination**

If you are using document sections, you can choose to apply page numbering that crosses over all the sections or you can number each section independently. In Exercise 5.4, you'll apply page numbering to a document that contains multiple sections, and then you'll change the numbering so that each section starts with the page number 1.

EXERCISE 5.4

Applying Page Numbering to Documents and Sections

1. Open 5-4.doc from the files you downloaded for this chapter.

   Note: 5-4.doc uses the endnotes feature that you will be learning about later in this chapter.

2. Choose Insert ➤ Page Numbers to open the Page Numbers dialog box.

   Word inserts page numbers in the header or footer of a document (see Chapter 2 if you need a review of headers and footers).

3. Select Bottom Of Page (Footer) from the Position drop-down list.

   You can choose Left, Center, Right, Inside, or Outside alignment from the Alignment drop-down list. Inside and Outside are used with documents that will be printed double-sided. With Outside, the page number appears on the left of even-numbered pages and the right of odd-numbered pages. With Inside, the page number appears on the right of even-numbered pages and the left of odd-numbered pages.

4. Select Center from the Alignment drop-down list.

If you want the number to appear on the first page of the document, leave the Show Number on First Page check box selected. If you prefer not to have page 1 numbered, clear this check box.

5. Leave the Show Number On First Page check box selected.

6. Click OK to apply the page numbering to the document.

7. Switch to Print Layout view, if you aren't already there, and scroll through the document to view the page numbering in the footer of each page.

You can change the format of the page numbers from the default Arabic numbers to Roman numbers or upper- or lowercase letters. If you are creating a long document, you can use heading styles (see Chapter 2 for more about heading styles) to have Word automatically recognize new chapters and number them according: 1-1, 2-1, 3-1, etc. And you can number each section of a document individually.

8. Scroll to the footer on page 4 of the document and double-click the footer area to switch to the Header And Footer view, showing the footer for Section 2 of the document. The Header And Footer toolbar also opens.

9. Click the page number in the footer to select it, and click the Format Page Number button on the Header And Footer toolbar. This opens the Page Number Format dialog box.

10. Click the Number Format drop-down list on the Page Number Format dialog box and choose - 1 -, - 2 -, - 3 -, ... as the number format.

11. Do not select the Include Chapter Number check box.

12. Select Start At in the Page Numbering section and accept the default of 1 in the spin box. This changes the page number of the second section to start at 1 rather than continuing from the previous section.

13. Click OK to accept the change.

14. Click the Show Previous button on the Header And Footer toolbar to show the page number in Section 1.

EXERCISE 5.4 *(continued)*

15. Select the page number in the Section 1 footer and click the Format Page Number button on the Header And Footer toolbar.

16. Click the Number Format drop-down list on the Page Numbering dialog box and choose - 1 -, - 2 -, - 3 -, ... as the number format.

17. Click OK to accept the change.

18. Click the Show Next button on the Header And Footer toolbar twice to show the page number in Section 3.

19. Select the page number in the Section 3 footer and click the Format Page Number button on the Header And Footer toolbar.

20. Click the Number Format drop-down list on the Page Number Format dialog box and choose - 1 -, - 2 -, - 3 -, ... as the number format.

21. Select Start At and enter **1** in the Start At text box.

22. Click OK to accept the change.

23. Click Close on the Header And Footer toolbar to close the Header And Footer view and return to the main document. Scroll through the document to see the page numbering change between sections.

24. Save and close the document.

If you already have a header or footer that you want to edit to include page numbers, switch to the Header And Footer view and use the options on the Header And Footer toolbar. You can click the Insert AutoText button and choose from the AutoText page numbering options or click the Insert Page Number button.

Creating and Applying Character and Paragraph Styles

In Chapter 1, "Creating Basic Documents," we showed you how to apply predefined character and paragraph styles to format text in a document. For the Word Expert exam, you also need to know how to create your own styles and then apply them to text and paragraphs in a document. Styles can include fonts, sizes, font attributes, alignment, character spacing, paragraph spacing, bullets and numbering, borders, indenting, and just about any other formatting you can think of. Styles can save you countless hours of reformatting, because once you've applied styles to your text, a simple change in the style changes all the text formatted in that style.

Microsoft
✓ *Exam*
Objective

Create and apply character and paragraph styles

After you start working with styles, it won't be long before you're dissatisfied with the basic selection of predefined styles and want to create your own. There are several ways to do so.

To quickly create a new paragraph style based on an existing style, follow the steps in Exercise 5.5.

EXERCISE 5.5

Creating a New Style the Easy Way

1. Open 5-5.doc from the files you downloaded for this chapter.

2. Double-click the section title, "Overview," and change the formatting to Arial, 12 pt, Bold, Italic, Blue. Change paragraph spacing on the Indents And Spacing tab of the Paragraph dialog box to 6 pt Before and 6 pt After (Format ≻ Paragraph). Use the Borders button on the Standard toolbar to apply a bottom border.

3. Click the Style text box on the Formatting toolbar to highlight the name of the current style.

4. Type **Section Titles** for the name of your new style and press Enter.

5. To apply the new style to other text, scroll down the page and select the other two section titles, "Services" and "Financial Considerations and Staffing." You can select them at the same time by selecting the first title and then holding down Ctrl as you select the second one. Click the down arrow on the Styles list and choose Section Titles from the drop-down list that opens.

6. Save and close the document.

You can also create a new character or paragraph style in the Styles And Formatting task pane. To do so, follow the steps in Exercise 5.6. In this example, you'll create a character style.

EXERCISE 5.6

Creating a New Character Style Using the Styles And Formatting Task Pane.

1. Open 5-6.doc from the files you downloaded for this chapter.

2. Click the Styles And Formatting button on the Formatting toolbar to open the Styles And Formatting task pane.

3. Click New Style to display the Style dialog box.

4. Create the new style by changing the following options:

    a. Type **Key Term** as a descriptive name for the new style in the Name text box.

    b. Select Character in the Style Type drop-down list. You could also choose Paragraph, Table, or List when you are creating other styles.

    c. Select the style on which you would like to base this style. If a similar style already exists, you could choose that style from the Style Based On list. If you are not certain, leave the Default Paragraph Font.

    d. If you are creating a paragraph style, you can choose to revert to another style in the paragraph following the new style. To do this, select the name of the style in the Style For Following Paragraph drop-down list. For example, if you apply the Heading 1 style, type a heading, and press Enter, Word automatically switches to the Normal style for the subsequent paragraph. This option is dimmed for character styles.

    e. To choose the formatting for the characters, use the controls in the dialog box. For this exercise, choose Bold, Italic, and change the font color to Blue.

EXERCISE 5.6 *(continued)*

For more options, especially when creating Paragraph styles, click the Format button (at the bottom) and then choose Font, Paragraph, Tabs, Border, Language, Frame, or Numbering to display the dialog box for that feature. Select any options you want in that dialog box to apply the new format. If you want to apply a style using a shortcut key combination, choose that option from the Format button choices.

5. The Add To Template check box stores the new style in the template on which the document is based, for example, Normal. If you do not check this box, the new style is stored only in the active document. Leave this box unchecked for this exercise.

If you are creating a paragraph style, you can also choose Automatically Update to redefine the new style with formatting you apply manually to the paragraph in your document. Every paragraph in the document to which this style is applied will also be updated to contain the new format.

6. Choose OK in the New Style dialog box.

7. Double-click "Homeless" in the first paragraph and then hold Ctrl and drag over "self-sufficiency" and "positive youth development" to also select them.

8. Click Key Term in the Pick Formatting To Apply list in the Styles And Formatting task pane.

9. Save and close the document.

Word does not inform you when you make changes to a paragraph style for which you've chosen Automatically Update. Unless you are very confident about the changes you are making, it is safer to keep this option turned off. Because the formatting of every paragraph to which the style is applied will also be changed, the Automatically Update option may give you some unexpected results.

To modify an existing style, rest your mouse pointer over the style in the Styles And Formatting task pane list, click the down arrow that appears, and choose Modify from the drop-down list. Make any changes you want to make, and click OK to close the Modify Style dialog box and save the changes.

You can use the Select All button to select any characters or paragraphs in a document that share the same style.

When you no longer need a style you created, you can delete it. When you do, Word automatically applies the Normal paragraph style to all paragraphs in the document to which the deleted style was applied. To delete a style from the current document, rest your mouse pointer over the style in the Styles And Formatting task pane list, click the down arrow that appears, and choose Delete from the drop-down list. In the message box that appears, choose Yes to confirm that you want to delete the style.

If the style you want to modify or delete does not appear in the Pick Formatting To Apply list in the Styles And Formatting task pane, click the down arrow on the Show text box and choose All Styles from the list. Scroll through the styles in the Pick Formatting To Apply list to find the style you want.

In the next section, you'll learn how to add references such as tables of contents and footnotes to your well-styled documents.

Creating References for Easy Navigation

Making long and complex documents less painful to wade through improves the likelihood that someone might actually read them. Word has a number of tools to make printed and online documents more accessible. For example, Word can automatically generate an index and tables of contents, figures, and authorities. You can create cross-references that let a reader jump from one section of a document to another. And you can add footnotes and endnotes without worrying about having to manually number and renumber them as you make changes to the document. Each of these tools adds usability and readability. In this section, we'll show you how to make documents more accessible using the reference tools.

Generating Indexes and Tables of Contents, Figures, and Authorities

Typically, tables of contents appear at the beginning of documents and indexes at the end. Between the two of them, readers should be able to find most anything they are looking for without having to read every page. If the document contains a number of figures, you can add tables of figures for quick reference. For the legal world, Word can generate tables of authorities faster than you can say "pro bono." In this section, we'll show you how to create indexes and then move on to tables of contents, figures, and authorities.

Microsoft ✓ *Exam* *Objective*

Create and update document indexes and tables of contents, figures, and authorities

Indexing for Easy Reference

You can make lengthy documents more user-friendly by creating an index of key words and phrases. Index entries can consist of individual words, phrases, or symbols that you select in your document, a topic that extends through several pages that you have named as a bookmark, or a topic that references another index entry.

Although marking index entries is a manual process, Word automates the creation of the index and updates it on request. You can either mark each entry individually or have Word mark every instance of the same entry. In Exercise 5.7, you'll create an index for an existing document by first marking the index entries and then generating the index.

EXERCISE 5.7

Creating an Index for a Document

1. Open 5-7.doc from the files you downloaded for this chapter.

2. This multi-page document already has a number of marked index entries. You can view these entries by clicking the Show/Hide ¶ button on the Standard toolbar.

Word inserts the XE (Index Entry) field code for each marked entry.

EXERCISE 5.7 *(continued)*

3. To mark an index entry for yourself, select the first occurrence of the name "Traverse City."

4. Press Alt+Shift+X (or choose Insert ➢ Reference ➢ Index and Tables and click the Mark Entry button on the Index tab) to display the Mark Index Entry dialog box.

The selected text appears in the Main Entry text box. You can edit the text if you want to change how the entry appears in the index. Or if you are satisfied with the entry, you can skip this step.

5. Type **Traverse City, Michigan** in the Main Entry text box.

To place subentries below the main index entry when the index is generated, type up to two entries, separated by a colon, in the Subentry text box. For example, when the main entry is Traverse City, Michigan, you would type **Grand Traverse Bay: National Cherry Capital** to include those topics below the Traverse City, Michigan topic in the index. For this exercise, leave the Subentry text box empty.

6. Choose Current Page in the Options section to automatically add the page number after the marked entry.

You have two other options in this section: Cross-Reference and Page Range. You'll create a cross-reference in step 12 of this exercise. Page Range shows the index entry as a span of pages. If you had previously named a bookmark that defines text that spans multiple pages, you could choose Page Range and select the bookmark in the adjacent drop-down list.

7. Leave the Bold and Italic check boxes unselected in the Page Number Format area—you could select these to add bold or italic formatting to the entry's page number. However, we don't recommend it because you'd have to remember to do it for every entry.

8. Click Mark All to label every occurrence of the selected text in your document. If you choose Mark, only the single occurrence of the selected text appears as an index entry.

The Mark Index Entry dialog box stays open while you return to your document and select the next text you want to appear in the index.

9. Select "Petosky" in the fourth line of the paragraph, and then click anywhere in the Mark Index Entry dialog box to move that entry into the Main Entry text box.

10. Click Mark All to create the index entries.

11. Select "Street Outreach" in the second paragraph, and then click anywhere in the Mark Index Entry dialog box to move that entry into the Main Entry text box.

12. Select Cross-Reference in the Options section. Type **Outreach** after *See* in the corresponding text box. When "Street Outreach" appears in the index, "See Outreach," rather than the page number, will be listed.

13. Mark the Street Outreach Index entry and close the Mark Index Entry dialog box.

You are now ready to generate the index.

14. Press Ctrl+End to move the insertion point to the last page of your document, and then enter a hard page break by pressing Ctrl+Enter or choosing Insert ➢ Break and choosing Page Break.

15. Type **Index** and format it as a Heading 1 style (this allows you to include this heading in the table of contents you will create later). Click to unselect it and press Enter twice to create space for the index.

16. Choose Insert ➢ Reference ➢ Index And Tables to display the Index And Tables dialog box.

17. Choose any of the following options to specify how you'd like to format the index. These are mostly a matter of personal preference, so play around a little bit here and see how your choices affect the preview.

EXERCISE 5.7 *(continued)*

   a. To specify how all subentries will appear below main entries, select one of the options in the Type area. The Indented option places subentries below main entries; the Run-In option places subentries on the same line as main entries.

   b. Adjust the value in the Columns text box to specify the number of columns that will appear in the index. Choose Auto to have the index appear with the same number of columns as the document.

   c. Select the language for the index in the Language drop-down list.

   d. Check the Right Align Page Numbers box to have Word place the entries' page numbers along the right margin of the page or column. Then select dots, dashes, underline, or none as the tab leader character that appears before the right-aligned page numbers.

   e. Select the styles to apply to the index in the Formats drop-down list. If you choose From Template, choose Modify to display the Style dialog box and then make any necessary changes to the selected index style.

18. When the sample index in the Print Preview area appears with the formatting you want for your index, choose OK to generate the index at the position of the insertion point.

Word gathers the marked index entries and then uses them to create the index. A continuous section break mark is automatically inserted after the index. Go through each entry in the index to make sure it says what you want it to say and that the references are accurate. If you find any errors, you can fix them in the index, but any changes made to the index itself will be lost if you regenerate the index. Instead, make any necessary changes in the Index Entry (XE) fields inserted in the document and then regenerate the index.

Note: You can't see marked index entries unless the Show/Hide ¶ button on the Standard toolbar is turned on.

19. To regenerate the index after making changes, choose Insert ➢ Reference ➢ Index And Tables and then click OK to regenerate the index. Word selects the existing index and displays a dialog box asking whether you want to replace it. Choose Yes. You can also regenerate the index by clicking anywhere in it and pressing F9.

20. Save and close the document.

If you know you want to create an index for a document, you can mark index entries as you are creating the document or you can wait to the end and mark them all at one time. It doesn't hurt to generate the index after you have marked the first few entries—that way, you get a feel for how the index is working and you can always regenerate it when you are ready for the final pass.

Generating a Table of Contents

Creating a table of contents (TOC) is similar to creating an index but a whole lot easier. Instead of marking entries to generate the table of contents, you apply Word's built-in heading styles to the text that is to appear in the TOC. Word automatically selects the document's headings and lists them in the table of contents. If you did not apply heading styles when you created the document, you can go through the document and apply them before you create the table of contents (you'll find heading styles in Chapter 2). In Exercise 5.8, you'll create a table of contents for the same document you worked with in the last exercise.

Creating a Table of Contents

1. Open 5-8.doc from the files you downloaded for this chapter. This file is already formatted using heading styles, so no changes need to be made to it.

2. With the insertion point at the beginning of the document, press Ctrl+Enter to insert a hard page break.

3. Press Ctrl+Home to move the insertion point to the top of the newly inserted page and type **Table of Contents**.

4. Press Enter twice and click the Align Left button on the Formatting toolbar to position the insertion point for the table of contents.

5. Choose Insert ➢ Reference ➢ Index And Tables to display the Index And Tables dialog box.

6. Click the Table Of Contents tab.

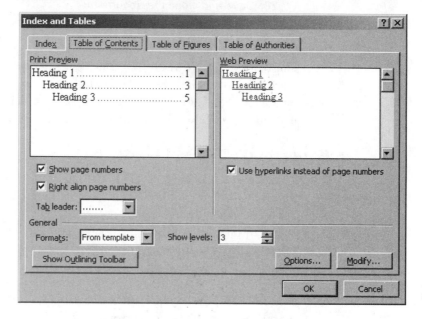

7. Leave the Show Page Numbers box checked so that page numbers appear when the document is viewed in Print Layout view or when the document is printed.

8. Leave the Right Align Page Numbers box checked so that displayed or printed page numbers align along the right margin of the page.

9. From the Tab Leader drop-down list, select your choice of none, dots, dashes, or underline as the character to appear before the page number.

10. Select the formatting you want for the table of contents in the Formats drop-down list. Select each option to view how it affects the preview. If you choose From Template, you can click Modify to display the Style dialog box and then make any desired changes to the TOC headings.

11. Adjust the value in the Show Levels text box to display the number of heading levels you want to appear in the table of contents. This document contains three heading levels, so you can leave it at 3. However, you could choose to display only the top level or the top two levels in the TOC if you wanted.

12. Leave the Use Hyperlinks Instead Of Page Numbers box checked so that online readers can click the link rather than scrolling to the page they want to read. In Print Layout view, page numbers appear, and readers can press Ctrl+click to use the hyperlinks.

13. Click OK to generate the table of contents.

If you want to change any of the entries in the table of contents, it's better to change the heading text in the document itself and then regenerate the TOC. Although you can directly edit the text in the table of contents, any changes you make will be lost if you regenerate the table or update the TOC field code.

14. Move the mouse pointer to "Group" and press Ctrl+click to move to that section of the document. Change the heading "Group" to **Group Counseling**.

15. Chose Insert ➢ Reference ➢ Index And Tables, and from the Table Of Contents tab, click OK to regenerate the TOC. If you want to make changes to the TOC options, you can do so before you click OK.

16. Click Yes when Word asks if you want to replace the selected table of contents.

Note: You can also update the table by moving the insertion point into the TOC, pressing F9, clicking the Update TOC button on the Outlining toolbar (if it is visible), or right-clicking and choosing Update Field. With each of these options, Word asks you if you want to update the page numbers only or the entire table. Choose the entire table unless you have made editing changes to the table itself that you don't want to lose.

17. Save and close the document.

For easy navigation in a document with a table of contents, turn on the Web toolbar (View ➤ Toolbars ➤ Web). You can use Ctrl+click to move to a section from the TOC and click the Back button on the Web toolbar to return to the TOC. You may find it even easier to view the document on the screen by switching to Web Layout view (View ➤ Web Layout or clicking the Web Layout button on the horizontal scroll bar).

Creating Tables of Figures

A table of figures is similar to a table of contents, but rather than referencing document headings, it references figures such as charts, drawings, bitmapped images, Word tables, or any other type of inserted object. To create a table of figures, you must first add captions to the objects. After the objects are captioned, you can use the Table Of Figures tab on the Index And Tables dialog box to create the table of figures in much the same way as you do a table of contents. To add a caption to an object, choose Insert ➤ Reference ➤ Caption. This opens the Caption dialog box.

Choose Figure, Equation, or Table from the Label drop-down list or click New Label to create your own. In the Caption text box, to the right of the label, e.g., "Figure," type the text of the label that applies to the specific object you are captioning. Click OK to create the caption. You can also turn on autocaptioning if you want Word to automatically caption every incidence of a particular type of object as you insert the object, for example, each chart or table you insert into a document.

When you are ready to run the table of figures, position the insertion point where you want the table to appear and choose Insert ➤ Reference ➤ Index And Tables and click the Table Of Figures tab. Make any desired changes to the appearance of the table and click OK to create the table.

Creating Tables of Authorities

If you are in the legal profession, then you know the importance of a comprehensive table of authorities. Marking citations in order to create a table of authorities is similar to marking index entries to create an index. To mark a citation, select the text that you want to cite, choose Insert ➤ References ➤ Index And Tables and click the Table Of Authorities tab. Click the Mark Citation button to open the Mark Citation dialog box.

Choose the category of the citation. The Short Citation box displays a list of short citations in the document. Choose one of the existing short citations

or enter text to create a new one. If you select one from the list, the corresponding long citation text appears in the Long Citation box. When you are
ready to mark the citation, click the Mark button or the Mark All button to
mark all occurrences of the same text in the document.

After you have marked all the citations in a document, you can create the
table of authorities by choosing Insert ➢ Reference ➢ Index And Tables.
Click the Table Of Authorities tab. Make any desired changes to the appearance of the table and click OK to create the table.

Creating Cross-References

When you created an index in Exercise 5.7, you saw an example of a cross-
reference used in an index. You can also create cross-references so readers
are directed to further information about a topic directly in the text of a
document. Word automatically updates cross-references when referenced
sections of the document are moved so that after you create the cross-reference,
you don't have to keep track of where everything is.

Microsoft
✓ *Exam*
Objective   **Create cross-references**

Cross-references can be linked to bookmarks, headings, numbered items,
footnotes, endnotes, equations, figures, and tables—and you can choose
how the reference appears in the document. For example, if you want to
refer to a heading, you can have the cross-reference indicate the actual text
of the heading, the page number where the text is found, or just the word
"above" or "below."

To insert cross-references to more than one document, change the documents
into subdocuments of a master document. See "Managing Large Projects with
Master Documents" later in this chapter for additional information.

In Exercise 5.9, you'll create cross-references in a document.

Creating Cross-References

1. Open 5-9.doc from the files you downloaded for this chapter.

2. Point to "Experience of the Organization" in the TOC and press Ctrl+click to move to that section.

3. Position the insertion point after "degreed professionals" near the end of the first paragraph.

4. Press the spacebar and type (**see**). Be sure to press the spacebar before entering the second parentheses. Then position the insertion point directly to the left of the closing parentheses.

5. Choose Insert ➢ Reference ➢ Cross-Reference to display the Cross-Reference dialog box.

6. Select the type of item to which the reference refers in the Reference Type drop-down list. A list of the items of the corresponding type in the document appears in the list box. For this exercise, choose Heading from the drop-down list.

7. From the Insert Reference To drop-down list, choose what you want to reference in the document. Choose Heading text to display the actual text of the heading.

8. Leave the Insert As Hyperlink check box enable to make the onscreen document easier to navigate.

9. Select the item in the For Which Heading list box to which the cross-reference will refer. Choose Supervision from the list of headings.

10. Choose Insert to insert the cross-reference and click Close to close the Cross-Reference dialog box.

You may decide that you'd like to include the page number of the cross-reference in addition to the heading.

11. Press the spacebar to insert a space after the cross-referenced heading.

12. Choose Insert ➢ Reference ➢ Cross-Reference to display the Cross-Reference dialog box.

13. Choose Page Number from the Insert Reference To drop-down list and select the Include Above/Below check box.

Note: In this example, Word doesn't show the words "above" or "below"—instead it displays "on page x" rather than just the page number. If you want to display the words "above" and "below," choose Above/Below from the Insert Reference To drop-down list.

14. Choose Supervision from the For Which Heading list.

15. Click Insert to insert the additional cross-reference.

(see Supervision on page 3)

16. Create additional cross-references in the document to practice using this feature.

17. Test each cross-reference by pointing to it and using Ctrl+click to navigate to the cross-referenced text.

18. Save and close the document.

If you make any changes to the document, you should manually update the results of the field codes created by the index, table of contents, other reference tables, and cross-references. To do so, follow these steps:

1. Choose Edit ➢ Select All to select the entire document.

2. Press F9, or right-click the reference, and then choose Update Field from the shortcut menu.

To have Word automatically update all the field codes in a document before you print it, choose Tools ➢ Options, display the Print page, check the Update Fields check box in the Printing Options area, and then choose OK.

Annotating with Endnotes and Footnotes

When you want to give your readers more information about your topic or a reference to the source of your information, Word gives you options for inserting both *footnotes*, which appear at the bottom of the page, and *endnotes*, which appear at the end of the document. Word automatically numbers the notes for you and calculates how much space footnotes will need at the bottom on the page.

Microsoft Exam Objective	**Add and revise endnotes and footnotes**

If you want to provide different kinds of references for your readers, you can insert both footnotes and endnotes in the same document. For example, you may want to insert footnotes to add comments to the text of a page and endnotes to add source information, such as a bibliography, at the end of a report.

In Exercise 5.10, you'll create and revise footnotes and endnotes.

EXERCISE 5.10

Creating and Revising Footnotes and Endnotes

1. Open 5-10.doc from the files you downloaded for this chapter.

2. Position the insertion point where you'd like the note reference mark to appear, in this case, position it just to the right of the period at the end of the first sentence.

3. Choose Insert ➤ Reference ➤ Footnote to display the Footnote And Endnote dialog box.

4. You can select Footnotes or Endnotes in the Location area to specify what type of note you want to insert. Choose Endnotes and choose End Of Document from the drop-down list to the right to designate the position of the note.

Additional position options are available depending on the type of note:

- For Footnotes, choose Bottom Of Page to place footnotes just above the bottom margin on the page that includes the note reference mark or choose Beneath Text to place the footnotes below the last line of text on a short page of text.

- For Endnotes, you can choose to display them at the end of the document or at the end of each section.

5. Choose a Number Format from the drop-down list or, if you prefer, type the character you wish to use in the Custom Mark field or click Symbol to select a character from Word's symbol fonts. For this exercise, choose 1, 2, 3, ...

6. Enter **1** as the Start At number and choose Continuous to have Word insert consecutive numbers or symbols using the numbering format selected. You could also choose one of the following numbering options:

   - Select Restart Each Section to restart footnote numbering, using the Start At number you specified, at each section break.

   - Choose Restart Each Page to restart numbering, using the Start At number you specified, at each page break.

7. Choose Whole Document in the Apply To drop-down list. If you wanted to use different footnote/endnote formats in different parts of the document, you could also apply changes just to the section you are positioned in or just to selected text.

8. Click Insert to close the Footnote And Endnote dialog box.

Word inserts the note reference mark you specified and then, in Print Layout view, the insertion point moves to the location where the note will appear in your document. Because this is only a one-page document, the endnotes appear on the same page as the text. Normally, the endnotes would appear at the end of the document.

9. Type the text of the note, **U.S. Census Bureau (2000), Census 2000**. Press Shift+F5 or double-click the note's reference number to return to the location where you inserted the note reference mark in your document.

In Normal view, the notes pane opens. Type the text of your note beside the note reference mark.

EXERCISE 5.10 *(continued)*

You can then press F6 to move the insertion point into the document pane in the position where you inserted the note. When you want to review your note, point to the reference mark. The mouse pointer changes to an I-beam with a note attached to it, and a second later the note text appears (the notes pane has to be open for the ScreenTip to appear). You can also choose Close to hide the notes pane and View ➢ Footnotes to redisplay it.

10. Position the insertion point to the right of the third sentence in the paragraph and choose Insert ➢ Reference ➢ Footnote to display the Footnote And Endnote dialog box.

11. Word remembers all of the previous choices, so unless you want to make a change, click Insert to close the dialog box. Type **Ibid.** for the second note.

12. Click to the right of the last sentence in the paragraph and reopen the Footnote And Endnote dialog box. Click Insert and enter **Bureau of Labor Statistics, 2001** for the third note.

13. To reposition a footnote reference to another location, select the reference and drag it or use cut and paste to move it to another location. Select the third reference mark (3) and drag it to the end of the previous sentence.

14. Position the insertion point at the end of the last sentence to now insert a footnote in the same document.

15. Reopen the Footnote And Endnote dialog box and choose Footnotes. Select Bottom Of Page for the footnote's position. The other option, Below Text, positions the footnote directly after the last line of text on the page.

16. Select i, ii, iii, ... from the Number Format drop-down list. Although you could use the same format for footnotes and endnotes, using a different format makes it easier for your readers to distinguish the notes.

17. Click Insert to create the footnote at the bottom of the page. Type the following text for the footnote:
Seasonal unemployment is affected by the amount of snow for winter sports and the economy, especially the price of gasoline.

18. When you have finished entering the text, scroll to the top of the page and click anywhere to reposition the insertion point.

If you decide you want to change the footnotes or endnotes after you have created them, you can change any of the options in the Footnote And Endnote dialog box, you can delete notes, and you can even convert endnotes to footnotes and vice versa.

19. To change the number format of the endnotes in the sample document, right-click the second or third endnote and choose Note Options from the shortcut menu to reopen the Footnote And Endnote dialog box.

Note: If a footnote or endnote is identified with a spelling or grammar error, you must deal with the spelling or grammar error before the shortcut menu will include options related to notes.

20. Choose a, b, c, ... from the Number Format drop-down list. Click Apply to apply the change and close the dialog box.

Note: Clicking the Apply button in any other dialog box does not close it—in fact, it is designed to apply the changes *without* closing the dialog box. The Apply button in the Footnote And Endnote dialog box does not follow this standard. If you click the Insert button, it applies the formatting changes and inserts another note number with no reference in the document. So use Apply when you want to make changes without creating a new note.

21. To edit a note in Normal view, double-click any reference mark in the document to open the notes pane at the bottom of the screen. Double-click the reference note for the footnote.

22. All notes of the same type appear in the pane—if the list is long, scroll to the one you want to edit and make your changes. In this example, double-click "affected" and replace it with **influenced**.

23. To view the endnotes, select All Endnotes from the notes pane drop-down list.

EXERCISE 5.10 *(continued)*

24. To delete a note, you must delete the reference mark in the document. Double-click before or after the reference mark and press the Backspace or Delete key twice—the first time selects the reference mark, and the second time deletes both the mark and the note. All the other affected notes are renumbered accordingly.

Note: Deleting the text inside the notes pane or at the bottom or end of the document does not delete the reference mark in the document.

25. Close and save the document.

Adding an index, table of contents, cross-references, and notes to your documents makes them more accessible to your readers. But what do you do when your documents become the size of this book? In the next section, you'll learn about how to break a very large writing project into smaller, bite-sized chunks with master documents and subdocuments.

Managing Large Projects with Master Documents

As a policy manual, personnel handbook, report, contract, or similar document gets longer, it uses more resources to open, save, or print. It takes forever to scroll down a couple of pages, and editing becomes a nightmare. With a little foresight, you can avoid this dilemma by starting with an outline and then dividing the entire document, called the *master document*, into various related documents, called *subdocuments*. You— and others in your work group—can then work with subdocuments as autonomous entities. However, at any point you can work with the entire master document so that you can have continuous page numbering, add headers and footers, create a table of contents, attach an index, and insert cross-references—all those things you cannot do with individual, unrelated documents.

Microsoft ✓ *Exam Objective*

Create and manage master documents and subdocuments

In Exercise 5.11, you'll create and work with a master document and subdocuments.

EXERCISE 5.11

Creating and Managing Master Documents and Subdocuments

1. To create a new master document from scratch, open a new blank document and display it in Outline view. To change to Outline view, choose View ➢ Outline or click the Outline View button next to the horizontal scroll bar.

The Master Document tools appear on the Outlining toolbar.

2. Enter the following titles, pressing Enter after each one. Be sure each title is formatted using the Heading 1 style:
   Employment Philosophy
   Hiring and Employment
   Employment Requirements
   Compensation
   Benefits
   Safety and Security

3. Select the headings and click the Create Subdocument button on the Outlining toolbar. Word creates individual subdocuments using the highest-level heading text you selected as the subdocument name. In this case, you entered only Heading 1s, so each heading you entered represents a separate document. The master document displays each subdocument in a box with a small subdocument icon in the upper-left corner when displayed in Master Document view (the default).

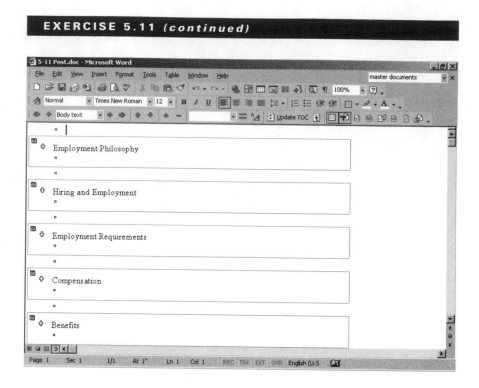

4. Save the master document and each of its subdocuments by clicking the Save button.

We recommend creating a folder to house all of the related documents and clearly identifying the master document to distinguish it from the subdocuments in the folder.

5. Click the Create New Folder button on the Save As dialog box toolbar and enter **Personnel Handbook** as the folder name. Click OK to create and open the new folder.

6. Type **Master – Personnel Handbook** in the File Name text box and click Save.

Word saves the master document and each of the subdocuments as separate documents in the folder. Now you can close the master document and open any of the subdocuments to work with them independently.

7. Close the master document by choosing File ➢ Close.

8. Choose File ➤ Open and navigate to the Personnel Handbook folder. Double-click Employment Philosophy to open it.

Remember the employment philosophy that you were working on in the last chapter? Well, we're going to insert it here to save you from typing new text.

9. Click to the right of "Philosophy" and press Enter twice. Choose Insert ➤ File and select 5-11.doc from the files you downloaded for this chapter. Delete the second "Employment Philosophy" title, and save and close the document.

10. Reopen the master document, Master - Personnel Handbook.

The document opens in Outline view. Each of the subdocuments appears as a hyperlink in the master document.

11. Click the Expand Subdocuments button on the Outlining toolbar to see the contents of each of the subdocuments, including the text we just inserted in Employment Philosophy.

Note: If you want to collapse the documents again, click the same button—it's now the Collapse Subdocuments button.

12. Click the Master Document View button on the Outlining toolbar to display the master document in Outline view. When you do, the subdocument icon and box no longer appear, and the display shows the section break marks that Word inserted before each selected heading when you created subdocuments. You can enter and edit text in individual sections and even switch to Normal or Print Layout view and work with the document just as you would a regular Word document. This includes adding page numbering, creating references, adding an index and a table of contents, and creating headers and footers. When you save changes, Word resaves each individual document.

13. The subdocuments of a master document can be locked, which makes them read-only files. Read-only files can be viewed, but no changes can be saved to them. To lock a subdocument, be sure you are in Master Document view and click the Lock Document button on the Outlining toolbar. Click the Lock Document button again to unlock a locked subdocument.

EXERCISE 5.11 *(continued)*

Note: In Master Document view, subdocuments are collapsed by default and always appear to be locked—the subdocument icons have padlocks—even if they are not. To see whether the subdocuments in a master document actually are locked, click the Expand Subdocuments button on the Outlining toolbar and look for the lock icon there.

14. To delete a subdocument, select it and press the Delete key. The subdocument is no longer a part of the master document but the file is not deleted from disk.

15. Save and close the document.

You should be pretty good by now at creating large documents and adding all the bells and whistles. But as your documents grow longer, getting around them becomes more of a challenge. In the next section, we'll show you some ways to navigate your documents.

Moving Around Documents

You probably know how to use scroll bars to move around a document. However, as documents become more complex, the scroll bar becomes less effective and can easily frustrate you as you watch pages and pages of text scroll by. In this section, we'll show you how to use the Browse Objects menu to help you navigate long documents.

Microsoft ✓ *Exam Objective*   **Move within documents**

To review specific features of a lengthy document, browsing a document is not only faster but much more accurate. You'll find the Select Browse Object button below the vertical scroll bar between the Previous [*Object*] and Next [*Object*] buttons. You can use the Select Browse Object menu, shown in Figure 5.1, to focus on just those parts of a document in which you are interested. *Objects* are files or documents created in another application and inserted into a document: for example, pictures, line art, or an Excel worksheet placed in a Word document. In this menu, the term also includes other document landmarks you might want to browse: Fields, Endnotes, Footnotes, Sections, Comments, Pages, Edits, Graphics, Headings, and Tables.

FIGURE 5.1 Select Browse Object menu

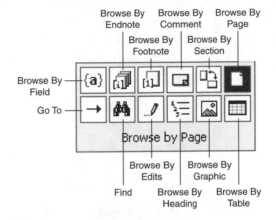

In Exercise 5.12, you'll use the Select Browse Object menu to browse by endnotes, sections, and pages and use the Go To option.

EXERCISE 5.12

Moving around a Document

1. Open 5-12.doc from the files you downloaded for this chapter.

2. Click the Select Browse Object button to open the Select Browse Object menu.

3. Click Browse By Endnote to move to the first endnote reference in the document.

4. To continue browsing to the next endnote reference, you don't have to open the menu again, just click the Next Endnote button below the Select Browse Object button. Click the Previous Endnote button to move back to the first endnote reference.

5. Click the Select Browse Object button and choose Browse By Section. This moves you to the second section in the document. Click the Next Section button to move to section 3, the last section in the document. Clicking the Next Section button again has no effect—you must click the Previous Section button to move back through the sections to the top of the document.

6. Click the Select Browse Object button and choose the Go To option. This opens the Go To tab of the Find And Replace dialog box. To go to a specific endnote reference, for example, select Endnote in the Go To What list and enter **32** in the Enter Endnote Number text box.

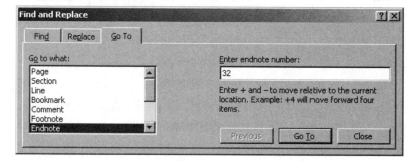

7. Click Go To to jump to the specific endnote. Click the Close button to close the Find And Replace dialog box.

8. Click the Select Browse Object button and choose Browse By Page.

9. Click Next Page and Previous Page to move through the pages of the document.

10. Close the document without saving the changes.

Using the Select Browse Object menu can make you more efficient as you move through long, complex documents. Another way to improve your efficiency is to create and distribute electronic user forms. In the next section, we'll show you how to create forms and then prepare those forms for distribution to others.

Standardizing with User Forms

A *user form* is a Word document that contains form fields in which users can enter data. Word's form controls make it possible to create text boxes, drop-down lists, and check boxes to make data entry easier.

WARNING Be aware, however, that without some programming code, data that a user enters in a Word form cannot be extracted and aggregated. If you need to collect data in a database format, you are better off using Access forms or Web forms.

Microsoft
Exam
Objective

Create and modify forms using various form controls

Word comes with the Forms toolbar, a set of tools used to create on-screen forms. The Forms toolbar includes buttons to insert form fields, to create tables and frames, to position questions and prompts on the page, to turn form-field shading on or off, and to protect the text and other objects on the form so that users can enter data only where you have placed form fields. The Forms toolbar has three types of form fields you can insert into a form:

- **Text** form fields are open fields of any length where users can enter text.

- **Check box** form fields are check boxes that a user can check or clear to indicate yes or no answers.

- **Drop-down** form fields allow users to choose a response from a list of choices you provide.

Figure 5.2 shows an example of an on-screen form that was created using a table. As you can see, the rows and columns aren't evenly distributed, and extra cells have been inserted to provide the appropriate spacing for items on the form.

FIGURE 5.2 On this protected form, users can enter text only where a form field is displayed.

In Exercise 5.13, we'll show you how to create a simpler version of the form shown in Figure 5.2.

EXERCISE 5.13

Creating a User Form Using Various Form Controls

1. Create a new blank document.

2. Activate the Forms toolbar by choosing View ➢ Toolbars ➢ Forms.

3. Click the Insert Table button on the Forms toolbar and create a table with four columns and six rows. (See Chapter 2 for an introduction to tables. Chapter 6 covers tables in more depth.)

4. Starting in the first cell in the first column, type the labels in the cells, as shown here:

Name:		Date of Request:	
Department:			
Beginning Date:		Return Date:	
	Approved		Disapproved
Comments:			
		Supervisor:	

5. Select the first column (position the pointer above the first column and click when you see a black downward-pointing arrow) and click the Align Right button on the Formatting toolbar. Repeat this step with the third column.

6. Click the cell in the first row, second column adjacent to "*Name.*" Click the first button on the Forms toolbar, Text Form Field, to insert a field into the cell.

7. Double-click the newly inserted form field to open the Text Form Field Options dialog box and set the options for the field.

8. Keep the default Regular Text in the Type drop-down list. You could choose from Regular Text, Number, Date, Current Date, Current Time, and Calculation.

9. Leave Default Text blank for this field. If you were creating a field that most users would answer a specific way, you could enter default text so users wouldn't have to enter anything unless their answer differed. For example, you could enter your state name in a State field and only users who didn't live in that state would have to re-enter an item into the field.

10. Leave Maximum Length set to Unlimited. However, if you wanted to control how many letters or numbers could be entered in a field, use the spin box controls or type a number to limit the field.

11. Select Title Case from the Text Format field. This assures that all first letters of the user's name will be in uppercase. You could also choose Uppercase, Lowercase, or First Capital. The items in this list change if you choose a different type of field from the Type list.

EXERCISE 5.13 *(continued)*

You could choose to run a macro when a user enters or exits this field by indicating the Entry or Exit macro. For example, you could have a macro that took users to another form if they answered a certain way.

12. Enter **Name** in the Bookmark field. This creates a bookmark for this field that you could reference in a macro, for example.

13. Leave the Fill-in Enabled check box selected so users can enter text into the field, and leave the Calculate On Exit check box cleared. You could check this check box if you wanted to have Word update and calculate all the fields after any exit macros run.

14. Click the Add Help Text button to add user help to the field.

15. On the Status Bar tab, choose one of the following options to specify what Help text will appear on the status bar when the field is selected:

   ▪ **None** provides no Help text on the status bar for the form field.

   ▪ **AutoText Entry** allows you to use a previously created AutoText entry as the Help text that appears on the status bar. Select the AutoText entry in the adjacent drop-down list.

   ▪ **Type Your Own** allows you to type up to 138 characters of Help text in the text box.

16. Choose Type Your Own and enter the following:
   Enter your full name, first name, and then last name.

17. On the Help Key (F1) tab, choose one of the following options to specify what Help text will appear in a message box when the field is selected and the user presses F1:

   ▪ **None** provides no Help text for the form field when the F1 key is pressed.

   ▪ **AutoText Entry** allows you to use a previously created AutoText entry as the Help text that appears when you press F1. Select the AutoText entry in the adjacent drop-down list.

   ▪ **Type Your Own** allows you to type up to 255 characters of Help text in the text box.

18. Select Type Your Own and enter the following:
   Enter your full name, first name, and then last name.

19. Click OK to close the Form Field Help Text dialog box and OK again to close the Text Form Field Options dialog box.

20. Repeat Steps 6 through 19 to create form fields next to "Comments" and "Supervisor." For the Comments field, you may want to leave the Text Format blank. Enter the following Status Bar Help text in the Comments field and create your own for the Supervisor field: **Supervisor Only: Enter comments about why the request was disapproved**.

21. Click the blank cell to the right of "Date of Request" and insert a Text form field.

22. Double-click the field to open the Text Form Field Options dialog box.

23. Choose Current Date as the Type and M/d/yyyy as the Date Format.

24. Enter **DateOfRequest** (no spaces are allowed in Bookmark names) in the Bookmark text box. Click OK to close the dialog box.

    Note: Because you chose Current Date, users won't be able to change the date and so there is no need to add help. Choose Current Date as the type only if you don't want users to be able to change it.

25. Click the cell to the right of "Beginning Date" and insert a Text form field.

26. Open the Text Form Field Options dialog box and choose Date as the Type and M/d/yyyy as the Date Format. Name the field **BegDate** and enter the following help text:
    Enter the first date you will not be at work.
    Close the Text Form Field Options dialog box by clicking the OK button.

27. Click the cell to the right of "Return Date" and insert a Text form field.

28. Open the Text Form Field Options dialog box and choose Date as the Type and M/d/yyyy as the Date Format. Name the field **ReturnDate** and enter the following Help text:
    Enter the date you will return to work.
    Close the Text Form Field Options dialog box by clicking the OK button.

29. Click the cell to the right of "Department" and click the Drop-Down Form Field button on the Forms toolbar.

30. Double-click the Drop-down form field to open the Drop-Down Form Field Options dialog box.

31. Type **Select Department** in the Drop-Down Item text box and click the Add button to add it to the items in the drop-down list.

    Note: "Select Department" is obviously not a choice you would like users to make. However, if you don't include it, the first department you enter appears as the default choice for every user. If a user fails to choose a department, you may just inadvertently reassign them. By including Select Department, you will know immediately if a user fails to select a choice.

32. Add the following additional items to the list: **Accounting**, **Info Tech**, **Sales**, and **Marketing**.

33. Click Marketing and click the Move Up button to move it before Sales.

34. Enter **Department** as the Bookmark name and **Select your department from the drop-down list.** as the Help text.

35. Close the Drop-Down Form Field Options dialog box by clicking the OK button.

36. Click the cell to the left of "Approved" and click the Check Box Form Field button on the Forms toolbar.

37. Double-click the check box to open the Check Box Form Field Options dialog box.

38. Leave the Check Box Size as Auto unless you want to control the specific size of the check box.

39. Leave the Default Value as Not Checked. Choose Checked if you want the users to click the check box to turn off a selection (No, I do not want to be on your mailing list!).

40. Enter **Approved** as the Bookmark name and **Supervisors Only: click to approve this request.** as the Help text. Click OK to close the Check Box Form Field Options dialog box when all options have been set.

EXERCISE 5.13 *(continued)*

41. Repeat Steps 36-40 to insert and set options for the Disapproved check box. Enter **Disapproved** as the Bookmark name and **Supervisors Only: click to disapprove this request**. as the Help text. Click OK to close the Check Box Form Field Options dialog box when all options have been set.

42. To give users more room to enter comments without the text wrapping, you can merge the three cells adjacent to Comments field. Select all three cells by dragging over them, and choose Table ➢ Merge Cells to merge them as one.

43. Save the form as **Time-Off Form**. You can close it if you have finished working for now or leave it open for the next exercise.

Your form is now complete. You may want to spruce up the form with borders and other formatting choices, but we'll leave that up to you. In the next section, we'll show you how to prepare the form to distribute it to others to use.

Preparing Forms for Distribution

Your form is almost ready to distribute. Before you do though, you'll want to take care of a few things to make sure the form functions the way you want it to. To make the form more attractive, you can turn off form field shading so users don't think they are restricted to the width of the form fields. You'll also want to lock it down and password-protect it so users can't make changes to it. Finally, you will want to save the form as a template, so each time the form is used, users are forced to save a copy of the form.

Microsoft ✔ *Exam Objective* | **Create forms and prepare forms for distribution**

While you are working on designing a form, you can click the Protect Form button on the Forms toolbar to work with the form as users will experience it. You can enter data in each of the fields to test that each field is set the way you want it to be. Notice that many of the toolbar buttons on the Standard and Formatting toolbars are no longer available when the form is protected. To unprotect the form, click the Protect Form button again.

After you unprotect a form, you can click the Reset Form Fields button to clear the entries you made in the form fields.

In Exercise 5.14, you'll prepare a form for distribution by finalizing its appearance, protecting the form, and saving it as a template.

EXERCISE 5.14

Preparing a Form for Distribution

1. Open 5-14.doc from the files you downloaded for this chapter or use the Time-Off Form you created in Exercise 5.13 if it is still open.

2. Click the Form Field Shading button on the Forms toolbar to turn off the form field shading.

3. Add or remove cell borders, as desired, using the Borders toolbar button on the Formatting toolbar. Make any other formatting changes. For example, you may want to add a heading such as "Time-Off Request Form" to the page.

   Note: To move the insertion point above a table on a page, press Ctrl+Home and then press Enter. The insertion point moves outside the table. Press Enter as many times as you want to create the space you need.

4. After you're sure that everything is exactly the way you want it, protect the form so the user can enter data only in the form fields. On the Tools menu, click Protect Document.

5. Select Forms.

6. Type a password of your choosing in the Password (Optional) box to assign a password to the form. Only users who know the password can remove the protection and change the form. Users who don't know the password can still enter information in the form fields. If you forget the password, you will not be able to make changes to the form either, so use a password you will remember.

7. Click OK to protect the form.

EXERCISE 5.14 *(continued)*

When you protect the form, the descriptive labels, formatting, and layout of the form cannot be changed. In addition, you will no longer have access to most toolbar and menu options.

8. The last step before distributing the form to users is to save the form as a template. Although many of the toolbar buttons and menu commands are no longer available, you can still save the template by choosing File ➢ Save As.

9. Choose Document Template from the Save As Type drop-down list. This opens the Templates folder. You can save the template here or navigate to a shared workgroup templates folder, if one is available in your organization.

10. If you want to change the name, enter a new name for the template in the File Name text box.

11. Click Save to save the template.

12. To test the form, close the template and create a new document based on the template. To create a new document, choose File ➢ New and choose the template from the New From Template section of the New Document task pane. Click General Templates to open the Templates dialog box to locate the template.

13. Enter data in the form just as a user would, pressing Tab between each field. When you have finished the form, save the document—Word requires that you enter a new name for the document.

Note: You might want to include instructions on the form for users to choose File ➢ Send To ➢ Mail Recipient (for review) to e-mail their completed form to their supervisor.

14. Save and close the document.

If you need to edit the form, be sure to open the form's template, not a document based on the template. You can do this by choosing File ➢ Open and navigating to the templates folder. After opening the template, choose Tools ➢ Unprotect Document and enter the document's password to unlock the document for editing.

If you are uncertain where templates are stored on your system, choose Tools ➢ Options and click the File Locations tab. Select either User Templates or Workgroup Templates and click the Modify button, and then click the Look In drop-down list to see the file path.

Summary

This chapter covered many advanced formatting tools that you can use with long and complex documents. In this chapter, we covered the following topics:

- Sorting paragraphs in tables and paragraphs
- Inserting new sections into documents and formatting sections differently
- Controlling pagination in a document
- Creating your own character and paragraph styles
- Generating an index for a document
- Producing a table of contents based on heading styles
- Creating tables of figures and authorities
- Adding cross references to a document
- Annotating documents with endnotes and footnotes
- Combining separate documents into one master document for page numbering and formatting
- Browsing a document using browse objects
- Adding form controls to create user forms
- Preparing a user form for distribution

Chapter 6

Customizing Tables and Graphics

MOUS WORD 2002 EXPERT EXAM OBJECTIVES COVERED IN THIS CHAPTER:

- ✓ Use Excel data in tables
- ✓ Perform calculations in Word tables
- ✓ Create, modify, and position graphics
- ✓ Create and modify charts using data from other applications
- ✓ Align text and graphics

Tables, graphics, and charts can turn a boring text document into an interesting and useful communication tool. Well-constructed tables can summarize paragraphs of text into a few lines that the reader can absorb in a single glance. Graphics can call attention to important points in the document, and charts can translate complex numeric data into easily understandable information. In this chapter, we'll present tools you can use to modify and position graphics of all kinds and to align text and graphics in tables and drawings.

If you have data in other applications, there is no sense re-creating it to incorporate into a Word document. We'll show you several ways to use data from other applications in Word tables and charts. We'll also show you how to import data from Microsoft Excel into a Word table and perform calculations on data in a table. In addition, you'll learn how to import data from Excel to create a chart in Word.

Before you begin this chapter, you should go to the Sybex website and download the file 4113Ch06.zip. This package contains the files necessary to complete some of the exercises in this chapter. In addition, it contains files of what most of the documents should look like after you complete the exercise. These files are affixed with the word *Post*.

Customizing Tables

If you are already a Microsoft Excel user, you know the benefits of creating tabular data in Excel. Just as Word is primarily designed for text, Excel is designed for tabular data—columns and rows of text and numbers. Although Word's Table feature is pretty powerful, it doesn't hold a candle to the power of Excel. Consequently, if you already have data in Excel, why reconstruct it in Word? Microsoft Office has several methods of incorporating Excel data into your Word documents.

Importing Data from Excel

When you decide to include data from a Microsoft Excel workbook in a Word document, you must first decide how important it is that the data retain some or all of its Excel functionality. In this section, we'll explore different ways to use Excel data in Word tables.

Microsoft ✓ *Exam* *Objective*	**Use Excel data in tables**

In Microsoft Office, you can make Excel data available to a Word document using three primary methods of importing data, depending on your needs for working with the data. These three methods are as follows:

- If you have simple data in an Excel worksheet that you just want to replicate in a Word document, you can simply copy and paste from Excel to Word. This method converts Excel data into a Word table and retains no relationship to the original Excel worksheet.

- If the data is a more complex and you would like to retain the option of using Excel tools to work with the data after it is copied into Word, you can embed the data as a Microsoft Worksheet object.

- If you want to be able to edit the data in Excel and have the changes automatically reflected in the Word document, you can create a dynamic link between the data and the Excel workbook.

In Exercise 6.1, you'll use each of the three primary methods to use Excel data in a Word table. Don't worry if you are unfamiliar with Excel; we'll walk you through anything you need to know about it.

EXERCISE 6.1

Using Excel Data in Tables

1. Open 6-1.doc from the files you downloaded from the Sybex website.

2. Launch Microsoft Excel (Start ➢ Programs ➢ Microsoft Excel) and choose File ➢ Open to open 6-1.xls from the Sybex website files.

3. Click cell A1 in the Revenue worksheet. Hold the mouse button down and drag down to row 5 and across to column D.

4. Click the Copy button on the Standard toolbar.

5. Switch to Word (6-1.doc) by clicking the Word taskbar button at the bottom of the screen.

6. Move the insertion point between the first two paragraphs to the line just before "The US Department...."

7. Click the Paste button on the Standard toolbar to convert the Excel data into a Word table.

   You can modify this table just as you would any other Word table. For example, you could select the cells that contain the dollar values in columns B and C and click the Align Right button on the Formatting toolbar to change their alignment.

8. Switch back to Excel (6-1.xls) by clicking the Excel taskbar button, and click cell A7. Drag the mouse pointer down to row 10 and across to column D to select the next set of data.

9. Click the Copy button on the Standard toolbar.

10. Switch to Word and position the insertion point between the second and third paragraphs and just before "The State of Michigan...."

11. Click Edit ➢ Paste Special to open the Paste Special dialog box.

EXERCISE 6.1 *(continued)*

12. Select Microsoft Excel Worksheet Object from the As list and click OK.

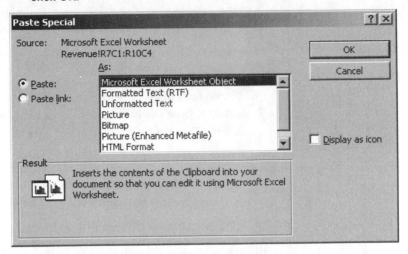

13. Double-click the table you just inserted to open the Worksheet object in Word. The worksheet retains its Excel functionality.

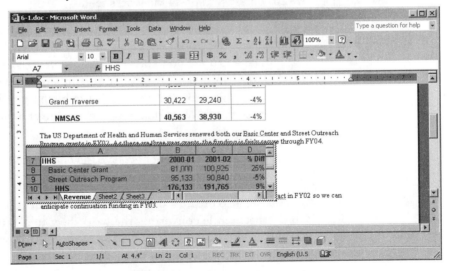

Notice that the application title bar still says Microsoft Word but the toolbar buttons and menus are those of Excel. In this mode you can edit the data, format it, and perform calculations by creating formulas (see "Performing Calculations in Word Tables" later in this chapter).

14. Click anywhere in the Word document to embed the Worksheet object into the Word document.

15. Switch back to Excel by clicking the Excel taskbar button, and click cell A12. Drag the mouse pointer down to row 14 and across to column D to select the next set of data.

16. Click the Copy button on the Standard toolbar.

17. Switch to Word and position the insertion point at the end of the document two lines down from the last paragraph.

18. Click Edit ➤ Paste Special to open the Paste Special dialog box.

19. Select Microsoft Excel Worksheet Object from the As list, and select the Paste Link radio button in the Paste Special dialog box.

20. Click OK to paste the worksheet.

21. Double-click the table you just inserted. Because it is linked to Excel, the worksheet opens directly in Excel. Any changes you make to it are immediately reflected in the Word document. For example, change the 2000-01 dollar amount by clicking cell B13 and typing **250,152**. Press Enter to input the new amount. Switch back to the Word document to see the changes reflected in the table.

22. Close the document and save the changes.

You can also create a dynamic link to the data contained in the cells of a worksheet while converting the worksheet to a Word table. You might use this method if you want to have more control over the formatting of the table while still being able to update the data. To do this, copy and paste the data into Word. After you click Paste, click the Paste Options button at the bottom right of the table and choose either Keep Source Formatting And Link To Excel or Match Destination Table Style And Link To Excel.

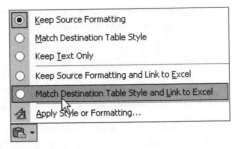

In this case, the table functions as a Word table, but when you click the cell, all of the cells' contents display a gray background. This is the telltale sign that the data is linked.

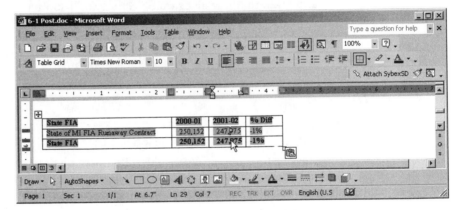

If you open the Excel workbook and make changes to the data, the changes are immediately reflected in the Word table.

WARNING Using this method of data linking is a one-way operation. If you change the data in the Word table, the changes are not reflected in the original Excel worksheet.

Performing Calculations in Word Tables

To do or not to do—that is the question when it comes to performing calculations in Word tables. Creating a table using the Word Table feature does not give it the functionality of an Excel worksheet. The most obvious negative implication of entering formulas to perform calculations in a Word table is that they do not automatically recalculate if you change the data. As you can imagine, this could have serious consequences—changing one number could throw off all of the calculations in a complex table. For this reason alone, we recommend that you never perform calculations in a Word table.

As you saw in the last section, you can insert an Excel Worksheet object into a Word document and retain all of the functionality of Excel, including automatically recalculating formulas. Or, better yet, you can link the table or the data to an Excel worksheet and do all your work directly in Excel, where you can be confident that all of Excel's functionality will be available to you.

Even the Microsoft Help files recommend that you use Excel to perform complex calculations. For more information about working with Excel and creating Excel formulas to perform calculations, see chapters 10–21.

That being said, it is possible to enter simple formulas into a Word table, and given that it is an exam objective, we'll show you how to do it.

Microsoft ✓ *Exam Objective*

Perform calculations in Word tables

If you have created formulas in Excel, then you already know a lot about creating formulas in Word tables. Because you don't have column letters and row numbers in Word tables, you have to do some counting to know how to refer to cells. Columns are designated by letters (A, B, C, etc.), and rows are designated by numbers (1, 2, 3, etc). So the cell at the intersection of the first column and the first row is referred to A1.

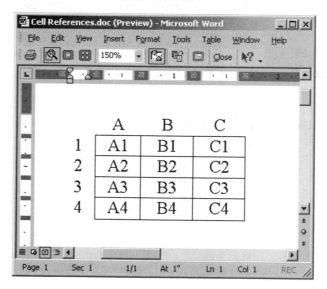

In Exercise 6.2, you'll create formulas that include addition, subtraction, multiplication, and division.

EXERCISE 6.2

Performing Calculations in Word Tables

1. Open the document 6-2.doc from the files you downloaded from the Sybex website. Activate the Tables And Borders toolbar by clicking the Tables And Borders button on the Standard toolbar.

2. Click cell B4—that is where you will enter the first formula to add the two numbers above it.

3. Click the AutoSum button on the Tables And Borders toolbar.

Word automatically enters the formula =Sum(Above) and displays the result in a field in the cell.

Warning: Because this formula does not identify a range of cells, e.g., B2:B3, it stops if it encounters an empty cell or a cell that contains text. If you are adding a column or row that contains empty cells, be sure to enter **0** in those cells.

4. Click cell D2 to enter a formula to subtract the 2002 column from the 2001 column.

5. Choose Table ➢ Formula to open the Formula dialog box.

6. Word automatically inserts the formula =Sum(Left). Select this formula leaving the equal sign (=) and enter the text **C2-B2**.

7. Select the number format, #,##0, from the Number Format drop-down list to display the result with a comma and no decimal places.

EXERCISE 6.2 *(continued)*

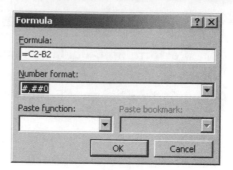

8. Click OK to enter the formula and display the result.

To calculate the percentage difference, you need to divide the number in the Difference column by the 2001 number and multiply by 100.

9. Click cell E2 and choose Table ≻ Formula to reopen the Formula dialog box.

10. Replace the existing formula with **=D2/B2*100** and select 0.00% as the number format. Click OK to enter the formula and display the result.

11. For practice, enter the remaining formulas in cells C4, D3, D4, E3, and E4.

12. Close the document and save the changes.

After you enter a formula, you can view the formula by right-clicking the field that contains the result and choosing Toggle Field Codes from the shortcut menu. This shows you the formula and any number formatting that you applied.

	2001	2002	Difference	% Increase /Decrease
Rent	17,500	19,000	{ =C2-B2 \# "#,##0" }	8.57%
Telephone	6,225	7,500		
	25,726			

Editing Formulas

You can edit the formula directly if, for example, you entered C3 and you meant C2. You can also edit the formula by returning to the Formula dialog box. To do this, right-click the formula and choose Edit Field. Click the Formula button on the Field dialog box to open the Formula dialog box.

Accessing Additional Functions

In addition to the four standard mathematical operations of addition, subtraction, multiplication, and division, you can access functions to calculate an average, count, show the minimum and maximum values, and even create IF statements in Word tables. From the Formula dialog box, select the function you want to use from the Paste Function drop-down list. Word automatically inserts the function in the Formula text box.

Recalculating Word Formulas

If you change a number that is used in a calculation, you must manually recalculate the formula since Word does not automatically recalculate formulas. To recalculate a formula, right-click the field that contains the formula and choose Update Field or press F9.

Modifying and Positioning Graphics

In Chapter 3, you learned how to create graphics using the Drawing toolbar and the drawing canvas. In this section, you'll learn how to reposition and resize graphics so they appear where you want them to be in your documents.

Microsoft *Exam* *Objective*	**Create, modify, and position graphics**

Positioning and Resizing Pictures

Finding the perfect clip art is more than half the battle. Positioning the clips in your document so they enhance rather than detract from your message is the rest. Word makes it easy to work with pictures, but knowing a few tricks will give you full control of how your clips appear in your documents.

When you insert a picture into a document, the bottom of the picture is aligned with the text at the location of the insertion point. This default layout position, In Line With Text, is rather limiting—you can move the clip only as if you were moving a block of text, one character or one line of text at a time. In Exercise 6.3, you'll insert and then reposition the clip art so that it appears exactly where you want it.

EXERCISE 6.3

Repositioning Clip Art

1. Open the file 6-3.doc from the files you downloaded from the Sybex website.

2. Position the insertion point roughly where you want the clip art to appear. For this exercise, position the insertion point at the end of the first paragraph.

3. Activate the Insert Clip Art task pane (Insert ➤ Picture ➤ Clip Art), or click the Insert Clip Art button on the Drawing toolbar. If the Drawing toolbar is not open, you can open it by clicking the Drawing button on the Standard toolbar).

4. Enter **business, computer** in the Search Text box, and click Search to repeat the search conducted in Exercise 3.1.

5. Click the first image that appears in the task pane to insert it into the document.

6. Click the image in the document to select it—the Picture toolbar should open automatically.

Note: The Picture toolbar may float over the document or may appear in line with the Standard and Formatting toolbars. If the Picture toolbar does not appear, you can open it by choosing View ➤ Toolbars ➤ Picture.

EXERCISE 6.3 *(continued)*

7. For more flexibility with how the clip integrates with the text and with how easy it is to move around the document, choose a different text-wrapping option. Click the Text Wrapping button on the Picture toolbar to open the Text Wrapping menu.

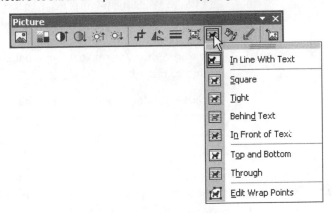

8. Choose Square or Tight if you want the text to wrap around the image. With Square, the text maintains a square around the image; with Tight, the text wraps more closely to the image. For this exercise, choose Square.

9. Point to the image, and with the four-headed arrow, move the image where you want it. For example, you may want it toward the right margin so the first and second paragraphs wrap around it.

10. Close the document and click Yes to save the changes.

Resizing Clip Art

When you click a picture (or any object) to select it, eight handles appear around the outside: one handle at each of the four corners and one on each side. When you point to any of these handles, the pointer changes to a two-headed resize arrow. Drag any handle to resize the object in the desired direction. Drag one of the corner handles if you want to resize the object while maintaining the object's original proportions.

EXERCISE 6.4

Resizing Clip Art

1. Open 6-4.doc from the files you downloaded from the Sybex website. This is the same document you saved in Exercise 6.3.

2. Click to select the picture. Point to the selection handle in the bottom-left corner of the image and drag the handle up and to the right to make the image smaller. Resize the graphic so that it fits in the first paragraph. If you make it too small, drag the selection handle down and to the left.

3. Close the document and save the changes.

As long as you resize a picture using a corner handle, Word 2002 automatically maintains the picture's original proportions. To turn this feature off, clear the Lock Aspect Ratio check box on the Size tab in the Format Picture dialog box (right-click the picture and choose Format Picture). You can still maintain proportions even with this option turned off by holding Shift while dragging a corner handle.

Modifying Pictures with the Picture Toolbar

Although Word does not have the features of photo-editing software such as Microsoft Photo Editor or a third-party photo-editing package such as Adobe PhotoShop, you still have some basic editing options available to you within Word. When you want to change a picture by adjusting the contrast or brightness, setting the transparency, or cropping it, the Picture toolbar may just have the tools you need. Table 6.1 describes the buttons you can find on the Picture toolbar.

The Crop and Set Transparent Color buttons are used with specific areas of the picture. All other buttons affect the entire picture.

TABLE 6.1   The Picture Toolbar Buttons

Button	Name	Use
	Insert Picture	Inserts a picture from a file.
	Color	Determines the appearance of the picture: Automatic (applies the most appropriate format, usually the defaults), Grayscale (converts each color to a shade of gray), Black & White (changes each color to black or white, converting the image to line art), or Washout (changes the picture to a bright, low-contrast format that can be placed behind document text—an excellent choice for creating a watermark).
	More Contrast	Increases color intensity.
	Less Contrast	Decreases color intensity.
	More Brightness	Adds white to lighten the colors.
	Less Brightness	Adds black to darken the colors.
	Crop	Trims rectangular areas from the image.
	Rotate Left	Rotates the picture 90 degrees to the left with each click.
	Line Style	Formats the border that surrounds the picture.
	Compress Pictures	Reduces the size of graphics, and thereby the size of document files, by changing the resolution of the picture for Web/Screen and Print uses, compressing the picture by applying jpeg compression to high-color pictures (may result in a loss of quality), and deleting cropped areas of a picture.

TABLE 6.1   The Picture Toolbar Buttons *(continued)*

Button	Name	Use
	Text Wrapping	Determines the way document text wraps around the picture.
	Format Picture/ Object	Displays the Picture page in the Format Object/Picture dialog box so you can change the format to exact specifications.
	Set Transparent Color	Used like an eyedropper to make areas of jpeg pictures transparent. Used extensively in web design.
	Reset Picture	Returns the picture to its original format.

Aligning Text and Graphics

You may be pretty good at eyeballing how high to hang a picture on the wall, but when it comes to printed or online documents, eyeballing may not give you the precision you need. In this section, we'll review how to align text, both in paragraphs and in the cells of tables, and introduce you to using the Drawing toolbar to align graphics on a page.

Microsoft ✓ *Exam Objective*   **Align text and graphics**

Aligning Text in Paragraphs and Table Cells

Aligning a paragraph between the left and right margins of a document is a simple matter of clicking the Align Left, Center, Align Right, and Justify buttons on the Standard toolbar.

Align Left aligns the paragraph with the left margin, Center centers the paragraph between the left and right margins, Align Right aligns the paragraph with the right margin, and Justify spreads out the characters in the paragraph so that the paragraph appears to be aligned evenly with the left and right margins. Refer to Chapter 1, "Creating Basic Documents," if you want to find more information on paragraph alignment.

To align text horizontally in the cells of a table, you use the same process. The difference is that the text aligns between the borders of the cell rather than the margins of the document. You can also align text vertically in the cell of a table. To align text vertically, however, you must first adjust the row height so the text has somewhere to go (see Exercise 2.6 for practice with setting row height). You can then choose from among a number of vertical and horizontal alignment combinations by clicking the drop-down arrow on the Cell Alignment button on the Tables And Borders toolbar.

Aligning Graphics

Whether you are inserting clip art or using the Drawing toolbar to create your own graphics, it's not always easy to line up everything so it looks intentional. Figure 6.1 shows a simple flowchart created with Word's AutoShapes. All in all, it looks pretty good, but the few shapes that are out of place detract from the entire flowchart. In Exercise 6.5, we'll show you how to use Word's alignment tools to put everything in its place.

FIGURE 6.1   This flowchart needs some help from Word's alignment tools.

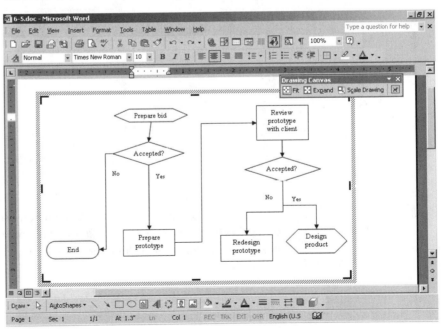

EXERCISE 6.5

Aligning Graphics

1. Open 6-5.doc from the files you downloaded from the Sybex website, and activate the Drawing toolbar by clicking the Drawing button on the Standard toolbar if it is not already visible.

2. Click the Draw button on the Drawing toolbar, and choose Align Or Distribute from the Draw menu.

Because you are going to use several tools on the Align Or Distribute menu, you might find it easier to convert it to a floating toolbar so it stays open as you work.

3. Point to the title bar of the Align Or Distribute menu and drag the menu into the document.

The Align Or Distribute toolbar contains a number of alignment tools. The first three buttons are used for horizontal alignment and the next three are for vertical alignment (in relation to the page margins).

4. Select the Prepare Bid, Accepted?, and Prepare Prototype boxes by holding the Shift key and clicking each shape. Each selected shape has selection handles around it.

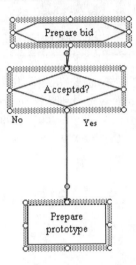

5. Click the Align Center button on the Align Or Distribute toolbar to align the boxes horizontally.

Note: If the Drawing Canvas toolbar appears, click the Close button to close it.

6. Select the No and Yes text boxes in the first column (holding Shift to select both boxes), and click the Align Middle button on the Align Or Distribute toolbar to align the boxes vertically.

7. Select the No and Yes text boxes in the second column and click the Align Top button on the Align Or Distribute toolbar to align the tops of these boxes vertically.

8. Select all four of the boxes at the bottom of the flowchart and click the Align Middle button to align the boxes vertically.

EXERCISE 6.5 *(continued)*

Note: If the connector line pointing to the Design Product box bugs you, you can line it up by clicking the line to select it and dragging the yellow diamond handle down until it lines up with the other connector line.

9. Close the document and save the changes.

The other alignment buttons on the Align Or Distribute toolbar work the same way as the ones demonstrated in the exercise. If you are unhappy with the results of your choice, click the Undo button on the Standard toolbar and try another option.

Using External Data to Create and Modify Charts

Just as you might import data from Excel to display in a Word table, you might also import Excel data to create a chart with Microsoft Graph. In Chapter 3, you learned how to create a chart by entering data into a Microsoft Graph datasheet. Microsoft Graph also accepts external data in a number of different file formats. Table 6.2 identifies the file types and corresponding file extensions that can be imported into Microsoft Graph.

TABLE 6.2 File Types That Can Be Imported into Microsoft Graph

File Extension	File Type
txt, csv	Text (delimited, that is, separated by tab characters, commas, or spaces)
wks, wk1	Lotus 1-2-3
xls	Microsoft Excel worksheet or workbook
xlw	Microsoft Excel version 4.0 workbook
xlc	Microsoft Excel version 4.0 or earlier chart

Microsoft
Exam
Objective

Create and modify charts using data from other applications

In Exercise 6.6, you will import data into Microsoft Graph from an Excel worksheet. You'll also modify the chart by excluding columns and rows of imported data and switching from plotting the data series in rows to plotting the data series in columns.

EXERCISE 6.6

Creating and Modifying a Chart with Imported Data

1. Create a new, blank Word document.

2. Choose Insert ➢ Picture ➢ Chart to start Microsoft Graph.

3. Click the Import File button on the Microsoft Graph Standard toolbar.

4. In the Import File dialog box, locate and select 6-6.xls from the files you downloaded from the Sybex website. Click Open.

5. Click OK in the Import Data Options dialog box to select the Revenue worksheet, to import the entire sheet, and to overwrite existing cells in the Microsoft Graph datasheet.

6. If the Picture toolbar opens, move it in front of the datasheet by pointing to the title bar and dragging it to a blank part of the document.

7. Resize the datasheet by dragging the resize handle in the bottom-right corner of the datasheet so you can see all of the imported data. You may need to move the datasheet up further within the Word window in order to be able to resize it to accommodate all the data.

8. Double-click the C column header to remove column C from the chart. The data in column C turns gray to indicate that it is not displayed in the chart.

EXERCISE 6.6 *(continued)*

9. Double-click the row headers for rows 1, 2, 3, 7, and 8 to remove these rows from the chart.

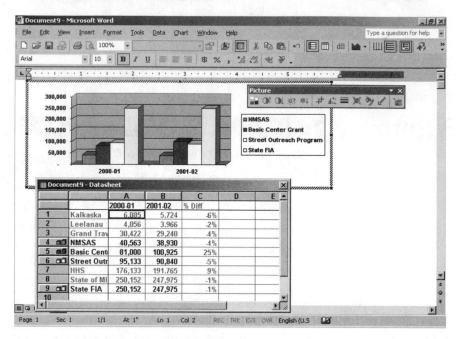

The chart currently displays the data by rows. Displaying the data by columns changes the chart. Rather than comparing funding sources in each fiscal year, it compares fiscal years for each funding source. The chart you choose to use depends on what information you want to communicate.

10. Click the By Column button on the Standard toolbar to switch to the column data series.

11. Drag the right border of the chart to extend the chart so that all of the data labels appear underneath the columns. If the datasheet is in your way, click the Close button to close it. You can reopen it by clicking the View Datasheet button on the Standard toolbar.

EXERCISE 6.6 *(continued)*

Note: If the data labels still do not display clearly, right-click the labels, choose Format Axis, and change the font size to 8 or 10 pt on the Font tab of the Format Axis dialog box.

12. Click outside the chart to embed the chart in the Word document.

13. Close and save the document.

Summary

Microsoft Word is part of the Microsoft Office suite, and it's the suite that makes Office so powerful. By learning how to integrate the applications in the Office suite, you can maximize the power of each of the Office tools.

In this chapter, we covered the following topics:

- Importing data from Excel into Word tables
- Entering formulas to perform calculations in Word tables
- Repositioning graphics
- Resizing clip art and other graphics
- Using the Picture toolbar in modifying pictures
- Aligning text and graphics
- Importing data from Excel to create a chart in Microsoft Graph

Customizing Word with Macros and Toolbars

MOUS WORD 2002 EXPERT EXAM OBJECTIVES COVERED IN THIS CHAPTER:

✓ Create, edit, and run macros

✓ Customize menus and toolbars

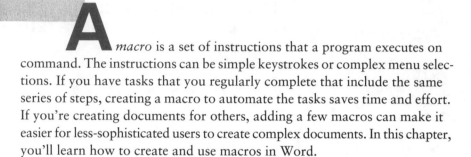

A *macro* is a set of instructions that a program executes on command. The instructions can be simple keystrokes or complex menu selections. If you have tasks that you regularly complete that include the same series of steps, creating a macro to automate the tasks saves time and effort. If you're creating documents for others, adding a few macros can make it easier for less-sophisticated users to create complex documents. In this chapter, you'll learn how to create and use macros in Word.

While you are saving time and effort, you might also want to consider creating customized menus and toolbars. You will find customized menus and toolbars especially useful when you create macros, but they can be used to make your life easier in a variety of other ways by putting just the tools you need at your fingertips. In this chapter, we'll also show you how to customize menus and toolbars so the tools you need are ready and waiting.

Before you begin this chapter, you should go to the Sybex website and download the file 4113Ch07.zip. This package contains the files necessary to complete some of the exercises in this chapter. In addition, it contains files of what most of the documents should look like after you complete the exercises.

Customizing Word with Macros

Whenever you find yourself repeating the same steps over and over again, it's time to think macros. Let's say, for example, that you regularly prepare documents for the board of directors that include line numbering so they can discuss the document by referring to the line numbers. In this document, you like to include standard text on the last page of a document that contains the date the document was created, the date the document was last printed, and the filename. By creating a macro that inserts line numbers and adds field codes with the variable data at the end of the document, you can prepare any document for board review at the click of a button. This is just one example of the usefulness of macros. Macros can be simple or complex, for your use or to share with others—the important thing is that macros can generally save you time and help you avoid costly mistakes.

Microsoft ✓ *Exam* *Objective*	**Create, edit, and run macros**

One of the great things about macros is that you don't need to know anything about programming languages such as Visual Basic to create one. Microsoft Office has a built-in macro recorder that you can use to record the steps you want to include in your macro. As you complete the tasks you want to accomplish, Office translates the recording into Visual Basic code for you. In this section, you'll use the macro recorder to create a couple of different macros.

Recording a Macro

Most macros complete repetitive tasks that involve several steps. You record (create) the series of steps you want to repeat. The next time you need to carry out the operation, you can run (play back) the macro to repeat the steps. Before recording a macro, you should practice the steps you want to record, because once you begin recording, all your actions are recorded, mistakes included. After you have the steps down, determine what conditions your macro will operate under and set them up. Will you always use the macro in a specific document? If so, open that document. Will the macro be used to change or format selected text? Then have the text selected before you begin recording the macro, just as you will when you play the macro back at a later time.

In Exercise 7.1, you'll walk through the steps of creating a macro using the macro recorder. This macro prepares a document for printing by inserting file-related information at the end of the document, automatically running the Spelling and Grammar feature and then sending the document to the printer. Later in this chapter, we'll show you how to replace the Print button on the Standard toolbar with a button that runs this macro. Remember that if you were creating this macro by yourself, you would want to practice all the steps you want to accomplish before you start recording. For the purposes of this exercise, we'll tell you what we're going to accomplish and then start recording. After you start recording, you can take your time executing each step because Word records only the steps—it is not concerned about the timing.

EXERCISE 7.1

Creating a Macro with the Macro Recorder

1. Open 7-1.doc from your downloaded files. Notice the spelling and grammar errors.

2. Choose Tools ≻ Macro ≻ Record New Macro to start the Macro Recorder. The Record Macro dialog box opens.

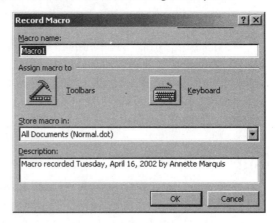

3. Enter **SpellAndPrint** in the Macro Name text box.

Note: Macro names can contain up to 80 letters and numbers but they must start with a letter and cannot contain spaces.

You can create a macro that is available in all documents based on the Normal template (Normal.dot) or you can choose to make a macro available only in the current document. In this case, we'll leave the Store Macro In section set to its default, All Documents.

4. If desired, you can enter a more detailed description of the macro in the Description text box.

Note: If other users will have access to the macro, include your name for reference. With the proliferation of macro viruses, anonymous macros are obviously suspect.

EXERCISE 7.1 *(continued)*

5. To make a macro easy to run, you can assign it to a toolbar or create a keystroke combination that runs the macro from the keyboard. In this example, we'll assign the macro to the toolbar, so click the Toolbars button.

6. The Customize dialog box opens, which is the regular dialog box you use to customize toolbars. To add the macro to the Standard toolbar, select Normal.NewMacros.SpellAndPrint in the Commands list on the Commands tab, and then drag and drop the macro to the right of the Print button. The entire name of the macro, Normal .NewMacros.SpellAndPrint, appears on the toolbar button.

Note: Later in this chapter, we'll return to the Customize dialog box and show you how to replace the text on this macro button with the image of the Print button and then remove the original Print button from the toolbar.

7. To begin recording the macro, click the Close button on the Customize dialog box. The dialog box closes and the Stop Recording toolbar opens.

From this point until you stop recording, every mouse click and keystroke are recorded by the macro recorder, so be sure to follow the instructions carefully.

a. Press Ctrl+End to move to the end of the document.

b. Press Enter three times.

c. Click the down arrow on the Borders button on the Formatting toolbar, and click the Top Border button.

d. Choose Insert ➢ AutoText ➢ Header/Footer and choose Created On.

e. Press Enter.

f. Choose Insert ➢ AutoText ➢ Header/Footer and choose Last Printed.

g. Press Enter.

h. Type **File Name:** and press the spacebar.

i. Choose Insert ➤ AutoText ➤ Header/Footer and choose Filename.

j. Press Ctrl + Home to move to the top of the document.

Note: Although it is not necessary to move to the top of the document to run Spelling and Grammar, doing so means that it always starts at the top and runs through to the end. This ensures that no text is selected and makes it easier for you to know where you are as you correct a long document.

k. Click the Spelling And Grammar button on the Standard toolbar. This opens the Spelling And Grammar dialog box and identifies the first error. In this case, it identifies the grammar error in the first sentence.

Note: Although the Macro Recorder records mouse clicks and keystrokes, it automatically pauses recording while the Spelling And Grammar dialog box is open. It just so happens that in this sample document, each error can be corrected with the top suggestion offered in the Suggestions list. So you can correct the error and move on to the next error by clicking the Change button. In another document, you may have to select a different choice, ignore the error, or make the correction manually.

l. To correct the errors, click the Change button in the Spelling And Grammar dialog box four times and then click OK to acknowledge the completion of the spelling and grammar check.

m. Click the Print button on the Standard toolbar to send the document to the printer.

8. Click the Stop Recording button on the Stop Recording toolbar to turn off the Macro Recorder.

9. To test the macro, close the document without saving changes and then reopen it. Click the Normal.NewMacros.SpellAndPrint button on the Standard toolbar. When the Spelling And Grammar dialog box opens, correct the spelling and grammar errors. After the errors are corrected, the document is automatically sent to the printer. When the macro has finished playing, it returns control back to you.

EXERCISE 7.1 *(continued)*

10. Close and save the document.

Note: For an even better test, open one of your own documents that contains spelling and grammar errors and run the macro. You'll know that the macro ran correctly if it prints after inserting the AutotText and allowing you to correct the errors.

If you create a macro and do not assign it to a toolbar or menu in the Record Macro dialog box, you can still run the macro by following these steps:

1. Choose Tools ➤ Macro ➤ Macros to open the Macros dialog box.

2. Select the macro you want to run from the list of available macros.

3. Click the Run button.

Opening a Document that Contains Macros

Because of the proliferation of macro viruses, Word notifies you if any macros exist in a document you are trying to open (unless you have changed the Security setting in Word's Options to Low).

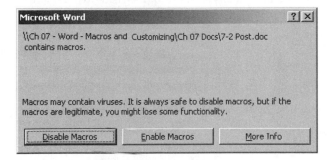

You can decide whether you want to open the document with macros enabled or to disable them. Disabling the macros gives you an opportunity to look at them in the Visual Basic Editor without endangering your computer. If you decide you want to enable the macros, just close and then reopen the file. If you are opening a document that contains macros and you know that you or a coworker created the macros, choose Enable. If, on the other hand, you received the document, unsolicited, as an e-mail attachment, consider disabling the macros or not opening the file.

Examining and Editing Macros

Word 2002 macros are stored in Visual Basic *modules* and edited in the Visual Basic Editor. To examine or edit a macro, choose Tools ➤ Macro ➤ Macros to open the Macros dialog box, select the macro you want to examine, and then click the Edit button to open the Visual Basic Editor, shown in Figure 7.1.

The Visual Basic Editor may contain a number of windows. In Figure 7.1, Project and Properties windows are open on the left and the actual code is displayed on the right. If you are new to VB programming, leave the Project and Properties windows alone for the time being and focus on the code. If a macro is longer than the window, you can scroll through the Visual Basic code window to see the information recorded in the macro.

The macro name and description always appear at the top of the macro. The macro code begins with the word Sub (for subroutine) and the macro name. The description appears on the following lines. If you know VB or VBA (Visual Basic for Applications), you can create macros and other procedures directly by typing VBA code into a module's code window. If you want to learn about Visual Basic, recording macros and studying the resulting code are a good way to begin. Even if you don't understand VB, you can do some simple editing here. In Exercise 7.2, you'll edit the SpellandPrint macro you created in Exercise 7.1.

FIGURE 7.1 Visual Basic Editor in Word displaying the SpellAndPrint macro

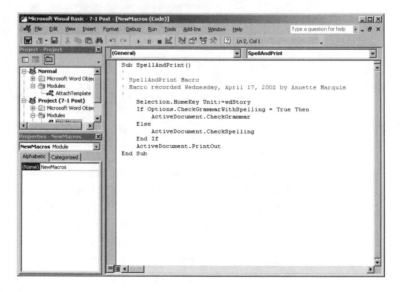

EXERCISE 7.2

Editing a Macro

1. Open 7-2.doc and choose Tools ➤ Macro ➤ Macros to open the Macros dialog box.

Note: So that the macro would be available for you to use, when this macro was created, we chose to store it in this document rather than in the default choice of All Documents. We made this choice in the Record Macro dialog box. Macros stored in a specific document are saved and can be distributed with the document, whereas the All Documents choice makes the macro available only to the user who created it. When you store a macro in All Documents, the macro loads every time you launch Word. If you plan to use a macro only with a specific document, it's better to store it with the document.

In the Macros dialog box, the default choice is to view macros in all active documents and templates. If you have a lot of macros, you can narrow down the list by choosing to see only the macros in the default template (normal.dot), the current document, or any other open template. You choose these options from the Macros In drop-down list.

2. For the purposes of this exercise, select All Active Templates And Documents from the Macros In drop-down list. Choose SpellAndPrint from the Macro Name list and click on the Edit button. This opens the Visual Basic Editor.

In the SpellAndPrint macro, visible in the right pane of the Microsoft Visual Basic Editor, you can see the commands the Macro recorder inserted as you followed the steps. In the first part of the macro, you see the end of document command: Selection.EndKey Unit:=wdStory, followed by the three hard returns: Selection.TypeParagraph. It then shows the insertion of the top border, the AutoText entries, and finally the spell checking and printing.

3. To change printed text that is inserted by a macro, scroll down to the end of the macro and in the line that reads Selection.TypeText Text:="File Name: ", replace File with **Document**.

4. Click the Save button to save the macro, and click the Close button to close the Visual Basic window.

Note: Word automatically saves the macro when you close the window, so you really don't need to click Save first. However, it's always a good habit to get into just to be on the safe side.

EXERCISE 7.2 *(continued)*

5. Click the Normal.NewMacros.SpellAndPrint button on the Standard toolbar to see the changes. Because you recently checked spelling, it sails through that part but the change to the AutoText entry is obvious in the new text at the end of the document.

6. Save and close the document.

Deleting Macros

You can delete a macro in two ways. If you have recorded a macro and are not pleased with the way it executes, you can record the macro again, using the same name. You will be asked if you want to overwrite (delete) the existing macro. You can also choose Tools ➤ Macro ➤ Macros, select the macro from the macro list, and click the Delete button to delete the macro from the template. If you delete a macro that has a command bar item, you also need to remove the macro's button from the toolbar. In the next section, you'll learn how to add and remove buttons from a toolbar and create custom toolbars.

Creating Customized Menus and Toolbars

Automating repetitive tasks with macros is one way to make Word work for you. Another valuable way to save time is to customize Word's toolbars and menus. You can add items to toolbars and menus, remove items you don't need, and move items to new locations that fit the way you work.

Microsoft ✓ *Exam* *Objective*	**Customize menus and toolbars**

Office XP is designed to create an environment that supports the way you use each application. When you initially launch an Office application, such as Word, it displays one row of buttons containing the most frequently used buttons from the Standard and Formatting toolbars. The menus show similarly limited options. In order to see all choices under a menu, you must pause a moment or click the Expand button at the bottom of the collapsed menu.

As you use an application, Office "personalizes" the toolbars and menus by displaying the commands you use. When an entire toolbar or menu is not displayed, the buttons you have used most recently are displayed and others are hidden. For many users, this is enough customization. And for some of us, spontaneously regenerating toolbars are a bit too much customization. If you want to control which menu options and toolbar buttons are visible, you can customize all of the menu bars and toolbars and most of the Office XP shortcut menus.

Changing Toolbar Options

Microsoft heard users' pleas to make certain toolbar settings available without having to open the Customize dialog box (see below). In Office XP, you can click the drop-down arrow at the end of any toolbar and choose Show Buttons On Two Rows.

For additional settings, you must access options for toolbars by right-clicking any toolbar or menu bar and choosing Customize from the shortcut menu. The Customize dialog box opens. Choose the Options tab to view the options for menus and toolbars, as shown in Figure 7.2.

FIGURE 7.2 You can change toolbar options on the Options tab of the Customize dialog box.

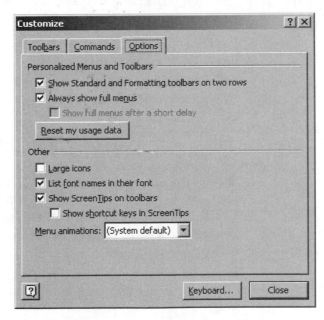

Two options in this dialog box are specific to the application: Show Standard And Formatting Toolbars On Two Rows and Reset My Usage Data. All the other options affect all of Office XP, regardless of which application you set them in. The following list includes all options:

Show Standard And Formatting Toolbars On Two Rows   You can turn on the check box to stack the toolbars, which gives more room to display buttons.

Always Show Full Menus   With this option turned off, each application shows you a personalized menu (short menu) with the commands you use frequently. Turn this on, and you'll see full menus in all applications.

Show Full Menus After A Short Delay   If you like personalized menus, you should probably leave this turned on. If you don't leave it on, then you must actually click the Expand icon at the bottom of a collapsed menu—as opposed to pausing a moment—to see the items you don't select often.

Reset My Usage Data   Office tracks and saves your usage data when you close each application. This button resets the buttons and the menu commands shown in the personalized menus and toolbars.

Large Icons   Intended for users with impaired vision, these are truly large. Just turn them on for a moment, and you'll either love them or rush to return them to their normal size.

List Font Names In Their Font   This option affects only the Font drop-down list on the Formatting toolbar. It makes it easier to choose a font, but you'll take a slight performance hit, particularly if you have a large number of fonts installed on your computer.

Show ScreenTips On Toolbars   Formerly called ToolTips, these are enabled by default; remember that turning them off here turns them off throughout Office.

Show Shortcut Keys In ScreenTips   Heads up keyboarders! Here's your opportunity to learn the keyboard shortcuts for toolbar buttons. Enable this setting and you'll see the shortcuts in the screen tips when you point to a button. Look at them enough and you'll have them memorized in no time.

Menu Animations   Although interesting initially, these effects (Unfold, Slide, and Random) can become cloying rather quickly. Animation is disabled by default.

After you've changed the options, click Close to close the Customize dialog box and apply the options you chose.

To make toolbars appear and behave as they did in Office 97, you need to enable two check boxes: Show Standard And Formatting Toolbars On Two Rows and Always Show Full Menus.

Customizing Built-in Toolbars

While the Customize dialog box is open, all displayed toolbars are open for editing. Drag menu items or buttons to new locations to rearrange them, or drop them in the document window to delete them. To add a toolbar button or menu command, click the Commands tab of the Customize dialog box. The Commands tab from Word is shown in Figure 7.3.

FIGURE 7.3   Drag commands from the Commands tab to a toolbar or menu.

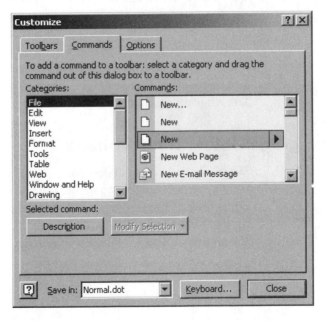

Commands are grouped into categories. Choose a category in the Categories pane, and then locate the command you want to add in the Commands pane. (Click the Description button to see a brief description of the selected command.) Drag the command onto a toolbar or the menu bar. To add a command to an existing menu, select and drag the command you want to add, point to the menu you want to add it to, and when the menu opens, place the command in the appropriate place.

You can also rearrange, delete, or display toolbar buttons and menu items without opening the Customize dialog box. Simply hold the Alt key while you drag the command.

Each toolbar has its own set of built-in buttons. To quickly add or remove built-in buttons on a toolbar, click the Toolbar Options drop-down arrow and choose Add Or Remove Buttons from the menu. Buttons displayed on the toolbar have a check mark. Click the button name to add or remove the button from the toolbar.

Creating New Toolbars

You aren't limited to the built-in toolbars. Creating a new toolbar gives you the opportunity to gather all the toolbar buttons you frequently use in one place. To create an entirely new toolbar, click the New button on the Toolbars tab of the Customize dialog box. You are prompted for a new toolbar name, and the application opens the toolbar. Drag buttons onto the toolbar from the Commands list. To copy a button from an existing toolbar, hold down the Ctrl key while dragging the button.

Changing Toolbar Item Options

While the Customize dialog box is open, you can change the properties of toolbar buttons and menu items. For example, you can change the text that appears in the macro buttons you added to the Standard and Formatting toolbars in Exercise 7.1. Exercise 7.3 walks you through the steps to replace the text on the macro buttons with images.

EXERCISE 7.3

Customizing Toolbar Options

1. From any document, right-click a toolbar and choose Customize from the shortcut menu.

If you recall from Exercise 7.1, the purpose of the macro we created was to ensure that you never send a document to the printer without checking spelling and grammar first. You can be most confident of this by replacing the standard Print button with a button that calls this macro. To replace the button, you'll first copy the image from the Print button and then remove the original Print button from the toolbar. You'll then paste the image to the macro button and turn off the text display so only the image appears.

2. Right-click the Print button and choose Copy Button Image from the shortcut menu of customization options.

3. Drag and drop the Print button off the Standard toolbar or choose Delete from the shortcut menu to remove the Print button.

4. Right-click the Normal.NewMacros.SpellAndPrint button to display the shortcut menu.

5. Choose Paste Button Image from the shortcut menu to add the Print button image to the macro button.

6. Choose Text Only (In Menus) from the shortcut menu to change the button from text to the print icon.

7. Click the Close button on the Customize dialog box to return to the document.

8. Point to the former Print button, and the ScreenTip now says SpellAndPrint. Clicking this button runs the SpellAndPrint macro.

Note: To reset the toolbar to its original state, right-click the toolbar and choose Customize. Click the Toolbars tab, select the Standard toolbar from the list of toolbars, and click the Reset button.

9. Close the document and close Word. Because toolbar changes are changes to the Normal template, you may be prompted to save changes to the Normal template. If so, click Yes.

Customizing menus and toolbars is an effective way to put the tools you need right at your fingertips. By combining toolbar buttons with macros, you can make Word work exactly the way you want it to. It may take a little forethought, but with careful planning, it is ultimately worth the investment.

Summary

In this chapter, you learned about how to take Word to the next level by automating repetitive tasks and creating toolbars that work they way you want them to. In this chapter, we covered the following topics:

- Creating macros using the Macro Recorder
- Assigning a macro to a toolbar button
- Running a macro
- Opening a document that contains macros
- Editing macros with the Visual Basic Editor
- Deleting macros
- Customizing toolbars and menus by adding and removing buttons and menu options
- Creating new toolbars
- Changing toolbar item options such as button images
- Replacing a standard toolbar button with a macro button

Chapter

8

Taking Collaboration to Another Level

MOUS WORD 2002 EXPERT EXAM OBJECTIVES COVERED IN THIS CHAPTER:

- ✓ Track, accept, and reject changes to documents
- ✓ Merge input from several reviewers
- ✓ Insert and modify hyperlinks to other documents and Web pages
- ✓ Create and edit Web documents in Word
- ✓ Create document versions
- ✓ Protect documents
- ✓ Define and modify default file locations for workgroup templates
- ✓ Attach digital signatures to documents

With Microsoft Word's collaboration tools, you can edit and revise documents, merge documents from multiple reviewers, post documents to the Web, save multiple versions of a document, protect a document from changes, share templates in a workgroup, authenticate a document with digital signatures, and even route documents. In this chapter, you'll learn about collaboration in the twenty-first century.

> **NOTE**   Before you begin this chapter, you should go to the Sybex website and download the file 4113Ch08.zip. This package contains the files necessary to complete some of the exercises in this chapter. In addition, it contains files of what most of the documents should look like after you complete the exercise. These files are affixed with the word *Post*.

Tracking Revisions in a Document

Word's Reviewing tools, including versioning and tracking changes, allow you to keep your online documents intact while inviting others' input. In addition, Word allows you to protect a document so that the tracked changes and comments cannot be edited. You can easily access all of the Reviewing tools from the Reviewing toolbar. To display the toolbar, right-click any toolbar, and then choose Reviewing.

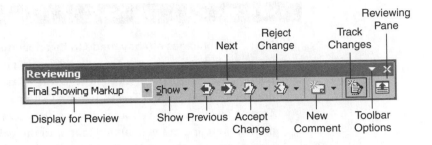

The Reviewing toolbar may open as a floating toolbar as shown here or as a docked toolbar with the Standard and Formatting toolbars.

Microsoft Exam Objective

Track, accept, and reject changes to documents

When Word's Track Changes feature is turned on, Word can track each change to a document and allow you to accept or reject individual revisions or all revisions in one fell swoop. Any changes to the document are indicated on your screen, and you can choose to print them when you print the document. In Exercise 8.1, you'll add your own revisions to a document that already contains some tracked changes.

EXERCISE 8.1

Tracking Changes to a Document

1. Open 8-1.doc from your downloaded files. If the Reviewing toolbar is not already visible, choose View ➤ Toolbars ➤ Reviewing to activate it. Track Changes should also be turned on. Look on the status bar for TRK. If TRK is black, Track Changes is active; if TRK is dimmed, double-click TRK to turn on Track Changes.

Note: You can also activate the Track Changes feature by choosing Track Changes from the Tools menu or by clicking the Track Changes button on the Reviewing toolbar.

Page 1   Sec 1   1/1   At 2.1"   Ln 7   Col 50   REC TRK EXT OVR English (U.S

Notice the changes already made to this document. In Print Layout view, each deletion, comment, and formatting change is noted by a balloon (for information about how to make insertions visible in the document, see "Setting Track Changes Options" later in this chapter. To display information about a change, just point to the small triangle at the beginning of the changed text or to the balloon describing the change to see a ScreenTip that indicates the type of change, who made it, and the time and date it was made.

As other people work with the document, any changes they make appear in different colors (up to eight authors can work on one document before the colors repeat).

2. Select the heading, "Executive Director," and change the formatting to Arial 12 pt bold. The change appears in a different color and shows your name as the reviewer.

Note: If your name does not appear as the reviewer, choose Tools ➤ Options and edit the Name text box on the User Information tab.

3. Select "agency" in the first paragraph and replace it with **organization**.

4. Replace "the" with **this** in the second line preceding "position."

5. Switch to Normal View (View ➤ Normal) to see how differently the revisions appear. Balloons are visible only in Print Layout and Web Layout views. In Normal and Outline view, deletions are represented by the Strikethrough font format. Formatting changes are not visible in Normal and Outline views. However, if you point to text that has been reformatted, a ScreenTip with the revision information appears.

6. Save the changes and close the document.

Setting Track Changes Options

Follow these steps to specify the formats and characters you want Word to use when tracking changes:

1. Click the Show drop-down list on the Reviewing toolbar and choose Options, or right-click the TRK icon on the status bar and then choose Options, or choose Tools ➤ Options and display the Track Changes page, shown in Figure 8.1.

2. In the Track Changes Options area:

  - Choose an option from the Insertions drop-down list. Select (none), Color Only, Bold, Italic, Underline, or Double Underline as the format to apply to inserted text. If you leave the default here, it is difficult to distinguish inserted text. We recommend choosing a format that easily identifies inserted text.

  - From the Formatting drop-down list, select (none), Color Only, Bold, Italic, Underline, or Double Underline as the format to apply to formatting changes.

3. Choose a Color option for revisions:

  - Select the color in which all revisions will appear or choose Auto to display all text changes in the default font color (usually black).

  - Choose the By Author option to have Word assign a different color to the first eight reviewers who insert text, delete text, or change the formatting applied to the document text (this is the preferred option so that it is easy to distinguish each reviser).

4. In the Balloons area:

  - Enable or disable the option to Use Balloons In Print And Web Layout.

  - If you leave balloons enabled, you can adjust the size of the balloons—use the spin control to select a Preferred Width and change the Measure In setting to reflect your preferred unit of measurement. Select whether to display the balloons in the right or left margin, and enable or disable the Show Lines Connecting To Text option depending, again, on your preference.

5. To set options for how Word prints with balloons, select a paper orientation from the drop-down list:

  - **Preserve** prints using the orientation specified in the Page Setup dialog box.

  - **Auto** lets Word print using the layout it deems best for the document.

  - **Force Landscape** prints the document in landscape orientation, leaving the most room for balloons.

These orientation options apply only if you choose Document Showing Markup in the Print dialog box. If you choose to print just the document, the regular page setup settings remain in effect.

6. In the Mark drop-down list, select (none), Left Border, Right Border, or Outside Border as the location for Word to insert a vertical line in the margin when any changes have been made to a line of text. Then choose a color for the line.

7. Click OK when you have finished adjusting the Track Changes options.

FIGURE 8.1   Display the Track Changes page when you want to modify the way changes to the document appear on-screen and in printed copies.

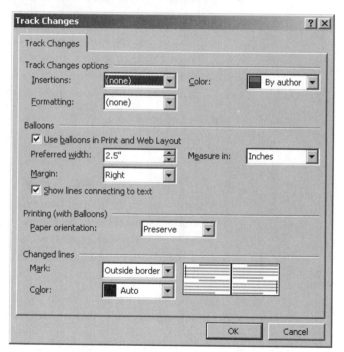

Accepting or Rejecting Changes

After all reviewers have edited a document, you can accept or reject the changes. The easiest way to accept or reject changes is to use the

Accept Change or Reject Change buttons on the Reviewing toolbar. In Exercise 8.2, you'll accept and reject changes in the document you revised previously.

Accepting and Rejected Revisions

1. Open 8-2.doc. Press Ctrl+Home to move to the top of the document. Switch to Print Layout view, if necessary.

2. Click the Next button on the Reviewing toolbar to move to the first change in the document, the reformatting of the heading.

You can use the Previous and Next buttons to move through each change in a document.

3. Click the Accept Change button to accept the formatting change. The balloon disappears.

4. Click the Next button to move to the next change, deleting "agency."

5. Click the Reject Change/Delete Comment button to undo this change. "Agency" is restored.

6. Click the Next button to move to the next change, inserting "organization."

7. Click the Reject Change/Delete Comment button to undo this change. "Organization" is deleted.

8. Continue through the remainder of the document accepting or rojecting changes as you see fit.

9. When you have accepted or rejected each of the changes, save the changes and close the document.

Click the Undo button on the Standard toolbar immediately after accepting or rejecting a change to return to the original edit.

Merging Input from Multiple Reviewers

In Chapter 4, "Collaborating in a Workgroup," we introduced you to Word's Compare and Merge feature. Using Compare and Merge (Tools ➢ Compare And Merge Documents), you learned how you can take two individual documents that have both been edited and merge the changes into one document. Word shows the differences between the documents as tracked changes, i.e., balloons (in Print Layout and Web Layout views) or revision marks (in Normal and Outline views).

Earlier in this chapter, you saw how multiple reviewers can review a single document using Track Changes. Each change is again marked with a balloon or revision mark. Whether a document has one contributor or several, Word randomly assigns a color to the reviewer that provides a visual clue to who made the revision. All of the changes made by one person are indicated by the same color balloon or revision mark.

Microsoft ✓ *Exam* *Objective*

Merge input from several reviewers

Using Compare and Merge, you can merge changes in multiple documents into a single document. Using Track Changes, you can distribute a single document to multiple reviewers. In either case, when you are ready to review the changes, you can review each change individually or you can choose to accept all changes in the document at one time.

Using the same process you learned in Chapter 4, you can use Compare and Merge to merge several documents into one target document. Open the target document and repeat the process outlined in Exercise 4.1 for each document you want to merge. Choose Into Current Document each time you click the Merge button on the Compare And Merge dialog box.

In Exercise 8.3, we'll show you how to take changes from multiple reviewers and accept them all at once to create a revised document that incorporates all of the changes.

EXERCISE 8.3

Merging Input from Multiple Reviewers

1. Open 8-3.doc from your downloaded files. This document contains revisions entered by four different reviewers. Turn on the Reviewing toolbar (View ➤ Toolbars ➤ Reviewing). Two of the reviewers made their revisions to this document using Track Changes and two worked on separate documents that were merged into this document. The document is in Normal view and the Color Only option is on (choose Show ➤ Options from the Reviewing toolbar) to mark insertions.

2. Scroll through the document and note each change that was made and who made it.

You can choose to review each change individually, or you can accept or reject all changes to the document.

3. Click the drop-down arrow next to the Accept Change button on the Reviewing toolbar and choose Accept All Changes In Document. To reject all changes in a document, click the drop-down arrow next to the Reject Change/Delete Comment button and choose Reject All Changes In Document. For the purposes of this exercise, accept all changes.

4. Save the changes and close the document. The resaved document incorporates all of the changes made by each of the reviewers.

Compare and Merge and Track Changes are two invaluable tools for incorporating input from others. The Web is another invaluable collaboration tool. And as the Web and web technologies grow in popularity, the tools become easier to use and more available for everyone. In the next section, we'll explore some of Word's tools for working on the Web.

Collaborating on the Web

The Web opens up a whole new world of collaboration opportunities. From publishing websites to web meetings, the Web takes the vision of virtual teams and makes it a reality. Word offers tools such as hyperlinks that can be used to connect related documents and simplify the process of sharing information. In addition, you can create actual web pages with Word 2002. With HTML as a default format, you can use Word to create web documents that you can post to your company's intranet, publish to the World Wide Web, or use to send documents to team members who don't use Word. Although we'll just scratch the surface here, we hope your wheels will start spinning as you begin to envision the possibilities of using the Web to collaborate within your organization.

Connecting Document with Hyperlinks

Hyperlinks are one of the key ingredients that make the Web so successful. When Tim Berners-Lee, CERN researcher, developed HTML and the Hypertext Transfer Protocol (HTTP), his primary interest was in being able to access related documents easily—without regard to computer platform or operating system—by connecting the documents through a series of links. Hyperlinks allow readers to pursue their areas of interest without having to wade through tons of material searching for specific topics, and hyperlinks take readers down paths they might never have traveled without the ease of clicking a mouse. Adding hyperlinks to your documents moves information down off the shelf, dusts it off, and makes it a living, breathing instrument that people can really use.

Microsoft *Exam* *Objective*	**Insert and modify hyperlinks to other documents and Web pages**

Creating a hyperlink in a Word document is surprisingly effortless. In Exercise 8.4, you'll create hyperlinks to other documents and to pages on the World Wide Web.

EXERCISE 8.4

Creating Hyperlinks

1. Open 8-4.doc from your downloaded files.

This document lists current course offerings from At Your Desk University. You would like people to be able to review the list and find out more information about a course they are interested in by clicking the course name.

2. Select the text "Introduction to Microsoft Word." Right-click the selection and choose Hyperlink from the shortcut menu or choose Insert ➢ Hyperlink. This opens the Insert Hyperlink dialog box.

All of the course descriptions are located in a folder called 8-4 Course Descriptions.

3. Double-click 8-4 Course Descriptions to open it. The folder name appears in the Look In text box.

4. Select the Introduction to Microsoft Word document. The folder and document name appear in the Address text box (8-4 Course Descriptions\Introduction to Microsoft Word.doc).

5. Click OK to create the hyperlink.

6. Repeat steps 2–5 to create hyperlinks for "Intermediate Microsoft Word," "Introduction to Microsoft Excel," and "Intermediate Microsoft Excel."

Creating a link to a site on the World Wide Web is just as easy. It's helpful to have a web connection when you create a link to the Web, but it is not necessary if you are sure about the website address.

7. Select "Sybex Books" and right-click and choose Hyperlink.

8. When the Insert Hyperlink dialog box opens, enter **http://www.sybex.com** in the Address text box.

Note: If you are uncertain about the address of a World Wide Web site, click the Browse The Web button in the Insert Hyperlink dialog box and navigate to the site in your browser. When you locate the site to which you want to link, click the Word button on the Windows Taskbar to return to Word. The web address appears in the Address text box automatically. You can then close your browser if you want to do so.

9. Click OK to create the link.

Word automatically creates a hyperlink when you type an address it recognizes as an Internet or file path address. If, for example, you type www.train2k.com in a Word document, Word creates a hyperlink to that address. To turn hyperlink automatic formatting on or off, choose Tools ➢ AutoCorrect Options. Click AutoFormat As You Type and check or clear the Internet And Network Paths With Hyperlinks check box.

Modifying Hyperlinks

To modify a hyperlink in a document, right-click the hyperlink, choose Edit Hyperlink, and make the appropriate changes in the Insert Hyperlink dialog box. If Edit Hyperlink does not appear on the shortcut menu when you right-click, it could be because the hyperlinked text contains a spelling or grammar error. Word displays the Spelling shortcut menu until you correct the spelling or grammar error.

If you want to remove a hyperlink, right-click the hyperlink (you do not need to select the hyperlink first) and choose Remove Hyperlink.

Creating and Editing Web Documents in Word

Your supervisor has just asked you to create a series of web pages for your corporate intranet. If you haven't created web pages but have heard the lunchroom rumors about HTML, this new assignment can be pretty intimidating. Fear no more: Office XP will put your anxiety to rest. All you need to do is add a few new skills to your extensive bag of Word tricks, and you'll be producing dazzling pages in no time.

Microsoft ✓ *Exam Objective*	**Create and edit Web documents in Word**

In Chapter 4, you leaned how to convert existing Word documents into web pages using the Save As Web Page option on the File menu. We also gave you a preview of applying a theme to a web page.

When you are ready to create a web page from scratch, Word provides seven templates and a Web Page Wizard to help get you started. The templates are single pages that provide some basic structure and suggestions for content. Unfortunately, previews of the templates are not available, so you have to create each one to see what the templates have to offer.

The Web Page Wizard creates not only web pages but also full *websites:* collections of pages with links between them. If the project you are undertaking involves multiple documents, the Web Page Wizard is generally the best choice, because it creates the web folder structure and links between the web's pages. It also gives your pages a consistent look and feel through the application of a theme to the entire web.

In Exercise 8.5, you'll learn to create web pages from a template and then modify the page by adding a theme and additional content.

EXERCISE 8.5

Creating and Editing Web Documents in Word

1. Choose File ➢ New to open the New Document task pane.

2. Use the scroll arrow at the bottom of the task pane, if available, to scroll down the list of documents and document types. Choose General Templates from the New From Template group.

3. Click the Web Pages tab in the Templates dialog box.

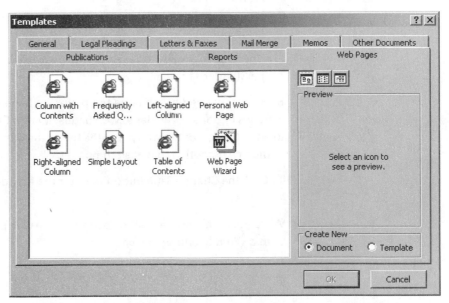

EXERCISE 8.5 *(continued)*

4. Select Personal Web Page from the list of choices, and click OK to create the document.

Note: The Personal Web Page template creates a web page with several built in hyperlinks. These hyperlinks, such as Work Informa are referred to as *bookmarks*. You can create a bookmark by selecting the text and choosing Insert ➢ Bookmark. Give the bookmark a descriptive name. When you want to create a hyperlink that takes readers to the bookmarked location, click Bookmarks in the Insert Hyperlink dialog box and select the bookmark from the list of choices.

5. To see how the Personal Web Page works before you modify it, choose File ➢ Web Page Preview to launch the document in a browser. Click each of the links to see where it takes you.

6. Click the Word button on the Windows Taskbar to return to Word.

7. If you are planning to apply a theme to the web page, choose Format ➢ Theme and select a theme from the list. You need to apply the theme before you make any formatting changes to the document. Otherwise, the formatting changes may be altered by the theme or all of the theme elements may not be applied to the document.

8. Edit the text in the document just as you would any other Word document.

9. When you are ready to save the web page, click the Save button on the Standard toolbar.

Because you used a web page template, the Save As dialog box includes options particular to web pages. It has a Change Title button to enter the title of the web page (the title is the name your visitors see in the title bar when they visit the page).

10. Click the Change Title button to enter the friendly name you want to use.

Word automatically saves the document as a web page (*.htm) rather than a Word document (*.doc).

EXERCISE 8.5 *(continued)*

11. Enter a filename in the File Name box—Word applies the appropriate extension—and click the Save button.

12. Close the document when you have finished modifying it.

Whether you use a template, convert an existing document, or create a web page completely from scratch, using Word to create your web documents turns web creation into a walk in the park.

For more about using Office XP's web development tools, you may want to check another of our books, *Mastering™ Microsoft® Office XP Premium Edition*, also from Sybex, Inc.

Saving Multiple Versions of a Document

When you work with others, one of Word 2002's most useful features is its capability to save multiple versions of a document. For example, if you are sending an online document to be reviewed by team members or supervisors, you can save the original version and then save the version that includes the changes suggested by reviewers.

Microsoft ✔ *Exam Objective*	**Create document versions**

Prior to versioning, if you wanted to change and save a document and keep the original intact, you had to remember to save the revised document using a different filename. If you're like most people, there were those inevitable times when you saved without thinking and, with one click of the mouse, wiped out any vestige of the original document. Word's versioning feature allows you to save multiple versions of a document within the document itself and open a different version to edit.

Word can automatically save a version of the document each time it is closed. This feature is useful if you need to keep track of who made changes to the document and when they were made. The most recently saved version of the document displays by default the next time you open the file.

Word also allows you to manage the versions in other ways. For example, you can see how many versions of the document have been saved, the date and time each was saved, and the name of the person who created each version. The most recent version appears highlighted at the top of the list in the Versions dialog box.

Any existing version can be saved to a separate file. When the version is in a separate file, you can make sure that the reviewers are evaluating the most recent version (by circulating only that version), or you can compare it to another file to find changes that were made with Track Changes (which you'll find earlier in this chapter) turned off. You can also delete a saved version, which is useful when your file becomes large and seems to take a long time to open and cause you to navigate more slowly.

In Exercise 8.6, you'll save three versions of the same document.

EXERCISE 8.6

Creating Multiple Versions

1. Open 8-6.doc from your downloaded files.

2. Click File ➤ Versions to open the Versions In *Document* dialog box. Previous versions (if any) appear in the list box with information about each saved version.

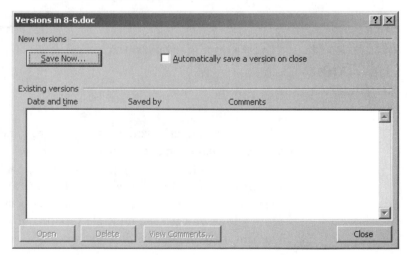

3. Click Save Now to open the Save Version dialog box. The date, time, and name of the person creating this version are displayed at the top of the dialog box.

4. Type any comments you want to make about this version of the document in the Comments On Version text box. For this exercise, type **Original**.

5. Click OK to save the version. The Versions icon appears on the right end of the status bar to let users know that this document contains a version.

Versions icon

Now you can change the document and always revert to the original version.

6. Format the subheadings, "Building Experience" and "Experience You Can Trust," using the Heading 2 style (select the headings and choose Heading 2 from the Style drop-down list).

7. Choose File ➤ Versions. Notice that the Original version is available in the list of Existing Versions. Repeat steps 3 and 4 to save a new version. Type **Reformatted subheadings** in the Comments text box. Click OK to save the version.

Make one more change so you have three versions to work with.

8. Insert **(AYDU)** after "At Your Desk University" in the first paragraph. Replace the two other occurrences of "At Your Desk University" with **AYDU**.

9. Choose File ➤ Versions. Notice that the two previously saved versions are available in the list of Existing Versions. Repeat steps 3 and 4 to save a new version. Type **Abbreviated AYDU** in the Comments text box. Click OK to save the version.

10. Save and close the document.

Use the following options to manage your versions and the size of the file:

- Check the Automatically Save A Version On Close check box in the Versions In *Document* dialog box to have Word save the document each time the file is closed.

- Highlight the version you want to manage in the Versions In *Document* dialog box, and then use any of the following options:

  - Choose Open to open the selected version in another window on your screen. (The currently active document is also open and appears in its own window.)

  - Choose Delete to delete the selected version when you no longer need it, and then choose Yes in the message box that appears to confirm the deletion.

  - Choose View Comments to display a message box containing all of the comments that were entered by the reviewer when the selected version was saved.

When you open a version from the Versions In *Document* dialog box, you can save the version as a separate file by choosing File ➤ Save and entering a name for the document. However, the version you open is still available in the document that contains the versions unless you delete it from the Existing Versions list in the Versions In *Document* dialog box.

When you delete a version of a document, you're only marking it for deletion. The version isn't actually deleted until you save the document that contains the versions.

Protecting Documents from Changes

Although you may not think there is much in your documents that anybody else would want, the gloomy truth is that your documents could become victims of corporate espionage or of unscrupulous colleagues out to pass your work off as their own. Add to that the risk that some well-meaning but misguided individual might revise one of your documents without your consent, and it's clear that it never hurts to be too careful when protecting your files and your work.

Microsoft ✓ ***Exam Objective***	**Protect documents**

Word 2002 provides the following options to protect your documents:

- You can require a password to open the document.

- You can require a password to modify the document. Users without the password can open a read-only copy of the document. If they make changes to the document, they can't overwrite your original document. They must enter another filename or location.

- You can suggest, but not require, that users open the document as read-only.

- You can prevent changes from being made to a document you route for review, except for comments or tracked changes.

- You can add a digital signature to a document.

WARNING   Word gives you a stern warning that password-protected documents cannot be opened if you forget the password. Take this warning seriously. If you forget the password to open a document, Word will not let you open the document.

Passwords, which are case-sensitive, must be at least one character but no more than 15 characters in length and can consist of letters, numbers, spaces, and symbols. A combination of upper- and lowercase letters with numbers, spaces, and symbols is best—**bl%Ack ?9** is an example of a password that would be difficult to break. When you choose a password option, the password will not be visible on the screen as you type it. Instead, Word asks you to reenter the password for verification.

To apply document protection when you save a document for the first time, follow the steps in Exercise 8.7

EXERCISE 8.7

Protecting a Document

1. Open 8-7.doc from the downloaded files for this chapter.

2. Click the Save button on the Standard toolbar to display the Save As dialog box.

3. Choose Tools ➢ Security Options in the Save As dialog box to display the Security dialog box.

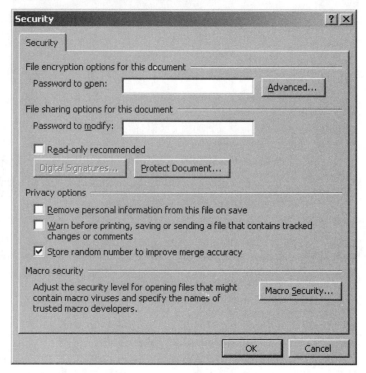

4. Add passwords to the document in the File Encryption Options For *This Document* area:

   a. Type a password in the Password To Open text box to limit access to those who know the password.

EXERCISE 8.7 *(continued)*

b. Type a password in the Password To Modify text box to allow those who know the password to open the document and edit it. Users who don't know the password can open the file as a read-only document if they know the Password To Open or if you don't specify a Password To Open.

c. Check the Read-Only Recommended box to have Word ask the user whether or not to open the document as a read-only document. You do not need to specify a password when you recommend that a document be opened as read-only, but you can't prevent users from ignoring the recommendation.

5. Click Advanced to choose a specific encryption type for your Password To Open. For example, if you wish to use a password longer than 15 characters, choose RC4. For this exercise, click Cancel to close the Encryption Type dialog box.

6. Click OK in the Security dialog box. Because you specified passwords in step 4, the Confirm Password dialog box appears.

7. Type the password again in the Confirm Password dialog box, and then choose OK.

You will be prompted to confirm each password you entered.

8. When you have entered all the passwords, choose Save in the Save As dialog box.

9. Save the changes and close the document.

10. To test the security, reopen the document. You should be prompted to enter a password.

To password-protect a file you've already saved, choose Tools ➢ Options and click the Security tab. Alternatively, choose File ➢ Save As and follow steps 2 through 4 above.

To change or delete a password, open the document and reenter or delete the password on the Security page.

Protecting a Document before Review

If you're sending a document to several people for review, you probably want to make sure that none of the reviewers, either by accident or intention, hides their changes by turning off the Track Changes option or by accepting or rejecting changes. You might want to make sure that the reviewers can insert comments but not insert or delete any of the document's text. If the document is a form, you probably want to protect the form by ensuring that users can enter data in the form's fields but cannot alter the structure or labels in the form.

Word can warn you before sending files with tracked changes. That way, you'll remember to turn document protection on. To enable the warning feature, click Tools ➤ Options ➤ Security and check the box that says Warn Before Printing, Saving, Or Sending A File That Contains Tracked Changes Or Comments.

Follow the steps in Exercise 8.8 to protect your document against such revisions.

EXERCISE 8.8

Protecting a Document before Review

1. Open the document that is to be sent for review, in this case, 8-8.doc.

Note: Check to see if the document contains more than one version by choosing File ➤ Versions. If it does, save the current version to a file with a different filename to prevent reviewers from seeing any previous versions of the document.

2. Choose Tools ➤ Protect Document or click the Protect Document button on the Security tab of the Options dialog box to display the Protect Document dialog box.

3. Choose one of the following options:

   - **Tracked Changes** tracks all changes made by reviewers and prevents reviewers from either turning off the Track Changes feature or from accepting or rejecting any changes. Reviewers can also insert comments in the document.

   - **Comments** prevents reviewers from making any changes to the document text. They can insert comments, however.

   - **Forms** prevents reviewers making any changes to a document except in form fields or unprotected document sections.

   For this exercise, choose Tracked Changes.

   If you choose Forms in step 4, choose Sections, enable the check box for each section in the document you want to protect, and then click OK. The sections are listed in the Protected Sections list box.

4. Type a password in the Password (Optional) text box, and then click OK to allow reviewers who know the password to turn off the Track Changes feature, accept or reject changes, edit regular document text, or edit the structure or labels in a form. Retype the password in the Confirm Password dialog box, and click OK.

5. Save and close the document.

When a password is required, users must enter the password before they can unprotect the document.

If you don't require a password, anyone can unprotect a document by simply choosing Tools ➤ Unprotect Document.

Certifying Documents with Digital Signatures

In an age where a virus can send e-mail from you to everyone in your address book, document authentication is more important than ever. With Word 2002, you can *digitally sign* your important documents to confirm through electronic encryption that the information originates from you, it is valid, and it has not been modified since signed.

Microsoft ✔ *Exam* *Objective*	**Attach digital signatures to documents**

In order to digitally sign a document, you must have a digital certificate. There are several ways to do this, each with its own set of considerations.

- **Commercial Certification Authorities** such as VeriSign issue digital certificates upon approval of an application submitted by you or your company. This process can be time consuming, as information on the application must be fully verified by the certification authority before your digital certificate is issued.

- **Information Technology Departments** in some companies are equipped to issue digital signatures using tools such as Microsoft Certificate Server. Sometimes companies contract with an outside group qualified as a certification authority. Contact your network administrator or IT department to learn about the availability of certification services in your company.

- **Selfcert.exe** and other tools like it allow you to create your own digital certificate, but since the certificate isn't issued by a formal certification authority, it is considered unauthenticated and won't get past most security settings in Office XP.

After you obtain and install your digital certificate, you can digitally sign files (and macros). To use a digital certificate, make sure you've finished all modifications to the file, and then follow these steps:

1. Click Tools ➢ Options ➢ Security.

2. Click Digital Signatures to open the Digital Signature dialog box. Previous signers, if any, appear in the list box.

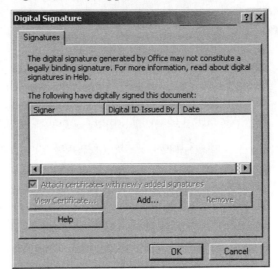

3. To add your own certification, click Add to open the Select Certificate dialog box. Word prompts you to save the document if it hasn't previously been saved.

4. Installed certificates appear in the Select Certificate dialog box. Click View Certificate to see details about the selected certificate. Then click the one you want to use, and click OK three times to close all dialog boxes.

   When a document is digitally signed, the title bar of the document displays the text "(Signed)," and after a certificate has been specified, the Status bar displays the Digitally Signed icon.

Sharing Workgroup Templates

In Chapter 2, "Working with Documents," you learned how to create documents and save them as templates. Templates become even more valuable when you can distribute them to others in your workgroup to use. If you work on a network and have access to a shared drive or directory, you can define a folder location for shared templates.

Define and modify default file locations for workgroup templates

Your server administrator may have already established a shared location for workgroup templates. You can review file locations for each of the file types that Word uses in the Options dialog box. To review and modify the location for workgroup templates, follow these steps:

1. Choose Tools ➢ Options and click the File Locations tab.

2. Review the location listed for workgroup templates. If a location is specified, this may be the location established by your server administrator. Do not change this setting unless instructed to do so by the server administrator. If the location is blank, you can define a location.

3. Select Workgroup Templates and click the Modify button to open the Modify Location dialog box.

4. Navigate to the desired folder location.

5. If you want to create a new folder, navigate to the parent folder location and click the Create New Folder button on the Modify Location dialog box toolbar. Name the folder, and click OK to create the new folder.

6. Click OK to close the Modify Location dialog box. This defines the location for the workgroup templates.

7. Click OK again to close the Options dialog box.

If at a later date, you want to modify this location, reopen the File Locations tab of the Options dialog box and repeat steps 3–7.

To save a template to the workgroup templates location so others have access to it, follow these steps:

1. Choose File ➢ Save As.

2. Select Document Template from the Save As Type drop-down list. This takes you to your local templates folder.

3. Navigate to the workgroup templates folder (you might want to add it to the Places bar—Tools ➢ Add to "My Places"—for easy access).

4. Enter a name for the template.

5. Click Save.

When others want to create a document based on this template, they need to follow these steps:

1. Choose File ➢ New.

2. Select Choose Document from the New From Existing Document group in the New Document task pane.

3. Navigate to the workgroup templates folder and select the template they want to use.

4. Click the Create New button. Word creates a document based on the template.

Summary

This chapter focused on additional collaboration tools that can take you from being an isolated worker to a true team player. It takes some coordination and communication to make these tools work, but the payoffs are immeasurable. This chapter covered the following topics:

- Tracking, accepting, and rejecting document changes
- Merging input from multiple reviewers
- Using the Web as a collaboration tool
- Creating and modifying hyperlinks
- Designing web documents in Word
- Saving multiple versions of the same document
- Protecting and certifying documents
- Sharing workgroup templates

Chapter

9

Merging to Create Letters and Labels

MOUS WORD 2002 EXPERT EXAM OBJECTIVES COVERED IN THIS CHAPTER:

- ✓ Merge letters with a Word, Excel, or Access data source
- ✓ Merge labels with a Word, Excel, or Access data source
- ✓ Use Outlook data as mail merge data source

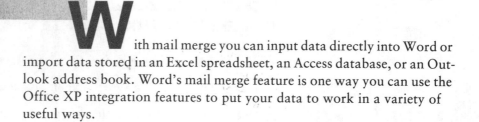

With mail merge you can input data directly into Word or import data stored in an Excel spreadsheet, an Access database, or an Outlook address book. Word's mail merge feature is one way you can use the Office XP integration features to put your data to work in a variety of useful ways.

Mail merge has been completely revised in Word 2002, so even if you are an old hand at mail merge, you'll want to spend time with this chapter to learn how to use Word's new Mail Merge Wizard.

In this chapter, we'll look at mail merge from a variety of perspectives. We'll show you how to use data that is stored in a Word table, an Excel spreadsheet, an Access database, and an Outlook contacts file to create customized letters and labels.

Before you begin this chapter, you should go to the Sybex website and download the file 4113Ch09.zip. This package contains the files necessary to complete some of the exercises in this chapter. In addition, it contains files of what most of the documents should look like after you complete the exercise. These files are affixed with the word *Post*.

Understanding Mail Merge

A mail merge requires two documents: a *data source* (also called a *recipient list*) in which the individual records are stored and a *main document* or form that contains text, formatting, and the fields in the data source.

These two documents then come together to create the final *merge document*, which uses the text and layout in the main document and the data in each record of the data source.

You can create six types of main documents:

- **Letters** are letters, memos, or reports you want to personalize.

- **E-mail messages** are electronic mail items sent through Outlook.

- **Faxes** use WinFax or another faxing program installed on your system.

- **Envelopes** are envelopes fed directly into your printer.

- **Labels** are address labels or any other kind of label, such as nametags, videotape or disk labels, and file folder labels.

- **Directories** are lists of data, such as phone lists, course catalogs, and membership directories.

Word's new Mail Merge Wizard helps you create a main document, create or select a data source, and then produce merged documents. You start the Mail Merge Wizard by choosing Tools ≻ Letters And Mailing ≻ Mail Merge Wizard. In Step 1 of the wizard, shown in Figure 9.1, you are asked to select what type of main document you want to create.

FIGURE 9.1 Word's new Mail Merge Wizard guides you through the steps to complete a mail merge.

A data source consists of a number of individual *records*. A record contains all the information gathered about the item. For example, a record about a person may contain a name, address, telephone number, and date of birth. Each record is made up of a series of *fields*; a field, such as first name, is the smallest amount of data collected. A record about a person probably contains quite a few fields. The person's name might consist of four fields in the record—SocialTitle, FirstName, MiddleInitial, and LastName. The address might contain a separate field for the StreetAddress, City, State, and PostalCode. Any item you might need to use by itself, for example, addressing a letter to someone by first name only, should have its own field. The ability to store data such as your personal or business contacts, product catalog information, or purchasing records puts extra power in your hands. Using Word, you can access the data stored in a data source file created using Word; a file created with other Microsoft Office products such as an Excel database (list), Outlook contacts, or an Access database; or a database file created using any type of software and saved in a supported file format or as a delimited text file.

Merging to Create Letters

Creating form letters or other documents that pull data from a data source is one of the most common uses of mail merge. Depending on the data contained in your data source and the information you want to convey, you can, for example, create personalized form letters to send to your clients, letters to employees about their salary increases, or student grade reports to parents.

Microsoft ✓ *Exam* *Objective*	**Merge letters with a Word, Excel, or Access data source**

In this section, we'll explore the similarities and differences in creating merge letters using various data sources.

Creating or Specifying the Main Document

You must create, or at least specify, which document is the main document before you create or select a data source. Your main document can be any document, including a new, blank document. In Step 2 of the wizard you are asked to select a starting document from the following choices:

Use The Current Document   This option allows you to work with the active document, whether it is a previously saved document you have already opened or a blank page you will edit later.

Start From A Template   This option lets you select from the Template's dialog box.

Start From Existing Document   This option allows you to open a previously created Word document.

If you are creating the letter or other document from scratch, then either the first or second option is the best choice depending on whether you plan to use a blank document or a template. If you previously created the letter you want to use as the main document, you can open it and choose the first option or you can wait to open it in the second step of the wizard by choosing the third option.

When you save a merge document, it's a good idea to indicate the type of document somewhere in the filename. We suggest that you begin main document filenames with the word Main and, when appropriate, the name of the data source it is linked to (Main-Acknowledgment Letter to Customers) so that you can identify your main documents easily.

In Exercise 9.1, you'll begin the process of creating a mail merge letter by specify a document type and creating a main document.

The exercises in this chapter flow together as we take you through the steps of the Mail Merge Wizard. We suggest reading the chapter first and then planning to do the practice exercises when you have enough time (an hour to an hour and a half) to complete them all in one sitting.

EXERCISE 9.1

Specifying and Creating a Main Document

1. Create a new blank document.

2. Choose Tools ➤ Letters And Mailings ➤ Mail Merge Wizard to display Step 1 of the Mail Merge Wizard. (If the task pane is already visible, you can choose Mail Merge from its selection menu.)

3. Choose a document type from the list that appears in Step 1 of 6. In this case, Letters is already selected, so you can leave the default choice.

4. Click Next: Starting Document at the bottom of the task pane to move to Step 2.

5. Choose a start option. Once again, the default choice, Use The Current Document, is the choice you want.

After choosing a start option you may, at any time, modify the document by adding text or changing formatting.

6. Change the font to Arial 14 pt.

7. Enter today's date in the blank document, and press Enter twice.

8. Enter the following text exactly as it appears:

   Time is drawing near. In just three short weeks, we will be arriving in City with our $1,000,000 prize notification team. What will it take for our team to be stopping at the LastName family home at Address? All you have to do is order 10 new magazines, purchase 22 hot-off-the-press books, and buy a lifetime membership in our dine and travel club. After that, you have a one-in-22 billion chance at winning one of our fabulous prizes.

9. Press Enter twice and type

   Good luck,

10. Press Enter three times and type

    $1,000,000 Prize Notification Team

Although Word doesn't prompt you to do so, if you've spent a fair amount of time on the main document, you should save it now.

EXERCISE 9.1 *(continued)*

11. Click the Save button and save the document as **Main-Come On to Customers**.

12. Click Next: Select Recipients at the bottom of the task pane.

Move on to Exercise 9.2.

In Step 3 of the Mail Merge Wizard, you can create a new data source or select an existing data source to use in the merge.

Creating a New Data Source in Word

If you haven't created a data source before you start the Mail Merge Wizard, Word provides the means to do so as part of the process. You can use the default address fields Word provides or create your own fields.

When you create a data source as part of the mail merge process, Word 2002 creates an Access database file (.mdb), not a Word document as in previous versions.

Word 2002 has made it possible to use just about any field name you can imagine. However, this newly available freedom in naming fields could have adverse effects if you share a data source with another user who isn't running Office XP. To be safe, it is a good idea to follow these rules, which are absolutes in earlier versions of Word and in other data applications:

- Field names should be less than 40 characters long. Some programs won't recognize larger names, and shorter is better for easy reference.

- Each field name must be unique—no two fields in a data source can have the same name.

- Field names should not contain spaces and should begin with a letter rather than a number. You can use the underscore (_) character to separate words, but it is easier to omit spaces and underscores and simply capitalize the first letter of each word in a name, such as StreetAddress or DateOfBirth.

- Stay away from using periods, commas, colons, semicolons, slashes, or backslashes in field names.

This is a good time to think about how you will use your data. If you use only one field, Name, for both first and last names, you can't open a letter with "Dear Joe." By separating names into FirstName and LastName fields, you have more options for how you can use the name in your main document. If you're feeling formal and might want to use "Dear Mr. Smith" as the salutation, you will want to include a Title or Honorific field for Mr., Mrs., Ms., and other social titles.

Addresses should be separated into StreetAddress or Address, City, State (or Province), and ZipCode or PostalCode. Later, you can choose to print labels that are sorted by ZipCode or print envelopes and letters only for clients in a particular state.

If you are creating several different data source files, it's helpful to use the same field names in each data source. For example, if you use First-Name in one data source, use this field name consistently—don't use FNAME or First in other source files. When you use the Mail Merge Wizard to create your data source, you can select many commonly used field names from a built-in list to help you keep your field names consistent. If you use the same field names, you'll often be able to use the same main documents with different data source files, rather than creating new main documents.

In Exercise 9.2, you'll create a new data source using Word.

EXERCISE 9.2

Creating a New Data Source Using Word

If you closed Word after completing Exercise 9.1, reopen Main-Come On to Customers and repeat steps 1–5 and step 12 in Exercise 9.1 before starting this exercise.

1. Choose Type A New List in Step 3 of the Mail Merge Wizard.

2. Click the Create icon to open the New Address List dialog box.

You'll see the list of commonly used address fields Word provides for you. If these fields are all you need, simply type the data you want in the appropriate field, and press Tab or Enter to move to another field. You don't have to enter data in every field, but if you're not going to use a field, consider deleting it as described below. And don't be disconcerted if the data you want to enter has nothing to do with names and addresses. You can delete all the fields if you choose to and then enter the fields you want to use.

3. Click the Customize button to add, delete, reorder, or rename fields. Word displays the Customize Address List dialog box.

4. Select Company Name and click the Delete button to remove it from the data source. Confirm the delete by clicking Yes in the message box, but be aware that if you've previously entered data in that field, you are deleting the data as well as the field. Also delete the Address Line 2, Country, and Work Phone fields.

In this dialog box you can also perform these tasks:

- Change the name of a field by selecting it and clicking the Rename button. Type a new name for the field in the Rename Field dialog box, overwriting its original name. Use this option to create a new field from a field you don't plan to use.

- Adjust the order of the fields by clicking the Move Up and Move Down buttons. This is particularly helpful if you are typing data from a written page and the fields are in a different order on the page than they are in the New Address List dialog box.

- Add another field by clicking the Add button and typing the name of the field you wish to add in the Add Field dialog box.

5. When you've adjusted the fields to your satisfaction, click OK to close the Customize Address List dialog box and proceed with entering data in those fields.

6. Type the information for the first field in the text box beside its name and then press Tab or Enter to move the insertion point to the next field's text box, until you've entered data for each field in the first record. Then choose New Entry or press Enter to place the current data in the data source and to display the next empty record. Continue entering data. Enter the following five records in the Title, First Name, Last Name, Address Line 1, City, State, Zip Code fields:

Mr. John Martin, 6000 Zue Rd., Buckley, MI, 49620

Ms. Martha Stewart, 4444 Home Lane, Traverse City, MI, 49685

Ms. Rosa Martinez, 3355 Rose St., Empire, MI, 49630

Mr. Jackson Browne, 7777 Motown St., Detroit, MI, 48000

Mrs. Indira Paku, 8787 Bayview Dr., Petosky, MI, 49770

Use the navigation buttons at the bottom of the New Address List dialog box to view the Next, Previous, First, and Last records. You can also type the number of a record and press Enter to display it. If you wish to remove a record, navigate to it and click the Delete Entry button.

EXERCISE 9.2 *(continued)*

7. When you have finished entering data in the records, click Close to return to the main document. Word prompts you to save the data source. Because Word creates the data source as an Access database, it prompts you to save it in the My Data Sources folder of My Documents. You can choose to save it here or to choose another folder location. Save the data source as **Customers**.

After you have saved the new data source, Word returns you to the main document. The task pane displays the filename and path of the data source you just created.

8. Click OK to close the Mail Merge Recipients dialog box.

9. Click Next: Write Your Letter at the bottom of the task pane to move on to the next step of the wizard, covered in Exercise 9.3.

If you wish to make changes to the data in the list, click Edit Recipient List to open the Mail Merge Recipients dialog box. In the Mail Merge Recipients dialog box you can search, sort, filter, and validate records, as shown in Figure 9.2. You can also select records you want to include in the merge. To enter, edit, or delete records, click the Edit button to reopen the data source form.

FIGURE 9.2 From the Mail Merge Recipients dialog box you can enter new records as well as edit, delete, sort, filter, and validate records.

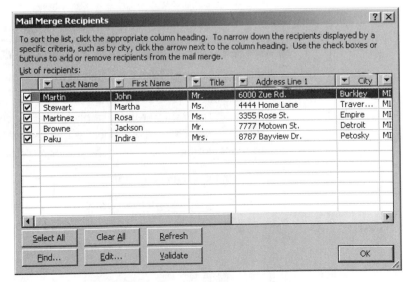

For more information about working with records in the Mail Merge Recipients dialog box, refer to our book, *Mastering™ Microsoft® Office XP Premium Edition,* © Sybex, 2001.

Regardless of the data source you choose for the merge, the steps in completing the merge do not vary much. After you complete a merge using a new Word data source, we'll show you the differences you'll encounter if you choose an existing data source such as a Word table, an Excel spreadsheet, an Access database, or an Outlook contacts folder.

Adding Merge Fields to a Main Document

After you have created or identified the data source, you are ready to add *merge fields* and any additional information you need to the main document. There are two kinds of text in a main document: *Regular text* is text that will be the same in each version of the merged document, such as the body text in a form letter. *Variable text* is text that will be different in each merged document and is represented by a merge field. Merge fields have the same names as the field names in the data source. For example, the recipient's name and address are variable text in the main document.

You can edit the regular text in your main document as necessary, using the same methods as those you use to edit any other document. Insert a merge field where you want text from the data source to appear in your final merged document.

In Exercise 9.3, you'll add merge fields to the letter you created in Exercise 9.2.

EXERCISE 9.3

Adding Merge Fields to the Main Document

If you closed Word after completing Exercise 9.2, reopen Main-Come On to Customers and repeat steps 1–5 in Exercise 9.1 before starting this exercise. Click Next: Select Recipients and Next: Write Your Letter to move you to Step 4 of the Mail Merge Wizard.

1. Click the blank row after the Date in the letter and press Enter.

Step 4 of the Mail Merge Wizard displays several choices for adding variable text.

2. Click Address Block in Step 4 of the wizard to display the options for addressing your letter.

In this dialog box you can choose if you want to include the recipient's name and then select a name format from the list if applicable. You can enable or disable the Insert Company Name check box. And if you want to include the postal address, enable that choice and then choose an option for including or excluding country and region data.

3. Click OK to accept the default Address Block options.

Word inserts a field code called Address Block in the letter at the position of the insertion point.

Note: Merge field codes must be entered using the options in the Mail Merge Wizard. You cannot simply type "<<" before the field name and ">>" after it to make it a merge field.

4. Press Enter twice and click Greeting Line in Step 4 of the wizard.

Here you can select the greeting line format you want to use and the greeting line for invalid recipient names.

5. Click OK to accept the default Greeting Line options. Press Enter.

You can now insert field codes into the body of the letter.

EXERCISE 9.3 *(continued)*

6. Double-click City in the body of the letter to select it, and click More Items in Step 4 of the wizard.

7. Choose City from the list of available merge fields in the Insert Merge Field dialog box and click Insert to insert the merge field in the document, replacing the existing text. Click Close in the Insert Merge Field dialog box and press the spacebar to insert a space after the field code.

8. Double-click Last Name in the letter and click More Items in Step 4 of the wizard, and then choose Last Name from the list of available field codes in the Insert Merge Field dialog box. Click the Insert button and then click Close to close the dialog box.

9. Double-click Address in the letter and click More Items in Step 4 of the wizard to choose Address Line 1 from the list of available field codes in the Insert Merge Field dialog box. Click the Insert button and then click Close to close the dialog box.

10. Click the Save button to resave the main document.

11. When you have finished setting up the main document, Word provides you with an opportunity to preview the merge results before completing the actual merge. Click Next: Preview Your Letters to move on to the next step of the wizard, covered in Exercise 9.5.

By default, merge fields appear with gray shading when the insertion point is anywhere in the field. To have them always appear with gray shading in your main document, choose Tools ➤ Options ➤ View Tab. In the Show area, choose Always in the Field Shading drop-down list and click OK.

Previewing and Merging Documents

When a form letter main document and data source are merged, Word generates a separate letter for each record in the data source, based on the layout of the main document. Before you perform the merge, it is a good idea to see a sample of how the merged document will appear. Step 5 of the Mail Merge Wizard provides preview and editing options.

In Exercise 9.4, you'll preview the merge and then complete the merge by merging to a new document.

Previewing and Merging to a New Document

1. On Step 5 of the Mail Merge Wizard, click the Next button (the double right arrow) to view each of the individual letters. The task pane shows which recipient number you're currently viewing. Click the double left arrow to see the previous record.

If necessary, you can make any additional edits to the main document while you're previewing the merged data. For example, if you did not place a colon or other punctuation after the greeting, you can insert it now. If you make any changes to the main document, be sure to save it again.

If you are content with the setup of both the main document and the data source, you're ready to complete the merge.

2. Click Next: Complete The Merge at the bottom of the task pane to move to Step 6 of the wizard.

The choices you see at Step 6 depend on which type of main document you are using. For each main document type, you will be able to perform at least one of the following:

- Click Print to open the Merge To Printer dialog box. Once again, you're given the choice to merge all records, the current record, or a range of records. When you click OK, Word sends the results of the merge directly to the printer. Therefore it is prudent to send the current record or a small range just to make sure everything goes as expected. If you send the entire merge results and something is wrong, the error is multiplied by the total number of records you have in your data source. Choose All only if you have previewed your merge and everything is in perfect order (check that nobody has left purple and green paper in the printer!).

- Click Edit Individual Letters (or Edit Individual Labels or Envelopes) to open the Merge To New Document dialog box. (It looks just like the Merge To Printer dialog box.) Choose which records you wish to merge and then click OK to have Word conduct the merge and create a new document with the results. Labels appear in columns, form letters and envelopes are separated by page breaks, and catalogs display each record. You can review the results of the merge (and even modify individual letters) before sending the merge document to the printer. Once the merge is printed, there is no reason to save the merge results. If you need to print it again at a later date, you'll want to do the merge again in case you've updated any of the records in the data source.

3. Choose Edit Individual Letters to open the Merge To New Document dialog box. Select All and click OK to create a new document with a new page for each letter.

4. Use the navigation buttons on the horizontal scroll bar to view each of the letters and make any personalized comments to individuals you wish to include.

Note: Do not make changes here that you want to affect all letters. If you find something that you want to change, close this document without saving the changes. Make the changes to the main document, and click Edit Individual Letters again to create a new merged document.

5. For this exercise, close the merge document without saving the changes and then resave and close the main document.

After you have your letters ready to go, it's time to create mailing labels to put on the envelopes. In the next section, you'll create mailing labels to go along with the letters.

Merging to Create Mailing Labels

Creating mailing labels is not a whole lot different from creating merge letters. You are already familiar with many of the steps because, just as in letters, you use the Mail Merge Wizard to create labels.

Microsoft
✓ *Exam*
Objective

Merge labels with a Word, Excel, or Access data source

Labels are another type of main document you can choose in Step 1 of the Mail Merge Wizard. Specialty labels are available at office supply stores, allowing you to create labels for any use. In Exercise 9.5, you'll create mailing labels for the individuals in the data source you created in Exercise 9.2.

EXERCISE 9.5

Merging to Create Labels

1. Create a new, blank document and display the Mail Merge Wizard (Tools ➢ Letters And Mailings ➢ Mail Merge Wizard).

2. Choose Labels in the Select Document Type options in Step 1.

3. Click Next: Starting Document.

4. Choose Change Document Layout from the Select Starting Document list to create a label set up from a blank document. If you already had a document with an existing label set up, you could choose Start From Existing Document.

5. Click Label Options to set up the label you want to use. The default product number selected, Avery 5160, is the product number for the most common type of mailing label—sheets with three columns of 10 labels each, or 30 to a page. If you want to use different labels, select the manufacturer of your labels in the Label Products drop-down list. (If the manufacturer of the labels you have is not listed, look on the label box for the Avery equivalent. If there is one, choose Avery. If there isn't an Avery equivalent listed, get different labels, if at all possible. It's a lot of work to enter all the measurements manually.) Select the product number (or Avery equivalent) that appears on your label package in the Product Number list box. Select Avery 5160 if it is not already selected.

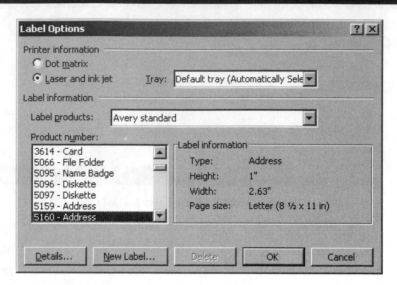

6. Click OK to create a page of blank labels.

7. Click Next: Select Recipients.

8. Because you already have a data source created, choose Browse. Navigate to the folder where you saved the data source you created in Exercise 9.2 and select Customers or select the Access database, Customers.mdb, from the list of files you downloaded from the Sybex website. Click Open to attach the data source.

9. Modify the recipient list, if desired, by clicking Edit Recipient List and then sorting or filtering, or by selecting individual records. Click OK to close the Mail Merge Recipients dialog box, and click Next: Arrange Your Labels to proceed to Step 4 of the wizard.

10. Set up the first label with the fields you want to use. In this case, click Address Block and click OK to select the default options in the Insert Address Block dialog box.

11. Click Update All Labels to place the Address Block fields on every label.

Note: Don't delete the Next Record field that Word automatically inserts on every label but the first. If you do, the first record will be repeated on every label!

12. Click Next: Preview Your Labels to get an idea of how the final merged document will appear.

13. Use the navigation buttons to browse through the labels in Preview mode. Just as with other main document types, you can also edit the recipient list at this point, if you wish.

14. Click Next: Complete The Merge when you are ready to proceed.

15. In the final step of the wizard, you can send the labels directly to the printer or you can choose to edit individual labels. For this exercise, choose Edit Individual Labels and click OK to merge all records to a new document.

Note: If you choose to edit individual labels, any changes you make are not saved in the original data source. If you are updating address or other merge data, edit the information in the Mail Merge Recipients dialog box that you can access in Step 5 of the wizard.

16. When you are ready to print the labels, click the Print button on the Standard toolbar. After printing, close the mail merge document without saving your changes.

17. If you plan to create these labels again, save the main label document. We recommend saving it so you'll know something about what the file contains, i.e., that it is labels, what label product it is based on, and what data source it is attached to. For example, for this exercise, which uses 5160 labels and attaches to the Customers data source, you can name this document **Labels – 5160 – Customers**. You can create these labels in the future by just opening the document and jumping to Step 6 of the Mail Merge Wizard.

18. Close any open documents.

Now that you know the basics of creating merge letters and labels, we'll show you how to use data from existing data sources.

Using Existing Data Sources to Create Letters and Labels

The key to using Word's mail merge feature most efficiently is to make it work with your data regardless of what format it is in. If you are most comfortable keeping your data in Excel, in Access, or in Outlook, leave it there. You can even access data in a dBASE, FoxPro, or delimited database. Word doesn't require you to move it or change it in any way. Whatever your choice for a data repository, the Mail Merge Wizard is at your disposal. In this section, we'll describe the steps to access your data in almost any format you have it in. In Exercise 9.6, we'll walk you through a mail merge using data from an Excel worksheet.

EXERCISE 9.6

Using an Existing Database As a Data Source

1. Open 9-6.doc. This is the same letter you created in Exercise 9.1, but we removed its attachment to a data source.

   Note: You can remove a document's attachment to a data source by opening the document and, from the Mail Merge toolbar (View ➢ Toolbars ➢ Mail Merge), clicking the Main Document Setup button and choosing Normal Word Document from the Main Document Type dialog box.

2. Start the Mail Merge Wizard (Tools ➢ Letters And Mailing ➢ Mail Merge Wizard).

3. In Step 1 of the wizard, choose the type of document you are creating, in this case, Letters. Click Next: Starting Document.

4. Choose Use The Current Document in Step 2 of the wizard. Click Next: Select Recipients.

5. Choose Use An Existing List and click Browse to open the Select Data Source dialog box.

   My Data Sources is the default folder selected in the Look In list. You can save your data sources here if you want but you are not required to. All Data Sources is selected in the Files Of Type drop-down list. To see all the types of data sources you can use, click the down arrow on the Files Of Type drop-down list.

6. Locate the data source you want to use. For this exercise, locate the Excel file, `Customers List.xls`, from the files you downloaded from the Sybex website. Select the file and click the Open button.

7. Because spreadsheets and databases can contain multiple worksheets or tables, you are immediately presented with the Select Table dialog box. Select the table that contains the data you want use, in this case, Customers, and click OK.

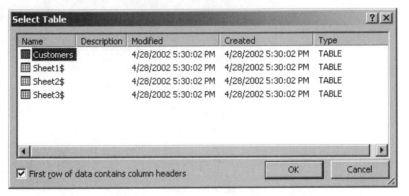

Note: If you're using spreadsheet data, be sure to enable or disable First Row Of Data Contains Column Headers as appropriate.

8. In the Mail Merge Recipients dialog box, you can select, sort, filter, and find records, but you cannot edit records. You must open the original data source to edit records.

If you plan to use most of the records, click Select All and clear the check marks from the ones you don't want. If you plan to use only a few of the recipients listed, click Deselect All and then check the ones you want.

9. Click OK when you've finished selecting recipients.

10. After you've selected recipients, Word closes the dialog box and displays the name of the data source in the task pane. Click Next: Write Your Letter to move on to Step 4 of the wizard.

11. Position the insertion point in the blank row directly above the body of the letter to begin entering field codes.

12. Click Address Block in Step 4 of the wizard.

EXERCISE 9.6 *(continued)*

External data sources are less likely to conform to the same naming conventions Word uses when you create a data source in Word. Consequently, you may have to tell Word how your fields correspond to the default Word fields.

13. Click the Match Fields button to check that the fields from your data source correspond appropriately.

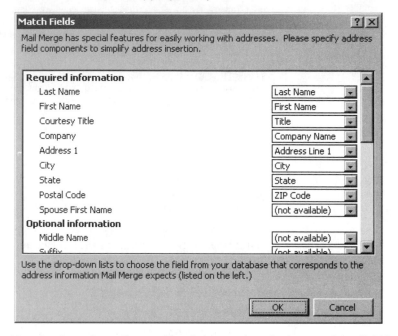

Use the drop-down lists on the right to select the name of the field in your data that corresponds with the address field Word displays on the left. For instance, Word uses the term Postal Code and many databases call this same field Zip Code. For the purposes of this exercise, you do not need to make any changes in this dialog box.

14. Click OK twice to close both dialog boxes.

15. Just as you did in steps 4–9 in Exercise 9.3, enter the additional field codes:

a. Press Enter twice and enter a Greeting Line.

EXERCISE 9.6 *(continued)*

b. Replace City, Last Name, and Address Line 1 in the body of the letter with the corresponding field codes from the More Items list. The easiest way to do this is to double-click the replaceable word in the text, for example, City, to select it and then click More Items to replace the text with the field code.

16. Click the Save button to save the main document as **Main - 2nd Come-On to Customers**.

17. Click Next: Preview Your Letters and Next: Complete the Merge to complete the Mail Merge Wizard.

18. Choose Edit Individual Letters to complete the merge in a new document.

19. Close the merged document without saving the changes, and resave the main document before closing it.

As you can see, only a few of the steps you need to follow are different depending on whether you are creating a data source in Word or using an existing data source. However, if you are using Excel data as your data source, you have to prepare the worksheet to be able to access the fields through the Mail Merge Wizard. This next section describes the changes you need to make.

Using an Excel Worksheet As a Data Source

Excel worksheets are also tables, which, as you've seen, can be used to create a data source. An Excel data source is called a *list*. In Excel, each column is described with a label (the field name), and each row contains an individual record.

There are several things to keep in mind when you are using an Excel worksheet as your data source:

- The list cannot contain any blank rows or columns. Excel uses a blank row or column to indicate the end of the list.

- The column labels (field names) must be in the first row of the list. You can add special formatting to the column labels to differentiate them from the data entered in each record.

- Items in the list can be sorted by multiple fields in Word when you're selecting recipients or in Excel when you're setting up the data.

If you typically use only *some* of the data in the worksheet as the data source, you may find it easier to name a range in Excel, rather than spend extra time selecting recipients in Word. In Excel, select the range of cells that contains the list items, including the column labels in the first row of the list, and then assign it a range name. Make sure you include the column labels as the first row in the named range, because Excel uses the data in the first row as the merge field names. Use one of the following methods to create a range name:

- Select the range of cells and then type the name you want for that range in the Name box at the left of the formula bar.

- Select the range of cells and then choose Insert ➤ Name ➤ Define to display the Define Name dialog box. Type the name in the Names In Workbook text box and then choose Add. Click OK when you have finished entering range names.

Make sure you resave the file after you name the range. When you're ready to use the named range as a data source, simply follow the same steps as you would in any merge. When Word displays the Select Table dialog box, the named range(s) appear in the list along with the sheet tab names. Select the one you want and click OK.

Using Outlook As a Data Source

If you store names, addresses, and other recipient data in Outlook, mail merge is easier than ever!

Microsoft ✓ *Exam* *Objective*	**Use Outlook data as mail merge data source**

You already know how to use the Mail Merge Wizard. Exercise 9.7 takes you through the first three steps of the wizard, where you can connect to your Outlook contacts folder as the mail merge data source. In this exercise, you'll be creating labels, but this time you'll be using Outlook data as the data source.

EXERCISE 9.7

Using Outlook Data As a Mail Merge Data Source

1. Create a new blank document and start the Mail Merge Wizard.

2. Click Labels as the document type in Step 1 of the wizard. Click Next: Starting Document to move to Step 2.

3. Select Change Document Layout and click Label Options to open the Label Options dialog box. Click OK to select the default labels.

4. Click Next: Select Recipients to move to Step 3 of the wizard.

5. In the Select Recipients section of the task pane, choose Select From Outlook Contacts, and then click Choose Contacts Folder.

6. If Outlook is not open, you may be prompted to choose an Outlook profile. Select the Outlook profile that contains the contacts folder you wish to use.

7. After you've chosen a profile, the Select Contact List Folder dialog box appears:

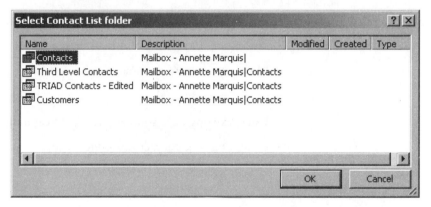

8. Select the appropriate contacts folder and then click OK.

9. The Mail Merge Recipients dialog box opens with Outlook contact data displayed. Proceed with selecting, sorting, and filtering as you normally would.

10. Click Next: Arrange Your Labels and continue as you would with any labels merge (see step 10 of Exercise 9.5 for a refresher).

11. Close the document and save the changes.

If you have any trouble accessing the Outlook contacts folder you want to use, be sure the folder is designated as an Outlook e-mail address book. You can check this by right-clicking the contacts folder in Outlook and choosing Properties. Select the Show This Folder As An E-mail Address Book on the Outlook Address Book tab of the Properties dialog box. When you return to the Select Recipients step of the Mail Merge wizard, the contacts folder should be available to use.

Summary

This chapter covered the essentials of Word's mail merge feature and showed how to use mail merge with a variety of data sources. We discussed the following topics:

- Understanding mail merge
- Creating a mail merge letter
- Creating a new data source in Word
- Adding merge fields to a letter using blocks of fields and individual fields
- Previewing the results of a mail merge
- Merging to a new document
- Creating mailing labels
- Using existing data sources such as Excel data to create a mail merge
- Using Outlook contacts as a data source

Microsoft
Excel 2002
Core Exam

PART

III

Chapter

10

Creating Worksheets and Workbooks

MOUS EXCEL 2002 CORE EXAM OBJECTIVES COVERED IN THIS CHAPTER:

- ✓ Insert, delete and move cells
- ✓ Enter and edit cell data including text, numbers, and formulas
- ✓ Check spelling
- ✓ Find and replace cell data and formats
- ✓ Work with a subset of data by filtering lists
- ✓ Manage workbook files and folders
- ✓ Create workbooks using templates
- ✓ Save workbooks using different names and file formats

Excel 2002 is both easy and challenging to use. Easy, because it behaves like the other applications in the Office XP Suite. This means you can quickly find commands on toolbars and menus. If you've worked with tables in Word, you'll be able to easily navigate in Excel. At the same time, Excel is challenging because as with any Office application, there are many ways to complete a task. The first method you figure out may not be the most efficient way to get the job done. The MOUS exams are timed, so efficiency is important to your success on the Excel exams.

In this chapter, we will discuss working with cells and cell data as well as managing workbooks. By the time you have finished this chapter, you will have more tools in your toolbox; choosing the proper tool will speed up your work and give you better results in this powerful spreadsheet application.

Before you begin this chapter, you should visit the Sybex website and download the file 4113Ch10.zip. This package contains the files necessary to complete some of the exercises in this chapter. Other files show the documents after the exercise has been successfully completed. These files are affixed with the word *Post*.

Working with Cells and Cell Data

When you launch Excel, the Excel application window opens with a new Excel *workbook*. A workbook is a multipage Excel document. Each page in the workbook is called a *worksheet*, and the active worksheet is displayed in the document window. By default, a new workbook has three worksheets, or *sheets*.

To access a worksheet, click the worksheet's tab at the bottom of the Excel application window. Worksheets consist of columns and rows separated by gridlines; the intersection of a column and row is a cell, the basic unit of an Excel worksheet. The first column is column A, and the letter A appears in the column heading. The horizontal rows are numbered. The row headings are the vertical numbers at the left edge of the worksheet. Each worksheet has 256 columns (A through IV) and 65,536 rows—plenty of room to enter all your data! See Figure 10.1 for features of the Excel 2002 application window.

FIGURE 10.1   The Excel 2002 application window

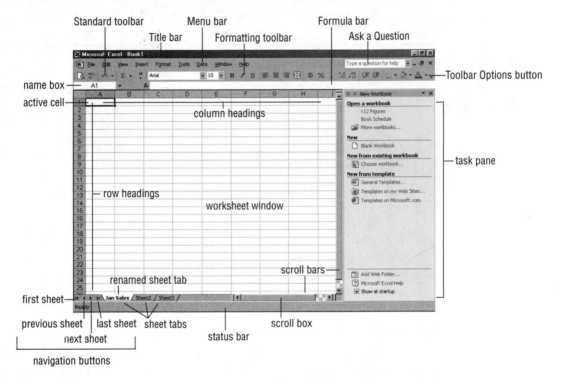

 To display the two default toolbars on separate rows, click the Toolbar Options button at the right end of either toolbar and choose Show Buttons On Two Rows.

The active cell, A1 in Figure 10.1, has a frame around it called the *cell pointer*, and the headings in the active cell's column (A) and row (1) are highlighted. When you enter data, it is always placed in the active cell.

Changing Worksheet Layout

A well-constructed Excel worksheet can have a long, useful life. As business rules or needs change, you can change the worksheet to reflect the current reality. You may, for example, need to insert a few rows for new categories in a budget worksheet, add a column of new calculations, or remove unused rows or columns you no longer require. The features you'll learn about in this section allow you to change worksheet layout quickly and easily.

Microsoft ✓ *Exam* *Objective*	**Insert, delete and move cells**

Although it may not be obvious at first glance, this objective expects you to know how to do each of the following things:

- Select cells, rows, columns, and ranges
- Delete the contents of a cell or range of cells
- Insert and delete cells and cell ranges
- Insert and delete rows and columns
- Move a selection using cut and paste or drag and drop

Selecting Cells, Rows, Columns, and Ranges

As with Word, you must select before you can insert, delete, or move a selection. Exercises 10.1, 10.2, and 10.3 focus on methods you can use to select one or more cells in Excel. In Exercise 10.1, you will select cells, rows, and columns.

EXERCISE 10.1

Selecting Cells, Rows, and Columns

1. Start Excel from the Programs menu. Excel opens with a new Excel workbook. Cell A1 is selected.

2. Click cell C5 to select it.

EXERCISE 10.1 (*continued*)

3. Press the down arrow on the keyboard to select cell C6.

4. Scroll vertically until you can see cell C35. Click cell C35 to select it.

5. Hold Ctrl and press Home to select cell A1, the "home cell."

6. Point to the column heading for column D. The mouse pointer changes to a column selection pointer (an arrow that points directly downward). Click the column heading for column D to select column D.

7. Point to the row heading for row 7. The mouse pointer changes to a row selection pointer. Click the row heading for row 7 to select row 7.

8. Select cell A1. Press PgDn to select the cell one screen down from cell A1. Press PgUp to return to the previous cell.

You can drag to select contiguous cells, rows, and columns, or hold Ctrl and click to select noncontiguous (nonadjacent) areas of the worksheet, as shown in Exercise 10.2.

EXERCISE 10.2

Selecting Multiple Columns and Rows

1. Using the same spreadsheet used in Exercise 10.1, hold down the mouse button and drag across the column headings for columns B, C, and D to select all three columns.

2. Drag across the row headings for rows 2, 3, 4, and 5 to select all four rows.

3. Click the column heading for column D to select the column. Hold the Ctrl key and click the column heading for column B to select columns B and D but not column C. Release the Ctrl key.

4. Click the row heading for row 2. Hold Ctrl and click the row heading for row 5 to select rows 2 and 5 but not rows 3 and 4.

5. With rows 2 and 5 selected, hold Ctrl and click the heading for column B to add column B to the selection. Notice that the selections overlap in cells B2 and B5.

Some commands, including the commands used to move, insert, and delete, are not available with overlapping selections. The formatting commands are available with overlapping selections.

To select the entire worksheet, hold Ctrl and press A on the keyboard, or click the Select All button at the left end of the worksheet's column headings.

One or more selected cells are called a *range*. A range is described with the addresses of the first and last cells in the range separated by a colon. For example, A1:A4 refers to cells A1, A2, A3, and A4. You can select ranges using the mouse or keyboard or a combination of the two. We will show you how to use all three methods in Exercise 10.3.

EXERCISE 10.3

Selecting Ranges

1. Using the same spreadsheet used in the previous two exercises, click cell A1.

2. Hold the mouse button and drag to cell B10 to select cells A1 through B10.

   You can also select this range using the keyboard. Hold Ctrl and press Home to move to cell A1. Hold the Shift key, and then use the arrow keys to move the cell pointer to B10 and select the range. If you hold Shift while moving to a new cell, the original cell, the ending cell, and all the cells in between are selected.

3. Using the mouse, select cell A1.

4. Hold the Shift key and click cell B10 to select cells A1 through B10.

5. Hold Ctrl and press Home to select cell A1.

6. Hold Shift and press the right arrow key twice to select cells A1 through C1.

7. Using the mouse, select cells A1:B5. Hold Ctrl and select cells C1:C11.

To select the area of the worksheet that contains entries, select the first cell with contents: usually cell A1. Hold Shift and Ctrl, and then press the down arrow key then the right arrow.

Deleting Cell Contents

In Excel, "delete" has two meanings. When you delete or *clear* the contents of a cell, the cell remains, but its contents are removed. When you delete a cell, the cell and its contents are removed from the worksheet. In Exercise 10.4, you'll clear the contents of cells.

EXERCISE 10.4

Deleting the Contents of a Cell

The first four steps create content that you will delete in the remaining steps:

1. Click the New button on the Standard toolbar to open a new workbook. Select cell A1. Type **123** in the cell. Press Enter to enter the number and move down one cell to A2.

2. Type **456** in cell A2. Press Tab to enter the number and move one cell to the right.

3. Type **789** in cell B2.

4. Using the mouse, select cell B3. Type **10** in the cell. Click the Enter button (with the green check mark) on the formula bar to enter the number and remain in cell B3.

Next, we'll delete the contents of a single cell:

5. Select cell B2. Press the Delete key or choose Edit ➢ Clear ➢ Contents from the menu. Note that cell B2 is still there, but the entry 789 has been removed.

6. Click the Undo button on the Standard toolbar to undo the last deletion.

EXERCISE 10.4 *(continued)*

To delete the contents of multiple cells, select the row, column, or range of cells you want to delete:

7. Select column A by clicking the column header. Press the Delete key or choose Edit ➢ Clear ➢ Contents from the menu. Column A is not removed, but the contents of all the column's cells are deleted.

Leave the worksheet open. You will use it in the next exercise.

Deleting a Cell or Range of Cells

When you delete a cell or range of cells, Excel removes the cells from the worksheet. Excel will prompt you to specify what should be done with the cells to the right of or below the deleted cells. In Exercise 10.5, you'll delete cells and cell ranges and instruct Excel how to handle placement of the remaining cells.

EXERCISE 10.5

Deleting a Cell or Range of Cells

1. Using the worksheet you used in Exercise 10.4, select cell A3 in the worksheet. Type **New** in the cell.

2. Select cell A2.

3. Choose Edit ➢ Delete from the menu. Excel opens the Delete dialog box:

4. Select Shift Cells Left to delete A2 and shift the contents from cell B2 to the left. Click OK.

5. Click the Undo button on the Standard toolbar or choose Edit ➢ Undo Delete to undo the last step.

6. Choose Edit ➢ Delete from the menu. In the Delete dialog box, choose Shift Cells Up to delete the contents of A2 and move the contents of A3 up. Click OK.

7. Undo the last step.

8. Choose Edit ➢ Delete from the menu. In the Delete dialog box, choose Entire Row to delete row 2.

9. Undo the last step.

Leave the worksheet open. You will use it in the next exercise.

Inserting and Deleting Rows and Columns

As you'll see in Exercises 10.6 and 10.7, there are three ways to insert or delete rows and columns in Excel. In this exercise, you'll insert rows and columns.

Inserting Rows and Columns

1. In the spreadsheet you used in Exercise 10.5, select row 1.

2. Choose Insert ➢ Rows from the menu to insert a new row 1 and shift the remaining rows down.

3. Select cell A1.

4. Choose Insert ➢ Cell from the menu to open the Insert dialog box.

5. Choose Entire Row and click OK to insert a new row.

6. Right-click the row 1 row heading. Choose Insert from the shortcut menu to insert a new row.

7. Right-click the column B heading. Choose Insert from the shortcut menu to insert a new column in column B and shift the contents of column B and columns that follow to the right.

8. Drag to select row headings 1 through 3. Right-click one of the selected headings and choose Insert to insert three rows.

Keep the workbook open for the next exercise.

There are 65,536 rows and 256 columns in a worksheet. If there are entries in row 65536 or column IV and you attempt to insert another row or column, Excel will warn you that it cannot insert the row or column. In Exercise 10.7, you'll delete rows and columns.

EXERCISE 10.7

Deleting Rows and Columns

1. In the spreadsheet you used in Exercise 10.6, click the column B heading to select column B.

2. Choose Edit ➤ Delete to delete column B.

3. Select cell A1.

4. Choose Edit ➤ Delete to open the Delete dialog box.

5. Choose Entire Row. Click OK to delete the selected row, row 1.

6. Right-click the row 1 heading. Choose Delete to delete row 1.

7. Drag to select row headings 1 through 4. Right-click one of the selected headings and choose Delete from the shortcut menu to delete the four rows.

Close the workbook without saving.

Obviously, the fastest way to insert or delete one or multiple rows or columns is to select and right-click the row or column headings.

Moving Using Cut and Paste or Drag and Drop

There are two ways to move a selection of cells in Excel: cut and paste and drag and drop. Cut and paste operate the same in Excel as in other Office applications. You can copy or cut a selection, perform other operations (such as inserting rows or columns), and paste later. The Office XP Clipboard holds the contents of up to 24 copy operations from any Office application, so you can copy or cut several selections and then begin pasting. The Clipboard task pane opens automatically when you cut or copy more than one item without pasting. You can also choose Edit ➤ Office Clipboard or hold Ctrl and press C twice to display the Clipboard task pane.

There are two clipboards: the Office XP Clipboard and the system (Windows) Clipboard. The last item you cut or copied is placed on the system Clipboard. When you paste using the Edit menu, Paste button, or the shortcut keys (Ctrl+V), you're pasting from the system Clipboard.

If you're familiar with cut and paste operations in Word, you'll have no trouble completing them in Excel. There are a few differences:

- If you paste cells on top of existing data, the existing data will be over-written. Before pasting, make sure that there are enough blank cells to accommodate the selection you want to paste. For example, if you want to move the contents of column E to the right of column A without overwriting column B, you can begin by inserting a blank column between columns A and B.

- When you cut a cell in Excel, it is copied to the system Clipboard but is not removed from its current location until you paste it in its new location by pressing Enter or clicking the Paste button.

- When you get ready to paste, just select the first cell, row, or column where you want pasted cells, rows, or columns to appear. If you select more than one cell to paste into, the selected destination range must be exactly the same size as the range on the Clipboard that you want to paste.

There are four ways to access the Cut and Paste commands. First, select the cell, range, column(s) or rows(s) you want to move. Then, to cut the selection, do one of the following:

- Click the Cut button on the Standard toolbar.

- Choose Edit ➤ Cut from the menu.

- Hold Ctrl and press X on the keyboard.

- Right-click in the selection and choose Cut from the shortcut menu.

To paste the selection, select the cell in the upper-left corner of the area where you want to paste the selection. When you copy a selection, you can paste it more than once. Use one of the following methods to paste all but the last copy. Press Enter to place the final pasted copy.

- Click the Paste button on the Standard toolbar.

- Choose Edit ➤ Paste from the menu.

- Hold Ctrl and press V on the keyboard.

- Right-click the selected cell and choose Paste from the shortcut menu.

Even if you plan to paste only once, there's a good reason to use Paste rather than simply pressing Enter. When you use Paste, Excel displays a Paste Options button at the bottom of the pasted selection. Click the button to choose to copy formatting only, to retain column widths and formatting, or to match the pasted cells' format to the format of the surrounding cells. (Other commands on the Paste Options menu are discussed in other chapters.)

You'll use several of the cut-and-paste techniques listed above to complete Exercise 10.8.

EXERCISE 10.8

Moving Cells with Cut and Paste

1. Open a new workbook.

2. In cell A1 type your name. Press Enter.

3. Select cell A1 and choose Edit ➢ Cut to cut the cell contents. The prompt Select Destination And Press ENTER Or Choose Paste appears in the status bar. The moving border surrounds cell A1, but the contents of cell A1 do not change.

4. Select cell C5. Hold Ctrl and press V to move the contents of A1 to C5.

Moving a selection with drag and drop is more straightforward, as you'll see in Exercise 10.9.

EXERCISE 10.9

Moving Cells with Drag and Drop

1. Open a new workbook (or use the one you used in Exercise 10.8) and select cell A1. Type your first name in A1 and click the Enter button on the formula bar.

2. Point to any border of the cell. The mouse pointer changes to a four-headed arrow.

3. Hold the mouse button down and drag to cell D7.

4. Release the mouse button to drop the selection.

5. Point to any border of D7.

6. Hold Ctrl and drag to cell A1.

7. Release the mouse button and then release the Ctrl button to copy the contents of D7 to A1.

Entering and Editing Cell Data

Two types of data can be entered directly into cells in a worksheet: numbers and text.

Numbers   *Numbers* are values you may want to use in calculations, including dates. Dates are often used in calculations to determine, for example, how many days to charge for an overdue video or how many months of interest you have earned on a deposit. *Formulas*, which are calculations, are a specific kind of number entry.

Text   *Text* is any entry that isn't a number.

Microsoft ✓ ***Exam Objective***	**Enter and edit cell data including text, numbers, and formulas**

To enter data in a cell, first select the cell, and then begin typing the data. As soon as you begin entering characters from the keyboard, an insertion point appears in the cell, the text you are entering appears in the cell and the formula bar, and the formula bar buttons are activated. If you make a mistake while entering data, click the Cancel Formula button (the red X) to discard the entry you were making and turn off the formula bar buttons. You can also cancel an entry by pressing the Esc key on the keyboard.

Clicking the Enter button (the green check mark) on the formula bar finishes the entry and turns off the formula bar buttons. Pressing the Enter key on the keyboard does the same thing but also moves the cell pointer down one cell. So if you are entering columns of data, the Enter key is more efficient than the Enter button. To finish an entry and move one cell to the right, press Tab. Moving to another cell always finishes an entry as if you had clicked the Enter button before you moved the cell pointer.

Some Excel features are disabled while you are entering data in a cell. Be sure you finish an entry by entering or canceling it before moving on to other tasks.

There is another way to finish an entry: Simply move to another cell by clicking the cell or using the arrow keys. Before Excel switches the focus to the new cell, it finishes the entry in the current cell. If your entry needs to be changed now or in the future, you'll want to know how to edit cell data.

Editing Cell Data

There are two ways to change an entry in a cell: typing over the entry or editing a portion of the entry.

Type over   Select the cell and type a new entry to overwrite the existing cell contents. This is the easiest way to change a number (for example, from 15 to 17) or to replace text with a short word.

Edit a portion   If the original entry is long and requires only minor adjustment, you might prefer to edit it. Click the cell and edit the entry in the formula bar, or double-click the cell or press F2 to open the cell for editing and edit directly in the cell. When you have finished, press Enter or click the Enter button to complete the entry.

In Exercise 10.10, you'll enter numeric and text data to create a worksheet.

EXERCISE 10.10

Entering Text and Numbers

1. Click the New button on the Standard toolbar to open a new workbook.

2. Enter the following labels. Press Enter to finish each entry and move down one cell:

   A1: **Williams Paint Corporation**

   A2: **Quarterly Sales (thousands)**

   A4: **Location**

A5: **North Chicago**

A6: **Schaumberg**

A7: **Hyde Park**

A8: **Rosemont**

A10: **Totals**

B4: **Jan-Mar**

C4: **Apr-Jun**

D4: **Jul-Sep**

E4: **Oct-Dec**

F4: **Totals**

3. Enter the following first-quarter sales numbers in column B. Press Enter after each entry to move down the column. Some data in column A may appear cut off. This is normal.

B5: **388**

B6: **319**

B7: **567**

B8: **217**

4. Enter the second-quarter sales numbers in column C:

C5: **421**

C6: **345**

C7: **566**

C8: **251**

5. Enter the third-quarter sales numbers in column D:

D5: **399**

D6: **333**

D7: **534**

D8: **264**

6. Enter the fourth-quarter sales numbers in column E:

   E5: **485**

   E6: **369**

   E7: **601**

   E8: **289**

7. Select cell A5. Double-click the cell to edit it.

8. Select and delete "North" to change the entry to "Chicago."

9. Finally, select cell C5. Enter **412** to overtype the existing entry.

   This is what your completed worksheet should look like.

	A	B	C	D	E	F
1	Williams Paint Corporation					
2	Quarterly Sales (thousands)					
3						
4	Location	Jan-Mar	Apr-Jun	Jul-Sep	Oct-Dec	Totals
5	Chicago	388	412	399	485	
6	Schaumber	319	345	333	369	
7	Hyde Park	567	566	534	601	
8	Rosemont	217	251	264	289	
9						
10	Totals					

10. Save the workbook as **Williams Paint Corporation Quarterly Sales** and close it. The workbook will be used later in the chapter.

Excel has an *AutoComplete* feature, which keeps track of text entered in a column and can complete other entries in the same column. For example, if you have already typed "Expenses" in cell A1 and then enter the letter "E" in A2, Excel automatically fills in "xpenses" to make "Expenses." If "Expenses" is the correct entry, finish the entry by simply pressing Enter, moving to another cell, or clicking the Enter button. If the AutoComplete entry is not correct, just continue entering the correct text to overwrite the AutoComplete entry. AutoComplete resets each time you leave a blank cell in a column.

AutoComplete is turned on by default. To turn it off, select Tools ➤ Options, choose the Edit tab, and clear the last check box on the tab: Enable AutoComplete For Cell Values.

Entering Formulas

You use a *formula* when you want to perform a calculation in Excel. You don't have to be a math major to use formulas, because Excel does the math correctly every time. Excel uses standard computer operator symbols for mathematical and logical operators, as shown in Table 10.1.

TABLE 10.1 Mathematical and Logical Operators

Operation	Symbol
Addition	+
Subtraction	–
Multiplication	*
Division	/
Exponentiation (to the power of)	^
Precedence (do this operation first)	Enclose in ( )
Equal to	=
Not equal to	<> (this is typed as two symbols)
Greater than	>
Less than	<

There are three ways to create formulas in Excel: using point and click, typing the formula using cell addresses, or copying/filling a formula from another cell. We'll begin with simple formulas that have one math operation. For example, the `Williams Paint Rosemont Payroll` worksheet, shown in Figure 10.2, needs formulas to calculate the total gross pay.

FIGURE 10.2 Williams Paint Rosemont Payroll worksheet

	A	B	C	D
1	Williams Paint			
2	Rosemont Payroll			
3				
4	Name	Pay Rate	Hours	Gross Pay
5	Benson	10	40	
6	Browning	9	41	
7	Lawrence	10.25	30	
8	Monroe	9	16	
9	Stephens	9.75	44	

Point and click is the highly reliable formula entry method that Excel is known for. You'll create formulas using point and click in Exercise 10.11. In this exercise, we'll enter the formula in cell D5 using the point-and-click method.

EXERCISE 10.11

Entering Point-and-Click Formulas

1. Open the file 10-11.xls and select the cell where you want the result of the formula to appear: cell D5.

2. Type an equal sign: =

3. Click the first cell you want to include in the formula: B5. A border called a *range finder* appears around cell B5.

4. Type the multiplication operator: *

Note that as you select cells and enter operators, you're building a formula in Excel's formula bar. The cell reference in the formula bar is the same color as the range finder surrounding the cell reference.

5. Click the next cell in the formula: C5.

    Excel applies a green range finder to the cell and colors the cell reference green in the formula bar.

6. Finish the formula by pressing Enter or clicking the Enter button on the formula bar. (Don't just click another cell—Excel will include it in the formula!)

7. Keep this workbook open for the next exercise, or save it as 10-12.xls.

Formulas are dynamic, so the results automatically change each time the numbers in the underlying cells are revised. In our worksheet, if Benson's hours or pay rate change, Benson's gross pay will also change because we created a formula based on the contents of two cells rather than typing in the values (=10 * 40) or an answer (400).

Cells that contain formulas display the formula results—the answer. To see the formula, click the cell and look at the formula bar, or double-click the cell to open it for editing.

The traditional spreadsheet approach is to type the formula using the cell addresses of each cell you want to include in the formula, for example =b6*c6. It's easier to type the wrong cell address than to click the wrong cell, so typing the entire formula is a less desirable way to create a formula. However, Exercise 10.12 provides an opportunity to create a formula by typing the cell references.

EXERCISE 10.12

Typing a Formula

1. Using the spreadsheet you completed in Exercise 10.11, or the file 10-12.xls, select the cell where you want the formula result to appear: cell D6.

2. Type an equal sign: =

3. Type the address of the first cell you want to include in the formula: **b6**

4. Type the multiplication operator: *

5. Type the address of the next cell in the formula: **c6**

6. Finish the formula by pressing Enter or clicking the Enter button on the formula bar.

7. Choose File ➢ Save or click the Save button on the Standard toolbar to resave the file, which you will use in the next exercise.

Complex formulas involve more than one operation: for example, adding two numbers and then multiplying the result by a third number as in the formula =(E7+F7)*G7. When you have more than one operation in a formula, you'll need to know about the *order of operations*, a short set of rules about how formulas are calculated:

1. Formulas are calculated from left to right.

2. Multiplication and division are always done before any addition or subtraction. Excel will make two left-to-right passes through a formula and do the multiplication and division on the first pass. Then it will come back through and complete any addition and subtraction operations.

3. To force Excel to add or subtract before it multiplies or divides, use parentheses. Any operation in parentheses is calculated first. If you want two numbers added before multiplying their total by a third number, just throw a set of parentheses ( ) around the addition part of the formula. Notice that you never need to include parentheses if you're doing only one operation, only when you need to tell Excel how to order two or more operations. If you include extra parentheses, Excel ignores them.

Exponentiations (operations "to the power of" such as squares and cubes) are performed after operations in parentheses and before multiplication and division.

Filling Formulas, Numbers, and Dates

In the `Williams Paint Rosemont Payroll` worksheet, the formula for each employee's gross pay is the same: the employee's hours multiplied by their pay rate. If you've already created one correct formula, all you need to do is fill it to the other cells to create the new formulas. Filling is a form of copying.

Begin by activating the cell that has the formula you want to copy. There is a square box in the lower-right corner of the cell pointer called the *fill handle*.

Move the mouse pointer toward the fill handle until the mouse pointer changes to the fill pointer shape: a skinny crosshair. Press the mouse button and drag the fill handle down to select the cells you want to copy the formula to. Release the mouse button, and the formula is filled to the other cells. If the content of the original cell includes a formula, Excel adjusts the formula relative to its new location. For example, if a formula is copied from row 5 to row 6, all row references are increased by 1. Fill a formula from column D to column E, and all column references are adjusted to reflect the change in position. In Exercise 10.13, you'll fill the Gross Pay formula in the Williams Paint Rosemont Payroll worksheet to other cells in the same column—this is both easier and faster than creating each formula separately.

EXERCISE 10.13

Filling Formulas

1. Open the Williams Paint Rosemont Payroll workbook you used in Exercise 10.12, and select the cell that contains the formula you want to copy to other cells: D6.

2. Point to the fill handle in the lower-right corner of the selection. The mouse pointer changes to a fill pointer.

3. Drag the fill handle to cell D9 to select the cells where you want the formula copied.

4. Release the fill handle to fill the formula.

5. Save and close the workbook.

The fill feature provides a fast way to enter numeric data as well. When you fill a number (like the number 1), Excel fills the destination cells with the same number. If you want to increment the number, hold Ctrl while you fill to create a series: 1, 2, 3, and so on, or use the Fill Options button that appears at the end of a fill operation, as you'll see later in this section.

If you're filling dates, you don't need to hold Ctrl to increment. Excel automatically increments dates by one day when you fill dates by dragging the fill handle. If you don't want to increment dates, you can use the Fill commands from the Edit menu. Select the cell you want to copy and the adjacent destination cells. Choose Edit ➢ Fill ➢ Down, Right, Up, or Left. Excel swiftly copies the source cell contents into all of the destination cells. The shortcut keystroke to fill down is Ctrl+D; Ctrl+R fills to the right. Exercise 10.14 provides practice using these fill methods.

EXERCISE 10.14

Filling Numbers and Dates

1. Open a new workbook.

2. In cell A1, enter the number **15**.

3. Select cell A1. Drag the fill handle to cell A5 to copy the contents of A1 to the other four cells:

	A	B
1	15	
2	15	
3	15	
4	15	
5	15	
6		▣
7		

4. Click the Undo button on the Standard toolbar.

5. Select cell A1. Hold Ctrl and drag the fill handle to cell A5 to fill the cells with a series. Or, drag the fill handle to A5, then select the Fill Options button, click the down arrow to open the menu, and choose Fill Series:

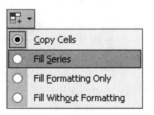

6. In cell B1, enter the date **3/1/2002**.

7. Select cell B1. Drag the fill handle to fill the date to cells B2:B5:

	A	B	C
1	15	3/1/2002	
2	16	3/2/2002	
3	17	3/3/2002	
4	18	3/4/2002	
5	19	3/5/2002	
6			▣
7			

8. Click Undo.

9. Select cells B1:B5. Hold Ctrl and press D to fill the range with the date in cell B1.

10. Click Undo.

11. Select cell B1. Drag the fill handle to fill the date to cells B2:B5.

12. Select the Fill Options button, click the down arrow, and choose Copy Cells:

13. Click Undo.

14. Fill B1 to B2:B5 again. Select the Fill Options button, click the down arrow, and choose Fill Months.

    You can select other options to increment the date by another period.

15. Close the workbook without saving your changes.

Creating Totals Formulas

While the basic mathematical operators work well for formulas that contain a few cell adzdresses, it would be cumbersome to create a formula to add one hundred cells if you had to use the point-and-click or traditional typing method.

The AutoSum button on the Standard toolbar provides quick access to these functions used to summarize data:

- **SUM** returns the total of all values in a range of cells.

- **AVERAGE** returns the arithmetic mean for a range of cells.

- **COUNT** returns the number of cells in a range that contain numbers.

- **MAX** returns the highest value from a range of cells.

- **MIN** returns the lowest value from a range of cells.

In Exercise 10.15, you'll use the SUM function to total columns. In this exercise, we'll add totals to the `Williams Paint Corporation Quarterly Sales` worksheet.

EXERCISE 10.15

Using AutoSum to Create Formulas

1. Open the `Williams Paint Corporation Quarterly Sales` workbook you created in Exercise 10.10, or open the file `10-15.xls`.

2. Select the cell where the result of the formula will appear: B10.

3. Click the down arrow on the AutoSum button.

4. Choose the type of summary formula you want to create: Sum.

   If you're creating a Sum, as you are in this exercise, you can just click the button instead of choosing Sum from the AutoSum button's menu.

5. Excel selects a nearby range of numbers to summarize: B5:B9. If the selection is not correct, select the numbers you wish to summarize.

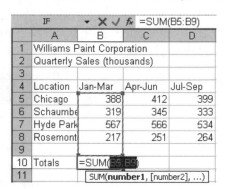

EXERCISE 10.15 *(continued)*

6. Press Enter to create the formula.

7. Select the formula in B10 and fill it to C10:F10.

	A	B	C	D	E	F	G
1	Williams Paint Corporation						
2	Quarterly Sales (thousands)						
3							
4	Location	Jan-Mar	Apr-Jun	Jul-Sep	Oct-Dec	Totals	
5	Chicago	388	412	399	485		
6	Schaumbe	319	345	333	369		
7	Hyde Park	567	566	534	601		
8	Rosemont	217	251	264	289		
9							
10	Totals	1491					
11							

8. Select cell F5.

9. Click the AutoSum button.

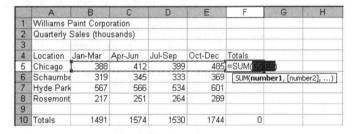

	A	B	C	D	E	F	G	H
1	Williams Paint Corporation							
2	Quarterly Sales (thousands)							
3								
4	Location	Jan-Mar	Apr-Jun	Jul-Sep	Oct-Dec	Totals		
5	Chicago	388	412	399	485	=SUM(B5:E5)		
6	Schaumbe	319	345	333	369	SUM(**number1**, [number2], ...)		
7	Hyde Park	567	566	534	601			
8	Rosemont	217	251	264	289			
9								
10	Totals	1491	1574	1530	1744	0		

10. Press Enter to create the formula.

11. Select the formula in F5 and fill it to F6:F8.

12. Save and close the workbook.

Checking Spelling in Your Worksheet

Misspelled words automatically cast doubt on the accuracy of an entire worksheet. Excel includes two tools to help you correct spelling errors. *AutoCorrect* automatically fixes common typos and *Spelling* checks all the text in a worksheet to ensure that it is error-free. If a cell other than A1 is selected when you begin checking, Excel will check from the cell pointer to the end of the worksheet and then ask if it should return to the top of the worksheet and finish checking. When Spelling is complete, Excel will notify you that it has finished checking the entire sheet.

Microsoft
Exam
Objective

Check spelling

Office comes with an extensive English dictionary and, if you install the Language Pack, dictionaries for other languages. There's a custom dictionary that contains words you've added to the dictionary. Spelling is a shared feature of all the Office XP products, so words you add to the dictionary or to AutoCorrect are added to the common custom dictionary you use with Excel, Word, PowerPoint, and Access. When you run the Spelling feature, Excel checks each word against these dictionaries. When it doesn't find a word, it flags it for you to verify. You have a number of ways of dealing with a word that isn't in any of the dictionaries:

- **Ignore Once** ignores the selected occurrence of the word.

- **Ignore All** ignores all occurrences of the word in this document.

- **Add To Dictionary** adds the word to the Custom dictionary so Excel will recognize it in the future.

- **Change** substitutes the correction you selected or entered for this occurrence of the misspelled word.

- **Change All** substitutes the correction for all occurrences of the word in this worksheet.

- **AutoCorrect** corrects the word and adds it to the AutoCorrect dictionary.

In Exercise 10.16, you'll use Excel's AutoCorrect and Spelling features to check spelling in a worksheet created with typographical errors.

EXERCISE 10.16

Checking Spelling

1. Open a new workbook.

2. In cell A1, type **Teh Gratest Show on Earth**. Excel's AutoCorrect feature automatically corrects "Teh" to "The."

3. In cell A2, type **Michigun**.

EXERCISE 10.16 *(continued)*

4. In cell A3, type **Expemdrd**.

5. Select cell A1.

6. Click the Spelling button on the Standard toolbar or choose Tools ➢ Spelling from the menu to check spelling.

7. Excel finds the first misspelled word (Gratest) and opens the Spelling dialog box.

8. Choose Greatest from the list of suggestions and click Change.

9. Excel finds the second misspelled word (Michigun).

10. Choose Michigan from the list of suggestions and click Change.

11. Excel finds the third misspelled word (Expendrd). The correct word, Expenses, does not appear on the list of suggestions.

12. Type the correct word, **Expenses**, in the Not In Dictionary text box.

13. Click Change to correct the misspelling.

14. Excel notifies you that the spelling check is complete. Click OK to close the dialog box.

15. Close the workbook without saving your changes.

Using Find and Replace

One of the fastest ways to locate text or make repetitive changes throughout a worksheet is to use Find and Replace. Find helps you locate a text string. Replace lets you substitute another text string for the string that is found.

Microsoft ✔ *Exam* *Objective*	**Find and replace cell data and formats**

In Exercise 10.17, you'll use Excel's Find feature to locate text and numbers in a worksheet.

EXERCISE 10.17

Finding Text in a Worksheet

1. Open the Williams Paint Corporation Quarterly Sales workbook you saved in Exercise 10.15.

2. Select cell A1. Choose Edit ➢ Find or hold Ctrl and press F to open the Find And Replace dialog box.

3. Enter **Chicago** in the Find What text box.

4. Click the Find Next button. The cell pointer moves to cell A5.

5. Click Find Next to find the next occurrence of Chicago. This is the only occurrence, so the cell pointer stays in cell A5.

6. Change the Find What entry to **3**.

7. Click Find All. Excel lists the location of all occurrences of 3 in the worksheet. Move to the fifth occurrence by clicking the fifth hyperlink in the list:

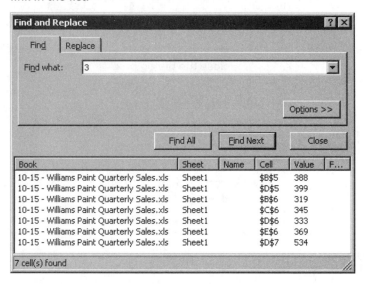

8. Click Close to close the Find And Replace dialog box. Keep the workbook open for the next exercise.

You use Replace to substitute one string for another in a worksheet, as you'll see in Exercise 10.18. In this exercise, we'll quickly convert formulas that calculate sums to those that calculate averages.

EXERCISE 10.18

Using Replace to Swap One String for Another

1. Open the `Williams Paint Corporation Quarterly Sales` workbook used in the previous exercise (`10-15.xls`). The worksheet contains sums in column F and row 10. We will replace the totals in row 10 with averages but keep the totals in column F.

2. Change the label "Totals" in cell A10 to **Averages**.

3. Select cell A1.

4. Choose Edit ➤ Replace from the menu or hold Ctrl and press H to open the Replace dialog box:

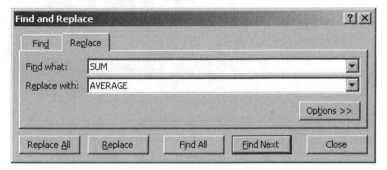

5. In the Find What text box, enter **SUM**.

6. In the Replace With text box, enter **AVERAGE**.

7. Click Find Next to move to the first occurrence of sum in cell F5. You do not want to replace this formula, so click Find Next. Click Find Next three more times to skip the occurrences of SUM in cells F6, F7, and F8 and find the formula in cell B10.

8. Click Replace to replace SUM in the formula with AVERAGE. The result in B10 changes to 372.75.

9. Click Replace four more times to replace the other formulas in row 10. Click Close to close the Find And Replace dialog box.

10. Select the formula in B10. Examine the formula in the formula bar: `=AVERAGE(B5:B9)`.

11. Choose File ➤ Save As. In the Save As dialog box, enter `Williams Paint Sales Averages` as the new filename. Save the file.

Find and Replace have a number of options worth tweaking. Click the Options button in the Find And Replace dialog box to reveal the choices shown in Figure 10.3 and detailed in Table 10.2.

FIGURE 10.3 Options in the Find And Replace dialog box

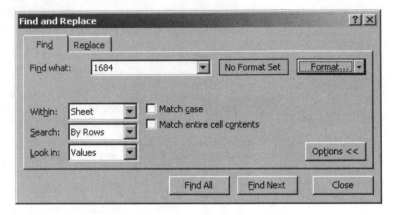

TABLE 10.2 Find and Replace Options

Option	Selection	Description
Within	Sheet	Find/replace in the active worksheet.
Within	Workbook	Find/replace in all sheets in the workbook.
Search	By Rows	Search the current row and then search the column below. With By Rows selected, hold Shift and click Find Next to search the current row and then search upward by rows.
Search	By Columns	Search the current column and then search the row to the right. With By Columns selected, hold Shift and click Find Next to search the current column and then search the column to the left.
Look In	Formulas	Search user-entered text and formulas.

TABLE 10.2 Find and Replace Options *(continued)*

Option	Selection	Description
Look In	Values	Search user-entered text and the results of formulas.
Look In	Comments	Search in comments.
	Match Case	Enable this check box to find only cells where the case of the string in the cell matches the case of the Find What string.
	Match Entire Cell Contents	Enable this check box to find only cells where the contents exactly match the Find What string.
Format	Format	Open the Find Format dialog box so you can specify formatting to find.
Format	Choose Format From Cell	Select and then click a cell that contains the formatting you want to find.

In Exercise 10.19 you'll use the Find and Replace options to replace formats in a worksheet. The first five steps of this exercise apply formatting that you will replace in the remaining steps.

EXERCISE 10.19

Finding and Replacing Formats

1. Open the Williams Paint Sales Averages workbook you created in Exercise 10.18, or open the file 10-19.xls.

2. Select row 4. Hold Ctrl and select row 10.

3. Click the Italic button on the Formatting toolbar.

4. Select cells A4, A10, F4, and F10.

EXERCISE 10.19 *(continued)*

5. Click the Bold button on the Formatting toolbar. Your worksheet should look like this:

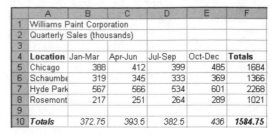

6. Select cell A1. Choose Edit ➤ Find or hold Ctrl and press F to open the Find And Replace dialog box.

7. Click the Options button.

8. Click the down arrow on the top Format button to specify the format you want to find. Select Choose Format From Cell.

9. Select cell A4 to choose the formatting (bold and italic) in cell A4. Delete the contents, if any, of the Find What text box to search for formatting regardless of cell contents.

10. Click Find All to find all four bold, italicized cells:

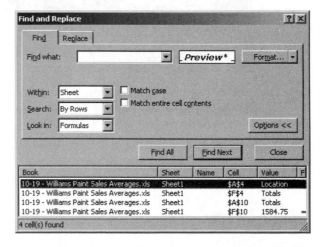

11. Click the Replace tab in the Find And Replace dialog box. Excel retains the formatting selected on the Find tab.

12. Click the down arrow on the Replace With Format button. Choose Format from the menu to open the Replace Format dialog box.

13. On the Font tab, choose Bold in the Font Style list.

14. Choose a color other than Automatic or Black from the Color palette.

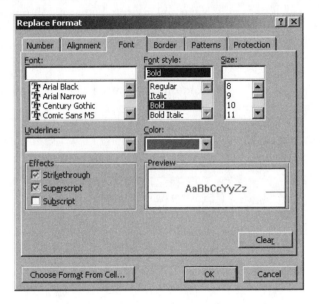

15. Click OK to close the Replace Format dialog box.

16. Click Replace All to replace all four occurrences of bold italic formatting with bold colored formatting. When you choose Replace All, Excel notifies you of the number of replacements made.

17. Click OK to close the message box. Click OK again to close the Find And Replace dialog box.

18. Close the workbook without saving your changes.

Filtering Lists

An Excel list, also known as a database, has a specific structure, defined by its *fields:* the categories of information it contains. In an Excel database, each *field* is a column. Each row is a *record* in the database, containing a single set of the fields. The `Aurora Borealis Writeoffs` worksheet (shown in Figure 10.4) is an Excel database. Each field is a separate column. Column labels (Date, Item #, Type, Quantity, Unit Cost, Reason, and Employee) are field names. Each individual row is a record.

There are construction rules for Excel databases:

- **Blank rows and blank columns** signal the end of a database. Don't leave a blank row between column headings and data records, or blank columns within the database. *Do* leave a blank row after all records and before totals or other summary rows, and between worksheet titles and column headings.

- **Column labels** must be unique within a database. Be consistent: Label every column.

FIGURE 10.4 An Excel list is a section of a worksheet bounded by empty rows and columns.

	A	B	C	D	E	F	G
1	Aurora Borealis Nursery						
2	Write Offs						
3							
4	Date	Item #	Type	Quantity	Unit Cost	Reason	Employee
5	1/7/2002	S9999-P	Poinsetta	37	2.99	Seasonal	AM
6	1/7/2002	S9998-P	Poinsetta	55	3.99	Seasonal	AM
7	1/7/2002	S9911-G	Chia Pet	15	3.75	Seasonal	CC
8	1/12/2002	E4412-J	Juniper	4	13.99	Damaged	AM
9	1/17/2002	X0101-6	6" clay pot	10	1.25	Damaged	GC
10	2/22/2002	E4422-F	Frazier Fir	1	17.45	Damaged	AM
11	3/17/2002	P1201-C	Columbine	120	3.79	Frost	GC
12	3/17/2002	P1201-C	Columbine	60	3.79	Frost	GC
13	3/17/2002	X0101-3	3" clay pot	3	0.66	Damaged	GC
14	3/17/2002	A2213-M	Marigolds	720	0.69	Frost	AM
15	3/17/2002	A5412-P	Phlox	224	2.49	Frost	CC
16	3/20/2002	X0120-H	Hoe	2	8.27	Damaged	GC
17	3/27/2001	H7722-S	Sage	12	0.89	Damaged	GC
18	4/1/2002	T6712-C	North Star	2	17.59	Damaged	GC
19	4/12/2002	T7717-B	Paper Birch	1	22.95	Infected	CC
20	4/19/2002	V8818-T	Early Girl	72	0.49	Damaged	CC
21	4/20/2002	V8172-P	Baby Bell	144	0.49	Damaged	GC
22	4/22/2002	H5917-L	Parsley	24	0.79	Damaged	AM

Any worksheet you've already created can be used as a database, but you might have to delete or add rows, delete columns, or edit column labels to meet these requirements.

In a well-constructed database, every column is *atomic:* it contains the smallest meaningful unit of data. For example, put First Names and Last Names in separate columns rather than combining them into a single Full Name column.

Microsoft ✓ *Exam* *Objective* | **Work with a subset of data by filtering lists**

There are many times when you'll want to work with a database *subset*: a group of records in the database. For example, you might want to print all sales records for one salesperson, all the orders from one client, or all the customers who haven't made a purchase this year. A *filter* is used to select records that meet specific criteria and temporarily hide all the other records in the list. Excel's AutoFilter tool, which you'll use in Exercise 10.20, is an easy-to-use tool for simple filters.

EXERCISE 10.20

Setting Up and Using an AutoFilter

1. Open the file 10-20.xls and save it as **Aurora Borealis Writeoffs.xls**. You will be using this file in a number of the following exercises.

2. Select any cell in the database: a column heading or a value. Do not select more than one cell.

3. Choose Data ➢ Filter ➢ AutoFilter from the menu.

   Excel reads every record in the database and creates a filter criteria list for each field. Click the filter arrow that appears next to the column label to access the field's criteria list. The default criteria setting in each field is All, which means that the contents of the field are not being used to filter the records. Top 10 is used in numeric fields to display the top or bottom 10, 5, or any other number or percentage of values. Custom prompts you to create a custom filter for choices that don't appear on the list.

4. Click the filter arrow on the Reason column. Choose Damaged from the list to filter the database and show goods written off because of damage:

	A	B	C	D	E	F	G
1	Aurora Borealis Nursery						
2	*Write Offs*						
3							
4	Date	Item #	Type	Quantity	Unit Cos	Reason	Employe
8	1/12/2002	E4412–J	Juniper	4	13.99	Damaged	AM
9	1/17/2002	X0101–6	6" clay pot	10	1.25	Damaged	GC
10	2/22/2002	E4422–F	Frazier Fir	1	17.45	Damaged	AM
13	3/17/2002	X0101–3	3" clay pot	3	0.66	Damaged	GC
16	3/20/2002	X0120–H	Hoe	2	8.27	Damaged	GC
17	3/27/2001	H7722–S	Sage	12	0.89	Damaged	GC
18	4/1/2002	T6712–C	North Star	2	17.59	Damaged	CC
20	4/19/2002	V8818–T	Early Girl	72	0.49	Damaged	CC
21	4/20/2002	V8172–P	Baby Bell	144	0.49	Damaged	GC
22	4/22/2002	H5917–L	Parsley	24	0.79	Damaged	AM

The number of records found and the total number of records in the list are displayed in the status bar. Each record retains its original row number; the row numbers of filtered records appear in blue. The drop-down arrow for the filtered field also turns blue.

5. To remove the filter and display all the records, click the filter arrow on the Reason column and choose All or choose Data ➢ Filter ➢ Show All from the menu.

6. Click the filter arrow on the Employee column. Choose AM from the list to show goods written off by employee AM:

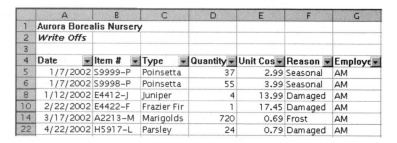

	A	B	C	D	E	F	G
1	Aurora Borealis Nursery						
2	*Write Offs*						
3							
4	Date	Item #	Type	Quantity	Unit Cos	Reason	Employe
5	1/7/2002	S9999–P	Poinsetta	37	2.99	Seasonal	AM
6	1/7/2002	S9998–P	Poinsetta	55	3.99	Seasonal	AM
8	1/12/2002	E4412–J	Juniper	4	13.99	Damaged	AM
10	2/22/2002	E4422–F	Frazier Fir	1	17.45	Damaged	AM
14	3/17/2002	A2213–M	Marigolds	720	0.69	Frost	AM
22	4/22/2002	H5917–L	Parsley	24	0.79	Damaged	AM

7. With the Employee filter still turned on, click the filter arrow on the Reason column. Choose Damaged from the list to display the goods written off by employee AM due to damage.

EXERCISE 10.20 *(continued)*

8. Choose Data ➤ Filter ➤ Show All to remove the filters and show all records.

   This workbook is used in the next exercise. You may close it now or leave it open.

In the previous exercise, you filtered for one or more precise values. Use other AutoFilter options, like Top 10, to filter for a range or percentage of items.

Using the Top 10 Filter

Top 10 filters display records based on their value. You can use Top 10 filters only with numeric fields. In Exercise 10.21, you'll use Top 10 filters to return the five highest values from a list column.

EXERCISE 10.21

Applying a Top 10 Filter

1. Open the Aurora Borealis Writeoffs workbook you used in Exercise 10.20, or open the file 10–20.xls.

2. If the AutoFilter is not turned on, choose Data ➤ Filter ➤ AutoFilter to turn it on.

3. Click the drop-down arrow for the Quantity column, and choose Top 10 to open the Top 10 AutoFilter dialog box:

4. Choose Top in the first drop-down list to filter for the highest values.

EXERCISE 10.21 *(continued)*

5. Enter **5** in the spin box control to see the five highest values.

6. Choose Items in the third control to display five records.

7. Click OK to apply the filter.

8. Choose Data ➤ Filter ➤ Show All to display all records.

This workbook is used in the next exercise, so you might want to leave it open.

Creating a Custom Filter

When you filter using the items on the filter lists, you are filtering for records that exactly equal specific criteria. Custom filters give you access to other ways to set criteria:

- All records with fields that are *not* equal to a criterion

- Records that are greater than a criterion

- Records that are less than a criterion

- A range of records that are greater than one criterion and less than another criterion

- Records that meet one condition *or* another

In Exercise 10.22, you'll create custom filters to filter the list for a range of dates, records that do not contain a specific string, and items that begin with a specific character.

EXERCISE 10.22

Applying a Custom Filter

1. Open the Aurora Borealis Writeoffs workbook you used in the last two exercises, or open the file 10-20.xls.

2. If the AutoFilter is not turned on, choose Data ➤ Filter ➤ AutoFilter to turn it on.

3. Click the filter arrow on the Date field, and choose Custom from the list to open the Custom AutoFilter dialog box.

EXERCISE 10.22 *(continued)*

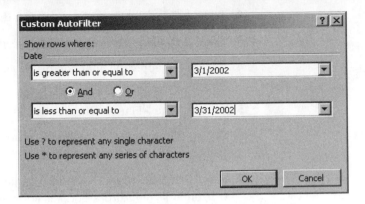

4. In the first drop-down list, select Is Greater Than Or Equal To.

5. In the first text box, enter **3/1/2002**.

6. Select the And option button so the filter will return only records that meet both conditions.

7. In the second drop-down list, select Is Less Than Or Equal To.

8. In the second text box, enter **3/31/2002**.

9. Click OK to apply the Custom filter and return the six records from March 2002.

10. Choose Data ➢ Filter ➢ Show All to display all records.

11. Click the filter arrow on the Reason column. Choose Custom to open the Custom AutoFilter dialog box:

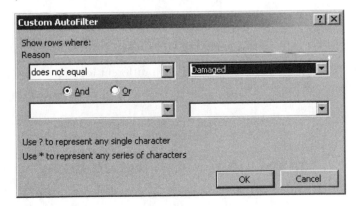

EXERCISE 10.22 *(continued)*

12. Choose Does Not Equal from the first drop-down list.

13. Choose Damaged from the second drop-down list.

14. Click OK to apply the filter and display goods that were written off for reasons other than damage.

15. Choose Data ➢Filter ➢ Show All to display all records.

16. Click the filter arrow on the Item # column. Choose Custom to open the Custom AutoFilter dialog box.

17. In the first drop-down list, choose Begins With. In the text box control, enter **A**, the Aurora Borealis code for annual flowers. Or choose Equals in the first control and type **A*** in the second control.

18. Click OK to apply the filter.

19. To turn the AutoFilter off, choose Data ➢ Filter ➢ AutoFilter. Close the workbook without saving.

Managing Workbooks

You've already created several workbooks. Workbook management focuses on the common tasks of the workbook life cycle:

- Creating folders
- Opening a file as read-only or as a copy
- Deleting, moving, and copying files
- Creating workbooks from templates
- Saving files in different locations
- Saving read-only versions of files
- Saving files using various formats

File Management in the Dialog Boxes

Excel's Open and Save As dialog boxes make it easy to manage workbooks from creation to storage (and eventual deletion). In the Open dialog box, you can open a workbook as read-only. Both the Open and Save As dialog boxes allow you to copy and delete files and create new folders.

Creating a New Folder

Windows' folder structure is a virtual version of a filing cabinet. Folders take the place of file drawers, and folders within those "drawers" are substitutes for hanging folders and file folders. Create a new folder when you're beginning a new project or saving a file related to a new client, budget year, or other type of endeavor.

Microsoft
✔ *Exam*
Objective

Manage workbook files and folders

You often discover the need for a new folder when you're in the middle of saving a file and realize that this file's contents don't really fit in any of the existing folders. As you'll see in Exercise 10.23, you can create a new folder for a file and future related files in the Save As or Open dialog boxes.

EXERCISE 10.23

Creating a New Folder

1. Choose File ➢ Open from the menu or click the Open button on the Standard toolbar to open the Open dialog box.

2. In the Look In drop-down list, select the folder that will contain the new folder. Select My Documents.

3. Click the Create New Folder button on the dialog box toolbar. The New Folder dialog box opens.

4. Type a name for the folder: **Core Exercises**

5. Click OK to create the folder and return to the Open dialog box.

6. Click Cancel to close the Open dialog box.

If the Save As dialog box is open, follow steps 2 through 6 in Exercise 10.23 to create a new folder.

Opening a Workbook As Read-Only or As a Copy

You can change a read-only file, but when you save the file, Excel prompts you to provide another name for the file. You cannot overwrite the original file accidentally or intentionally. Open a workbook as read-only when you want to make sure that you retain the original workbook.

When you open a workbook as a copy, Excel opens a copy of the workbook and precedes the original filename with Copy (1), creating a new filename. Open a workbook as a copy when you want to work with a new copy of the file. You can either save the copy as a separate workbook or, by choosing File ➢ Save As from the menu, save the copy with the original filename to overwrite the original workbook with the copy. In Exercise 10.24, you'll open a workbook as a copy.

EXERCISE 10.24

Opening a Workbook As Read-Only or As a Copy

1. Choose File ➢ Open or click the Open button on the toolbar to open the Open dialog box.

2. Locate and select the workbook you want to open. Choose the Aurora Borealis Writeoffs workbook created earlier in this chapter.

3. Click the down arrow on the Open button.

4. Choose Open As Copy to open a copy of the workbook. (Choose Open Read-Only to open a read-only copy.)

5. Close the Copy (1) Aurora Borealis Writeoffs workbook.

Deleting, Moving, and Copying Workbooks

You can delete, move, and copy workbooks from Excel's Open and Save As dialog boxes, which is much quicker than launching My Computer or Windows

Explorer simply to perform these housekeeping tasks. In Exercise 10.25, you'll delete the workbook copy created in the previous exercise.

EXERCISE 10.25

Deleting a Workbook

1. Choose File ➤ Open or click the Open button to open the Open dialog box.

2. Select the workbook you want to delete: Copy (1) Aurora Borealis Writeoffs.xls.

3. Press the Delete key on your keyboard, or right-click the workbook and choose Delete from the shortcut menu.

4. Click Yes to confirm the deletion.

5. Press Esc on the keyboard or click the Cancel button in the Open dialog box to close the dialog box.

In Exercise 10.26, you'll move and copy workbooks in the Open dialog box.

EXERCISE 10.26

Moving or Copying a Workbook

In this exercise, we'll move the Aurora Borealis Writeoffs workbook to the Core Exercises folder created earlier in this chapter. After completing this exercise, move the other workbooks you've created for this chapter to the same folder.

1. Open the Open dialog box.

2. Locate the Aurora Borealis Writeoffs workbook.

3. Right-click the workbook and choose Cut from the shortcut menu. (To copy a workbook, choose Copy rather than Cut.)

4. In the Look In drop-down list, locate and select the Core Exercises folder.

5. Right-click the open pane and choose Paste from the shortcut menu to move the Aurora Borealis Writeoffs workbook to the Core Exercises folder.

6. Click the Cancel button to close the dialog box.

Creating a Workbook from a Template

Templates are workbooks that are used to create other workbooks. Templates let you quickly construct workbooks that are identical in format, giving your work a standard look. An Excel template can include text, numbers, formatting, formulas, and all the other features you already use. When you create a new document based on a template, Excel opens a copy and the original template is not altered. This protects the original from accidental changes—yet another reason to save workbooks you created for others to use as templates.

Microsoft ✓ *Exam Objective*

Create workbooks using templates

Excel 2002 includes predesigned templates that you can use or modify, but the Office XP installation CD isn't the only source for existing templates. There are templates on the Microsoft Office Update website, and you can purchase third-party templates or create your own.

The New button on the Standard toolbar opens an empty Excel workbook based on the default template, bypassing the task pane. In Exercise 10.27, you'll learn how to create workbooks based on other templates.

EXERCISE 10.27

Creating a Workbook from a Template

1. Choose File ➢ New from the menu bar to display the New Workbook task pane. Template sources are listed in the New From Template section of the task pane:

New from template

- General Templates...
- Templates on my Web Sites...
- Templates on Microsoft.com

2. Click the General Templates link to open the Templates dialog box. Shortcuts to the built-in templates are on the Spreadsheet Solutions tab.

3. Select any template icon to preview the template.

   You would click Templates On My Web Sites to locate templates stored on a local intranet or Internet site. To locate more templates, click Templates On Microsoft.com.

4. To open the Sales Invoice template, double-click the icon or select it and click OK. If the template is not installed, Excel will install it. You may be prompted for the Office XP CD.

5. Close the workbook without saving your changes.

Most templates on Microsoft.com are Word templates, but there's an adequate selection of Excel templates for Finance and Accounting and Business Forms. Unlike the templates in Excel 2000, most Excel 2002 templates don't have a separate Customize This Template worksheet. Instead, non-customizable ranges are protected, and customization is done directly in the template.

The Sales Invoice1 template, shown in Figure 10.5, is a typical Excel template. The cells with standard text and formulas are protected; you can't select, for example, the Total cells in column M. Select a cell with an italicized placeholder—*Insert Company Information Here*—to view a screen tip. Some templates include comments; commented cells have a red triangular comment indicator. To view a comment, move the mouse over the cell.

If you're going to use the template again, you should resave the template with a new name so you don't have to enter the company information the next time you open it. Choose File ➤ Save As and choose Template from the Save As Type drop-down list. Change the filename—for example, Company Sales Invoice instead of Sales Invoice1—to indicate that the template has been modified by adding your company information.

FIGURE 10.5 The Sales Invoice1 template is a typical Excel template.

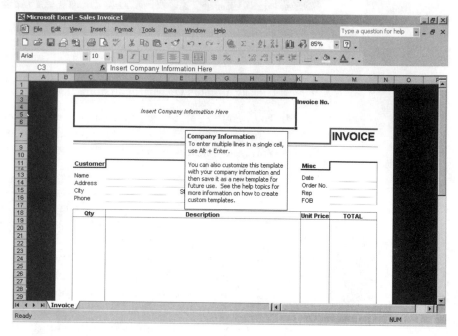

Saving Workbooks Using Different Names and File Formats

The final objective in this chapter requires you to demonstrate your file-saving versatility.

Microsoft
✓ *Exam*
Objective

Save workbooks using different names and file formats

Use Save As to save a copy of a previously saved workbook with different options: a different name, different location, or different format. The original workbook remains in its original location. If, for example, you open the Aurora Borealis Writeoffs workbook, add three entries, and save it in a different folder using Save As, the original workbook without the three new entries will remain in the Core Exercises folder. To save the three entries in the original workbook, save the workbook using File ➤ Save prior to the Save As operation. In Exercise 10.28, you will save the Aurora Borealis

`Writeoffs.xls` file with a different name. You will delete the file at the end of the exercise.

EXERCISE 10.28

Saving a File Using a Different Name

1. Open the Aurora Borealis `Writeoffs.xls` workbook in the Core Exercises folder.

2. Choose File ➢ Save As from the menu to open the Save As dialog box.

3. Select a location for the workbook in the Save In drop-down list or by using the Places bar on the left side of the dialog box. Click the Desktop icon in the Places bar.

4. Enter a name for the workbook—**Aurora Copy**—in the File Name text box.

5. Click Save to save the workbook. Note that the filename is changed on the Excel application title bar.

6. Choose File ➢Close to close the Aurora Copy workbook.

7. Delete the file by following the steps in Exercise 10.25.

Within a folder, each filename must be unique. However, if you're saving the file in a different location, you can use the same filename.

Saving a Workbook or Worksheet in a Previous Excel Format

Excel 2000 and 2002 share a file format that is very similar to the format used in Excel 97. You can save a workbook in versions of Excel earlier than these. Excel versions 2.1, 3, and 4 were single-sheet workbooks. When you save using one of these formats, you will save only the active sheet. In Exercise 10.29, you'll save the Aurora Borealis `Writeoffs` workbook as an Excel 5.0/95 workbook for a fictional colleague, John, who uses Excel 95.

EXERCISE 10.29

Saving a Workbook in a Previous Excel Format

1. Open the workbook you want to save in a previous format: Aurora Borealis `Writeoffs`.

EXERCISE 10.29 *(continued)*

2. Choose File ➢ Save As from the menu.

3. In the Save As dialog box, click the down arrow to open the Save As Type drop-down list.

4. Select Excel 5.0/95 from the list.

5. In the File Name text box control, enter **Aurora Writeoffs for John**.

6. Click Save to save the workbook.

7. Choose File ➢ Close to close Aurora Writeoffs for John.

8. Delete the file by following the steps in Exercise 10.25.

Saving a Workbook in a Non-Excel File Format

Excel has a reputation as a great translator. Excel can open a wide range of file formats, and you can save Excel workbooks in many different formats. One caveat: Most of the file formats you can use do not support all the features of Excel. For example, text file formats such as the comma-separated value (CSV) format do not support multiple pages or charts. When you save a workbook as a CSV file in Exercise 10.30, Excel will warn you that only the active sheet will be saved. If the active sheet is a chart, the CSV file format will not appear on the list of formats that you can use to save the file. With most formats, some text and numeric formatting are lost.

In Exercise 10.30, we'll save the Aurora Borealis Writeoffs workbook as a CSV file to send to our fictional friend Jane, who uses an application that can open CSV files.

EXERCISE 10.30

Saving a Workbook in the CSV Format

1. Open the workbook you want to save in another file format: Aurora Borealis Writeoffs.xls.

2. Choose File ➢ Save As from the menu.

3. In the Save As dialog box, click the down arrow to open the Save As Type drop-down list.

EXERCISE 10.30 *(continued)*

4. Select Comma Delimited (*.CSV) from the list.

5. In the File Name text box control, enter **Aurora Writeoffs for Jane**.

6. Click Save to save the workbook. Click OK when prompted to save only the active worksheet and again when prompted to save without features that are not compatible with the format (comma delimited) you selected.

7. Choose File ➢ Close to close Aurora Writeoffs for Jane.

8. Delete the file by following the steps in Exercise 10.25.

Summary

In this chapter, you learned how to work with cells and cell data and to manage workbooks. We covered the following topics:

- Inserting, deleting, and moving cells

- Entering and editing text, numbers, and formulas

- Using Excel's Spelling feature

- Finding and replacing cell data and formats

- Filtering lists

- Managing files and folders using the Open and Save As dialog boxes

- Creating a workbook from a template

- Saving workbooks using different names, locations, and file formats

Chapter

11

Formatting and Printing Worksheets

MOUS EXCEL 2002 CORE EXAM OBJECTIVES COVERED IN THIS CHAPTER:

- ✓ Apply and modify cell formats
- ✓ Modify row and column settings
- ✓ Modify row and column formats
- ✓ Apply styles
- ✓ Use automated tools to format worksheets
- ✓ Modify Page Setup options for worksheets
- ✓ Preview and print worksheets and workbooks

ormatting in Excel is more than cosmetic. Number formats, for example, are used to make a worksheet readable by aligning decimal points and using commas to delineate thousands and millions. When cell contents are wider than the cell, the contents are truncated until you change the formatting for the cell or column. This chapter focuses on the formatting skills used to enhance worksheet appearance, both onscreen and in print.

NOTE Before you begin this chapter, you should go to the Sybex website and download the file 4113Ch11.zip. This package contains the files necessary to complete some of the exercises in this chapter. In addition, it contains files of what most of the documents should look like after you complete the exercise. These files are affixed with the word *Post*.

Formatting Worksheets

In this section, you'll apply formats to cells, columns, and rows using the toolbars, menu, and Excel's automated formatting tools.

Applying and Modifying Cell, Row, and Column Formats

Excel has several types of formats. Many of the text formats, such as fonts, font styles, text color, and borders, are the same as the familiar formatting from Word, PowerPoint, and other Windows applications. In addition, Excel includes number formats for numeric entries, including dates and times as well as currency.

Microsoft ✓ *Exam* *Objective*	**Apply and modify cell formats**

Number Formats

Number formats identify numbers as currency or percentages and make numbers easier to read by aligning decimal points. You format selected cells with two tools:

- The Formatting toolbar
- The Format Cells dialog box, accessible from the Format menu and the shortcut menu

In even the simplest worksheets you'll want to do some formatting to align numbers and their corresponding labels. The default format, General, results in left-aligned text entries and right-aligned numbers. The General format doesn't display zeros that have no effect on the value of the number. For example, if you enter 10.50 in a cell, the cell displays 10.5, without the extra, or *trailing*, zero. Unless all your numbers have the same number of decimal places, you'll need to format the numbers to make them easier to visually compare.

Using the Formatting Toolbar

To format cells with the Formatting toolbar, select the cells and then click a button to apply one of the formats shown in Table 11.1.

TABLE 11.1 Numeric Formatting from the Formatting Toolbar

Button	Style	Effect
$	Currency	Displays and lines up dollar signs, comma separators, and decimal points: 75.3 as $75.30. Excel uses the currency symbol (for example, the $) selected in Regional Settings in the Windows Control Panel.
%	Percent	Displays number as a percentage: .45 as 45%.

TABLE 11.1 Numeric Formatting from the Formatting Toolbar *(continued)*

Button	Style	Effect
	Comma	Same as Currency, but without dollar signs: 12345.6 as 12,345.60.
	Increase Decimal	Displays one more place after the decimal: .45 as .450.
	Decrease Decimal	Displays one less place after the decimal: .452 as .45. If decreasing the number of digits eliminates a nonzero digit, the displayed number will be rounded. For example, if you format 9. 50 with no digits following the decimal, Excel will display 10. If you format 9.49 with the same format, Excel will display 9.

When you format a number, you change its appearance, not its value. For example, if you format the number 10.575 for two decimal places, the number will be displayed in the cell as 10.58. To view the unformatted contents of a cell, click the cell and look at the formula bar. The number entered in the cell appears in the formula bar exactly as entered regardless of the format you have applied to the cell. The actual value, not the displayed value, is the value used when you refer to the cell in a formula.

In Exercise 11.1, you will apply formats to cells and ranges.

EXERCISE 11.1

Applying and Modifying Formatting with the Formatting Toolbar

1. Open the file 11-1.xls.

2. Click the column heading for column E to select the column.

3. Click the Comma Style button on the Formatting toolbar to apply the comma style. The decimals in column E will be lined up.

EXERCISE 11.1 *(continued)*

4. Click the Decrease Decimal button on the Formatting toolbar. Notice that the numbers in column E are rounded to one decimal place.

5. Select cell E5. In the formula bar, notice that the value in the cell (2.99) remains the same, although the cell format displays 3.0.

6. Select column E. Click the Increase Decimal button to display two digits following the decimal to the values in column E.

7. Save the file. Keep the workbook open for Exercise 11.2.

Using the Format Cells Dialog Box

The Format Cells dialog box has more numeric formats that don't appear on the Formatting toolbar. These formatting options include other number formats, alignment options, and border colors.

In Exercise 11.2, you'll use the Format Cells dialog box to apply formatting.

EXERCISE 11.2

Applying Formatting with the Format Cells Dialog Box

1. In the 11-1.xls workbook saved in the previous exercise, select column A. Then either choose Format ➢ Cells from the menu bar, press Ctrl+1, or right-click in the selection and choose Format Cells from the shortcut menu to open the Format Cells dialog box. Click the Number tab, shown here:

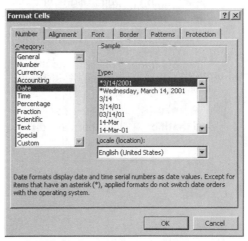

2. In the Category list, choose Date.

3. In the Type list, choose the Short Date format with the two-digit year (3/14/01):

4. Click OK to apply the format and close the Format Cells dialog box.

5. Save the workbook. This workbook is used again in Exercise 11.3.

The Format Cells dialog box has separate tabs for Number, Alignment, Font, Border, Patterns, and Protection. The Number tab contains a list of format categories (see Table 11.2) and controls for the number of decimal places, thousands separator, and treatment of negative numbers.

TABLE 11.2 Numeric Formatting in the Format Cells Dialog Box

Category	Description
General	The default format.
Number	Like General, but with set decimal places, a thousands separator, and formatting for negative numbers.
Currency	Numbers can be preceded with a dollar sign immediately before the first digit. Zero values are displayed.
Accounting	Dollar signs and decimal points line up. Dollars signs are lined up one space from the left edge of the cell. Zero values are shown as dashes.
Percentage	The same as the Percent toolbar button. Numbers are displayed as if multiplied by 100 and followed by a percent sign.
Scientific	Numbers are displayed in scientific notation, for example, 1.01E+03.

If you point to the button on the Formatting toolbar with the dollar symbol, the ScreenTip indicates that it is the Currency Style button. However, when you apply this button's format, Excel applies the Accounting format, with dashes for zeros and the dollar signs lined up. Microsoft has decided not to fix this discrepancy, which was introduced in a much earlier version of Excel, because it could confuse existing users.

The Format Cells dialog box includes six more specialized formatting categories:

Date formats　Used for displaying dates and dates/times in a variety of formats.

Time formats　Includes options for mixed date and time displays, 24-hour clock times, and stopwatch results.

Fraction formats　Choose from formats based on either the number of digits to display in the divisor (1, 2, or 3) or the fractional unit (halves, quarters, tenths, and so on).

Special formats　Includes formats for different types of numbers that aren't mathematical values: Zip Code, Zip Code + 4, Phone Number, and Social Security Number.

Text formats　Changes a number to text without adding other formatting. This is useful for numeric labels that may include leading zeros, such as employee ID numbers. All the regular numeric formats strip off leading zeros. You must apply the Text format *before* entering the cell's contents: Numbers entered and later formatted as Text will always be treated as numbers.

Custom formats　Select from or make an addition to a list of formats for numbers, dates, and times. Custom formats are discussed in Chapter 17, "Automating and Customizing Excel."

Formatting Text

Even if you're new to Excel, you already have most of the skills you need to format text from your previous experience in other applications. Select the cells you want to format and then choose a formatting option from the Formatting toolbar. Fonts, font weights (bold, italic, underline), font size, and font colors work the same way in Excel as they do in Word and PowerPoint. In this section, we'll focus on text formatting unique to Excel.

Aligning Text

By default, Excel left-aligns text and right-aligns numbers. The default settings reflect common-sense rules about worksheet construction:

- Columns of text should be left-aligned because we're used to reading left-aligned text.

- Columns of numbers should be kept in the default (right) alignment and formatted so that the decimal points align and numbers can be easily visually compared—unless the numbers are actually text such as item numbers, seat assignments, or social security numbers.

- Column labels should appear over the contents of the column. If the column is filled with numbers, manually adjust the heading so it is right-aligned or centered. Labels for text columns should be left-aligned or centered.

 Use the alignment buttons on the Formatting toolbar to override the defaults and align text and numbers at the left, center, or right within cells. Excel's fourth alignment, called Merge and Center, *merges* selected adjacent cells into one cell and centers the contents of the top-left selected cell across the newly merged cell. Worksheet titles are often merged and centered. To merge and center a title, select the cell containing the title and the cells in the same row for all the used columns in the worksheet, and then click the Merge And Center button. Excel centers only the text in the top-left cell of the selection, so if your worksheet's title is in more than one row, you'll need to merge and center each title row separately.

In Exercise 11.3, you will format and align column labels and merge and center the worksheet labels.

EXERCISE 11.3

Applying Alignments, Font Size, and Bold

1. Open the 11-1.xls workbook saved in the previous exercise.

2. Select the titles by selecting rows 1, 2, and 4.

   Hold the Ctrl key to select noncontiguous ranges, rows, or columns.

EXERCISE 11.3 *(continued)*

3. Click the Bold button on the Formatting toolbar to turn off the Bold font style. Click the button again to bold the selected cells.

4. Select the labels in A4, D4, and E4. Hold Ctrl to select noncontiguous cells.

5. Click the Align Right button on the Formatting toolbar.

6. Select cells A1:G1.

7. Click the Merge And Center button on the Formatting toolbar to center the title over the worksheet.

8. Select cells A2:G2. Merge and center the second row of the title.

9. Select row 1. Change the Font Size to 16 using the Font Size drop-down list on the Formatting toolbar.

10. Save the workbook. It will be used in the next exercise.

There are more alignment options that don't appear on the Formatting toolbar. To see all the alignment options, select the cells you want to format and open the Format Cells dialog box. The Alignment page of the Format Cells dialog box is shown in Figure 11.1.

FIGURE 11.1   The Alignment tab of the Format Cells dialog box

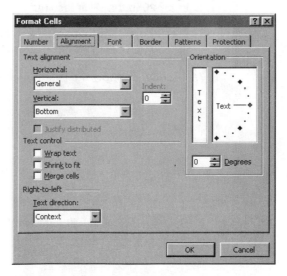

Rotating, Merging, Shrinking to Fit, and Wrapping Text

Formatting that you apply to a cell or range can also be applied to a row or column. For example, you can use the rotation tools to orient rows or columns vertically or to rotate text to a specific orientation. Consider rotating column labels when you have wordy column headings for columns with relatively small values.

Microsoft ✓ ***Exam Objective***   **Modify row and column formats**

In Exercise 11.4, you will rotate label text.

EXERCISE 11.4

Rotating Text

1. If necessary, open the file 11-1.xls saved in the previous exercise.

2. Select the column labels in row 4.

3. Right-click the selection and choose Format Cells from the shortcut menu to open the Format Cells dialog box.

4. Click the Alignment tab.

5. Enter **90** in the Degrees spin box:

6. In the Text Alignment section, choose Center from the Horizontal drop-down list to center the labels in their cells.

7. Click OK to apply the rotation and alignment changes.

8. Click Undo to undo the changes you applied in this exercise.

9. Save the file. You will use it in the next exercise.

To orient text vertically, click the pane with the vertical word *Text* on the Alignment tab.

There are other alignment options in the Format Cells dialog box. Wrap Text wraps the contents of a cell if it would exceed the cell's boundaries. Shrink To Fit reduces the display size of the type within selected cells so the contents fit. Both Shrink To Fit and Wrap Text use the current column width to determine how much to shrink and where to wrap the selection. (See Exercise 11.6: Adjusting Column Width and Row Height and Wrapping Text, later in this chapter.)

Use the Merge Cells check box on the Alignment tab to merge cells without centering the contents.

Applying Borders and Color

Borders and colors, when used effectively, make worksheets easier to understand. A *border* is a line drawn around a cell or group of cells. *Fill color* is used to highlight the background of part of a worksheet; *font color* is applied to text. Bordering or filling totals or other summary cells provides visual cues that users appreciate.

The Borders, Fill Color, and Font Color buttons are on the Formatting toolbar. All three buttons are combination buttons that include menus opened by clicking the down arrows attached to the buttons. Select an item from the menu to apply it to the selected cells and make it the default for the button.

In Exercise 11.5, you'll apply borders and color to selected cells.

EXERCISE 11.5

Applying Borders and Color

1. If the 11-1.xls workbook is not open from Exercise 11.4, open it now.

2. Select cells A4:G4.

EXERCISE 11.5 *(continued)*

3. Click the drop-down arrow on the Fill Color button.

4. Choose a light yellow fill.

5. With the same cells selected, click the drop-down arrow on the Borders button.

6. Click the Bottom Border button to apply a border below the selected cells.

7. Select rows 1 and 2.

8. Click the drop-down arrow on the Font Color button.

9. Choose Blue from the palette.

10. Save the workbook and keep it open for the next exercise.

Adjusting Worksheet Layout

As your workbook grows, you'll want to modify its layout so that it's easier to use both onscreen and as a publication on paper or the Web. Excel's column and row structure makes it easy to change the appearance of a worksheet in a few simple steps.

Microsoft
✓ *Exam*
Objective

Modify row and column settings

Adjusting Column Width and Row Height

By default, Excel columns are slightly more than eight characters wide. If the data in a worksheet is wider or much narrower than the column, you'll want to adjust the *column width* so it is wide enough to contain the data but not so wide that data seems lost. Some users simply leave blank columns rather than adjusting column widths, for example, skipping column B because the entries in column A are too wide for column A. Don't leave blank columns in Excel. Blank columns and rows identify the limits of a database, so data on the "other side" of the blank column will not be sorted, mixing up the data.

You can adjust the column width either manually, by dragging the right edge of the button, or by double-clicking the column heading button to AutoFit the column width to the existing data. You can also select several columns and either adjust them manually to a uniform width or AutoFit each one to its contents.

In Exercise 11.6, you'll adjust the column width and row height, as well as wrap text to fit the column width.

EXERCISE 11.6

Adjusting Column Width and Row Height and Wrapping Text

1. If 11-1.xls used in Exercise 11.5 is not open, open it.

2. Move the mouse pointer to the right edge of the column E header.

3. When the pointer shape changes to the double-headed column adjustment pointer, double-click to size the column to its contents. Repeat to adjust the width of column C.

4. Select column A.

5. Choose Format ➢ Column ➢ Width from the menu to open the Column Width dialog box.

6. Enter **15** in the Column Width text box, and click OK.

7. Select column A if it is not already selected.

8. Point to the right edge of the column A header.

9. Drag the column header to make the column wide enough for the column data in rows 4–26. It does not need to be wide enough to accommodate the title.

10. Point to the lower edge of the row header for row 5. Drag the header down to make the row taller, providing space between the labels in row 4 and detail entries.

11. Adjust the width of column E so that it is slightly narrower than the text in cell E4 (with the text Unit Cost). The Unit Cost title will appear cut off.

12. Select cell E4.

EXERCISE 11.6 *(continued)*

13. Right-click E4 and choose Format Cells, or choose Format ≻ Cells from the menu to open the Format Cells dialog box.

14. On the Alignment tab, enable the Wrap Text check box. Click OK to apply the format.

15. Save and close the workbook.

If you narrow or widen a column after you shrink or wrap a label, you'll need to reshrink or rewrap the formatted cells.

Applying AutoFormats and Styles

Excel includes a number of canned worksheet designs, including formal business designs, designs for reports and lists, and 3-D formats. These AutoFormats offer a quick way to apply a standard format to all or part of a worksheet. Before you AutoFormat, you must select the cells to be formatted. These will usually include all the text and numbers in the worksheet, but you may wish to apply an AutoFormat to titles or data only.

Microsoft *Exam* *Objective*	**Apply styles**
	Use automated tools to format worksheets

In Exercise 11.7, you will use AutoFormat in a worksheet.

EXERCISE 11.7

Applying an AutoFormat

1. Open the file 11-7.xls.

2. Select the range A1:F2.

EXERCISE 11.7 *(continued)*

3. Choose Format ➢ AutoFormat from the menu to open the Auto-Format dialog box.

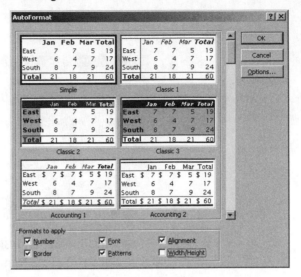

4. Click the Options button to expand the dialog box to display all the formatting elements you can apply.

5. In the Formats To Apply section, turn off the Width/Height and Alignment check boxes so that Excel won't adjust column A to fit the selection in cell A1 and to prevent alignment changes in the title cells.

6. Select the Classic 3 format. Click OK to apply the format.

7. Select the range A4:F10.

8. Open the AutoFormat dialog box.

9. Click the Options button. Turn off the Alignment option. Leave Width/Height enabled so that column A will be adjusted to fit the contents in the selected range.

10. Choose the Classic 3 format. Click OK to apply.

11. Resave the workbook. Keep it open for the next exercise.

AutoFormats are composed of styles—specifications about one or more formatting options. In Exercise 11.8, you will create and apply styles.

EXERCISE 11.8

Creating and Applying Styles

1. In the 11-7.xls workbook you saved in Exercise 11.7, select cell A4 (with the text "Location").

2. Choose Format ➢ Style from the menu to open the Style dialog box.

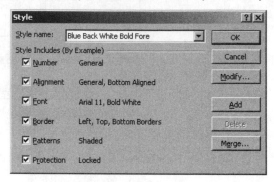

3. Enter a Style Name for the style: **Blue Back White Bold Fore**. If you wanted to exclude any of the formatting elements, you would deselect their check boxes at this point.

4. Click Add to add the style. Click OK to close the Style dialog box.

5. To apply the style, select the range you wish to format: A10:F10.

6. Choose Format ➢ Style to open the Style dialog box.

7. Select the style Blue Back White Bold Fore from the Style Name drop-down list.

8. Click OK to apply the style to the selected cells.

9. Save and close the workbook.

Previewing and Printing

Print Preview, Page Setup, Page Break Preview, and Print are all inter-related. Print Preview, Print, and Page Setup function much as they do in the other Office XP applications. Page Break Preview, a view available only in Excel, displays the current page breaks and allows you to adjust them.

Changing Page Setup

To change page setup, choose File ➤ Page Setup from the menu bar to open the Page Setup dialog box. (If you're already in Print Preview, click the Setup button; from Page Break Preview, right-click and choose Page Setup from the shortcut menu.) The Page Setup features are divided into four tabbed pages: Page, Header/Footer, Margins, and Sheet.

Microsoft ✓ *Exam* *Objective*   **Modify Page Setup options for worksheets**

Setting Page Options

Use the Page options of the Page Setup dialog box to set page orientation, scaling, paper size, and print quality.

Orientation   This is the direction of print in relation to the paper it is printed on. Portrait, the default setting, places the short edge of the paper at the top and bottom. If your worksheet is wider than it is long, consider using Landscape orientation.

Scaling   This option is used to reduce or enlarge the print. If you simply need to make the print larger, use the Adjust To control and choose a size greater than 100 percent. The Fit To control instructs Excel to reduce a worksheet so it will print on a specific number of pages.

Paper Size   This option lets you choose a paper size other than the $8\frac{1}{2} \times 11$ inch default (for example, legal-size paper).

Print Quality   This is measured in dots per inch (dpi). Higher dpi means clearer print quality but slower printing.

First Page Number   This option is used to start printing from a page number other than 1.

The Options button appears on every page of the Page Setup dialog box. The button opens the Windows Properties sheet (or the manufacturer's Properties sheet) for the printer that's currently selected.

In Exercise 11.9, you'll change page settings and see their effect in Print Preview.

Changing the Page Settings

1. Open the 11-1.xls workbook you saved in Exercise 11.6.

2. Choose File ➢ Print Preview or click the Print Preview button on the Standard toolbar to see how the workbook will print with the current settings.

3. Click the Close button to close Print Preview.

4. Open the Page Setup dialog box by choosing File ➢ Page Setup.

5. Change the Orientation setting to Landscape.

6. In the Scaling section, choose Adjust To and enter **150** to enlarge the print job by 50 percent.

7. Click OK to apply the Page Setup options.

8. Click the Print Preview button to return to Print Preview. View your changes.

9. Click the Setup button at the top of the Preview window to open the Page Setup dialog box.

10. Choose Portrait orientation to return to the original Orientation setting.

11. Click OK to apply the changes.

12. Close the Print Preview window.

13. Save the changes and keep the workbook open. You'll use it in the next three exercises.

Setting Margins in the Page Setup Dialog Box

The preview in the Margins tab of the Page Setup dialog box (see Figure 11.2) displays the margins as dotted lines. You can change the margins here using the spin arrows for each margin.

FIGURE 11.2   Set margins, including space for headers and footers, on the Margins tab of the Page Setup dialog box.

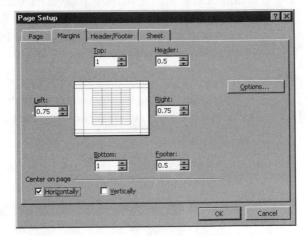

Use the Center On Page controls to center the printed worksheet horizontally between the left and right margins or vertically between the top and bottom margins. As you change settings on the Margins page, the Preview will change to reflect the new margin settings.

In Exercise 11.10, you'll change margins in the Page Setup dialog box.

EXERCISE 11.10

Changing Margins

1. In the 11-1.xls workbook, choose File ➤ Page Setup to open the Page Setup dialog box.

2. In the Page Setup dialog box, select the Margins tab.

3. Using the spin box controls, set the left margin to 1.5 inches.

4. Set the right margin to 1 inch.

5. Set the footer margin to 1 inch.

6. Set the bottom margin to 1.5 inches.

7. Enable the Center On Page Horizontally check box.

8. Click the OK button to apply the changes.

9. Click the Print Preview button to preview the margin changes. Close the Print Preview window.

Setting Headers and Footers

A header is printed at the top of each page of a document. Footers are printed at the bottom of each page. In Excel 2002, there are no default headers and footers. If you want a header or footer, you must choose or create it from the Header/Footer tab in the Page Setup dialog box, shown in Figure 11.3.

You can access the Header/Footer tab of the Page Setup dialog box directly by choosing View ➤ Headers/Footers from the menu.

FIGURE 11.3 Create page headers and footers on the Header/Footer tab of the Page Setup dialog box.

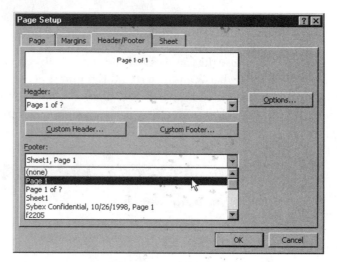

In Exercise 11.11, you'll set headers and footers on the Header/Footer tab of the Page Setup dialog box.

EXERCISE 11.11

Setting Headers and Footers

1. In the 11-1.xls workbook, choose File ➤ Page Setup to open the Page Setup dialog box.

2. Click the Header/Footer tab. The current header and footer settings are displayed in the two preview panes. Both header and footer are blank.

3. To choose a different predesigned header, click the Header drop-down list. Choose the Header that includes the author's name (Gini Courter) followed by the page number and today's date.

4. Click the Custom Header button to open the Header dialog box.

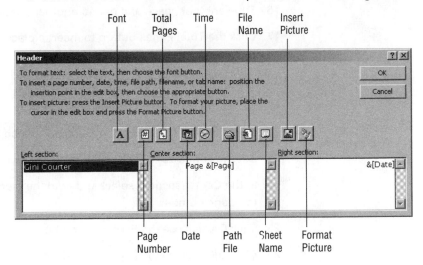

Font   Total   Time   File   Insert
Pages   Name   Picture

Page   Date   Path   Sheet   Format
Number   File   Name   Picture

5. Select the contents of the Center Section: Page &[Page]. Press Del to delete the page number in the center section.

6. In the left section, type your name. Select your name and click the Font button to open the Font dialog box.

7. Italicize your name. Change the Font Size to 8.

8. Click OK to close the Font dialog box.

9. In the Right Section, click at the right end of the &[Date] place-holder. Press Enter to move to the second line.

10. Click the Time button to insert a placeholder for the time.

11. Click OK to close the Header dialog box and return to the Header/Footer tab of the Page Setup dialog box.

12. Click the Custom Footer button to open the Footer dialog box, which is much like the Header dialog box.

EXERCISE 11.11 *(continued)*

13. Click the Center Section.

14. Type the word **Page** and a space.

15. Click the Page Number button to insert a placeholder for the page.

16. Type another space and **of** and another space.

17. Click the Total Pages button to insert a placeholder for the total number of pages.

18. Type a space and the word **Pages**.

19. Select the contents of the Center Section.

20. Click the Font button to open the Font dialog box.

21. Set the Font Size to 8. Click OK to close the Font dialog box.

22. In the Center section, select and bold the placeholder &[Page] for the page number.

23. Click OK to close the Footer dialog box.

24. Click OK to close the Page Setup dialog box.

25. Choose File ➢ Print Preview to preview the page, including the header and footer.

26. Close the Preview window.

27. Save the file. You will use it in the next exercise.

Changing Sheet Settings

The Sheet settings shown in Figure 11.4 control the worksheet features that will appear in the printed copy, including the print area, repeating rows and columns, and gridlines.

FIGURE 11.4 Use the settings on the Sheet tab to repeat rows or columns on each printed page.

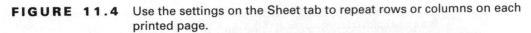

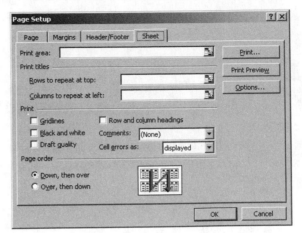

Figure 11.4 shows the Sheet tab when the Page Setup dialog box is opened from the File menu. All the controls on the tab are enabled. The Print Area, Rows To Repeat At Top section, and Columns To Repeat At Left section controls are enabled only when you open the Page Setup dialog box from the menu (File ➢ Page Setup or View ➢ Header And Footer). If you go to Page Setup from Print Preview, you won't be able to change the first three settings on this page.

Print Area   By default, Excel prints from the home cell A1 to the last occupied cell in the active worksheet. To specify a different range, click the Collapse button in the Print Area text box to collapse the Page Setup dialog box, select the area you want to print, and then click the Expand button to expand the Page Setup dialog box. If the Print Area includes noncontiguous ranges, each range of contiguous cells will print on its own page.

Print Titles   This option repeats columns or rows on each page of the printout. Specify these rows or columns in the Rows To Repeat At Top and Columns To Repeat At Left text boxes. Excel requires a range for these entries (such as A:A to print column A on each page) even if you're selecting only a single row or column.

Gridlines This check box indicates whether gridlines will be printed but does not affect their display in the worksheet. Turning off the print gridlines gives your worksheet a cleaner appearance and may make it easier to read.

To turn off screen gridlines, choose Tools ➤ Options and clear the check mark in the Gridlines option on the View tab of the Options dialog box.

Black And White If you used colors in the worksheet but won't be printing on a color printer, click this control to speed up the print process.

Draft Quality This control prints the worksheet without gridlines or graphics.

Row And Column Headings This control prints the row numbers and column letters. This is a useful feature when you are editing or trying to locate an error in a worksheet.

Comments If the print area contains comments, you can choose to print them as they appear or on a separate page at the end of the print job. By default, comments are not displayed, so if you wish to print them as they appear, you'll also need to show them. Right-click the cell that contains the comment and choose Show Comment from the shortcut menu.

Cell Errors As This drop-down list is used to hide error values (for example #NAME and ####) in the printed version of the worksheet. See Chapters 16, "Checking for Errors," and 19, "Summarizing Data."

Page Order This control group establishes the order in which multipage worksheets are printed.

In Exercise 11.12, you'll change sheet settings in the Page Setup dialog box.

EXERCISE 11.12

Changing Sheet Settings

   1. If necessary, open the 11-1.xls workbook you saved in Exercise 11.11.

2. Choose File ➤ Page Setup to open the Page Setup dialog box. Click the Sheet tab.

3. Click the Print Area text box.

4. Select A2:G26—the entire worksheet with the exception of the company name in row 1.

5. Click the Rows To Repeat At Top text box.

6. In the worksheet, click the header for row 4 to repeat row 4 at the top of each printed page. The selection is entered as an absolute range: $4:$4.

7. In the Columns To Repeat At Left control, type **A:A** to repeat column A at the left edge of each printed page.

8. In the Page Setup dialog box, switch to the Page tab. Verify that the Adjust To setting is 150% Normal Size.

9. Click the Print Preview button to preview the printed page with the current settings. Note that column A appears on the left side of each printed page.

10. Click the Setup button at the top of the Preview window. On the Sheet tab, notice that the Print Area, Rows To Print At Top, and Columns to Print At Left text boxes are not enabled because you accessed the Page Setup dialog box from the Preview window.

11. In the Print section, enable the Row And Column Headings and Gridlines check boxes.

12. Click the Print Preview button. Preview the changes from these two settings.

13. Close the Preview window.

14. Choose File ➤ Page Setup to open the Page Setup dialog box.

15. On the Sheet tab, turn off the two check boxes in the Print section. Click OK to close the Page Setup dialog box.

16. Save the workbook. You'll use it in the next section.

Setting Print Options

Excel offers flexible page breaks so you can print unwieldy spreadsheets on standard-size paper. The Page Break Preview feature is a good tool for managing the printable areas of a spreadsheet, while the Print dialog box delivers complete control over which pages to print.

Microsoft ✓ *Exam* *Objective*	**Preview and print worksheets and workbooks**

Using Page Break Preview

Page Break Preview is a worksheet view that displays the print area with page breaks and the page order. In Exercise 11.13, you'll use Page Break Preview to adjust the area of your worksheet that will print.

EXERCISE 11.13

Using Page Break Preview

1. If necessary, open the 11-1.xls workbook that you resaved in Exercise 11.12.

2. To turn on Page Break Preview, click the Print Preview button and then click the Page Break Preview button in Print Preview, or choose View ➢ Page Break Preview from the menu bar. If the Welcome To Page Break Preview dialog box opens, click OK to close it.

In Page Break Preview, areas that will be printed are white; cells that won't be printed are gray.

3. Drag the dashed line separating page 1 and page 2 one column to the left to move the page break. The dashed line is replaced with a solid line.

4. Drag the top edge of the print area line to the top of the worksheet to include row 1 in the print area.

5. Click the Print Preview button to preview your changes.

EXERCISE 11.13 *(continued)*

6. Click the Close button to return to Page Break Preview.

7. Drag the line separating page 1 from page 2 so that page 1 includes the entire print area:

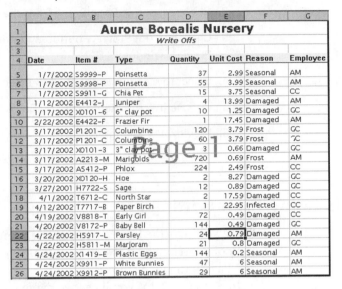

8. Choose File ➢ Page Setup to open the Page Setup dialog box. Note that the Adjust To percentage has changed.

When you extend the page break for any page (making it wider or longer than the default setting), Excel will change the scaling on all pages, reducing the print type so the page still fits on the paper specified in the Page Setup dialog box.

9. Click the Sheet tab. Set the Print Area to (once again) exclude row 1.

10. Click the OK button to close the Page Setup dialog box.

11. Choose View ➢ Normal to return to Normal view.

12. Save the workbook. You will use it in the next exercise.

Inserting Manual Page Breaks

You insert page breaks in order to print a worksheet on multiple pages when it will fit on one page. In Exercise 11.14, you'll insert a page break to print the rows for the second quarter (starting in April) on a new page.

EXERCISE 11.14

Inserting and Removing Page Breaks

1. If necessary, open the 11-1.xls workbook you saved in Exercise 11.13 and select row 18.

2. Choose Insert ➢ Page Break from the menu.

3. Click the Print Preview button and preview the change. Close the Preview window.

4. Select row 18 if it is not already selected.

5. Choose Insert ➢ Remove Page Break to remove the page break.

6. Preview the change in the Preview window.

7. Close the Print Preview window. Save the file.

Changing Print Settings

When you click the Print button on the Standard toolbar, Excel prints one copy of the selected worksheet(s) using the current settings from the Print and Page Setup dialog boxes.

In Exercise 11.15, you'll change the print settings.

EXERCISE 11.15

Changing Print Settings

1. If necessary, open the 11-1.xls workbook you saved in Exercise 11.14.

2. Select the titles and the rows of data for January through March: A1:G17.

3. To adjust print settings, choose File ➢ Print to open the Print dialog box.

4. Click the Preview button in the dialog box. In the Preview window, notice that the entire worksheet except row 1 will be printed because you excluded it in the print area you set in Exercise 11.12. Click Close to close Print Preview. Choose File ➢ Print to reopen the Print dialog box.

5. In the Print What section, choose Selection.

EXERCISE 11.15 *(continued)*

6. Click the Preview button. Notice that the print area now includes A1:G17.

Choosing Selection overwrites the Print Area setting.

7. Click Close, then choose File ➢ Print to return to the Print dialog box.

8. Change the Number Of Copies to 2.

9. Click OK to print two copies of the worksheet with the specified print settings.

10. Save and close the workbook.

Use the Print Range controls to print some, but not all, of the pages of a multiple-page print job. In Excel, you cannot specify noncontiguous pages as you can in Word, so if you want to print pages 1–4 and 6–8, you either have to print twice or choose the cells on those pages and specify them as your print area. To print all the sheets you have used in this workbook, choose Entire Workbook in the Print What section of the Print dialog box.

Summary

In this chapter, you learned how to work with cells and cell data and to manage workbooks. We covered the following topics:

- Applying and modifying cell formats
- Modifying row and column height and width settings
- Modifying row and column formats
- Applying styles
- Using automated tools to format worksheets
- Modifying Page Setup options for worksheets
- Previewing and printing worksheets and workbooks

Chapter

12

Enhancing and Revising Workbooks

MOUS EXCEL 2002 CORE EXAM OBJECTIVES COVERED IN THIS CHAPTER:

- ✓ Insert and delete worksheets
- ✓ Modify worksheet names and positions
- ✓ Use 3-D references
- ✓ Create and revise formulas
- ✓ Use statistical, date and time, financial, and logical functions in formulas

n previous chapters, you've created, formatted, and printed worksheets. In this chapter, you'll modify the structure of a workbook by inserting, deleting, and rearranging worksheets within a workbook. With the workbook's structure in place, you'll create complex formulas that span worksheets and that use more advanced functions.

> **NOTE** Before you begin this chapter, you should go to the Sybex website and download the file 4113Ch12.zip. This package contains the files necessary to complete some of the exercises in this chapter. In addition, it contains files of what most of the documents should look like after you complete the exercise. These files are affixed with the word *Post*.

Modifying Workbooks

Excel's default workbook includes three worksheets: Sheet1, Sheet2, and Sheet3. In this section, you'll radically reconfigure your workbook by adding and removing sheets, moving and copying sheets, and renaming worksheets.

Microsoft ✓ *Exam* *Objective*   **Insert and delete worksheets**

Inserting Worksheets

You can insert a worksheet from the application menu or by using the worksheet shortcut menu. You'll use both of these methods in the Exercise 12.1.

EXERCISE 12.1

Inserting Worksheets

1. Open a new blank workbook.

2. From the menu choose Insert ➤ Worksheet to insert a new worksheet.

   Excel inserts a worksheet and names it Sheet*n*, where *n* is the first unused positive integer: Sheet4 in this case.

3. Right-click any sheet tab to open the shortcut menu.

4. Choose Insert to open the Insert dialog box.

5. Select Worksheet from the General tab.

6. Click OK to insert the new worksheet, automatically named Sheet5. You'll use this workbook in the remaining exercises in this section, so leave it open.

The first method, shown in step 2 above, is obviously quicker if you're inserting a default worksheet. You would use the second method (steps 3 through 6) to insert a specialized worksheet, for example, a chart sheet or a customized template.

Deleting Worksheets

Every new Excel workbook contains the same number of worksheets (three by default). If you're creating a workbook for other users, you should delete the unused sheets before passing the workbook to others. You might also delete worksheets if the data on the sheets is no longer valid. As you'll see in Exercise 12.2, there are two ways to delete worksheets: using the menu bar or the worksheet shortcut menu.

EXERCISE 12.2

Deleting Worksheets

1. In the workbook you used in the last exercise, right-click the Sheet5 tab.

EXERCISE 12.2 *(continued)*

2. Choose Delete from the shortcut menu to delete Sheet5. If you've entered data or formatted the sheet, you'll be prompted to confirm the deletion.

3. Select Sheet4 by clicking its tab.

4. From the menu, choose Edit ➤ Delete Sheet to delete Sheet4. Leave the workbook open; you'll use it in the next exercise.

Modifying Worksheet Names and Positions

Worksheets are like documents within a workbook. In Excel 2002, you can rename the worksheets, giving them useful names that describe their contents, and reorder the worksheets so they are in a logical sequence.

Microsoft ✔ *Exam Objective*   **Modify worksheet names and positions**

Renaming Worksheets

The default worksheet names—Sheet1, Sheet2, and so on—describe the original order of the sheets. You should rename the sheets with text, including spaces, that describes their contents to make it easier to navigate in the workbook. You have up to 32 characters to name a worksheet, and the name can include spaces, underscores, and hyphens. In Excel 2002, you can also set the color of sheet tabs. Choose the same color for two or three worksheets to visually group the sheets within the workbook. In Exercise 12.3, you'll rename, select, and set tab color for worksheets.

EXERCISE 12.3

Renaming, Selecting, and Coloring Worksheet Tabs

1. In the workbook you used in Exercise 12.2, right-click the Sheet1 tab.

2. Choose Rename from the shortcut menu to edit the sheet tab.

EXERCISE 12.3 *(continued)*

3. Type a new name for Sheet1: Communications Budget. Press Enter.

4. Double-click the Sheet2 tab to edit the sheet tab.

5. Type a new name for Sheet2: Info Tech Budget. Press Enter.

6. Right-click the navigation buttons at the left end of the sheet tabs to open the shortcut menu.

7. Select the Communications Budget sheet from the menu to move to that worksheet.

8. Right-click the Info Tech Budget tab. Choose Tab Color from the shortcut menu to open the Format Tab Color dialog box. Choose a color from the palette and click OK.

9. Right-click the Communications Budget tab. Apply a different color to the sheet tab. Leave the workbook open for the next exercise.

Moving and Copying Worksheets

You can move and copy worksheets within a workbook using drag and drop or the Move And Copy dialog box and between workbooks using the Move And Copy dialog box. In Exercise 12.4, you'll see how to move worksheets within a book to rearrange the sheets in a sensible order. Then you'll practice copying worksheets within a workbook to create a new worksheet based on an existing worksheet and copying sheets between workbooks when you need to send one sheet from a workbook to another user who doesn't need the other sheets in the book.

EXERCISE 12.4

Moving and Copying Worksheets within a Workbook

For this exercise, use the blank workbook you used in Exercise 12.3.

1. In the workbook you used in Exercise 12.3, select the Communications Budget sheet tab if necessary.

EXERCISE 12.4 *(continued)*

2. Drag the sheet tab to the right of the Info Tech Budget tab. A triangle indicator appears to the right of the Info Tech Budget tab:

3. Release the mouse button to move the Communications Budget sheet after the Info Tech Budget sheet.

4. Right-click the Info Tech Budget sheet tab and choose Move Or Copy from the shortcut menu, or select the Info Tech Budget tab and choose Edit ➤ Move Or Copy Sheet from the menu to open the Move Or Copy dialog box:

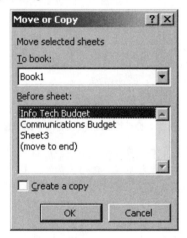

5. In the Before Sheet list, choose Sheet3.

6. Click OK to move the Info Tech Budget sheet before Sheet3.

7. Select Sheet3. Drag Sheet3 before the Communications Budget sheet. Do not release the mouse button.

8. Hold Ctrl on the keyboard while releasing the mouse button to create a copy of Sheet3 before the Communications Budget sheet.

Within a workbook, each sheet name must be unique, so Excel names the copy Sheet3 (2).

9. Double-click the Sheet3 (2) sheet tab and rename the sheet **Sheet4**.

10. Right-click the Sheet4 tab and choose Move Or Copy from the shortcut menu to open the Move Or Copy dialog box.

11. In the Before Sheet list, choose (Move To End).

12. Enable the Create A Copy check box.

13. Click OK to create a copy of Sheet 4 at the end of the workbook.

14. Save the workbook as **Worksheet Practice**. Leave the workbook open for the next exercise.

You can use the same Move Or Copy dialog box to move and copy worksheets from one workbook to another open workbook or to a new workbook. In Exercise 12.5, you'll move and copy sheets between workbooks.

EXERCISE 12.5

Moving and Copying Worksheets between Workbooks

1. If necessary, open the workbook Worksheet Practice, which you saved in Exercise 12.4.

2. Open the file 12-5.xls.

3. In the 12-5 workbook, rename Sheet1 as **2002 Writeoffs**.

4. Right-click the 2002 Writeoffs sheet.

5. Choose Move Or Copy from the shortcut menu to open the Move Or Copy dialog box.

6. In the To Book list, choose Worksheet Practice.

7. In the Before Sheet list, choose Communications Budget.

8. Enable the Create A Copy check box.

9. Click OK to copy the 2002 Writeoffs sheet to the Workbook Practice workbook.

10. Save and close the 12-5 workbook.

11. In the Worksheet Practice workbook, select the 2002 Writeoffs sheet.

EXERCISE 12.5 (continued)

12. Right-click the sheet tab and choose Move Or Copy from the short-cut menu.

13. In the To Book list, choose (New Book).

14. Click OK to move the 2002 Writeoffs sheet to a new workbook. Excel automatically switches you to the new workbook, which contains only one sheet: 2002 Writeoffs.

15. Close the new workbook. Do not save the changes.

16. Save and close the Worksheet Practice workbook. Close the new workbook without saving the changes.

Creating Complex Formulas

Excel formulas can be simple formulas that add one cell to another or complex formulas that use cell contents from several worksheets and statistical, financial, or other functions. You worked with simple formulas in Chapter 10, "Creating Worksheets and Workbooks." In this section, you'll create more advanced formulas using complex cell references and functions.

Using 3-D References

In Excel formulas, you can refer to ranges of cells that occur in the same cell or group of cells on two or more worksheets with a single reference. If you're unfamiliar with 3-D references, an analogy may help. Imagine a five-story office building with the same floor plan on each floor. The building is like a workbook, each floor is a worksheet, and each office is a cell. If you're referring to the office in the northwest corner of the fifth floor of the building, that's similar to a cell reference: 5NW. If, on the other hand, you want to refer to the northwest office on every floor, that's a 3-D reference: 1-5NW. The office is the same, but the floor numbers span several floors.

Here's the Excel example: Figure 12.1 shows four worksheets from the same workbook, 2003 Service Team Budget. The three team worksheets and the summary worksheet have exactly the same layout. The Budget_Summary worksheet summarizes the figures from the three team worksheets.

Because all three worksheets have exactly the same layout, you can total all worksheets at one time with formulas that use 3-D cell references. For example, the formula in cell B16 in the Budget_Summary worksheet refers to cell B16 in the other three worksheets: =SUM(Communications:Info_Tech!B16).

Microsoft
✓ *Exam*
Objective

Use 3-D References

FIGURE 12.1 Three team budget worksheets are combined in a summary budget worksheet using formulas with 3-D cell references.

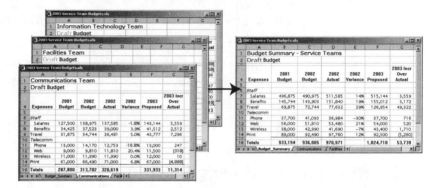

In Exercise 12.6, you'll create 3-D cell references using the workbook shown in Figure 12.1.

EXERCISE 12.6

Creating Formulas with 3-D References

1. Open the file 12-6.xls.

2. On the Budget_Summary worksheet, select cell B7: the 2001 Budget for Salaries.

3. Click the AutoSum button to create a SUM formula.

4. Click the Communications sheet tab.

5. Select cell B7.

6. Hold Shift and click the Info_Tech sheet tab to select the Communications, Facilities, and Info_Tech worksheets. The formula in the formula bar will read =SUM('Communications:Info_Tech'!B7) All four sheet tabs will be selected: the Budget_Summary worksheet with the formula, and the three sheets referenced in the formula.

7. Press Enter to enter the formula.

If you want more practice, you can follow steps 2–7 to create the other formulas in column B. Formulas with 3-D references can be filled and copied like other formulas.

8. Use the fill handle to fill the formula in B7 to the other cells in the Budget_Summary worksheet.

9. The numbers in the Budget_Summary sheet are wider than those in the other sheets, so you may need to adjust column widths in the Budget_Summary sheet.

10. Save and close the 12-6 workbook.

Creating and Modifying Formulas

Many worksheets contain similar formulas. You already know how to save time by filling formulas across columns and down rows. In this section, you'll learn how to create and revise formulas.

Microsoft ✓ *Exam Objective*   **Create and revise formulas**

Figure 12.2 shows a customer service report that summarizes performance-resolving issues raised by customers. Column B contains the number of customer issues reported each month in 2001. Columns C, E, and G contain the number of issues resolved within three different time frames.

FIGURE 12.2 The Customer Issues worksheet

	A	B	C	D	E	F	G	H
1	Customer Issues							
2					Resolution			
3		# of Issues	Same Day	Same Day %	Next Day	Next Day %	Three Plus Days	Three Plus %
4	January	31	19		6		6	
5	February	14	9		2		3	
6	March	27	21		6		0	
7	April	26	20		4		2	
8	May	19	19		0		0	
9	June	33	20		6		7	
10	July	11	10		0		1	
11	August	18	15		2		1	
12	September	27	21		5		1	
13	October	32	22		6		4	
14	November	30	21		9		0	
15	December	20	19		0		1	
16								
17	Total	288	216		46		26	
18	Average							
19	Minimum							
20	Maximum							
21	Variance							
22	Stan Dev							

The number of customer issues per month varies. Expressing performance as a percentage makes it easier to compare performance between months. In Exercise 12.7, you'll create and modify percentage formulas in columns D, F, and H of the worksheet.

EXERCISE 12.7

Entering and Revising Formulas

For this exercise, create the worksheet shown in Figure 12.2 or download the 12-7.xls workbook from the Sybex website. You'll use this workbook in this exercise and Exercises 12.8 and 12.9.

1. Open the file 12-7.xls, and select cell D4: the Same Day % for January.

2. Type an equal sign: =

3. Click cell C4.

4. Type a division symbol: /

5. Click cell B4. The formula in the formula bar should read =C4/B4.

6. Press Enter to finish the formula.

If you format cell D4 before filling the results, the fill operation will copy both the formula and the formatting.

7. Select cell D4. Click the Percent Style button on the formatting toolbar.

8. Fill cell D4 to cells D5:D15.

9. Select cell D4. Click the Copy button on the Standard toolbar to copy the cell's formula and formatting.

10. Select cell F4.

11. Press Enter to paste the formula and format from cell D4.

In the formula bar, the formula in cell F4 is =E4/D4. The reference to E4 is correct, but you need to divide the contents of E4 by the total number of issues in B4. Therefore, you need to edit the formula slightly.

12. Double-click cell F4 to open the cell for editing. Excel places a *range finder*—a border with handles and a unique color—around each range of cells referenced in the formula. You can drag the range finder handles to include more or fewer cells in the reference or drag the range finder border to move the reference:

13. Point to the range finder around cell D4. The pointer will change to a four-headed arrow. Drag the range finder to cell B4 to change the formula to =E4/B4.

14. Press Enter.

15. With cell F4 selected, double-click the fill handle to fill the formula to the other cells in column F.

EXERCISE 12.7 *(continued)*

16. Repeat steps 9 through 15 to copy, modify, and fill the formulas for column H.

	A	B	C	D	E	F	G	H
1	Customer Issues							
2						Resolution		
3		# of Issues	Same Day	Same Day %	Next Day	Next Day %	Three Plus Days	Three Plus %
4	January	31	19	61%	6	19%	6	19%
5	February	14	9	64%	2	14%	3	21%
6	March	27	21	78%	6	22%	0	0%
7	April	26	20	77%	4	15%	2	8%
8	May	19	19	100%	0	0%	0	0%
9	June	33	20	61%	6	18%	7	21%
10	July	11	10	91%	0	0%	1	9%
11	August	18	15	83%	2	11%	1	6%
12	September	27	21	78%	5	19%	1	4%
13	October	32	22	69%	6	19%	4	13%
14	November	30	21	70%	9	30%	0	0%
15	December	20	19	95%	0	0%	1	5%
16								
17	Total	288	216		46		26	
18	Average							
19	Minimum							
20	Maximum							
21	Variance							
22	Stan Dev							

17. Save the file as Customer Issues.xls. You'll use this workbook in Exercises 12.8 and 12.9.

Constructing Formulas with Functions

Functions, such as the SUM function introduced in Chapter 10, are used to calculate results used in statistics, finance, engineering, math, and other fields. *Functions* are programs that calculate a specific result: a total, an average, the interest rate for a loan, or the geometric mean of a group of numbers. Most of Excel's hundreds of functions are included in the typical installation, but others, like the engineering functions, must be installed separately. Each function has a specific order, or *syntax*, that must be used for the function to work properly.

Microsoft ✓ *Exam* *Objective*

Use statistical, date and time, financial, and logical functions in formulas

Functions are formulas, so the syntax of all functions begins with the equal sign (=). The equal sign is followed by the *function name*, followed by one or more *arguments* separated by commas and enclosed in parentheses. For example, if you're adding the cells B10 through B50, the formula is =SUM(B10:B50). SUM is the function name; the reference to the range B10:B50 is the only argument. Excel's functions are grouped into the 10 categories listed in Table 12.1.

TABLE 12.1 Excel Function Categories

Category	Examples
Financial	Calculates interest rates, loan payments, depreciation amounts, and so on.
Date & Time	Returns the current hour, day of week or year, time, or date.
Math & Trig	Calculates absolute values, cosines, logarithms, and so on.
Statistical	Includes common functions used for totals, averages, and high and low numbers in a range; advanced functions for t-tests, Chi tests, and deviations.
Lookup & Reference	Searches for and returns values from a range; creates hyperlinks to network or Internet documents.
Database	Calculates values in an Excel database table.
Text	Converts text to upper- or lowercase; trims characters from the right or left end of a text string; concatenates text strings.
Logical	Evaluates an expression and returns a value of TRUE or FALSE, which is used to trigger other actions or formatting.
Information	Returns information from Excel or Windows about the current status of a cell, object, or the environment.
Engineering	Included with Office, but must be installed separately from the Analysis Toolpack. These functions are not included in either Excel MOUS exam.

You don't have to learn all the functions—but you should know the common functions thoroughly. SUM and the other simple aggregate functions are the only functions included on the Standard toolbar. (See Exercise 10.15 for practice creating formulas using the AutoSum button.) You can access all the functions (including SUM) using the Insert Function dialog box.

When you begin entering a function, make sure the cell where you want the results to be displayed is active. There are three ways to enter a function:

- The SUM, AVERAGE, MIN, MAX, and COUNT functions are on the AutoSum button on the Standard toolbar.

- The 10 functions you used most recently are available in a drop-down list that appears in the Name box when you type an equal sign (=).

- All installed functions are available when you choose More Functions from the AutoSum button's drop-down list or the Function list in the Name box, or when you click the Insert Function button on the formula bar.

Using Statistical Functions

Excel includes many Statistical functions. Everyday functions that you may not think of as Statistical functions are also included in the list:

- **AVERAGE** sums the numbers in a range and divides the total by the number of numbers.

- **COUNT** returns the number of numbers in a range.

- **COUNTA** returns the number of entries, including text entries, in a range.

- **MAX** returns the largest value in a range.

- **MEDIAN,** another kind of average, is used to calculate the value in the middle of a range.

- **MIN** returns the smallest value in a range.

- **MODE** returns the value that occurs most frequently.

The Statistical functions are some of the most commonly used functions. Five of these functions are accessible from the AutoSum button's drop-down list. In Exercise 12.8, you'll use two different methods to enter Statistical functions in formulas.

EXERCISE 12.8

Using Simple Statistical Functions

1. Open the `Customer Issues.xls` file you saved in Exercise 12.7 if it is not already open, and select cell B18 to create a formula for the average number of customer issues.

2. Click the AutoSum button's drop-down arrow and select Average from the menu:

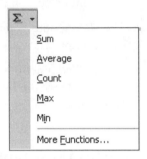

3. Select the # of Issues data in B4:B15.

4. Press Enter to enter the formula.

5. Select cell D18.

6. Type an equal sign: =

7. Select AVERAGE from the drop-down Functions list (where the Name box is normally located). The functions you've used recently are at the top of the list.

Excel opens the Function Arguments dialog box. The Number1 text box is selected:

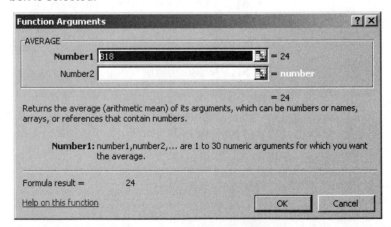

8. Select the Same Day % data in cells D4:D15. (Use the collapse button in the Number1 text box to collapse the dialog box if it is in the way.)

9. Press Enter to enter the formula.

10. Select cell D18 if it is not already selected.

11. Click the Copy button on the Standard toolbar to copy the formula to the Clipboard.

12. Select cell F18 and click Paste or right-click and choose Paste from the shortcut menu to paste the formula and formatting and leave the copy on the Clipboard.

13. Select cell H18 and press Enter to paste the formula again and clear the Clipboard.

14. Select cell C18. Repeat steps 6 through 13 to create and copy the Average formula in cells C18, E18, and G18.

15. Hold Ctrl and select cells C18, E18, and G18. Use the Decrease Decimal button on the Formatting toolbar to format the cells for one decimal place.

16. Use the drop-down list on the AutoSum button to create MIN and MAX formulas for rows 19 and 20.

17	Total	288	216		46		26	
18	Average	24	18.0	77%	3.8	14%	2.2	9%
19	Minimum	11	9	61%	0	0%	0	0%
20	Maximum	33	22	100%	9	30%	7	21%
21	Variance							
22	Stan Dev							

17. Resave the workbook.

There are other, less-frequently-used Statistical functions that are most easily accessed from the Insert Function dialog box. In Exercise 12.9, you'll create formulas using some of these functions.

EXERCISE 12.9

Using Other Statistical Functions

1. Open the Customer Issues worksheet you saved in Exercise 12.8 if it is not already open, and select cell B21, the Variance for # of Issues.

2. Click the Insert Function button in the formula bar to open the Insert Function dialog box.

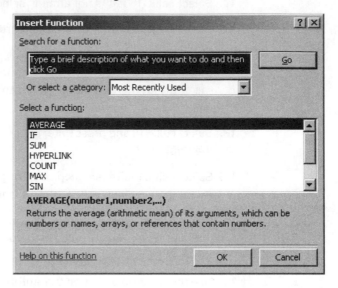

3. In the Search For A Function text box, enter **variance**. Click the Go button.

4. In the Select A Function list box, choose VARP. Note that in the MOUS exam, you'll be told which function to use.

5. Click OK to open the Function Arguments dialog box.

6. In the Number1 text box, select the range B4:B15.

7. Click OK to enter the formula.

8. Select cell B22, the Standard Deviation for # of Issues.

9. Click the drop-down arrow on the AutoSum button.

10. Choose More Functions from the list.

11. In the Or Select A Category drop-down list, choose Statistical.

12. Enter **s** to scroll to the functions that begin with the letter *S*. Scroll to and select STDEVP.

13. Click OK to open the Function Arguments dialog box.

14. In the Number1 text box, select B4:B15.

15. Click OK to enter the formula.

16. Format cells B21 and B22 for two decimal places.

17. Save and close the workbook.

Using Date and Time Functions

Excel includes time/date conversion and mathematical functions. The conversion functions convert or extract date and time data and include tools to handle dates and times stored as text. The mathematical functions are used for addition and subtraction to calculate, for example, the length of time or number of days between two time or date values.

When you enter dates, Excel generally recognizes them as dates. If, for example, you enter 1/1/2003, 1-1-2003, or January 1, 2003, Excel will recognize it as a date.

Table 12.2 lists commonly used date and time functions.

TABLE 12.2 Common Date and Time Functions

Function	Description	Syntax
DATE	Creates a serial value (which you can format using any of the date formats) from three numbers: the year, month, and day.	=DATE(year,month,day)
TIME	Creates a decimal number time in the range 0 – 0.99999999 from three numbers: the hour, minute, and second. 0 is midnight, and .99999999 is 11:59:59 P.M.	=TIME(hour,minute,second)

TABLE 12.2 Common Date and Time Functions *(continued)*

Function	Description	Syntax
NOW	Returns the serial value for the current date and a decimal fraction for the current time from your computer's system clock.	`=NOW()`
TODAY	Returns the serial value for the current date from the computer's system clock.	`=TODAY()`
DAY	Returns the day number (1–31) from a text string, date, or value.	`=DAY(date or number or string)`
MONTH	Returns the month value (1–12) from a text string, date, or value.	`=MONTH(date or number or string)`
YEAR	Returns the year value (1–9999) from a text string, date, or value.	`=YEAR(date or number or string)`
HOUR	Converts a text string or decimal fraction to an hour.	`=HOUR(string or number or fraction)`
MINUTE	Converts a text string or decimal fraction to a minute.	`=MINUTE(string or number or fraction)`

The NOW and TODAY functions have no arguments. Both consult the computer's system clock. TODAY returns the current date; NOW returns the current date and time. Functions like NOW and TODAY that return different results each time are called *volatile* functions. In Exercise 12.10, you'll use several volatile and nonvolatile date and time functions.

EXERCISE 12.10

Using the Date and Time Functions

1. Open the file 12-10.xls, and select cell B2.

2. Type the formula **=TODAY()** and press Enter to insert the current date.

3. Select cell B3 if it is not already selected.

4. Click the Insert Function button on the formula bar to open the Insert Function dialog box.

5. In the Or Select A Category list, choose Date & Time.

6. Select NOW from the Function list:

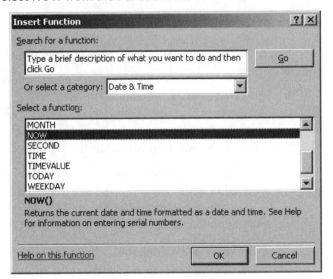

7. Click OK to select the function and open the Function Arguments dialog box.

8. The NOW function has no arguments. Click OK to enter the function.

9. In cell B4, enter your birth date using the mm/dd/yyyy format (for example, **2/28/1946** or **02/28/1946**).

10. In cell B5, use the Insert Function dialog box or type this formula, which uses the YEAR function: **=YEAR(B4)**

EXERCISE 12.10 *(continued)*

11. In cell B6, use the Insert Function dialog box or type this formula, which uses the MONTH function: `=MONTH(B4)`

12. In cell B7, enter this formula, which uses the DAY function: `=DAY(B4)`

13. In cell B8, enter this formula, which uses the DATE function: `=DATE(B5,B6,B7)`

14. Save and close the file.

Using Financial Functions

Excel has more than 50 built-in financial functions, and you don't have to be an accountant to find ways to use many of them. You'll find functions for a variety of essential operations, including the following:

- Five ways to calculate depreciation on assets or inventory

- Tools to manage the profits you invest

- Functions that help you determine the cost of borrowing against your business line of credit

The amounts of a periodic payment, present value, interest rate, and the total number of payments have a fixed relationship to one another. If you know any three of these, you can use one of the Excel financial functions to calculate the fourth:

- **NPER** calculates the number of periods.

- **PMT** calculates the payment amount.

- **PV** returns the present value for the amount loaned or invested.

- **RATE** returns the interest rate.

With these four functions, you can determine how much interest you paid on a loan or how much income you would receive from an annuity. When you work with the financial functions, you need to make sure that all the arguments in a function are based on the same period: a day, month, or year. If the interest rate is an annual rate, divide it by 12 to use it in a formula that calculates or includes a monthly payment.

In Exercise 12.11, you'll use the PMT, RATE, and NPER functions to determine the monthly payment, interest rate, and number of periods for three different loans.

EXERCISE 12.11

Using the Financial Functions

1. Open the 12-11.xls workbook and select cell B6.

2. Click the drop-down arrow on the AutoSum button. Choose More Functions to open the Insert Function dialog box.

3. In the Or Select A Category drop-down list, choose Financial.

4. In the Select A Function list, choose the payment function PMT. Click OK to open the Function Arguments dialog box. The dialog box with arguments entered is shown here:

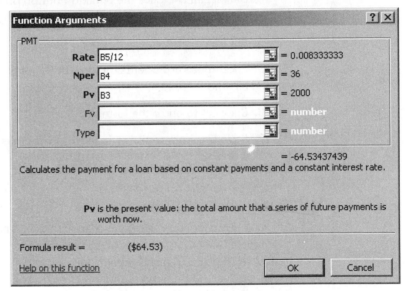

5. In the Rate text box, enter **B5/12**—the annual interest rate divided by 12 to convert it to a monthly rate.

6. Click the Nper text box, and then click cell B4 to enter the number of payment periods.

7. Click the Pv text box, and then click cell B3 to enter the present value of the loan.

8. Click OK to enter the formula.

The payment is a negative number because the principal was entered as a positive number. If the money coming in is positive, the money going out to repay the principal must be negative.

EXERCISE 12.11 *(continued)*

9. Select cell C5. Choose More Functions from the AutoSum button drop-down list to open the Insert Function dialog box.

10. In the Or Select A Category list, choose Financial.

11. In the Select A Function list, choose RATE. Click OK to open the Function Arguments dialog box.

12. Enter the following arguments for the RATE function: Nper is **C4**, Pmt is **C6**, and Pv is **C3**. Click OK to enter the function in the worksheet.

13. Select cell D4. Click the Function button on the formula bar.

14. Choose NPER in the Insert Function dialog box. Click OK to open the Function Arguments dialog box.

15. Enter these arguments for the NPER function: Rate is **D5/12**, Pmt is **D6**, and Pv is **D3**.

16. Click OK to enter the formula.

17. Save the workbook as `Financial Functions.xls`. Close the workbook.

Using Logical Functions

Logical operators, such as greater than, less than, and not equal to, allow you to compare two or more values or text strings to filter or sort in Word, Access, and Excel. Excel's Logical functions place that selection power inside a formula. Use Logical functions (sometimes called the IF functions) when you want to take different actions based on the contents of a cell, such as these:

- Applying an overtime pay formula if hours worked are more than 40

- Calculating different sales commissions for different sales volumes

- Applying different sales tax rates to orders from different states

The syntax of the IF function is =IF(`test`, `result if true`, `result if false`). In the payroll worksheet in Figure 12.3, there are two employees who worked more than 40 hours who must be paid time-and-a-half for hours in excess of 40. Without the IF function, you would need two separate formulas—one for employees who worked overtime and another for those who did not—applied on a case-by-case basis.

FIGURE 12.3 Use the IF function to apply the proper Gross Pay formula for each employee based on the number of hours worked.

	A	B	C	D
1	Williams Paint			
2	Rosemont Payroll			
3				
4	Name	Pay Rate	Hours	Gross Pay
5	Benson	10	40	
6	Browning	9	41	
7	Lawrence	10.25	30	
8	Monroe	9	16	
9	Stephens	9.75	44	

In Exercise 12.12, you'll use the IF function to have Excel apply one of two formulas based on the number of hours an employee worked.

EXERCISE 12.12

Using the IF Function

1. Open the file 12-12.xls and select cell D5.

2. Click the Insert Function button on the formula bar to open the Insert Function dialog box.

3. Choose the Logical category.

4. Select the IF function and click OK to open the Function Arguments dialog box. The Function Arguments dialog box with the arguments for this formula is shown here:

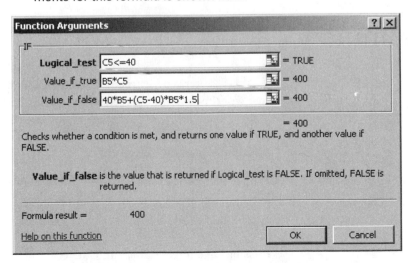

EXERCISE 12.12 *(continued)*

5. Enter the arguments for the function.

   - The Logical_test argument checks to see if the employee worked 40 hours or less: **C5<=40**

   - If the result of the Logical_test argument is true (hours are 40 or less), the Value_if_true formula will be applied: **B5*C5**

   - If the result of the Logical_test argument is false (hours are more than 40), the Value_if_false formula is applied, paying 40 hours at the regular rate and hours over 40 at 1.5 times the rate: **40*B5+(C5-40)*B5*1.5**

6. Click OK to enter the formula.

7. Format cell D5 for two decimal places. Fill D5 to the other cells in the column.

8. Save and close the file.

There's always more than one way to write an IF statement. Rather than testing to see if an employee worked less than or exactly 40 hours, you can test to see if the hours are more than 40 and then swap the two formulas within the IF function: =IF(C5>40, 40*B5+(C5-40)*B5*1.5, B5*C5).

Summary

In this chapter, you learned how to work with cells and cell data and to manage workbooks. We covered the following topics:

- Inserting and deleting worksheets

- Renaming worksheets

- Moving and copying worksheets within and between workbooks

- Using 3-D cell references

- Creating and revising formulas

- Using functions: Statistical, Date & Time, Financial, and Logical

Chapter

13

Creating Charts and Graphics

MOUS EXCEL 2002 CORE EXAM OBJECTIVES COVERED IN THIS CHAPTER:

✓ Create, modify, position, and print charts

✓ Create, modify, and position graphics

n this chapter, you'll break past Excel's numeric barrier, using graphic tools like charts and clip art that help you make the numbers approachable and easy to understand.

> **NOTE** Before you begin this chapter, you should go to the Sybex website and download the file 4113Ch13.zip. This contains the file 13-1.xls, which you will use in a number of exercises in this chapter.

Working with Charts

Charts are graphical representations of numerical data. Charts, sometimes called graphs, make it easier for users to compare and understand numerical values. Charts highlight information that can be lost in a long list of numbers. Every chart tells a story; a well-designed chart provides context and focus so the story you want to tell is easily understood. Charts are constructed with *data points*, which are the individual numbers in a worksheet, bundled into *data series*, which are the groups of related data points within a column or row.

Microsoft ✓ Exam Objective	Create, modify, position, and print charts

For example, Figure 13.1 shows the `Williams Paint Corporation Quarterly Sales` worksheet (`11-7 Post.xls`) from Chapter 11, "Formatting and Printing Worksheets." In this chapter's exercises, you'll use the data in the worksheet to create charts. Each of the numbers in the worksheet is a data point. There are many possible sets of data series in this worksheet: One set includes four data series—one for each city's row. Another set includes a data series for each quarter's column. Each column or row of numbers is a series.

FIGURE 13.1   Each number in this worksheet is a data point, and each row or column is a potential data series.

	A	B	C	D	E	F
1	Williams Paint Corporation					
2	Quarterly Sales (thousands)					
3						
4	Location	Jan-Mar	Apr-Jun	July-Sept	Oct-Dec	Totals
5	Chicago	388.00	412.00	399.00	485.00	1,684.00
6	Schaumberg	319.00	345.00	333.00	369.00	1,366.00
7	Hyde Park	567.00	566.00	534.00	601.00	2,268.00
8	Rosemont	217.00	251.00	264.00	289.00	1,021.00
9						
10	Averages	372.75	393.50	382.50	436.00	1,584.75

Excel supports a broad selection of chart types. Your data and the story you want to illustrate determine the type or types of chart that best illustrate the data. In this chapter, we'll focus on the chart types used most frequently for business charts in North America and, therefore, most likely to turn up on the MOUS exam.

Creating Pie Charts

You use *pie charts* to show the relationships between pieces of an entity. The implication is that the pie includes *all* of something: for example, all sales, all expenses, or all donations. In the 3-D pie chart shown in Figure 13.2, the pie shows the Total Sales by location. The pie chart type isn't appropriate for illustrating only *some* of anything, so if there's not an obvious "all" in the data you're charting, don't use a pie chart.

A pie chart can include only one data series. If you select more than one data series, Excel uses the first series and ignores all others. No error message appears, so you won't necessarily know that the chart doesn't show the data you intended to include, unless you examine the chart carefully.

FIGURE 13.2 A pie chart created from sales data in the Williams Paint Corporation Quarterly Sales worksheet.

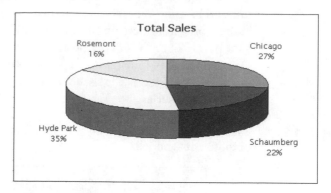

When you create a pie chart, you don't need to create worksheet formulas to calculate percentages. Excel totals the data points in the series and then divides the value of each data point into the series total to determine how large each data point's pie slice should be. Don't include a total from the worksheet as a data point; this would double the total Excel calculates, resulting in a pie chart with one large slice that represents exactly 50 percent of the pie.

You create pie charts using the Chart Wizard button on the Standard toolbar. In Exercise 13.1, you'll create a pie chart like the chart shown in Figure 13.2.

EXERCISE 13.1

Creating a Pie Chart

1. Open the file 13-1.xls and select the ranges you want to include in the chart: Select cells A4:A8 and then hold Ctrl and select F4:F8.

2. Click the Chart Wizard button on the Standard toolbar.

    If the Office Assistant's Help With Wizards option is turned on, the Office Assistant appears at this point. The Assistant is helpful with charts, providing information on each step of the wizard. It is your choice to accept Clippit's offer of help or hide the Office Assistant.

3. In the first step of the Chart Wizard, select Pie in the Chart Type list and the Pie With A 3-D Visual Effect subtype. The description of the subtype appears in the label below the subtypes. Click Next.

EXERCISE 13.1 (continued)

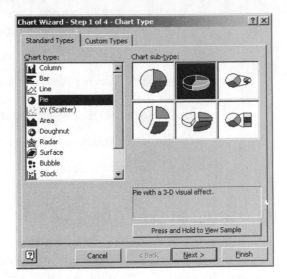

4. In Step 2 of 4 of the Chart Wizard, verify that you have selected the correct ranges (A4:A8 and F4:F8) and choose the Series In option By Columns. Click Next.

   With a pie chart, if the wrong Series In option is selected, you'll have a pie with one large slice rather than individual slices.

5. In Step 3 of 4 of the Chart Wizard, set options for the chart, including titles, legend placement, and data labels:

   a. On the Titles tab, select the text in the Chart Title text box and enter the title **Total Sales.**

   b. On the Legend tab, turn off the Show Labels check box.

   c. On the Data Labels tab, enable the Category Name and Percentage check boxes. Turn off the Show Leader Lines check box.

6. Click Next.

7. In the fourth step, select a location for the chart. Leave the default option, placing the chart as an object in the same worksheet as the chart's data.

EXERCISE 13.1 *(continued)*

You'll save a chart in a new sheet in Exercise 13.4 so you'll be able to compare the two location options.

8. Click Finish to create the Chart object in the worksheet.

   The Chart object is placed in a separate layer in front of the worksheet. To make changes to the worksheet, you need to select the sheet rather than the Chart object.

9. Save the workbook as `Williams Paint Sales Charts.xls`.

10. Don't close the workbook yet—you'll use it in the next exercise.

Moving, Sizing, and Printing Chart Objects

If you place the chart as an object in the current worksheet, you'll inevitably need to resize and move it so it will print well with the existing data. The Chart object floats on a layer above the worksheet, so it may cover part of the worksheet data or fall across a page break. When the Chart Wizard closes, the chart displays square *sizing handles* on the corners and sides to show that it is selected. In Exercise 13.2, you'll use the handles to resize and position the chart in the worksheet.

EXERCISE 13.2

Moving and Sizing Charts

For this exercise, use the `Williams Paint Sales Charts.xls` workbook saved in Exercise 13.1.

1. If necessary, open the `Williams Paint Sales Charts.xls` workbook. If the chart isn't selected, click once on the chart to select it.

2. Point to an empty area in the Chart object. Drag the chart directly below the worksheet data; the mouse pointer changes to a four-headed arrow as you begin to drag.

3. Move the mouse pointer to one of the chart's corner handles. Hold the mouse button and drag the handle to resize the chart so that it is slightly narrower than the worksheet data area. Dragging diagonally

by a corner handle maintains the proportions between the chart height and width by resizing in two dimensions. Dragging a handle that isn't on a corner changes the proportions of the Chart object.

4. Move the mouse pointer to the center handle on the right side of the Chart object. Drag to the right to make the chart the same width as the worksheet data without changing its height.

5. Click anywhere in the worksheet to deselect the chart.

6. Choose View ➤ Page Break Preview on the menu to locate the page breaks. If necessary, click the chart to select it, and resize the chart so that it is within the page breaks.

7. Choose View ➤ Normal to return to Normal view.

   You can't return to Normal view when the Chart object is selected. You must have one or more worksheet cells selected to switch between views in Excel.

8. Resave the workbook. Keep the workbook open for the next exercise.

Printing Charts As Objects or Worksheets

If you placed your chart as an object in the current worksheet, you can still print it separately. When the worksheet is selected, the worksheet and the objects on it print. When the Chart object is selected, only the Chart object prints. We'll demonstrate this in Exercise 13.3.

Printing Charts and Worksheets with Chart Objects

1. Using the Williams Paint Sales Charts workbook you resaved in Exercise 13.2, select the Chart object.

2. Click the Print Preview button. In the Preview window, note that only the chart prints when the chart is selected.

3. Close the Preview window.

4. Click anywhere in the worksheet to deselect the chart.

5. Click the Print Preview button. In the Preview window, note that the worksheet, including the Chart object, prints when the worksheet is selected.

6. Close the Preview window.

Creating Series Charts

In a *series chart*, you can chart more than one data series. Series charts let you compare the data points in the series, such as sales for Jan–Mar versus Apr–Jun, Hyde Park sales compared to the sales in Rosemont. Series charts are open-ended; there is no requirement that the data shown is all the data for a month or year. There are several types of series charts, so you can often improve the usefulness of a series chart simply by changing the chart type. In Exercise 13.4, you'll create a commonly used series chart, the column chart.

EXERCISE 13.4

Creating a Column Chart

1. In the Williams Paint Sales Charts worksheet you resaved in Exercise 13.2, select A4:D8, which contain the location names and sales data for all locations for the first three quarters.

2. Click the Chart Wizard button on the Standard toolbar.

3. In the first step of the wizard, choose Column in the Chart Type list and Clustered Column With A 3-D Visual Effect in the Sub-Type list. Click Next.

4. In the second step, choose Series In Rows. Click Next.

5. In the third step, set the following options:

- Titles: Chart Title: Williams Paint Quarterly Sales
- Titles: Value (Z) Axis: Sales
- Data Table: Enable the Show Data Table check box.

Click the Next button.

6. In the final step, select the As New Sheet option.

EXERCISE 13.4 *(continued)*

7. Enter **Chart - Quarterly Sales** as the sheet name.

8. Click Finish to create the chart on its own sheet.

9. Resave the workbook.

The Quarterly Sales column chart created in Exercise 13.4 is shown in Figure 13.3. The data table appears below the chart. Data tables are useful when users need both the chart and the underlying data, but the worksheet includes data that you don't want to display with the chart. Unlike the worksheet, the data table includes only the data presented in the chart.

FIGURE 13.3 The Quarterly Sales column chart

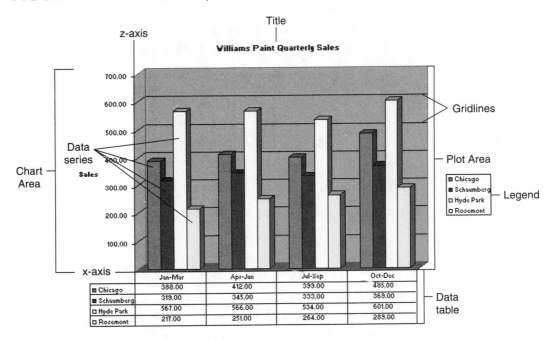

The Chart Area includes the entire chart. To select the Chart Area, click any unoccupied area of the chart.

Modifying Charts

You can modify the chart by changing any of the options you selected in the Chart Wizard. The four steps of the Chart Wizard are four separate dialog boxes. To return to a specific dialog box, right-click in the Chart Area and choose from the following options:

- Chart Type to return to the first step of the Chart Wizard

- Source Data to return to the second step

- Chart Options to return to the third step

- Location to return to the fourth step

In the Exercise 13.5, you'll modify the chart and change the chart's location, converting it from a chart sheet to a Chart object.

EXERCISE 13.5

Changing Chart Type, Source Data, Chart Options, and Location

1. In the Williams Paint Sales Charts workbook you resaved in Exercise 13.4, select the Chart - Quarterly Sales sheet.

2. Right-click in a blank portion of the Chart Area.

3. Choose Chart Type from the shortcut menu to open the Chart Type dialog box.

4. Choose the Stacked Column With 3-D Visual Effect chart subtype. Click OK to apply the chart type change.

5. Right-click in the Chart Area to open the Chart Area shortcut menu.

6. Choose Source Data from the shortcut menu to open the Source Data dialog box.

7. In the worksheet, select A4:E8 to include the fourth-quarter sales figures. If necessary, collapse the Source Data dialog box to select the range.

8. Click OK to close the Source Data dialog box and re-create the chart with the new data.

9. Right click in the Chart Area, and choose Chart Options from the shortcut menu.

10. On the Data Table tab, turn off the Show Data Table check box.

11. On the Titles tab, enter a Category (X) Axis Title: **Quarter.**

EXERCISE 13.5 *(continued)*

12. On the Legend tab, choose the Bottom placement option.

13. Click OK to apply the changes.

14. Switch to the 2002 Sales worksheet.

15. Right-click the Chart object and choose Location from the shortcut menu.

16. Select the As New Sheet option.

17. Name the sheet **Chart - Pie**. Click OK to convert the Chart object to a chart sheet.

18. Resave the workbook. Keep the workbook open for the next exercise.

Editing and Formatting Charts

A chart's plot area is bounded by the axes and contains the columns, lines, wedges, or other objects used to represent the data points. The Plot Area includes the axes, the axis labels, and the data labels. To select the Plot Area, click to the right of the X-axis labels.

To select the Plot Area on a pie, imagine that the pie is surrounded by a square box that the pie touches at the top, bottom, left, and right sides. Point to one of the four corners of the box and click when the Screen Tip reads "Plot Area."

Objects that form the boundaries of the plot area have fixed location areas and cannot be moved or individually sized. For example, the X-axis labels must be located near the X-axis.

Resizing and Deleting Objects in a Chart

You can, however, resize all the objects in the Plot Area by increasing or decreasing the Plot Area itself. Objects outside the Plot Area and axes such as the legend and title can be sized or moved to other locations in the Chart Area. The title and legend can be placed above, below, or in the Plot Area.

Any object in a chart can be selected and then formatted or deleted, with the exception of individual data points. Data points can be formatted, but only data *series* can be added or deleted. To select a data point, first select the data series. A data series will have handles when it is selected. With the data series selected, click the data point once. Handles will appear on the data point.

Formatting the Chart with the Chart Toolbar

Common formatting options are available on the Chart toolbar (choose View ➤ Toolbars ➤ Chart if the toolbar is not displayed). The first item on the toolbar is the Chart Objects drop-down list, used to select one of the objects in the chart; the other buttons format the entire chart or selected objects or text. See Table 13.1 for descriptions of the buttons on the Chart toolbar.

TABLE 13.1   Chart Toolbar Buttons

Button	Button Name	Function
Chart Area	Chart Objects	Selects the object chosen from the list.
	Format Object	Opens the Format dialog box for the selected object.
	Chart Type	The drop-down arrow opens a menu of chart types; clicking the button applies the chart type indicated on the button face.
	Legend	Displays or hides the legend.
	Data Table	Displays or hides the data table.
	By Row	Uses the selected worksheet rows as a data series.
	By Column	Uses the selected worksheet columns as a data series.
	Angle Clockwise	Angles selected text downward.
	Angle Counter-clockwise	Angles selected text upward.

In Exercise 13.6, you'll use the Chart toolbar to format individual objects in a chart.

EXERCISE 13.6

Formatting Individual Objects

1. If it's not already open, open the Williams Paint Sales Charts workbook you resaved in Exercise 13.5, and select the Chart – Pie worksheet. If the Chart toolbar is not displayed, right-click any toolbar and choose Chart or choose View ➢ Toolbars ➢ Chart.

2. On the Chart toolbar, click the Legend button to display the legend.

3. Click the Legend button again to hide the legend.

4. Click once on the pie chart to select the data series.

5. Click once on the Hyde Park slice to select the Hyde Park data point.

6. Drag the slice away from the center of the pie to "explode" the slice.

   You explode a pie slice to emphasize the data represented by the slice.

7. Click a blank area of the Chart Area.

8. Click the Format Object button on the Chart toolbar to open the Format Chart Area dialog box.

9. On the Font tab, choose Tahoma to change the font used in the chart.

10. Click one of the data labels. All data labels will be selected.

11. Click the Format Object button on the Chart toolbar to open the Format Data Labels dialog box.

12. On the Patterns tab, choose Automatic in the Border section.

13. On the Font tab, choose Bold in the Font Style list.

14. Click OK to apply the formatting changes.

15. Click once on the chart title to select it.

16. Use the Font Size menu on the Formatting toolbar to change the font size to 18.

17. Save and close the workbook.

To quickly format an object, select it, right-click, then select Format *Object-name* from the shortcut menu.

Working with Graphics

This section focuses on inserting and positioning pictures in workbooks.

Microsoft Exam Objective	Create, modify, and position graphics

Inserting and Positioning a Picture

In Excel, there are a variety of reasons to use graphics. You insert a picture from a file when you want to add an image, such as a company logo, to a worksheet. You use the clip art that's included with Microsoft Office XP to add interesting graphic elements to attract or focus your user's attention on the worksheet.

The charts you created earlier in this chapter are also graphics. For more practice moving and sizing graphics in a worksheet, see Exercise 13.2: Moving and Sizing Charts.

In Exercise 13.7, you'll insert and position a graphic from a file.

EXERCISE 13.7

Inserting and Positioning a Picture from a File

1. Open a blank workbook and select the cell where you want to place the picture. Choose cell B3.

2. To insert a picture from a file, choose Insert ➢ Picture ➢ From File to open the Insert Picture dialog box.

3. Locate the picture you want to insert. Choose sample.jpg in the My Documents\My Pictures folder or, if you prefer, another picture file.

4. Select the picture file, and then click the Insert button to insert the picture in the worksheet.

5. With the picture selected, drag the picture to move it.

6. Use the green Free Rotate handle to rotate the picture. If the picture file format does not support rotation, there will be no Free Rotate handle.

7. Drag a handle to resize the image.

8. Close the workbook without saving the changes.

On the exam, you may be asked to insert a picture or any of the graphic elements created using the Drawing toolbar, such as:

- Conceptual diagrams
- Organization charts
- AutoShapes
- WordArt
- Textboxes, lines, ovals, and rectangles

If you are not familiar with the Drawing toolbar, complete the exercises in Chapter 3 as part of your preparation for the Excel Core Exam.

Summary

In this chapter, you learned how to create, modify, position, and print charts and graphics. We covered the following topics:

- Creating pie charts
- Changing chart options
- Creating series charts
- Formatting and positioning charts

Additionally, you should know how to complete the following tasks, which are covered in Chapter 3:

- Inserting graphics from files and clip art and using the Drawing tools
- Creating conceptual diagrams
- Creating organization charts
- Positioning graphics

Collaborating in Excel

MOUS EXCEL 2002 CORE EXAM OBJECTIVES COVERED IN THIS CHAPTER:

- ✓ Convert worksheets into Web pages
- ✓ Create hyperlinks
- ✓ View and edit comments

This chapter focuses on three Excel features that support collaboration: converting worksheets into web pages, creating hyperlinks, and adding comments to workbooks. Every version of Excel since Excel 95 has included new web and collaboration functionality, and Excel 2002 is no exception. Using Excel's web tools, you can publish static and interactive spreadsheets, charts, and pivot tables. In this chapter, you'll learn to convert worksheets and workbooks into static web pages. Interactive web pages are discussed in Chapter 15, "Managing Workbooks and Data."

Before you begin this chapter, you should go to the Sybex website and download the file 4113Ch14.zip. This package contains the file necessary to complete some of the exercises in this chapter.

Web Publishing in Excel

When you save or publish Excel 2002 worksheets as web pages, the pages you create are either interactive or noninteractive. *Noninteractive*, or *static*, pages are created so users can examine data. These are the same pages you've been able to publish in earlier versions of Excel. Users can look at the pages, but they can't rearrange data on the page. *Interactive* pages include the *Office Web Components*, which empower users by letting them work directly with Excel data in their browser using Excel tools, turning Internet Explorer into a decent ad hoc report and analysis tool. For example, users can sort and filter data in an interactive page.

Microsoft✓*Exam**Objective*	**Convert worksheets into Web pages**

In Excel, saving and publishing are not synonymous. Saving creates static (noninteractive) web pages. Interactive pages must be published. In Exercise 14.1, you'll create a static web page from a worksheet. For this exercise, use the 2003 Service Team Budget workbook you created in Chapter 12, "Enhancing and Revising Workbooks," or open 14-1.xls from the downloaded zip file for this chapter.

EXERCISE 14.1

Saving a Worksheet As a Web Page

1. Open the workbook 14-1.xls.

2. Select any cell in the worksheet you want to publish. In this exercise, you'll publish the Budget_Summary worksheet.

3. Choose File ➢ Save As Web Page to open the Save As dialog box.

4. Select your My Documents folder as the Save In location for the web page. Enter a filename: **2003 Service Team Budgets**

EXERCISE 14.1 *(continued)*

5. Click the Selection: Sheet option button in the Save options.

6. Click the Change Title button to open the Set Title dialog box.

7. Enter a title that will appear in the browser title bar, **2003 Budget Summary - Draft**, and click OK to close the Set Title dialog box.

8. Click the Save button to save the worksheet as a web page.

9. In Windows, choose Start ≻ Documents to open the Documents menu. Choose the My Documents folder.

10. Double-click the 2003 Service Team Budgets.htm file to open the web page in your default browser.

11. Close the browser window to return to Excel.

Leave the workbook open for the next exercise.

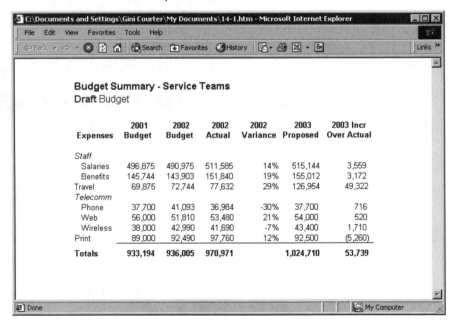

You can save more or less than a worksheet as a static web page, as you'll see in Exercise 14.2. For this exercise, use the 14-1.xls workbook used in Exercise 14.1.

EXERCISE 14.2

Saving a Selection or Workbook As a Web Page

1. In the Budget_Summary worksheet in the 14-1.xls workbook, select the range A1:E16—the columns for 2001 and 2002.

2. Choose File ➢ Save As Web Page to open the Save As dialog box, shown in the previous exercise.

3. Select My Documents as the location for the web page. Enter the filename **Budget 2001-2002** for the HTML file.

4. Click the Selection: Range ($A$1:$E$16) option button in the Save options.

5. Click the Change Title button to open the Set Page Title dialog box. Enter the title **2001-2002 Budget Summary**, and click OK to close the Set Page Title dialog box.

6. Click the Save button to save the selection as a web page.

7. In Windows Explorer, open the Budget 2001-2002.htm web page. The web page contains only the selection.

8. Return to Excel. Choose File ➢ Save As Web Page to open the Save As dialog box.

9. Select a location for the web page. Enter the filename **2003 Team Budgets**.

10. Click the Change Title button. Title the page **2003 Team Budgets**.

11. Click the Entire Workbook option button in the Save options.

12. Click Save to save the workbook as a web page.

13. In Windows Explorer or My Computer, locate and open the 2003 Team Budgets.htm web page. In your browser, click the sheet tabs for each of the worksheets in the workbook.

14. Close the browser window. Save and close the workbook.

Creating Hyperlinks

You can create four types of hyperlinks in Excel. You can link to the following:

- An existing file or web page
- A range in the current workbook
- A new workbook
- An e-mail address

Excel creates links to web URLs and e-mail addresses automatically. When you type an e-mail address (for example, `authors@triadconsulting.com`) or a web address (`www.sybex.com`), Excel converts the text to a hyperlink.

Microsoft ✓ Exam Objective

Create hyperlinks

In Exercise 14.3, you'll enter text that Excel will automatically format as hyperlinks.

EXERCISE 14.3

Creating Hyperlinks By Typing Text

1. Open a new workbook.

2. In cell A1, type **www.microsoft.com** and press Enter to create a hyperlink.

3. In cell A2, type **support@sybex.com** and press Enter to create a hyperlink.

4. Click the hyperlink in cell A1. Excel will open your browser and navigate to the home page on the Microsoft website.

5. Close your browser.

6. Click the hyperlink in cell A2. Excel will launch Outlook and open a new mail message form addressed to support@sybex.com. Close the message.

EXERCISE 14.3 *(continued)*

If your e-mail client doesn't support automation, the hyperlink in cell A2 will not work.

7. Save the workbook as **Links.xls**. Leave the workbook open for the next exercise.

Typing a hyperlink works fine if you want to display the actual URL or e-mail address in the workbook. If, however, you want the user to click text that reads "Click here to visit the Microsoft site," you need to create the hyperlink in the Insert Hyperlink dialog box, shown in Figure 14.1.

FIGURE 14.1 Create and customize hyperlinks in the Insert Hyperlink dialog box.

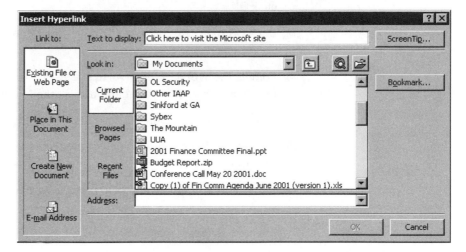

In Exercise 14.4, you'll create two customized hyperlinks.

EXERCISE 14.4

Inserting a Hyperlink

For this exercise, use the Links.xls workbook saved in the previous exercise.

1. In cell A4, type the text **Click here to visit the Microsoft site**. Press Enter.

EXERCISE 14.4 (continued)

2. With cell A4 selected click the Insert Hyperlink button on the Standard toolbar, or choose Insert ➤ Hyperlink from the menu, or hold Ctrl and press K to open the Insert Hyperlink dialog box. The text from cell A4 appears in the Text To Display text box.

3. In the Links bar on the left side of the dialog box, select the type of hyperlink you want to create: Existing File Or Web Page.

4. Type the URL www.microsoft.com in the Address text box.

5. Click the ScreenTip button to open the Set Hyperlink ScreenTip dialog box.

6. Enter **Microsoft home page** in the ScreenTip Text field and then click OK.

7. Click OK to create the hyperlink and close the Insert Hyperlink dialog box.

8. Point to the hyperlink in cell A4 to see the ScreenTip. Click the hyperlink to launch your browser and display the Microsoft home page.

9. Select cell A6. Open the Insert Hyperlink dialog box.

10. In the Links bar on the left side of the dialog box, choose Place In This Document.

11. In the Text To Display text box, type **Go to Sheet2**.

12. In the Or Select A Place In This Document area, choose Sheet2. Click OK to create the hyperlink.

13. Click cell A6 to navigate to Sheet2.

14. Save the workbook. Leave it open for the next exercise.

Using Comments

Comments enhance collaboration by making it easy to communicate questions and answers about worksheet values or formulas. Or, you can insert comments to help other users understand how to use a worksheet. Comments are also useful for your own worksheets. For example, you can use comments to note the source for a figure in a budget or annotate the reason why the markup value in a sales estimate is 25 percent.

Microsoft ✓ Exam Objective   **View and edit comments**

In Exercise 14.5, you'll insert a comment into a workbook.

EXERCISE 14.5

Inserting a Comment

For this exercise, use the workbook used in the previous exercise.

1. Enter the number **595** in an empty cell. Then right-click that cell to open the shortcut menu.

2. Choose Insert Comment. Excel inserts a comment with your user-name on the first line.

   If the user name is incorrect, you can fix it. Choose Tools ➤ Options. Change the User Name entry at the bottom of the General tab.

3. Type the text for your comment: **Miscellaneous expenses are included in this figure**.

4. Click any cell in the worksheet to close the comment.

5. Point to the cell indicator (the red triangle in the upper-right corner) of the cell containing the comment to display the comment.

6. Save the workbook. Keep it open for the next exercise.

As you'll see in the Exercise 14.6, you can edit a comment, making it easy to correct an annotation or add more information as new information is available.

EXERCISE 14.6

Editing a Comment

Use the same worksheet you used in the previous exercise.

1. Right-click the cell containing the comment.

EXERCISE 14.6 *(continued)*

2. Choose Edit Comment from the shortcut menu to open the comment for editing.

3. Add the following sentence at the end of the comment text: **Travel-related expenses are included in Entertainment.**

4. Drag the comment border to resize the comment to display all the text, and then click any cell to close the comment.

5. Point to the comment indicator in the cell containing the comment to display the comment.

6. Save the workbook. Leave it open for the next exercise.

You can delete comments from worksheets if they are no longer relevant. In Exercise 14.7, you'll delete the comment you just edited.

EXERCISE 14.7

Deleting a Comment

Use the workbook you used in the previous exercise.

1. Right-click the cell containing the comment.

2. Choose Delete Comment from the shortcut menu.

3. Save and close the workbook.

Summary

In this chapter, you learned how to use workbook features that support collaboration. We covered the following topics:

- Converting worksheets into web pages
- Converting workbooks into web pages
- Saving a selection as a web page
- Creating hyperlinks
- Viewing and editing comments

Microsoft Excel 2002 Expert Exam

Chapter

15

Managing Workbooks and Data

MOUS EXCEL 2002 EXPERT EXAM OBJECTIVES COVERED IN THIS CHAPTER:

- ✓ Import data to Excel
- ✓ Export data from Excel
- ✓ Publish worksheets and workbooks to the Web
- ✓ Create, edit, and apply templates
- ✓ Create workspaces
- ✓ Use data consolidation

In this chapter, you'll learn the skills that extend Excel to work with other file formats, such as importing data from a variety of sources, creating new workbooks from templates, and exporting data to formats including HTML, the language of the World Wide Web. The chapter ends with two workbook-management tools: workspaces and data consolidation.

Before you begin this chapter, you should visit the Sybex website and download the file 4113Ch15.zip. This package contains the files necessary to complete some of the exercises in this chapter.

Importing and Exporting Data

Excel is more than an outstanding spreadsheet application. Excel is also used extensively to work with data saved using other file formats. In this section, you will practice importing to Excel and exporting Excel workbooks to other formats.

Excel 2002 and Excel 2000 use the same file format, so if you want to work with an Excel 2000 workbook, just open it as you would an Excel 2002 workbook.

Importing Data

You import whenever you want to use Excel to work with data saved in other file formats. Importing saves the time (while preventing potential errors) that would be needed to retype the data in Excel. There are two different Excel features referred to as *importing*. The first meaning of import, covered in this chapter, is to directly open a file created in another application using the File ➤ Open command. The second import command (called Get External Data in previous versions of Excel) is found on the Data menu: Data ➤ Import External Data. The external data-importing feature creates a connection to a data source and returns data as a *query*, which is a refreshable link to the data. External data importing is discussed in Chapter 19, "Summarizing Data."

Microsoft ✓ *Exam Objective*	**Import data to Excel**

Importing Workbooks Created in Other Versions of Excel

Excel 97, 2000, and 2002 share a common file format. A workbook saved in Excel 2002 can be opened in any of the three versions. Excel 2002 converts files saved in prior Excel formats: Excel 3, 4, 5, and 95. If you save the converted file, you can resave it in its original format or "update" it by saving it in the current format. In Exercise 15.1, you'll learn how to import workbooks saved in Excel 5.0/95.

EXERCISE 15.1

Importing Workbooks Saved in Excel 5.0/95

1. In Excel, choose File ➤ Open to open the Open dialog box.

2. Locate and open the 15-1 Risk and Reward Plan.xls workbook.

3. Choose File ➤ Save or click the Save button to save the workbook:

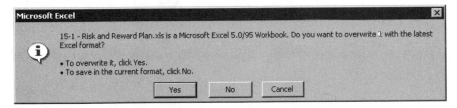

4. Click No to save the workbook in the Excel 5.0/95 format. Close the workbook.

EXERCISE 15.1 *(continued)*

5. Open the workbook again.

6. Choose File ➢ Save or click the Save button.

7. Click Yes to save the workbook in the Excel 97/2000/2002 format.

8. Save and close all open workbooks.

Importing Data from Other Applications

Excel users sometimes need to import data stored in files created with other spreadsheet programs such as Lotus 1-2-3 and Quattro—although this need occurs less frequently as the percentage of Lotus and Quattro users decreases. Excel readily opens files saved in a variety of formats. And Excel 2002 supports HTML and XML as native formats, so web files open as readily as Excel workbooks.

In some instances, an attempt to open a file results in a "file not valid" error message. There are two possible reasons for this message: Excel doesn't support the file type, or the type is supported but the converter is not installed. For example, the Lotus 1-2-3 converter is installed by default; the Quattro Pro converter is installed only in a custom installation.

The file types Excel imports directly are listed in Table 15.1.

TABLE 15.1 Import File Types Supported by Excel 2002

File Type	File Extensions
Data Interchange	.dif
dBASE	.dbf
Lotus 1-2-3	.wk, .wj
Microsoft Access	.mdb, .mde
Microsoft Excel	.xls
Microsoft Works 2.0	.wks

TABLE 15.1   Import File Types Supported by Excel 2002 *(continued)*

File Type	File Extensions
Quattro Pro (DOS)	.wq1
SYLK	.slk
Text files	.csv, .txt, .prn
Web pages/Web	.htm, .html, .asp, .mht, .mhtml, .xml

If the file type you want to open isn't included on Excel's list, request the file in one of the common text formats supported by Excel. Almost all data applications (spreadsheets and databases) can save files as comma-separated or tab-separated files. Comma-delimited text files use commas to represent the breaks between columns and carriage returns to represent breaks between rows. Comma-delimited files have the file extension .csv or, less frequently, .txt.

In Exercise 15.2, you'll open a comma-delimited text file, first in Notepad (its native application) and then in Excel. The file 15-2 – Volunteer Data.csv is shown in Notepad in Figure 15.1.

FIGURE 15.1   A comma-delimited text file shown in Notepad

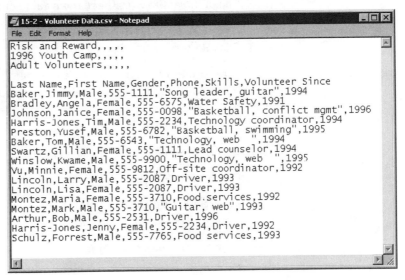

EXERCISE 15.2

Importing a Comma-Delimited Text File

1. From the Windows Start menu, choose Start ➤ Programs ➤ Accessories ➤ Notepad to launch Notepad.

2. Choose File ➤ Open from the Notepad menu. In the Open dialog box, change the Files Of Type entry to All Files (*.*).

3. Locate and open the 15-2 - Volunteer Data.csv file.

   Notice that commas separate the values in this file. Where a value includes a comma, the value is surrounded by quotation marks. For example, the value 22 Twain Dr, Apt. 13 would be surrounded by quotation marks.

4. Close Notepad. If prompted, do not save the file.

5. In Excel, choose File ➤ Open to display the Open dialog box.

6. In the Files Of Type list box, select the relevant source file type: Text Files (*.txt; *.prn, *.csv).

7. Locate and select the 15-2 - Volunteer Data.csv file and click Open. Excel opens and converts the CSV file to an Excel format.

8. Select the entire worksheet and double-click the right edge of any column heading to adjust the column widths to fit the contents.

9. Click Save on the Standard toolbar.

   Excel prompts you to choose Yes to save the file in the original text format or choose No to cancel the save and save it as an Excel file. You are warned that the file may contain features that are not supported by the CSV format.

10. Click Yes to resave the file as a CSV file.

11. Choose File ➤ Save As from the Excel menu.

12. In the Save As dialog box, choose Microsoft Excel Workbook in the Save As Type drop-down list.

13. Save the file with the suggested name, 15-2 - Volunteer Data.xls.

EXERCISE 15.2 *(continued)*

14. Close 15-2 - Volunteer Data.xls.

15. Reopen the text file, 15-2 - Volunteer Data.csv, from the list of recent files on the File menu. Notice that the column width formatting was not retained.

16. Close the file without saving changes.

17. Reopen the Excel file, 15-2 - Volunteer Data.xls, from the list of recent files on the File menu. Note that the column widths were retained. Close the file.

Using the Text Import Wizard

Comma-delimited files open directly in Excel. Other text file types do not. When Excel can't import a text file directly, you can use the Text Import Wizard to open the file and parse it into an Excel spreadsheet. When you *parse* a file, Excel examines it, converts text items to appropriate data types, and places the data in rows and columns.

In order to be parsed successfully, a text file must contain either delimited or fixed-width data:

- **Delimited:** These are text files where data fields are separated by commas, tabs, or another consistent symbol or character.

- **Fixed-width:** These are non-delimited files in which each field is a specific length; the space between fields is padded with zeros or spaces.

In Exercise 15.3, you'll use the Text Import Wizard to parse a file. The file has the same content as the file used in Exercise 15.2 but was saved using the .txt extension.

EXERCISE 15.3

Importing a Text File with the Text Import Wizard

1. In Excel, select File ➢ Open or click the Open button and select Text Files in the Files Of Type list box.

EXERCISE 15.3 *(continued)*

2. Locate and select the 15-3 - Volunteer Data.txt file. Click Open.

   The wizard attempts to determine whether the file is delimited or fixed width.

3. Verify that the Delimited option is selected.

4. Leave the Start Import At Row spin box control at 1 to import the file beginning with row 1.

5. Click Next to move to the second step of the wizard.

6. The file is tab delimited, so in the Delimiters section, make sure Tab is selected. Excel adds the column boundaries so that each column contains data from only one field. Click Next.

7. In the final step in the Text Import Wizard, choose the format for each of the newly defined columns. Select the first column, and then hold Shift and select all other columns except the last column. Choose Text as the Column Data Format. For the last column, leave the default General option:

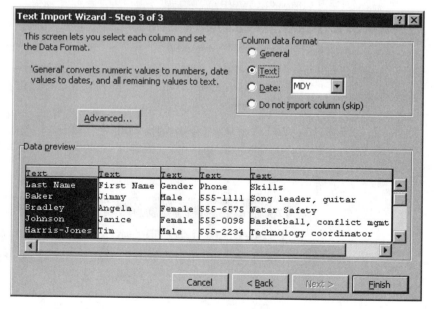

EXERCISE 15.3 *(continued)*

8. Click Finish to import the data beginning with the first row.

9. Choose File ➢ Save As and save the imported data using default name in the Microsoft Excel Workbook format. Close the file.

Eurodata alert: Click the Advanced button to choose separators if you're importing data that uses decimal and thousands separators other than the period and comma.

Importing a Web Page

Excel 2002 has native support for HTML, MHTML (Web archive), and XML. Native support means files in these web formats open as easily as Excel workbooks. In Excel 2002, you don't really import web pages; you simply open them, as you'll see in Exercise 15.4.

EXERCISE 15.4

Importing a Web Page

1. Choose File ➢ Open from the Excel menu.

2. Locate and select the 15-4 - Meeting Agenda.htm file.

3. Click Open to open the web page.

4. In cell D14, enter **Everyone** as the WHO assigned to the 10:00 AM Break.

5. Click Save to save the web page. Close the file.

Exporting Data

You export Excel data when you want to save data in a file type other than the Excel workbook file format used in Excel 97/2000/2002.

Microsoft ✓ *Exam Objective*

Export data from Excel

Excel exports to even more formats than it can import from. The file types Excel can export to are listed in Table 15.2.

TABLE 15.2 Export File Types Supported by Excel 2002

File Type	Extensions
Data Interchange	.dif
dBASE II, III, IV	.dbf
Lotus 1-2-3	.wks, .wk1, .wk3, .wk4
Microsoft Excel 2.1 worksheet	.xls
Microsoft Excel 3.0 worksheet	.xls
Microsoft Excel 4.0 workbook	.xls
Microsoft Excel 4.0 worksheet	.xls
Microsoft Excel 5.0 and 95	.xls
Microsoft Excel 5.0–2002	.xls
Quattro Pro (DOS)	.wq1
SYLK	.slk
Text - Comma-delimited	.csv
Text - Mac, DOS, Unicode	.txt
Text - Space-delimited	.prn
Web archive	.mthm, .mhtml

TABLE 15.2 Export File Types Supported by Excel 2002 *(continued)*

File Type	Extensions
Web page	`.htm`, `.html`
XML spreadsheet	`.xml`

The "tool" used to export Excel files is the Save As dialog box—the same tool you used in Chapter 14, "Collaborating in Excel," to export (save) workbooks as web pages. In Exercise 15.5, you'll export a workbook and its sheets in four different formats.

EXERCISE 15.5

Exporting Files in Excel

1. Open the 15-1 - Risk and Reward Plan.xls workbook you used earlier in this chapter.

2. Select the 1997 Plan - Draft worksheet.

3. Choose File ➢ Save As to open the Save As dialog box.

4. From the Save As Type menu, choose CSV (Comma Delimited) (*.csv).

5. Click Save to save the file as 15-1 - Risk and Reward Plan.csv. Excel notifies you that the CSV format can only be used for a single worksheet.

   The CSV file format is plain text, so formatting will be lost when the file is saved.

6. Click OK to save the active worksheet as a CSV file and switch to the CSV file.

7. Close the CSV file. When prompted to save changes, choose No.

8. Reopen the 15-1 - Risk and Reward.csv comma-delimited file. Notice that the file contains only one worksheet with no formatting. Close the file.

EXERCISE 15.5 *(continued)*

9. Reopen the 15-1 - Risk and Reward Plan.xls Excel workbook. Choose File ➤ Save As.

10. From the Save As Type menu, choose the WK4 (1-2-3) (*.wk4) file format. Enter **Risk and Reward Lotus Format** in the File Name text box. Click Save.

    The selected Lotus 1-2-3 file format supports multiple-worksheet workbooks, so all worksheets will be saved. However, Excel notifies you that the Lotus 1-2-3 format may not support all the features included in the workbook.

11. Click Yes to save the workbook as a Lotus 1-2-3 workbook.

12. Close the workbook without saving changes (again).

13. Reopen the Risk and Reward Lotus Format.wk4 Lotus workbook. Notice that the file includes all three worksheets with only minimal changes from the original (for example, borders around the chart titles). Close the Lotus workbook without saving the changes.

14. Reopen the 15-1 - Risk and Reward Plan.xls Excel workbook. Choose File ➤ Save As.

15. From the Save As Type drop-down list, select Microsoft Excel 5.0/95 Workbook (*.xls). Click Save.

    All versions of Excel use the same file extension, so you're notified that the file already exists. Excel notifies you that if you save the file with this name, you will overwrite the original file.

16. Click No to return to the Save As dialog box.

17. Enter a new name for the file: **Risk and Reward Excel 5 Format**. Click Save.

Publishing Worksheets and Workbooks

Interactive web pages let users add formulas, sort and filter data, analyze data, and edit charts. In this section, you will learn to publish workbooks and worksheets as web pages.

For information on creating static (noninteractive) pages, see Chapter 14.

Microsoft Exam Objective   **Publish worksheets and workbooks to the Web**

Excel 2002 includes three Office Web Components, and each supports specific kinds of interactivity. They're called Office Web Components (OWCs) because they can be used in web pages created with other Office applications such as FrontPage, but the functionality is all Excel. The components are as follows:

- **The Spreadsheet component** inserts a spreadsheet where users can add formulas, sort and filter data, and format the worksheet. Use the Spreadsheet component to present unsummarized data.

- **The Chart component** is linked to data in the Spreadsheet component so that the chart can display changes when the data in the spreadsheet changes.

- **The PivotTable component** lets users analyze database information using most of the sorting, filtering, grouping, and subtotaling features of PivotTable reports.

There's a fourth component that works in the background: the Data Source component, the data retriever for the PivotTable and Chart components. In this section, you'll publish web pages with the Spreadsheet and Chart components.

Pivot tables and the PivotTable component are discussed in Chapter 20, "Analyzing Data."

The Office Web Components are interactive only if the user's browser supports ActiveX components. You, and your users, need to run Internet Explorer 5.0 or better to use the interactive features of the page. If a user has an older browser, they'll still see the spreadsheet, chart, or pivot table, but they will not be able to manipulate it in their browser. You can download the newest version of Internet Explorer from the Microsoft website.

The Office Web Components have another requirement: Your user must have a Microsoft Office 2002 license to use the components. The Office licensing and browser requirements make the OWCs a better choice for an intranet, where they were intended to be used, rather than the Internet.

In Exercise 15.6, you'll practice publishing an interactive web page from a worksheet.

EXERCISE 15.6

Publishing an Interactive Web Page from a Sheet

1. Open the 15-1 - Risk and Reward Plan.xls workbook used in Exercises 15.1 and 15.5.

2. Select the 1997 Plan - Draft worksheet.

3. Choose File ➢ Save As Web Page to open the Save As dialog box:

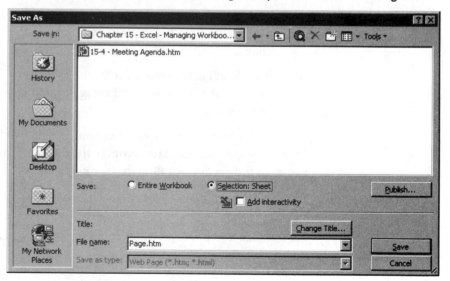

4. Choose a location for the web page.

5. In the Save area, choose the Selection: Sheet option.

6. Enter the filename **1997 Plan - Proposed** in the File Name text box.

7. Enable the Add Interactivity check box and then click the Publish button to open the Publish As Web Page dialog box:

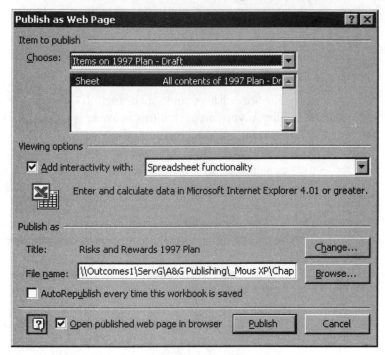

8. Choose Spreadsheet Functionality from the drop-down list.

9. Click the Change button to open the Set Title dialog box. Enter **Risks and Rewards 1997 Plan** as the page title, and then click OK to close the Set Title dialog box.

10. Click Browse, select the folder in which you want to publish, and click OK.

In Excel 2002, you can select the AutoRepublish Every Time This Workbook Is Saved check box to take the hassle out of remembering to republish the worksheet every time you make a change.

11. Enable the Open Published Web Page In Browser check box.

EXERCISE 15.6 *(continued)*

12. Click the Publish button, and Excel creates the web page, including the spreadsheet component, and displays it in your default browser.

13. Close your browser. Keep the Excel workbook open for the next exercise.

Using the Spreadsheet Component

The Spreadsheet component includes about as much spreadsheet functionality as you can pack into a browser window. With the static page created in Chapter 14, you created one report available in a browser. With the interactive page, you created a report tool with sorting, filtering, and formatting capabilities. Changes are retained during a browser session, so you can switch from the browser to other applications while you work with the spreadsheet in the browser.

Excel users will immediately know how to use most of the buttons on the Spreadsheet component toolbar, shown in Figure 15.2.

FIGURE 15.2   The Spreadsheet component toolbar provides spreadsheet functionality in a browser window.

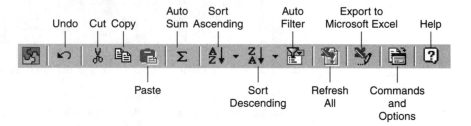

Most of the toolbar buttons are familiar. There are two additions: the Export To Excel button and the Commands And Options button. The Export To Excel button creates the Excel worksheet in a user-specified folder so the user can manipulate it as much as they wish without changing the original data in the web page. The Commands And Options button opens the Commands And Options dialog box with additional user tools, shown in Figure 15.3. Use this dialog box to change the format of a worksheet, work with formulas in the sheet, find worksheet data, and change worksheet and workbook options.

FIGURE 15.3 You change the format and other properties of component cells with the Commands And Options dialog box.

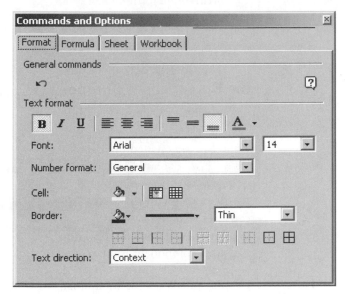

Because data values persist through a browser session, another good use of a spreadsheet component is to create a small application that collects values from a user, performs a few calculations, and then displays the results.

Publishing a Page with the Chart Component

The Chart component displays both the chart and the underlying data. Users manipulate the data to change the chart, just as they would in Excel. In Exercise 15.7, you'll learn how to publish an interactive chart page, using the 15-1 Risk and Rewards Plan.xls workbook you saved in the previous exercise.

EXERCISE 15.7

Publishing an Interactive Chart Page

1. In the 15-1 - Risk and Reward Plan.xls workbook, select the 1997 Expenses Chart worksheet.

EXERCISE 15.7 *(continued)*

2. Click once on the chart but outside the plot area to select the Chart Area. The name Chart_Area appears in the Name Box at the left end of the formula bar.

3. Choose File ➢ Save As Web Page to open the Save As dialog box.

4. In the Save section, choose the Selection: Chart option. Enable the Add Interactivity check box.

5. Select a Save In location and change the File Name entry to **1997 Expenses Chart**.

6. Click Publish to open the Publish As Web Page dialog box:

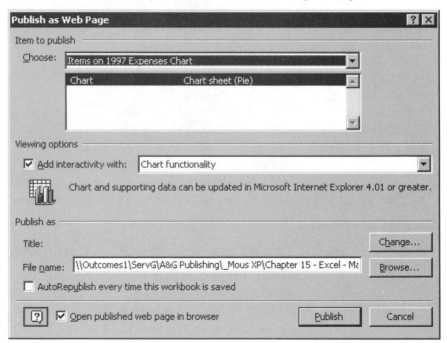

7. Click the Change button and change the page title to **Risks and Rewards 1997 Expenses**.

8. Click the Publish button to publish and open the web page, shown below:

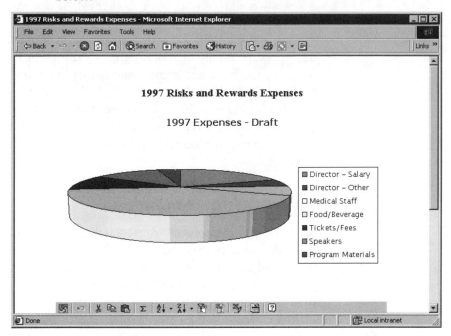

9. Close the browser and close the Excel workbook.

Don't spend a lot of time formatting your chart before publishing it. Most chart features are supported, but Drawing objects (such as callouts and other annotations) and the placement of chart elements are not. If, for example, you've neatly positioned the title and data labels and resized the plot area, you've wasted your time. They'll all snap back to their default positions in the Chart component. If you already have a published spreadsheet and you'd like to add another web component such as a chart or a pivot table to it, you can append the data to the existing page. To place a second component on a page, choose File ➢ Save As Web Page and then click Publish to reopen the Publish As Web Page dialog box. Enter the name of the existing HTML file in the File Name text box. When you click Publish, you'll be prompted to replace or add to the page. Choose Add To File to display more than one component on the page.

Managing Workbooks

The workbook is the basic storage unit in Excel. The number of workbooks you can open simultaneously is limited only by your computer's resources. While the default number of sheets in a new workbook is three, the number of sheets in a workbook is also limited only by system resources, primarily memory. Other workbook features including custom formats, toolbars, and menus, and names are likewise limited only by the available hardware. Workbooks "rule," so managing workbooks is a necessary skill in Excel 2002. In this section, you'll learn how to create new workbooks from templates, save all the open workbooks as a workspace, and summarize multiple worksheets in a workbook using a feature called *consolidation*.

Creating and Applying Templates

You can create a template from scratch or base it on an existing workbook. If you're using an existing workbook, first make sure that all the formulas work and that numbers and text are formatted appropriately. Remove the text and numbers that will be entered each time the template is used. Don't remove formulas—although the results of the formulas change, the formulas themselves remain the same. If you're creating a template from scratch, you still need to enter (and then remove) values to test the template's formulas before saving the template.

A template differs from a regular workbook in three specific ways:

- The file is saved as a template (.xlt file extension) rather than a regular workbook (.xls) so that Excel opens a copy when you use the template.

- The template is saved in the Templates folder or a shared folder for others to use.

- The workbook contains only the text, formulas, and formatting that remain the same in each workbook.

Every workbook and worksheet are based on a template. A template can include values, formulas, formatting, macros, and custom toolbars or form features. Workbooks created based on a template include the template's contents, so templates are the best way to make sure workbooks have a uniform look and feel. Template files use the file extension .xlt.

NOTE   The default workbook template (the Excel equivalent of Word's Normal.dot template) is Book.xlt; the default template for worksheets is Sheet.xlt.

Microsoft
Exam
Objective

Create, edit, and apply templates

Applying a Template

In the Exercise 15.8, you'll create a workbook using the Sales Invoice template that is included with Excel 2002.

EXERCISE 15.8

Applying a Template

For this exercise, you may be prompted to insert the Office XP CD if the Excel templates included with Office XP are not installed on your computer.

1. In Excel, choose File ➢ New to open the New Workbook task pane.

2. In the New From Template section, click the General Templates hyperlink to open the Templates dialog box. Click the Spreadsheet Solutions tab to view the Excel templates.

3. Double-click the Sales Invoice icon to create a new workbook named Sales Invoice1.xls based on the template. If the template is not installed, you'll be prompted to insert the Office XP CD.

4. Click the Insert Company Information Here text box.

5. Type your name or your organization name, and then hold Alt and press Enter to move to the next line.

6. Type your address, using Alt+Enter to move from the street address to the second line of the address.

7. Click the cell for the Invoice Number and enter **3300**.

8. Enter the following information in the Customer area:

   - Name: **Train2K.com**
   - Address: **607 Kensington Ave.**
   - City: **Flint**
   - State: **MI**
   - Phone: **(810) 555-3333**

9. Enter the following information in the Misc area:

   - Date: ***Today's date***
   - Order No.: **313**

10. In the body of the invoice, enter these two items:

    - Qty: **5**
    - Description: **Stick Pens (box 12)**
    - Unit Price: **7.99**
    - Qty: **2**
    - Description: **CD Spindle - 50**
    - Unit Price: **32.95**

11. Choose File ➢ Save As to save the invoice. Name the invoice **3300-Train2K**. Note that Excel applies the workbook file extension, .xls, to the file.

12. Close the invoice.

Editing a Template

If you're going to use a template frequently, it's tedious to enter the stock information—your company name and address, for example—each time you use the template. In Exercise 15.9, you'll edit the template and save it as a template, which you can use as the basis for future workbooks.

Editing and Saving a Template

1. In Excel, choose File ➢ New to open the New Workbook task pane.

2. In the New From Template section, click the General Templates hyperlink to open the Templates dialog box. Click the Spreadsheet Solutions tab.

3. Double-click the Sales Invoice icon to create a new workbook based on the template.

4. Click the Insert Company Information Here text box.

5. Type your name or your organization name, and then hold Alt and press Enter to move to the next line.

6. Type your address, using Alt+Enter to move from the street address to the second line of the address.

7. Choose File ➢ Save As from the menu.

8. Choose Template from the Save As Type drop-down list. Note that Excel changes the Save In location to the Templates folder, where Excel templates are stored.

9. Change the filename—for example, *YourCompanyName* Sales Invoice—to indicate that the template has been modified by adding your company information.

10. Close the template.

11. Choose File ➢ New to open the New Workbook task pane.

12. Click the General Templates hyperlink.

13. In the Templates dialog box, click the General tab.

14. Select and open your new template.

15. Close the file without saving the changes.

Creating a Template

Any workbook can be turned into a template, and your frequently created workbooks should be. Why create a new workbook that includes formatting, formulas, named ranges, charts, and other predictable elements each time you do the same basic task? Examine the Excel files on your drives to see how many of them are variations of the same few workbooks.

In Exercise 15.10, you'll create a new template using the Risk and Reward Plan workbook used earlier in this chapter.

EXERCISE 15.10

Creating a Template

1. Open the 15-1 - Risk and Reward Plan.xls workbook.

2. Select cell A3. Change "1997" to **Year.**

3. In row 5, change all occurrences of "1996" to **Prior Year** and "1997" to **Year.**

   You want to delete values that will change in each workbook but retain the formulas.

4. Select the range B7:D30.

5. Choose Edit ➢ Go To to open the Go To dialog box.

6. Click the Special button to open the Go To Special dialog box. Choose the Constants option:

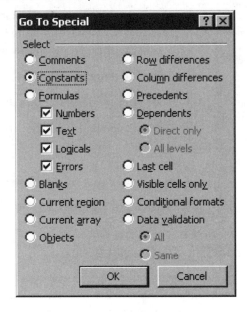

7. Click OK to select the cells in the range that do not contain formulas:

56	60	72
$30	$30	$35
16	18	18
$ 1,680	$ 1,800	$ 2,520
10,000	10,000	13,000
320	400	300
2,000	2,800	2,500
$ 14,000	$ 15,000	$ 18,320
$ 3,000	$ 3,000	$ 3,300
810	819	891
1,000	1,000	1,100
5,600	6,000	7,200
1,440	1,560	1,800
1,500	1,700	2,000
640	600	720
$ 13,990	$ 14,679	$ 17,011
$ 10	$ 321	$ 1,309

8. Press Delete or choose Edit ➢ Delete to delete the contents but preserve the formatting of the selected cells.

9. Choose File ➢ Save As from the menu.

10. In the Save As dialog box, choose Template as the file type.

11. Name the file **Risk and Rewards Planning**.

12. Click Save to save the template.

13. Close the template.

14. Choose File ➢ New and then open the template from the list of templates in the Templates dialog box. If you open the template from the list of recent files on the File menu, you're opening the template, not a new workbook based on the template.

15. Close the workbook without saving the changes.

Working with Workspaces

A workspace includes one or more worksheets opened simultaneously and saved as a group. The workspace file doesn't contain the workbooks;

instead, it contains the settings for each workbook, including print area, the size of each workbook's window, and display settings. When you open the workspace file, Excel opens each workbook in the workspace with the saved settings. When you're working on a project that involves two or more workbooks, save them as a workspace when you finish work for the day. When you want to resume work on the project, simply open the workspace.

Microsoft ✓ *Exam* *Objective*	**Create workspaces**

In Exercise 15.11, you'll learn how to create a workspace.

EXERCISE 15.11

Creating a Workspace

1. Open each of the workbooks you want to save in the workspace. For this exercise, open the following workbooks:

   15-1 - Risk and Reward Plan.xls, 15-8 Meeting Agenda.xls.

2. Arrange the workbooks the way they should appear when you open the workspace the next time. Choose Window ➤ Arrange to open the Arrange dialog box. Choose Horizontal.

3. Choose File ➤ Save Workspace from the menu to open the Save Workspace dialog box.

4. Enter a name for the workspace: **Resume**

   Workspace files are saved with the .xlw extension.

5. Click Save to save the workspace.

6. Hold Shift and choose File to open the File menu. Choose Close All.

   Holding Shift while you open the menu changes the default menu command, Close, to Close All.

7. Choose File ➤ Open or click the Open button.

8. Open the Resume.xlw workspace file.

9. Close the workspace.

Consolidating Data

If two or more worksheets have identical layouts or use the same row and column labels, you can consolidate them using the Consolidate command on the Data menu. You can use consolidation to, for example, summarize four quarterly worksheets, as you'll see in Exercise 15.12.

Microsoft ✓ *Exam* *Objective*	**Use data consolidation**

If two or more worksheets have identical row/column layouts, you can consolidate them into another worksheet using summary formulas with 3-D cell references, which are discussed in Chapter 12, "Enhancing and Revising Workbooks."

EXERCISE 15.12

Consolidating Data

1. Open the 15-12 - Quarterly Sales Summaries.xls workbook. The workbook contains five worksheets: a worksheet named Consolidation and four worksheets with the same labels and layout.

	A	B	C	D	E	F
1			**RetroLunch, Inc.**			
2			Quarterly Sales Summary			
3						
4			**Division**			
5			DVD	Video	CD	Tape	Totals
6	Rochester	3,300	1,980	3,960	1,782	**11,022**
7	New Albany	1,290	774	1,548	697	**4,309**
8	Worchester	1,311	787	1,573	708	**4,379**
9	Norwalk	1,923	1,154	2,308	1,038	**6,423**
10	Kingsley	950	570	1,140	513	**3,173**
11						
12	Totals	**8,774**	**5,264**	**10,529**	**4,738**	**29,305**
13						
14						
15						
16	Questions? Click to email the accounting staff.					

EXERCISE 15.12 *(continued)*

2. Select the Consolidation worksheet tab.

3. Select and delete the range B6:E10 in the Consolidation worksheet to remove the values.

4. Select cell B6.

5. Choose Data ➢ Consolidate from the menu to open the Consolidate dialog box.

6. Choose Sum from the Function drop-down list.

7. Click the Reference text box.

8. Click the Qtr1 sheet tab. Select the range B6:E10.

9. Click the Add button to add the range to the list of All References.

10. Click the Qtr2 tab. Click Add to add the same range from the Qtr2 worksheet.

11. Repeat steps 8 and 9 for the Qtr3 and Qtr4 worksheets.

12. Enable the Create Links To Source Data check box so that the Consolidation sheet will be automatically updated if any of the four underlying worksheets change.

13. Click OK to consolidate the worksheets.

14. Save and close the workbook.

Summary

This chapter has focused on the skills required to work on the "macro" level with Excel: importing and exporting to other file formats and the Web, creating and using templates, creating workspaces, and consolidating sheets. In the next chapter, you'll learn how to help ensure that the contents of those workbooks are accurate.

Chapter

16

Checking for Errors

MOUS EXCEL 2002 EXPERT EXAM OBJECTIVES COVERED IN THIS CHAPTER:

✓ **Audit formulas**

✓ **Locate and resolve errors**

✓ **Identify dependencies in formulas**

n this chapter, you'll learn to check worksheets for errors. You'll use the Auditing toolbar to audit worksheets, learn to locate errors, and find dependencies in formulas.

Before you begin this chapter, you should visit the Sybex website and download the file 4113Ch16.zip. This package contains the files necessary to complete some of the exercises in this chapter.

Auditing Formulas

Reviewing your data is important. But as with proofreading, it's difficult to catch all your own errors: It's easy to overlook errors because you "see" what you think should be there, rather than the actual contents. Excel includes tools that help you audit formulas to ensure your formulas are accurate.

Microsoft ✓ *Exam* *Objective*	**Audit formulas**

Formula auditing mode displays the worksheet formulas rather than the results of the formulas. In Exercise 16.1, you'll switch to formula auditing mode.

EXERCISE 16.1

Using Formula Auditing Mode

For this exercise, use the 16-1.xls workbook you downloaded from the Sybex website.

1. Open the 16-1.xls workbook.

2. Select any cell on the Error Worksheet sheet.

3. Choose Tools ➢ Formula Auditing ➢ Formula Auditing Mode to switch to formula auditing mode.

The formulas in the worksheet are displayed.

4. Hold Ctrl and press ` (to the left of the number 1 on the keyboard) to turn off formula auditing mode.

Leave the workbook open for the next exercise.

Other auditing and error-checking tools are found on the Formula Auditing toolbar, shown in Figure 16.1. The toolbar is not accessible from the list of toolbars on the shortcut menu; you turn it on from the Tools menu.

FIGURE 16.1 The Formula Auditing toolbar

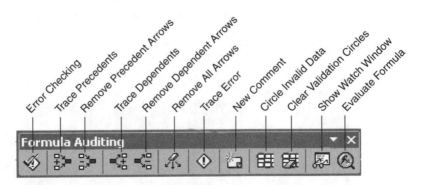

The Watch Window is a separate window that lets you see the formulas and the results in cells. With the Watch Window, you can see the results of several cells without scrolling to the cells. In Exercise 16.2, you'll turn on the Formula Auditing toolbar and use the Watch Window to watch several cells.

EXERCISE 16.2

Using the Watch Window

For this exercise, use the 16-1.xls workbook used in the previous exercise.

1. On the Error Worksheet sheet, select cell E4.

2. Choose Tools ➤ Formula Auditing ➤ Show Formula Auditing Toolbar to display the Formula Auditing Toolbar, shown previously in Figure 16.1.

3. Click the Show Watch Window button on the Formula Auditing toolbar to open the Watch Window.

4. Click the Add Watch button in the Watch Window to open the Add Watch dialog box:

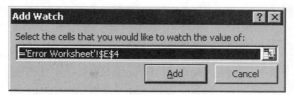

5. Click Add to add E4 to the Watch Window.

6. Repeat steps 4 and 5 to add cells E10, H4, and H11 to the Watch Window.

7. Select cell D4. Type **45** and press Enter.

The values of all four cells are updated in the Watch Window:

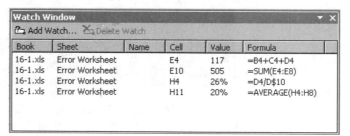

8. Close the Watch Window. Save the workbook. Leave it open for the next exercise.

Locating and Resolving Errors

Many errors are obvious in an Excel worksheet. Some errors appear with an error code. For example, when a numeric entry is wider than the column width, the number does not appear. Instead, Excel displays an error value, filling the cell with the # symbol to indicate that the number cannot be displayed in the current format and column width. Table 16.1 describes the Excel error values, conditions that cause the error value, and what you can do to fix the error. Error values with multiple causes are listed more than once in the table.

Microsoft ✓ *Exam* *Objective*	**Locate and resolve errors**

TABLE 16.1 Excel Error Values

Error Value	Common Causes	Corrective Action
#######	The column is not wide enough. Note: This error value is anomalous; when you select cells with errors, cells with this error are not selected.	Increase column width or switch to a more compact format (for example, omitting dollar signs).
#######	The cell contains a negative date or time.	If the content is a value, delete the minus symbol. If the content is a formula, check to ensure the result is greater than or equal to zero.
#VALUE!	One of the formula arguments is the incorrect type, for example, entering an IF formula where the first argument is text rather than a condition that returns TRUE or FALSE, or entering a range for a function that requires a single value.	If the formula is correct, use the Trace Precedents feature to locate the cells referenced in the formula. Check each precedent to make sure the data in the precedent cell is the required type for the argument.

TABLE   16.1   Excel Error Values *(continued)*

Error Value	Common Causes	Corrective Action
#DIV/0!	A formula is trying to divide by zero, an empty cell, or a nonnumeric entry, for example, =20/0 or =20/Jones. This error is often found in worksheets where formulas are entered prior to entering data. For example, if a formula divides each row into a total, the formula will return an error if the total is 0.	Use the Trace Precedents feature to find the precedent divisor (the number being "divided by"). If the formula points to the correct cell, and 0 (or blank) may be a legitimate entry in the cell, modify the formula by adding an IF function so that the division operation is completed only if the divisor is a nonzero value.
#NAME?	The formula includes unidentifiable text, often a misspelled function name, for example, =ABERAGE(B5:B10), or a range without the colon, such as B5B10 rather than B5:B10.	Select the formula. If it is a function, click the Insert Function button on the formula bar to see if the function name is spelled correctly or is identified as Undefined in the Function Arguments dialog box. Check each item in the formula to ensure that text entries are enclosed in quotation marks. If the formula includes a range name, choose Insert ➢ Name ➢ Define to double-check the name.
#NAME?	The workbook was created on another computer, and the cell includes a formula using a function that is not installed on your computer—usually a function from the Analysis Toolpak.	Choose Tools ➢ Add-Ins and install the Analysis Toolpak.
#NAME?	The formula relies on column or row labels, and support for labels in formulas is not turned on. This feature was turned on by default in Excel 2000 and is off by default in Excel 2002.	Examine the formula. If it uses column or row labels, either change the formulas or choose Tools ➢ Options to open the Options dialog box. On the Calculation tab, enable the Accept Labels In Formulas check box.

TABLE 16.1 Excel Error Values *(continued)*

Error Value	Common Causes	Corrective Action
#N/A	A value used by a lookup is blank. (See Chapter 18, "Making Excel Even Easier.")	If the cell contains a lookup function, use the Trace Precedents command to identify the cell's precedents. Make sure that the cell referred to in the first argument is not blank.
#N/A	Too few arguments are supplied for a function.	Click the Insert Function button on the formula bar to open the Function Arguments dialog box. Make sure you have entered all required (bold) arguments.
#N/A	A precedent cell has the error value #N/A.	Use the Trace Precedents command to examine all precedents.
#REF!	There is an invalid cell reference, often caused by deleting cells or pasting a selection over cells referred to in a formula.	If this just happened, click Undo. If it's too late to undo the change, you'll need to re-create the formula.
#NUM!	Text is used as an argument when a number is required.	Click the Insert Function button to open the Function Arguments dialog box. Examine the output at the right end of the text box for each argument to find the error.
#NUM!	A formula returns a number that is incredibly large or incredibly small that cannot be represented by Excel.	Change the formula.
#NULL!	A formula includes the intersection of two ranges that have no common cells, for example, =(B9:B10,C9:C10). This error is most often created when you insert a second range when editing an existing formula, rather than replacing the original range.	Use the range finder to identify the ranges in the formula. Modify the formula.

You can find and select all the error values in a worksheet using the Go To Special dialog box. Exercise 16.3 demonstrates how to find and select error values.

Finding and Selecting Error Values

For this exercise use the `16-1.xls` workbook saved in the previous exercise.

1. Select the `Error Worksheet` sheet.

2. Click the Select Worksheet button (in the upper-left corner of the worksheet) or hold Ctrl and press A to select the entire worksheet.

3. Choose Edit ➤ Go To to open the Go To dialog box.

4. Click the Special button to open the Go To Special dialog box.

5. Choose the Formulas option. Turn off the check boxes on Numbers, Text, and Logicals, leaving the Errors check box selected:

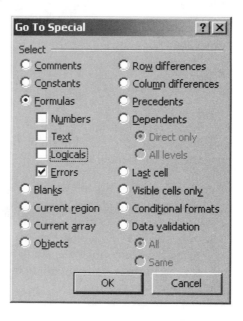

6. Click OK to select all cells with error values.

EXERCISE 16.3 *(continued)*

7. Click the down arrow on the Fill Color button on the Formatting toolbar. Apply a yellow fill to the selection.

8. Save the workbook. Leave it open for the next exercise.

Using the Formula Checker to Find Errors

Excel 2002 has an error checker for formulas. Like Word's grammar checker, the error checker works by applying rules to the formulas in the worksheet. By default, the error checker runs in the background as you enter formulas in the worksheet. If a formula violates one or more rules, a green triangle indicator appears in the upper-left corner of the cell. Select the cell, and an Error Options smart tag appears. Click the drop-down arrow on the Error Options tag to open a menu and deal with the error by selecting one of the menu options, including ignoring the error:

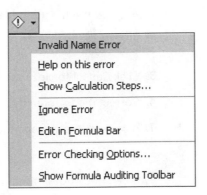

If you ignore the error, the Error Options tag is removed. In Exercise 16.4, you'll use the formula checker feature to find the errors in the worksheet.

EXERCISE 16.4

Finding Errors Identified by the Formula Checker

For this exercise, use the 16-1.xls workbook, which contains errors.

1. Select the Error Worksheet sheet. Select cell B10 with the #NAME? error.

EXERCISE 16.4 *(continued)*

2. Click the Insert Function button on the formula bar to open the Function Arguments dialog box:

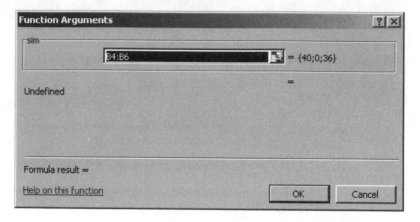

Notice that the function description reads "Undefined." This means that either the function name is misspelled or the function is not available to Excel.

3. Click Cancel to close the Function Arguments dialog box.

4. Correct the formula by changing "sim" to **sum**.

This corrects the dependent formulas in column F.

5. Select cell E5.

This cell does not contain an error value, but the formula checker indicator shows that the formula may be incorrect.

6. Point to the Error Options button, and click the down arrow to open the menu.

The menu is titled Inconsistent Formula. The formulas above and below this formula are the same, but this formula is different.

7. Choose Copy Formula From Above from the menu to correct the formula.

8. Save and close the workbook.

Finding Precedents and Dependents

Precedents are cells referred to in a formula. For example, if the active cell, E5, contains the formula =C5*D5, then cells C5 and D5 are precedents of E5. Dependents are cells that contain formulas that rely on another cell. In our example, E5 is a dependent of both C5 and D5. The next three exercises show you two ways to find precedents and one method to identify dependents.

When you create a formula, Excel color-codes each cell reference. When you double-click the cell, each referenced cell or range is bordered by a range finder of the same color as the reference in the formula. The range finder shows the immediate precedents for a cell.

Microsoft *Exam* *Objective*	**Identify dependencies in formulas**

In Exercise 16.5, you will use the range finder to find immediate precedents.

EXERCISE 16.5

Using the Range Finder to Find Immediate Precedents

1. Open 16-5.xls, which contains the Risk and Reward workbook.

2. Select cell B17. Double-click cell B17 to open the range finder:

	A	B	C	D
11	**Income**			
12	Participant Fees	$ 1,680	$ 1,800	$ 2,520
13	Grant Funding	10,000	10,000	13,000
14	T–Shirt Sales	320	400	300
15	Donations	2,000	2,800	2,500
17	**Total Income**	=SUM(B12:B15)		$ 18,320

Excel selects the immediate precedents for this cell: B12:B15.

3. Press Esc to close the range finder.

4. Double-click cell B30. The range finder selects the immediate precedents B17 and B28. Press Esc to close the range finder.

5. Keep the workbook open for the next exercise.

From this exercise, you know that one of the precedent cells for B30 is B17, which also has precedents. Excel includes other commands to expose multiple layers of precedents and dependents. In Exercise 16.6, you'll learn another method to find precedents.

EXERCISE 16.6

Finding Precedents

For this exercise, use the 16-5.xls workbook used in the previous exercise.

1. Select cell B17.

2. Choose Tools ➢ Formula Auditing ➢ Trace Precedents. Excel uses an arrow to trace the precedents for cell B17:

Income		
Participant Fees	$	1,680
Grant Funding		10,000
T–Shirt Sales		320
Donations		2,000
Total Income	$	14,000

3. Choose Tools ➢ Formula Auditing ➢ Remove All Arrows to turn off the tracing arrow.

4. Select cell B30.

5. Choose Tools ➢ Formula Auditing ➢ Trace Precedents to show the immediate precedents.

6. Choose Tools ➢ Formula Auditing ➢ Trace Precedents again to show the next level of precedents:

Income		
Participant Fees	$	1,680
Grant Funding		10,000
T–Shirt Sales		320
Donations		2,000
Total Income	$	14,000
Expenses		
Director – Salary	$	3,000
Director – Other		810
Medical Staff		1,000
Food/Beverage		5,600
Tickets/Fees		1,440
Speakers		1,500
Program Materials		640
Total Expenses	$	13,990
Net Gain/Loss	$	10

EXERCISE 16.6 *(continued)*

7. Choose Tools ➤ Formula Auditing ➤ Remove All Arrows to turn off the tracing arrows.

Leave the workbook open for the next exercise.

In Exercise 16.7, you'll use the Formula Auditing menu commands to identify dependents.

EXERCISE 16.7

Finding Dependents

For this exercise, use the 16-5.xls workbook used in the previous exercise.

1. Select cell B7.

2. Choose Tools ➤ Formula Auditing ➤ Trace Dependents. Excel uses an arrow to trace the three immediate dependents for cell B7:

Participants		56
Individual Fee		$30
Adult Volunteers		16
Income		
Participant Fees	$	1,680
Grant Funding		10,000
T-Shirt Sales		320
Donations		2,000
Total Income	$	14,000
Expenses		
Director – Salary	$	3,000
Director – Other		810
Medical Staff		1,000
Food/Beverage		5,600
Tickets/Fees		1,440
Speakers		1,500
Program Materials		640
Total Expenses	$	13,990
Net Gain/Loss	$	10

3. Choose Tools ➤ Formula Auditing ➤ Trace Dependents again to add the next level of dependents, cell B28.

EXERCISE 16.7 *(continued)*

4. Choose Tools ➢ Formula Auditing ➢ Trace Dependents again to add the next level of dependents, cell B30.

Participants		56
Individual Fee		$30
Adult Volunteers		16
Income		
Participant Fees	$	1,680
Grant Funding		10,000
T–Shirt Sales		320
Donations		2,000
Total Income	$	14,000
Expenses		
Director – Salary	$	3,000
Director – Other		810
Medical Staff		1,000
Food/Beverage		5,600
Tickets/Fees		1,440
Speakers		1,500
Program Materials		640
Total Expenses	$	13,990
Net Gain/Loss	$	10

5. Choose Tools ➢ Formula Auditing ➢ Trace Dependents again. No new dependents are displayed, so you have now traced all dependents.

6. Choose Tools ➢ Formula Auditing ➢ Remove All Arrows to turn off the tracing arrows.

7. Close the workbook.

There are other commands on the Formula Auditing toolbar that aren't discussed in this chapter but that are of great value. The Circle Invalid Data and Clear Validation Circles commands are used with data validation, which is discussed in Chapter 19, "Summarizing Data." The New Comment button inserts a comment in the active cell so you can make notes about the cell's formula or value.

The Evaluate Formula command is used with nested formulas to see how the formula is evaluated by Excel and is used to help "break down" a formula to find which part of the formula returns a result you may not anticipate.

Summary

This chapter introduced the tools used to locate and correct errors in Excel workbooks, including:

- Evaluating formulas
- Using the Watch Window
- Tracing precedents and dependents
- Finding and correcting errors

Automating and Customizing Excel

MOUS EXCEL 2002 EXPERT EXAM OBJECTIVES COVERED IN THIS CHAPTER:

- ✓ Create and apply custom number formats
- ✓ Use conditional formats
- ✓ Customize toolbars and menus
- ✓ Create, edit, and run macros

Excel 2002 is more than just a spreadsheet, chart creator, or data analysis tool. This chapter focuses on some of the most powerful Excel tools: the tools that allow you to customize and automate Excel, redefining the application so that the tasks you perform frequently can be performed more efficiently. The chapter begins with two types of formatting: custom (user-defined) number formatting and conditional formatting. Then you'll learn to record, edit, and run macros, which are programming code you create and use to automate tasks in Excel. The last section of the chapter focuses on customizing toolbars and menus to run Excel's built in commands and macros that you've created.

NOTE Before you begin this chapter, you should visit the Sybex website and download the file 4113Ch17.zip. This package contains the files necessary to complete some of the exercises in this chapter. Other files show the documents after the exercise has been successfully completed. These files are affixed with the word *Post*.

Advanced Number Formatting

Excel includes lots of number formats. Currency, Comma, and Percent formats are available on the Formatting toolbar, and you apply additional formatting choices from Number tab of the Format Cells dialog box. You use custom formatting to create additional number formats based on the formats included in Excel. Conditional formatting is a different beast altogether. You apply conditional formatting to have Excel apply text formatting based on a cell value or formula.

Creating Custom Formats

Custom formats are number formats created using placeholders. If the Format Cells dialog box doesn't include the number format you need, you can create a custom format.

Microsoft ✓ *Exam* *Objective*	**Create and apply custom number formats**

We've found a number of uses for custom formats, including the following:

- For a real estate appraisal firm, a format that includes the text "/sq ft": for example, "$15.51/sq ft"

- A format that omits the last three digits of a number to present budget figures in thousands of dollars (e.g., 1,500,000 as 1,500) or omits the last six digits for figures in millions

- A format that appends the text "Net Gain" to a positive number and "(Net Loss)" to a negative number for use in income statements

Custom formats are created by stringing together codes, shown in Table 17.1. Each code is a placeholder for a digit or character. If a number has more digits to the right of the decimal than there are placeholders, the number will be rounded so it fits the number of placeholders. For example, if the format has two placeholders to the right of the decimal, 5.988 will be rounded to 5.99.

TABLE 17.1   Custom Format Codes

Code	Use	Example
#	Displays significant digits.	###.## formats 3.50 as 3.5 and 3.977 as 3.98.
0	Displays all digits; placeholders to the right of the decimal are filled with trailing zeros if required.	##0.00 formats 3.5 as 3.50 and 57.1 as 57.10.

TABLE 17.1 Custom Format Codes *(continued)*

Code	Use	Example
?	Displays significant digits and aligns decimal or slash placeholders.	???.?? displays 3.50 as 3.5, 57.10 as 57.1, and 3.977 as 3.98, and aligns decimals.
/	Displays a number as a fraction.	# ??/?? displays 7.5 as 7 1/2.
,	Thousands separator, also used to format numbers as if they were divided by a thousand or a million.	##,### displays 99999 as 99,999. ##, displays 9,000 as 9. ##,, displays 9,000,000 as 9.
( )	Parentheses, usually used to format negative numbers.	(##,###) formats -99999 as (99,999).
-	Hyphen, used to place a hyphen in a number.	000-000 formats 123456 as 123-456.
" "	Indicates a text string.	### "/per hour" formats 100 as 100/per hour.

Excel differentiates between significant digits and insignificant digits. A significant digit is part of a number's "real value." In the value 3.70, the 3 and 7 are significant; the zero is an insignificant digit because removing it doesn't change the real value of the number. Only zeros can be insignificant. Insignificant zeros after the decimal are called trailing zeros. The # placeholder hides insignificant zeros. The 0 placeholder displays them.

A number format includes up to four sections separated by semicolons. Each section is composed of the codes listed in Table 17.1. The first section is applied to positive numbers and the second to negative numbers. The third section is applied to only one value: zero. The fourth section is used to specify a format for text. The syntax for a complete format is positive_format;negative_format;zero_format;text_format.

This is the format that's used when you apply the Accounting format with two decimal places:

_($* #,##0.00_);_($* (#,##0.00);_($* "-"??_);_(@_)

When Excel applies this format, the following values are used:

- _($* #,##0.00_) is used for positive numbers.

- _($* (#,##0.00) is used for negative numbers.

- _($* "-"??_) is used for the value 0.

- _(@_) is used to format text entries.

You don't need to create all four sections of a format. If there's only one section, it is applied to all numbers. If you want to skip a section (to create, for example, a format that includes only sections for numbers and text), be sure to include the semicolons that let Excel know what each section is used for.

In Exercise 17.1, you'll see how to create a custom format.

EXERCISE 17.1

Creating a Custom Format

In this exercise, you'll create custom formats that will display two decimal places for positive numbers but no decimal places for negative numbers.

1. Open a new workbook.

2. Enter the following values:

   - A1: **-55.75**

   - A2: **0**

   - A3: **6.375**

   - B3: **8.1256**

   - C3: **12**

   - A4: **300.5**

   - A5: **300.05**

   - A6: **3000.005**

   - A7: **3000000**

- A8: **5500000**

- A9: **String**

- A10: **Another String**

3. Select A1:C10.

4. Choose Format ≻ Cells to open the Format Cells dialog box.

5. On the Number tab, choose the format that most closely resembles the format you want to create: Number, 2 Decimal Places, with a comma as the thousands separator and a minus sign preceding negative values.

6. Select Custom from the Category list. The format #,##0.00 is placed in the Type text box.

This custom format has only one section, which will be applied to all numbers. The format requires one digit prior to the decimal and two after it.

7. In the Type text box, click at the right end of the format and add the following section for negative numbers: ;-#,##0

As you enter the format, the Sample reflects your changes.

8. Click OK to create the custom format and apply it to the selection.

Leave the workbook open for the next exercise.

When you're comfortable with the codes, you can skip step 5 of the previous exercise. Just choose Custom from the Category list, select the currently active format in the Type text box, and begin typing a format from scratch.

Custom formats are saved in the workbook, so you don't need to re-create a format that you've used elsewhere in the workbook. The formats you've created are shown at the bottom of the Custom Type list. To delete a custom format, select it from the Type list, and then click the Delete button in the Format Cells dialog box.

You can add one of eight colors to a format. The colors come from the two default RGB color palettes used in old PC applications, so for some of us, these colors are a trip down memory lane. Don't smack your monitor—that's really what green used to look like. You type the name of the color in brackets at the beginning of the format: [BLUE], [GREEN], [RED], [MAGENTA], [CYAN], [YELLOW], [BLACK], or [WHITE]. Type the color code at the beginning of the format: for example, [BLUE]00.0;[RED]00.0 to format positive numbers blue and negative numbers red.

You can enter a condition in brackets, followed by the two formats to be used based on whether the condition is true or false. A common use for a conditional custom format is formatting U. S. zip codes when some have nine digits and others have five. The condition [>99999] will be true for nine-digit zip codes, so the format [>99999]00000-0000;00000 will format both nine-digit and five-digit zip codes correctly, including leading zeros.

Spacing Codes

You'll use spacing codes for two reasons: alignment and filling. In some formats, negative numbers are surrounded by parentheses. If you use parentheses in a custom format, you need to add a space to the end of the positive format that will line up with the right parenthesis in a negative value. (This keeps the decimal points aligned.) To create a one-character space in a format, include an underscore, for example ##,##0.00_.

You can fill any empty space in a cell by entering an asterisk (*) and then a fill character in the number format. For example, the accounting format begins with an underscore and a dollar sign, followed by an asterisk and a space before the digit placeholders: _$* #,##0.00. The underscore ensures that the dollar sign is one space from the left edge of the cell. The asterisk and space ensure that all the room between the dollar sign and digits is filled with spaces.

Codes for Dates and Times

Use the format codes shown in Table 17.2 to create date and time formats. The *m* code is used for both months and minutes. Excel treats the *m* as a month code unless it appears directly after a code for hours or before a code for seconds.

If you don't include one of the versions of am/pm, Excel bases time on the 24-hour clock.

TABLE 17.2 Date and Time Format Codes

Code	Use	Examples
m	Months as ##	Formats January as 1 and December as 12.
mm	Months as 00	Formats January as 01 and December as 12.
mmm	Months as three-letter abbreviation	Formats January as Jan.
mmmm	Month named spelled out	Formats Jan as January.
mmmmm	Month's first letter	Formats January as J and December as D.
d	Days as ##	Formats 1 as 1 and 31 as 31.
dd	Days as 00	Formats 1 as 01 and 31 as 31.
ddd	Days as weekday abbreviation	Formats 1/1/99 as Fri.
dddd	Days as weekday	Formats 1/1/99 as Friday.
yy	Years as 00	Formats 1999 as 99.
yyyy	Years as 0000	Formats 1/1/99 as 1999.
h, m, s	Hours, minutes, and seconds as ##	Formats 3 as 3.
hh, mm, ss	Hours, minutes, and seconds as 00	Formats 3 as 03.
AM/PM	12-hour clock, uppercase	H AM/PM formats 3 as 3 AM.
am/pm	12-hour clock, lowercase	hh am/pm formats 3 as 03 am.
a/p	12-hour clock, short form	hh:mm a/p formats 3 as 3:00 a.

In Exercise 17.2, you'll see how to create a custom date format.

EXERCISE 17.2

Creating a Custom Date Format

Excel doesn't include a number format with four-digit years that also uses two digits for all month and day numbers: 01 for January, 02 for February, and so on. In this exercise, you'll create and apply such a format; for example, the date March 8, 1957 will be formatted 03/08/1957.

1. In the workbook used in Exercise 17.2, enter the following values:

   - A11: **3/8/1957**

   - A12: **2/28/1946**

   - A13: **5/5/1955**

2. Select A11:A13.

3. Choose Format ➢ Cells to open the Format Cells dialog box.

4. On the Number tab, choose the short date format from the Date Category that includes leading zeros: 03/14/01.

5. Choose Custom in the Category list. The format mm/dd/yy;@ appears in the Type text box.

6. Edit the format, changing the yy for year to **yyyy** for a four-digit year.

7. Click OK to create and apply the custom format to the selection.

Leave the workbook open for the next exercise.

Codes for Text

If you want to include text along with a number in a cell, put quotes around the text string. If you want to include a format for text entered in a cell, make it the final section in your format. If you don't include a text format, text entered in the cell is formatted according to the defaults or the formatting applied with the toolbar and Format Cells dialog box. In Exercise 17.3, you'll create a custom format with text.

EXERCISE 17.3

Creating a Custom Format with Text

In this exercise, we'll create a custom format that appends the label /pound to the number that appears in a cell.

1. Select cells A3:C3.

2. Right-click the selection and choose Format Cells from the short-cut menu.

3. Select the Number category, and set 2 decimal places.

4. Choose Custom in the Category list. The format 0.00 appears in the Type text box.

5. Add the text **"/pound"** after the existing format: 0.00**"/pound"**

6. Click OK to create and apply the format.

7. Save and close the workbook.

Using Conditional Formatting

With *conditional formatting*, you can apply formats to selected cells based on a condition. You can apply font attributes, borders, or patterns to cells based on whether the condition is true or false to highlight, for example, above-average performance or dates outside a specified range. Conditional formatting is one of Excel's more amazing features. Before conditional formatting became available, users would manually format worksheets, selecting, for example, each cell with a value over 200 and applying a fill or border. Of course, when the values changed, the user had to unformat some cells and apply formatting to others. With conditional formatting, the formatting is automatically applied or removed when the value changes.

Microsoft ✓ ***Exam*** ***Objective***   **Use conditional formats**

There are two types of conditional formats: formatting based on a cell value and formatting based on a formula.

Conditional formatting overrides other formatting of the same type in a cell. If, for example, you create a custom format that includes colors, they will be replaced with colors in a conditional format whenever the condition is met.

In Exercise 17.4, you will apply conditional formatting based on cell value.

EXERCISE 17.4

Conditional Formatting Based on Cell Value

For this exercise, you'll use the 17-4.xls workbook you downloaded from the Sybex website. You'll apply a conditional format to the higher cost items in the list.

1. Open the workbook. The workbook contains macros, so you may be prompted to enable macros.

2. Select cells E5:E22, the Unit Cost values.

3. Choose Format ≻ Conditional Formatting from the menu bar to open the Conditional Formatting dialog box:

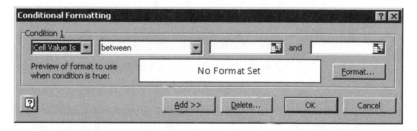

4. You want to format cells based on the values in the cells, so choose Cell Value Is in the first drop-down list.

5. In the second drop-down list, choose Greater Than.

6. In the Condition text box, enter **10**.

The format will be applied to cells with a value greater than 10.

7. Click the Format button to open the Format Cells dialog box.

EXERCISE 17.4 *(continued)*

8. On the Patterns tab, choose the Yellow fill in the second row from the bottom of the palette.

9. On the Font tab, set the Font Style to Bold.

10. Click OK to close the dialog box and return to the Conditional Formatting dialog box.

11. Click OK to apply the conditional formatting to the selection.

12. Save the workbook and leave it open for the next exercise.

You can apply up to three conditional formats to a cell. When you apply the formats, Excel works down the list in order. If the cell's value meets the first condition, Excel applies the first condition and ignores the second and third conditions. If the cell's value does not meet the first condition, Excel tests the value against the second condition and, if it fails that test, then the third. In Exercise 17.5, you'll modify the conditional format to apply one of two formats to the selected cells.

EXERCISE 17.5

Modifying and Deleting a Conditional Format

This exercise also uses the 17-4.xls workbook.

1. Select E5:E22.

2. Choose Format ➢ Conditional Formatting to open the Conditional Formatting dialog box.

3. The condition you created in Exercise 17.4 is displayed.

4. Click the Add button to add another condition.

5. Choose Greater Than in the second drop-down list for the second condition.

6. Enter **5** in the Condition 2 text box.

7. Click the Format button in the Condition 2 section to open the Format Cells dialog box.

EXERCISE 17.5 *(continued)*

8. On the Patterns tab, choose a green fill on the bottom row of the palette. Click OK to return to the Conditional Formatting dialog box.

9. Click OK to apply the conditional format. Examine the results.

10. Select E5:E22.

11. Choose Format ➢ Conditional Formatting to open the Conditional Formatting dialog box.

12. Click the Delete button to open the Delete Conditional Format dialog box:

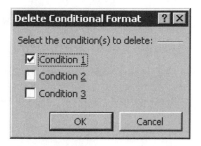

13. Select the Condition 1 check box. Do not select Condition 2.

14. Click OK to close the dialog box, and then click OK again to close the Conditional Formatting dialog box. Examine the results.

15. Save the workbook. Leave it open for the next exercise.

You don't have to apply conditional formatting to all the cells in a range at once. Create one or more conditional formats for a single cell and tweak them until they're exactly what you want, and then select the entire range you want to format, including the formatted cell. Choose Format ➢ Conditional Formatting, and the dialog box will open, displaying the format you created. Just click OK, and the format will be adjusted and applied to the other selected cells.

Using Formulas As Conditions

Now you can add one more flourish, very useful in databases like the Aurora Borealis Writeoffs workbook: You can compare a cell to a formula. In the Conditional Formatting dialog box, you can use the Formula Is option, rather than Cell Value Is, when you want to format all the cells in a row based on the value in one cell.

For example, in the Aurora Borealis Writeoffs workbook, you can apply a fill color format to all the rows in the list where Damaged is the reason for the write-off. This is even more useful when the data is wider than a single screen—the formatting is visible even when the user scrolls past the cell that the formatting is based on. In Exercise 17.6, you'll apply conditional formatting based on a formula.

EXERCISE 17.6

Conditional Formatting Based on a Formula

For this exercise, use the 17-4.xls workbook.

1. Select A5:G22—the database without the column labels.

2. Choose Format ➢ Conditional Formatting.

3. Select the Formula Is format type from the first drop-down list.

4. Click the text box. Type an equal sign: =

Even though the entire database is selected, you are building the condition for the first row, row 5.

5. Click cell F5.

6. Click at the right end of the text box and add ="**Damaged**".

When you create a conditional format, Excel automatically makes all references absolute references, so when you click F5, Excel enters $F$5. This works for the first row but not for rows 6, 7, 8, and so on. You must modify the reference so the row number changes when the format is applied to the other rows.

7. Delete the $ symbol between the F and 5 in the formula. The completed formula looks like this: =$F5="Damaged"

When the formula is applied to the entire database, it will always refer to column F ($F), but the row number in the cell address will be relative.

8. Click the Format button to open the Format Cells dialog box.

9. On the Patterns tab, choose a light blue color.

10. Click OK to close the Format Cells dialog box and return to the Conditional Formatting dialog box.

11. Click OK to apply the format. Save and close the workbook.

The criteria formula can include functions. For example, you can use the TODAY function to format cells or database rows that contain the current date: =$A5=TODAY( ), where A5 is the first cell in the column of dates.

Creating Macros in Excel

Macros are programs that perform a series of steps. Macros are written in the Visual Basic for Applications programming language, but you don't need to be a programmer to write macros. In Excel 2002, as in Word, PowerPoint, and previous versions of Excel, you can use the Macro Recorder to create macros. You turn on the recorder, complete the steps you want to repeat, and save the macro. The next time you need to complete the steps, you "play back" the steps by running the macro. In this section, you'll record, edit, and play back macros.

Microsoft ✓ *Exam Objective*   **Create, edit, and run macros**

Recording a Macro

Before recording a macro, you should practice the steps you want to record, because once you begin recording, *all* your actions are recorded. Take note of the conditions your macro will operate under and set up those conditions. Will you always use the macro in a specific workbook? If so, open the workbook. Will the macro always be used to change or format a selected range?

Then have a range selected before you begin recording the macro, just as you will when you run the macro later.

Naming Macros

When you create a macro, you must name it. Here are the rules and some suggestions about naming macros:

- The default macro name is Macro1 just as the name of a blank workbook is Book1.

- Visual Basic names, including macro names, can be up to 255 characters long, and they can contain numbers, letters, and underscores but not spaces or other punctuation.

- Names must begin with a letter and can include numbers and letters.

Visual Basic will preserve your capitalization style, but it is not case sensitive: It won't recognize FixMyName and fixmyname as different names.

If your organization uses a naming convention, you'll probably prefix the macro name with mcr for macro or bas for Visual Basic code. Check the standards for your organization to determine the appropriate prefix.

Storing Macros

When you create a macro, you select a workbook where you want to store the macro. The storage location determines how you'll be able to access and run the macro later:

- If you select the current workbook (or another workbook), the macro will be directly available only in that workbook. If you want to use the same macro somewhere else, you'll have to copy or re-create it or insert Visual Basic code that loads the workbook before the macro can be run. Macros that are stored in a workbook or template are called *local macros*.

- Storing an Excel macro in the Personal Macro Workbook creates a *global macro*, which is available to all workbooks you create in Excel.

If you're not sure where to store a macro, err on the conservative side and store it locally. While global macros are convenient, all global macros are loaded each time you launch Excel, consuming valuable resources. And macro names you use globally can't be reused in individual workbooks. Unless a macro is going to be widely used, it's best to store it locally.

Assigning a Shortcut Key

In the Record Macro dialog box, you can assign a shortcut keystroke combination to a macro. In practice, this is not a very good idea; most of the Ctrl combinations and many of the Ctrl+Shift combinations are already in use. It is better practice to assign frequently used macros to a menu or a toolbar button; you have more control over menus and toolbars, which can be turned on and off programmatically. However, you may be asked to assign a macro to a shortcut key on the exam.

In Exercise 17.7, you'll learn how to create local and global macros.

EXERCISE 17.7

Recording Macros

In this exercise, you will create two macros: The first, a local macro, sorts the database by the Reason column. The second macro, a global macro, applies formatting to a selected range so you can easily apply the same format to titles in all worksheets.

Before beginning the exercise, you need to check the security level in Excel to make sure you can open workbooks that contain macros. Choose Tools ➤ Macro ➤ Security. On the Security Level tab, choose the Medium option and then click OK.

For this exercise, use the 17-4.xls workbook used in previous exercises.

1. Select any cell in the database.

2. Choose Tools ➤ Macro ➤ Record New Macro from the menu to open the Record Macro dialog box:

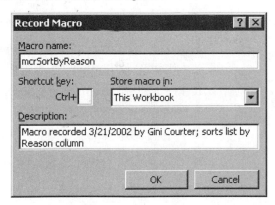

EXERCISE 17.7 *(continued)*

3. Enter **mcrSortByReason** as the macro name.

4. Modify the description by appending the following text: **; sorts list by Reason column**

5. In the Store Macro In drop-down list, select This Workbook.

6. Do not set a shortcut key.

7. Click the OK button to begin macro recording.

The message *Recording* is displayed at the left end of the status bar, and the Stop Recording toolbar opens. You may have to look for it—it's a small toolbar with just two buttons.

8. Choose Data ➢ Sort from the menu.

9. In the Sort By drop-down list, choose Reason.

10. Click OK.

11. Click the Stop Recording button on the Stop Recording toolbar:

The Stop Recording toolbar closes.

12. Select cell A1.

13. Choose Tools ➢ Macro ➢ Record New Macro from the menu to open the Record Macro dialog box.

14. Enter **mcrFormatTitle** as the macro name.

15. Modify the description by appending the following text: **Applies company formatting for titles.**

16. In the Store Macro In drop-down list, select Personal Macro Workbook.

17. Enter **t** as the shortcut key.

18. Click the OK button to begin macro recording.

EXERCISE 17.7 *(continued)*

The message *Recording* is displayed at the left end of the status bar, and the Stop Recording toolbar opens.

19. Choose Format ➢ Cells to open the Format Cells dialog box.

20. On the Font tab, choose the Tahoma font, size 12, Dark Red color.

21. On the Alignment tab, choose Left (Indent) Horizontal Alignment.

22. Click OK to close the dialog box.

23. Click the Stop Recording button on the Stop Recording toolbar.

When you format text in a macro, choose the formatting options from a Format dialog box rather than clicking toolbar buttons to select font style and alignment. If you use the toggle buttons, the results when you run the macro are unpredictable: If, for example, selected cells are already italicized, clicking the Italics button turns italics off.

Absolute and Relative Cell References in Macros

In Excel macros, all cell references are absolute by default. If you click a cell during macro recording, the macro will select that cell each time you play it back. This is not always useful. For example, you might want the macro to format selected cells and move to the cell below the selection. For example, when you record the macro, the cell below the selection is J22. But each time you play the macro, you don't want Excel to select J22; you want to select the cell below the cells you just formatted.

To use relative cell references, click the Relative References button on the Stop Recording toolbar. The macro will record references relative to the current cell until you click the button again to turn relative references off. Then you can record other actions using absolute references.

Editing Macros

Excel 2002 macros are written in the Visual Basic programming language and are directly accessible in the Visual Basic Editor. The Visual Basic Editor (also called the Integrated Development Environment, or IDE) is shown in Figure 17.1.

FIGURE 17.1   The Visual Basic IDE includes a code window, the Project Explorer, and a Properties window.

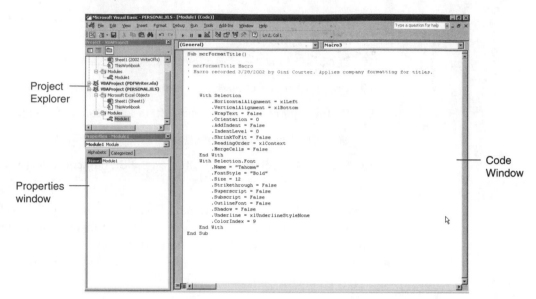

In Figure 17.1, the Project Explorer and Properties window are open to the left of the Code Window. The Project Explorer shows all the open VBA projects. Every workbook can have one VBA project associated with it; the project is stored with the workbook. Projects contain *Application objects* (worksheets and a workbook) and one or more *modules*. A module is a container for VB code. Each macro you create with the Macro Recorder is placed in a new module. Projects can include other types of objects, including forms for user interaction and references to templates or other documents.

The Properties window displays the properties for the object selected in the Project Explorer.

The Code Window displays code from the active component in the Project Explorer, and it's where you actually edit your macros. Double-click a module or select the module and click the View Code button in the Project Explorer to display the module's code in the Code Window. The green lines of code that begin with apostrophes (') are *remarks* that explain the code. The code itself is displayed in the default text color, black.

In Exercise 17.8, you will edit the second macro you created.

EXERCISE 17.8

Editing a Macro

For this exercise, you can use any open workbook. The macro you are editing is a global macro, so it is accessible whenever an Excel workbook is open. There's only one catch...the Personal Macro Workbook is hidden.

1. Choose Window ➢ Unhide to open the Unhide dialog box:

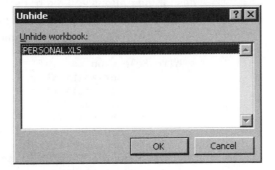

2. Choose PERSONAL.XLS and click OK to unhide the Personal Macro Workbook.

Excel opens the PERSONAL.XLS workbook.

3. Choose Tools ➢ Macro ➢ Macros to open the Macro dialog box:

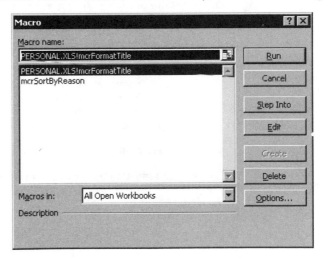

EXERCISE 17.8 *(continued)*

4. Select the PERSONAL.XLS!mcrFormatTitle macro and click the Edit button to open the Visual Basic Editor.

The selected macro appears in the Code Window. The macro begins with the word Sub followed by the macro name and ends with End Sub. When you use the Macro Recorder, it records every setting on every tab you use in a dialog box, so the macro includes lots of extra code describing options you did not set in the macro. For example, you selected only one option on the Alignment tab: left horizontal alignment. However, the Macro Recorder captured every setting on that tab:

```
With Selection
        .HorizontalAlignment = xlLeft
        .VerticalAlignment = xlBottom
        .WrapText = False
        .Orientation = 0
        .AddIndent = False
        .IndentLevel = 0
        .ShrinkToFit = False
        .ReadingOrder = xlContext
        .MergeCells = False
    End With
```

When you play the macro, it will change all these settings, which could remove formatting you want to keep.

5. Using the mouse, carefully select these lines in the Code Window:

```
        .VerticalAlignment = xlBottom
        .WrapText = False
        .Orientation = 0
        .AddIndent = False
        .IndentLevel = 0
        .ShrinkToFit = False
        .ReadingOrder = xlContext
        .MergeCells = False
```

6. Press Delete on your keyboard to delete the extra lines.

Extra code was also generated on the Font tab.

7. Using the mouse, select these lines in the Code Window:

```
        .Strikethrough = False
        .Superscript = False
```

```
.Subscript = False
.OutlineFont = False
.Shadow = False
.Underline = xlUnderlineStyleNone
```

8. Press Delete on your keyboard to delete the extra lines. The edited code looks like this:

```
Sub mcrFormatTitle()
'
' mcrFormatTitle Macro
' Description that includes your name, etc.
'
'
    With Selection
        .HorizontalAlignment = xlLeft
    End With
    With Selection.Font
        .Name = "Tahoma"
        .FontStyle = "Bold"
        .Size = 12
        .ColorIndex = 9
    End With
End Sub
```

9. Choose File ➢ Close And Return To Microsoft Excel to save your changes, close the VB IDE, and return to Excel.

Running a Macro

Excel takes control when you run a macro. You can't enter text or choose menu options while the macro is executing. When the macro has finished playing, Excel will return control to you. It's a good idea to save any open workbooks before you run a new macro. If you've made a mistake during recording, the playback results may not be what you expected.

 If there is an error, you can record the macro again using the same name or delete the macro in the Macro dialog box. You may also have to click Undo a few times to back out of any problems the macro created.

In Exercise 17.9, you'll practice running a macro you created.

EXERCISE 17.9

Running Macros

For this exercise, use the 17-4.xls workbook.

1. Select any cell in the database.

2. Sort the database by date in ascending order.

3. Choose Tools ➢ Macro ➢ Macros to open the Macro dialog box.

4. Select the mcrSortByReason macro from the list.

5. Click the Run button.

The macro executes, and the list is sorted by the Reason column.

6. Select cell A2.

7. Choose Tools ➢ Macro ➢ Macros to open the Macro dialog box.

8. Select the mcrFormatTitle macro.

9. Click Run.

The macro executes, formatting the second line of the title.

10. Select cell A2. Change the font to Times New Roman and the font size to 18.

11. Hold Ctrl and press **t**, the shortcut combination for mcrFormatTitle.

The macro executes, and the second line of the title is formatted.

12. On the Window menu, choose the Personal.xls workbook.

13. Choose Window ➢ Hide to rehide the workbook.

When a macro doesn't end on its own, you need to be able to terminate it. If you need to stop a macro during execution, press Ctrl+Break. A Visual Basic dialog box will open, offering you options to end program execution or debug the macro in the Visual Basic Editor.

Opening a File That Contains Macros

If you can add code to an Excel workbook, so can the people who write viruses. Viruses are self-replicating programs. When you open a workbook that contains a virus, the virus copies its code into the default Excel template, effectively becoming a global virus. From that point forward, every workbook you save using the template will be infected, which means that every file you give to someone else on a disk or via the Internet will also contain the virus.

Office XP does not include virus-detection software; you're responsible for installing anti-virus software on your computer. However, Excel scans workbooks to see if they contain macros. (The exception is macros that have a Visual Basic signature that can be authenticated by Excel.) Based on your security settings, Excel 2002 disables the macros (High security), notifies you that the workbook has macros (Medium security), or does nothing (Low security). With security set at Medium, you'll be prompted to choose an action when opening a workbook that contains unsigned macros:

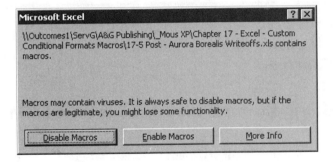

Decide whether you want to open the workbook with macros enabled or to disable them. (Clicking the More Information button doesn't give you more information about the macros in the workbook; it opens the Excel help topic on macros and security.)

If you know that the workbook contains macros that you or a coworker put there, choose Enable. If, on the other hand, you received the workbook unsolicited in an e-mail message from a friend who just loves to pass along the latest hot item from the Internet, you should disable the macros or simply delete the file. Disabling the macros gives you an opportunity to look at them in the Visual Basic Editor without endangering your computer. If you decide the macros are legitimate, close the Visual Basic Editor, reopen the workbook, and choose Enable Macros.

To change your security level, choose Tools ➤ Macros ➤ Security.

Customizing Toolbars and Menus

Part of what makes Excel a powerful application is the fact that it can be customized. You can make Excel work better for you by changing the interface to reflect the way you work—the buttons you use, the menu selections you need to see. In this section, you'll learn how to customize toolbars and menus to reflect your work style and preferences. You'll also find out how to run the macros you created in this chapter from toolbars and menus rather than using the Macro dialog box.

Microsoft *Exam* *Objective*	**Customize toolbars and menus**

Adding Commands to Toolbars and Menus

From Excel's point of view, there are few differences between menus and toolbars. Menus and toolbars are both members of the command bar family of objects. Menu items and toolbar buttons are generically referred to as commands or command items. From the user's point of view, there is one major difference between the menu bar and toolbars: You can hide toolbars, but you can't hide the menu bar.

For the exercises in this section, you'll use a blank workbook and the 17-4.xls workbook used earlier in this chapter. In Exercise 17.10, you'll add commands to a toolbar and menu.

EXERCISE 17.10

Adding Commands to a Toolbar and Menu

1. Open a new workbook.

2. Choose View ➤ Toolbars ➤ Customize, or Tools ➤ Customize to open the Customize dialog box. Click the Commands tab.

EXERCISE 17.10 *(continued)*

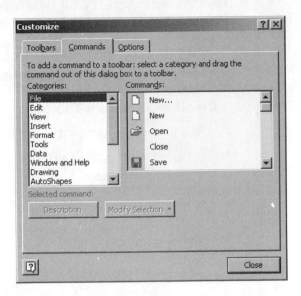

3. Choose the Edit category. Scroll down the Commands list to Select Visible Cells.

4. Drag the Select Visible Cells command from the Commands list and drop it near the middle of the Formatting toolbar.

5. Drag Select Current Region from the Commands list. Point to the Edit menu and pause for the menu to open.

6. Drop the command on the menu directly above the Fill command.

7. Close the Customize dialog box. Open the Edit menu to view the Select Current Region command.

8. Right-click the Standard toolbar and choose Customize from the shortcut menu.

9. Drag the Select Visible Cells button from the Formatting toolbar and drop it in the worksheet to remove it from the toolbar.

10. Open the Edit menu. Drag the Select Current Region button into the worksheet and drop it to remove the command from the menu.

11. Click Close to close the Customize dialog box.

12. Close the workbook without saving the changes.

Creating a Custom Toolbar

If you have a number of buttons you want to add to toolbars, it makes sense to create a custom toolbar with the buttons you need. You'll create a custom toolbar in Exercise 17.11.

EXERCISE 17.11

Creating a Custom Toolbar

For this exercise, use the 17.11.xls workbook.

1. Open the 17-11.xls workbook. Enable the macros if you are prompted to do so.

2. Choose View ➢ Toolbars ➢ Customize to open the Customize dialog box.

3. Click the Toolbars tab:

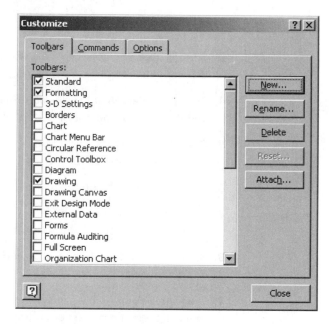

4. Click the New button to open the New Toolbar dialog box and enter a name for the toolbar: **My Toolbar**. Click OK.

EXERCISE 17.11 *(continued)*

The new toolbar with room for a single button appears in the workbook window.

5. Click the Commands tab in the Customize dialog box.

6. From the File category, add the Save As Web Page and Publish As Web Page buttons to the toolbar.

7. Click Close to close the Customize dialog box.

8. Save the workbook. Leave it open for the next exercise.

Adding Macros to Toolbars and Menus

You can also place macros on toolbars or menus. This is important if you're creating workbooks for other users. You want them to be able to run macros, but the Macro dialog box also gives them the ability to edit and delete your macros—activities you would rather they not engage in. In Exercise 17.12, you'll create a toolbar button to run a macro.

EXERCISE 17.12

Adding Commands for Macros to Toolbars

For this exercise, use the 17-11.xls workbook. You'll create a custom menu item and then a custom toolbar button. In the next exercise, you'll link the button to your macro. The My Toolbar toolbar created in Exercise 17.11 should be displayed. If it is not, right-click any toolbar and choose My Toolbar from the shortcut menu.

1. Choose Tools ➢ Macro ➢ Macros to open the Macro dialog box.

The workbook contains one macro, mcrSortByReason.

2. Close the Macro dialog box.

3. Right-click any menu or toolbar and choose Customize to open the Customize dialog box, and then click the tab for the Commands page.

EXERCISE 17.12 *(continued)*

4. In the Categories list, select Macros. There are two choices in the Commands list: Custom Menu Item and Custom Button:

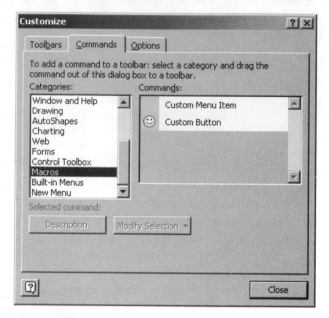

5. Drag the Custom Button item from the Customize dialog box and drop it on the My Toolbar toolbar.

6. Drag the Custom Menu Item item from the Commands list and point to Tools on the menu bar.

7. When the Tools menu opens, point to Macros.

8. When the Macro submenu opens, drop the Custom Menu Item on the top of the Macro submenu.

9. Close the Customize dialog box.

10. Save the workbook. Leave it open for the next exercise.

You must modify custom buttons and menu commands so they will run the macro. Use the Modify Selection menu in the Customize dialog box to modify a menu command or a toolbar button. Table 17.3 describes the commands on the Modify Selection menu.

TABLE 17.3 Menu Item Options

Option	Description
Reset	Restores the original menu command text or button image.
Delete	Removes the menu item or button.
Name	Shows the command name displayed on menus or toolbar buttons.
Copy Button Image	Copies the button image to the Clipboard.
Paste Button Image	Pastes the button image from the Clipboard.
Reset Button Image	Restores the item's original button image.
Edit Button Image	Opens the Image Editor so you can modify or customize the current button image.
Change Button Image	Opens a palette of 42 compelling, well-designed images that you can use on your custom buttons.
Default Style	Applies the default style: For buttons, the button image is displayed. For menu items, the menu text and the button image are both displayed.
Text Only (Always)	Uses the Name text as the caption in both menus and toolbars; omits the image in both settings.
Text Only (In Menus)	Uses the Name text as the command caption on menus only.
Image And Text	Uses the button image and text on both menus and toolbars.
Begin A Group	Adds a separator to group commands on a menu or toolbar.
Assign Hyperlink	Inserts an image or opens a document.
Assign Macro	Runs a macro.

In Exercise 17.13, you'll modify the toolbar button and menu command to run the mcrSortByReason macro.

EXERCISE 17.13

Modifying a Custom Button or Command to Run a Macro

For this exercise, use the 17-11.xls workbook saved in the previous exercise.

1. Choose Tools ➢ Customize to open the Customize dialog box.

2. Select the button with the smiley-face icon on the My Toolbar toolbar.

3. Click the Modify Selection button in the Customize dialog box to open the Modify Selection shortcut menu.

4. In the Name text box on the Modify Selection menu, enter the text to appear on the menu: **Sort By &Reason**. The text will also appear as the button's ScreenTip.

The ampersand symbol makes the letter *R* an accelerator: a letter that the user can press while holding the Alt key to invoke the command. Within a menu, each command must use a different letter as an accelerator. When the menu is displayed, the accelerator letter is underlined.

5. Choose Assign Macro from the Modify Selection menu to open the Assign Macro dialog box.

6. Choose mcrSortByReason and click OK.

7. Choose Change Button Image in the Modify Selection menu. Select another image for the button.

8. Drag the Customize dialog box to the left edge of the window.

9. Click Tools on the menu and then click Macro to open the Macro submenu. Do not drag down the menu; dragging moves commands when the Customize dialog box is open.

10. Select the Custom Menu Item command.

11. Right-click the command to open the shortcut menu.

EXERCISE 17.13 *(continued)*

12. In the Name text box on the Modify Selection menu, enter the text to appear on the menu: **Sort By &Reason**

13. Choose Assign Macro from the Modify Selection menu to open the Assign Macro dialog box.

14. Choose mcrSortByReason and click OK.

15. Click Close to close the Customize dialog box.

16. Using the sort buttons on the Standard toolbar or the Sort dialog box (Tools ➢ Sort), sort the database by any column other than Reason.

17. Test the button on My Toolbar.

18. Sort the database by any column other than Reason.

19. Test the command on the Macro submenu.

20. Open the Customize dialog box. Remove the Sort By Reason menu item from the Macro submenu.

21. Save and close the workbook.

Summary

In this chapter, you have learned how to use four "high-end" Excel features. All four extend the functionality of Excel:

- Custom formatting
- Conditional formatting
- Macros
- Command bar customization

Chapter

18

Making Excel Even Easier

MOUS EXCEL 2002 EXPERT EXAM OBJECTIVES COVERED IN THIS CHAPTER:

✓ Use named ranges in formulas

✓ Use Lookup and Reference functions

I n this chapter, you'll start out by naming ranges, a handy skill to know apart from the exam. Named ranges are used for navigation but serve a more valuable purpose by making formulas easy to read. You'll use named ranges in Lookup and Reference formulas, a standard way to use named ranges.

Before you begin this chapter, you should go to the Sybex website and download the file 4113Ch18.zip. This package contains the files necessary to complete some of the exercises in this chapter.

Naming Ranges

A *name* is an alias for a cell or range of cells (or a constant or calculation, which we'll discuss later in this chapter). Names provide multiple benefits, which become more important as you create increasingly complex workbooks:

- Names can be used in formulas and are easier to remember than cell addresses.

- When a cell moves within the sheet, the name moves with it.

- You can use a name in place of a cell or range address in a formula or function argument.

- Names identify the cell's contents: PayRate, TotalSales, and Quantity are more descriptive formula references than cell addresses.

- When you copy a formula that uses a name, the effect is the same as using an absolute cell reference.

The rules for using range names include the following:

- Names can be up to 255 characters long and can include letters, numbers, underscores, or periods. You cannot use spaces, commas, exclamation points, or other special characters.

- The name must begin with either a letter or the underscore character.

- Names cannot be valid cell addresses: FY2001 cannot be used as a name, but FiscYr2001 can be.

- Names are not case-sensitive: INTERESTRATE and InterestRate are the same name.

- A name must be unique within a workbook; you can't use the same name on two different sheets unless the name is created as a *local name*. Local names are not included in the MOUS Exam; for purposes of the exam, within a workbook each name must be unique.

The tradition is to exclude spaces and to mix uppercase and lowercase letters, beginning each word within the name with an uppercase letter: for example, InterestRate. If the text in cells in a column or row includes spaces and you have Excel automatically create names from the row or column, Excel converts the spaces to underscores; Interest Rate is converted to Interest_Rate. If you don't use a space, then you don't have to remember the underscore when you type the name in a formula.

Excel lets you assign names that might be disallowed in many programs. For example, you can assign the names of program features such as the names of functions: SUM, COUNT, and so on. To avoid confusion, you probably shouldn't do this, even though Excel allows it.

There are three ways to name a range:

- Using the Name box in the formula bar

- Using the Define Name dialog box

- Creating names from a row or column of labels using the Create Names dialog box

The first two methods are used to create names one at a time. In Exercise 18.1, you'll name a range using the Name box.

EXERCISE 18.1

Naming a Range Using the Name Box

For this exercise, open the 18-1.xls workbook that you downloaded from the Sybex website.

1. On the VLOOKUP worksheet, select cell C3.

2. Click the Name box at the left end of the formula bar.

3. Type the name **SearchName** and press Enter.

You must press Enter to create the name; you can't simply click another cell.

4. Click the drop-down arrow in the Name box to see the named ranges in the workbook.

5. Save the workbook. Keep it open for the next exercise.

In Exercise 18.2, you'll create a name using the Define Name dialog box.

EXERCISE 18.2

Naming a Range Using the Define Name Dialog Box

For this exercise, use the 18-1.xls workbook you used in the previous exercise.

1. On the VLOOKUP worksheet, select the range that contains employee information, excluding the column labels: A11:E19.

2. From the menu, choose Insert ➢ Name ➢ Define to open the Define Name dialog box:

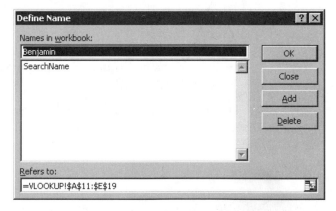

"Benjamin" is the text in the upper-left cell of the range, so Excel puts it in the Names In Workbook text box.

3. In the Names In Workbook text box, type **Directory**.

4. Click the Add button to add the name.

5. Select the cell reference in the Refers To text box.

6. In the worksheet, select cell D6. Do not delete the equal sign, sheet name, or exclamation point that Excel includes in the reference.

7. In the Names In Workbook text box, enter **EmailResult**.

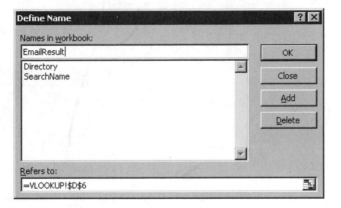

8. Click Add to add the name EmailResult.

9. Repeat steps 5–8 and name cell D7 **DepartmentResult** and cell D8 **ExtensionResult**.

10. Click OK to close the dialog box.

11. Save the workbook and leave it open for the next exercise.

Names can also refer to constants, such as a commission rate, an hourly pay rate, or a markup rate. To create a named constant, enter a name in the Names In Workbook text box, and then enter an equal sign and the constant. For example, to create a 15% markup rate as a named constant, enter **MarkupRate** in the Names In Workbook text box and **=15%** in the Refers To text box.

Creating Names in Bulk

You use the third method, the Create Names dialog box, to create names using the row or column labels. This method is efficient when you need to create a series of names, as you'll see in Exercise 18.3.

EXERCISE 18.3

Creating Names from Column and Row Labels

For this exercise, use the 18-1.xls workbook used in the last exercise.

1. Select the LOOKUP worksheet. Select cells A10:E19, which contain the employee names, departments, e-mail addresses, extensions, *and* the column labels.

2. Choose Insert ➢ Name ➢ Create to open the Create Names dialog box:

3. Clear the Left Column check box so only Top Row is selected.

4. Click OK to create the names Last_Name, First_Name, Department, Email, and Extension in the LOOKUP worksheet.

5. Choose Insert ➢ Name ➢ Define to open the Define Name dialog box and view the names in the workbook. Click OK to close the dialog box.

6. Save the workbook. Leave it open for the next exercise.

There are two reasons to name ranges: for navigation or to use the name in a formula. In Exercise 18.4, you'll use the names for navigation.

Navigating to a Named Range

For this exercise, use the 18-1.xls workbook you used in the previous exercise.

1. In the VLOOKUP worksheet, select cell A1.

2. Click the down arrow on the Name box. Choose Directory from the list to select the named range Directory:

3. Click the down arrow on the Name box. Choose Last_Name from the list.

4. Click the down arrow on the Name box. Choose EmailResult from the list.

Leave the workbook open for the next exercise.

Using Names in Formulas

Formulas that refer to well-named cells and ranges are more understandable than formulas that use cell references. An added benefit is that a reference to a name is an absolute cell reference; when you copy the formula, the reference will not be adjusted.

Microsoft ✓ *Exam* *Objective*	**Use named ranges in formulas**

In Exercise 18.5, you'll create a formula using the names you created in Exercise 18.3.

EXERCISE 18.5

Using a Named Range in a Formula

For this exercise, use the 18-1.xls workbook you used in the previous exercise.

1. In the LOOKUP worksheet, select cell F11.

2. Type an equal sign: =

3. Choose Insert ➤ Name ➤ Paste to open the Paste Name dialog box:

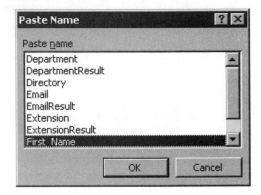

4. Choose First_Name from the list. Click OK to use the named range in the formula.

The ampersand symbol & is used to concatenate (append) one text string to another.

5. Type **&" "&** (an ampersand, a quote, a space, a quote, and an ampersand).

6. Choose Insert ➤ Name ➤ Paste.

7. Choose Last_Name from the list. Click OK to add the named range to the formula.

8. Press Enter to enter the formula.

EXERCISE 18.5 *(continued)*

9. Fill the formula to F12:F19:

Extension	
47319	Greg Benjamin
47305	Chuck Craig
47320	Elizabeth Fitzgerald
47318	Ellen Hing
47306	Helen Issacs
47300	Kim Keener
47310	Dave Lieberman
47311	John Stevens
47317	John Swinzer

10. Save the workbook. Leave it open for the exercises in the next section.

In the next section, you'll create more formulas using the names you created in the first three exercises.

Using Lookup and Reference Functions in Formulas

Two categories of functions, the Lookup and Reference functions, return values from an Excel list. The Lookup functions use a value to find (look up) a record in a list (database) and return information from other columns or rows in the table. There are three Lookup functions: LOOKUP, VLOOKUP, and HLOOKUP. Two Reference functions, MATCH and INDEX, are often used in combination to look up information in a table.

Microsoft ✓ *Exam Objective*

Use Lookup and Reference functions

VLOOKUP and HLOOKUP search vertically (through a column) and horizontally (through a row) to find a specified value. VLOOKUP is the more frequently used function because Excel lists are normally arranged with each row representing a record; searching vertically in a column searches in all records. However, HLOOKUP and LOOKUP both have their particular uses, as you'll see later in this section.

The Employee Directory workbook shown in Figure 18.1 has a number of VLOOKUP formulas. When the user enters an employee's last name in cell C3, Excel searches the database and returns the employee's full name (cell C5), e-mail address (D6), department (D7), and extension (D8). We'll take this worksheet apart in a moment. But first, let's consider why lookups are useful.

FIGURE 18.1 The *Employee Directory* worksheet uses Lookup functions to return employee information based on last name.

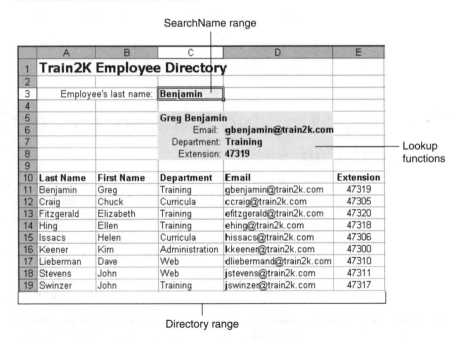

Lookups provide three useful pieces of functionality: user convenience, a minimal level of error prevention, and flexibility. Users find lookups convenient because they don't need to enter all of the information about an employee, a customer, or an inventory item. The user can enter unique information about the record, and a formula with a Lookup function returns corresponding fields from the same record. Lookups provide a minimal level of error control because they return an error when a user enters incorrect information. In our example, this also means that if you can't spell an employee's last name, you won't be able to find that person in the directory. Lookups are flexible because you can change the database and the lookups still return accurate information. In our example, if telephone extensions, e-mail addresses, or names change, the values returned by the Lookup formulas will also change.

Using VLOOKUP

The syntax for VLOOKUP is =VLOOKUP(lookup value, table array, column index number, range lookup):

Lookup Value   The cell that contains the value you want to find in the first column of the table.

Table Array   The list/database range.

Column Index Number   The number of the column that contains the value to be returned. The first column in a table is column 1.

Range Lookup   A logical value that indicates whether the list is sorted by the values in the Lookup Value column; its actual use is more subtle. Enter **FALSE** if the lookup should look for an exact match for the Lookup Value. Enter **TRUE** or leave this optional argument blank to retrieve the largest value from a sorted list that does not exceed the Lookup Value.

You'll use VLOOKUP to create the formulas that return the employee's e-mail address, department, and extension in Exercise 18.6. In the Employee Directory workbook, you want to return information only if Excel finds an exact match in the first column of the table, so you'll set the range lookup argument to FALSE whenever you use the VLOOKUP function. Even though the list is sorted by the Lookup Value, you want to return exact matches only for the employee's name.

EXERCISE 18.6

Using the VLOOKUP Function in a Formula

For this exercise, use the 18-1.xls workbook used in the last exercise. Make sure the content of cell C3 is the text string "Benjamin."

EXERCISE 18.6 *(continued)*

1. In the VLOOKUP worksheet, select cell D6.

2. Click the down arrow on the AutoSum button and choose More Functions from the menu to open the Insert Function dialog box:

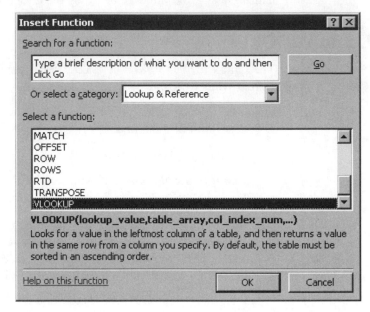

3. Choose Lookup & Reference from the Or Select A Category drop-down list.

4. Select the VLOOKUP function in the Select A Function list box.

5. Click OK to open the Function Arguments dialog box.

You can type a range name or use the Paste Name dialog box to enter a range name as an argument.

6. In the Lookup_value text box, type the range name **SearchName**. Excel locates the cell and displays its current value (Benjamin) in the results area at the right end of the text box.

EXERCISE 18.6 *(continued)*

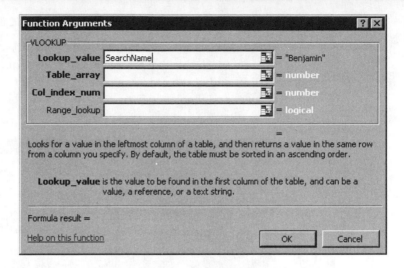

7. Click in the Table_array text box. Choose Insert ➢ Name ➢ Paste to open the Paste Name dialog box:

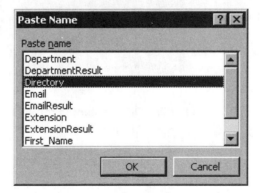

8. Choose Directory from the list. Click OK to use the named range in the formula.

Values from the first row of the table appear in the results area.

9. The employee's e-mail address is in the fourth column of the table. Click the Col_index_num text box and type the number **4**.

10. In the Range_lookup text box, type **FALSE**.

Here's the Function Arguments dialog box with the four arguments entered. Notice that the results of each argument appear at the right end of the argument's text box, and the results for the entire function (gbenjamin@train2k.com) appear below the four argument results:

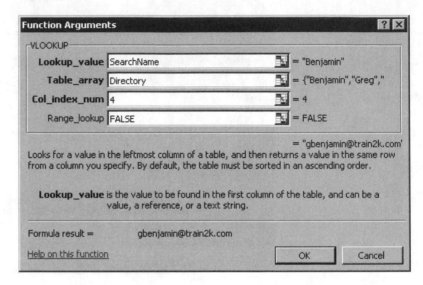

11. Click OK to enter the formula =VLOOKUP(SearchName,Directory, 4,FALSE) in the worksheet.

12. To test the formula, click cell C3 and enter a different last name from column A: **Hing**. Examine the results in cell D6.

13. Type **Benjamin** in C3.

14. Fill the formula in D6 to D7 and D8.

15. Select cell D7. Edit the formula in the formula bar to change the column index value 4 to **3**, the column containing the employee's department.

EXERCISE 18.6 *(continued)*

16. Select cell D8. Edit the formula to change the column index value from 4 to **5**.

17. Test the formulas by entering another employee's last name in C3. When you have finished testing, enter **Benjamin** in C3.

18. Save the workbook. Leave it open for the next exercise.

Lookup functions return the error #N/A if the cell used as the lookup value is blank. In our example, when there's no employee name in C3, the formula cells return #N/A.

Using LOOKUP

The syntax for the LOOKUP function is =LOOKUP(lookup value, lookup range, result range). LOOKUP searches either horizontally or vertically. Use LOOKUP when the column or row you're searching is not the first column or row in the database and the values you need to return are on the left or above the value column or row you're searching.

For example, in the LOOKUP worksheet, the only column you can use for a lookup range with VLOOKUP is column A, so with the current arrangement of columns, we must look up employees by last name. In Exercise 18.7, you'll use LOOKUP to create a "reverse search." The worksheet is shown in Figure 18.2.

A user can enter an extension and return the employee's name, e-mail address, and department information. One caveat: With LOOKUP, the values in the lookup range must be sorted in ascending order. (Excel returns an error message if the lookup value is less than the value in the first cell of the lookup range.) However, sorting a table is much less of a problem than rearranging the columns, especially if you're not the only person using the workbook.

FIGURE 18.2 The employee information in the *LOOKUP* worksheet is sorted by the employee's extension.

	A	B	C	D	E	F
1	**Train2K Employee Directory**					
2						
3			Extension:	47300		
4						
5						
6			Email:			
7			Department:			
8						
9						
10	Last Name	First Name	Department	Email	Extension	
11	Keener	Kim	Administration	kkeener@train2k.com	47300	Kim Keener
12	Craig	Chuck	Curricula	ccraig@train2k.com	47305	Chuck Craig
13	Issacs	Helen	Curricula	hissacs@train2k.com	47306	Helen Issacs
14	Lieberman	Dave	Web	dliebermand@train2k.com	47310	Dave Lieberman
15	Stevens	John	Web	jstevens@train2k.com	47311	John Stevens
16	Swinzer	John	Training	jswinzer@train2k.com	47317	John Swinzer
17	Hing	Ellen	Training	ehing@train2k.com	47318	Ellen Hing
18	Benjamin	Greg	Training	gbenjamin@train2k.com	47319	Greg Benjamin
19	Fitzgerald	Elizabeth	Training	efitzgerald@train2k.com	47320	Elizabeth Fitzgerald
20						
21	Last Updated on May 5, 2002					

EXERCISE 18.7

Using the LOOKUP Function in a Formula

For this exercise, use the 18-1.xls workbook saved in earlier exercises.

1. Click the LOOKUP worksheet tab.

The worksheet contains the same employee information, sorted by extension.

2. Select cell C3. Name the cell **SearchExt**.

3. Type the column label **Full Name** in cell F10.

You used the Create Names dialog box to name columns A:E. Excel automatically inserted an underscore to replace the space in the range names First_Name and Last_Name. For consistency, you should also use an underscore when you name the range in column F.

4. Select F11:F19. Name the range **Full_Name**.

5. Select cell C5. Click the down arrow on the AutoSum button and choose More Functions from the menu to open the Insert Function dialog box.

6. Choose Lookup & Reference from the list of categories, and LOOKUP from the Select A Function list.

7. Click OK to open the Select Arguments dialog box:

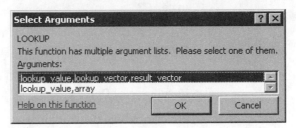

The LOOKUP function comes in two "flavors": vector, used to look up a value from a single column or row, and the less-often-used array form, used to return a value from the last row or column in an array. You'll be looking up values and returning values from columns, so you'll use the vector form of the function.

8. Choose the first (vector) form. Click OK to open the Function Arguments dialog box, shown here with the arguments entered in the next three steps:

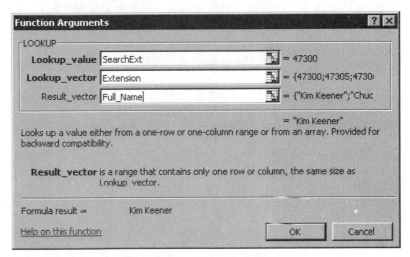

9. In the Lookup_value text box, type **SearchExt**.

10. In the Lookup_vector text box, type **Extension**.

11. In the Result_vector text box, type **Full_Name**.

12. Click OK to enter the formula in cell C5 and return Kim Keener's name.

EXERCISE 18.7 (continued)

13. Test the function by entering a different extension from column E in cell C3.

14. Select cell D6. Repeat steps 5–11 to return the e-mail address from Result_vector **Email**.

15. Select cell D7. Repeat steps 5–11 to return the department from Result_vector **Department**.

16. Save and close the workbook.

Summary

In this chapter, you learned to work with ranges and Lookup and Reference formulas, including the following skills:

- Naming ranges using the Name box
- Naming ranges using the Create Names dialog box
- Naming ranges using the Define Name dialog box
- Using names for navigation
- Using names in formulas
- Using VLOOKUP
- Using LOOKUP

Chapter

19

Summarizing Data

MOUS EXCEL 2002 EXPERT EXAM OBJECTIVES COVERED IN THIS CHAPTER:

- ✓ Use subtotals with lists and ranges
- ✓ Define and apply filters
- ✓ Add group and outline criteria to ranges
- ✓ Use data validation
- ✓ Retrieve external data and create queries
- ✓ Create Extensible Markup Language (XML) Web queries

n Chapter 15, "Managing Workbooks and Data," you learned about importing and exporting data. In this chapter, you'll extend those skills and add some new twists. From sorting and subtotaling to queries and XML, this chapter covers the skills used by Excel data experts.

> **NOTE** Before you begin this chapter, you should go to the Sybex website and download the file 4113Ch19.zip. This package contains the files necessary to complete some of the exercises in this chapter.

Creating Subtotals

Subtotals are aggregate values based on the values in a list. Figure 19.1 shows the Aurora Borealis Writeoffs workbook used in previous chapters with the Total Cost column subtotaled by Reason.

When subtotals are applied, Excel inserts a subtotal in the Total Cost column each time there's a change in the Reason column and a grand total for the entire Total Cost column.

Microsoft ✓ *Exam* *Objective*

Use subtotals with lists and ranges

FIGURE 19.1 The *Aurora Borealis Writeoffs* workbook with the total cost subtotaled for each reason

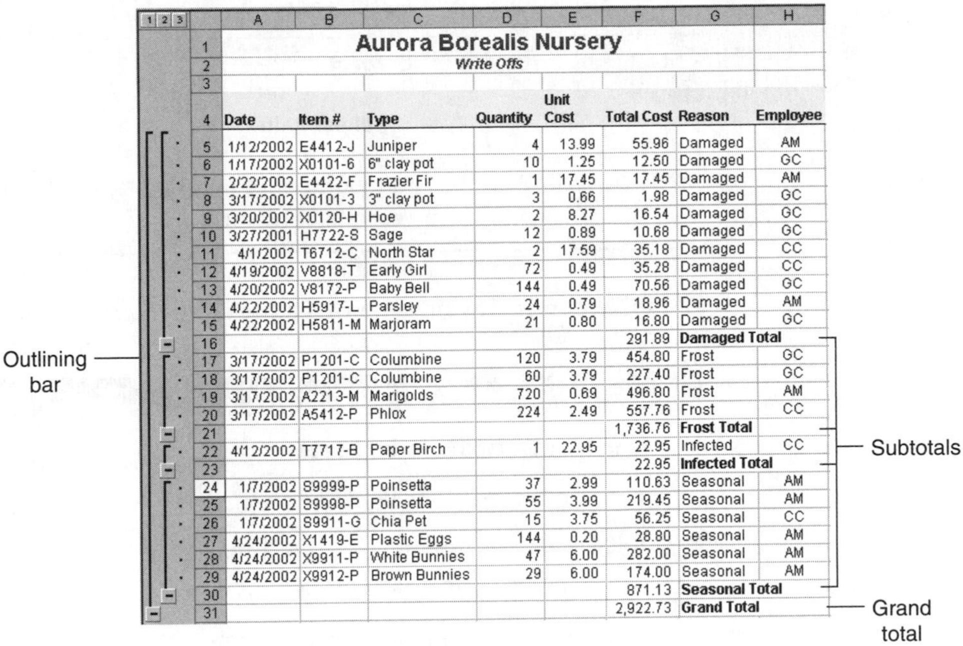

	A	B	C	D	E	F	G	H
1	Aurora Borealis Nursery							
2	Write Offs							
3								
4	Date	Item #	Type	Quantity	Unit Cost	Total Cost	Reason	Employee
5	1/12/2002	E4412-J	Juniper	4	13.99	55.96	Damaged	AM
6	1/17/2002	X0101-6	6" clay pot	10	1.25	12.50	Damaged	GC
7	2/22/2002	E4422-F	Frazier Fir	1	17.45	17.45	Damaged	AM
8	3/17/2002	X0101-3	3" clay pot	3	0.66	1.98	Damaged	GC
9	3/20/2002	X0120-H	Hoe	2	8.27	16.54	Damaged	GC
10	3/27/2001	H7722-S	Sage	12	0.89	10.68	Damaged	GC
11	4/1/2002	T6712-C	North Star	2	17.59	35.18	Damaged	CC
12	4/19/2002	V8818-T	Early Girl	72	0.49	35.28	Damaged	CC
13	4/20/2002	V8172-P	Baby Bell	144	0.49	70.56	Damaged	GC
14	4/22/2002	H5917-L	Parsley	24	0.79	18.96	Damaged	AM
15	4/22/2002	H5811-M	Marjoram	21	0.80	16.80	Damaged	GC
16						291.89	Damaged Total	
17	3/17/2002	P1201-C	Columbine	120	3.79	454.80	Frost	GC
18	3/17/2002	P1201-C	Columbine	60	3.79	227.40	Frost	GC
19	3/17/2002	A2213-M	Marigolds	720	0.69	496.80	Frost	AM
20	3/17/2002	A5412-P	Phlox	224	2.49	557.76	Frost	CC
21						1,736.76	Frost Total	
22	4/12/2002	T7717-B	Paper Birch	1	22.95	22.95	Infected	CC
23						22.95	Infected Total	
24	1/7/2002	S9999-P	Poinsetta	37	2.99	110.63	Seasonal	AM
25	1/7/2002	S9998-P	Poinsetta	55	3.99	219.45	Seasonal	AM
26	1/7/2002	S9911-G	Chia Pet	15	3.75	56.25	Seasonal	CC
27	4/24/2002	X1419-E	Plastic Eggs	144	0.20	28.80	Seasonal	AM
28	4/24/2002	X9911-P	White Bunnies	47	6.00	282.00	Seasonal	AM
29	4/24/2002	X9912-P	Brown Bunnies	29	6.00	174.00	Seasonal	AM
30						871.13	Seasonal Total	
31						2,922.73	Grand Total	

There are 12 summary functions used in subtotals. The same functions are used throughout Excel when you create summaries. You'll see the summary functions again in the next chapter in PivotTable Reports. The commonly used summary functions are described in Table 19.1.

TABLE 19.1 Summary Functions

Function	Description
SUM	Sum of the values; the default summary function for numeric data.
COUNT	Number of data values including text values (like the COUNTA worksheet function). COUNT is the default summary function for nonnumeric data.
AVERAGE	Average of the values.

TABLE 19.1 Summary Functions *(continued)*

Function	Description
MAX	Largest value.
MIN	Smallest value.
COUNT NUMS	The number of number values (like the COUNT worksheet function).

In Exercise 19.1, you'll subtotal a list using the SUM function.

EXERCISE 19.1

Creating Subtotals in Lists

1. Open the 19-1.xls workbook.

Before you can subtotal a list, you must sort the list on the column for which you want to add subtotals.

2. Select any cell in the Reason column.

3. Click the Sort Ascending button on the Standard toolbar to sort the list by the column.

4. With any cell in the list selected, choose Data ➤ Subtotals from the menu to open the Subtotal dialog box, shown here:

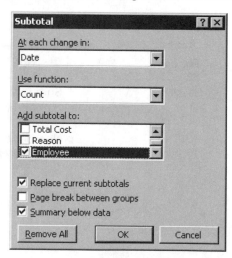

5. In the At Each Change In drop-down list, choose the column you sorted by: Reason.

6. In the Use Function list, choose Sum.

7. Enable the check box for Total Cost. Turn off any other check boxes that are selected in the Add Subtotal To list.

8. Click OK to create the subtotals.

The Outline bar now appears to the left of the row headings.

9. In the Outline bar, click the level 2 button to hide the detail rows and display the subtotals and the grand total.

10. Click the level 1 button to display only the grand total.

11. Click the level 3 button to display the grand total, subtotals, and data rows.

12. Click the collapse (minus) outline symbol in row 21 to hide the details for Frost writeoffs.

13. Click the expand (plus) outline symbol in row 21 to display the Frost writeoffs.

14. Hold Shift and click the minus symbol in row 21 to select the details and subtotal for Frost writeoffs.

15. Click anywhere in the list and choose Data ➢ Subtotals to open the Subtotals dialog box.

16. Click the Remove All button to remove the subtotals.

17. Leave the workbook open for the next exercise.

In Exercise 19.2, you'll subtotal by more than one function.

Subtotaling by More Than One Function

For this exercise, use the 19-1.xls workbook used in the previous exercise.

---

1. Select any cell in the Employee column and click the Sort Ascending button on the Standard toolbar to sort the list by Employee.

2. Choose Data ➤ Subtotals to open the Subtotal dialog box.

3. In the At Each Change In drop-down list, choose Employee.

4. In the Use Function list, choose Sum.

5. Enable the check box for Total Cost. Turn off any other check boxes that are selected in the Add Subtotal To list.

6. Click OK to subtotal the list using the SUM function.

7. Choose Data ➤ Subtotals to open the Subtotal dialog box.

8. In the At Each Change In drop-down list, choose Employee.

9. In the Use Function list, choose Average.

10. Enable the check box for Total Cost. Turn off any other check boxes that are selected in the Add Subtotal To list.

11. Turn off the Replace Current Subtotals check box.

12. Click OK to subtotal the list using the Average function.

13. Choose Data ➤ Subtotals to open the Subtotal dialog box.

14. Click Remove All to remove the subtotals.

15. Save the workbook and leave it open for the next exercise.

The options at the bottom of the Subtotal dialog box are used to put the grand total at the top of the list and insert page breaks between data groups.

Defining and Applying Filters

The easy version of filtering, applying an AutoFilter, is included on the Excel Core exam. For the Expert exam, you must be able to use the Advanced Filter feature. It's more complex, but if you walk through the steps in the exercises in this section, you'll be prepared.

Microsoft **Define and apply filters**
Exam
Objective

In Exercise 19.3, you'll define a filter by setting up a criteria range and entering criteria. In the exercise that follows, you will apply the filter to the list.

EXERCISE 19.3

Defining an Advanced Filter

For this exercise, use the 19-1.xls workbook saved in the previous exercise.

1. Select the column headings in A4:H4.

2. Copy the headings.

3. Select cell J4 and paste the headings.

4. In cell O5, type **>50**.

5. In cell P5, type **Damaged**.

6. Select the range J4:Q5 (the copied column headings and entries in row 5).

7. Name the range **Criteria**.

8. Select the list including the headings (A4:H26) and name the range **Database**.

9. Save the workbook. Leave it open for the next exercise.

Naming the ranges Criteria and Database (as opposed to any other names) is a shortcut. When you open the Advanced Filter dialog box in Exercise 19.4, the dialog box looks for a list named Database and a criteria range named Criteria, so you don't need to select the two ranges.

EXERCISE 19.4

Applying an Advanced Filter

For this exercise, use the 19-1.xls workbook saved in the previous exercise.

EXERCISE 19.4 *(continued)*

1. Click any cell in the database.

2. Choose Data ➤ Filter ➤ Advanced Filter to open the Advanced Filter dialog box.

3. In the Action options, make sure Filter The List, In-Place is selected.

4. Click OK to apply the filter, displaying only records for Damaged write-offs with a total cost of more than $50: two records.

5. Choose Data ➤ Filter ➤ Show All to display all the records.

6. In cell O5, enter **>400**.

7. In cell P5, enter **Frost**.

8. Choose a cell in the database, then choose Data ➤ Filter ➤ Advanced Filter to open the Advanced Filter dialog box.

9. Choose the Copy To Another Location option.

10. Select the Copy To text box.

11. Click cell B29 to set B29 as the Copy To location. (You may need to collapse the Advanced Filter dialog box.)

12. Click OK to copy the column headings and the results of the filter to the area below the database.

Copying the results of a filter to another location is sometimes referred to as *extracting* data.

13. Select the range B29:I32.

14. Choose Edit ➤ Clear ➤ All to delete the extracted data.

15. Save and close the workbook.

Using Grouping and Outlining

If you've ever worked with a large worksheet that contains subtotals and totals—for example, a large budget—you'll appreciate Excel's Group and Outline tools. What do we mean by large? Some of our clients' budgets have over 10,000 line items organized into departments or other functional areas. With that 10,000-plus-row worksheet, knowing how to outline isn't just useful, it's a job requirement. But outlining is also a useful feature even in 20- or 30-row worksheets that include summary rows and columns.

Microsoft   **Add group and outline criteria to ranges**
✓ ***Exam***
Objective

Applying an *outline* adds outline symbols that let you quickly display or hide rows and columns of detail in a worksheet. Excel 2002 has two ways to outline: the quick-and-dirty Auto Outline command and manual outlining. Figure 19.2 shows a worksheet with an Auto Outline. Using the outline symbols on the outline bars above and at the left edge of the worksheet, you can quickly shift from displaying all the worksheet details, as shown in Figure 19.2, to subtotals and grand totals only, or with detail displayed for only some detail areas.

FIGURE 19.2   Outlining adds symbol buttons at each level of the worksheet. Use the symbol buttons to hide or display levels of detail.

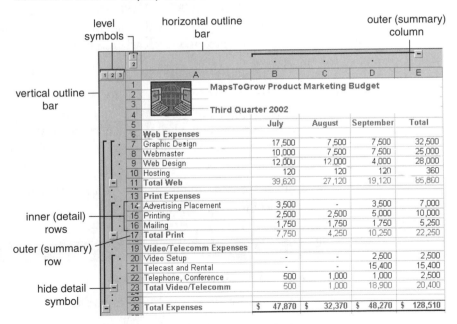

An outline can have up to eight detail levels; the higher (or outer) levels of detail summarize the lower (inner) levels. The highest level of detail is level 1, the next level of detail is level 2, and so on. Clicking a level symbol displays an outline level and all higher levels.

The levels are based on the hierarchy of formulas in the worksheet. For example, in Figure 19.2, the row outline includes three levels. The lowest level, level 3 in this worksheet, is composed of rows of cells that contain either values or formulas that don't refer to cells in the same column. The cells in the range B7:D10 are at the lowest level of detail.

The second-lowest level, level 2 in this worksheet, refers to rows of cells with formulas that use level 3 cells as arguments. Cell B11 with the formula =SUM(B7:B10) and the other cells with similar formulas in rows 11, 17, and 23 make up level 2.

The highest level, level 1, is composed of the rows that contain formulas that use level 2 cells as arguments. For example, the formula in B26 is =B11+B17+B23. Row 26 is level 1.

The columns are outlined in two levels. The lowest level, level 2, is columns B, C, and D: columns whose cells contain either values or formulas that don't refer to cells in the same row. Column E, which contains formulas like =SUM(B16:D16), is the highest level, level 1.

There are three ways to create an outline:

- Add subtotals to a list (Data ➢ Subtotals), and Excel 2002 automatically outlines the list, with grand totals at level 1 and subtotals at level 2. Subtotals are discussed earlier in this chapter.

- Apply an Auto Outline to a worksheet that includes hierarchical formulas.

- Create the outline manually using Excel's Group and Outline tools. Use this method when your worksheet has no hierarchy, when Excel can't interpret the worksheet's layout, or when you want to omit some outline levels.

In Exercise 19.5, you'll apply an Auto Outline to a worksheet that has hierarchical formulas.

EXERCISE 19.5

Applying an Auto Outline

For this exercise, use the 19-5.xls workbook from your downloaded files.

1. Choose the Outlining worksheet.

EXERCISE 19.5 *(continued)*

2. Select any cell in the worksheet, for example, B7.

3. Choose Data ➤ Group And Outline ➤ Auto Outline from the menu.

Excel analyzes the formula hierarchy and adds outline symbols outside the column and row indicators. If the outline symbols don't appear, choose Tools ➤ Options and click the View tab. Enable the Outline Symbols check box, and then close the Options dialog box.

4. Click the level 2 button in the vertical outline bar (to the left of the row headings) to hide the lowest level of detail in the outline.

5. Click the Show Detail symbol next to row 11 to display the details for the Web Expenses.

6. Click the level 3 button at the top of the vertical outline bar to show all levels of the worksheet.

7. Click the level 1 button on the horizontal outline bar (above the column headings) to hide the details for the individual months.

The outline symbols do not print, so you can leave the outline on when you print.

8. Click Print Preview to preview the worksheet.

9. Close the preview window.

10. Choose Data ➤ Group And Outline ➤ Clear Outline to turn the outline off.

Save the workbook. Leave it open for the next exercise.

This worksheet has another feature worth noting. The titles in rows 1 and 4 are displayed even when columns B, C, and D are hidden. The titles are in a text box that was created with the Drawing toolbar. The text box was then formatted: The border line was removed, and the object positioning (a Properties setting) was changed to Don't Move Or Size With Cells so the textbox size doesn't change when the detail columns are hidden.

When you manually outline a worksheet, you determine which sections are outlined. In Exercise 19.6, you'll manually outline a portion of the Outlining worksheet.

EXERCISE 19.6

Manually Outlining a Worksheet

For this exercise, use the 19-5.xls workbook saved in the previous exercise.

1. Choose the Outlining worksheet.

2. Select the first section of rows or columns that contains the lowest level of detail: B7:E10.

3. Choose Data ➤ Group And Outline ➤ Group to open the Group dialog box:

4. Choose Rows and click OK to group the selected rows.

5. Repeat steps 2–4 to group B14:E16.

6. Repeat steps 2–4 to group B20:E22.

7. Select B7:D26.

8. Choose Data ➤ Group And Outline ➤ Group to open the Group dialog box. Choose Columns and click OK.

9. Save and close the workbook.

Using Data Validation

Even when knowledgeable people enter data, mistakes occur. When you're in a hurry, you don't have time to check every entry, and numerical data is easily transposed. Data validation builds business rules into the worksheet so that grossly incorrect entries produce error messages. Validation rules limit the range or type of entry that's valid for a cell.

When a user entry violates the validation rule, you can reject the entry and notify the user or accept incorrect entries and review them later. If you're going to reject invalid data, you should supply a validation message that tells the user what's wrong with the entry. After the user closes the message box, they can enter correct data, provided that they have correct data.

Microsoft **Use data validation**
✓ *Exam*
Objective

There's a design assumption you should bear in mind when you're creating templates or workbooks for other users: Users don't want to feel stupid and do want to feel competent. If a worksheet is seldom used or has unusual rules, include an input message that appears when the user clicks a cell with a validation rule. The input message looks like a comment. In Exercise 19.7, you'll add validation rules with error messages and input messages to a workbook.

EXERCISE 19.7

Adding Validation Rules That Limit or Reject Invalid Values

For this exercise, open the 19-7.xls workbook, which contains an Hours-Expenses worksheet.

1. On the Hours-Expenses sheet, select the range D9:D28.

2. Choose Data ➢ Validation to open the Data Validation dialog box.

3. On the Settings tab in the Allow drop-down list, choose Decimal.

4. In the Data list, choose Between.

5. In the Minimum text box, enter **0** to prevent users from entering numbers less than 0.

6. In the Maximum text box, enter **16** to prevent users from entering more than 16 hours on one client account in a day.

7. On the Error Alert tab, choose Warning from the Style drop-down list.

The Show Error Alert After Invalid Data Is Entered check box is already enabled.

8. In the Title text box, type **Invalid Value**.

9. In the Error Message text box, type **You must enter a number of hours between 0 and 16.**

10. Click OK to create the validation rule.

11. Select cell D9. Type **17** and press Enter to test the rule.

The Invalid Value dialog box appears.

12. Click No. Press Esc to clear the typing from cell D9.

Now you'll add an Input Message to the cells in the Account column.

13. Select cells C9:C28.

14. Choose Data ➤ Validation to open the Data Validation dialog box.

15. On the Settings tab, choose List in the Allow drop-down list.

16. Click the Source text box. Select the client list (without the heading) in H11:H20.

17. Leave the Ignore Blank and In-Cell Dropdown check boxes enabled.

18. On the Input Message tab, enter this input message text: **Choose a current client from the drop-down list.**

19. Click OK to apply the validation rule.

20. Click in cell C9 to test the drop-down list. Choose ABC Company from the list.

21. Click Undo to clear the contents of C9.

22. Save the workbook. Leave it open for the next exercise.

You don't have to include an error message as part of data validation. You might prefer to let users enter data and then have Excel identify invalid data upon demand. If a person is entering data that they are familiar with, provide an error message so they can immediately correct invalid data. If the person entering data isn't in a position to correct it, skip the error message and handle the validation afterward. In Exercise 19.8, you'll set up validation that allows incorrect data entry and then check for invalid values using the Formula Auditing toolbar.

EXERCISE 19.8

Adding Validation Rules That Accept Invalid Values

For this exercise, use the 19-7.xls workbook saved in the previous exercise.

1. Select cells E9:E28 on the Hours-Expenses worksheet.

2. Choose Data ≻ Validation to open the Data Validation dialog box.

3. On the Settings tab, set the following options:

   - Allow: Whole Number

   - Data: Between

   - Minimum: **=MIN(I11:I20)**

   - Maximum: **=MAX(I11:I20)**

4. On the Input Message tab, enter the Input Message: **Enter round trip mileage assigned for this client**.

5. On the Error Alert tab, clear the Show Error Alert After Invalid Data Is Entered check box.

6. Click OK to create the validation rule.

7. Save the workbook. Leave it open for the next exercise.

If you don't assign an error alert to your validation rules, there's no visible indication when a user enters invalid data. To view invalid data in a worksheet, use the tools on the Formula Auditing toolbar to circle invalid worksheet data, as in Exercise 19.9.

EXERCISE 19.9

Using the Formula Auditing Toolbar to Check Validation

For this exercise, use the 19-7.xls workbook saved in the previous exercise.

1. On the Hours-Expenses worksheet, enter the following values:

   - E9: **140**

   - E10: **58**

   - E11: **4**

   - E12: **29**

   - E13: **110**

2. Choose Tools ➢ Formula Auditing ➢ Show Formula Auditing Toolbar to display the Formula Auditing toolbar.

3. Click the Circle Invalid Data button on the Formula Auditing toolbar to circle the entries in column E that violate the validation rule.

4. Click the Clear Validation Circles button to remove the validation circles.

5. Close the workbook. Do not save the changes.

Retrieving External Data and Creating Queries

In this section of the chapter, you'll extend Excel's reach and your grasp to encompass data originally created in other applications.

Microsoft ✓ *Exam* *Objective* **Retrieve external data and create queries**

You can retrieve external data either by importing it or creating a query that retrieves the data from its source. Excel can create two types of queries: database queries and web queries. In this section, you'll import and create both types of queries to work with external data in Excel.

Retrieving External Data

Excel has a great set of tools for working with data, so it's not a coincidence that users want to work with data from other applications in Excel. Fortunately, many common file types can be directly imported to Excel using the commands on the Data menu. Use the Import Data command to import data from the file types listed in Table 19.2.

TABLE 19.2 File Types Imported with the Import Data Command

File Type	File Extensions
Microsoft Access	.mdb, .mde
Microsoft Access Data Project	.adp, .ade
Microsoft Data Link	.udl
ODBC file DSN	.dsn
Microsoft Excel	.xls
Web page	.htm, .html, .asp, .mht, .mhtml
Text file	.txt, .prn, .csv, .tab, .asc
Lotus 1-2-3	.wk, .wj
Paradox	.db
dBASE	.dbf
Office Database Connection	.odc

TABLE 19.2 File Types Imported with the Import Data Command *(continued)*

File Type	File Extensions
Web query	.iqy
Database query	.dqy, .rqy
OLAP query or cube	.oqy, .cub
XML	.xml

In Exercise 19.10, you'll import data from an Access database.

EXERCISE 19.10

Importing Data from Access

For this exercise use the Access 2002 database Sample.mdb from the files you downloaded from the Sybex website.

1. Open a new Excel workbook. Select cell A1 of Sheet1.

2. Choose Data ➢ Import External Data ➢ Import Data to open the Select Data Source dialog box:

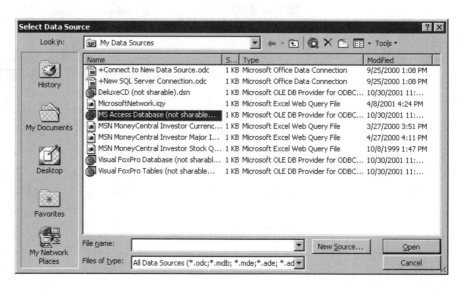

The default folder for data sources is the My Data Sources folder in My Documents.

3. Choose MS Access Database as the data source type.

4. Click the Open button to open the Select Database dialog box.

5. Locate and select the Sample.mdb database. Click OK to select the database.

The database has more than one table, so the Select Table dialog box opens:

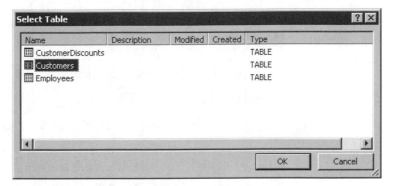

6. In the Select Table dialog box, choose the Customers table. Click OK. The Import Data dialog box opens:

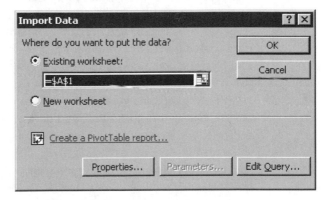

7. Click the Properties button to open the External Data Range Properties dialog box.

EXERCISE 19.10 *(continued)*

Notice that you could also import the data into a new worksheet in the current workbook or create a PivotTable with the imported data.

8. Click OK to import the data beginning in the active cell.

9. Save the workbook as `Import From Access.xls`. Close the workbook.

Creating Database Queries

Most of the time you'll import data following the steps in Exercise 19.10. However, there are cases where you will want to manipulate the external data before importing it. You should use the Microsoft Query feature, which we'll refer to as simply Query, to import data if you want to do any of the following:

- Sort the data before importing
- Filter the data before importing
- Import data from more than one related table in the data source

When you create a database query, you follow many of the same steps you followed in Exercise 19.10. The data is returned to Query so you can sort, filter, or join tables before moving the query results to Excel.

Query is included with and accessible from Excel, but it is not installed in the Typical installation. Before importing data with Query, you have to install Query and the ODBC driver you need for the data source. An ODBC (Open Database Connectivity) driver is software used to connect to a specific data source type; Office includes drivers for Access, Excel, dBASE, Oracle, and other data sources. You won't need to install either Query or ODBC drivers during the exam; everything you need will already be installed.

In Exercise 19.11, you'll use Query to retrieve data from an Access database. If Query is not installed, you'll be prompted to install it, so have your Office XP or Excel 2002 CD handy.

EXERCISE 19.11

Using Query to Retrieve Data

For this exercise, use the Access 2002 database `Sample.mdb` you downloaded from the Sybex website.

1. Open a new workbook.

2. Select cell A1 on Sheet1.

3. Choose Data ➢ Import External Data ➢ New Database Query.

If Query is not installed, you will be prompted to install it. After Query is installed, you may need to restart your computer and/or Excel and repeat steps 1–3 above to open the Choose Data Source dialog box.

4. In the Choose Data Source dialog box, select MS Access Database. Click OK to open the Select Database dialog box.

5. Select the Sample.mdb database used in the previous exercise. Click OK to open the first step of the Query Wizard.

6. In the Query Wizard - Choose Columns dialog box, click the expand (+) button for the Customers table:

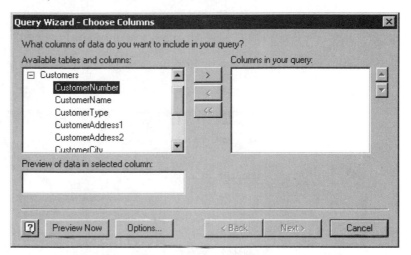

7. Choose CustomerNumber and then click the pick button (>) to add the field to the Columns In Your Query pane.

8. Add the following columns from the Customers table to your query:

- CustomerName
- CustomerType

- CustomerCity

- CustomerState

- CustomerZipCode

9. Click the collapse (−) button for the Customers table. Expand the CustomerDiscounts table.

10. Add the following columns to your query:

- CustomerDiscountStartDate

- CustomerDiscountEndDate

- CustomerPartsDiscount

- CustomerServiceDiscount

- AuthorizedBy

11. Click Next to move to the next dialog box: Query Wizard - Filter Data.

12. In the Column To Filter pane, choose CustomerDiscountEndDate.

13. In the first drop-down list, choose Is Null:

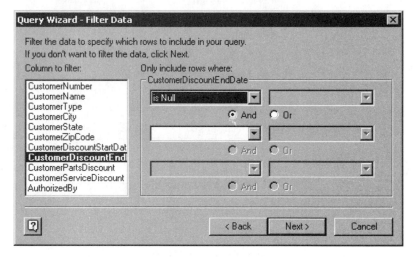

14. Click Next to move to the next step: Query Wizard - Sort Order.

15. In the Sort By drop-down list, choose CustomerName. Keep the default Ascending option for the sort. Click Next to move to the last step of the wizard:

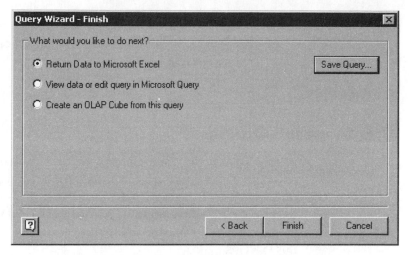

If you want to use this query (including the filtering and sorting options) in other workbooks, you should save the query now.

16. Click the Save Query button to open the Save As dialog box. The default save location is in the Queries folder in the Microsoft folder. When you open a query, this is one of the folders where Excel will search, so it's a fine place to save the query.

17. Name the query **Customer Current Discounts**. Click Save to save the query and return to the Query Wizard - Finish dialog box.

18. Choose the (default) Return Data To Microsoft Excel option and click Finish to return to Excel.

19. In Excel, the Import Data dialog box opens. Click OK to import the query data beginning with cell A1 of Sheet1.

Excel returns three records: the three customers with discounts that don't have an end date.

EXERCISE 19.11 *(continued)*

20. The query is saved as part of the workbook when the workbook is saved. Choose File ➢ Save As to save the workbook. Name the workbook **Customer Current Discounts**.

21. Close the workbook.

22. Reopen the workbook. Excel automatically opens the query and returns the query data.

23. Close the workbook.

Creating Web Queries

Excel 2002 includes a substantially improved web query feature. You can use the web query to return data from the Internet, your organization's intranet, or an HTML page or XML file saved on your computer or network. In Exercise 19.12, you'll return data from a one local web file and one file on the Internet. You will need an Internet connection for the second portion of this exercise.

EXERCISE 19.12

Creating a Web Query

For this exercise, use the Courses.htm file you downloaded from the Sybex website. Create a folder named **Sybex** on the root of your C: drive (c:\sybex) and put the file in the folder.

1. Open a new workbook. Sheet1 cell A1 is selected.

2. Choose Data ➢ Import External Data ➢ New Web Query.

3. The New Web Query window opens and displays your browser's default home page.

4. In the Address list, enter **c:\sybex\courses.htm**. Click Go to load the file:

EXERCISE 19.12 *(continued)*

A yellow arrow appears in the upper-left corner of each table you can query.

5. In the open pane, click the second yellow arrow to select the data table.

6. Click Import to open the Import Data dialog box.

7. Click OK to import the data.

8. Select cell A1 on Sheet2.

9. Choose Data ➢ Import External Data ➢ New Web Query.

10. The New Web Query window opens and displays your browser's default home page.

11. In the Address list, enter www.msn.com. Click Go to load the file.

12. Using the selection arrows, select any table displayed in the pane.

13. Click Import to open the Import Data dialog box.

EXERCISE 19.12 *(continued)*

14. Click OK to import the data.

15. Save the workbook as **Web Queries**. Leave the workbook open for the next exercise.

Creating XML Queries

XML (Extensible Markup Language) is a web markup language for structured data, such as information in an Excel list or Access database table. XML, like HTML, uses tags; in HTML, tags are usually used for formatting. In XML, tags are used to define the structure of the data. XML files that are internally consistent (with appropriate start tags and end tags) are referred to as "well formed." Excel can open any well-formed XML file, or you can create a web query for an XML file.

Microsoft ✓ *Exam Objective*	**Create Extensible Markup Language (XML) Web queries**

In Exercise 19.13, you'll create an XML web query. You'll find that it is much like creating an HTML query, with one exception: Unlike a web page, which can contain many data sets, an XML file contains only one data set. You'll open the XML file directly in the Excel workbook.

EXERCISE 19.13

Creating an XML Query

For this exercise, use the Web Queries.xls workbook and the WNBA_ Draft.xml file you downloaded from the Sybex website. Place the XML file in the Sybex folder on your C: drive.

1. Open the Web Queries workbook saved in the last exercise. Select cell A1 in Sheet3.

2. Choose Data ➢ Import External Data ➢ New Web Query.

3. The New Web Query window opens and displays your browser's default home page.

EXERCISE 19.13 *(continued)*

4. In the Address list, enter **c:\sybex\wnba_draft.xml**. Click Go to load the file.

The XML displayed in the pane isn't a table per se, but the description used to create a data table.

5. In the open pane, click the yellow arrow to select the data table.

6. Click Import to open the Import Data dialog box.

7. Click OK to import the data.

8. Save and close the workbook.

9. Choose File ➢ Open to open the Open dialog box.

10. Select the WNBA_Draft.xml file (you may need to change the Files Of Type list to display All Files).

11. Click Open to open the XML file directly in Excel.

12. Close the workbook without saving the changes.

Summary

In this chapter, you learned a number of Excel Expert skills related to importing and manipulating data, including the following:

- Using subtotals to sum and average lists
- Defining and applying advanced filters
- Using data validation
- Importing data from external data sources
- Using Microsoft Query
- Creating database queries
- Creating web queries
- Creating XML queries
- Opening XML files

Chapter

20

Analyzing Data

MOUS EXCEL 2002 EXPERT EXAM OBJECTIVES COVERED IN THIS CHAPTER:

✓ Create a Microsoft PivotTable®, Microsoft PivotChart®, and PivotTable/PivotChart Reports

✓ Forecast values with what-if analysis

✓ Create and display scenarios

This chapter focuses on advanced data analysis features that truly test your Excel Expert skills. First, you'll create PivotTables and Pivot-Charts to summarize information in an Excel list. Then you will turn to the what-if analysis tools used to forecast the future values of business variables such as budget, sales, and per-unit costs. Finally, you'll learn to create and use scenarios to quickly switch a worksheet between two layouts or two sets of assumptions created with the what-if analysis tools.

Creating PivotTables and PivotCharts

The PivotTable Report, Excel 2002's equivalent of an Access cross-tab query, is a powerful data-summarization tool. A *PivotTable* summarizes the columns of information in a database in relation to one another. A *Pivot-Chart* is the graphical representation of a PivotTable. When you need to present thousands of rows of data in a meaningful fashion, you need a Pivot Table. The `Aurora Borealis WriteOffs` workbook used in earlier chapters contains a small database, but it would still take several subtotal operations to answer the following questions:

- What was the total cost of write-offs for each month?

- What was the value of seasonal goods write-offs for all employees? For individual employees?

- What is the damage total per employee?

You could sort the list and then add subtotals to answer any one of these questions. Then, to answer any other question, you would have to sort and subtotal again. A single PivotTable, shown in Figure 20.1, allows you to answer all of these questions and more. On the exam, you may be asked to create and/or modify either a PivotTable or PivotChart.

FIGURE 20.1 This PivotTable Report of the Aurora Borealis Writeoffs list summarizes write-offs by Employee and Reason and can be filtered by Date.

Page field button · Data field button · Column field button

	A	B	C	D	E	F
1	Date	(All)				
2						
3	Sum of Total Cost	Reason				
4	Employee	Damaged	Frost	Infected	Seasonal	Grand Total
5	AM	92.37	496.8		330.08	919.25
6	CC	70.46	557.76	22.95	56.25	707.42
7	GC	112.26	682.2			794.46
8	Grand Total	275.09	1736.76	22.95	386.33	2421.13

Row field button · Data area

Microsoft ✓ ***Exam Objective***

Create a Microsoft PivotTable®, Microsoft PivotChart®, and PivotTable/PivotChart Reports

---

Not all Excel lists are good candidates for PivotTable analysis. Lists contain many different types of information. PivotTables focus on two broad types of information:

- Data fields that can be summarized, such as the Cost field in the Aurora Borealis Writeoffs database

- Text fields that describe the data, such as the Employee, Date, and Reason fields

Numeric data fields can be summarized using SUM, AVERAGE, MAX, MIN, and the other aggregate functions including COUNT, which can also be used to summarize text fields.

While PivotTables are often associated with reporting data in two dimensions—for example, sales by month and county or registrations by term and academic major—you can create one-dimensional PivotTables, too. The PivotTable shown in Figure 20.2 summarizes write-offs by Reason.

FIGURE 20.2   A one-dimensional PivotTable, reporting write-off costs by Reason

	A	B
1	Date	(All) ▼
2		
3	Sum of Total Cost	
4	Reason ▼	Total
5	Damaged	275.09
6	Frost	1736.76
7	Infected	22.95
8	Seasonal	386.33
9	Grand Total	2421.13

You can easily extract this same information from the list using the subtotals feature, but the PivotTable has three distinct advantages over subtotals:

- Subtotals require a database sorted on the field by which you wish to subtotal. We didn't need to change the sort order of the database to create the PivotTable. If another user sorts the database, it won't affect the PivotTable.

- The subtotals feature inserts rows in the database, which makes it temporarily useless as a data source for mail merges, queries, and analysis. The PivotTable is created separate from the subtotals.

- The most exciting aspect of PivotTables is that they are dynamic. After you create a PivotTable, you can rearrange the columns and rows, add and remove data fields, and add calculated fields and items to glean more information from the data. You can pivot the summaries around the detail data, providing different points of view of the details—hence the name *PivotTable*.

Excel 2002's PivotTable feature is a simple, and simply incredible, tool. So fasten your seatbelt, open the 20-1.xls workbook, and let's go to work.

Creating a PivotTable with the Wizard

Use the PivotTable and PivotChart Wizard to create an Excel PivotTable. In Exercise 20.1, you'll create the two-dimensional PivotTable shown in Figure 20.1.

EXERCISE 20.1

Creating a PivotTable Report

1. Open the 20-1.xls workbook and choose Enable Macros.

2. Select any cell in the list (for example, A5).

3. Choose Data ➢ PivotTable And PivotChart Report to launch the wizard:

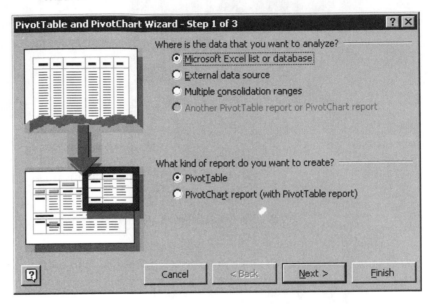

4. In the first step of the wizard, select the type of data you want to work with: Microsoft Excel List Or Database.

5. Select the kind of report you want to create: PivotTable. Click Next to move to the second step of the wizard.

6. In the second step of the wizard, verify the range of the database. If there is no range selected, or if the range is incorrect, select the correct range. The correct range includes the column labels as well as the data in the list.

EXERCISE 20.1 *(continued)*

7. Click Next to move to the third step of the wizard:

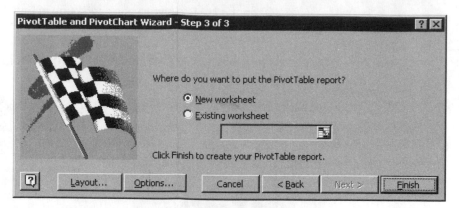

In the third step, you specify the destination. The default destination is a new worksheet. To place the PivotTable in an existing worksheet, click Existing Worksheet. Then identify a cell address for the upper-left corner of the PivotTable.

8. Choose New Worksheet. Click Finish to create an empty PivotTable Report.

9. Save the workbook. Leave it open for the next exercise.

Adding Items to the PivotTable

When you complete the wizard, Excel displays the PivotTable, the Pivot Table toolbar, and the PivotTable Field List (which we'll simply refer to as the Field List), as shown in Figure 20.3. A PivotTable contains four areas, which are clearly labeled: the Page area, the Column area, the Row area, and the Data area.

You create a PivotTable by placing fields in each of the areas. You place text fields you want to compare in the Row and Column areas. When the table is created, Excel will examine the fields you've chosen. Each unique entry becomes a row or column heading—an *item*—in the PivotTable. If one of the fields has fewer entries than the other, it's a better candidate for the Column area so you don't have to scroll horizontally to view the table.

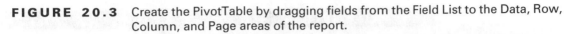

FIGURE 20.3 Create the PivotTable by dragging fields from the Field List to the Data, Row, Column, and Page areas of the report.

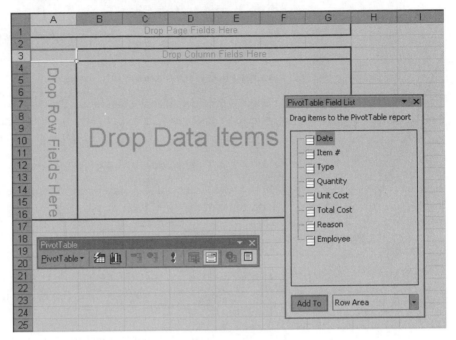

While you can filter items in the Row area and Column area, the Page area is used specifically to filter the entire PivotTable. If you need to create separate reports for values in one or more columns, drag their field buttons to the Page area.

Information in the Data area is summarized (SUM, AVERAGE, COUNT), so numeric fields are generally placed there. If you place a text field in the Data area, you can only COUNT the number of entries for each column and row. As you drop a field button into the Data area, Excel indicates the default summary type for the data. SUM is the default for numeric values; COUNT is the default for text entries, dates, or times.

In Exercise 20.2, you'll use the Field List controls or drag and drop from the Field List to place fields in the report.

If you need more room, you can drag the PivotTable Field List to the left or right edge of the window to dock it as a task pane.

Adding Items to the PivotTable

For this exercise, use the 20-1.xls workbook saved in the previous exercise.

1. In the Field List, select the Employee item.

2. Make sure Row Area is selected in the Add To drop-down list, and then click the Add To button to add the Employee item to the Row area.

3. In the Field List, select the Date item.

4. In the Add To drop-down list, choose Column Area. Click Add To to add the dates to the Column area.

5. Drag the Date button in cell B3 to cell A1 and drop it to move the Date item to the Page area.

6. In the Field List, choose the Reason item. Drag the item and drop it in the Column area (for example, B3) to add the Reason item to the table.

7. In the Field List, choose the Total Cost item. Drag the item and drop it in the Data area (C8, for example) to add the Total Cost item to the Data area.

8. Save the workbook. Leave it open for the next exercise.

If a column of numbers includes text entries, you're limited to the COUNT function, even if most entries are numeric—a good reason *not* to use text values like None or NA to indicate the absence of a value. Use Replace (Edit ➢ Replace) to replace text entries like NA with blanks; simply leave the Replace With text box blank. Blanks are also easier to filter than the text entries used to indicate blanks. To quickly locate all the blank entries in a column, turn on an AutoFilter (Data ➢ Filter ➢ AutoFilter) and choose Blanks from the list of values on the column's filter list.

Modifying Table Layout

What you learn from one PivotTable often raises questions that another PivotTable can easily answer. Rather than create a new PivotTable, you can change the layout of an existing PivotTable by dragging a field button to another area. Excel 2002 automatically updates the PivotTable.

You can place more than one field in each area to create a richer analysis. In Figure 20.4, for example, the Row area contains both the Employee and Reason fields so you can see the breakdown by employee.

FIGURE 20.4 Each PivotTable area can include multiple fields.

	A	B	C
1	Date	(All) ▼	
2			
3	Sum of Total Cost		
4	Employee ▼	Reason ▼	Total
5	AM	Damaged	92.37
6		Frost	496.8
7		Seasonal	330.08
8	AM Total		919.25
9	CC	Damaged	70.46
10		Frost	557.76
11		Infected	22.95
12		Seasonal	56.25
13	CC Total		707.42
14	GC	Damaged	112.26
15		Frost	682.2
16	GC Total		794.46
17	Grand Total		2421.13

In Exercise 20.3, you'll modify the table layout to create the table shown in Figure 20.2 and then the table shown in Figure 20.4.

EXERCISE 20.3

Modifying Table Layout

For this exercise, use the 20-1.xls workbook saved in the previous exercise.

1. Point to the Employee item button in cell A4. Drag the field button out of the PivotTable area. A large *X* appears on the button. Release the mouse button to drop and delete the field.

2. Drag the Reason button from the Column area to the Row area and drop it to move the Reason field to the Row area.

3. Drag the Employee item from the Field List and drop it on the Reason button to display two items in the Row area.

4. Save the workbook. Leave it open for the next exercise.

The PivotTable toolbar and Field List are displayed only when you select one or more cells in a PivotTable. If one or more cells in the table are selected and the toolbar is not displayed, right-click any toolbar and select PivotTable from the list.

Filtering PivotTable Items

You can filter the table to display one or more values in a field. In Exercise 20.4, you'll filter the table to hide the write-offs due to frost damage and seasonal reasons.

EXERCISE 20.4

Filtering a PivotTable

For this exercise, use the 20-1.xls workbook used in the previous exercise.

1. Click the down arrow on the Reason item button:

2. Clear the check boxes for Frost and Seasonal.

3. Click OK to apply the filter.

4. Click the down arrow on the Reason button again.

5. Enable the Show All check box.

6. Click OK to remove the filter.

7. Drag the Employee item button to the Column area in cell C3.

8. Drag the Reason item button from the PivotTable and drop it outside the PivotTable to remove it from the table.

9. Save the workbook. Leave it open for the next exercise.

Grouping PivotTable Items

Grouping combines items and is usually used to combine date fields into months or years. If you drop the Date item from the Aurora Borealis Writeoffs worksheet into the Row area, there are almost as many rows as there are in the original database.

To analyze by month, quarter, or year, you need to group the data in the Date field, as you'll see in Exercise 20.5.

EXERCISE 20.5

Grouping Dates in a PivotTable

For this exercise, use the 20-1.xls workbook saved in the previous exercise.

1. Drag the Date item from the Page area and drop it into the Row area.

2. Right-click the Date item button and choose Group And Show Detail ➢ Group from the shortcut menu to open the Grouping dialog box:

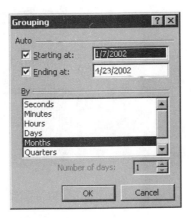

3. Choose Months from the By list.

EXERCISE 20.5 *(continued)*

4. Click OK to group the dates in the table.

5. Save the workbook. Leave it open for the next exercise.

The By list box in the Grouping dialog box is a multipick list; choose Months if you want to group by month regardless of year, for example, if details from March 2001 and March 2002 should be combined into a single row. Choose both Months and Years if the same month in different years should be in separate rows.

Changing the Summary and Format for Data Fields

By default, Excel totals number values placed in the Data area and counts text items. If you want to count numeric values or average numbers, you must change the summarization method, as you'll see in Exercise 20.6.

EXERCISE 20.6

Changing Field Settings

For this exercise, use the 20-1.xls workbook saved in the previous exercise.

1. Double-click the Sum Of Total Cost button in cell A3 to open the PivotTable Field dialog box for the Total Cost item:

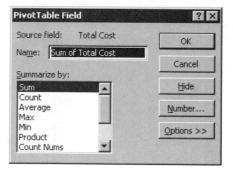

2. Choose Average in the Summarize By list.

EXERCISE 20.6 *(continued)*

You can change the name displayed on the item button in the table. Names can include spaces. You cannot, however, change the name to the name of an item in the table. For example, you can't change Sum Of Total Cost to Total Cost.

3. Edit the text in the Name text box to read **Average Total Cost**.

4. Click OK to change the summarization method and the field name in the table.

5. Drag the Employee item button from the Column area and remove it from the table. Drag the Reason item from the Field List to the Column area to show the average by month by Reason.

The default number format in a PivotTable is General, so the averages are pretty ugly.

6. Double-click the Average Total Cost item button to reopen the PivotTable Field dialog box.

7. Click the Number button in the PivotTable Field dialog box to open the Format Cells dialog box.

8. Choose Accounting, 2 decimal places, $ symbol.

9. Click OK to return to the PivotTable Field dialog box.

10. Click OK to close the dialog box and apply the format to the Average Total Cost data.

11. Save the workbook. Leave it open for the next exercise.

Applying an AutoFormat

There are 22 different AutoFormats designed specifically for PivotTables. The first 10 AutoFormats captioned Report 1 through Report 10 are indented formats designed to resemble traditional printed database reports, which were, in turn, based on outlines used in text documents. These Pivot-Table Reports look very little like PivotTables and a lot like reports you'd spend a fair amount of time creating and formatting in Access or a reporting application. Table 1 through Table 10 and the Classic PivotTable formats resemble tables more than reports. In Exercise 20.7, you'll apply an Auto-Format to the PivotTable.

EXERCISE 20.7

Applying an AutoFormat

For this exercise, use the 20-1.xls workbook saved in the previous exercise.

1. Select any cell in the PivotTable.

2. Choose Format ➢ AutoFormat from the menu or click the Format Report button on the PivotTable toolbar to open the AutoFormat dialog box:

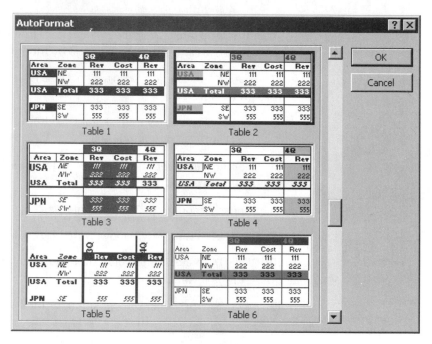

3. Choose Table 7 from the sample formats. Click OK to apply the format.

The Report AutoFormats may change the layout of the table as part of the formatting.

4. Click the PivotTable, and then choose Format ➢ AutoFormat from the menu or click the Format Report button on the PivotTable toolbar to open the AutoFormat dialog box.

5. Choose Report 7 from the sample reports. Click OK to apply the format.

EXERCISE 20.7 *(continued)*

6. Click Undo to return to the Table 7 format.

7. Double-click the Sheet1 sheet tab. Name the sheet that contains the PivotTable **PivotTable**.

8. Save the workbook. Leave it open for the next exercise.

Creating PivotCharts

PivotCharts help users understand data in a way that conventional database reports cannot. You can base a PivotChart on an existing PivotTable or a database. If you base a PivotChart on a database, Excel creates an associated PivotTable before creating the chart, so if you need to create a table and a chart, you can save a step by simply creating the chart.

If you select any cell in a PivotTable and click the Chart Wizard button on the PivotTable toolbar, Excel creates a PivotChart.

In Exercise 20.8, you'll create a new PivotTable and PivotChart.

EXERCISE 20.8

Creating a PivotChart

For this exercise, use the 20-1.xls workbook saved in the previous exercise.

1. Select the 2002 WriteOffs worksheet. Click anywhere in the database, and then select Data ➢ PivotTable And PivotChart Report.

2. In the first step of the wizard, select PivotChart Report (With Pivot-Table Report) and click Next.

3. In the second wizard step, verify that the correct data range is selected and click Next.

You previously created a PivotTable with the selected data range, so Excel prompts you to create a chart based on the existing PivotTable. Basing one PivotTable on another saves file size and memory, so this is a good idea unless you intend to change the data source for the existing PivotTable in the future.

EXERCISE 20.8 *(continued)*

4. Click Yes to base this report and chart on the existing PivotTable.

5. Excel prompts you to select a PivotTable. Click Next.

6. In the third step in the wizard, choose a location (New Worksheet) for the associated PivotTable. Click Finish to create the empty PivotTable and PivotChart:

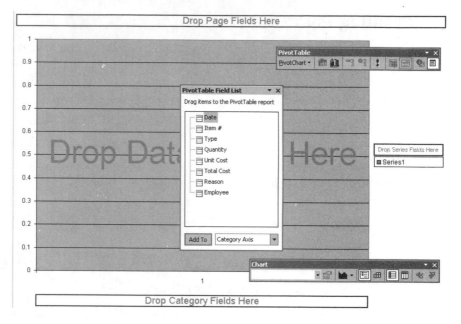

Note: Excel uses the default chart type to create the PivotChart. To change the chart type, choose Chart ➤ Chart Type from the menu and choose Column and the Clustered Column subtype.

7. Rename the new worksheet (Sheet2) **Supporting Table**.

8. Rename the new chart sheet (Chart1) **Column Chart**.

The new PivotTable worksheet and PivotChart chart sheet are linked, so you can add elements to the chart using either the table or the chart sheet.

9. In the PivotTable in the Supporting Table worksheet, drag the Reason item from the Field List into the Row area.

EXERCISE 20.8 (continued)

10. Drag the Total Cost item into the Data area.

11. Switch to the Column Chart sheet.

12. Drag the Employee item from the Field List and drop it on the legend, which is labeled Drop Series Fields Here.

13. Click Print Preview to preview the chart.

14. Save and close the workbook.

The PivotChart fields have many of the same properties as PivotTable fields. Use the filter drop-down lists to filter chart items, or double-click a data button to change the summarization method. Use the Chart toolbar and menu to modify the chart elements as you would any Excel chart.

Using Business Analysis Tools

You already know how to use many of the business analysis tools: Excel's functions and formulas. For more advanced work, Excel includes specialized forecasting tools, often referred to as what-if tools.

Using the What-If Tools

There are three tools used in what-if analysis: data tables, Goal Seek, and Solver. Data tables are the least complex, and Solver the most complex.

Microsoft
Exam
Objective

Forecast values with what-if analysis

Creating Data Tables

Data tables are used to show the results of changing either one or two variables used as arguments in a formula. The worksheet in Figure 20.5 uses the square root function (SQRT) to return the square root of a series of values. The syntax of the function is =SQRT(value). To create a single-variable data table, you enter the series of values in a row or, as shown in Figure 20.5, in a column.

FIGURE 20.5 The Squares worksheet uses a single formula to calculate the square root of each value in column A.

	A	B	C
1			
2			
3			
4		=SQRT(B1)	
5	1	SQRT(**number**)	
6	2	1.414214	
7	3	1.732051	
8	4	2	
9	5	2.236068	
10	6	2.44949	
11	7	2.645751	
12	8	2.828427	
13	9	3	
14	10	3.162278	
15	11	3.316625	
16	12	3.464102	
17	13	3.605551	
18	14	3.741657	
19	15	3.872983	

The data table feature uses an *input cell* to temporarily store each value from the data series as it calculates results. Rather than creating nine formulas that refer to cells A4 through A12, you create one formula that refers to the input cell. Excel changes the value of the input cell as it creates the table, so the input cell should be an empty cell. In Exercise 20.9, you'll create this data table that uses a single variable.

EXERCISE 20.9

Creating a Single-Variable Data Table

For this exercise, use the 20-9.xls workbook downloaded from the Sybex website.

1. On the Squares worksheet, select the cell directly above the first cell that will return results: B4.

2. Enter the formula to calculate the square root of the input cell, B1: =SQRT(B1)

3. Select the data table range, including the formula, data series, and results cells: A4:B19. Do not include the input cell. Do not hold Ctrl and select multiple ranges. Do not include extra cells.

4. With the cells selected, choose Data ➢ Table to open the Table dialog box:

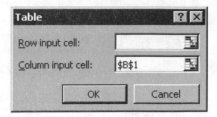

5. Click the Column Input Cell text box and then click cell B1. (You enter the input cell in the Row Input Cell text box if your data is in a row.)

6. Click OK to create the data table.

7. Save the workbook. Keep it open for the next exercise.

Now you'll create a data table that uses two sets of variables: the simple Multiplication Table shown in Figure 20.6.

FIGURE 20.6 The Multiplication Table was created using a two-variable data table.

	A	B	C	D	E	F	G	H	I	J	K
1	**Multiplication Table**										
2	**Two-Variable Data Table**										
3											
4	**0**	**1**	**2**	**3**	**4**	**5**	**6**	**7**	**8**	**9**	**10**
5	**1**	1	2	3	4	5	6	7	8	9	10
6	**2**	2	4	6	8	10	12	14	16	18	20
7	**3**	3	6	9	12	15	18	21	24	27	30
8	**4**	4	8	12	16	20	24	28	32	36	40
9	**5**	5	10	15	20	25	30	35	40	45	50
10	**6**	6	12	18	24	30	36	42	48	54	60
11	**7**	7	14	21	28	35	42	49	56	63	70
12	**8**	8	16	24	32	40	48	56	64	72	80
13	**9**	9	18	27	36	45	54	63	72	81	90
14	**10**	10	20	30	40	50	60	70	80	90	100
15	**11**	11	22	33	44	55	66	77	88	99	110
16	**12**	12	24	36	48	60	72	84	96	108	120
17	**13**	13	26	39	52	65	78	91	104	117	130
18	**14**	14	28	42	56	70	84	98	112	126	140
19	**15**	15	30	45	60	75	90	105	120	135	150
20	**16**	16	32	48	64	80	96	112	128	144	160
21	**17**	17	34	51	68	85	102	119	136	153	170
22	**18**	18	36	54	72	90	108	126	144	162	180
23	**19**	19	38	57	76	95	114	133	152	171	190
24	**20**	20	40	60	80	100	120	140	160	180	200

In the two-variable table, layout is critical. The formula cell must be directly above the column of data and directly to the left of the row of data. The column and row cannot share common cells. The process to create the table is the same, but two input cells are required, as you'll see in Exercise 20.10.

EXERCISE 20.10

Creating a Two-Variable Data Table

For this exercise, use the 20-9.xls workbook you used in the previous exercise.

1. On the Multiply worksheet, select cell A4. Cell A4 contains a formula that refers to the two input cells: =D1*E1

2. Select the range A4:K24.

3. Choose Data ➢ Table from the menu to open the Table dialog box.

4. Select D1 as the Row Input Cell and E1 as the Column Input Cell.

   The formula uses multiplication, so you can assign either cell as the Row or Column Input Cell. Just make sure you refer to both cells.

5. Click OK to create the data table.

6. Save the workbook and leave it open for the next exercise.

The formulas in a data table are an array. You can format the values (including conditional formatting), but you can't delete one value from the table. If you try, you'll see this message:

To delete the results, select the entire array of results (not the original row and column of data) and press Delete, or choose Edit ➢ Clear ➢ Contents.

Forecasting and Modeling Using Goal Seek and Solver

Business forecasts try to simulate future behavior of variables such as gross profit based on information gathered from a variety of sources. In Excel, forecasting always involves creating a model—one or more worksheets with formulas to show how different variables interrelate—and then applying Goal Seek or Solver to the model to forecast values.

Excel's analysis tools require something to analyze. We'll use a fictitious company, Rack 'Em Up Products Corporation, to work with Excel's analysis tools. The company makes a variety of kits for the do-it-yourselfer. The Wood Rack Kits division makes kits to hold firewood. The RackEmUp Goal Seek sheet in the 20-9.xls workbook, shown in Figure 20.7, contains a model that includes information on the income generated by wood rack kit sales and the expenses involved in manufacturing the kits. The Goal column, column F, is a duplicate of column E.

FIGURE 20.7 This model shows income, expenses, and gross profit at different levels of production.

	A	B	C	D	E	F
1	Rack 'Em Up Products					
2	Wood Rack Kits					
3						
4	Income	Current	High	Medium	Low	Goal
5	Units Produced	41,390	52,000	45,000	40,000	40,000
6	Unit Price	13.72	11.60	13.00	14.00	14.00
7	Total Income	567,954	603,200	585,000	560,000	560,000
8						
9	Expense					
10	Fixed Expense	80,000	80,000	80,000	80,000	80,000
11	Labor Expense	248,340	324,000	270,000	240,000	240,000
12	Material Expense	69,121	86,840	75,150	66,800	66,800
13	Total Expense	397,461	490,840	425,150	386,800	386,800
14						
15	Gross Profit	170,492	112,360	159,850	173,200	173,200

Some of the expenses are *fixed expenses:* expenses that are the same amount no matter how many firewood holders are manufactured. Other expenses (like labor and materials) that vary based on production are *variable expenses.*

The RackEmUp Goal Seek sheet contains a number of comments. This is typical in worksheets used for forecasting. Every number or formula in the model has some basis, but it's not always easy to reconstruct the source in six months or a year.

Columns B, C, D, and E show results for four different levels of production (row 5). We could continue adding columns and copying formulas until we arrived at an answer. Fortunately, there's a better way. You'll use Excel's Goal Seek and Solver features to forecast values outside the current model. Use Goal Seek analysis when you want to find a specific solution by changing one variable. Solver, a linear programming tool, supports multivariate analysis and is the tool designed for most real-world problems where more than one variable can change or when you're looking for an optimal value rather than a specific numerical goal.

Using Goal Seek

Goal Seek is used to calculate backwards—to determine the values necessary to reach a specific goal. Goal Seek changes an underlying value until the value in the goal cell is equal to the goal. Excel will begin by trying an upper and lower value for the underlying value. If the goal falls between the initial values, Goal Seek then narrows the value in small increments until the goal value is within 0.01 of the goal. If the goal value is outside the initial range, Goal Seek will try larger values. Each attempt to meet the goal is an *iteration*.

The default settings (Tools ➤ Options ➤ Calculation) instruct Excel to cycle through 100 iterations before giving up.

If you have a worksheet model, you can use Goal Seek to get a specific answer. For example, one of the Rack 'Em Up managers wants to know how many units must be manufactured and sold to result in gross profits of exactly $150,000 per month. In Exercise 20.11, you'll use Goal Seek to find the answer.

EXERCISE 20.11

Using Goal Seek to Find a Specific Value

For this exercise, use the 20-9.xls workbook saved in the previous exercise.

1. Open the RackEmUp Goal Seek worksheet.

2. Choose Tools ➤ Goal Seek from the menu bar to open the Goal Seek dialog box.

EXERCISE 20.11 *(continued)*

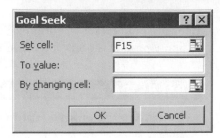

3. Enter references or values in all three controls of the Goal Seek dialog box:

   - Set Cell: The cell that will contain the goal result. There must be a formula in this cell. Enter **F15** as the Set Cell.

   - To Value: The target value. Enter **150000** as the value.

   - By Changing Cell: The cell that contains the value that will be incrementally changed to try to reach the goal in the Set Cell. This cell must contain a value rather than a formula. Enter **F5** as the cell to change.

4. Click OK to start Goal Seek.

Goal Seek returns a solution in the Goal Seek Status dialog box:

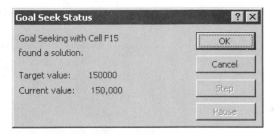

5. To accept the solution, click OK in the Goal Seek Status dialog box.

When you choose to accept the Goal Seek solution, the solution over-writes the existing values with the solution values. In this case, the match is exact.

6. Save the workbook and keep it open for the next exercise.

Goal Seek was able to find a value for Units Produced that resulted in a Gross Profit of exactly $150,000. Clicking the OK button replaced the figures in the Set Cell and Changing Cell with the Goal Seek results. Clicking Cancel would retain the original figures.

Some problems don't have a solution, as you'll see in Exercise 20.12.

EXERCISE 20.12

Using Goal Seek to Rule Out a Solution

For this exercise, use the 20-9.xls workbook saved in the previous exercise.

1. Open the RackEmUp Goal Seek worksheet.

2. Choose Tools ➢ Goal Seek from the menu bar to open the Goal Seek dialog box.

3. Enter references or values in all three controls of the Goal Seek dialog box:

   - Set Cell: **F15**

   - To Value: **250000**

   - By Changing Cell: **F5**

4. Click OK to start Goal Seek.

Goal Seek returns a message in the Goal Seek Status dialog box:

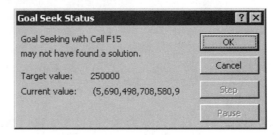

The target value entered for Gross Profit was 250,000. Goal Seek has already tried 100 numbers. The last number tested—a very large number—is displayed as the Current Value; the other numbers in column F are so large that they can't be displayed in the current column width. Goal Seek has already tried both positive and negative numbers as large as the Current Value shown in the dialog box. It's unlikely that additional iterations would result in a solution.

EXERCISE 20.12 *(continued)*

5. To reject the solution, click Cancel in the Goal Seek Status dialog box to retain the original values.

6. Save the workbook and keep it open for the next exercise.

Even when Goal Seek can't find a solution, however, you know more than you knew before. Given the values for price, fixed expenses, and variable expenses, Rack 'Em Up cannot make $250,000 a month from the Wood Rack Kits division no matter how many kits they manufacture (or fail to manufacture).

Using Solver

Solver is used to find an *optimal* solution: the largest or smallest value rather than a specific value goal such as 150,000. Optimization has many business applications. Solver can be used to find the least-expensive solution to a problem or a solution that maximizes income. You also use Solver rather than Goal Seek when you need to change values in multiple cells or apply constraints to the range of solutions. Solver can also be used, like Goal Seek, to find a specific value. As with Goal Seek, a Solver solution overwrites existing data.

If you don't see Solver on the Tools menu, click Tools ➤ Add-Ins and choose Solver Add-In in the Add-Ins dialog box. Excel may prompt you for the CD to install this feature.

In Exercise 20.13, you'll use Solver to find the highest possible gross profit for the Rack 'Em Up Wood Rack Kits division.

EXERCISE 20.13

Using Solver to Find an Optimal Solution

For this exercise, use the 20-9.xls workbook saved in the previous exercise.

1. Open the RackEmUp Solver worksheet.

2. Select the cell where the results should appear: F15

EXERCISE 20.13 *(continued)*

3. Choose Tools ➢ Solver. Click OK to clear the message box and open the Solver Parameters dialog box:

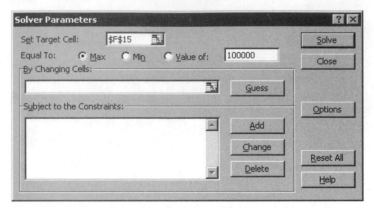

4. Enter references or values in the following controls:

- Set Target Cell: Solver's Target Cell is the same as Goal Seek's Set Cell: the cell that the final result should appear in. Enter **F15** for the Target Cell.

- Equal To: Set the Max, Min, or Value Of option to solve for the largest or smallest possible number or a set value. Choose the Max option.

- As with Goal Seek, the By Changing Cells value is the cell that Solver is to change to find the solution indicated. Enter **F5** as the Changing Cell.

5. Click the Solve button to look for a solution.

Solver reports success or failure in the Solver Results dialog box:

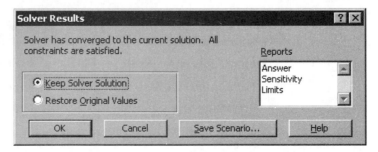

EXERCISE 20.13 *(continued)*

6. Choose Keep Solver Solution. Click OK to replace the original values with the Solver solution values.

7. Save the workbook. Leave it open for the next exercise.

 There's more you can do with Solver, including solving for multiple variables, but this is the limit of what will appear on the exam. For more information on the what-if tools in Excel, see *Mastering Excel 2002* from Sybex.

Working with Scenarios

Wouldn't it be nice if you could save models that reflect different scenarios: best case, worst case, current, and most likely? Excel has just the tool for this type of what-if analysis! You can create and save different groups of values using Excel's Scenarios feature and then switch between scenarios within the same workbook.

Microsoft ✓ *Exam Objective*   **Create and display scenarios**

In Exercise 20.14, you'll create various scenarios.

EXERCISE 20.14

Creating Scenarios

For this exercise, use the RackEmUp Solver worksheet in the 20-9.xls workbook.

1. Choose Tools ➢ Scenarios to open the Scenario Manager.

2. Click the Add button to open the Add Scenario dialog box.

3. In the Scenario Name text box, type the name for the scenario: **Optimal Production**

4. Enter the address of the cell or cells you wish to change in the Change Cells field: **F5**

5. Enter additional details about the scenario in the Comment field. Include your name and the text **Optimal production calculated using Solver**.

6. Click OK to open the Scenario Values dialog box. The value from cell F5 is already entered in the dialog box. Click OK to return to the Scenario Manager dialog box.

7. Click Add to open the Add Scenario dialog box.

8. In the Scenario Name text box, type a name for the scenario: **July 2002**

9. Enter the address of the cell or cells you wish to change in the Change Cells field: **F5**

10. Enter additional details about the scenario in the Comment field. Include your name and the text **Actual production for July 2002**.

11. Click OK to open the Scenario Values dialog box and enter the value **39050** for this scenario.

12. Click OK to return to the Scenario Manager.

13. Click Close to close the Scenario Manager.

14. Change the label in cell F4 to **Forecast**.

15. Save the workbook. Leave it open for the next exercise.

If you're sharing a workbook with other users, you can protect the scenario by preventing changes or hiding it in the Add Scenario dialog box. The scenario is not protected until you protect the worksheet (Tools ➤ Protection ➤ Protect Sheet).

In Exercise 20.15, you'll display the scenarios you just created.

Displaying Scenarios

For this exercise, use the 20-9.xls workbook saved in the previous exercise.

1. Open the Scenario Manager (Tools ➤ Scenarios) and choose the July 2002 scenario from the list.

2. Click the Show button to display the scenario results in your worksheet.

3. Open the Scenario Manager if necessary and choose the Optimal Production scenario from the list.

4. Click the Show button to display the scenario results.

5. Close the Scenario Manager. Save and close the workbook.

Goal Seek and Solver both support scenarios. To save the results of an analysis operation as a scenario, click the Save Scenario button in the Solver Or Goal Seek Results dialog box before you accept or reject the results.

As with Goal Seek and Solver, there is much more you can do with scenarios, including summarizing scenarios in a single worksheet to show a series of alternatives. For more information on scenarios, see *Mastering Excel 2002*.

Summary

In this chapter, you learned to use high-end data analysis and forecasting tools, including the following:

- PivotTable Reports
- PivotCharts
- Data tables
- Goal Seek
- Solver
- Scenarios

Chapter

21

Sharing Excel Data with Others

MOUS EXCEL 2002 EXPERT EXAM OBJECTIVES COVERED IN THIS CHAPTER:

- ✓ Modify passwords, protections, and properties
- ✓ Create a shared workbook
- ✓ Track, accept and reject changes to workbooks
- ✓ Merge workbooks

Effective collaboration is the key to any successful business today. In this chapter, we'll explore Excel's collaboration tools such as sharing workbooks, tracking changes in workbooks, and merging workbooks. First, you'll learn how to use passwords and protection to safeguard workbooks you share—or would rather not share—with others.

Before you begin this chapter, you should visit the Sybex website and download the file 4113Ch21.zip. This package contains the files necessary to complete some of the exercises in this chapter.

Modifying Passwords, Protections, and Properties

You can protect workbooks, worksheets, and ranges within a workbook in Excel 2002. You protect a workbook, worksheet, or range by specifying a password that must be entered to work in or view the workbook, view or modify the worksheet, or alter data in the protected range.

Microsoft ✓ *Exam Objective*

Modify passwords, protections, and properties

Setting a Workbook Password

The most general form of protection is setting a password that the user must supply to view and/or edit a workbook. You create a workbook password when you save the workbook, as you'll see in Exercise 21.1.

EXERCISE 21.1

Setting a Workbook Password

For this exercise, use the 21-1.xls workbook you downloaded from the Sybex website.

1. Open the 21-1.xls workbook.

2. Choose File ➤ Save As from the menu.

3. From the Save As dialog box toolbar, click the Tools button and choose General Options from the menu to open the Save Options dialog box:

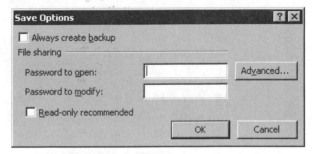

4. In the Password To Open text box, type **open**.

5. In the Password To Modify text box, type **sesame**.

6. Click OK.

7. When the Confirm dialog box opens, type **open** to confirm the open password:

8. When the Confirm dialog box opens again, type **sesame** to confirm the modify password and return to the Save As dialog box.

EXERCISE 21.1 *(continued)*

9. Click Save.

10. Click Yes to overwrite the existing file.

11. Close the workbook.

12. Open the 21-1.xls workbook again.

13. Excel prompts you to enter the password to open the workbook. Type **open** and click OK:

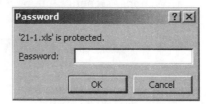

14. You are then prompted to provide the password to modify the workbook. Type **sesame** and click OK to open the workbook with permission to modify the workbook:

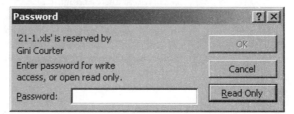

15. Save the workbook. Leave it open for the next exercise.

Protecting Workbooks

You can further protect a workbook to prevent other users from changing the structure of the workbook so that worksheets can't be hidden, unhidden, renamed, moved, inserted, or deleted. Or, you can protect the workbook's windows to lock in the windows that can be displayed. In Exercise 21.2, you'll protect the structure of a workbook.

EXERCISE 21.2

Protecting Workbook Structure

For this exercise, use the 21-1.xls workbook you saved in the previous exercise. If you need to open the workbook, see steps 13 and 14 of Exercise 21.1 for the passwords.

Before protecting the workbook, you'll hide the Lookups worksheet.

1. In the 21-1.xls workbook, select the Lookups worksheet.

2. Choose Format ➢ Sheet ➢ Hide from the menu to hide the worksheet.

3. Choose Tools ➢ Protection ➢ Protect Workbook from the menu to open the Protect Workbook dialog box.

4. Make sure the Structure check box is enabled.

5. To prevent other users from turning off the protection, type the password **prevent** in the Password textbox and then click OK.

6. When prompted, confirm the password by typing it again. Click OK.

7. Choose Format ➢ Sheet from the menu. Notice that the Hide and Unhide commands are both disabled.

8. Save the workbook. Leave it open for the next exercise.

Protecting Worksheets and Ranges

Each cell in a workbook has a Locked property, which is enabled by default. Although the cell is locked, the Locked property is enforced only when you protect the cell's worksheet. Before protecting a worksheet, you must unlock all cells where you'll want users to enter data. In Excel 2002, there are two ways to do this:

- Unlock the range by turning off the cells' Locked property. This unlocks the range for all users, so anyone who can edit any sheet in the workbook can enter, edit, or delete data in these cells.

- Use the Allow Users To Edit Ranges feature to provide specific users with permission to edit the cells.

With either option, the remaining worksheet cells are locked only after you protect the worksheet.

Unlocking Ranges

In the Exercise 21.3, you'll unlock ranges and then protect the worksheet. All the cells you will unlock in this exercise have a yellow or green fill.

EXERCISE 21.3

Unlocking Ranges

For this exercise, use the 21-1.xls workbook saved in the previous exercise.

1. On the Hours-Expenses worksheet, select cells B3 and B5.

2. Choose Format ➢ Cells to open the Format Cells dialog box. On the Protection tab, turn off the Locked check box.

3. Click OK to unlock cells B3 and B5.

4. Select cells B8:D27 and F8:H27.

5. Right-click in the selection and choose Format Cells from the shortcut menu to open the Format Cells dialog box.

6. On the Protection tab, turn off the Locked check box. Click OK to unlock the cells.

7. Select cells A8: A27.

8. Right-click and choose Format Cells from the shortcut menu. On the Protection tab, turn on the Hidden check box to hide the formulas in the cells.

9. Click OK to hide the formulas in the selected cells.

10. Choose Tools ➢ Protection ➢ Protect Sheet to open the Protect Sheet dialog box.

EXERCISE 21.3 *(continued)*

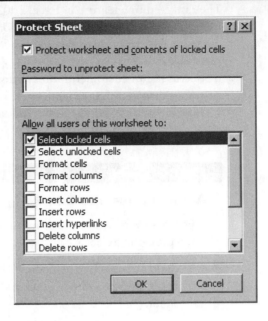

11. Scroll the list of user actions you can allow. Leave the first two check boxes turned on to allow users to select locked and unlocked cells.

12. In the Password text box, enter **protect**. Click OK.

13. When prompted, reenter the password **protect**. Click OK.

14. Select cell E8. Note that the formula is visible in the formula bar.

15. Select cell A8. The formula is hidden.

16. Attempt to enter data in A8. Do not remove protection when prompted to do so.

17. Save the workbook as **Hours and Expenses.xls**. Leave it open for the next exercise.

Allowing Users to Edit Ranges

The range-editing feature in Excel 2002 provides two new types of security: user-based and range-based. Permission can be granted based on either passwords or network authentication, and different permissions can be granted for specific ranges of cells. For example, in a customer table, you might let one user edit customer address information and another user edit only customer discount data. This feature is operating system–dependent and works only with Windows 2000. In Exercise 21.4, you'll allow users to edit ranges of cells.

EXERCISE 21.4

Allowing Users to Edit Ranges

For this exercise use the Hours and Expenses.xls workbook saved in the previous exercise.

1. Choose Tools ≻ Protection ≻ Unprotect Sheet. When prompted, enter the password **protect** and click OK to unprotect the worksheet.

2. In the Name box, choose Clients_Miles to select the named range.

3. Choose Tools ≻ Protection ≻ Allow Users To Edit Ranges to open the Allow Users To Edit Ranges dialog box:

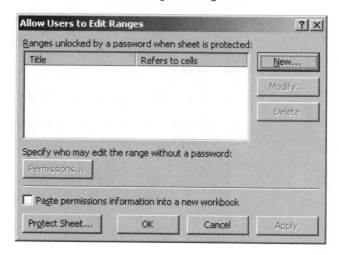

EXERCISE 21.4 *(continued)*

4. Click the New button to open the New Range dialog box:

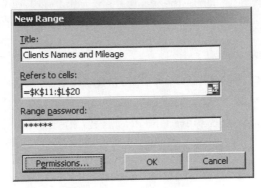

5. In the Title text box, enter a descriptive name for the selected cells: **Client Names and Mileage**

6. Verify the selection in the Refers To Cells text box.

7. Enter the password **unlock** for this range of cells. Click OK.

8. Reenter the password **unlock**. Click OK to return to the Allow Users To Edit Ranges dialog box.

   The Client Names and Mileage range appears in the list of ranges.

9. Click Apply to apply the change.

10. Click the Protect Sheet button to open the Protect Sheet dialog box.

11. Enter the password **protect**. Click OK, and then reenter the password. Click OK again to protect the worksheet.

12. Select cell K11. Begin typing the corrected company name: **ABC Limited**

13. Excel opens the Unlock Range dialog box, prompting you to enter a password. Enter **unlock** and click OK.

14. Change the value in K11 to **ABC Limited**.

15. Save the workbook. Leave it open for the next exercise.

If all users with range-editing permission have accounts on your network, you can authenticate them with their login. Click the Permissions button to use network authentication rather than a password.

Setting Workbook Properties

Every file has properties. When you open My Computer or Windows Explorer and display the file list in the Details view, you see some of the file properties, including the date the file was created, the file type, and the file size. These properties are updated by Windows. In Office documents, including Excel workbooks, there are other properties that are user-updateable, including the workbook's author and company name.

The properties include personal information, such as your name. In Exercise 21.5, you'll remove personal information from your workbook and then set specific workbook properties.

EXERCISE 21.5

Setting Workbook Properties

For this exercise, use the Hours and Expenses.xls workbook saved in the previous exercise. When prompted, enter the passwords to open the workbook (**open**) and modify the workbook (**sesame**).

1. Choose File ➤ Properties to open the Hours and Expenses.xls Properties dialog box.

2. Review the information on the Summary and Statistics tabs.

3. Close the Properties dialog box.

4. Choose Tools ➤ Options to open the Options dialog box.

5. On the Security tab, enable the Remove Personal Information From This File On Save check box.

6. Click OK to close the Options dialog box.

7. Save the workbook.

8. Choose File ➤ Properties to open the Properties dialog box. Note that your user name and company name have been removed.

9. On the Summary tab, enter the following properties:

   - Title: **Hours and Expenses**
   - Company: *Your organization name*
   - Category: **Employee Worksheets**

10. Click OK to close the Properties dialog box.

11. Save and close the workbook.

Collaborating with Others

Excel's sharing and tracking features make it easy for you to collaborate with others by sharing the same workbook file among multiple users. Excel's workgroup features are powerful, allowing you to distribute copies of workbooks and merge changes from the copies into a single file. Excel minimizes the potential for problems by giving you control over how the changes made by all of the users are merged into a single, error-free file.

Creating a Shared Workbook

Excel is designed to allow multiple users to view and modify a single workbook simultaneously. If you want others to be able to use a workbook while you have it open, you need to share the workbook and ensure that it is stored on a shared drive that other users can access.

Microsoft
✓ *Exam*
Objective

Create a shared workbook

When you share a workbook, Excel automatically tracks the changes made by each user. As the workbook owner, you can then review the changes and accept or reject each change made. You can set options for tracking changes and resolving conflicts on the Advanced tab of the Share Workbook dialog box, shown in Figure 21.1.

FIGURE 21.1   Use the Advanced tab of the Share Workbook dialog box to set up the rules for the shared workbook.

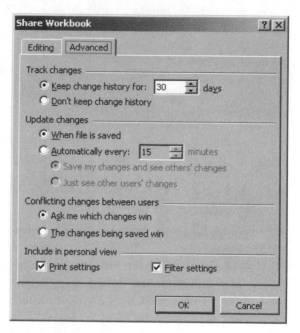

The Advanced options give you, the owner of the shared workbook, control over the changes made to the workbook:

Track Changes   Choose Keep Change History For *n* Days if you'd like Excel to maintain a history of changes so that you can review the changes and merge multiple copies of the same document for a specified interval. You must keep a change history to review changes or merge changes from multiple copies of the same workbook.

Update Changes   You can choose to update changes either when the file is saved or automatically at the interval you specify. If you choose the automatic update option, you can also choose whether you want to see your changes along with everyone else's or see only others' changes.

Conflicting Changes Between Users   If more than one user changes the same cell of the shared workbook, you can choose to have Excel ask you which changes should be saved or you can have Excel automatically keep the changes as they are when you save the workbook.

Include In Personal View   Enable the Print Settings and Filter Settings check boxes so you can save any personal print or filter settings that you choose without affecting others who are sharing the workbook.

In Exercise 21.6, you'll create a shared workbook.

EXERCISE 21.6

Sharing a Workbook

For this exercise, open the 21-6.xls workbook you downloaded from the Sybex website.

1. Choose Tools ➢ Share Workbook from the menu to open the Share Workbook dialog box.

2. On the Editing tab, enable the Allow Changes By More Than One User At The Same Time check box to make the file accessible to other users.

3. On the Advanced tab, set the Keep Change History For setting to 365 days.

4. Click OK.

5. Excel prompts you to save the workbook. Click OK again.

After saving, notice that the filename in the Title Bar indicates that the file is shared.

Leave the workbook open for the next exercise.

Even though you can track changes only in a shared workbook, that doesn't mean you have to give any one else access to it. If you want to simply track the changes that you make, save the workbook to a private folder or password-protect the shared workbook and don't give anyone the password.

Highlighting, Accepting, and Rejecting Changes

When Highlight Changes is enabled, each change made is noted in a ScreenTip similar to a comment, and changed cells are flagged with a cell indicator in the upper-left corner. Excel assigns a different triangle color to each user who modifies the workbook, so you can visually inspect the workbook to find all the changes made by each user. Hover over the cell, and Excel displays a ScreenTip to show you the changes that have been made.

Microsoft *Exam* *Objective*	**Track, accept and reject changes to workbooks**

In Exercise 21.7, you'll learn how to highlight changes in workbooks.

EXERCISE 21.7

Highlighting Changes

For this exercise, use the 21-6.xls workbook saved in the previous exercise.

1. Choose Tools ➢ Track Changes ➢ Highlight Changes to open the Highlight Changes dialog box:

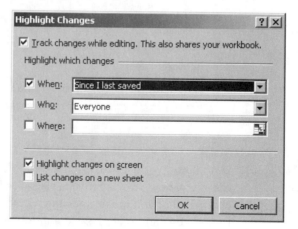

2. In the When drop-down list, choose All. Click OK to close the Highlight Changes dialog box. If a message box appears, click OK to close it.

EXERCISE 21.7 *(continued)*

3. Enter the following values in the worksheet:

   - D6: **450**
   - D7: **72**
   - D8: **150**
   - D9: **225**
   - D10: **180**

4. Hover over each cell and note the changes.

5. Change the value in D6 to **500**. Notice the change comment.

6. Save the workbook. Leave it open for the next exercise.

You can review a workbook and accept or reject changes in bulk or individually as you do in Microsoft Word. In Exercise 21.8, you'll accept and reject changes made in Exercise 21.7.

EXERCISE 21.8

Accepting and Rejecting Changes

For this exercise use the 21-6.xls workbook saved in the previous exercise.

1. Select cell A1.

2. Choose Tools ➤ Track Changes ➤ Accept Or Reject Changes to open the Select Changes To Accept Or Reject dialog box.

3. Click OK to open the Accept Or Reject Changes dialog box using the default settings.

Excel selects the first cell with changes: D7.

4. Click Accept to change D7 to its previous value and move to the change in D8.

5. Click Reject to reject the change in D8.

6. Click Accept All to accept all remaining changes.

7. Click Close to close the dialog box.

8. Save and close the workbook.

Merging Workbooks

If you anticipate many conflicting changes in a shared workbook, or if you want users to be able to make changes independently and then review all changes at once, you must make and distribute copies of the shared workbook. To create the copies, use Save As and give each copy of the workbook a different name—for example, the filename with the user's initials appended. Then you can merge the copies when users have finished with their changes.

You can merge only workbooks that have the same change history, so it's important that none of the users turns off sharing while using the workbook. The history must be complete when you merge the workbooks. If, for example, you set the number of days for the history at 30 days and users keep the workbooks for 32 days, you won't be able to merge the workbooks. Before you make copies of the shared workbook, make sure you set the history to allow enough time for changes and merging. If you're uncertain, set the history to 1000 days or an equally ridiculous length of time.

Microsoft ✓ *Exam* *Objective*	**Merge workbooks**

In Exercise 21.9, you'll merge three workbooks.

EXERCISE 21.9

Merging Workbooks

1. Open the workbook that you want to merge the other workbooks into: 21-9 My Workbook.xls.

2. Choose Tools ➢ Compare And Merge Workbooks. Save the workbook if prompted to do so.

3. In the Select Files To Merge Into Current Workbook dialog box, choose the copies of the shared workbook containing the changes you wish to merge. Choose 21-9 User1.xls and then hold Ctrl and choose 21-9 User2.xls.

EXERCISE 21.9 *(continued)*

You can merge the workbooks separately or both workbooks at the same time.

4. Click OK to merge both workbooks into 21-9 My Workbook.xls.

5. Save and close the workbook.

Summary

This chapter focused on the workgroup features included on the Excel Expert exam, including the following:

- Setting workbook passwords
- Protecting workbook structure
- Unlocking cells
- Protecting worksheets
- Allowing users to edit ranges
- Sharing workbooks
- Tracking, accepting, and rejecting changes
- Merging workbooks

Microsoft PowerPoint 2002 Core Exam

Chapter 22

Getting Started with PowerPoint

MOUS POWERPOINT 2002 CORE EXAM OBJECTIVES COVERED IN THIS CHAPTER:

- ✓ Create presentations (manually and using automated tools)
- ✓ Add slides to and delete slides from presentations
- ✓ Modify headers and footers in the Slide Master
- ✓ Import text from Word
- ✓ Insert, format, and modify text

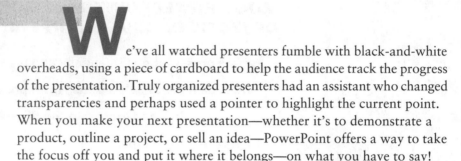

We've all watched presenters fumble with black-and-white overheads, using a piece of cardboard to help the audience track the progress of the presentation. Truly organized presenters had an assistant who changed transparencies and perhaps used a pointer to highlight the current point. When you make your next presentation—whether it's to demonstrate a product, outline a project, or sell an idea—PowerPoint offers a way to take the focus off you and put it where it belongs—on what you have to say!

In this chapter, we'll focus on the text of your presentation. You'll learn about several different possibilities for starting a new presentation, adding text, editing text, and deleting text from your presentations.

Before you begin this chapter, you should go to the Sybex website and download the file 4113Ch22.zip. This package contains the files necessary to complete some of the exercises in this chapter. In addition, it contains files of what most of the slides should look like after you complete the exercise. These files are affixed with the word *Post*.

Creating a Presentation from Scratch

Every PowerPoint presentation consists of a series of *slides*, which contain text or objects displayed on a graphic background, as shown in Figure 22.1. You create your presentation by adding text and objects (like a chart, image, sound file, or video clip) to slides. Once you complete this chapter, you should be fairly comfortable with adding and editing text. Chapter 23, "Adding Color and Graphics to Presentations," introduces you to some of the graphic objects available in PowerPoint.

FIGURE 22.1 A PowerPoint slide

For every presentation you create in PowerPoint, you'll go through these steps:

1. Plan the presentation and gather materials you'll want to include: clip art, tables, charts, and other graphic objects.

2. Create the presentation by creating slides, entering and editing text, and arranging slides.

3. Apply a presentation design: the background colors and graphics that appear on every slide. Modify the design if necessary.

4. Format individual slides if you wish: Add bold or italic formatting to text as needed, adjust text outline levels, remove bullets where they aren't needed, and adjust line spacing.

5. Add objects to the presentation: charts, tables, and pictures.

6. Apply and modify transitions, animation effects, and links for electronic presentations.

7. Create audience materials and speaker notes.

8. Rehearse the presentation and add slide timings.

9. Deliver the presentation.

You don't have to work through all the steps sequentially. With Power-Point, you can create and modify a few slides, adding objects, animation, and speaker notes, and then insert more slides. If you find the slides distracting, you can create your presentation's content as an outline and then work on the aesthetics.

Starting a New Presentation

Ah...where to start? That question gets asked by the manager of the marketing team with a newly won contract, by the author beginning a new book, by the teenager cleaning his room for the first time in six months, and by the novice PowerPoint user faced with the task of creating her first presentation. Fortunately, PowerPoint 2002 makes getting started a snap. You have essentially three choices: start with a blank slide, start with a wizard, or start with a template.

Microsoft ✓ *Exam Objective*   **Create presentations (manually and using automated tools)**

Starting with a Blank Slide

When you launch PowerPoint, the task pane at the right automatically displays the New Presentation options, as shown in Figure 22.2.

FIGURE 22.2   When you launch PowerPoint, the options for starting a presentation appear in the task pane.

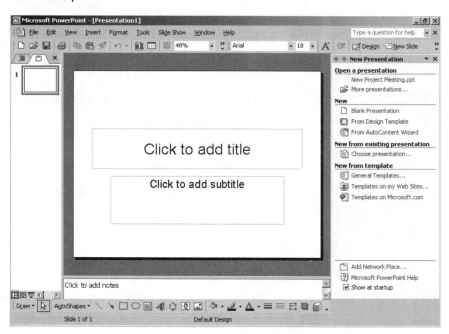

You can open an existing presentation or create a new presentation using one of several listed options. The blank slide in the center of the window is set up as a title slide, ready and waiting for your text. Exercise 22.1 walks you through the process of adding text.

EXERCISE 22.1

Adding Text to a Blank Slide

1. Launch PowerPoint from the Windows Start menu or from the Windows Desktop. A blank slide is displayed in the main part of the application window.

2. Click the Click To Add Title text box. A cursor appears, centered within the text box.

3. Type the title of your presentation. For this exercise, let's keep it simple and type **My Presentation**.

4. Click the Click To Add Subtitle text box. Once again, a centered cursor appears.

5. Type your name. Then press Enter.

6. Type some additional information about yourself: your company name or job title, for example.

7. Close the file without saving the changes.

As evidenced in Step 5 of Exercise 22.1, pressing Enter in a text box allows you to create a new line of text within that text box. PowerPoint also supports *word wrap*. If the content you enter is longer than the width of the text box, the text wraps to the next line automatically, just as it does when it reaches the right margin in a Word document.

When you add text to a slide, the text also appears on the slide miniature in the slide pane at the left side of the application window (see Figure 22.2).

Using the AutoContent Wizard

The AutoContent Wizard is helpful for beginning users of PowerPoint because it generates an outline and applies a considerable amount of slide formatting automatically. It's also a good tool for a more advanced user whose presentation matches one of the AutoContent templates or who wants some help structuring a presentation. As its name implies, it is designed to suggest content.

The AutoContent Wizard works like any of the other wizards in Microsoft Office. You move through a series of steps that help you design your presentation. In each step, you click Next to advance to the next step or Back to return to a previous step. For practice with the AutoContent Wizard, try Exercise 22.2.

EXERCISE 22.2

Using the AutoContent Wizard

1. If you closed PowerPoint in our last exercise, launch it from the Windows Start menu or from the Windows Desktop. A blank slide is displayed in the main part of the application window.

2. Choose From AutoContent Wizard from the task pane to start the wizard. (If the task pane isn't visible, turn it on by clicking View ≻ Task Pane. Then, if necessary, click the task pane drop-down arrow and choose New Presentation to display the options for beginning a presentation.) The first step of the wizard explains the purpose of the wizard. Click Next.

Note: You may wish to close the Office Assistant if it's in your way. Just choose No Don't Provide Help Now.

3. In the second step of the wizard, choose the PowerPoint presentation type that most closely matches your topic. You can click the All button at the top of the button list (as shown here) and scroll through all the presentation types. If you prefer to narrow your choices, select a category from the button list. For this exercise, select the Generic presentation type and click Next.

4. Select a style for your presentation. Will this presentation be displayed on the Internet? Will you be using black-and-white overheads? The choice you make now will not prohibit you from switching to another style later, but it limits the options PowerPoint displays in the wizard. Choose On-screen Presentation and click Next.

Note: If you are creating an online presentation, refer to Chapter 25, "Preparing and Delivering the Final Product," for more on Power-Point's dynamic web features.

5. In the fourth step of the wizard, click the Presentation Title text box and enter the title that you want to appear on the first slide. If there is additional information you would like to include on every slide, such as a company, project, or department name or the current date, activate those features here. Enter your information and click Next to continue.

6. The Finish step lets you know you have completed the steps of the wizard. Just click Finish to create the presentation.

7. Save the presentation as **AutoContent Wizard Practice.ppt**.

The AutoContent Wizard uses the information you have provided to create the first slide of your presentation and an outline for the rest of it, all on an attractive background, complete with graphic accents. Figure 22.3 shows the presentation produced by the wizard in Exercise 22.2.

FIGURE 22.3   The AutoContent Wizard produces the first slide in a presentation and a suggested outline for additional slides.

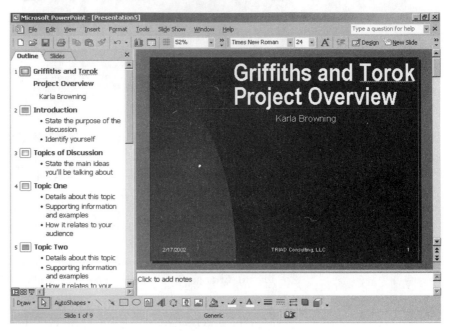

Using a PowerPoint Template

Thus far, we have introduced you to two possibilities for starting a Power-Point presentation. You can start with a blank slide and create your outline from scratch. This method helps you to focus on text without the distraction of backgrounds, graphics, and placeholder text supplied by the wizard. Or you can use the AutoContent Wizard when you want PowerPoint to suggest content based on the type of presentation you're planning to give. Now here's a third possibility: Choose from dozens of PowerPoint's built-in templates.

If you choose to start with a template, you get the backgrounds, graphics, and, depending on the template, varying amounts of placeholder text. Follow the steps in Exercises 22.3 and 22.4 to learn two different ways to start a presentation using a template.

EXERCISE 22.3

Starting a Presentation by Choosing a Template from the Task Pane

1. Display the New Presentation task pane (Choose View ➤ Task Pane from the menu, and then click the task pane's drop-down menu and choose New Presentation). The New Presentation task pane shows four categories of choices: Open A Presentation, New, New From Existing Presentation, and New From Template.

2. In the New area of the task pane, choose From Design Template. The task pane now shows Slide Design options. Templates are displayed in categories: Used In This Presentation and Available For Use. A third category, Recently Used, appears once you've used Slide Design options.

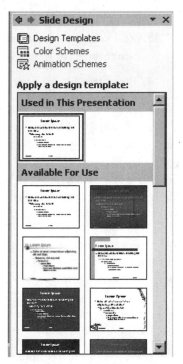

3. By default, templates are displayed as thumbnails. To enlarge them, position your mouse over one of the thumbnails, click its drop-down arrow, and choose Show Large Preview.

4. Point to a template to see its filename.

EXERCISE 22.3 *(continued)*

5. Resize the task pane to make it wider, displaying more templates at once.

6. Locate the Pixel template.

7. Click anywhere on the miniature Pixel template to apply it (or click the drop-down arrow and choose Apply To All Slides).

8. Close the task pane to allow more working room.

9. Click the Title text box and type **New Project Meeting**.

10. Click the Subtitle text box and type today's date.

11. Press Enter.

12. Type your name and job title.

13. You will use this presentation for future exercises, so save it as **Starting With A Template Practice.ppt**.

14. Close this file for now.

PowerPoint 2002 offers another option for starting a presentation using a design template. If you prefer to work from a dialog box rather than the task pane, you may do so from the New Presentation task pane. In the New From Template area, click General Templates. The Templates dialog box opens to the Design Templates tab. Just click one of the templates to see its preview.

If a preview does not appear, it means the template was not included in your Office installation. In most cases, you can just click OK and Office will install the template you're after. You may be prompted to insert the Office XP CD, however.

The Templates dialog box has three tabs, each with its own set of choices. Feel free to explore them.

General   This tab contains the Blank Presentation template as well as the AutoContent Wizard. Here's another way to access those choices that also appear in the New Presentation task pane.

Design Templates   This tab includes the new 2002 templates and a few holdovers from PowerPoint 2000. You'll find over a dozen striking new designs, including Eclipse, Fireworks, Network, Orbit, and Pixel. Try Crayons for a fun and informal look.

Presentations   This tab holds designs with placeholder text from the AutoContent Wizard presentation types. Choose Company Meeting, Financial Overview, or Marketing Plan to get you started. Save yourself some steps by using one of the online templates if you're planning to display the presentation on the Web.

Applying a New Template

Sometimes the text works well in your presentation, but the background, colors, and graphics just don't "fit" with your particular client or situation. Good news! You can give your presentation a whole new look and feel with just a couple of clicks. Keep the text and ditch the design template any time the urge strikes. Exercise 22.4 tells you how. In this exercise, you will apply the Proposal template to the Starting With A Template Practice presentation you created in Exercise 22.3. You will also create an additional slide and then reapply the Pixel template.

EXERCISE 22.4

Choosing a New Template

1. Open Starting With A Template Practice.ppt or open 22-4.ppt.

2. Display the Slide Design Templates task pane. (Click the drop-down menu at the top of the task pane and choose Slide Design – Design Templates.)

3. Scroll through the templates to locate and select the Proposal template. The title slide changes dramatically with the new template:

4. Scroll through the Slide Design Templates task pane and reapply the Pixel template.

5. No need to save the changes; you're right back where you started.

Navigating the PowerPoint Application Window

In order to work comfortably in PowerPoint 2002, it is necessary to have a general understanding of the multipaned PowerPoint application window and each of the following topics specifically:

- Viewing slides

- Navigating from slide to slide

- Selecting a slide (or slides)

In this section, you'll learn about PowerPoint views and how to switch between them. You'll practice navigating through a presentation as well as selecting slides one at a time and in multiples.

Viewing Slides

As you're well aware, the MOUS exams are timed. Completing each question correctly is important, but equally important is your ability to complete the questions efficiently. And you can't work comfortably and efficiently in PowerPoint without understanding its views.

The term *view* refers to how you look at and work on your presentation. PowerPoint 2002 offers several different views, three of which are accessible from the View menu and view buttons: Normal view, Slide Sorter view, and Slide Show view. The other views, Master view and Notes Pages view, have special features that we will discuss at length in Chapters 24 and 25. While you'll quickly adopt one view as your favorite, you'll probably work in all of the views while you're building your presentation.

Normal View

When you click Finish, the AutoContent Wizard closes and the presentation is displayed in Normal view, as shown previously in Figure 22.3. The outline (with text suggested by the AutoContent Wizard) is displayed on the left; your first slide is shown in the main part of the application window. The smaller pane at the bottom of the window allows you to add notes for this slide. (See Chapter 25 for more on speaker notes.)

Normal view is a *tri-pane view* that allows you to see three different aspects of your presentation within one window. The sections of the tri-pane window are resizable so you can choose the element(s) of the presentation you wish to focus on.

The Drawing toolbar, at the bottom of the application window, is on by default. You can hide it by choosing View ➢ Toolbars ➢ Drawing from the menu (or by right-clicking any toolbar and choosing Drawing) if you need a little extra room for the document window.

The outline pane in Normal view has two tabs: Outline and Slides. When the AutoContent Wizard finishes, the Outline tab, which shows the text on each slide, is displayed by default. For those of us who are visually oriented, it helps to display the slides themselves rather than the text of the slides. To see slide miniatures in the left pane, as shown in Figure 22.4, click the Slides tab.

FIGURE 22.4 Normal view lets the user display slide miniatures in the left pane.

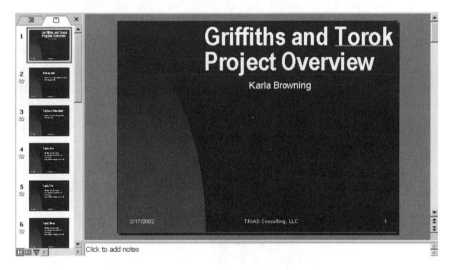

When you're viewing slide miniatures in the left pane, the tabs at the top of the pane show icons rather than words. Click the Outline View icon to show slide text in the left pane.

If you accidentally close the left pane that displays outline and slide miniatures, you can bring it back by clicking View ➢ Normal (Restore Panes).

Three view buttons appear at the left end of the horizontal scroll bar; in Figure 22.5, the Normal View button is boxed in.

You can change to Slide Sorter view or Slide Show view by clicking the appropriate view button at the bottom-left of the PowerPoint window or by choosing the view name from the View menu.

Slide Sorter View

Slide Sorter view, shown in Figure 22.5, allows you to see many slides at once. The number of slides shown depends on the zoom setting, your monitor size, and the screen resolution. PowerPoint defaults to 66% zoom, which allows you to see approximately 12 slides with display resolution settings of 800×600 pixels. If you wish to see more or fewer slides, you can adjust the zoom level higher or lower, or you can seize this opportunity to request a larger monitor from the appropriate person in your organization.

The focus in Slide Sorter view is on entire slides: selecting, deleting, moving, etc. You can't edit text on a slide in Slide Sorter view.

FIGURE 22.5   Slide Sorter view displays multiple slides.

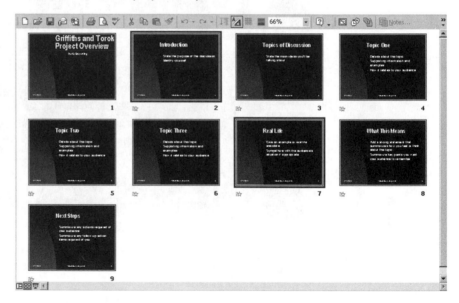

Slide Show View

Click the Slide Show (From Current Slide) button to see how a slide will look in full-screen mode when you display your presentation. Click the mouse or press Enter to move from one slide to the next; if a slide has multiple lines of text, you might have to click once for each line. After the last slide, PowerPoint returns to the previous view. Press Esc if you want to end the slide show before the last slide.

When you switch from one view to another, the current slide remains current, regardless of view. For example, if you are on the fifth slide in Normal view and switch to Slide Sorter view, the fifth slide will be selected. Clicking the Slide Show button starts the slide show with the fifth slide.

Slide Sorter view is discussed in more depth in Chapter 24, "Producing Exciting Presentations." For more information about Slide Show view, see Chapter 25.

Adjusting Panes in Normal View

With the Outline displayed in Normal view, presentation text is in the left pane of the tri-pane window. The selected slide is shown in the main part of the application window. Below the slide is an area for notes if you choose to use them. Notes are hidden from the audience in an electronic presentation and are displayed in online or NetMeeting presentations only if you choose to display them. You can also print notes for your own use at the podium. Unless you're adding notes to a web presentation, think of the notes as somewhat private—the perfect place to put a reminder to distribute a handout or tell a specific joke or to enter the full text that you intend to present while the slide is displayed. (For more on notes, see Chapter 25.)

 For efficiency's sake, you may wish to resize the panes in Normal view so that the one you're working in is larger. Simply point to any of the gray pane dividers and your mouse pointer changes to the resize tool (the double-headed arrow). Click and drag to move the pane divider.

If you don't see the notes pane, point to the pane divider directly above the Drawing toolbar. Click and drag upward to open the notes pane.

Navigating from Slide to Slide

There are several different ways to move between slides in Normal view. You can click any slide in the outline to move to that slide. Or, if slide miniatures are displayed in the left pane, simply click the one you want to view. You can also use the vertical scroll bar to move forward and backward through your slides or use the PgUp and PgDn keys to move through the slides. As you drag the vertical scroll box, the slide number and slide title are displayed in a ScreenTip.

If you wish to advance to the next or previous slide, you can use the Next Slide and Previous Slide buttons located at the bottom of the vertical scroll bar.

Selecting a Slide

You must select a slide in order to edit or delete it. The selected slide also determines the placement of new slides you add to your presentation. In Normal view, the slide displayed in the main part of the application window is the selected slide. In Slide Sorter view, the selected slide(s) show a darker border around the outside like Slides 2 and 7 in Figure 22.5 shown previously in this chapter.

In Exercise 22.5, you'll learn to select slides so you can move them, delete them, or apply transitions to them.

EXERCISE 22.5

Selecting Slides

1. Open 22-5.ppt or one of your own presentations, and switch to Slide Sorter view.

2. Click Slide 3 to select it (note the dark border around the outside of the slide).

3. Click any other slide to select it while simultaneously deselecting Slide 3.

4. To select several contiguous (adjacent) slides, click the first (let's choose Slide 1), and then hold Shift and click the last (use Slide 5 for this exercise). Slides 1 through 5 are now selected, and you may release the Shift key.

5. Click in the white space below or between slides to deselect Slides 1–5.

6. To select multiple *noncontiguous* slides, click the first (use Slide 1 again), and then hold Ctrl and click each additional slide you wish to select (choose Slides 3, 4, and 6 for this exercise).

7. Release the Ctrl key when you've finished selecting. If you've done this exercise correctly, slides 1, 3, 4, and 6 should have the dark border.

8. Click in the white space below or between slides to deselect them all.

9. Switch to Normal view and select the Slides tab in the outline pane.

10. Try selecting multiple contiguous and noncontiguous slide minia-
    tures using the same keyboard/mouse combinations you used in
    steps 4 and 6 above.

11. There's no need to save the presentation again, as we haven't
    made substantial changes to it.

Adding and Deleting PowerPoint Slides

Now that you're off to a running start, it's time to rid the presentation of
unnecessary slides and add some of your own. The following sections show
you how to add slides in a variety of ways and how to delete those slides you
no longer need.

Microsoft ✓ *Exam* *Objective*   **Add slides to and delete slides from presentations**

Adding Slides to a Presentation

Once you've mastered PowerPoint 2002's application window, you're ready
to begin customizing the presentation for use as you originally intended.
Whether you have created the presentation using a blank slide, the Auto-
Content Wizard, or a PowerPoint template, you have the same choices for
adding slides:

- Adding slides by typing in the outline pane

- Adding slides by clicking the New Slide button on the Formatting
  toolbar or by choosing Insert ➢ New Slide

- Adding slides from another presentation using the Slide Finder

Working with a PowerPoint Outline

Most users work in the outline pane when it's necessary to concentrate on
text rather than objects or entire slides. You can't work with objects directly
in the outline pane, and the text-only interface helps you focus on content
rather than format. Remember, you can resize the outline pane to give you
more room to work, yet you can still see in the right pane how the text fits

on the slide. In Normal view the Outlining toolbar, shown in Figure 22.6 appears by default. If you don't see the toolbar, choose View ➢ Toolbars ➢ Outlining from the menu.

In a PowerPoint outline, there are five text levels below the slide title. Text entered at any level other than the title level is a point or a subpoint. Each level in the outline has a unique bullet.

Slide Title

- Level 1
  ◆ Level 2
    ⋆ Level 3
      • Level 4
        – Level 5

FIGURE 22.6   The Outlining toolbar is helpful in working with text.

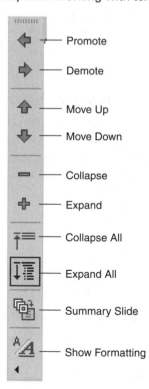

Exercise 22.6 provides an introduction to outline levels. In this exercise, you will work with a PowerPoint outline, moving text from level to level using the buttons on the Outlining toolbar shown previously in Figure 22.6. (For more on working in outlines, see "Working with Text in a Presentation," later in this chapter.)

EXERCISE 22.6

Working with a PowerPoint Outline

1. If you just completed Exercise 22.5, the presentation we've been using should be open and ready to go. If not, open 22-6.ppt or one of your own presentations, and switch to Normal view.

2. Click the Outline tab to display the outline pane; then resize that pane to make it approximately two inches wider, as shown here:

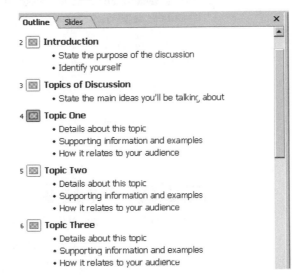

3. Click at the end of any bullet point and press Enter to create a new line. The new line is on the same level as the previous line, and a blank bullet point appears. The assumption is that you'll type some text for the new bullet point, but we'll skip that for purposes of this exercise. (Adding and editing text are covered under a different exam objective later in this chapter.)

4. Press Backspace twice to return the insertion point to the end of the previous line.

EXERCISE 22.6 *(continued)*

5. Turn on the Outlining toolbar by clicking View ➤ Toolbars ➤ Outlining. If you haven't previously moved the Outlining toolbar, it displays vertically to the left of the outline pane.

6. In step 4 above, we left the insertion point at the end of a bullet point. Press Enter once again to move to a new line and create a new blank bullet.

7. Click the Demote button on the Outlining toolbar to move the new bullet point to a lower level.

8. Click the Promote button on the Outlining toolbar to move the new bullet point back to its original level.

9. Press Backspace twice to delete the bullet and return the insertion point to the end of the previous line.

Note: You can also use the Tab key to demote and Shift+Tab to promote.

10. Again, there's no need to save. We haven't made any savable changes.

In Exercise 22.7, you'll learn how to add slides using the outline pane.

EXERCISE 22.7

Adding Slides Using the Outline Pane

1. If you just finished Exercise 22.6, the file you're currently using is the one you need. If not, open 22-7.ppt.

2. If necessary, display the outline pane in Normal view.

3. When you're working in a PowerPoint outline, pressing Enter at the end of an outline level gives you a new line at the same level. So pressing Enter at the end of a slide title gives you a new slide. Let's try it. Click at the end of Slide 3's title (Topics of Discussion).

4. Press Enter. A new Slide 4 icon appears, as shown here. You've added a new Slide 4 that includes the subpoint that was originally part of Slide 3.

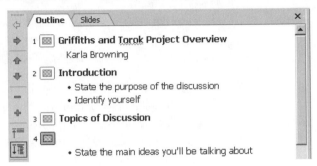

5. Press Backspace once to get rid of the new slide and return the sub-point to Slide 3.

6. To add a new slide without stealing bullets from another slide, simply click at the end of the last bullet on the slide that precedes where you want the new slide to go. For this exercise, let's click at the end of the bullet point on Slide 3 (Topics of Discussion).

7. Press Enter. A new bullet appears.

8. Click the Promote button on the Outlining toolbar. A blank Slide 4 title icon appears, and the remaining slides are renumbered.

9. Press Backspace once to get rid of the new slide. The outline should look exactly like it did when you started this exercise.

The keyboard and Outlining toolbar provide one way to insert a new slide in Outline view. Exercise 22.8 offers an alternative.

Adding Slides Using the New Slide Button

1. If you just finished Exercise 22.7, use that presentation. If not, open 22-8.ppt.

EXERCISE 22.8 *(continued)*

2. Click at the end of the bullet point (or slide title) that precedes where you want the new slide to go. For this exercise, click at the end of the bullet point on Slide 3 (Topics of Discussion).

3. Click the New Slide button on the Standard toolbar.

4. A blank Slide 4 title icon appears in the outline, and the task pane displays slide layout choices. The insertion point in the outline pane is positioned so that you can type the title for your new slide. Skip that for now; we'll address it later in the chapter under the appropriate exam objective.

Note: The slide layouts that appear in the task pane allow you to choose positions for text and other objects on your new slide. We'll cover slide layouts along with the discussion of graphic elements in Chapter 23.

5. Close the task pane by clicking the Close button (the X) in its upper-right corner.

6. Press Backspace once to get rid of the new slide and return the outline to its original form.

Using Slides from an Existing Presentation

Why reinvent the wheel? If you have great slides you've used in other presentations or if your company has existing presentation slides you would like to recycle, you can quickly insert them into your own presentation. Exercise 22.9 shows you how.

EXERCISE 22.9

Adding Slides from Another Presentation

1. Use the presentation we just worked with in Exercise 22.8 or, if you didn't complete Exercise 22.8, just open 22-9.ppt.

2. Switch to Slide Sorter view. Although you can follow these same steps in Normal view, the visual impact of the Slide Sorter's graphic view is helpful for most users in sorting through slides once they've finished inserting them.

3. In Slide Sorter view, click in the white space after the slide where you want the new slides to appear. For this exercise, click between Slides 1 and 2. A large, flashing insertion point appears between those slides.

4. Choose Insert ➢ Slides From Files. The Slide Finder dialog box opens.

5. Click the Browse button, and then select and open the presentation that contains the slides you want to add to your presentation. We're using the 22-9 New Project Meeting.ppt presentation, which you downloaded from the Sybex website. When you open the presentation, thumbnails of the slides appear in the Slide Finder dialog box:

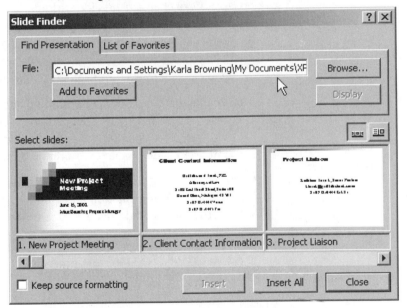

Note: If thumbnails don't appear, click the Display button in the Slide Finder dialog box.

6. The thumbnails show each slide's number and title below the slide. Use the horizontal scroll bar to move through the slides in order. To work more quickly, click the Show Titles button in the Slide Finder dialog box to display a list of slide titles with a single preview pane.

7. Click the Show Slides button to return to the thumbnails if you wish.

Select the slide or slides you want. For this exercise, just select slides 1 and 2.

Note: You do *not* have to hold Shift or Ctrl to select multiple slides!

8. Then do one of the following:

   a. When you click Insert in the Slide Finder dialog box, the selected slides appear in your presentation. The text and any objects (like a picture or chart) on the slide are imported. The slide's design is *not* imported into the current presentation. Instead, each slide is reformatted upon being imported so that it matches the design of the presentation you are currently working on. This is the choice we'll make for purposes of this exercise.

   b. Enable the Keep Source Formatting check box and then click Insert. Imported slides are positioned following the slide that was selected when you opened the Slide Finder dialog box. Imported slides retain their original formatting.

9. The Slide Finder dialog box remains open so you can browse to select another presentation and continue inserting slides. Click Close to close the Slide Finder and return to the current presentation.

10. Save the presentation as **Adding Slides from Another Presentation Practice.ppt**.

If you frequently use slides from a particular presentation, open it in the Slide Finder and click Add To Favorites. Confirm your decision to do so in the message box that appears. The next time you wish to insert slides from that presentation, you don't have to browse to select it. Just click the List Of Favorites tab in the Slide Finder dialog box.

Deleting Slides from a Presentation

As you might expect, there are multiple possibilities for deleting slides from a presentation. Exercise 22.10 introduces you to several methods. Use the one that makes the most sense, depending on which view you're working in when you need to delete.

EXERCISE 22.10

Deleting Slides from a Presentation

1. If you just completed Exercise 22.9, use that presentation. If not, open 22-10.ppt.

2. Switch to Slide Sorter view.

3. Select the slide(s) you wish to delete. For this exercise, select Slides 2 (New Project Meeting) and 3 (Client Contact Information).

4. Press Delete on the keyboard or choose Edit ➢ Delete Slide to remove the slides from the presentation.

5. Click the Undo button on the Standard toolbar to bring the slides back.

6. Switch to Normal view and display the outline pane. Click the slide icon preceding the title of Slide 2 (New Project Meeting).

7. Hold Shift and click the slide icon preceding the title of Slide 3 (Client Contact Information). Now release the Shift key. The text on both slides is selected.

8. Press Delete on the keyboard or choose Edit ➢ Delete Slide from the menu. Both slides are removed from the presentation.

Note: As another alternative, you can display slide miniatures in the left pane (rather than the outline) and then select and delete slides just as you did in the Slide Sorter.

9. Save the presentation as **Deleting Slides Practice.ppt**.

Working with Slide Headers and Footers

Often, there are certain elements you wish to appear on every slide: your company's name, the current date, or the slide number, for example. If the item appears near the top of the slide, such as a company logo, we call it a *header*. Items that appear near the bottom of every slide, such as slide numbers, are *footers*.

Microsoft
Exam
Objective

Modify headers and footers in the Slide Master

PowerPoint's *Slide Master* contains placeholders for items that appear on every slide. You can move these placeholders, modify their contents, or even delete them.

> **NOTE** The Slide Master is discussed in more detail in Chapter 24.

If you are familiar with the header and footer feature in Word, you'll be pleased to note that PowerPoint's feature is even easier to learn. Exercise 22.11 takes you through the process of modifying a slide footer.

EXERCISE 22.11

Modifying a Slide Footer

1. For this exercise, we'll create a dummy presentation using the AutoContent Wizard. Launch the wizard from the New Presentation task pane. (Click View ➢ Task Pane and choose New Presentation from the drop-down menu at the top).

2. Proceed through the wizard, as you learned earlier in this chapter. Please make the following choices:

    a. At step 2, choose the Recommending A Strategy presentation type.

    b. At step 3, leave the default selection of On-screen Presentation.

    c. At step 4, enter a title and text for the slide footer.

    d. When you finish with the wizard, the presentation is displayed in Normal view. You should see the slide number, current date, and, if you used our settings in Step c above, the word *Confidential* at the bottom of the title slide and each subsequent slide. Display Slide 2 and then Slide 3 to verify this.

EXERCISE 22.11 *(continued)*

3. From any slide, click View ➢ Master ➢ Slide Master. Notice the footer, slide number, and date placeholders at the bottom of the master:

4. For this exercise, we'll remove the slide number (the text box with the # sign.) Click once on the slide number placeholder to activate its contents. You could now enter something at the insertion point and it would appear on every slide. Instead, click the frame of the placeholder again to select the placeholder itself. The frame of the placeholder changes from diagonal lines to dots.

5. Press Delete on the keyboard.

6. Return to Normal view by clicking the Normal View button. The slide number is gone from all slides. Browse them to verify this.

7. Close this practice presentation without saving.

You can also modify header and footer settings in the Header And Footer dialog box. Just click View ➢ Header And Footer to get there.

Inserting and Modifying Text

Although PowerPoint sets the stage for creating eye-catching slides with stunning graphics and animation, it's the text that forms the backbone of the presentation. No matter how you dress it up, poorly written and badly placed text leaves your audience with a negative impression. PowerPoint slides are meant to display main points and subpoints, not paragraphs of text. Choose and place text carefully for maximum visual appeal. Supplement with details as you speak or, in the case of web presentations, add notes in the notes pane.

Importing Text from Word

If your presentation text originated in a Word outline, there's no need to retype it in PowerPoint. Simply import the outline. Each level 1 outline heading in Word becomes a PowerPoint slide title. Levels 2 and below become subpoints.

Microsoft ✓ *Exam* *Objective*	**Import text from Word**

You can use text from a Word outline to create a brand-new presentation or to create new slides in a presentation you're already working on. The outline is inserted into the active presentation, so if you have just started, you can use the outline as the entire presentation. You may also use an outline as additional content in a partially completed presentation. If you choose to insert an outline into an existing presentation, each first-level heading becomes a new slide. To do this, follow the steps in Exercise 22.12. In this exercise, you will insert outline text from Word into your Choosing A New Template Practice presentation. Note: You can use a Word outline of your own or use 22-12 Outline For Import.doc, which you downloaded with the other files for this chapter.

EXERCISE 22.12

Adding Slide Text from a Word Document

1. Open Choosing A New Template Practice.ppt or use 22-12.ppt.

2. In Normal or Slide Sorter view, select the slide you want the inserted text to follow. Select Slide 1 for this exercise.

3. Choose Insert ➢ Slides From Outline.

4. Change the Look In field so it points to the folder where you saved the Word outline you downloaded with the other files for this chapter. Select 22-12 Outline For Import.doc.

5. Click Insert. You may be prompted to install a converter to complete the import. Click Yes to proceed with the installation.

EXERCISE 22.12 *(continued)*

6. If you used our 22-12 Outline For Import document, eight additional slides have been inserted into your presentation, for a total of nine slides.

7. Save the presentation as **Adding Text From Word Practice.ppt** for use in a later exercise. Close it when you've finished saving.

When you insert a Word outline, the complete document appears as part of your presentation. If you want only part of the outline, delete the extra slides after importing. If you have a rather lengthy outline from which you need only a few slides, consider copying those sections to a new Word document and importing from there.

If you're already working in Word, you can create a presentation from the active document by choosing File ➤ Send To ➤ Microsoft PowerPoint from the Word menu bar.

Working with Text in a Presentation

In the early stages of your presentation's development, you'll probably want to work in Normal view, which provides you with the most editing flexibility and allows you to see the text from multiple slides at one time—a bird's-eye view of your presentation. Resize the outline pane as needed to make it easier to work with text while keeping an eye on the slide pane to check text position.

Microsoft
Exam
Objective

Insert, format, and modify text

In PowerPoint, you can type text in the outline or directly on the slide. We'll focus first on the outline and then discuss entering text in the slide pane.

Inserting and Modifying Text

If you've created a presentation using the AutoContent Wizard, you'll need to replace suggested content in the slides created by the wizard as well as add text of your own. It makes sense to tackle these tasks before making substantial formatting changes.

You'll recall that PowerPoint slides have five text levels available below the slide title level. Each level in the outline has a unique bullet character. In the outline pane, all bullet characters appear the same, but take a peek at the slide pane as you're working through Exercise 22.13. You'll see that bullets on different outline levels usually have different characters. To edit in the outline pane, simply select the line of text you want to change by clicking the bullet or slide icon in front of that line. Overtype the selected text with new text. To move a bullet point to a lower outline level, select and demote it. To move to a higher level, select and promote it.

Outline levels, promoting, and demoting were discussed earlier in this chapter. See Exercise 22.6: Working with a PowerPoint Outline.

In PowerPoint 2002 outlines, the font size appears the same at each level. However, if you glance at the slide pane, you'll notice that PowerPoint automatically adjusts font size depending on the number of items contained on a slide, the available space in the text box, and the level at which the text is placed. This means that the text size for any given level can vary from slide to slide.

You can disable the feature that automatically adjusts font size by choosing Tools ➢ AutoCorrect Options ➢ AutoFormat As You Type. In the Apply As You Type settings, disable the AutoFit Body Text To Placeholder check box. Note the similar option for Title text.

Selecting Text, Lines, and Slides

Many of the methods used to select text in Word and Excel work here as well. Double-click a word to select it. To select a block of text, click at the beginning to place the insertion point and mark the start of the selection. Then hold Shift and click at the end. All text between the click and the Shift+click is selected. To select an entire bullet point, click the bullet or icon in front of the text or triple-click anywhere within the point.

If you select a first-level point that has second-level points underneath it, the second-level points are also selected. Click and drag to select only the main point. In the outline pane, selecting the title using any method other than dragging selects the entire slide.

Exercise 22.13 lets you practice replacing the wizard's placeholder text and adding text of your own. In this exercise, you will select and overwrite wizard-generated placeholder text on a slide. You'll also practice adding and deleting text on another slide to begin customizing this presentation as if a VP of Sales were planning to use it in introducing new clients to their project team.

EXERCISE 22.13

Selecting and Modifying Outline Text

1. Open AutoContent Wizard Practice.ppt, which you created in Exercise 22.2 earlier in this chapter, or open 22-13.ppt from the Sybex downloads.

2. Display the presentation in Normal view with the outline showing in the left pane.

3. Resize the outline pane so that it's about two inches wider, giving you more room to work.

4. If the Outlining toolbar is not visible, turn it on by choosing View ➢ Toolbars ➢ Outlining from the menu.

5. On Slide 2 (Introduction), place your mouse over the bullet character that precedes the first bullet point. Notice that the mouse pointer changes to a four-headed arrow.

Click once to select the bulleted text.

6. Type the text you wish to replace the selected text: **Welcome To Our New Clients**

7. Click the bullet icon to select the second bullet point on Slide 2.

8. Type the following text and press Enter: **Karla Browning, VP Sales**

EXERCISE 22.13 *(continued)*

9. Click the Demote button to move the next bullet to a lower level. Enter the following text: **Matt Bratcher, Project Manager**

10. Press Enter again to move to the next line. Type the following text: **Chad Cooke, Technical Liaison**

11. Dispense with the placeholder text on Slide 3 (Topics of Discussion) and add the following four bullet points: **Overview of the Project**, **Scope and sequence**, **Initial task assignments**, **Timeline**

12. Select the Timeline bullet point on Slide 3. Press Delete on the keyboard to remove it from the slide. Click anywhere in Slide 2 and see if your work matches the following graphic:

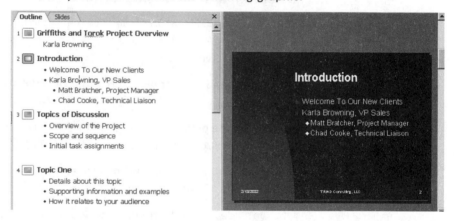

13. Resave this presentation as `Select and Modify Outline Text Practice.ppt`.

PowerPoint's Outlining toolbar provides additional tools for moving slides, points, and subpoints. You can also expand and collapse the outline to see as much or as little detail as you need for the task at hand.

You can collapse and expand sections of the outline by using the Collapse and Expand buttons on the Outlining toolbar or by right-clicking a slide title and choosing Collapse or Expand from the shortcut menu.

To collapse or expand multiple slides, select them and then right-click anywhere in the selection. Choose Collapse or Expand from the shortcut menu. You can also use the Collapse All and Expand All buttons to collapse or expand the entire outline.

Moving Points and Subpoints in the Outline

The Outlining toolbar has buttons for moving selected text to another location. Select a bullet point and click the Move Up button to move the text one line higher. Click the Move Down button to bring selected text one line lower. Exercise 22.14 helps familiarize you with these and other tools on the Outlining toolbar. In this exercise, you will change the order of bulleted text in the outline and move a bullet point from one slide to another.

EXERCISE 22.14

Moving Outline Text

1. Open 22-14.ppt, or use the Select and Modify Outline Text Practice presentation you created in Exercise 22.13.

2. Display the presentation in Normal view with the outline showing in the pane at the left.

3. Select the second bullet point on Slide 3 (Scope and sequence).

4. Click the Move Down button on the Outlining toolbar to make it the last bullet point on that slide.

5. On Slide 1, delete the text "Karla Browning."

6. On Slide 2, select the text "Karla Browning, VP Sales."

Note: You'll have to drag the mouse to select the text you want. If you just click the bullet preceding the text, the subpoints are selected along with the main point.

7. Click the Move Up button three times to move the selected text to Slide 1. The revised outline should look like this:

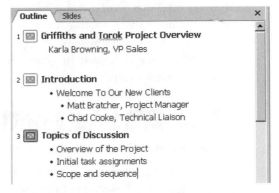

8. Save the presentation as **Moving Outline Text Practice.ppt**.

There are faster alternatives for moving text, but it may take a few tries to get the hang of it. Use drag and drop to move text just like you would in a Word document. Remember, as you mouse over a bullet or slide icon in the outline, the pointer shape changes to a four-headed arrow, the tool for moving text and objects. To move a point and all the subpoints beneath it, drag the bullet preceding that point (that is, hold down the left mouse button while moving the mouse).

As you drag the selection toward its new location, a two-headed arrow replaces the four-headed arrow, and a horizontal line appears in the outline. If you drag and drop the horizontal line, the selected point(s) move to the new location.

When you use drag and drop to rearrange points, be sure to move the mouse vertically. Horizontal dragging causes the selected text to change levels. If you drag a bullet point horizontally to the right, a vertical line appears in the outline. Drag and drop the horizontal line to the right to demote the text or to the left to promote the text.

Adding and Modifying Points and Subpoints in the Slide Pane

If you focus only on the outline, it's easy to put too much text on one slide, causing some lines of text to run off the bottom of the slide. Luckily, you can catch this mistake in the slide pane and quickly make the necessary adjustments. But the slide pane isn't just for viewing slides. You can insert, edit, move, and delete text directly on the slide. In fact, you may find it easier than working on the outline. While you can work with only one slide at a time, this view gives you a better feel for how the slide will actually look when complete.

Most slides include two text boxes: one for the title and one for the body text. When you click the title or body, a frame appears around the text box.

To add text to a slide, place your insertion point at the desired location in the text box. You promote or demote points and subpoints just as you would in the outline pane: Select the text first and either use the Promote or Demote buttons on the Outlining toolbar or press Tab or Shift+Tab. Practice modifying text in the slide pane by completing Exercise 22.15. In this exercise, you will insert, modify, move, and delete text on a slide.

EXERCISE 22.15

Modifying Text Directly on the Slide

1. Open 22-15.ppt, or use the Moving Outline Text Practice presentation you created in Exercise 22.14.

EXERCISE 22.15 *(continued)*

2. Display Slide 4 (Topic One) in the slide pane of Normal view.

3. Click and drag to select the placeholder text in the title text box, and type a new title for the slide: **Overview of the Project**

4. Revise the bullet points so the finished slide appears as follows:

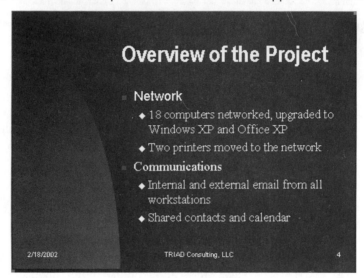

5. Move the last bullet point (Shared contacts and calendar) up one line, making it the first subpoint under Communications.

6. Resave the presentation as **Modify Text on Slide Practice.ppt**.

Formatting Text

In general, you can navigate to any slide and format the text by selecting it and changing formats using the Formatting toolbar or Format menu. It isn't any different than formatting text in Word 2002.

If you're planning to make the same formatting changes to every slide in a presentation, don't do it one slide at a time. PowerPoint has tools for making global changes with just a few clicks. See "Working with Slide Masters" in Chapter 24.

Earlier in this section, we imported a Word outline to create eight new slides in a presentation. Although importing the text is much faster than retyping it, there is still some cleanup work to be done. In Exercise 22.16, you'll use various buttons on the Standard and Formatting toolbars to edit the text in the Adding Text From Word Practice presentation. If you're comfortable editing in Word, you'll breeze through editing text in PowerPoint.

When you begin your first presentation after installing PowerPoint, the toolbars are displayed on one row. Click the Toolbar Options drop-down arrow at the end of the toolbar to see more buttons, or choose Show Buttons On Two Rows to see all buttons on both toolbars at once

The Adding Text From Word Practice presentation could be used by a project manager to kick off a project and introduce each team member to his assigned role. In Exercise 22.16, we'll clean up the slides we imported from the Word outline in Exercise 22.12.

EXERCISE 22.16

Formatting Text on a Slide

1. If you saved the Adding Text From Word Practice presentation from Exercise 22.12, open it. If not, open 22-16.ppt.

2. Display Slide 2 (Client Contact Information) in Normal view.

3. Select all the bulleted text and click the Bullets button on the Formatting toolbar to remove the bullets from each line.

4. Immediately click the Center button, also on the Formatting toolbar, to center the selected text on the slide. Much better, don't you think?

5. Repeat steps 3 and 4 above on Slide 3 (Project Liaison).

6. Select all the bulleted text on Slide 6 (Project Goals) and click the drop-down arrow on the Font Size control.

Change the font size to 28 pt. Now the text actually fits on the slide!

7. Click once inside the text box on Slide 6 to deselect the text. Then point to the frame around the text box. The pointer becomes a 4-headed arrow. Click and drag the arrow upward just enough to adjust the placement of the text on the slide, leaving a bit more room at the bottom.

8. Slide 7 has a similar problem with text overflow. We'll handle this one in a slightly different way. Click once to activate the text frame with the bulleted list on Slide 7 (Implementation and Timeline).

9. Overflowing text frames automatically display the AutoFit Options button.

Point to the button, and a drop-down arrow appears. Click the drop-down arrow to see a menu of choices:

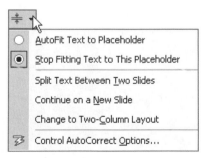

10. Choose AutoFit Text To Placeholder from the menu.

11. Save this presentation as **Formatting Text Practice.ppt**. Close it when you've finished saving.

Summary

In this chapter, you learned several options for starting a PowerPoint presentation. You also learned to work with text on slides. We covered the following topics:

- Creating a presentation from scratch, from a wizard, and from a template
- Navigating the PowerPoint application window
- Adding and deleting PowerPoint slides
- Modifying header and footer placeholders in the Slide Master
- Using a PowerPoint template
- Inserting and modifying text
- Importing text from Word
- Formatting text in a presentation

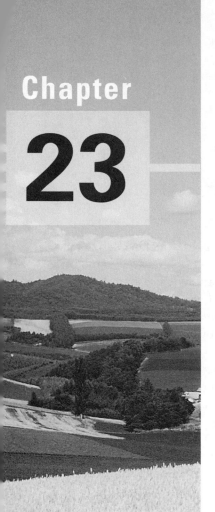

Chapter

23

Adding Color and Graphics to Presentations

MOUS POWERPOINT 2002 CORE EXAM OBJECTIVES COVERED IN THIS CHAPTER:

✓ Add tables, charts, clip art, and bitmap images to slides

✓ Customize slide backgrounds

✓ Add OfficeArt elements to slides

✓ Apply custom formats to tables

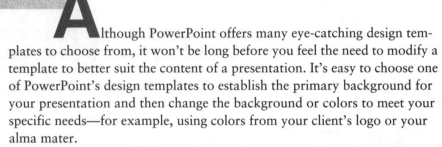

Although PowerPoint offers many eye-catching design templates to choose from, it won't be long before you feel the need to modify a template to better suit the content of a presentation. It's easy to choose one of PowerPoint's design templates to establish the primary background for your presentation and then change the background or colors to meet your specific needs—for example, using colors from your client's logo or your alma mater.

No matter how well you've executed the design, it's the presentation content that makes the difference between professional or amateur, selling or not selling, a high grade or a low one. In this chapter, we'll focus on the graphic elements in your presentation. You'll learn how to add pictures, clip art, tables, and other graphic objects to slides. You'll also learn to change slide backgrounds and colors and choose from numerous options to customize your presentation. And each new tool provides another way to make sure you look good at the podium!

Before you begin this chapter, you should go to the Sybex website and download the file 4113Ch23.zip. This package contains the files necessary to complete some of the exercises in this chapter. In addition, it contains files of what most of the slides should look like after you complete the exercises. These files are affixed with the word *Post*.

Inserting and Modifying Visual Elements

After your presentation's content is under control, it's time to think about ways to add visual impact that supports and extends your message. Objects add interest that text cannot; well-chosen graphics provide another way for the audience to understand your message. Why not include your company logo on the introductory slide? Consider displaying those month-end sales figures in a table. Emphasize a particularly important point with a graphical bullet. This is your opportunity to add the design elements that turn a good presentation into a great presentation.

Working with Objects on Slides

PowerPoint treats each item placed on a slide as an object. Even the text typed in the outline is placed in a text box. Most slides have at least two text boxes—one for the title and one for the bulleted text—and each text box is an object. We covered the title box and text box in Chapter 22, "Getting Started with PowerPoint." In this chapter, we'll focus on other, catchier objects that support content, such as colorful backgrounds and graphics. The PowerPoint Online Help uses the term *text boxes* to refer to both title boxes and text boxes (or simply text boxes) and uses the term *objects* to refer to objects other than the title box and text box. We'll use the same convention in this chapter. To add objects to slides, switch to Normal view.

If an object should appear on every slide (like a company logo or custom background), add it to the Slide Master (see Chapter 24, "Producing Exciting Presentations.")

Using Slide Layouts with Object Placeholders

The easy way to insert an object is to begin with a slide layout that includes the object, whether the object is text, clip art, a table, a chart, a sound or video clip, or any other object. Figure 23.1 shows several examples of slide layouts that include text and objects.

In the next several sections, you will learn how to work with different slide layouts to insert tables, charts, clip art, and other graphic images on slides.

Exam ***Objective***	**Add tables, charts, clip art, and bitmap images to slides**

FIGURE 23.1 You can choose a layout that includes an object in the Slide Layout task pane.

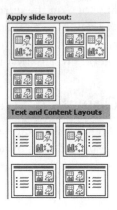

Inserting Tables

Use a table when you want to display information in columns and rows. You won't want to overwhelm your audience with facts and figures, so it's a good idea to keep the information in a table rather simple. Some users shy away from tables because they don't like the "grid" look. Once you're familiar with the feature, however, you can use the table's structure to position text and then turn off the visible borders to render the structure invisible. Figure 23.2 shows an example of a slide with a table that has the interior grid borders turned off.

FIGURE 23.2 Table slides display information in columns and rows.

In Exercise 23.1, you'll learn how to create a simple table and enter information in each column and row. Later in the chapter, we'll explore editing and formatting in tables, under a different exam objective.

EXERCISE 23.1

Creating a Table

1. Open 23-1.ppt from the zip file you downloaded from the Sybex website.

2. Navigate to Slide 2 and type a title: **Phone List**.

3. Double-click the table placeholder. You'll be prompted to enter the number of rows and columns:

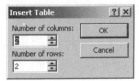

4. Use the spin boxes to choose 2 columns and 4 rows. Then click OK.

5. Your table appears with an insertion point in the first cell. If the Tables And Borders toolbar is in your way, drag its title bar to move it or click the X to close it. Type **Name**.

6. Press Tab to move one cell to the right.

7. Type **Phone Number**.

8. Press Tab to move to the next row.

9. Continue entering names and phone numbers, pressing Tab to move to the next cell. When you have finished, click away from your slide, and it should look something like this:

10. Save the file as **Creating A Table Practice.ppt**.

You can insert a table on any slide, even if it doesn't have the table layout. In the absence of the placeholder that the layout provides, just choose Insert ➢ Table to begin the process.

Creating Charts

Charts provide you with the visual means to display numeric data. An audience could easily lose sight of the main point when presented with a large table of numbers. In many cases, the visual impact of a chart draws attention to the figures you want them to remember. In Figure 23.3, the chart makes it very clear which region is improving sales, which region is declining, and which region has been up and down.

FIGURE 23.3 Charts help your audience decipher numeric data.

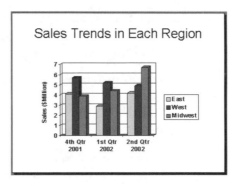

In order to create a chart, you must have numeric data from which to create it. In Exercise 23.2, we'll create a simple bar chart that compares the number of boxes of cookies sold by a local Girl Scout troop over the last four years.

You can insert a chart on any slide, regardless of layout. Just choose Insert ➢ Chart from the menu.

EXERCISE 23.2

Creating a Chart

1. Open your Creating A Table Practice presentation from Exercise 23.1. If you don't have this file, just use 23-2.ppt from your download.

2. Insert a new slide to follow Slide 2. Choose the Title And Chart layout for the new slide. (You'll have to scroll to the bottom of the Slide Layouts and look in the Other Layouts section.)

3. Enter a title for the slide: **Troop 477 Cookie Sales.**

4. Double-click the chart placeholder. The task pane closes and the chart's datasheet appears, complete with sample data:

		A	B	C	D	E
		1st Qtr	2nd Qtr	3rd Qtr	4th Qtr	
1	East	20.4	27.4	90	20.4	
2	West	30.6	38.6	34.6	31.6	
3	North	45.9	46.9	45	43.9	
4						

5. We'll delete the sample data we don't need and overtype the rest to suit our needs. First, let's get rid of the extra two rows. Select rows 2 and 3 by dragging your mouse over row headings 2 and 3. The selected data appears as shown:

| 2 | West | 30.6 | 38.6 | 34.6 | 31.6 |
| 3 | North | 45.9 | 46.9 | 45 | 43.9 |

6. Press the Delete key. The data disappears and the chart looks markedly different.

7. Click the cell that currently displays 1st Qtr. Enter **1998**.

8. Replace the text in the 2nd, 3rd, and 4th Qtr cells with **1999**, **2000**, and **2001**, respectively.

9. Enter the number of boxes sold in the cell below each year. 1998: **330**, 1999: **402**, 2000: **519**, 2001: **510**. The completed data sheet should look like this:

		A	B	C	D	E
		1998	1999	2000	2001	
1	East	330	402	519	510	
2						
3						
4						

EXERCISE 23.2 *(continued)*

10. Click the X in the Title bar of the datasheet to close it.

11. To delete the unnecessary legend (that's the part on the chart that displays the word *East* with a colored box in front of it), just click the legend to select it. Then press the Delete or Backspace key on the keyboard.

    Warning: Do not use the Del key on the numeric keypad when you are trying to delete a legend.

12. Click away from the chart to deselect it. The task pane reappears and the completed slide looks like this:

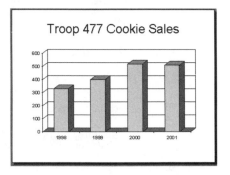

13. Save the presentation as **Creating a Chart Practice.ppt**.

Adding Clip Art and Other Images

It's standard practice in business to put the company logo on most anything that goes out of the office, including PowerPoint presentations. And just about any presentation can benefit from photos and clip art that help break up the monotony of text without detracting from its message. Yes, there's nothing like the perfect graphic to emphasize that critical point. There are two different ways to add art to a slide. You can start with a placeholder slide and go from there, or you can use any slide and search the Clip Organizer task pane. Exercise 23.3 teaches you how to insert a graphic using a placeholder slide.

EXERCISE 23.3

Inserting Clip Art from a Placeholder

1. Open your Creating A Chart Practice.ppt file from Exercise 23.2, or open 23-3.ppt.

2. Insert a new slide to follow Slide 3. Choose either of the Title, Text, And Clip Art layouts. Both are located in the Other Layouts section of the task pane:

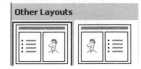

3. Enter a title in the Title text box: **Inserting Clip Art**

4. Enter three bulleted points in the other text box:

   - Clip Art spices up your slides

   - Clip Art adds emphasis

   - Clip Art is easy and fun!

5. Double-click the Clip Art placeholder. The Select Picture dialog box opens:

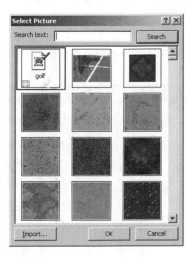

6. Although you could scroll to browse the available art, it would take quite a while to find something appropriate. Instead, type a keyword in the Search Text text box. Try entering the word **apple**, and then click Search.

7. To insert the picture you want, just click it (a blue box appears around the selected clip), and then click OK. The clip appears on the slide, and the Picture toolbar opens with options for editing, as shown here:

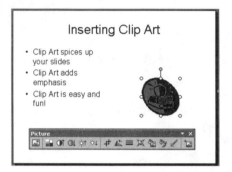

8. Save this presentation as `ClipArt From Placeholder Practice.ppt`.

In Exercise 23.4, we will search Microsoft's Clip Organizer to find and insert appropriate clip images on a slide.

Inserting Clip Art without a Placeholder

1. If you completed Exercise 23.3, open your `ClipArt From Placeholder Practice` presentation, or just open `23-4.ppt` from your downloaded files.

2. Insert a new slide to follow Slide 4. Choose the Title Only layout (from the Text Layouts section of the task pane).

3. Enter a title: **Inserting Clip Art on Any Slide.**

EXERCISE 23.4 *(continued)*

4. If your Drawing toolbar is on, just click the Insert Clip Art button to display the Insert Clip Art task pane.

If you prefer, you can click the drop-down arrow at the top of the task pane and choose Insert Clip Art. In any case, the Insert Clip Art task pane is displayed:

Note: The first time you open this task pane, you will be prompted to catalog your media files. You'll have better luck searching for clips if you let Office do this, and it takes only a few minutes.

5. To search for a specific type of clip, follow these steps:

    a. Enter a keyword or two in the Search Text text box. (See Table 23.1 for tips on what to enter.) For this exercise, enter **business, computer**.

    b. Choose which collection(s) you wish to search by selecting from the Search In drop-down list. Select Everywhere to search all collections for this exercise.

    c. Choose the type of file you're looking for in the Results Should Be list. This time, we'll just select Clip Art. That means you have to deselect Photographs, Movies, and Sounds.

    d. Click the Search button to display clips that meet your criteria.

EXERCISE 23.4 *(continued)*

6. Scroll through the search results until you find the clip you'd like to use. Click the clip's icon to insert it on the slide and display the Picture toolbar.

7. Save the presentation as **ClipArt on Any Slide Practice.ppt**.

Not all of the clips visible in the Clip Gallery are installed in a typical Office installation. When you insert a clip that was not installed, you may be prompted to insert the Office CD-ROM that contains the clip.

Microsoft assumes that you are probably too busy to spend time going through hundreds of images to find the one you want. Rather than relying on luck to find the perfect graphic, users are directed to the Clip Gallery's built-in Search feature. Search saves time, frustration, and that inevitable feeling of hopelessness that comes from browsing through the vast clip collection. Table 23.1 offers tips for getting the results you want.

TABLE 23.1 Search Tips

Search For	Results to Expect
A particular word: **school**	Clips that are cataloged with **school** as a keyword
Multiple words separated by commas: **school, teacher**	Clips that have one or both of the keywords you typed
Words in quotes: **"school teacher"**	Clips that have **school teacher** as a keyword
Multiple words without quotes or commas: **school teacher**	Clips that have both keywords you typed
Filenames with wildcards: **sc*.jpg**	Media clips with filenames such as school.jpg and scooter.jpg

In addition to using Clip Organizer as a source of art, you can insert pictures into your document from any file you can access. Exercise 23.5 shows you how to insert a bitmap image on a slide.

EXERCISE 23.5

Inserting a Bitmap Image

1. Open `ClipArt on Any Slide Practice.ppt` from Exercise 23.4, or open `23-5.ppt`.

2. Insert a new slide to follow Slide 5. Choose the Title Only layout.

3. Enter a title: **Inserting A Bitmap Image**.

4. Click in the white space on the slide and choose Insert ➢ Picture ➢ From File, or display the Picture toolbar and click the Insert Picture button to open the Insert Picture dialog box.

5. Locate and select the file you want to insert. Then click the Insert button.

6. Drag a resizing handle to make the picture bigger (if necessary). If you wish, drag the entire picture (by pointing to the middle of it) to position it where you want it.

7. Save the presentation as **`Inserting a Bitmap Practice.ppt`**.

Now that you know how to insert different types of objects, let's revisit the tables feature to learn about editing and formatting information you choose to present in rows and columns.

Customizing Your Slides

In a perfect world, the objects we create would look just like we envisioned them as soon as we insert them. Unfortunately, modifying, enhancing, and tweaking objects is the norm. In this section, we'll talk about changes you can make to your tables and slide backgrounds.

Formatting Tables

Earlier in this chapter, we created a rather utilitarian table. Now it is time to see what we can do to jazz it up. You'll learn to resize rows and columns, adjust text alignment, and change the look and feel of a table by adjusting borders and shading.

Exam	**Apply custom formats to tables**
Objective	

Before you can modify a table, it will be helpful to know how to select different parts of a table. Exercise 23.6 walks you through those steps.

EXERCISE 23.6

Selecting Parts of a Table

1. If you completed Exercise 23.5, open `Inserting a Bitmap Practice.ppt`. Or open `23-6.ppt`.

2. Navigate to Slide 2 to display the Phone List table.

3. Display the Tables And Borders toolbar if it isn't already onscreen. Just click View ➤ Toolbars ➤ Tables And Borders.

4. To select a row of cells, just drag over them. Alternatively, you can click anywhere in that row. Then click the Table menu button on the Tables And Borders toolbar and choose Select Row.

5. To select a column of cells, just position the mouse pointer above it until the column selection tool appears:

Then click once to select the column you are pointing to. Drag across the top of the columns to select multiple columns.

Selecting the appropriate cells in a table is important if you want to get the results you expect when you are formatting. Next you'll learn how to format text in a table. Exercise 23.7 shows you how.

EXERCISE 23.7

Formatting Text in a Table

1. If you just completed Exercise 23.6, you're right where you need to be. If not, open 23-7.ppt.

2. Navigate to Slide 2 to display the Phone List table.

3. Display the Tables And Borders toolbar if it isn't already onscreen. Just click View ➤ Toolbars ➤ Tables And Borders.

4. Select the first row in the table (the cells Name and Phone Number).

5. Select an appealing font from the Font drop-down list on the Formatting toolbar. For this exercise, we're using Arial Black.

6. Select all the cells in the table and click the Center Vertically button on the Tables And Borders toolbar.

7. Save the presentation as **Formatting in Tables Practice.ppt**.

By default, text wraps within the confines of the column in a table. We haven't produced this effect because we just haven't typed in enough text in our Tables exercises. At times we must adjust the column width to change how text wraps, or even to improve visual appeal. We can also adjust the row height if it suits what we're trying to do. For instance, row height must be decreased of you want to fit more than about eight rows on a slide. Exercise 23.8 walks you through adjusting row height and column width.

EXERCISE 23.8

Adjusting Row Height and Column Width

1. Open Formatting in Tables Practice.ppt from Exercise 23.7, or open 23-8.ppt from your downloaded files.

2. Navigate to Slide 2 to display the Phone List table.

EXERCISE 23.8 *(continued)*

3. Point to the vertical border that divides the table into two columns. Your mouse changes to the column adjustment tool.

4. Drag to the right to make the second column just a bit narrower.

Note: If you drag too far, you'll see the phone numbers wrap within the cell. Just drag back a bit to "unwrap" them.

5. Point to any of the horizontal borders that divide the rows. The mouse pointer changes to the row adjustment tool.

6. Drag upward to make the rows narrower. Drag downward to make them taller. For this exercise, let's make each of the rows just a bit narrower.

7. To ensure equal row height, select the rows in the table and click the Distribute Rows Evenly button on the Tables And Borders toolbar.

8. After these adjustments, your table should look much like this one:

Name	Phone Number
Mike Fallis	(904) 239-4700
Megan Browning	(305) 468-9502
Kirby Browning	(305) 468-2774

9. You may decide that the table is placed too close to the Title text box. Click it once to select it and then drag its border to move it, just as you would a text box.

10. Save the presentation as **Adjusting Rows and Columns Practice.ppt**.

For a cleaner look, you can completely remove the table's borders. Or just remove the interior borders. To the extent that you decide to keep borders, you can choose from over a dozen styles to give your table that professional look. If your goal is to draw attention to certain areas of the table, try shading those cells. Exercise 23.9 shows you how to accomplish all these tasks.

EXERCISE 23.9

Customizing Borders and Shading

1. Open Adjusting Rows and Columns Practice.ppt if you completed Exercise 23.8. If not, open 23-9.ppt from your downloaded files.

2. Navigate to Slide 2 to display the Phone List table.

3. Select all table cells.

4. Click the drop-down arrow next to the Borders button on the Tables And Borders toolbar. You'll see a menu of border choices.

5. Click the Inside Borders button to remove the inside borders from the selected cells.

6. Now let's adjust the remaining outside border, including its color. Select all table cells, and then click Table ➤ Borders And Fill from the Tables And Borders toolbar to open the Format Table dialog box, shown here:

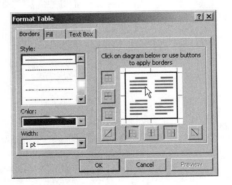

7. Scroll through the Style list and click the one you want to use. We chose the dash–double dot–dash style.

8. Select a border color from the Color drop-down list. We chose blue.

9. Select the width you'd like to use for your new border. We chose 3 pt.

EXERCISE 23.9 *(continued)*

10. Next, click directly on the existing borders in the preview window to replace them with the border selections you just made. If you prefer, you may click the buttons surrounding the preview window. We applied our changes to the outside borders only.

11. When you've finished selecting border changes, click OK to apply them to the table. Your table should now look similar to this:

Name	Phone Number
Mike Fallis	(904) 239-4700
Megan Browning	(305) 468-9502
Kirby Browning	(305) 468-2774

12. Next, we'll apply shading (fill color) to the first row in the table. Of course, you must select it first.

13. Now, click the drop-down arrow on the Fill Color button (it's on the Tables And Borders toolbar).

    Select one of the colors from there, or click More Fill Colors to open the Colors dialog box. Click the Standard tab to display these color choices:

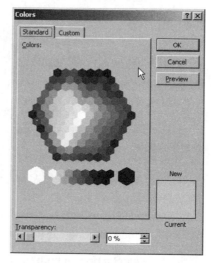

14. Select a color from the palette and click OK to apply it to the selected cells. Then click the slide once again to deselect the table

cells. For this exercise, we chose light gray. Our results are displayed below:

Name	Phone Number
Mike Fallis	(904) 239-4700
Megan Browning	(305) 468-9502
Kirby Browning	(305) 468-2774

15. Close the Tables And Borders toolbar and save this presentation as **Customizing Tables Practice.ppt**.

Now that you've learned how to use tables and other graphics on your slides, you're ready for some real design work. In the following section, you'll learn how to make some subtle and not-so-subtle changes to the background of your slides.

Designing Slide Backgrounds

Now that PowerPoint has become so common in sales departments, marketing groups, classrooms, boardrooms, and offices throughout the world, there's a new focus in presentation design. Increasingly, users are looking for ways to make their presentations stand out. Different is better.

In Chapter 22, we saw the many eye-catching design templates PowerPoint offers. However, it won't be long before you feel the need to modify a template to better suit the content of a presentation. There are two primary ways to change a template: modifying the background or modifying the color scheme.

Exam Objective — **Customize slide backgrounds**

Modifying the Slide Background

When you choose to apply a design template, the template includes, among other things, the color scheme and background color. Often, the background is more than just a solid color. It may have a shaded effect, a pattern, or a texture. A picture or graphic object may be part of the background. All these characteristics—shading, patterns, textures, and objects—form the background of the slide. Text and objects that you place on the slide are positioned on top of the background. Exercise 23.10 offers choices for changing the background of a slide.

EXERCISE 23.10

Modifying the Slide Background with Gradients

1. If you completed Exercise 22.9, open Customizing Tables Practice.ppt. If not, use 23-10.ppt from your downloaded files.

2. Display the Slide Design – Design Templates task pane and apply the Edge design. Browse through your slides to see the formatting changes that occurred when you applied the template. Then navigate your way back to Slide 1.

3. To change the background, choose Format ➤ Background, or in Normal view right-click the slide background and choose Background from the shortcut menu to open the Background dialog box:

4. To change the background, click the drop-down arrow in the Background Fill area of the Background dialog box to open a drop-down list of the color scheme options.

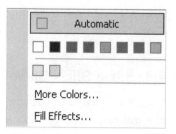

5. Choosing Automatic fills the background with the default fill color. You can also select one of the color-scheme colors or choose More

Colors (which opens the Colors dialog box) to select a solid background color. We're going to take a walk on the wilder side and choose Fill Effects to open the Fill Effects dialog box.

6. In this dialog box, you can select a background from four different types of fills, as demonstrated by the four tabs: Gradient, Texture, Pattern, or Picture. The Gradient page of the Fill Effects dialog box is shown here:

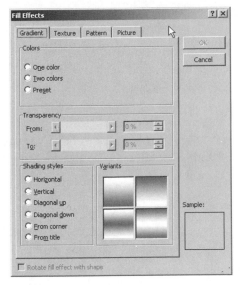

7. To apply a gradient, select one of the gradient options: One Color, Two Colors, or Preset. We chose Preset and then selected Parchment.

8. If you have chosen the two-color option, select the two colors you wish to use to create a custom gradient. If you're using a Preset, go to step 9.

9. Select a shading style to determine the direction of the gradient (Horizontal, Diagonal Up, From Title, etc.). If you chose Parchment in step 7, PowerPoint selects From Title as the default shading style. We accepted the default.

10. Click OK to return to the Background dialog box, and then click either Apply (to apply to the current slide only) or Apply To All.

11. Save the presentation as **Background Gradients Practice.ppt**.

In the Fill Effects dialog box, you probably noticed four tabs of choices for customizing the slide background.

Gradient A variegated color mix. The preset gradient schemes use two or more colors to create effects such as Early Sunset, Moss, and Parchment.

Texture A photo-like fill ranging from wood and mineral textures to a fossil fish.

Pattern A repeated pattern such as diagonal lines or vertical stripes.

Picture An image in one of the many graphic formats PowerPoint supports.

Pictures used as backgrounds can be stunning. Landscapes and group photos are particularly effective. You don't need to worry about sizing the image—it fills the entire slide. You should, however, change the font on the slide to a contrasting color so text will be legible. Figure 23.4 shows a slide that uses Horseshoe Falls (Niagara Falls, Canada) as the background graphic. This was one of many geographically specific background photos in a presentation for an audience that included decision makers from the U.S. and Canada.

FIGURE 23.4 The right picture can make an excellent background image.

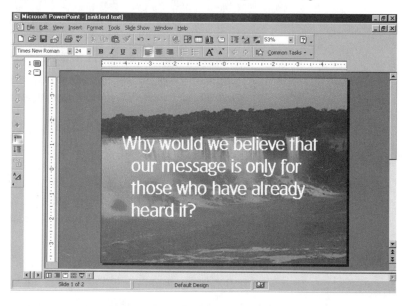

Exercise 23.10 took you through the steps for applying a gradient as a background. In Exercise 23.11, you'll learn how to use textures, patterns, and pictures.

EXERCISE 23.11

Modifying the Slide Background with Textures, Patterns, and Pictures

1. Open Background Gradients Practice.ppt from Exercise 23.10, or open 23-11.ppt from your downloaded files.

2. Insert three new slides to follow Slide 6. Use the Title Only layout from the Text Layouts section.

3. Enter titles in the Title text box. Slide 7: **Slide With Textured Background**; Slide 8: **Slide With Patterned Background**; Slide 9: **Slide With Picture As Background.**

4. In Normal view, select Slide 7 and click Format ➤ Background.

5. Click the drop-down arrow in the Background Fill area and choose Fill Effects. Click the Texture tab.

6. Select one of the textures and click OK. We chose White Marble for this exercise.

7. When you're using a "busy" background, graphic elements from the template may detract from the overall look of the slide. To remove the graphic lines from the Edge template, enable the Omit Background Graphics From Master check box in the Background dialog box. Then click Apply to apply the changes to this slide only.

8. Navigate to Slide 8 and click Format ➤ Background.

9. Click the drop-down arrow in the Background Fill area and choose Fill Effects. Click the Pattern tab.

10. Select contrasting foreground and background colors. The foreground color forms the pattern on top of the background color. Make your color selections from the default scheme or choose More Colors for additional options. For this exercise, we chose a white background and dark gray foreground.

11. Click one of the pattern styles displayed in the dialog box and click OK. We chose 10% polka dots as the pattern.

EXERCISE 23.11 *(continued)*

12. Enable the Omit Background Graphics From Master check box in the Background dialog box. Then click Apply.

13. Navigate to Slide 9 and click Format ➤ Background.

14. Click the drop-down arrow in the Background Fill area and choose Fill Effects. Click the Picture tab.

15. Click the Select Picture button to select a picture to apply to a background. We used keyboard.jpg, included with the zip files you downloaded at the beginning of this chapter. Once you select a picture, click OK to return to the Background dialog box.

16. Enable the Omit Background Graphics From Master check box in the Background dialog box. Then click Apply.

17. Sometimes the title text is hard to read when you change the background. We changed the font color of the title to white for more contrast. The three slides with background changes are displayed below:

18. Save this presentation as **More Background Practice.ppt**.

An easy way to build immediate rapport with your audience is to include pictures that are meaningful to them. When you use an image of a customer's building as the background to a presentation, it's a powerful way to say, "We visited your manufacturing facility." When you're collecting information for a proposal, use a digital camera to take photos of client sites for use in project and sales presentations (however, don't include images of people unless you have obtained their written permission). If you don't have a digital camera with good resolution, you can take 35mm photos and scan them on a high-resolution scanner.

Modifying the Slide Color Scheme

It's easy to choose one of PowerPoint's design templates to establish the primary background for your presentation and then change the background or colors to meet your specific needs—for example, using colors from your client's logo or your alma mater.

Consider the environment for your presentation when changing colors or backgrounds. For overheads, the lighter the background the better. Dark backgrounds work well for electronic or online presentations, but if you need to show a presentation with the room lights on, choose a light background and dark text. Follow the steps in Exercise 23.12 to learn about changing the slide color scheme.

EXERCISE 23.12

Modifying the Slide Color Scheme

1. Open 23-12.ppt. If you worked through the exercises in Chapter 22, you'll recognize this New Project Meeting.ppt presentation.

2. In Normal or Slide Sorter view, click Format ➢ Slide Design to display the Slide Design task pane.

3. If color schemes are not currently displayed, you must click the Color Schemes link in the task pane or choose Slide Design – Color Schemes from the task pane drop-down menu.

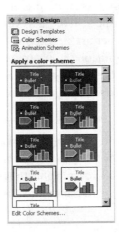

EXERCISE 23.12 *(continued)*

4. For most templates, PowerPoint displays several standard schemes and gives you the ability to edit them, creating your own custom color schemes. To apply a new color scheme to all slides in a presentation, just click the thumbnail of the color scheme you like. With PowerPoint 2002, color scheme changes are made in real time so you can see modifications immediately and undo any you don't like. We chose the standard scheme with the dark blue background.

5. Now let's try changing only selected slides in the presentation. First, display the presentation in Normal view with slide miniatures showing in the left pane.

6. Select the slides to be modified. We chose 2, 4, 6, and 8. Remember, hold Ctrl to select multiple, noncontiguous slides.

7. Click the drop-down arrow on the color scheme you want to use. Choose Apply To Selected Slides. We chose the last scheme: white background and blue accents.

8. Save the presentation as **Modifying Color Scheme Practice.ppt**.

Some design professionals think it's a bad idea to use multiple color schemes within a presentation. For continuity's sake, you may want to use only one scheme. However, every workplace has a design expert. Whether it's an entire marketing department or just the boss's assistant, there's usually someone you can go to who knows when things "look good." If you have doubts about your own design work, get another opinion from the expert(s) in your workplace.

You can't change the color scheme in a blank presentation because there's no scheme to change. Furthermore, some templates (Whirlpool, for example) have a large graphic that covers most of the background. When you make changes to the color scheme, you can't see them.

Edit Color Schemes... If none of the standard schemes trips your trigger, create your own scheme. Select the scheme that's closest to the scheme you want and click the Edit Color Schemes link at the bottom of the task pane. This opens the Edit

Color Scheme dialog box to the Custom page, as shown in Figure 23.5. Select the element color you want to change, and click the Change Color button to open the Colors dialog box. Choose a color from the array of colors presented, or if you want to mix your own, select the Custom tab to open the Color Picker.

FIGURE 23.5 Change the colors used in the selected scheme to create custom color schemes.

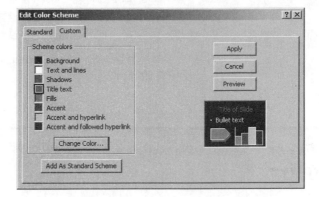

If you wish, you can save the color scheme of the current design for future use by clicking the Add As Standard Scheme button on the Custom tab of the Edit Color Scheme dialog box. Added schemes are displayed on the Standard tab of the Edit Color Scheme dialog box and in the Slide Design – Color Schemes task pane.

Creating Art with the Drawing Toolbar

If you want to design your own graphic objects, the Drawing toolbar has a bundle of tools for you to use. You can unleash your creativity and have loads of fun drawing your own graphics using these drawing tools.

Drawing is available in Word, Excel, and PowerPoint, and the drawing tools are available in the Access Toolbox. You use the same methods to create a drawing with the drawing tools no matter which application you are using.

The Drawing toolbar is displayed by default in PowerPoint. If yours isn't visible, just click View ➤ Toolbars, and then select Drawing in the toolbar list. This toolbar, shown in Figure 23.6, includes two broad categories of menus and buttons. The first set, beginning with the AutoShapes drop-down list button and ending with the Insert Picture button, is used to create drawing objects. The remaining buttons on either side of this set are used to select and format existing objects. For this exam objective, we'll focus on the first set of buttons.

FIGURE 23.6 The Drawing toolbar allows you to design your own slide graphics.

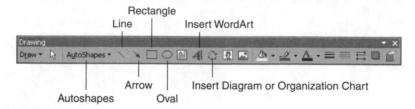

Exam Objective ✓   **Add OfficeArt elements to slides**

Inserting AutoShapes

AutoShapes are stars, hearts, banners, block arrows, lightening bolts, and other typical shapes you might want to add to give some pizzazz to a slide. When you click the AutoShapes button on the Drawing toolbar, a menu appears with a list of AutoShape categories:

AutoShapes consist of lines; basic shapes such as triangles, cylinders, hearts, and braces; block arrows; flowchart shapes; and many more. Choose the More AutoShapes option to see the complete list. Exercise 23.13 walks you through inserting and sizing a basic AutoShape.

EXERCISE 23.13

Inserting and Resizing an AutoShape

1. Open 23-13.ppt. Insert a new slide to follow the current Slide 9. Choose the Title Only layout from the Text Layouts section.

2. Enter a title on your new Slide 10: **Inserting AutoShapes**.

3. Click the AutoShapes drop-down list button on the Drawing toolbar, and then highlight a category to display its menu of AutoShapes. For this exercise, choose Basic Shapes.

4. Click an AutoShape from the Basic Shapes menu. Let's choose the diamond. As soon as you choose the diamond, the mouse pointer changes to a crosshair.

5. Position the crosshair where you want to place the AutoShape, and then click the slide to create the shape in its default size, filled with its default color.

6. Resize your AutoShape by dragging one of its corner handles (the small circles that surround a selected AutoShape) to increase or decrease its size. Hold the Shift key while you drag to resize proportionally.

7. If you wish to move your AutoShape, just position the mouse in the center of the shape and drag it to the new position. Your new Slide 10 should look something like this:

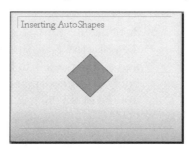

8. Save this file as **AutoShapes Practice.ppt**.

If you intend to add a lot of AutoShapes in the same category, you can drag the title bar at the top of the menu and place the menu in the document as a floating toolbar. For example, when creating a flowchart, you can drag that menu's title bar so the AutoShapes on it are easily available while you work.

Callout AutoShapes are text boxes used for annotating other objects or elements. When you insert a callout in your document, the insertion point automatically appears inside the callout. To place text in any closed AutoShape except those created using the Lines category, right-click the AutoShape and choose Add Text from the shortcut menu. When you do, the insertion point appears in the object, ready for you to type your text.

Curve, Freeform, and Scribble objects are AutoShape line objects that consist of multiple line segments you create individually. The line segments are extremely small in Curve and Scribble objects; in fact, they are so small that the lines appear to be curved. You can easily see the various line segments in a Freeform object. To create a Curve, Freeform, or Scribble AutoShape, follow the steps in Exercise 23.14.

EXERCISE 23.14

Creating Curve, Freeform, and Scribble Objects

1. Open 23-14.ppt. Insert a new slide to follow the current Slide 10. Choose the Title Only layout.

2. Enter a title on your new Slide 11: **Inserting AutoShape Lines**.

3. Click the AutoShapes drop-down list button and highlight Lines to display its menu of AutoShapes.

4. In the menu, click Curve, Freeform, or Scribble. For this exercise, we'll try a curve.

5. Position the mouse pointer where you want to begin the line, and then click to start it. Gradually move your mouse to a different location and click again to form the first segment of the line. Continue until the line appears as you want, and then double-click to form the end of the line.

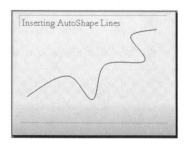

6. Save this presentation as **Line Objects Practice.ppt**.

Adding Other Line Art Objects

Line art objects include AutoShapes, lines, arrows, rectangles, ovals, and text boxes. You can easily insert any of these objects in your document by using the appropriate tool on the Drawing toolbar. Try Exercise 23.15 for some practice inserting other types of line art.

EXERCISE 23.15

Inserting Other Line Art Objects

1. Open 23-15.ppt. Insert a new slide to follow the current Slide 11. Choose the Title Only layout.

2. Enter a title on your new Slide 12: **Other Line Art**

3. Click the Line button or the Arrow button.

4. Move the pointer, which now appears as a crosshair, to one end of the line you want to draw.

5. Hold down the left mouse button and drag to draw the line.

6. Release the button to create the line. Now try it again with the button you didn't choose the first time.

7. Now we'll try two other line art tools. Click either the Rectangle or Oval button.

8. Move the pointer, which now appears as a crosshair, to the top-left corner or edge of the object you want to draw.

9. Hold down the left mouse button and drag down and to the right to draw the object.

10. Release the button to create the rectangle or oval and turn off the Drawing tool.

11. Now try the process with the button you didn't use the first time. Your slide with four new objects might look something like this:

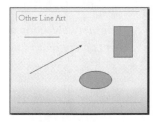

12. Save this file as **More Line Art Practice.ppt**.

If you want a line or arrow that is absolutely horizontal or vertical in relation to the page, hold the Shift key while dragging. Holding the Shift key while drawing a rectangle or oval creates an exact circle or square.

Because both the rectangle and oval are closed objects, you can add text in them just as you can in the closed AutoShapes. Right-click the object, and then choose Add Text from the shortcut menu to position the insertion point inside the object.

If you need a series of identical objects, create and copy one object and then paste as many copies of that object as necessary in the locations you want.

Designing WordArt

WordArt is used to create a text graphic object. You can use WordArt to create text logos, emphasize titles, and add excitement to a presentation. For example, you can create a vibrantly colored title slide and print it as a title page for a hard-copy proposal. Follow the steps in Exercise 23.16 to learn how to create WordArt.

EXERCISE 23.16

Inserting WordArt

1. Open 23-16.ppt. Insert a new slide to follow the current Slide 12. Choose the Title Only layout.

2. Enter a title on your new Slide 12: **Creating WordArt**

3. Click away from the Title text box to deselect it, and then click the Insert WordArt button on the Drawing toolbar to open the WordArt Gallery dialog box.

   Alternatively, choose Insert ➢ Picture ➢ WordArt to open the Word-Art Gallery dialog box, shown here.

4. Click the style you want for your text graphic in the Select A Word-Art Style area. Then click OK.

5. Next, you'll see the Edit WordArt Text dialog box:

6. Type your text in the Text area of the dialog box. Type your name for this exercise.

7. If you're feeling adventurous, you can apply the following formatting to the text in the Text area:

- Select a different font in the Font drop-down list.

EXERCISE 23.16 *(continued)*

- Select a different font size in the Size drop-down list.

- Click the Bold and/or Italics button to apply that formatting.

For this exercise, we italicized the text.

8. Choose OK to place the WordArt object on the slide. We sized ours a bit larger to make it look like this:

9. Save the presentation as **Inserting WordArt Practice.ppt**.

Constructing Diagrams and Organization Charts

An organization chart can provide an unambiguous, easy-to-understand graphical representation of

- your organization's leadership structure

- a decision making process, or

- the steps necessary to complete a project.

Microsoft Organization Chart has been available as an add-in application for many versions of Office. For the first time, however, you can create organization charts as a built-in feature of Office. In addition, you can create other types of diagrams such as Cycle and Venn diagrams. Exercise 23.17 focuses on the steps necessary to create an organization chart. For more on other types of diagrams, see the following section.

EXERCISE 23.17

Inserting an Organization Chart

1. Open 23-17.ppt. Insert a new slide to follow the current Slide 13. Choose the Title Only layout.

2. Enter a title on your new Slide 14: **Creating an Organization Chart**.

EXERCISE 23.17 *(continued)*

3. Click the Insert Diagram Or Organization Chart button on the Drawing toolbar.

This opens the Diagram Gallery, from which you can choose a diagram type:

4. Select the Organization Chart from the Diagram Gallery, and then click OK. Office creates an Organization Chart object with four boxes: one manager and three subordinates. The Organization Chart toolbar opens by default:

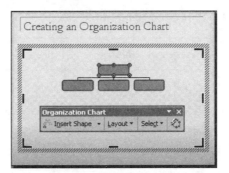

5. Select a box and begin typing. You can add up to two lines of text. See if you can reproduce our organization chart:

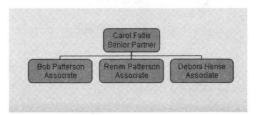

You can use the buttons on the Organization Chart toolbar to create additional boxes, delete boxes, and reposition boxes to fit your specific needs.

To insert additional boxes, select the boxes to which the new box is related and choose Insert Shape from the Organization Chart toolbar. If you click the down arrow to the right of the Insert Shape button, you can choose to add a subordinate, coworker, or assistant. To delete a box, click its border to select it and then press Delete.

If you work in a company that has a nontraditional organizational structure, i.e., shared leadership, partnership, or other less-hierarchical structure, you have to be creative to represent your structure with this tool. You cannot position an additional box at the top level. In this case, you might want to use the top level to represent your overall company, board, or maybe even your customers. Another option is to create your organization chart using AutoShapes and connectors.

The other five types of diagrams available from the Diagram Gallery can be used interchangeably to represent a process or related concepts. Select the type of diagram that most closely resembles the message you want to communicate. Table 23.2 shows the types of diagrams and how they can be used.

TABLE 23.2   Conceptual Diagrams

Diagram	Name	Use
⟳	Cycle diagram	Represents a process that has a continuous cycle.
✴	Radial diagram	Shows relationships of multiple entities/concepts to a central point.
▲	Pyramid diagram	Illustrates entities or concepts that are based on a foundation.
◉	Venn diagram	Demonstrates entities that overlap.
◎	Target diagram	Identifies steps toward a central goal.

Summary

In this chapter, you learned how to add pizzazz to your presentation with tables, graphics, and OfficeArt and by making changes to the background and color scheme. We covered the following topics:

- Using slide layouts with object placeholders
- Inserting tables, charts, clip art, and other images
- Formatting tables
- Modifying the slide background
- Modifying the slide color scheme
- Creating art with the Drawing toolbar

Chapter

24

Producing Exciting Presentations

MOUS POWERPOINT 2002 CORE EXAM OBJECTIVES COVERED IN THIS CHAPTER:

- ✓ Apply formats to presentations
- ✓ Apply animation schemes
- ✓ Apply slide transitions
- ✓ Customize slide formats
- ✓ Customize slide templates
- ✓ Manage a Slide Master
- ✓ Rehearse timing
- ✓ Rearrange slides
- ✓ Modify slide layout
- ✓ Add links to a presentation

In this chapter, we focus on setting up the presentation for delivery. You'll learn how to display slide objects one at a time or all at once. You'll learn how to transition slides so there's an interesting visual effect when you switch from one to another. And you'll learn how to make global formatting modifications that change all slides at once, rather than going through the tedious process of individually formatting each one.

Before you begin this chapter, you should go to the Sybex website and download the file 4113Ch24.zip. This contains files necessary to complete some of the exercises in this chapter as well as files that show how most slides should look once an exercise is completed. Files that show a completed exercise are affixed with the word *Post*.

Modifying Presentations

There are literally hundreds of different ways you can set up your presentation. Each creates a different "attitude," which can appear subtle (like using top-down text animations for a more authoritative voice) or extremely obvious (like sound bytes with each transition to create a more playful atmosphere). Have some fun with this chapter. It's a great place to use your imagination and experiment a bit.

Applying Presentation Formats

In Chapter 22, "Getting Started with PowerPoint," we discussed starting a presentation with a design template. Templates provide the quickest and easiest way to apply presentation formats: background color, background graphics, font size, font color, and title placement.

Apply formats to presentations

Exercise 24.1 walks you through applying a design template.

EXERCISE 24.1

Applying a Design Template to Change Presentation Formats

1. Open 24-1.ppt.

2. Display the Slide Design – Design Templates task pane.

3. Scroll through the available templates in the task pane. Point to one of the template miniatures to see its name. Click the Profile template to apply that template to the presentation. Notice that the template varies slightly from title slide to bulleted list:

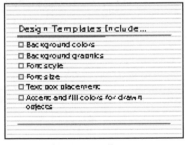

1   2

4. Try several of the templates. Now is a good time to experiment.

5. PowerPoint XP allows you to use multiple design templates within one presentation. In Normal view, display the title slide.

6. Place the mouse over the Network template miniature. Click the arrow that appears on the right. Choose Apply To Selected Slides.

7. Display Slide 2 in Normal view. Position the mouse over the Capsules template miniature. Click the arrow that appears on the right, and choose Apply To Selected Slides.

EXERCISE 24.1 *(continued)*

8. Display the presentation in Slide Sorter view:

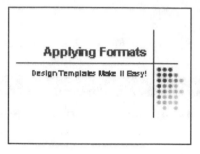
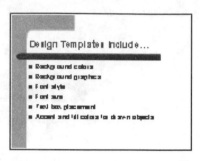

1   2

9. Save the presentation for future use if you wish. Name it `Practice Applying A Design Template.ppt`. Then close the file.

Most design experts would contend that the purpose of a template is to lend continuity to the presentation, tying slides together with common colors, fonts, and backgrounds. In this context, it doesn't make much sense to apply a different design to each slide.

However, there are times and places where multiple designs *do* make sense. We've seen a kindergarten teacher create an "All About Us" presentation where each student created a slide to represent himself or herself. As you might expect, each student chose a different template and the result was very powerful.

Animating Slide Objects with Animation Schemes

Slide *animation* is the term we use to describe how individual elements are added to the slide during a presentation. Do the bullet points fly in one at a time? Which direction do they fly from? Do they arrive automatically or on mouse click? Before or after the clip art appears? Animation settings determine the answers to all of these questions.

Microsoft ✓ *Exam Objective*   **Apply animation schemes**

In PowerPoint 2002, animation has been streamlined with new preset animation *schemes* that include separate effects for the slide title and bulleted paragraphs. You can apply a scheme to multiple slides with just a few clicks. You can apply preset animation schemes from Slide Sorter or Normal view. Exercise 24.2 walks you through the steps for using these new schemes.

EXERCISE 24.2

Applying an Animation Scheme

1. Open 24-2.ppt. If you completed Chapter 23, "Adding Color and Graphics to Presentations," you'll recognize the New Project Meeting presentation from Exercise 23.13.

2. Display the task pane (View ➤ Task Pane) in Normal view.

3. If the task pane is in Slide Design mode, click the Animation Schemes link to display preset schemes.

Animation Schemes

   If not, click the task pane selection menu and choose Slide Design - Animation Schemes.

4. Select the slide(s) you want to animate. For this exercise, don't select any slides. We're going to apply our changes to the entire presentation, but we're going to streamline the process a bit.

5. Choose a scheme from the Apply To Selected Slides list in the task pane. Schemes are categorized as Recently Used, No Animation, Subtle, Moderate, and Exciting. Let's choose the Ascend scheme from the Moderate category.

6. Schemes are applied to selected slides in real time. You'll see a preview as soon as you choose a scheme from the list. (If you don't see the preview, enable the AutoPreview check box at the bottom of the task pane.) Click Apply To All Slides to use the selected animation scheme on all slides.

7. Save this presentation as Animation Schemes Practice.ppt.

It's possible (and very easy) for your presentation to come across as a bit *too* exciting. Keep transitions simple and occasionally throw in something different. If you use too many effects, you could wind up obscuring your message rather than enhancing it.

If you apply an animation scheme in Slide Sorter view, you'll immediately see the animation icon below the left corner of the slide. From Slide Sorter view, click the icon to view animation. In Normal view, select a slide and click Play (in the task pane).

When you animate some but not all elements on a slide, Slide Show view opens the slide and displays those objects and graphics that are *not* animated. Click (or press Enter on the keyboard) to display the first slide element. Click again for each additional object.

Adding Transitions between Slides

An electronic presentation, or slide show, is a presentation displayed on a computer screen or projected with an LCD projector. Since slides are "changed" by the computer rather than by hand, you can add computerized special effects to a slide show that aren't possible when you use regular overheads for a presentation (unless you're an incredibly talented presenter who moonlights as a magician). A *transition* is a special effect added to the slide's initial appearance on-screen. The slide can appear from the right, dissolve in gradually, or fade through the background of the previous slide.

Microsoft ✓ *Exam Objective*   **Apply slide transitions**

When a presentation doesn't have transitions, each slide simply appears in place of the previous slide—very plain-vanilla. Many of the Power Point 2002 design templates include transitions so there is more pizzazz.

If you started your presentation with the AutoContent Wizard or specific templates, your slides may already have transitions and/or animation assigned. Think of these as default settings. You can easily modify these transitions or add transitions. In all previous versions of PowerPoint, the way to do this was switch to Slide Sorter view and use the tools on the Slide Sorter toolbar, shown below.

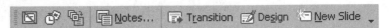

You can still use Slide Sorter view to apply and edit slide transitions. But why not take advantage of one of the new features of PowerPoint 2002? Now you have the ability to apply and preview transitions without ever leaving Normal view. Follow the steps in Exercise 24.3 to learn how.

EXERCISE 24.3

Applying and Modifying Transitions

1. If you just completed Exercise 24.2, you're right where you need to be. If not, open 24-3.ppt.

2. Switch to Normal view, if you're not already there.

3. We suggest displaying thumbnails (rather than the outline) for ease of selecting multiple slides. PowerPoint does so by default when you open the Slide Transition task pane. Display the task pane (View ➤ Task Pane).

4. Click the task pane selection list and choose Slide Transition. The task pane displays the current transition settings, as shown here:

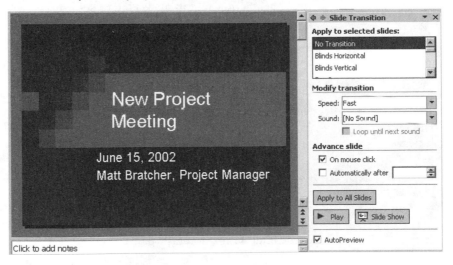

EXERCISE 24.3 *(continued)*

5. Select the slide(s) you want to transition. For this exercise, we'll select all slides. Just click the first slide in the slides pane on the left, then scroll down, hold Shift, and click the last slide.

6. Choose an effect from the Apply To Selected Slides list box. Let's try one of the new 2002 transition effects: Shape Circle.

7. Click the Slide Show button in the task pane to view your presentation, including animations and transitions. Each click of the mouse advances the presentation to the next animation or transition.

8. When you're through with the slide show, save this presentation as **Transitions Practice.ppt**, and then close the file.

Many of the transitions listed differ only in direction—for example, Cover Up, Cover Down, and Cover Up-Left. PowerPoint 2002 has several new transition effects as well. Check out Newsflash, Comb, Wedge, and Wheel. Any time you select a transition from the list, PowerPoint provides a preview of the transition using the selected slide. (Look fast—it doesn't take long.) To see the transition again, click Play at the bottom of the task pane. If you don't like seeing the automatic preview each time you make a transition selection, disable the AutoPreview check box at the bottom of the task pane. You can still click Play to see a preview when *you* decide it's appropriate.

If you prefer to add transitions in Slide Sorter view, click the Transition button on the Slide Sorter toolbar to display the Slide Transition task pane. Choose the effect you wish to use from the list box in the task pane.

In Slide Sorter view, the animation icon below the lower-left corner of a slide indicates that the slide has an assigned transition or animation. You can't tell from looking at the icon whether it has transitions, animations, or both. Click the icon to see a preview in the slide miniature.

Setting Transition Speed and Sound

Each transition has a default speed. You can change the speed for transitions, choose a different transition, or add sound effects to accompany a transition in the Slide Transition task pane.

Select the slide(s) you want to adjust. Choose a new transition effect (if you wish) and then choose one of the Speed options from the drop-down list in the Modify Transition area of the task pane. If you assign a transition sound from the Sound drop-down list, you can choose to have the sound loop until another sound begins playing. The last choice on the drop-down list, Other Sounds, opens a dialog box so that you can select a sound file. PowerPoint uses wave sounds (`.wav` extension). You'll find some wave files in the `Media` folder in the `Windows` folder, but you can purchase CDs of wave files at many computer stores and download free sound bytes from the Internet.

The Advance Slide settings are used to enter timings for automatic slide advances. For now, leave the default On Mouse Click setting to require human intervention to change slides (see "Adding Slide Timings Through Rehearsal" later in this chapter for information on automatic timings).

Any settings you choose are applied immediately to selected slides. If you wish, you can choose Apply To All Slides to apply the transition settings to every slide in the presentation. Effects, including sound, can be previewed by clicking the Play button in the task pane.

Customizing Slide Formats to Your Specifications

Sometimes it's the little things that make the difference between a great slide and one that's just so-so. A well-placed quote, for example, can produce a potent addition to your message. But do you really want a bullet character in front of that text? Probably not.

In this section, we'll explore several ways to adjust slide formatting to create that perfect presentation you had in mind.

Microsoft *Exam* *Objective*	**Customize slide formats**

When you format text on individual slides, the formatting takes precedence over formatting from the design template. Even if you apply a new design to the master, formatting applied to individual slides won't change, so you should make sure you are pleased with the overall design before formatting individual slides. You can apply standard Office text enhancements to text in your PowerPoint slides. Select the text to be formatted and then change the font typeface, size, and attributes using the Formatting toolbar or the Format menu. Exercise 24.4 shows you how.

EXERCISE 24.4

Modifying Slide Formatting

1. Open 24-4.ppt.

2. Switch to Normal view, if you're not already there.

3. Navigate to the title slide and select the subtitle: "Making the most of your text."

4. Choose Format ➤ Font from the menu to open the Font dialog box.

5. Select another font from the Font list. For this exercise, let's go with something a bit less formal: Comic Sans MS.

6. Change the Font Style to italic.

7. Change the Size to 28.

8. Change the Color to yellow.

9. Deselect the Shadow effect and then click OK.

10. Navigate to Slide 2 and select all the bullet points.

11. Choose Format ➤ Line Spacing to open the Line Spacing dialog box.

12. The three controls in the Line Spacing dialog box seem similar at first, so it is important that you understand the subtle differences among them:

    - **Line Spacing** controls the amount of vertical space between lines in each selected paragraph. If a bullet point has multiple lines, the line spacing setting applies to the lines within the bullet point and also to line spacing between bullet points.

    - **Before Paragraph** does just what it says it does: controls the amount of space between the selected paragraph and the one above it. Use this setting to move bullet points away from each other while keeping the lines within the bullet point single-spaced.

    - **After Paragraph** is the opposite of Before Paragraph, but you can use it in the same way. It provides space between bullet points while keeping multiline bulleted text single-spaced.

EXERCISE 24.4 *(continued)*

For this exercise, adjust the Before Paragraph setting to .6 lines and then click OK. Note: You can also use points to set line spacing (1 point = 1/72 inch).

13. Navigate to Slide 3.

14. Click anywhere in the line of text that reads "It's 100 meters...".

15. Click the Bullets button on the Formatting toolbar.

The bullet character for that line disappears.

16. Select the remaining two bullet points on that slide and remove those bullets. The completed slides from this exercise should appear as follows:

1   2   3

PowerPoint designers spend a considerable amount of time putting together templates with colors, fonts, and other attributes that provide a coordinated look. If you sometimes arrive at work wearing a striped shirt and plaid pants and still want to experiment with your own designs in PowerPoint, ask a colleague to review your presentation after you make formatting changes.

Aligning Text

Text can be left-aligned, centered, right-aligned, or justified. Left, Center, and Right alignment are options on the Formatting toolbar. To justify text, choose Format ➢ Alignment ➢ Justify from the menu bar. The paragraph containing the insertion point will be justified. If you wish to justify multiple paragraphs, select them before choosing the menu commands.

Replacing Fonts

Use the Replace Font dialog box to substitute one font for another globally in a presentation. You might choose to replace fonts to change the look of a presentation, but there is sometimes a more pressing reason. If you open a presentation on a computer that doesn't have the presentation's fonts installed, another font is automatically substituted—unless the fonts were embedded in the presentation. (See Chapter 25, "Preparing and Delivering the Final Product," for pointers on saving presentations for use on another computer.) This substitute font may not be good looking, and occasionally it isn't even readable. Rather than changing various levels of the master, you can have PowerPoint change each occurrence of the missing font by following the steps in Exercise 24.5.

EXERCISE 24.5

Replacing Fonts Globally

1. If you just finished Exercise 24.4, you're right where you need to be. If not, open 24-5.ppt.

2. In Normal view, select the text box that includes the font you want to replace. For this exercise, we'll select all the bulleted text on Slide 2.

3. Choose Format ➤ Replace Fonts to open the Replace Font dialog box.

4. Select a replacement font. We chose Calisto MT from the With drop-down list.

5. Click Replace. The Replace Font dialog box stays open so you can view your changes and modify them if necessary.

6. Click Close to close the Replace Font dialog box. Save the file as **Practice Replacing Fonts.ppt** and close it.

To replace fonts for *all* text boxes on *all* slides, switch to Slide Sorter view, select all slides (Ctrl+A is the fastest way), and follow steps 3–5 above.

Adjusting Tabs and Indents

The distance your insertion point moves when you press the Tab key is preset at one-half inch. You can see the default tab stops on the ruler in Normal view. Choose View ➢ Ruler to turn your ruler on, if necessary. To change the default tab settings for your presentation, do the following:

1. Switch to Normal view and display the ruler (View ➢ Ruler).

2. Select the text for which you want to change the tabs.

3. On the ruler, drag the first tab stop to its new position. All other tab stops will adjust so that the distance between each tab stop remains the same.

If you click a text box, you will see indent markers appear on the ruler, as shown in Figure 24.01. Each level of points has its own set of three indent markers. If you have only first-level bullets, you will see only three markers. If you have first- and second-level bullets, you will see six, and so on. You can use these indent markers to move text and bullets to the left or right, or you can indent just the text, moving it farther from the bullet that precedes it.

FIGURE 24.1   You can use indent markers on the ruler to move bullet points or indent text.

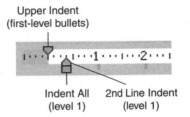

Upper Indent
(first-level bullets)

Indent All   2nd Line Indent
(level 1)   (level 1)

The upper indent marker moves the bullet character on selected paragraph(s). Just drag the upper indent marker to the right or left to move the bullet.

When you drag the triangular part of the lower indent marker, it adjusts all lines in each selected paragraph. If the first and subsequent lines of the paragraph are at the same setting (alignment), dragging this marker moves the entire paragraph in relation to the bullet. (The rectangular portion of the marker also moves when you drag the triangular portion.)

Drag the rectangular part of the lower marker to move the entire paragraph while maintaining the relationship between the first-line indent and the rest of the lines.

PowerPoint 2002 has buttons on the Formatting toolbar for increasing and decreasing the indent setting on selected text. Click the Increase Indent button to move text to the right one level at a time. Click Decrease Indent to move text to the left one level at a time. If you think this sounds just like promoting and demoting, you're correct! The buttons do essentially the same thing.

Working with Slide Masters

Every design includes one or more *Slide Masters* that identify the position of the text and graphic objects, the style of the fonts, the footer elements, and the background for all slides. Every design has a Slide Master; most designs include a separate Title Master as well. Templates from earlier versions of PowerPoint usually have only one master.

Microsoft ✓ *Exam* *Objective*	**Manage a Slide Master**

When you're ready to make global changes to your slides, do it on the Slide Master and the changes are applied to every slide based on that master. For example, if you want a graphic object (a company logo, perhaps) to appear on every slide, place it on the master rather than inserting it on each slide. In Exercise 24.6 you'll learn how to make changes to a Slide Master.

EXERCISE 24.6

Working with a Slide Master

1. Open 24-6.ppt.

2. Switch to Normal view, if you're not already there, and select Slide 2.

3. To open the Slide Master, click View ➢ Master ➢ Slide Master. The Slide Master pane opens to the left. Note the two masters: one Slide Master and one Title Master. When you're working on the Slide Master, the Slide Master View toolbar displays by default:

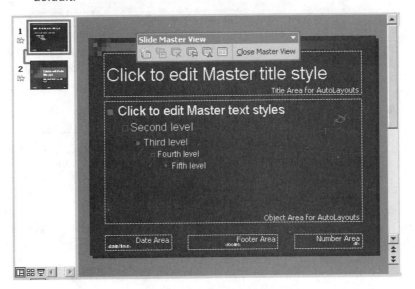

4. On the master, select any text box to modify its format. Use the buttons on the Formatting toolbar to format text or choose Format ➢ Font to change text color, size, or style. For this exercise, select the text in the slide title text box and italicize it.

5. Click the Close Master View button on the Slide Master View toolbar to return to Normal view.

6. Navigate through your slides to see their now-italicized titles.

7. Resave this presentation and close the file.

While you're working with the Slide Master, you can select and move or delete placeholders, including graphic objects and text boxes. You insert logos or other graphics you want to appear on every slide just as you would on any slide. (See Chapter 23 if you've forgotten how).

Microsoft has enhanced the Slide Master View toolbar for Power Point 2002. Not only can you close the master and return to your slides, there are options for inserting, deleting, renaming, and preserving Slide and Title Masters. Table 24.1 describes the other functions of the Slide Master View toolbar.

When you insert a new master, the design appears in the Used In This Presentation category of the Slide Design task pane. You can easily apply it to any new slides when you are working in Normal view.

TABLE 24.1   The Slide Master View Toolbar

Button	Button Name	Function
	Insert New Slide Master	Adds a blank Slide Master to the presentation. You can insert and arrange placeholders, graphics, fonts, bullets, color schemes, and other slide elements to create your own master from scratch.
	Insert New Title Master	Adds a blank Title Master to the presentation. Enabled only if you add a regular Slide Master first and apply a design to it. Modify design elements on the new Title Master to create your own Title Master from scratch.
	Delete Master	Removes the selected master from the presentation. Reformats slides based on those masters to match one of the remaining masters.

TABLE 24.1 The Slide Master View Toolbar *(continued)*

Button	Button Name	Function
	Preserve Master	Prevents PowerPoint from automatically deleting a master when no slides are based on that master or when you apply a new design to slides that were originally based on that master.
	Rename Master	Opens the Rename Master dialog box, where you can type a new name for the selected master. Renaming one master in a Slide-Title Master pair also renames the other.
	Master Layout	Opens the Master Layout dialog box, where you can enable or disable certain elements (date, footer, slide number) on the selected master.

If you want to save slight modifications to a master while retaining the original, PowerPoint now lets you copy any slide, including a master. Choose Insert ➢ Duplicate Master Slide, make your modifications to the copy, and then rename the copy if you wish.

Tailoring Slide Templates

If you've spent considerable time adjusting a template, you may want to save it for future use. Walk through Exercise 24.7 to learn about saving changes to a template.

Microsoft
✓ *Exam*
Objective

Customize slide templates

Modifying a Template

1. For this exercise, we'll start a new presentation based on the Watermark template. Refer back to Chapter 22, "Getting Started with PowerPoint" if you need a refresher on starting a presentation with a template.

2. Choose View ➢ Master ➢ Slide Master.

3. Select the miniature Slide Master (rather than the Title Master) in the pane on the left. The Slide Master is the one on top.

4. Select the slide title text and change the font to another color. We chose dark gray for this exercise. You can make additional changes, if you wish: add a company logo, change bullet characters, etc.

5. Choose File ➢ Save As to open the familiar Save As dialog box.

6. In the Save As Type area, choose Design Template (.pot).

7. Name the template. We called ours Watermark Revised. Click Save.

8. Close the presentation.

9. To use the revised template, start a new presentation and display the Slide Design – Design Templates task pane.

10. Click the Browse icon at the bottom of the task pane.

11. Your revised template should appear in the Apply Design Template dialog box. Select and apply it.

12. Save the file as **Modifying A Template Practice.ppt** and close it.

Note: If you can't find your modified template, try the following path: C:\Documents and Settings\Your Name\Application Data\Microsoft\Templates. And, if you want to replace the old template with your modified one, give it the same name as the original template and save it to C:\Program Files\Microsoft Office\Templates\Presentation Designs.

Fine-Tuning the Presentation

Once your slides are largely done, you'll want to give some thought to how you want them to run for your audience. The next section teaches you how to set up the slides so that they advance automatically. This works nicely for web presentations and those that run at trade-show kiosks.

Adding Slide Timings through Rehearsal

There are two ways to advance an electronic presentation. If the presentation is designed to run on its own—for example, in a booth at a trade show—you'll want to advance slides automatically. If your finished presentation will be used to illustrate a verbal presentation or will be posted on an intranet, you'll probably prefer to advance slides manually. If slides should advance automatically, only a bit more work is required to set the timings for each animation and transition.

You can always manually advance slides in a presentation, even if it includes slide timings. Choose Slide Show ➢ Set Up Show from the menu and choose an Advance Slides option: Manually or With Timings.

Microsoft ✓ *Exam* *Objective*	**Rehearse timing**

You can set slide timings in two ways: through rehearsal or manually in the Slide Transition task pane. For this objective, we'll focus on using rehearsal. Before setting timings, it's a good idea to run through the entire slide show two or three times. Try not to advance slides and animations too quickly for your audience because they will be seeing the slides for the first time. Make sure that your audience will have time to read the title, read each point, and see how a graphic illustrates the points. It helps to read the contents of each slide out loud, slowly, while rehearsing and setting the timings. When you're ready to practice recording timings, walk through Exercise 24.8.

EXERCISE 24.8

Adding Timings through Rehearsal

1. Open 24-8.ppt.

2. Switch to Slide Sorter view.

3. Click the Rehearse Timings button on the Slide Sorter toolbar or choose Slide Show ➤ Rehearse Timings.

The first slide appears, and the Rehearsal toolbar opens:

4. The dialog box has two timers. The timer on the right shows the total time for the presentation. The timer on the left is the elapsed time for the current slide. Click anywhere on the slide for your next animation or your next slide. The timers automatically record the number of seconds that pass between transitions and animations.

5. The Rehearsal toolbar has three additional buttons: Next, Pause, and Repeat. Click the Next button (or anywhere on the slide) to move to the next slide or animation.

6. If you are interrupted in the middle of rehearsal, click the Pause button, and then click Pause again to resume.

7. If you make a mistake while rehearsing a slide, click Repeat to set new timings for the *current* slide. If you don't catch a mistake before a slide has been advanced, you can either finish rehearsing and then edit the slide time manually or press Escape and begin again. Try clicking the Repeat button to retime a slide.

EXERCISE 24.8 *(continued)*

8. When you complete the entire rehearsal for a presentation, you'll be prompted to save the timings.

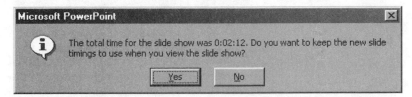

9. Choose Yes to save the timings as rehearsed. You can always adjust them later or choose to advance slides manually without the timings. In Slide Sorter view, the total time for each slide appears below the slide:

10. Save this presentation as **Rehearse Timings Practice.ppt**.

Editing Slide Timings

To edit an individual transition time, select the slide and click the Transition button on the Slide Sorter toolbar. The rehearsed time, which you can edit, is displayed in the Advance Slide area of the task pane.

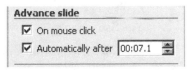

In Exercise 24.9, you'll learn how to edit rehearsed timings for one or more slides.

EXERCISE 24.9

Editing Rehearsed Timings

1. If you completed Exercise 24.8, open Rehearse Timings Practice.ppt. If not, open 24-9.ppt.

2. Choose Slide Show ➢ Set Up Show from the menu to open the Set Up Show dialog box:

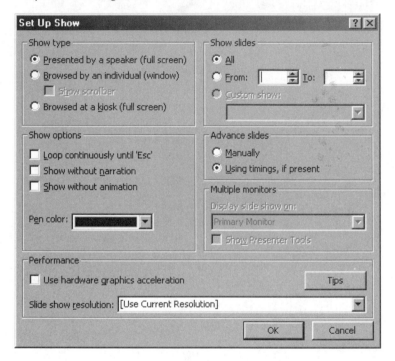

3. In the Show Slides section, set the From and To controls to the range of slides you wish to change animation timings for. For this exercise, choose Slides 1–3.

4. Click OK to close the dialog box.

5. Choose Slide Show ➢ Rehearse Timings, or click the Rehearse Timings button on the Slide Sorter toolbar, to rehearse new timings for the selected slides.

6. Save the new timings when prompted.

EXERCISE 24.9 *(continued)*

7. Choose Slide Show ➢ Set Up Show and set the Show Slides option to All. Click OK.

8. Save this presentation as `Editing Timings Practice.ppt`.

Rearranging Slides

Moving slides is fairly easy in both Normal and Slide Sorter view. For an overall balanced presentation, drag and drop allows you to distribute slides with graphic objects quickly and evenly among those that are text only. (You may want to review the outline to confirm that the text flows logically from slide to slide.)

Microsoft
✓ *Exam*
Objective

Rearrange slides

Exercise 24.10 teaches you how to rearrange slides in Slide Sorter view.

EXERCISE 24.10

Rearranging Slides

1. If you completed Exercise 24.9, open `Editing Timings Practice .ppt`. If not, open `24-10.ppt`.

2. Switch to Slide Sorter view.

3. Click a slide once to select it. Use Shift+click to select multiple contiguous slides or use Ctrl+click to select multiple noncontiguous slides. For this exercise, we'll select Slide 2. After selecting, it should have a dark border around it.

4. To move a selected slide, drag the slide toward its new location. A gray vertical line appears. Drag and drop to move the line and the selected slide to the new location. We'll place the current slide 2 after slide 3. (Be sure to drag the slide in front of slide 4 to put it after slide 3.).

EXERCISE 24.10 *(continued)*

5. Now, for additional practice, move the slide back to its original location.

6. No need to resave the presentation this time. We haven't changed it.

To rearrange slides in Normal view, just display slide miniatures in the pane at the left and use drag and drop, just as we did in Slide Sorter view.

Changing Slide Layouts

Your presentation would be pretty boring if all you had were slides with titles and bullet points. You'll want to spice things up a bit by varying the *layout* (arrangement of text and objects) on your slides.

Microsoft
✓ *Exam*
Objective

Modify slide layout

We touched on the concept of slide layouts in Chapter 23, where we discussed inserting new slides with placeholders for graphics. Exercise 24.11 takes you through changing the layouts of an existing slide. We'll adjust the text into a two-column bulleted list, rather than a one-column list.

EXERCISE 24.11

Modifying Slide Layout

1. If you just completed Exercise 24.10, you're right where you need to be. If not, open 24-11.ppt.

2. Display Slide 6 in Normal view.

EXERCISE 24.11 *(continued)*

3. Open the Slide Layout task pane. (Choose View ➤ Task Pane, and then choose Slide Layout from the task pane selection menu.)

4. In the task pane, choose Title And 2-Column Text. (You'll find it grouped near the top of the task pane in the Text Layouts category.) As soon as you apply this layout, the text runs off the slide:

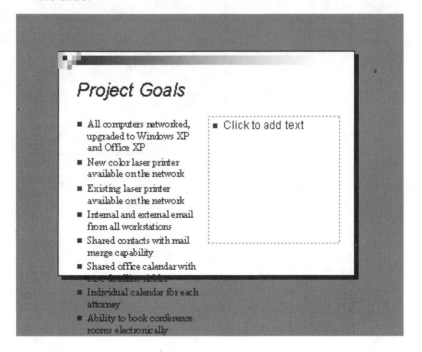

5. Select the last four bullet points. Just drag the mouse over the text, starting with the first paragraph.

6. Click Edit ➤ Cut. The text disappears from your slide.

7. Click the empty text box to the right of the bulleted list.

8. Click Edit ➢ Paste. Voila! Your slide is now arranged with two columns of bullet points:

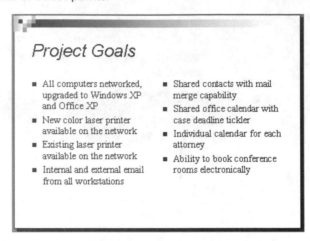

9. Save the presentation as **Changing Layouts Practice.ppt** and close the file.

Often when you change the layout of existing text slides, you have to reformat or rearrange the text to accommodate the new layout. So it's more efficient if you decide on layouts before you type your text—not always practical, but helpful when possible.

Adding Hyperlinks to Slides

A *hyperlink* is a connection between two areas of a presentation or a presentation and another location in a file or on the Web. If you've been online at all, you've probably clicked numerous hyperlinks and you know how quickly you jump to another location.

PowerPoint supports hyperlinks to other slides, other presentations, and URLs. Clicking a hyperlink moves the user from the current slide to another slide, another presentation, or a site on the Internet. Hyperlinks can provide the user with a means for navigating the presentation in your absence. Or they can provide you, the presenter, with access to back up slides, data in files, data on the Web, and a myriad of other resources that are just a click away when you need them.

Microsoft
✓ **_Exam_**
Objective

Add links to a presentation

There are a couple of different ways to create a hyperlink. Exercise 24.12 takes you to the Action Settings dialog box. But you can also create hyperlinks in the Insert Hyperlink dialog box (see Exercise 24.13).

EXERCISE 24.12

Adding Hyperlinks through Action Settings

1. Open 24-12.ppt.

2. Switch to Normal view and select the text that will be used as a hyperlink. Often, this text tells the user where they're going to end up: "Click Here to Exit the Presentation," for example, or "Click to View More Options." For this exercise we'll use Slide 3. Select the text "Kathleen Torok, Senior Partner."

3. Right-click the selected text and choose Action Settings from the shortcut menu, or choose Slide Show ➤ Action Settings from the menu bar, to open the dialog box shown here:

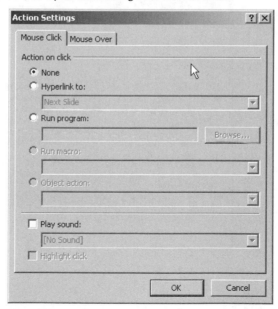

4. There are two ways to activate a hyperlink: clicking it or moving the mouse over it. Both tabs of this dialog box are identical—choose a tab based on which mouse action you want to trigger the hyperlink. For this exercise, we'll stay on the Mouse Click tab.

5. Click the Hyperlink To option and select Other File from the drop-down list.

6. In the Hyperlink To Other File dialog box, select the Torok bio.doc, which was included with the files you downloaded at the beginning of this chapter. Click OK to return to the Action Settings dialog box.

7. Click OK to close the Action Settings dialog box and apply the hyperlink. The text you selected for the hyperlink changes color, and PowerPoint automatically underlines it.

8. Now run the slide show (click Slide Show ➢ View Show). When you get to Slide 3, click the hyperlink to open a Word document that gives biographical information about the project liaison:

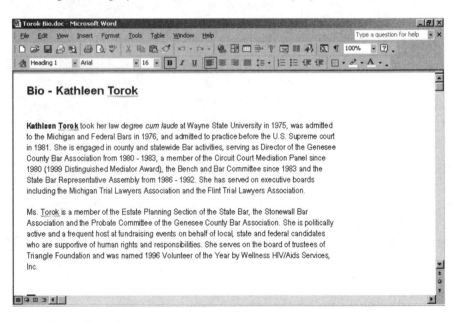

EXERCISE 24.12 *(continued)*

9. Close Word to return to the presentation and pick up where you left off.

10. Save this presentation as `Action Settings Practice.ppt`.

If you want to camouflage hyperlinks, you can change their colors to match surrounding text by using the Custom tab of the Slide Color Scheme dialog box (discussed earlier in Chapter 23).

WARNING Don't change the hyperlink color scheme to match surrounding text if you are creating a kiosk presentation for users to click through themselves. They won't know there's a hyperlink if it doesn't stand out. (And if you're presenting a slide show you created a few months ago, it's possible to forget the hyperlink without a visual cue.)

If you prefer, you can apply hyperlinks directly by selecting text and clicking Insert ➢ Hyperlink or clicking the Insert Hyperlink button on the Standard toolbar. Both of these actions open the Insert Hyperlink dialog box. In Exercise 24.13, we'll use this dialog box to insert a hyperlink to a website.

EXERCISE 24.13

Using the Insert Hyperlink Dialog Box

1. If you completed Exercise 24.12, open `Action Settings Practice.ppt`. If not, just open `24-13.ppt`.

2. Navigate to Slide 6 and select the text "Windows XP."

3. Choose Insert ➢ Hyperlink (or click the Insert Hyperlink button on the Standard toolbar) to display the Insert Hyperlink dialog box.

4. Make sure Existing File Or Web Page is selected in the Link To bar at the far left.

EXERCISE 24.13 *(continued)*

5. When Existing File Or Web Page is selected, PowerPoint provides you with three choices for where to look to get your link: Current Folder, Browsed Pages, or Recent Files. If the page you want to link to is one you've recently browsed, you can just click the Browsed Pages choice and a list of web pages you've visited recently appears in the window, as shown here:

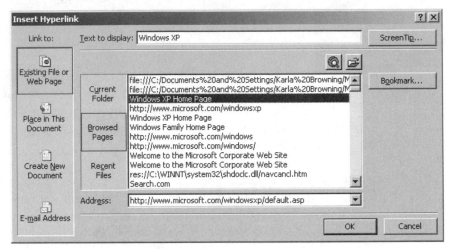

You can also click the Browse The Web button and actually go to the website you wish to link to.

For this exercise, click Browse The Web and navigate to the Windows XP home page. (Type **www.microsoft.com** into your browser's address bar, and then go to the Windows product family and then Windows XP.)

6. Once you arrive at the page you wish to link to, minimize the browser window to return to PowerPoint, and click the Browsed Pages choice in the Insert Hyperlink dialog box. The page you just visited should appear at the top of the list. Select it, and the proper URL appears in the Address area of the dialog box, as shown in the previous graphic.

7. Click OK to close the Insert Hyperlink dialog box and return to the slide.

8. Now repeat the process, but select the text "Office XP."

EXERCISE 24.13 *(continued)*

---

9. Create a hyperlink to a website that provides information about Office XP by doing the following:

   a. Click the Insert Hyperlink button on the Standard toolbar.

   b. Click Browse The Web.

   c. Go to Microsoft's home page (www.microsoft.com).

   d. In the list of Product Family links at the left, click Office.

   e. Follow the link that makes the most sense based on the information you want to get. We scrolled down to the Upgrade Center and clicked the Product Overview link:

   > **Upgrade Center**
   >
   > ▸ Product overview: Get the fast facts about Office XP
   >
   > ▸ Compare Office XP with your version of Office
   >
   > ▸ See how Office XP outpaced Office 2000 in a productivity study
   >
   > ▸ Students and Teachers: Get a huge discount on Office XP

   f. Minimize or close your browser window and return to PowerPoint.

   g. Choose Browsed Pages in the Insert Hyperlink dialog box.

   h. Choose the Office XP link at the top of the list of pages you've recently visited.

   i. Click OK to close the Insert Hyperlink dialog box and create the link.

10. It's always a good idea to test your hyperlinks in the slide show. Do so now.

11. Save this presentation as **Creating Hyperlinks Practice.ppt** and close the file.

There are four different types of hyperlinks you can create. We've practiced with only two of them. To clarify:

- **Existing File Or Web Page** allows you to link to files or web pages. Just type the path to the file or the address of the web page in the Address text box. Alternatively, adjust the Look In control and select one of the files or web pages that appears in the list box. The addresses in the list box change depending on which option (Recent Files, Browsed Pages, or Current Folder) is selected.

- **Place In This Document** allows you to link to another slide in the current presentation (see Figure 24.2).

- **Create New Document** allows you to link to another presentation file you're creating on the fly. You'll be prompted to type a filename for the document and choose whether you wish to edit the new document now (PowerPoint displays the blank presentation immediately) or later (PowerPoint saves the blank presentation and inserts the hyperlink—you can open the blank presentation and edit it at any time).

- **E-mail Address** lets you create a hyperlink that opens your default e-mail program and creates a new message addressed to the person you specify when you create the link. You'll be prompted to enter the address in the E-mail Address field (or select one from the list of recently used e-mail addresses).

FIGURE 24.2 You can link to the next slide, previous slide, or any slide in your presentation using the Insert Hyperlink dialog box.

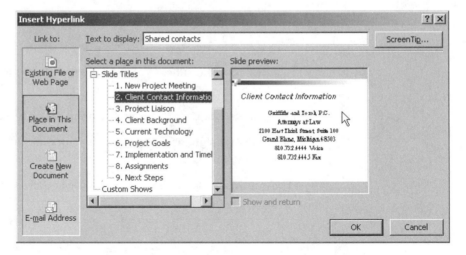

 You can also select an object (rather than text) to create a hyperlink. This is a handy way to camouflage a hyperlink, as there is no noticeable change to the object after you create the link.

Summary

In this chapter, we explained some more about slide formatting and then talked at length about controlling movement of slides, text, and objects in a presentation. Specifically, you learned about the following:

- Applying presentation formats
- Using animation schemes
- Creating transitions between slides
- Setting transition speed and sound
- Customizing slide formats
- Working with Slide Masters
- Tailoring slide templates
- Adding slide timings through rehearsal
- Editing slide timings
- Rearranging slides
- Changing slide layouts
- Adding hyperlinks to slides

Preparing and Delivering the Final Product

MOUS POWERPOINT 2002 CORE EXAM OBJECTIVES COVERED IN THIS CHAPTER:

- ✓ Preview and print slides, outlines, handouts, and speaker notes
- ✓ Import Excel charts into slides
- ✓ Add sound and video to slides
- ✓ Insert Word tables on slides
- ✓ Export a presentation as an outline
- ✓ Set up slide shows
- ✓ Deliver presentations
- ✓ Manage files and folders for presentations
- ✓ Work with embedded fonts
- ✓ Publish presentations to the Web
- ✓ Use Pack and Go
- ✓ Set up a review cycle
- ✓ Review presentation comments
- ✓ Schedule and deliver presentation broadcasts

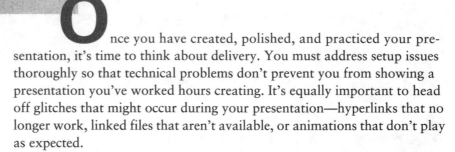

Once you have created, polished, and practiced your presentation, it's time to think about delivery. You must address setup issues thoroughly so that technical problems don't prevent you from showing a presentation you've worked hours creating. It's equally important to head off glitches that might occur during your presentation—hyperlinks that no longer work, linked files that aren't available, or animations that don't play as expected.

In this chapter, we'll talk about the final product and how you can deliver it. On-screen presentations are fairly common now, but with some audiences, you may wish to stick to printed materials. We'll cover the miscellaneous details you'll need to address to ensure that your presentation is delivered smoothly.

Before you begin this chapter, you should go to the Sybex website and download the file 4113Ch25.zip. This package contains the files necessary to complete some of the exercises in this chapter.

Preparing Handouts and Notes

*H*andouts are pictures of the slides or the outline from a presentation that you give to participants. You can arrange handouts so they have one, two, three, four, six, or nine slides to a page, or you may choose to create a handout from your outline.

The *Notes* feature can be used in several different ways:

- As speaker notes for a presenter to refer to during a presentation. You can include a list of specific items you want to cover or even a note to remind yourself to tell that audience-winning joke before you present the materials on a particular slide.

- To keep track of information about particular slides as you're creating a presentation. For example, there may be data that needs to be verified or alternative information you've considered adding to the slide.

- As a means to expand on the bullet points displayed on the slide. For example, a teacher may print notes to "flesh out" main points for students who miss the original presentation due to absence.

Your audience at a live slide show never sees the text you have entered in the notes pane unless you intentionally print your notes and hand them out. In web presentations, you can choose whether to display the notes.

In order to fully meet the requirements of the next exam objective, we must teach you how to create handouts and speaker notes. Once you know how to create them, we'll show you how to print them.

The Handout Master

Since handouts are miniature pictures of your slides, your job in preparing them is to choose a layout. Use the Handout Master to view and select the handout layouts. Follow the steps in Exercise 25.1 to learn how to work with the Handout Master.

EXERCISE 25.1

Using the Handout Master

1. Open 25-1.ppt.

EXERCISE 25.1 *(continued)*

2. From any slide, choose View ➢ Master ➢ Handout Master to open the master, shown here. The Handout Master View toolbar opens automatically:

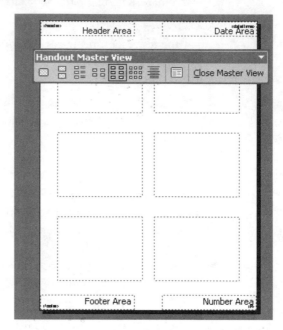

3. The unlabeled placeholders (rectangles with dotted-line borders) show where slides are positioned in the layout selected in the Handout Master View toolbar. Click the appropriate button on the Handout Master View toolbar to select the number of slides you'd like to display on each page of the handout. PowerPoint 2002 now lets you choose one slide per page in addition to the choices that were available in previous versions. For this exercise, choose 3 slides per page.

4. The Handout Master contains placeholders for the footer, header, date, and page number. If you have previously used the Header And Footer dialog box to include headers/footers on handouts, the Handout Master also includes these fields. Since we haven't

EXERCISE 25.1 *(continued)*

included a date/time field on these slides, let's do so on our handouts.

a. Click the Date Area placeholder to select it. Then change your zoom setting to 75% so you can see what you're doing:

b. Click where it says Date/Time to select that text, as shown in the above graphic.

c. Choose Insert ➢ Date And Time from the menu to open the Date And Time dialog box.

d. Choose a date format from the list. Use the fourth format (shown above) for this exercise.

e. Click OK to close the dialog box and insert the date.

Note: The words "Date Area" do not print on the handouts.

5. Save this presentation as **Handout Master Practice.ppt**.

 Settings for the masters, including the Slide Master and Handout Master, are saved as separate workspaces within PowerPoint. If you close, for example, the Handout Master toolbar before switching out of the Handout Master, the next time you open the Handout Master the toolbar will not be displayed. Right-click any toolbar or choose View ➢ Toolbars to display toolbars that were turned off in an earlier session.

If you wish to delete a placeholder on the Handout Master, just select it as you would any object (click the edge of it) and press Delete on the keyboard. The placeholder disappears from the master.

 If you delete a placeholder and later change your mind about the deletion, PowerPoint offers a quick and easy way to bring it back. Just click the

Handout Master Layout button to display the Handout Master Layout dialog box:

Enable the check box next to any placeholder you wish to restore. If the placeholder already exists on the master, it is grayed out in the dialog box. We deleted the Header placeholder before opening the dialog box in the above graphic so you could see the difference.

You can insert art or other graphics (a company logo, for example) on the Handout Master just as you would on a slide. (Choose Insert ➢ Picture ➢ Clip Art or Insert ➢ Picture ➢ From File.) You can format the background of your handouts by choosing Format ➢ Handout Background from the menu. To modify the slide color scheme for handouts, do the following:

1. Display the color scheme options in the task pane. (Choose View ➢ Task Pane, and then choose Slide Design - Color Schemes from the task pane selection menu.)

2. Click the arrow next to the color scheme you want to use.

3. Choose Apply To Handout Master.

Adding Notes to a Presentation

With the outline displayed in Normal view, presentation text is in the left pane of the tri-pane window. The selected slide is shown to the right of the outline. Below the slide is an area for notes if you choose to use them (see Figure 25.1). Notes are hidden from the audience in a live electronic presentation and are displayed in online or NetMeeting presentations only if you choose to display them.

Unless you're adding notes to a web presentation, think of the notes as somewhat private—the perfect place to put a reminder to distribute a handout or tell a specific joke or to insert the full text that you intend to present while the slide is displayed. For large presentations you create over a period of weeks, it's a good idea to use notes to remind yourself about details to address while you're working on the presentation. You can delete each note as you accomplish the task.

If you don't see the notes pane, point to the window divider directly above the Drawing toolbar. Click and drag upward to open the notes pane.

FIGURE 25.1 One way to enter notes is by typing them in the lower pane of PowerPoint 2002's Normal view.

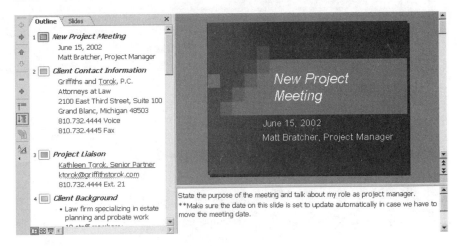

In Exercise 25.2, we'll reproduce the notes you see in Figure 25.1 above.

EXERCISE 25.2

Adding Notes to a Presentation

1. If you just completed Exercise 25.1, use that presentation. If not, open 25-2.ppt.

2. Switch to Normal view if necessary and navigate to Slide 1.

3. Click in the notes pane and type the following text: **State the purpose of the meeting and talk about my role as project manager.**

4. Press Enter and type the following: ****Make sure the date on this slide is set to update automatically in case we have to move the meeting date.** As you type, a scroll bar appears in the notes pane.

EXERCISE 25.2 *(continued)*

5. Resize the notes pane to make it larger. Just drag the horizontal divider between the slide pane and the notes pane.

6. Scroll the notes pane so that all the text is in view. The final result should look just like Figure 25.1 above.

7. Save the file as **Adding Notes Practice.ppt**.

PowerPoint lets you add Speaker Notes from Slide Sorter view and Slide Show view as well. In the Slide Sorter, just click the Speaker Notes button on the Slide Sorter toolbar. In Slide Show view, right click any slide and choose Speaker Notes.

Printing Presentations

When you click the Print button on the Standard toolbar, PowerPoint prints the entire presentation in the default setting—usually the slide pane from Normal view. If the slides have a background, this can take some time, even on a laser printer. More important, it's rarely what you intended to print. In PowerPoint, it's always best to choose File ➢ Print to open the Print dialog box so you can select whether to print slides, handouts, notes, or an outline.

Using Print Preview

In the previous section, you learned how to add notes and how to work with the Handout Master to select an appropriate layout for slide miniatures that print on handouts. Now we'll focus on the finished product: printed copies for your audience.

Microsoft ✓ *Exam Objective*   **Preview and print slides, outlines, handouts, and speaker notes**

Before you print, it's always a good idea to preview your work, particularly with notes and handouts. Print Preview just became available in PowerPoint 2002, so it might be helpful to complete Exercise 25.3 and explore this new feature.

EXERCISE 25.3

Using Print Preview

1. If you just completed Exercise 25.2, use your Adding Notes Practice presentation. Or just open 25-3.ppt.

2. From any slide, click the Print Preview button on the Standard toolbar (or choose File ➤ Print Preview) to display the presentation with the current print settings.

3. The default is to print slides, so the above graphic shows one slide per page. To preview another print option—Notes Pages, for example—choose that option from the Print What drop-down list in the Print Preview toolbar. The preview changes to reflect your choice:

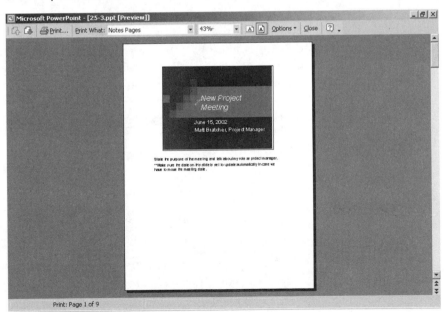

4. Click the Close button on the Print Preview toolbar to return to the view you just left.

5. Save this presentation as **Print Preview Practice.ppt**. Your print preview settings are saved along with the file.

While you're in Print Preview view, you can use the scroll bar to browse the document preview, but there are also buttons on the toolbar for viewing previous and next pages. The Print Preview toolbar, shown in Figure 25.2, provides several options for changing settings. We'll discuss some of these settings in the next section.

FIGURE 25.2   The Print Preview toolbar offers options for changing the preview and adjusting some print settings.

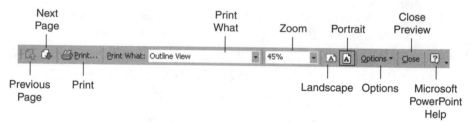

Printing Outlines, Handouts, Speaker Notes, and Slides

In PowerPoint 2002, you can print from any view by choosing File ➤ Print from the menu to open the Print dialog box. You can also open this dialog box from Print Preview, which is the safest thing to do because you can see the print results onscreen before opening the dialog box. For practice adjusting print settings from Print Preview, complete Exercise 25.4. In Exercise 25.5, we'll walk through the steps to actually print.

EXERCISE 25.4

Adjusting Print Settings in Print Preview

1. If you just completed Exercise 25.3, use your Print Preview Practice presentation. Or just open 25-4.ppt.

2. From any slide, click the Print Preview button on the Standard toolbar (or choose File ➤ Print Preview).

3. As you know, you can change what you're previewing by choosing from the Print What drop-down list. Choose Handouts – 3 Slides Per Page.

4. Click the Options button to display the menu shown here:

5. We're going to change our print settings to Grayscale—a good idea if you're just going to photocopy the handouts on a black and white copier or if your presentation has a dark background and you want to save some printer toner. Choose Options ➢ Color/Grayscale ➢ Grayscale. The preview immediately changes to Grayscale.

6. For an interesting change, click the Landscape button on the Print Preview toolbar to adjust the handout orientation:

EXERCISE 25.4 *(continued)*

Note: You can't change the orientation if Print What is set to Slides. See the next section for information about printing slides using a different orientation.

7. Click Close to leave the preview and return to Normal view.

8. Save the file as **Preview Settings Practice.ppt**.

The Print Preview Options menu allows for adjusting other settings that we didn't cover in Exercise 25.4. If you're printing handouts with multiple slides per page (and no lines for audience notes), you must choose either a vertical or horizontal printing order. Click the Frame Slides check box to print a simple box around each slide; this is a good idea if the slides themselves don't include a border. If there are hidden slides in your presentation, the default is to print them. You can disable that option by clearing its check box.

If there are no hidden slides in a presentation, that option is disabled.

You can also choose how many slides per handout page to print in the Print dialog box. If you previously used the Handout Master to choose the number of slides per page, you can override that choice here.

Now that you're familiar with print settings, let's actually print some handouts and explore the options for printing notes and the outline. Exercise 25.5 shows you how.

EXERCISE 25.5

Printing Notes, Handouts, and the Outline

1. If you just completed Exercise 25.4, you're right where you need to be. If not, open 25-5.ppt.

2. Click the Print Preview button on the Standard toolbar (or choose File ➤ Print Preview). It's always a good idea to print from Print Preview to make sure our settings are correct. We're printing Handouts, 3 per page. We've chosen a Landscape orientation and we're printing in Grayscale.

EXERCISE 25.5 *(continued)*

3. Click the Print button on the Print Preview toolbar. This opens the Print dialog box, with current print settings.

4. If you change your mind and decide to print slides or notes, you can select either one from the Print What drop-down list (bottom left in the dialog box) to override the choices we made in Print Preview. For this exercise, let's leave that setting alone.

5. You can also adjust the slides that print by changing the settings in the Print Range area of the dialog box. Choose Slides, and then type **1-3** in the text box.

6. Click OK to print the handout we saw earlier in Print Preview.

7. When the handout finishes printing, close the preview and save the presentation as **Print Practice.ppt**.

Working with Data from Other Sources

It's quite common to use PowerPoint as a vehicle to deliver data and information from a variety of sources. Perhaps the Accounting department has financial information in Excel while Marketing has data in Word. Of course, there is no need to redo your colleagues' work. This section explores how to bring in information from other applications.

Working with Excel Charts

In Chapter 24, "Producing Exciting Presentations," you learned how to create charts on slides. With small amounts of data it makes sense to do it this. Charts from larger data sets and certain types of custom charts work best when you create them in Excel. And often, charts for your presentation come from another person or another department. So why redo work someone else has done well? Simply import what you need into PowerPoint.

Microsoft ✓ *Exam* *Objective*   **Import Excel charts into slides**

In Exercise 25.6, you will learn how to insert an Excel chart into a slide in your presentation.

EXERCISE 25.6

Importing an Excel Chart

1. If you completed Exercise 25.5, open Print Practice.ppt. If not, open 25-6.ppt.

2. Insert a new slide to follow the current Slide 7, Implementation and Timeline. Use the Title Only layout.

3. Display the Slide Design – Color Schemes task pane and choose the white background/blue accent scheme for this slide.

4. Click the Title text box and type **Projected Costs**.

5. Launch Excel and open the Excel file we included with this chapter's downloads: Exercise 25-6 Chart For Import.xls.

6. Click once on the Chart object to select it, if necessary.

7. In Excel, click the Copy button on the Standard toolbar.

8. Switch back to PowerPoint and click the new Slide 8 (Projected Costs).

9. Click Paste to place the chart on the slide. Resize and reposition as necessary.

Note: If you don't want the white background behind the chart, before you copy and paste, you must change the formatting of the Chart Area (in Excel) to No Fill. Or, you can change the color scheme on the slide to the same background color as the chart. That's what we did for the above graphic.

10. To keep this slide consistent with the others in the presentation, we should add a slide timing to it. Switch to Slide Sorter view to do so. Select the slide with the chart (Slide 8) and open the Slide Transition task pane. In the Advance Slide area of the task pane, disable On Mouse Click and enable Automatically After. Set the spin box to 5 seconds and click Apply.

11. Close the task pane and save this file as **Chart Import Practice .ppt**. You may also close Excel if you wish.

Although this is the easiest method for transferring an Excel chart, there are other methods with which you should familiarize yourself before taking the MOUS exam. You can also choose Insert ➢ Object on any slide. Power-Point displays the Insert Object dialog box shown here:

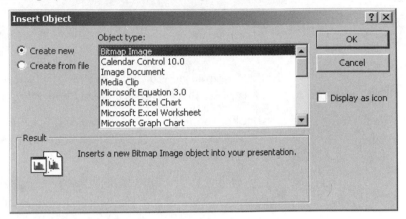

If you'd like to create the Excel object as you go, choose the Create New option at the left of the Insert Object dialog box. To use an existing Excel object, choose the Create From File option and then browse to find and select the Excel file with the chart you wish to import.

Adding Audio-Visual Elements

PowerPoint includes sounds and animated GIFs (collectively referred to as media clips) that you can play during your slide shows. Some sounds, like the typewriter or laser sound, are accessed from Animation Effects, which we covered in Chapter 24. Other sounds and motion clips are in the Microsoft Clip Gallery. Just as with clip art, you may find it easiest to insert media clips by choosing a slide layout that includes a media clip placeholder. Simply double-click the Insert Media Clip icon to open a dialog box with available clips. But you can insert media clips on any slide, as you'll see in Exercise 25.7 below.

Microsoft ✓ *Exam Objective*

Add sound and video to slides

In Exercise 25.7, you'll insert an animated GIF on one of your slides.

Inserting a Media Clip

1. If you completed Exercise 25.6, open Chart Import Practice.ppt. If not, open 25-7.ppt.

2. In Normal view, display the slide to which you want to add a media clip. For this exercise, choose Slide 3 (Project Liaison).

3. Choose Insert ➤ Movies And Sounds ➤ Movie From Clip Organizer. The Insert Clip Art task pane opens with available media clips displayed:

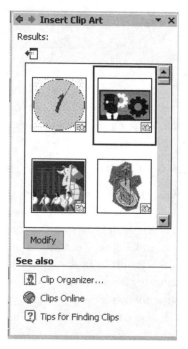

4. You can browse the available media clips or click Modify to search them (see Chapter 24 if you forgot how). To preview a clip, mouse over it until the drop-down arrow displays. Click the drop-down arrow and choose Preview/Properties. For this exercise, we chose the second clip displayed in the task pane. Your media clips may appear differently, depending on how Office was installed on your PC. Just click the clip's icon to insert it on the slide.

EXERCISE 25.7 *(continued)*

Interestingly, when we inserted this new movie clip, PowerPoint resized the existing text. Just click Undo if you have this same problem. The text returns to its original size and the clip is placed in the middle of the slide.

5. Move and resize the clip as necessary.

6. The clip plays automatically when you switch to Slide Show view. Try it.

7. Save the presentation as **Inserting A Movie Practice.ppt**.

If you're inserting a media clip from a placeholder, the task pane doesn't open. Instead, you must use the Media Clip dialog box to search for and select the clip you want.

To insert a sound or video that isn't in Clip Organizer, choose the From File menu option (Insert ➤ Movies and Sounds ➤ Movie From File, for instance). Locate, select, and open the file. Animated GIFs don't play in views other than Slide Show view. Click the Slide Show View button to preview the animated GIF on your slide.

Inserting Other Sound and Video Files

Microsoft provides a fine selection of sound clips, and you can download more sound and video clips from the Clip Gallery online. But you're not limited to the Microsoft clips. You can download royalty-free sounds and video from a number of websites, or you can grab a camera or microphone and hit the field to interview customers. Or you can use the Windows applets to capture sound and video from your PC. To insert a sound or video file stored on your computer or network, follow these steps:

1. Choose Insert ➤ Movies And Sound ➤ Sound From File or Movie From File.

2. Locate the file you wish to insert.

3. Click OK to insert the file.

If you need video for a presentation and don't have a video capture card, don't despair. Most computer graphics companies and many full-service camera shops can create video files from your video or 8mm tape.

The optimal size for a video depends on your screen resolution. To have Power Point estimate the best video size, right-click the video object and choose Format Picture to open the Format Picture dialog box. On the Size tab, enable the Best Scale For Slide Show check box, and then choose the resolution for the monitor or projector you'll use for playback from the drop-down list. When you click OK, PowerPoint will resize the object.

To hide the media clip icon from your audience, drag it off the slide in Normal view. In this case, you'll probably want to use Custom Animation to have the media clip play automatically when the slide is displayed.

Using Word Tables

In Chapter 22, "Getting Started with PowerPoint," you learned to create a Word table by choosing Insert ➤ Table or by using a Table AutoLayout from the task pane. If you've already created a table in Word that you want to use in a presentation, you can copy it in Word and paste it onto a slide or use the Insert ➤ Object command we discussed earlier in "Working with Excel Charts." As we mentioned earlier, larger tables may not show up clearly on a slide, so keep them simple.

Microsoft ✓ *Exam* *Objective*   **Insert Word tables on slides**

In Exercise 25.8, we'll bring a Word table into the presentation we've been working on.

EXERCISE 25.8

Inserting a Table from Word

1. If you completed Exercise 25.7, open Inserting A Movie Practice.ppt. If not, open 25-8.ppt.

2. In Normal view, display the slide to which you want to add the table. For this exercise, choose Slide 9 (Assignments).

3. Delete the existing empty text box from the slide. Click its border and then press Delete on the keyboard.

Note: If you forget to delete the text box in step 3, PowerPoint may paste your table as text. You'll lose the row and columns and defeat the purpose of pasting.

4. Launch Word and open the Word file we included with this chapter's downloads: Exercise 25-8 Table For Import.doc.

5. Select the Table object by clicking once on the four-headed arrow in the upper-left corner of the table. (Alternatively, you can hold the Alt key and double-click anywhere in the table.)

6. In Word, click the Copy button on the Standard toolbar.

7. Switch back to PowerPoint and click the new Slide 9 (Assignments).

8. Click Paste to place the table on the slide. If necessary, resize the table using the handles, or reposition the table by dragging it to a new location.

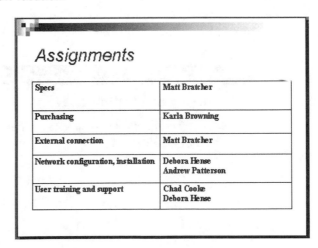

EXERCISE 25.8 *(continued)*

9. Save this file as **Table Import Practice.ppt**.

10. You may close Word if you wish.

Edit the table using the tools you learned about in Chapter 23. Remember, you can choose View ➤ Toolbars ➤ Tables And Borders to turn on the Tables and Borders toolbar, which provides most of the tools you'll need to edit.

Exporting a Presentation to Word As an Outline

You can use the power of Office automation to create handouts and reports for a PowerPoint presentation in Word. The Send To Microsoft Word feature transfers the text and/or slides from the current presentation to a Word document, which you can then edit (adding titles and additional text), format, and print to use as handouts. This tool uses a lot of system resources, so begin by closing other applications.

Microsoft ✓ *Exam Objective*   **Export a presentation as an outline**

In Exercise 25.9, you'll export a presentation to Word as an outline. Keep in mind you can use this same feature to export the slides themselves.

EXERCISE 25.9

Exporting an Outline to Word

1. If you completed Exercise 25.8, open Table Import Practice.ppt. If not, open 25-9.ppt.

EXERCISE 25.9 *(continued)*

2. Choose File ➤ Send To ➤ Microsoft Word to open the Send To Microsoft Word dialog box, shown here:

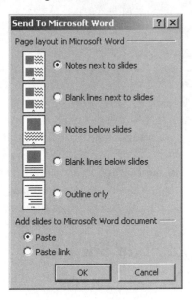

3. Select how you want the presentation to appear: in one of the four handout-style layouts or as an outline. For this exercise, choose Outline Only.

4. Click OK. PowerPoint launches Word and exports your outline:

Note: If you export slides (instead of an outline), it may take a few minutes because each slide is exported as a Graphic object.

5. Edit and print the document as you would any Word document.

EXERCISE 25.9 *(continued)*

6. For this exercise, you may close Word without saving. The Power-Point file remains unchanged, so there's no need to save it before you close it.

Managing and Delivering Presentations

You've designed a good presentation, had it reviewed by a colleague, and practiced moving through the slides. Now you're ready to specify the settings that you'll use to deliver the show. If you're setting up a kiosk, you'll probably want the presentation to loop continuously. If the animations look choppy or seem slow, you may want to adjust resolution settings. You can accomplish all this and more in the Set Up Show dialog box.

Setting Up a Slide Show

To access slide show settings, choose Slide Show ➢ Set Up Show, or hold Shift and click the Slide Show button, to open the Set Up Show dialog box, shown in Figure 25.3.

FIGURE 25.3 The Set Up Show dialog box lets users choose settings for a presentation.

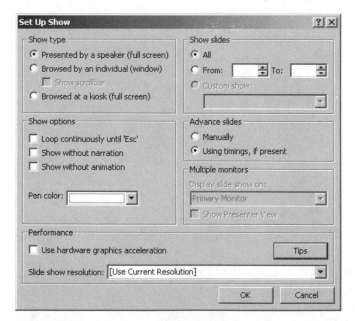

Microsoft ✓ *Exam* *Objective*	**Set up slide shows**

In Exercise 25.10, you'll learn about most of these settings and practice changing a few of them.

EXERCISE 25.10

Changing Slide Show Settings

1. If you completed Exercise 25.8, open Table Import Practice.ppt. If not, open 25-10.ppt.

2. Choose Slide Show ➢ Set Up Show.

3. In the Show Type area, you have three choices. For this exercise, we'll leave the default choice, Presented By A Speaker (Full Screen). When you choose Browsed By An Individual (Window), the presentation displays in a browser-like window, which may be easier for some users to navigate. The Browsed At A Kiosk (Full Screen) choice makes the presentation a self-running show where users can click hyperlinks or other action buttons if you have them. Users can't modify the show, and it restarts after five minutes of inactivity.

4. Show Options include looping continuously and showing without narration and/or animation. For this exercise, enable the Loop Continuously Until 'Esc' check box. Since the presentation already has timings, this means you can walk away from the computer during the slide show and it will continue on without you. You can also choose to show presentations without narrations (there aren't any in this presentation anyway) and without animations. If you're stuck with antiquated hardware to run the show, omitting the animations might be a good idea. The Pen Color drop-down list lets you choose a color for the Pen tool that allows you to draw on slides with your mouse during the show.

5. In the Show Slides area, you can choose to show the entire presentation, certain slide numbers, or a custom show (we haven't created any). Leave this setting on All slides.

6. When we added timings to this presentation back in Chapter 24, PowerPoint automatically selected Using Timings, If Present in the Advance Slides area. If you change the setting back to Manually, you must click for each new paragraph or object to be added to the slide—a good idea if you're speaking while showing the presentation. For this exercise, leave the Using Timings setting selected.

7. Click OK to close the Set Up Show dialog box.

8. Start the slide show (Slide Show ➢ View Show) and sit back while it plays automatically a couple of times.

9. Press the Esc key to discontinue the slide show.

10. Open the Set Up Show dialog box again and change the Advance Slides setting to Manually.

11. Save the presentation as **Set Up Show Practice.ppt**.

The other two options in the Set Up Show dialog box—Performance and Multiple Monitors—might come in handy in certain situations.

By tweaking the Performance settings, you can achieve smoothly running presentations when your processor speed may not be up to it. Click Slide Show ➢ Set Up Show to display the Set Up Show dialog box shown previously in Figure 25.3. If your video card supports it, enable the Use Hardware Graphics Acceleration check box to improve animation speed. Choose a resolution from the Slide Show Resolution list:

Use Current Resolution This option does just as it says. The slide show runs at the screen resolution of the computer it's on. If the presentation isn't displaying properly, make sure the projector's resolution matches the computer's resolution.

640 × 480 (Fastest, Lowest Fidelity) This setting causes the projector to use a lower resolution, but animations may run more smoothly (as opposed to "choppy"). This setting uses less of the computer's resources to display the slide show, so text and graphics may not display as sharply; nevertheless, choose 640 × 480 if your presentation is running too slowly.

800 × 600 (Slowest, Highest Fidelity)   This setting displays text and graphics in better resolution, but if your animations lurch haltingly across the screen, you'd better use the lower resolution setting or enable Graphics Acceleration and try again.

You may have additional resolution options, depending on the display hardware and operating system software settings.

If you're running PowerPoint 2002 under Microsoft Windows 98 or better, you can get the benefits of online broadcasting even if you're doing a live presentation to a group. PowerPoint's View On Two Screens option allows you to set up a show with one computer (say, your laptop) as the presenter and the other (a computer with a large monitor) for the audience. You get to see slides and notes while the audience sees only the slides.

First, your computer must have dual-monitor software installed (Windows 98 or better). Second, connect the two computers using a direct-connect serial cable. Then, on the primary computer (the laptop in this instance), choose Slide Show ➢ Set Up Show to open the Set Up Show dialog box. In the Multiple Monitors section of the Set Up Show dialog box, choose the monitor you want to use for the slide show. The other monitor displays your presentation in Normal view. Enable the Show Presenter View check box to see a navigation panel on one screen, making the presentation easier to navigate during the show.

Delivering a Slide Presentation

The audience is in place, the computer is fired up, and the pressure is on. Obviously, you'll want to practice delivering the presentation many times before the actual event—enough times that it becomes automatic to you, in fact.

Microsoft ✓ *Exam* *Objective*   **Deliver presentations**

Although clicking through slides isn't exactly rocket science, you'd be surprised at how tricky it becomes when you're nervous during the presentation. Exercise 25.11 walks you through delivering the presentation. We recommend hitting this one a few times.

Delivering the Slide Show

1. If you completed Exercise 25.10, open Set Up Show Practice.ppt. If not, open 25-11.ppt.

2. Navigate to Slide 1 and click the Slide Show From Current Slide button, or choose Slide Show ➢ View Show from any slide, to start the presentation on Slide 1.

3. To advance to the next slide or animation, click anywhere on the slide background or, if you're using a keyboard, press Enter, Page Down, the down arrow, or N (for Next). In a presentation with animation, you must click multiple times to advance to the next slide—once for each animation and once to switch slides.

4. A menu button appears in the lower-left or lower-right corner of the slide (depending on the template used in the presentation).

Click the button to open the Navigation shortcut menu:

5. The shortcut menu provides additional options for navigating through your presentation. From the menu, you can move to the

Previous or Next slide. To move to a specific slide, choose Go ➢ By Title and choose the slide you want to display. Choose Slide 9 (Assignments).

6. You can also navigate using the Slide Navigator. Open the Navigation shortcut menu and choose Go ➢ Slide Navigator to open the Slide Navigator:

7. Select a slide to move to (Slide 2 for this exercise) and click Go To.

8. Proceed through the rest of the presentation, moving forward and, occasionally, moving backward.

9. When you click past the last slide, PowerPoint begins the presentation again on Slide 1. That's because we have the Loop Continuously feature enabled (in the Set Up Show dialog box). Press the Esc key to leave the slide show and return to one of the working views.

10. There's no need to save the presentation, as we haven't made changes to it.

Keeping Track of Presentations

Putting together a brilliant presentation does you no good if you can't remember where you saved it. It pays to invest a few minutes to learn the basics of setting up a folder structure to manage your presentation files.

Microsoft
Exam
Objective

Manage files and folders for presentations

Storing and retrieving electronic presentations is analogous to keeping a paper filing system (something many of us deliberately avoid!). It might help to know that you don't have to be a Windows expert to organize your work. You can do it all from within PowerPoint. In Exercise 25.12, we'll create a subfolder in the My Documents folder and save a presentation into it.

EXERCISE 25.12

Creating and Saving into a Folder

1. If you just completed Exercise 25.11, you are right where you need to be. If not, open 25-12.ppt.

2. Choose File ➢ Save As from the menu. The Save As dialog box appears.

3. The Save As dialog box automatically opens the default folder (often My Documents) or the folder you last saved to. If the Save In setting at the top of the dialog box does not show My Documents, then click the My Documents icon on the Places bar at the left side of the Save As dialog box.

4. Click the Create New Folder button to open the New Folder dialog box. Type **PowerPoint Practice Folder** and click OK.

5. The Save As dialog box now displays PowerPoint Practice Folder as the Save In setting. Select the text in the File Name text box and overtype it with **Exercise 25-12**.

6. Click the Save button to save the file into the folder you just created.

7. Close the file.

There are several other useful buttons in the Save As dialog box. Understanding and using these buttons can make the difference between smoothly navigating folders and fumbling about. Table 25.1 explains the function of each button.

TABLE 25.1 Save Tools

	Button	Function
	Back	Takes you to the previous folder.
	Up One Level	Takes you to the main folder (or drive) directly above the selected folder.
	Search The Web	Opens your default browser to connect to the Internet.
	Delete	Sends the selected file or folder to the Recycle Bin. (If the selected item resides on a nonlocal drive, this command deletes the file for good, bypassing the Recycle Bin.)
	Create New Folder	Creates a new folder in the selected location, just like we practiced in Exercise 25.12.
	Views	Allows you to select a means for displaying files and folders in the Save As dialog box.
	Tools	Offers options for deleting, renaming, securing with a password, and other file and folder settings.

If you're saving the file to the computer you'll ultimately use to show the presentation, you can usually rehearse. That means you can probably discover and correct technical problems before you're standing in front of an audience. However, often you create a presentation on one computer and show it on another. In the following sections, we'll address some issues that might occur in the transition.

Embedding Fonts for Flawless Design

Fonts can be a big issue in a PowerPoint presentation. All users spend time choosing a design that includes fonts they think are attractive. Sometimes you go the extra mile and modify the presentation's fonts on the Slide Master. Imagine getting the text just like you want it and then taking the presentation to another computer that won't display your font settings. Fortunately, there are steps you can take to prevent that from happening.

Microsoft ✓ *Exam* *Objective*	**Work with embedded fonts**

If you try to show a presentation on a computer that doesn't have the fonts you used to create the presentation, PowerPoint substitutes a font that is "supposed" to be close. Do you want to take that chance? Thought not. Try Exercise 25.13; it will take you through *embedding* fonts, so that they'll be with the saved presentation regardless of the computer you show it from.

EXERCISE 25.13

Embedding Fonts

1. Open 25-13.ppt, or you can use a presentation of your own if you wish.

2. Click File ➤ Save As from the menu. The Save As dialog box opens.

3. In the Save As dialog box choose Tools ➤ Save Options to open the Save Options dialog box.

4. Enable the Embed TrueType Fonts check box.

5. Choose the Embed Characters In Use Only option. Click OK.

6. Navigate to the new folder we made in Exercise 25.12 (PowerPoint Practice Folder).

7. Select the text in the File Name text box and overtype it with **Exercise 25-13 With Embedded Fonts**.

8. Click Save and then close the file.

Making Presentations Available on the Web

Looking to go global? You can always use the Web to give others access to your presentation. Once it is published, any user with the ability to surf the net can view the presentation in their browser. When you publish a presentation, a copy of it is created in a file location you choose (in this case, a web server).

Microsoft ✓ *Exam* *Objective*	**Publish presentations to the Web**

In order to actually publish your presentation, you must have permission to save to a web server. Your company may have one. If this is the case, see your network administrator for information on how to access it. If you're on your own, check with your ISP. These days, most ISP accounts come with free web space. All you have to do is give them a call or visit their website to *activate* or set up your web space. Once that's done, it's a snap to publish. Exercise 25.14 walks you through the process.

EXERCISE 25.14

Publishing a Presentation to the Web

1. Open 25-14.ppt, or you can use a presentation of your own if you wish.

2. Click File ➢ Save As Web Page from the menu. The Save As dialog box opens with a few changes.

3. In the File Name box, type a name for the web page. We're going to leave our filename as 25-14.htm, but if you're doing this with a file of your own, it would be a good idea to make the filename more descriptive.

4. In the Save As Type list, you have two publishing choices (together with a number of other choices for nonpublished presentations).

   ▪ If you select Web Page, the presentation is saved separately from its supporting files. A newly created folder contains those files—bullets, background textures, and graphics. This is the best choice if you're saving to a location that already has published files and folders.

EXERCISE 25.14 *(continued)*

- If you select Web Archive, the presentation and supporting files are saved together in the location you specify.

Choose the setting that makes sense for your own purpose. We're choosing the Web Page option.

5. Click the Change Title button to set the titlebar text for your web page. We're leaving the default choice of New Project Meeting. Change yours if it makes sense to do so. Click OK.

6. Click Publish to open the Publish As Web Page dialog box:

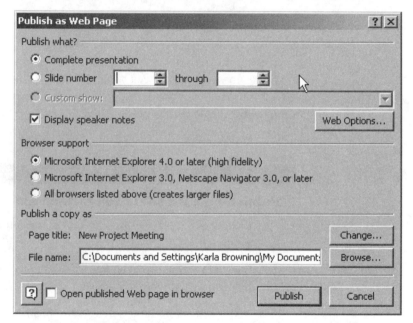

7. You can specify the slides you want to publish (we chose Complete Presentation) and optimize for a particular browser (we left the default setting, shown in the above graphic).

8. If you explore the Web Options button, you'll find settings that adjust navigation controls, appearance of text and graphics, and organization of supporting files, among other things. We left these settings at their defaults.

EXERCISE 25.14 *(continued)*

9. Back in the Publish As Web Page dialog box, click Browse to open the Publish As dialog box and either navigate to or type the http:\\ address of the web server where your presentation will reside. (Your network administrator or ISP can help with this part, or you can save to a folder on your hard drive for purposes of this exercise.)

10. Click OK to return to the Publish As Web Page dialog box. Then click Publish to publish and view it later, or enable Open Published Web Page In Browser (as we did) and then click Publish to see the published presentation:

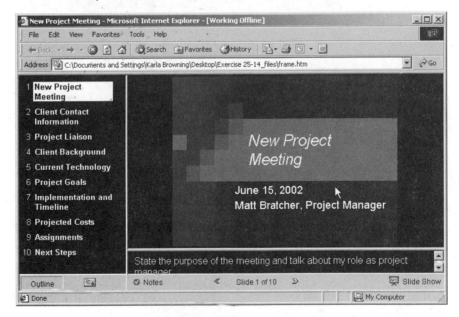

11. You may close your web browser and your PowerPoint file when you've finished.

You can disable the speaker's notes, navigation tools, and navigation frame under Web Options in the Save As Web Page dialog box. Then you must republish the presentation.

Using Pack and Go

Office includes a PowerPoint Viewer, which is used to display a presentation on a computer that doesn't include PowerPoint. To bundle your presentation and the viewer in one easy, compressed package, use the Pack and Go utility that comes with PowerPoint.

Even if there are no issues with available PowerPoint software, Pack and Go can be helpful in compressing the normally huge presentation files to save space on your storage media.

Microsoft ✓ *Exam* *Objective*

Use Pack and Go

Pack and Go is a two-part operation: the packing (covered in Exercise 25.15) and the unpacking (covered in Exercise 25.16).

EXERCISE 25.15

Packing a Presentation Using Pack and Go

1. Open 25-15.ppt, or use a presentation of your own if you wish.

2. Choose File ➢ Pack And Go to launch the Pack and Go Wizard:

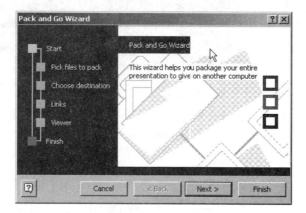

3. Click Next to proceed past the introductory step. Step 2 (Pick Files To Pack) allows you to choose which presentation you want to work with. Leave Active Presentation selected and click Next.

4. At Step 3 (Choose Destination) you must select where to pack the presentation. The default is to pack it to floppies, but you can also browse to find another location. For example, you may wish to pack it directly on the C: drive to make it smaller for e-mailing. Choose the location you want to use. If you have floppies, give it a try along with us. Click Next.

5. Step 4 (Links) allows you to include files you've linked and embed TrueType fonts (discussed earlier in this chapter).

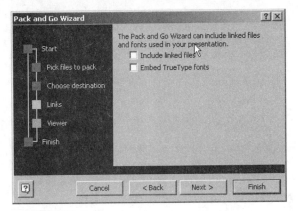

We disabled both options for this exercise. When you embed fonts and include linked files, even compressed files can become very large, requiring five, ten, or even more standard floppy disks. Packing time for these large files is considerable. You may want to use a Zip disk or other high-capacity medium to transport the presentation file between computers. Click Next.

6. At Step 5 (Viewer) you can include the PowerPoint Viewer if you're taking the presentation to a machine that doesn't have PowerPoint. We left the default setting of Don't Include The Viewer. Click Next.

7. The Finish step tells you what the settings are. You can click Back to return to any step of the wizard and change these settings. If all looks well, click Finish. (Make sure there's a floppy disk in drive A: if you're packing to a floppy as we are.)

8. PowerPoint displays a dialog box with the files being copied and prompts you for additional disks if needed. (We didn't need any in this instance.) When the wizard finishes, you'll return to the same PowerPoint view you were in when you started the wizard.

When it's time to unpack the presentation, take the steps outlined in Exercise 25.16.

EXERCISE 25.16

Unpacking a Presentation

1. If you used portable media, insert the disk created by Pack and Go (use Disk 1 if you have several). Then open Windows Explorer or My Computer.

2. In Windows Explorer or My Computer, select the drive and/or folder where the disk is located and then double-click the Pngsetup.exe file. The Pack And Go Setup dialog box opens:

3. Select a destination for the unpacked presentation (and viewer if applicable). We're going to unpack to the PowerPoint Practice Folder in My Documents.

4. Click OK. PowerPoint displays an overwrite warning message:

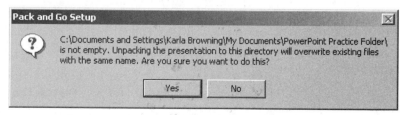

EXERCISE 25.16 *(continued)*

This just lets you know that if there's an existing file with the same name as the presentation you're unpacking, the unpacked presentation will overwrite it. Click Yes to proceed.

5. You'll be prompted for additional disks (if applicable), and you'll see this message when the unpacking process is finished:

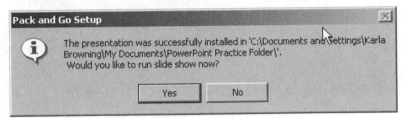

6. Choose Yes to view the show immediately, or choose No to open the presentation later from within the PowerPoint application window.

7. Close Windows Explorer (or My Computer) and your PowerPoint file.

If you go directly to the show from the Pack and Go Wizard, a copy of your presentation is created in `C:\Windows\Temp`. Delete this temporary file after the show, particularly if you're using someone else's computer.

Collaborating with Workgroups

Most of us wouldn't deliver new sales materials to a client without first having a colleague proofread them. Nor should you give a presentation that hasn't been scrutinized by someone else whose opinion you trust. The spelling checker catches most mistakes, but it can't do anything about a misspelled company name you've told it to ignore. And there's nothing quite like the feeling you get when you and a few hundred of your closest friends notice a spelling or grammatical error projected in five-foot-high letters in an auditorium.

Nearly all presentations can benefit from others' input. Have a colleague check your presentation for spelling and grammar errors the Office tools can't catch. Get a second opinion about the appropriateness of your transitions and animations. Have someone outside your field of expertise check the presentation for jargon and general clarity.

The people who proof your presentation don't have to be in the next office. They could be anywhere in the world! Attach your PowerPoint presentation to an e-mail message so others' comments can be added, or use online collaboration where you actually build your presentation with the help of a person or team at another location. Either way, you're getting suggestions from a second or third person as you're polishing your presentation.

Preparing a Presentation for Review

Use any MAPI-compliant e-mail program to send a PowerPoint file to reviewers. If e-mail hasn't made it to your corner of the office yet, save the file in a shared network location. No network? Then use sneaker net. (Put the document on a floppy disk and walk it over to a colleague for review!)

Microsoft ✓ *Exam Objective*	**Set up a review cycle**

There are several different ways you can set up a review cycle in PowerPoint. The method you choose depends on several variables:

- E-mail software: The exercises in this section use Outlook 2002, but we also include suggestions for using review features with other e-mail clients.

- Connectivity: We're assuming most of our readers are on an intranet or the Internet. However, suggestions for standalone computers are included.

- The number of reviewers.

- Whether you want reviewers to add their feedback all at once or one at a time.

Exercise 25.17 walks you through the steps for sending the presentation to one or more reviewers for simultaneous feedback. This is the simplest way of sending a presentation for review. In Exercise 25.18, we'll introduce you to *routing*, a process where you can send the presentation to multiple reviewers, in the order you specify, and have it returned to you at the end of the cycle.

Sending a Presentation for Review

1. Open 25-17.ppt, or use a presentation of your own.

2. Choose File ➤ Send To ➤ Mail Recipient For Review. Outlook automatically creates a review request message—flagged for follow-up—with the presentation attached. It is important to send the file this way if you want to take advantage of PowerPoint's automatic change tracking.

3. Address the e-mail message to reviewers. You can type an e-mail address in the To field or click the To button to open your default address book and then select recipients.

4. PowerPoint automatically places the text "Please review the attached document" in the message window. You can add text if you wish.

5. If your presentation has linked objects, you must also attach those files or the recipients won't be able to see them when they open the presentation. Just click the Insert File button in the e-mail message to open the Insert File dialog box. Locate, select, and insert any linked files.

6. Click Send to e-mail the presentation to all recipients.

7. There's no need to save the presentation. We haven't made changes to it.

8. Close the file when you've finished.

You can still send a presentation for review, and take advantage of automatic change tracking, even if you're not using Outlook. To do so, follow these steps:

1. Click File ➤ Save As and choose Presentation For Review in the Save As Type drop-down list. Name the file and select a location as you normally would, and then click Save. (If you're using floppy disks or

a shared network folder to distribute the presentation to reviewers, be sure to make enough copies for all reviewers, and that's it. Until the reviewed copies come back to you, that is!)

2. Attach the file to an e-mail message using the procedures established by your e-mail program. Don't forget to attach linked files as well.

3. Send the e-mail.

Combining Presentations from Multiple Reviewers

If you're not using routing (discussed in the next section) to distribute a presentation to multiple reviewers, you will wind up with presentation changes in separate files. Fortunately, PowerPoint 2002's Compare and Merge feature automatically handles this issue by incorporating modifications from several reviewers' files into one presentation. Each reviewer's changes show up in a different color. You can browse to apply or reject those changes all in one place. Although Compare and Merge is not a skill required for the MOUS exam, it makes sense to know it if you're going to be sending documents for review without using routing. If you used Outlook to e-mail the presentation for review, it works like this:

1. In Outlook, open the presentation sent back to you by the reviewer.

2. PowerPoint displays a message alert and prompts you to merge the document with the original one.

3. Click Yes.

If you didn't use Outlook to send the presentation for review, you still have the ability to compare and merge.

1. In PowerPoint, open the original presentation you sent for review.

2. Choose Tools ➤ Compare And Merge Presentations.

3. Select the reviewed presentations that you want to combine with your original presentation, and then click Merge.

EXERCISE 25.18

Routing a Presentation

1. Open 25-18.ppt, or use a presentation of your own.

2. Choose File ➤ Send To ➤ Routing Recipient. Depending on which version of Outlook you're running, you may see an access warning from Outlook. If so, click Yes to allow access and open the Add Routing Slip dialog box.

3. Click the Address button to display your e-mail system's address book. Select the name of your first reviewer and click To to place the name in the Message Recipients list box. Choose the name of each reviewer this way and then click OK to return to the Add Routing Slip dialog box. Each name you selected appears in the To list box.

4. Type a subject for the message in the Subject text box. By default, PowerPoint uses the word "Routing" followed by a colon and the title as entered in the document's properties. Overwrite this subject with your own if you wish.

5. Type the e-mail message you want to send with the attached document in the Message Text box. Our subject, message, and other settings are shown here:

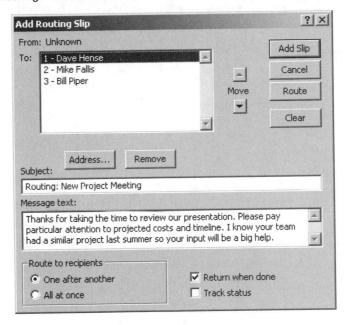

EXERCISE 25.18 *(continued)*

6. Choose the One After Another option so reviewers receive the presentation in the order you listed them in the To list box. (You can adjust this order by clicking the up and down arrow buttons.)

7. Enable the Return When Done check box if necessary to have the routed document sent back to you when the last reviewer closes it.

8. Click Route to add the slip and send the document.

Note: If you just click Add Slip, the routing information is added to the presentation file. You can continue working on the file and send it for review later by choosing File ➢ Send To ➢ Next Routing Recipient.

9. Close the file when you've finished.

Reviewing Others' Comments

Once you send the presentation out for review, others add their comments and return the presentation to you. Recipients of a presentation you send for review need only double-click to open the file, make their changes, and return the file to you. Depending on how they received the file, recipients should do one of the following:

- Outlook recipients using PowerPoint 97 or 2000: When finished making modifications in PowerPoint, they should choose File Send To ➢ Mail Recipient As Attachment and then address and send the e-mail as usual.

- Outlook recipients using PowerPoint 2002: They should choose File ➢ Send To ➢ Original Sender.

- Recipients of e-mail in a program other than Outlook and those who have reviewed the file from a shared network folder: They should make their changes and click Save. E-mail users should return the file to the original sender as an attachment. Shared-folder users should notify the original author when they have finished their review.

- Reviewers using a floppy disk: They should make their modifications in PowerPoint and click Save. Then they should close PowerPoint and walk (or mail) the disk back to the original author.

Only the original author sees a reviewer's changes. And reviewers needn't worry about overwriting the original presentation file. PowerPoint presents reviewers' modifications for approval. The original author still has the ability to reject any or all modifications.

Microsoft ✔ *Exam Objective*

Review presentation comments

PowerPoint 2002 offers some very robust reviewing features. When you send a presentation for review, PowerPoint tracks changes in content, color schemes, animation settings, transitions, layout, formatting of text and objects, and much more! For the MOUS exam, you need only understand how to examine reviewer's comments. However, it makes sense to discuss all changes as part of the review cycle since that's what you're most likely to see in your own working situation.

If you didn't use routing, you have to use the Compare and Merge feature to combine all of the versions when the presentations come back to you. See "Combining Presentations from Multiple Reviewers" in the previous section of this chapter. Routing distributes only one presentation, so the reviewer's changes and comments are all in one place automatically. In either case, follow the steps in Exercise 25.19 to look at the comments and changes made by your reviewers. You'll use the buttons on the Reviewing toolbar shown in Figure 25.4.

FIGURE 25.4 The Reviewing toolbar offers tools to examine and act on changes.

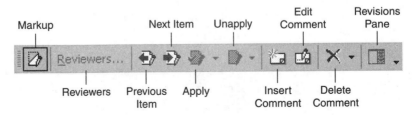

EXERCISE 25.19

Examining Reviewers' Comments and Changes

1. Open 25-19.ppt, or open a presentation you've routed yourself. The Revisions Pane opens automatically when you retrieve a reviewed presentation.

2. If you're using our presentation, navigate to Slide 4 to see revisions for that slide listed in the Revisions Pane.

3. PowerPoint 2002 displays markers next to the slide objects that have been changed. Comment markers show the individual's initials and sequential comment number in a small rectangle, usually located at the top left of the slide (unless the reviewer dragged it to a different location).

   Change markers show a slightly different icon (notepad with pen). Point to a marker to see the reviewer's name and comment or a description of the change. Use the Previous and Next buttons at the bottom of the Revisions Pane to browse markers in a presentation.

4. For each change marker you see, you must decide whether to keep or discard the reviewer's changes. Click the Apply button on the Reviewing toolbar to keep the selected change, or click Unapply to reject it.

   The drop-down lists on these buttons offer options for applying/unapplying all changes to a particular slide or all changes in the active presentation. After you have chosen Apply or Unapply, you may wish to delete a change marker. To do so, click it and press Delete on the keyboard. For this exercise, apply all changes to Slides 3 and 4.

5. Comment markers (see Slides 4 and 7) don't require you to apply or unapply anything. Generally, you read them and decide whether to take action. We usually delete the comment markers from a presentation as we address them. Just click them once to select them and then press Delete on the keyboard. Read and then delete the comment markers from Slides 4 and 7.

Note: Be sure to address the issue discussed in the change marker by clicking Apply or Unapply before deleting it.

EXERCISE 25.19 *(continued)*

6. Click the Reviewers button if you wish to review changes by one or more particular reviewers. Disable the check boxes next to the reviewers whose changes you don't want to see. This presentation only has one reviewer.

7. The Revisions Pane button toggles the Revisions Pane on and off. If you prefer to see changes and comments in a list, turn it on. You can select reviewers, browse changes, apply changes, and reject changes in the Revisions Pane.

8. If you've finished looking at changes for a particular reviewer, switch to the Gallery tab of the Revisions Pane, locate a miniature slide with changes from that reviewer, and then click the down arrow on that slide and choose Done With This Reviewer. Any remaining change markers from that reviewer are removed from the selected slide. Do this for Slides 3 and 4.

9. Save and close the presentation.

Ending a Review Cycle

As soon as you combine a reviewed presentation with your original, an End Review button appears on the Reviewing toolbar. Click it when you have finished reviewing file modifications.

Confirm the End Review command in the message box, keeping in mind the following:

- You can no longer combine reviewed presentations with the original.

- Any unapplied changes remain unapplied, and you can't view them again.

If you have applied (or unapplied) all reviewer modifications, deleted all change markers, and saved your presentation, PowerPoint ends the review automatically.

Broadcasting a Presentation

Rather than publishing a presentation and waiting for users to access it, you can schedule a web broadcast over the Internet or an intranet and have everybody view it at the same time. Presentation Broadcasting is often used in place of a face-to-face meeting or conference call when you have participants at remote locations, reducing the time and expense of traveling. Unlike a published presentation that users browse at their leisure, a broadcast occurs in real time, so you must schedule the broadcast and invite participants in advance using Outlook or another e-mail program. However, you can also record the broadcast and save it so that participants who could not attend or wish to review the presentation can do so.

Broadcasts come in two sizes: 1 to 10 participants and 11 or more participants. (This assumes that participants need their own Internet connections. If two people are sitting in front of the same monitor, count them as one participant.) You can use Internet Explorer 4 or 5 to broadcast to up to 10 people. For 11 participants or more, you'll need access to Windows Media Services, so talk to your web administrator. Windows Media Services, which is available to download free from Microsoft and runs on Windows 2000 Server, is also required if you include live video, regardless of audience size.

There are three steps required to get ready for the actual broadcast:

- Selecting the broadcast options
- Selecting a shared folder and server
- Scheduling the broadcast

Microsoft ✓ *Exam Objective*

Schedule and deliver presentation broadcasts

Exercises 25.20 and 25.21 take you through setting up and broadcasting a presentation. We'll assume that our audience has fewer than 10 participants and we're not using audio or video. To complete these exercises, you will need access to a shared network location.

EXERCISE 25.20

Scheduling a Presentation Broadcast

1. Open 25-20.ppt, or open a presentation you've created yourself.

2. Choose Slide Show ➤ Online Broadcast ➤ Settings to open the Broadcast Settings dialog box. You may be prompted to install the feature; if so, insert the Office XP CD (if you need it) and click Yes.

3. Change the Audio/Video setting to None.

4. Enter the server folder and path (this must be a shared location) in the File Location area.

5. Click OK to close the dialog box and schedule the presentation.

6. Choose Slide Show ➤ Online Broadcast ➤ Schedule A Live Broadcast to open the Schedule Presentation Broadcast dialog box. Fill out the information in this dialog box carefully. It appears on the Lobby (welcome) page of the presentation broadcast.

7. Click the Schedule button to open an Outlook appointment form so you can set a time and date for the meeting and e-mail invitations to participants.

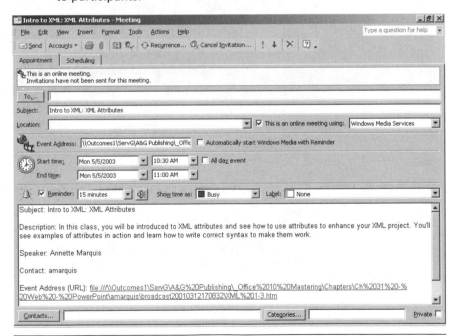

A few minutes before presentation time, you'll want to prepare yourself and set up the presentation for broadcast. Follow the steps in Exercise 25.21.

EXERCISE 25.21

Broadcasting the Presentation

1. Open a presentation you've previously scheduled for broadcast. You may use 25-20.ppt if necessary.

2. Choose Slide Show ➤ Online Broadcast ➤ Start Live Broadcast Now.

3. Click the Broadcast button in the Live Presentation Broadcast dialog box to begin the presentation. But don't get nervous just yet. You still have some setup steps.

4. PowerPoint displays the Broadcast Presentation dialog box and shows you the status of the presentation as it prepares it for broadcast:

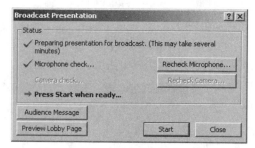

5. If you're using audio/video, PowerPoint guides you through microphone and camera checks. Just follow the instructions on the screen.

6. Click the Audience Message button in the Broadcast Presentation dialog box to write the audience a message that appears at the top of the Lobby page. (Preview the Lobby page at any time by clicking the button at the bottom of the dialog box. Switch back to Power-Point using the Taskbar button.)

7. When you're ready to start for real, click Broadcast again. The first slide of the presentation appears either in full screen or in a resizable window, depending on the settings you chose in the original setup (Exercise 25.20).

8. Proceed through the presentation broadcast.

9. Close the file when you've finished.

Summary

In this chapter, you learned how to take a presentation beyond your local machine, adding data from other sources and making your work available to a larger audience. Specifically, we addressed the following skills:

- Previewing and printing slides, outlines, handouts, and speaker notes
- Importing Excel charts, Word tables, and sound and video files into slides
- Exporting a presentation as an outline in Word
- Setting up a slide show
- Delivering a presentation
- Keeping track of presentations in folders
- Embedding fonts
- Publishing presentations to the Web
- Using Pack and Go
- Collaborating with colleagues for presentation review
- Scheduling and delivering presentation broadcasts

Microsoft
Access 2002
Core Exam

PART
VI

Chapter

26

Creating an Access Database

MOUS ACCESS 2002 CORE EXAM OBJECTIVES COVERED IN THIS CHAPTER:

✓ **Create Access databases**

✓ **Open database objects in multiple views**

✓ **Move among records**

✓ **Format datasheets**

Access 2002 is a database program designed to help you organize a collection of common information: for example, your organization's inventory, customer contact data, or product catalog, or your personal address book or home inventory. An Access database contains one or more *tables*. Each table is like an Excel list. The columns in an Excel list are called *fields* in Access, and the Excel rows are Access *records*. Access databases differ from Excel lists in several ways, but the most important distinction is this: An Access database can include more than one table, and the tables can be related. Figure 26.1 shows the Access application window displaying the database window for the Northwind database, which is included with Access. On the left edge of the database window is the Objects bar, used to navigate to different objects in the database: Tables, Queries, Forms, Reports, Pages, Macros, and Modules.

The seven types of Access objects are described below:

- **Tables** contain the data in your database. Almost all Access databases have at least two tables that contain data about different but related entities, such as classes and instructors, customers and orders, or inventory, warehouse locations, and suppliers.

- **Queries** retrieve information from one or more tables. You use queries when you need to view data from multiple related tables and when you want to sort or filter data from one or more tables.

- **Forms** are used to enter information in tables and display information from tables and queries on screen. Your database's *user interface* is comprised of all the forms in the database.

- **Reports** are printed output from the database tables and queries.

- **Pages** are the HTML (web) versions of reports and forms.

- **Macros** are user-created programs that execute one or more commands.

- **Modules** contain user-created Visual Basic code that executes commands.

FIGURE 26.1   Access 2002 application window

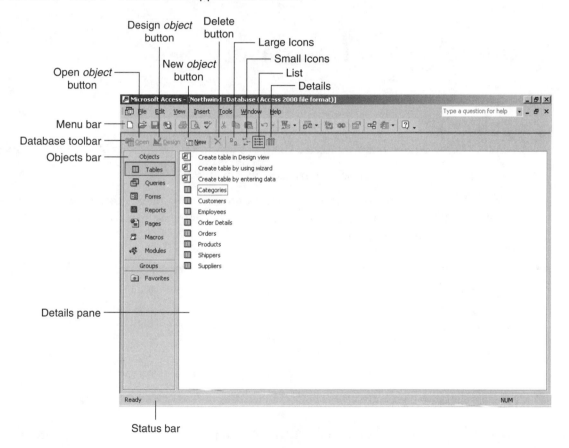

To pass the Access MOUS exam, you need to be comfortable with the first five objects. Macros and modules are not included in the exam objectives.

Before you begin this chapter, you should go to the Sybex website and download the file 4113Ch26.zip. This package contains the files necessary to complete some of the exercises in this chapter. In addition, it contains files of what most of the objects should look like after you complete the exercises. These files are affixed with the word *Post*.

Creating a New Database

There are three ways to create a database:

- Using a database wizard or other predesigned template
- Using an Access Project to connect to an existing SQL Server database
- From scratch by creating a blank database

If there is not a database wizard or template that corresponds to your data, you must design and create your database from scratch, which is how most databases are created.

Microsoft ✓ *Exam* *Objective*	**Create Access databases**

To meet this exam objective, you must able to create a blank database and create a database using a template.

Starting with a New Blank Database

To create a blank database, click the New button on the Database toolbar, choose File ➤ New, or hold Ctrl and press N, then click the Blank Database link in the task pane. In Exercise 26.1, you'll create a database using a blank database template.

Creating a Database Using a Blank Database Template

1. Open Microsoft Access 2002. The New File task pane should be displayed. If it is not, click the New button on the Standard toolbar to open the task pane.

2. In the New section of the task pane, click the Blank Database link to open the File New Database dialog box.

Unlike other types of Office documents, Access databases are saved *before* you enter any information, and the File New Database dialog box looks a lot like the Save dialog box.

3. Type **Sample** in the File Name text box.

4. Accept the default file location: My Documents.

5. Click the Create button to create the Sample.mdb database and open its database window.

Using a Database Template

The blank database created in Exercise 26.1 needs a lot more work before you can use it to enter data. Using a template can save precious time in the development of the database, so you should check the templates that are included with Access as well as those available on the Microsoft site. The templates included with Access all use wizards to create the database tables, forms, and reports. In Exercise 26.2, you'll create a database using a template.

Creating a Database Using a Template

1. Choose File ➢ New from the menu to open the New File task pane.

2. Click the General Templates link on the task pane to open the Templates dialog box.

3. Click the Databases tab in the Templates dialog box.

4. Select the Order Entry template and click OK to open the File New Database dialog box.

5. Type *Your Name* **Order Entry** in the File Name text box.

6. Choose a location for the database, and then click Create to launch the Database Wizard.

7. The first step of the wizard describes the Order Entry database template. Click Next.

The wizard displays the tables that will be created. Required and optional fields (in italics) are listed for each table.

8. Select the Customer Information table in the Tables In The Database list.

9. Scroll through the Fields In The Table list to the Email Address field. Enable the check box for the field to include this optional field in the table.

10. Select the Information About Employees table in the Tables In The Database list.

11. Enable the Home Phone field to include it in the table. Click Next.

In the third step of the wizard, you choose a style for all the forms in the database. The default style, Standard, relies on the Windows system settings for color choices and the appearance of controls like labels and text boxes.

12. Click Next to use the default Standard style.

The fourth step of the wizard focuses on reports. There is no Windows default for reports, but the default style, Corporate, is frequently used.

13. Make sure Corporate is selected and click Next to continue.

14. In the fifth step of the wizard, accept or enter a title for the database. Enter **Order Entry System** as the title and then click Next.

15. In the last step of the wizard, leave the Yes Start the Database check box enabled and click Finish to create and open the database.

The Database Wizard displays progress bars while the tables, forms, and reports are created. When the database objects have been created, a message box notifies you that you need to enter company information before using the application.

16. Click the OK button on the message box to open the My Company Information form.

17. Enter the company information specified below:
Company: **BCB Garden Supplies**
Address: **123 Dawson Street**
City: **Watsonville**
State/Province: **California**
Postal Code: **92431**
Country/Region: **USA**
Sales Tax Rate: **8.00%**
Default Terms: **Net 30**
Invoice Descr:
Phone Number: **(831) 555-1234**
Fax Number: **(831) 555-1111**

18. Click the Close button to close the My Company Information form and display the Main Switchboard for the database.

The Switchboard form helps users work in the database. All the databases created with the Database Wizard include switchboards.

19. Choose File ➢ Close to close the Switchboard form. Then choose File ➢ Close from the menu to close the only object that is still open, the database window.

Working with Database Objects

Database objects have at least two views. Tables and queries have Datasheet view, which is used to view the records in the table or query, Design view, which is used to modify the design of the table or query object, and two new views in Access 2002: PivotTable view and PivotChart view. Queries also have a SQL view, which displays the SQL code for the query. Forms have the four views that tables and queries share and a fifth view: Form view. Reports have three views: Design view, Print Preview, and Layout Preview. Pages have two views: Design view and Page view. In this section, you'll learn to work with database objects in multiple views.

Microsoft ✓ *Exam Objective* | **Open database objects in multiple views**

You can open database objects in a specific view, or switch views in an open object.

Exploring Database Objects

Object exploration begins with the Objects bar. The Objects bar lists all the types of objects available in Access 2002. Click an icon in the bar to display the objects of that type in the current database in the details pane. Select an object—for example, a table—in the details pane and then click the View buttons above the Object bar to open the table (in Datasheet view) or design the table (in Design view).

When an object is open in any view, you can switch between views using the View button on the toolbar. Click the down arrow on the View button to choose from the views for the current object:

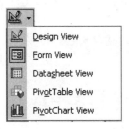

As with the other Office applications, you can also switch between views of the current object using commands on the View menu.

In Exercise 26.3, you'll explore the various database objects.

EXERCISE 26.3

Exploring Database Objects

1. Open the Northwind database by selecting Help ➢ Sample Databases ➢ Northwind Sample Database. The Northwind Traders "splash screen" form opens. Click OK to close the form and open the Switchboard form.

2. Click the Close button to close the Switchboard form and display the database window.

There is no Standard toolbar in Access. Each object view has its own toolbar, so as you switch between objects and views of an object, the default toolbar also changes. The Database toolbar is displayed now because the Database window is the active window.

3. Click the Tables icon in the Objects bar to display the tables in the database in the details pane.

When you double-click an object in the database window, it opens in its default view: Datasheet view for tables and queries, Form view for forms, and Print Preview for reports.

4. Double-click the Customers table to open the table in Datasheet view. In Datasheet view, you can browse, sort, filter, and edit the existing records and enter new records:

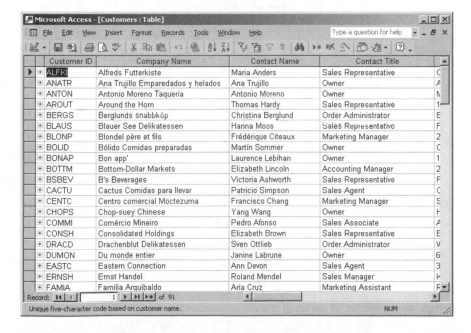

When you open a table in Datasheet view, the Database toolbar is hidden and the Table Datasheet toolbar is displayed.

5. Choose View ➢ Design View from the menu to switch to Design view. In this view, you can add, delete, or modify fields in the Customers table:

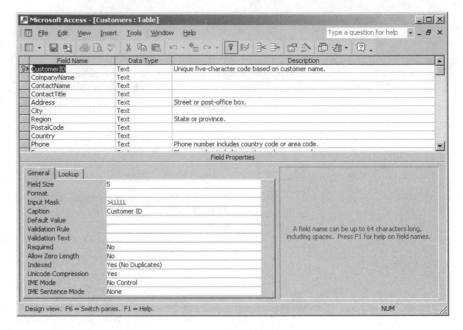

6. Click the View button to return to Datasheet view.

7. Choose File ➢ Close on the menu to close the table.

8. Click the Reports icon on Objects bar.

9. Double-click the Customer Labels report in the details pane to open the Customer Labels report in its default view, Print Preview.

10. Click the Close button on the Print Preview toolbar to close the report.

11. Click the Forms icon on the Objects bar to view the forms for this database.

12. In the details pane, double-click the Customers form to open the form in Form View.

EXERCISE 26.3 *(continued)*

13. Switch to Datasheet view by clicking the down arrow on the View button and selecting Datasheet View. This view is similar to the Datasheet view for a table.

14. Switch to Design view by clicking the View button on the Form View toolbar.

15. Choose View ➢ Form View on the menu to switch back to Form View.

16. Close the Customers form.

Leave the Northwind database open for the next exercise.

Opening Database Objects Using the Shortcut Menu

When you double-click an object in the details pane, it opens in its default view. Alternatively, you can right-click an object and select the view you would like to display from the context menu, as you'll see in Exercise 26.4.

EXERCISE 26.4

Opening Database Objects

For this exercise, use the Northwind database used in the previous exercise.

1. Click the Reports icon on the Objects bar.

2. Double-click the Summary Of Sales By Year report to open the report in the default view, Print Preview.

3. Click the View button on the Print Preview toolbar to switch to Design view of the Summary Of Sales By Year report.

4. Close the Summary Of Sales By Year report.

5. Select the Summary Of Sales by Year report in the details pane. Don't double-click—if you do, you'll open the report in Print Preview. Right-click the report and choose Design View from the shortcut menu to open the report in Design view.

6. Close the Summary Of Sales By Year report.

EXERCISE 26.4 *(continued)*

7. Right-click the Invoice report. Choose Print Preview from the shortcut menu.

8. Click the Close button on the Print Preview toolbar to close the Invoice report.

Leave the Northwind database open for the next exercise.

Moving among Records

You move between records in a form, table, or query using the mouse, the keyboard, or the navigation buttons at the bottom of the form, table, or query window.

Microsoft ✓ *Exam Objective*   **Move among records**

When navigating through the records in a database, you can use the mouse to quickly position the cursor in the desired field. You can scroll using the horizontal and vertical scroll bars until the desired field or record is displayed. You can also use the mouse to click the navigation buttons to move from one record to the next. The navigation buttons are shown in Figure 26.2.

FIGURE 26.2 The navigation buttons are used to navigate between records in tables, queries, and forms and between pages in reports.

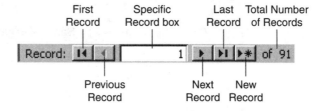

In Exercise 26.5, you'll navigate through records in the Customers table using the mouse and navigation buttons.

EXERCISE 26.5

Navigating with the Mouse and Navigation Buttons

1. With the Northwind database open, click the Tables icon on the Objects bar.

2. Double-click the Customers table to open the table in Datasheet view.

3. Use the vertical scroll bar to navigate through the table until you see the company name The Big Cheese.

4. Position the pointer over the company name The Big Cheese and click. The insertion point appears in the field, and the record number of the selected record appears in the Specific Record box in the navigation buttons section.

Record: ◀◀ ◀ [77] ▶ ▶▶ ▶✱ of 91

5. Enter **5** in the Specific Record box and press Enter to move to record 5: Berglunds snabbköp.

6. Click the Next Record button to move to record 6.

7. Click the First Record button to move to record 1.

8. Click the Last Record button to move to the last record in the table.

Leave the Customers table and the database open for the next exercise.

When you are entering data, you'll usually navigate using the keyboard. Press the Tab key to move to the next field; hold Shift and press Tab to move to the previous field. When the last field in a record is selected, pressing Tab moves to the first field of the next record. In Exercise 26.6, you'll navigate using the keyboard.

EXERCISE 26.6

Navigating Using the Keyboard

For this exercise, use the Customers table in the Northwind database.

1. Click the First Record button to move to record 1.

2. Press the Tab key to move to and select the next field.

EXERCISE 26.6 *(continued)*

3. Press the Tab key again to move to and select the next field.

4. Hold Shift and press Tab to move back to the previous field.

5. Close the Customers table. Leave the database open for the next exercise.

The New Record button is available in tables, queries, and forms to add records to the database. Some queries cannot be used to add records to a table. When you open one of these non-updateable queries, the New Record button is disabled.

Formatting Datasheets

Many Access users spend a lot of time working in Datasheet view, which looks a lot like an Excel worksheet. You can format the view by changing column widths as you would in Excel or by rearranging columns, setting background and gridline colors, and modifying the cell effects.

Microsoft ✓ *Exam Objective* | **Format datasheets**

As with Excel worksheets, formatting applied to a datasheet applies only to the current datasheet. In Exercise 26.7, you'll format the Datasheet view of the Categories table.

EXERCISE 26.7

Formatting the Datasheet View

1. Open the Categories table in the Northwind database in Datasheet view.

2. Point to the right edge of the Category ID column header and drag it to the left to adjust the column width so that it is slightly wider than the data in the column.

3. Drag the right edge of the Description column header so that some of the data in the column is cut off.

4. Double-click the right edge of the Description column header to adjust the column width to fit the contents of the column.

5. Point to the center of the Category Name column header. The pointer will change to a downward-pointing arrow. Click once to select the column.

6. Drag the column to the left of the Category ID column header and drop it to rearrange the first two columns in the datasheet.

7. Select the Category ID header and drag it to the left of the Category Name header so that Category ID is the first column again.

8. Choose Format ➢ Datasheet from the menu to open the Datasheet Formatting dialog box, shown here:

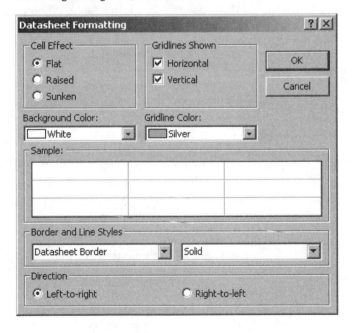

9. In the Cell Effect section, choose the Sunken option. The Sample updates to show you a preview of the effect.

EXERCISE 26.7 *(continued)*

10. Click OK to close the Datasheet Formatting dialog box and apply the changes.

11. Select Format ➢ Datasheet again.

12. In the Cell Effect section, choose the Flat option.

13. In the Background Color drop-down list, choose Silver.

14. In the Gridline Color drop-down list, choose Blue.

15. In the first Border And Line Styles drop-down list, select Horizontal Gridline.

16. In the second drop-down list, choose the Sparse Dots line style.

17. In the Gridlines Shown section, turn off the Vertical check box.

18. Click OK to apply the changes to the current datasheet.

19. Close the Categories table. When prompted, do *not* save the changes. This will discard the formatting.

20. Close the Northwind database.

Summary

This chapter focused creating and using databases. We covered the following topics:

- Creating a blank database
- Creating a database using the Database Wizard
- Working with database objects
- Switching between object views
- Navigating among table records using the mouse, the navigation buttons, and the keyboard
- Formatting the Datasheet view of a table

Chapter

27

Building Tables and Queries

MOUS ACCESS 2002 CORE EXAM OBJECTIVES COVERED IN THIS CHAPTER

- ✓ Create and modify tables
- ✓ Add a predefined input mask to a field
- ✓ Create Lookup fields
- ✓ Modify field properties
- ✓ Create and modify Select queries
- ✓ Add calculated fields to Select queries

Tables and queries are the most important objects in your database. The tables store your data and the queries allow you to retrieve and analyze the data.

Tables are the foundation of a database. When you design a table, you set properties for each field. The properties constrain the type and format for data that can be entered in the field. Other properties include default field values, validation rules, and input masks that help ensure that the information entered is accurate.

The queries you'll create in this chapter, Select queries, are used to display information from one or more tables. You can specify sorting and filtering criteria for the query results set and add calculated fields to queries.

Before you begin this chapter, you should go to the Sybex website and download the file 4113Ch27.zip. This package contains the files necessary to complete some of the exercises in this chapter.

Creating and Modifying Tables

When you initially create a blank database, the database contains no objects. The first objects you must create are tables.

Microsoft ✓ Exam Objective

Create and modify tables

Creating a New Table in Design View

You can create tables by importing existing data, by entering new data, by using a Table Wizard, or in Design view. Design view gives you the most control over the table's design and is the most commonly used table-creation method. Figure 27.1 shows Table Design View.

FIGURE 27.1 New blank table in Design view

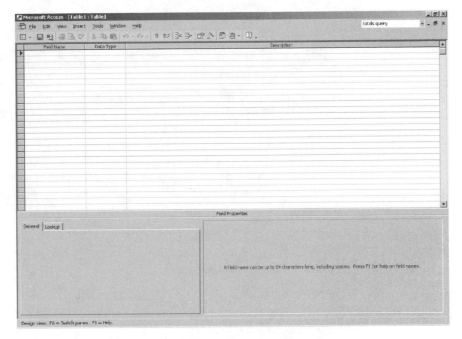

In Exercise 27.1, you'll create a new table in Design view.

EXERCISE 27.1

Creating a New Table in Design View

1. With Access 2002 open, click the New button on the Standard toolbar. The task pane will open.

2. Click the Blank Database link on the task pane.

3. Accept the default location, My Documents, and save the database as **Book Store**.

> **EXERCISE 27.1** *(continued)*
>
> 4. Click the Create button. A blank database window will be displayed.
>
> 5. Click the Tables icon in the Object bar. Double-click the Create Table In Design View option in the details pane. A blank table will be displayed.
>
> 6. Leave the blank table open for the next exercise.

Naming Database Objects Using the Reddick Naming Convention

The most common naming convention used in database development is the Reddick (aka "Leszynski/Reddick") convention. Each object within the database has a descriptive tag prefixing the object's name. You can find the Reddick convention tags on a number of web sites, including ours: `http://www.triadconsulting.com/resources/reddick.html`

Adding Fields to a Table

You create a table by entering field names, choosing a data type for each field, and setting field properties. Field names can include spaces, underscores, and hyphens.

Access allows spaces in field names, and the field names used in the exam include spaces, but we don't recommend using spaces. If you add code to a database, there are times you will need to enclose field names in quotations if the names include spaces. Instead of using spaces, capitalize the first letter of each word in a field name: for example, CustomerLastName.

Assigning Data Types to Fields

Table 27.1 describes the Access data types.

TABLE 27.1 Data Types

Data Type	Explanation
Text	The default data type. Holds up to 255 characters. Used for non-value numbers like phone numbers as well as words.
Memo	Allows you to enter sentences or paragraphs. You are not restricted by size, but you cannot easily filter the contents of memo fields. Commonly used for comments.
Number	Used for positive and negative numeric values.
Date/Time	Used for dates, times, and date/times.
Currency	Used for currency, but can also be used for numbers.
AutoNumber	Access automatically enters a value that increments by one when you enter a new record.
Yes/No	Entries limited to Yes/No, True/False, or On/Off. Commonly represented by a checkbox control.
OLE Object	Used for objects like pictures or documents that are not created in Access.
Hyperlink	Used for URLs, including file URLs and web URLs.
Lookup Wizard	Creates a drop-down list from a link to a value list or another table. The data type is derived from the data type of the data used in the lookup.

Entering Field Descriptions

Field descriptions can be used as a passive help system. When a user clicks a field, the description appears in the status bar. Field descriptions are optional, and you can turn off their status bar display so that, if you prefer, you can use the description for your own notes or internal documentation.

In Exercise 27.2 you will enter field names, data types, and descriptions to add fields to the table created in Exercise 27.1.

The remainder of the exercises for this chapter require the Book Store database created in Exercise 27.1.

EXERCISE 27.2

Adding Fields, Assigning Data Types, and Entering Field Descriptions for a Table

1. The insertion point should be in the first column, first row of the blank table created in Exercise 27.1. If it is not, click the first column/row.

2. In the Field Name box, type **First Name**.

3. Press the Tab key to move to the Data Type list.

4. Press Tab to accept the default data type, Text, and move to the Description column.

5. Type the Description **Enter the customer's first name**. Press Tab to move to the next field.

6. Repeat steps 2–5 to enter the remaining fields in the Table Design view:

   Field Name: **Last Name**
   Data Type: **Text**
   Description: **Enter the customer's last name**
   Field Name: **Company**
   Data Type: **Text**
   Description: **Enter the company name**
   Field Name: **Address**
   Data Type: **Text**
   Description: **Enter the customer's address**
   Field Name: **City**
   Data Type: **Text**
   Description: **Enter the customer's city**
   Field Name: **State**
   Data Type: **Text**
   Description: **Enter the customer's state**

EXERCISE 27.2 *(continued)*

Field Name: **Zip Code**
Data Type: **Text**
Description: **Enter the customer's zip code**
Field Name: **Phone Number**
Data Type: **Text**
Description: **Enter the customer's phone number**
Field Name: **Extension**
Data Type: **Text**
Description: **Enter the customer's phone extension**
Field Name: **Fax Number**
Data Type: **Text**
Description: **Enter the customer's fax number**
Field Name: **E-Mail**
Data Type: **Text**
Description: **Enter the customer's e-mail address**
Field Name: **Web Page**
Data Type: **Hyperlink**
Description: **Enter the customer's web page URL**

7. Click the View button on the Table Design View toolbar. You will be prompted to save the table. Click Yes to open the Save As dialog box.

8. Enter the table name **tblCustomers** and click OK.

9. A message box notifies you that the table has no primary key:

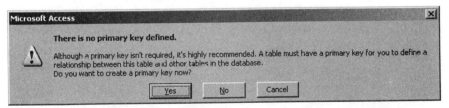

10. Click the No button to save the table without a primary key. (You'll set the primary key later in the chapter.) The table opens in Datasheet view, waiting for records to be added.

11. Close tblCustomers. Leave the database open for the next exercise.

Deleting and Rearranging Fields

While you're designing your database, you may need to rearrange a table's fields or add or remove fields. Even after a database is being used, a change in your organization's business rules may require modification of database tables. To modify a table, you must open the table in Design view.

Rearranging fields is a simple task. In Design view, you select a field by clicking the field selector (the gray button to the left of the Field Name column). Move the selected field by dragging the field to a new location. To delete the selected field, press Delete on the keyboard. If the table contains data, you will be prompted to confirm the deletion.

WARNING   When you delete a field, the data in the field is discarded. You cannot undo this deletion.

In Exercise 27.3, you will delete and rearrange fields in the tblCustomers table.

EXERCISE 27.3

Deleting and Rearranging Fields

1. Open the tblCustomers table in the Book Store database in Design view.

2. Select the Extension field by clicking the field's row selector. The entire row will be selected.

3. Click the Delete Rows button on the Table Design toolbar or press Delete on the keyboard to delete the field.

There is no data in this table, so you are not prompted to confirm the deletion.

4. Select the E-Mail field.

5. Drag the E-Mail row selector and drop it after the Web Page field to move the E-Mail field below the Web Page field.

EXERCISE 27.3 *(continued)*

Field Name	Data Type	Description
ID	AutoNumber	The Customer ID will automatically be generated. Please press Tab
First Name	Text	Enter the customer's first name
Last Name	Text	Enter the customer's last name
Company	Text	Enter the company name
Address	Text	Enter the customer's address
City	Text	Enter the customer's city
State	Text	Enter the customer's state
Zip Code	Text	Enter the customer's zip code
Phone Number	Text	Enter the customer's phone number
Fax Number	Text	Enter the customer's fax number
Web Page	Hyperlink	Enter the customer's web page URL
E-Mail	Text	Enter the customer's e-mail address

Field Properties

General | Lookup

Field Size	Long Integer
New Values	Increment
Format	
Caption	
Indexed	Yes (No Duplicates)

A field name can be up to 64 characters long, including spaces. Press F1 for help on field names.

6. Save the changes to tblCustomers.

7. Click the View button to view the datasheet.

8. Close the tblCustomers table.

Assigning Key Fields for a Table

In relational databases like Access databases, each table needs a primary key. Each record's primary key field contains a value that uniquely identifies it; therefore, no two records can have the same value in the primary key field. A primary key can be composed of one or more fields. The primary keys of the tables are used to relate tables to each other and to create a primary sort order and index.

Some tables have readily identifiable primary keys: UPCs for retail products, social security numbers for employees, or membership numbers for clubs. If the data in a table doesn't have a field (or combination of fields) that will have unique values, you can add an AutoNumber field to the table and set it as the primary key. In Exercise 27.4, you'll add a Customer ID field to tblCustomers and set it as the primary key.

EXERCISE 27.4

Assigning a Table's Primary Key

1. Open tblCustomers in Design view.

2. Select the first row of the grid. Click the Insert Rows button on the Table Design toolbar or press Insert on the keyboard to insert a new field row.

3. Click in the Field Name column in the new row. Name the field **ID**. Press Tab.

4. Set the Data Type to AutoNumber.

5. Type the following description: **The Customer ID will automatically be generated. Please press Tab**.

6. With the ID field active, click the Primary Key button on the Table Design toolbar.

Notice that the Primary Key image has been added to the Record Selector box, indicating that this field has been set to the Primary Key.

7. Save the tblCustomers table. Leave the table open for the next exercise.

Using Input Masks to Control Field Entry

Input masks help users enter data by minimizing the number of key-strokes required as well as formatting data in a consistent manner. For example, when you enter a phone number, it is time consuming to enter the parentheses and dashes. If the field includes an appropriate input mask, the user need only enter the digits in the phone number. All other formatting is supplied by the input mask.

Microsoft
✓ Exam
Objective

Add a predefined input mask to a field

Input masks, like other field properties, are changed in Design view. In Exercise 27.5, you will set the input mask property for the Phone Number and Fax Number fields.

EXERCISE 27.5

Set an Input Mask

1. Open tblCustomers in Design view if it is not open.

2. Select the Phone Number field.

3. In the Field Properties (lower) pane, click the Input Mask property text box. A Build button with three dots appears at the right end of the property.

4. Click the Build button to open the Input Mask Wizard.

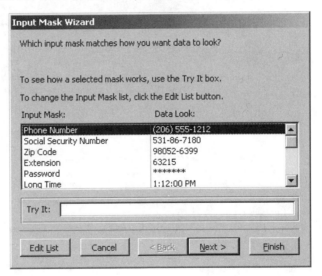

5. Select the Phone Number input mask from the list of predefined input masks.

6. Click the Next button to move to the next step.

7. Click Next to accept the input mask placeholder defaults.

8. Click Next to accept the default storage option.

9. Click the Finish button to set the input mask property and return to the table design. The Phone Number field properties should be updated to match the graphic below:

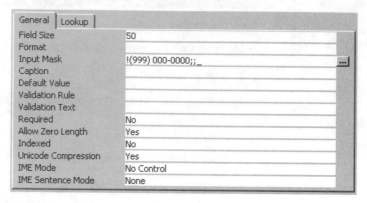

10. Select the Fax Number field.

11. Follow steps 3–9 to set the same input mask for the Fax Number field. Click the Yes button when prompted to save the table.

12. Click the View button on Table Design toolbar.

13. Click Yes when prompted to save the changes.

14. Click the Phone Number field. Notice that the parentheses and dash appear automatically.

15. Close tblCustomers. Leave the database open for the next exercise.

Creating Lookup Fields for Easy Entry

There are times when a field will use a specific set of entries. For example, there are only 50 possible entries in a State field, two in a Gender field, and a short list in a Credit Card field. When you can predict a field's range of entries, or want to force users to choose from a list, you want a Lookup field. A Lookup field promotes consistency and minimizes typing errors—and users like them, too!

Microsoft
Exam
Objective

Create Lookup fields

The Data Type drop-down list contains the Lookup Wizard option. When you choose Lookup Wizard, the wizard guides you through the process of creating the lookup list. In Exercise 27.6, you will define a lookup list for the City field in the tblCustomers table.

EXERCISE 27.6

Creating a Lookup Field

1. Open tblCustomers in Design view.

2. Select the City field.

3. In the Data Type column of the City field, choose Lookup Wizard.

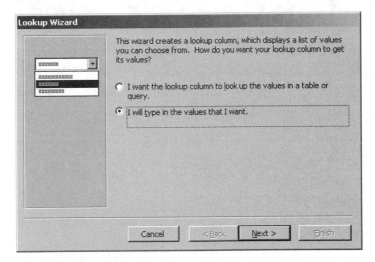

4. In the first step of the wizard, choose the I Will Type In The Values That I Want option. Click Next.

EXERCISE 27.6 *(continued)*

5. In the second step of the wizard, enter the list of values for the lookup: Leave the Number Of Columns setting at 1, and enter the following values in Col1, pressing Tab after each value to move to the next: **Monterey, Carmelle, Big Sur, Watsonville**.

6. Click the Next button to move to the last step of the wizard.

7. Click Finish to accept the default label (City) and close the wizard.

8. Click the View button on the Table Design toolbar.

9. Save the changes to the table when prompted.

10. Click the City field. Click the drop-down arrow to display the lookup list.

11. Close the table.

Modifying Other Field Properties

The Input Mask property is only one of many field properties. Field properties vary based on the field's data type. All properties appear in the Field Properties pane at the bottom of the window when the field is selected in Table Design view.

Microsoft ✓ *Exam Objective*	**Modify field properties**

In Exercise 27.7, you will modify several field properties.

EXERCISE 27.7

Modifying the Field Properties

1. In the Book Store database window, double-click Create Table In Design View.

2. Define the following fields:

   Field Name: **ID**
   Data Type: **AutoNumber**
   Description: **The ID field will automatically be generated. Press Tab to move to the next field.**
   Field Name: **Book Title**
   Data Type: **Text**
   Description: **Enter the Book Title**
   Field Name: **Author**
   Data Type: **Text**
   Description: **Enter the Author of the Book**
   Field Name: **Category**
   Data Type: **Text**
   Description: **Enter the Book's Category**
   Field Name: **Num Pages**
   Data Type: **Number**
   Description: **Enter the number of pages in the book**

3. Set the ID field as the primary key.

4. Save the table as **tblBooks**.

5. Select the Book Title field and set the Field Size property to **75** to allow users to enter a title up to 75 characters in length.

6. Select the Num Pages field and set the Format field property to **Fixed**.

7. Select the Num Pages field and set the Decimal Places field property to **0** (zero). Setting the Format as Fixed and Decimal Places at 0 forces users to enter whole numbers for this field.

8. Save and close the tblBooks table.

Creating and Modifying Queries

Queries help you find specific information from one or more tables. As with tables, you can create queries using a wizard or in Design view. To add criteria to a query, you modify the query in Design view. Figure 27.2 shows the query window in Design view.

FIGURE 27.2 Query in Design view

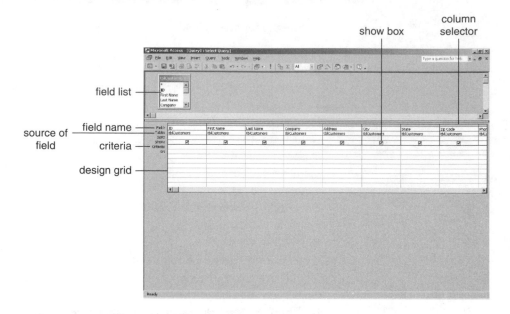

Microsoft ✓ Exam Objective

Create and modify Select queries

Creating a Select Query

Select queries, so named because they select information from one or more tables, let you display all the records and fields in a table, limit the fields and records that are displayed, or display data from multiple related tables. In Exercise 27.8, you will create a Select query based on the tblCustomers table.

EXERCISE 27.8

Creating a Select Query

1. Click the Queries icon on the Objects bar in the Book Store database.

2. Double-click the Create Query In Design View option in the details pane.

The Show Table dialog box is automatically displayed so you can add a table to the query.

EXERCISE 27.8 *(continued)*

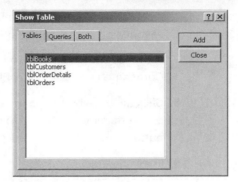

3. Select the tblCustomers table and click the Add button.

4. Click the Close button to close the Show Table dialog box.

The field list for the tblCustomers table is added to the query design.

5. Select the ID field in the field list and drag it into the first blank column of the design grid.

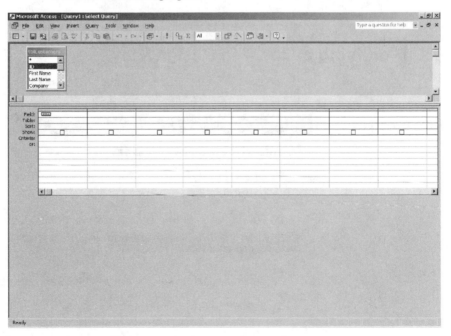

EXERCISE 27.8 *(continued)*

6. Double-click the First Name field in the field list to add it to the second column of the design grid.

7. Add the following fields to the design grid using either method: Company Name, Zip Code, Phone Number, Web Page, and E-Mail.

8. Click the Save button on the Query Design toolbar. Type the name **qryContactInformation** in the Save As dialog box and click the OK button.

9. Leave the query open for the next exercise.

Criteria are frequently used to restrict the records returned in a query. They are used to minimize the number of records in the current view so you can locate specific information. The operators available when setting your criteria are <, >, =, <>, <=, >=, And, Or, Not, Is Null, Is Not Null, Like, and Between.

Modifying a Query in Design View

In Exercise 27.9, you will modify the query created in the previous exercise.

EXERCISE 27.9

Modifying a Query in Design View

1. Open the qryContact Information query in Design view if it is not open.

2. Point to the column selector above the Zip Code field. The pointer changes to a downward-pointing black arrow. Click to select the column.

3. Press the Delete key to remove the Zip Code field.

4. Select the E-Mail column.

5. Click the column selector for the E-Mail column and drag the field to the left of the Web Page field.

6. Click the Criteria row of the Last Name field.

7. Type **> M** and press Enter.

Access 2002 automatically wraps quotation marks around the text.

8. Switch to Datasheet view. The query results set should include only records where the Last Name begins with *M* or a letter later in the alphabet.

9. Save and close the query. Close the Book Store database.

Adding Calculated Fields to Select Queries

Calculated fields perform calculations based on the data in one or more query fields. You can include the calculated fields in forms or reports that have been based on the query.

Microsoft ✓ ***Exam Objective***

Add calculated fields to Select queries

A calculated field begins with the field name followed by a colon. The colon indicates to Access that the text preceding the colon is a field name for the calculated field. Fields used within the calculation are enclosed in square brackets. Calculations can include typical mathematical operators like addition (+), subtraction (−), multiplication (*), and division (/), as well as functions. For example, if you want to determine the sales price of a product that is 150 percent higher than the value in the record's Purchase Price field, you would multiple the purchase price by 150%: Sales Price: [Purchase Price]*1.5

In Exercise 27.10, you will create a calculated field to determine the updated price of the items being sold.

EXERCISE 27.10

Creating Calculated Fields

1. Open the Northwind sample database. Close any open forms, including the switchboard, and maximize the database window.

2. Click the Queries icon in the Objects bar.

3. Create a new query in Design view.

4. Add the Products table.

5. Add the Product Name and Unit Price fields to the design grid.

6. Click in the blank Field cell to the right of the Unit Price column.

You will create a calculated field named New Price to calculate a price increase of 15 percent for each product. To accomplish this, the calculated field should multiply the Unit Price by 15% and add the original Unit Price to the field.

7. Type the following in the Field box: **New Price:[UnitPrice]*0.15+ [UnitPrice]**

8. Click the View button on the toolbar. Notice that the New Price field is not formatted as Currency.

9. Switch back to Design view.

10. Click the New Price field column heading to select the field.

11. Click the Properties button on the Query Design toolbar, or right-click the New Price field column selector and choose Properties from the shortcut menu to open the Properties dialog box for the field.

12. In the Format property, select Currency.

13. Close the Properties sheet and switch to Datasheet view. You should see the New Price field with the updated price for the products formatted as currency.

14. Save the query as **qrySuggestedPriceIncrease**.

15. Close the query and the Northwind database.

Summary

In this chapter, you learned the how to build tables and queries. Specifically, we addressed the following skills:

- Creating tables in Design view by adding fields to a table, assigning data types, and entering field descriptions

- Rearranging field order and deleting fields from a table; assigning a primary key to a table

- Adding a Lookup field to a table

- Setting field properties, including input masks

- Creating and modifying Select queries, including using criteria and calculated fields in queries

Organizing Access Data

MOUS ACCESS 2002 CORE EXAM OBJECTIVES COVERED IN THIS CHAPTER:

- ✓ Create and display forms
- ✓ Modify form properties
- ✓ Enter, edit, and delete records
- ✓ Create queries
- ✓ Sort records
- ✓ Filter records

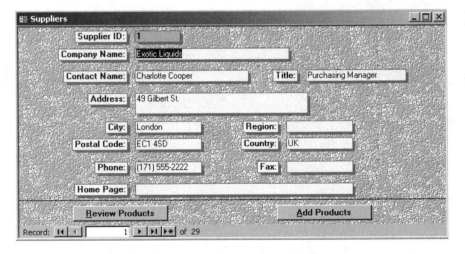

You can enter and edit data directly in tables or in queries, but most databases have forms for these purposes. Forms simplify data entry because a form can display all the data in a table in the order and arrangement that's convenient for users. Forms can include data from one table or related tables. Figure 28.1 shows a form from the `Northwind` database used in previous chapters.

FIGURE 28.1 Forms provide an interface for users to enter, view, and edit data.

Creating and Modifying Forms

As with other database objects, there is more than one way to create a form. You can create a form from scratch in Design view, but with the exception of forms such as dialog boxes that aren't linked to database data automatically, almost all forms are initially created as AutoForms or with the Form Wizard and then modified if necessary in Design view.

Creating Forms for Painless Data Entry

AutoForms are forms created using all the fields, in order, from a single table or query. The Form Wizard guides you through the form-creation process by asking some simple questions to determine the contents and appearance of your form. Use the Form Wizard when you want to choose specific fields from one or more tables or use fields in an order other than the table order.

Microsoft ✓ *Exam* *Objective*	**Create and display forms**

In Exercise 28.1, you will create forms using the Form Wizard and AutoForms.

EXERCISE 28.1

Creating Forms

1. Open the Northwind.mdb database by selecting Help ➢ Sample Databases ➢ Northwind Sample Database. Click OK to close the initial "splash screen" form that opens.

2. Close the Switchboard to view the main database window.

3. Click the Tables icon in the Object bar. Select the Categories table.

4. On the Database toolbar, click the down arrow on the New Object button and choose Form from the list to open the New Form dialog box.

5. Choose AutoForm: Columnar and then click OK to create the columnar AutoForm for the Categories table.

6. Save the form as **frmCategories**. Close the form.

7. In the Database window, click the Forms icon in the Object bar.

EXERCISE 28.1 *(continued)*

8. Double-click the Create Form By Using Wizard option in the details pane to open the Form Wizard.

9. In the first step of the wizard, choose Table: Products from the Tables/Queries drop-down list.

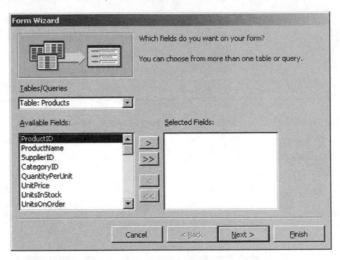

10. Click the Select All (>>) button to move all available fields to the Selected Fields list. Click the Next button.

11. In the second step of the wizard, choose a layout for the form. Accept the default style, Columnar, and click Next.

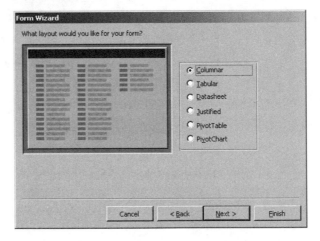

12. In the next step of the wizard, select a style for the form: Expedition. Click the Next button.

13. In the final step of the wizard, enter a form name: **frmProducts**. Click the Finish button.

14. Close the frmProducts form and return to the main database window. Leave the database open.

Modifying Form Properties

The form's properties determine how the form will open and function. You modify form design in (you guessed it!) Design view. A form is shown in Design view in Figure 28.2.

FIGURE 28.2 Design view of a form

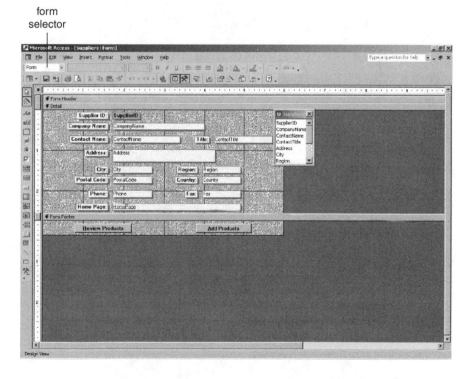

To view a form's properties, you must first select the form. Click the form selector button in the upper-left corner of the form, and then either right-click the form selector button and choose Properties from the shortcut menu or click the Properties button on the Form Design toolbar to open the Properties sheet for the form. Figure 28.3 shows some of the properties for a form.

FIGURE 28.3 Form Properties sheet

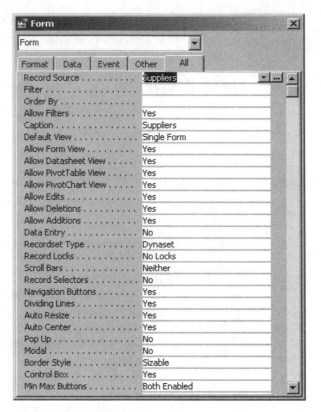

Microsoft ✔ **Exam** **Objective**

Modify form properties

In Exercise 28.2, you will modify some properties of the frmProducts form created in Exercise 28.1.

EXERCISE 28.2

Modifying Form Properties

1. Open the frmProducts form in Design view.

2. Click the form selector button to select the form.

3. Click the Properties button on the Form Design toolbar to open the Properties sheet for the form.

4. On the All tab, scroll to locate the Data Entry property.

5. Click the drop-down arrow for the Data Entry property and select Yes from the list to modify the form so it will appear as a blank form.

6. Click the Allow Deletions field and type **No**.

7. Close the Properties sheet.

8. Click the View button (or choose View ➢ Form View from the menu) to switch to Form view and observe the changes. Notice that with the Data Entry property set to Yes, the form does not contain any records.

9. Press the Tab key and type **Sample Product Name** in the Product Name field. Notice that the New Record button is available, but the Delete Record button is grayed out on the Form View toolbar because deletions are not allowed.

10. Press the Esc key twice to clear the record you entered.

11. Choose View ➢ Design View from the menu to switch to Design view. Set the Data Entry property back to No and the Allow Deletions property to Yes. Save the form changes, close the Properties sheet, and then close the form.

Viewing and Organizing Information

With tables and forms in place, it's time to enter and, inevitably, edit database data. After your initial data has been correctly entered, you can begin the work for which the database was designed: retrieving data using different filter criteria and sort orders.

Working with Database Records

In this section of the chapter, you'll learn how to enter and retrieve data.

Microsoft ✓ *Exam* *Objective*	**Enter, edit, and delete records**

In Exercise 28.3, you will enter and edit new records using a form and delete a record.

EXERCISE 28.3

Entering, Editing, and Deleting Records

1. Open the frmProducts form in Form view.

2. Choose Records ➢ New Record from the menu to enter a new record. If necessary, tab to the Product Name field. Type **Mozzarella di Giovanni**. Press Tab to move to the Supplier field.

3. Select Formaggi Fortini s.r.l. from the Supplier drop-down list.

4. Select Dairy Products from the Category drop-down list.

5. Type **10 – 500 g pkgs.** in the Quantity Per Unit field.

6. Type **21.5** in the Unit Price field.

7. Type **26** in the Units In Stock field. Your completed record should look like the following graphic.

8. Close the frmProducts form. The new record is automatically saved when you navigate to a new record, click the Save button, or close the form.

9. Open frmProducts again.

10. Navigate to record number 78 by entering the number **78** in the Specific Record box in the navigation buttons.

11. With record number 78 displayed, press the Delete Record button on the toolbar. When prompted, confirm the deletion.

12. Click the First Record navigation button to move to the first record within the database, Chai.

When you tab to a field, the field's contents are selected.

13. Tab to the Reorder Level field and enter **40**.

14. Update the Units On Order to 10 by selecting the text in the Units On Order field and typing **10**.

15. Close frmProducts. Leave the database open for the next exercise.

Creating Queries

The next two exam objectives use both tables and queries. If you're not familiar with creating and modifying queries, you should review the information in Chapter 27 and then return to the material in this chapter.

Microsoft ✓ *Exam* *Objective*	Create queries

Sorting and Filtering Records

If the primary objects in a database are the data tables, the primary functionality in a database is sorting and filtering that data. Sorting records places them in ascending (alphabetical) or descending order (reverse alphabetical) based on the values in one or more fields. Filtering returns records that meet a particular criterion.

Microsoft ✓ *Exam* *Objective*	Sort records

To sort your data, click any entry in the field you would like to sort by and click the Sort Ascending or Sort Descending button on the toolbar. The table or query display will be sorted. If you close the table or query without saving the changes, the sort order will be discarded. To save the sort order, you must save the table or query.

In Exercise 28.4, you will sort table records using several techniques.

EXERCISE 28.4

Sorting Records in Tables and Queries

1. With the Northwind database open, open the Products table in Datasheet view.

2. Select the Product Name column.

3. Click the Sort Ascending button on the Table Datasheet toolbar to sort the database by product name in alphabetical order.

4. Select the Units In Stock column.

5. Choose Records ➤ Sort ➤ Sort Descending from the menu to sort the database by Units In Stock.

EXERCISE 28.4 *(continued)*

6. Right-click the Units In Stock column and choose Sort Ascending from the shortcut menu.

7. Close the table without saving changes.

Filtering quickly displays specific records within the table or query. The filter is temporary, but a query that includes filter criteria can be saved for later use. There are two methods to apply a filter using the toolbar: Filter By Selection and Filter By Form. Figure 28.4 shows the Filter buttons available in the table and query Datasheet views as well as the Form view for forms.

FIGURE 28.4 Filter buttons

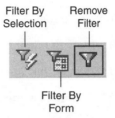

To use the Filter By Selection button, first select an entry you want to use as a filter to set it as your criterion. When you Filter by Form, Access opens a criteria grid so you can enter one or more criteria, as shown in Figure 28.5. With the criteria in place, you apply the filter.

FIGURE 28.5 Filtering by form

Product ID	Product Name	Supplier	Category	Quantity Per Unit	Unit Price	Units In Stock

Microsoft
Exam
Objective   **Filter records**

In Exercise 28.5, you will filter tables and queries by selection and by form.

EXERCISE 28.5

Filtering Tables and Queries

1. Open the Products table in Datasheet view.

2. Click in the Category field (Beverages) of record 1.

3. Click the Filter By Selection button on the Table Datasheet toolbar to show only the records in the Beverages category.

4. Click the Remove Filter button on the Table Datasheet toolbar to show all records.

5. Click the Filter By Form button on the Table Datasheet toolbar.

6. If the criterion Beverages is displayed in the Category field, delete the text.

7. Enable the check box in the Discontinued field.

8. Apply the filter to show the discontinued products.

9. Remove the filter by clicking the Remove Filter button on the toolbar.

10. To view only the records where the Unit Price is greater than 25, type **> 25** in the criteria for Unit Price.

11. Apply the filter.

12. Close the table without saving changes. Close the database.

Summary

In this chapter, you learned to organize Access data. We covered the following topics:

- Creating forms using AutoForms and the Form Wizard
- Changing form properties
- Entering and editing table data
- Sorting and filtering data

Chapter

29

Defining Relationships

MOUS ACCESS 2002 CORE EXAM OBJECTIVES COVERED IN THIS CHAPTER:

- ✓ Create one-to-many relationships
- ✓ Enforce referential integrity

The difference between an Access database and an Excel list is Access' support for relationships: links between records in separate tables. In this chapter, you'll learn to create the most common type of relationship, a one-to-many relationship, and use referential integrity settings to specify the nature of the relationship between tables.

Before you begin this chapter, you should go to the Sybex website and download the file 4113Ch29.zip. This package contains the file necessary to complete some of the exercises in this chapter.

Creating Relationships

When two tables are related, one or more records in one table are logically linked to one or more records in the related table. For example, in the Northwind database used in previous chapters, customers place orders, so records in the Customers table are related to records in the Orders table. There are three types of relationships: one-to-one, one-to-many, and many-to-many. We'll use two abstract tables, named Table A and Table B, to describe the three types of relationships.

In a one-to-one relationship, one record in Table A is related to no more than one record in Table B, and vice versa: Table B is really an extension of Table A. Most databases have no tables with one-to-one relationships because it's easier to include all the fields in one table.

In a one-to-many relationship, one record in Table A may be related to many records in Table B, but each record in Table B is related to only one record in Table A. For example, one customer may place many orders, but each order is placed by only one customer. To relate the two tables, the primary key field for

Table A is included as a field (called a foreign key) in Table B, and a relationship is created between the two fields.

In a many-to-many relationship, one record in Table A may be related to many records in Table B, and vice versa. For example, one employee may enter orders placed by many customers, and one customer may place orders through many different employees. In Access, you can't create many-to-many relationships directly. You must create a *linking table* (in this example, an orders table) that includes the primary key fields from both tables and create two one-to-many relationships: employees to orders and customers to orders.

Microsoft ✓ *Exam* *Objective*	**Create one-to-many relationships**

With very few exceptions, the relationships you'll create will be one-to-many relationships: one such relationship for two tables with a one-to-many relationship, and two one-to-many relationships for two tables with a many-to-many relationship. In Exercise 29.1, you'll create one-to-many relationships between tables in the 29-1.mdb database. The database contains four tables: tblCourses, tblRegistrations, tblTrainees, and tblTrainers. Here are the relationships required for this database:

- Trainers are assigned to teach multiple courses and each course is taught by only one trainer, so there is a one-to-many relationship between tblTrainers and tblCourses.

- Trainees can register for multiple courses, and a course can have multiple trainees. The tblRegistrations table is a linking table between tblTrainees and tblCourses, so there is a one-to-many relationship between tblTrainees and tblRegistrations and another one-to-many relationship between tblCourses and tblRegistrations.

EXERCISE 29.1

Setting One-to-Many Relationships

For the exercises in this chapter, use the 29-1.mdb database downloaded from the Sybex website.

1. Open the 29-1.mdb database.

2. Choose Tools ➢ Relationships from the menu or click the Relationships button on the Database toolbar to open the Relationships window. The Show Table dialog box is automatically displayed:

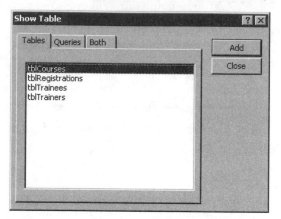

3. Select the first table, and then hold Shift and select the last table. Click Add to add all four tables to the Relationships window, and then close the Show Table dialog box.

4. Use drag and drop to arrange the four tables in this order from left to right: tblTrainers, tblCourses, tblRegistrations, and tblTrainees. Drag the table title bar to move the table.

5. Drag the borders of each table so each table's entire field list is visible:

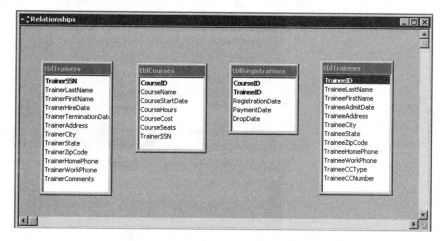

6. To create the one-to-many relationship between tblTrainers and tb!Courses, select the TrainerSSN field in tblTrainers (the primary or "one" table). Drag and drop it on the TrainerSSN field in tblCourses (the related or "many" table). The Edit Relationship dialog box opens automatically:

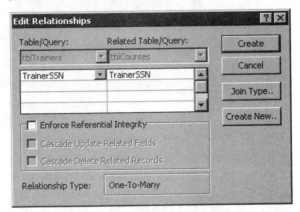

7. Verify that the TrainerSSN field is selected for each table, that tblTrainers is displayed in the first column and tblCourses in the second column, and that the relationship type listed in the dialog box is One-To-Many. Click Create to create the relationship.

When you create a one-to-many relationship, you drag a primary key field and drop it on a field that is either not a primary key or is one field in a multifield primary key (a composite key). If the relationship type is listed as Indeterminate, either the primary keys are set incorrectly in the tables you're relating or you dragged the wrong fields.

8. To create the one-to-many relationship between tblCourses and tblRegistrations, drag the CourseID field from tblCourses and drop it on CourseID in tblRegistrations. Click Create to create the relationship and close the Edit Relationship dialog box.

9. To create the one-to-many relationship between tblTrainees and tblRegistrations, drag the TraineeID field from tblTrainees and drop it on TraineeID in tblRegistrations. Click Create to create the relationship and close the Edit Relationship dialog box.

10. Click Save to save the layout in the Relationships window. Close the Relationships window. Leave the database open for the next exercise.

The Relationships window with all one-to-many relationships created is shown in Figure 29.1.

FIGURE 29.1   The 29-1.mdb database relationships

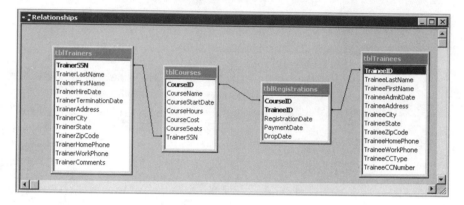

Setting Referential Integrity

Referential integrity settings ensure the validity of relationships between records in related tables. You set referential integrity for each relationship, so your database can include relationships where referential integrity is enabled while it is not enabled in other relationships.

Microsoft *Exam* *Objective*	**Enforce referential integrity**

When you turn on referential integrity, Access enforces rules in the related tables. For the examples below, assume that you have enforced referential integrity in the relationship between tblTrainers and tblCourses in the 29-1.mdb database:

- You can't enter a value in the related table's foreign key field unless the value already exists in the primary key field of the primary table. In the 29-1 database you can't assign a trainer to a course unless the trainer's social security number already appears in tblTrainers.

- You can't delete a trainer from tblTrainers if they've been assigned to a course in tblCourses.

- You can't change a trainer's social security number in tblTrainers if the trainer is assigned to a course in tblCourses.

You can set exceptions to the second and third rules by enabling cascade deletes and cascade updates. With cascade deletes enabled, if you delete a trainer from tblTrainers, all the courses they were assigned to in tblCourses are also deleted. (Clearly not a good idea in this case.) With cascade updates enabled, if you change the trainer's social security number in tblTrainers, Access will update the trainer's social security number everywhere it appears in tblCourses. (This might be a good idea; otherwise, you won't be able to edit a social security number after a trainer has been assigned to courses.)

In Exercise 29.2, you'll set referential integrity, including cascade update and delete settings.

EXERCISE 29.2

Setting Referential Integrity

For this exercise use the 29-1.mdb database used in the previous exercise.

1. Choose Tools ➢ Relationships to open the Relationships window.

2. Select the relationship line between tblTrainers and tblCourses.

3. Double-click the line to open the Edit Relationship dialog box.

4. Enable the Enforce Referential Integrity check box. This will prevent users from entering a trainer social security number in tblCourses that does not exist in tblTrainers.

5. Enable the Cascade Update Related Fields check box so changes in the trainer's social security number in tblTrainers result in updates to the related records in tblCourses.

6. Do not enable the Cascade Delete Related Records check box. This means you will not be able to delete a trainer who has been assigned to at least one course unless you first delete the course.

7. Click OK to enforce referential integrity.

Two symbols are added to the relationship line. The 1 near the primary table and the google (infinity symbol) near the related table indicate that referential integrity is enforced in the one-to-many relationship.

8. Double-click the relationship line between tblCourses and tblRegistrations.

9. Enable the Enforce Referential Integrity check box. This will prevent users from creating registrations for nonexistent courses.

10. Enable the Cascade Update Related Fields check box so changes in the CourseID in tblCourses result in updates to the related records in tblRegistrations.

11. Enable the Cascade Delete Related Records check box. If a course is deleted from tblCourses, the corresponding registrations will be deleted from tblRegistrations.

12. Click OK to enforce referential integrity.

13. Double-click the relationship line between tblTrainees and tblRegistrations.

14. Enable the Enforce Referential Integrity check box. This will prevent users from creating registrations for nonexistent trainees.

15. In the primary table, tblTrainees, TraineeID is an AutoNumber field that cannot be changed, so there is no reason to enable the Cascade Update Related Fields check box.

16. Do not enable the Cascade Delete Related Records check box. We do not want to delete trainees if they have ever registered for a course.

17. Click OK to enforce referential integrity.

18. Close the Relationships window. Save changes if prompted to do so.

19. Close the database.

Summary

In this chapter, we focused on defining relationships. You learned the following skills:

- Creating one-to-many relationships
- Setting referential integrity

Chapter

30

Reporting and Exchanging Data

MOUS ACCESS 2002 CORE EXAM OBJECTIVES COVERED IN THIS CHAPTER:

- ✓ Create and format reports
- ✓ Add calculated controls to reports
- ✓ Preview and print reports
- ✓ Import data to Access
- ✓ Export data from Access
- ✓ Create a simple data access page

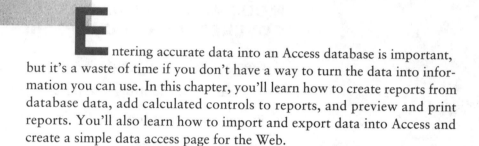

Entering accurate data into an Access database is important, but it's a waste of time if you don't have a way to turn the data into information you can use. In this chapter, you'll learn how to create reports from database data, add calculated controls to reports, and preview and print reports. You'll also learn how to import and export data into Access and create a simple data access page for the Web.

NOTE Before you begin this chapter, you should go to the Sybex website and download the file 4113Ch30.zip. This package contains the files necessary to complete some of the exercises in this chapter.

Producing Reports

A report pulls together data from Access tables and displays it in useful ways. A report can present raw data as it appears in database tables or it can aggregate, group, and calculate data to turn the data into information—information that can be used to identify trends, see results, and make decisions. In this section, you'll learn to create and format reports and add calculated controls to reports.

Creating and Formatting Reports

Access provides six ways to create a report:

- **Design view** gives you total flexibility in designing a report. You control which data to include and how you want it laid out and formatted.

- **Report Wizard** designs a report for you but still gives you choices about which tables and fields to include, how you want the report grouped and sorted, and which layout and style you want to use.

- **AutoReport: Columnar** displays every field of each record in a column down the page. An AutoReport can be based only on a single table or query, and you cannot select which records or fields to include in the report—it displays them all.

- **AutoReport: Tabular** displays each record in a table format with fields displayed in columns across the page.

- **Chart Wizard** creates graphical charts of numerical data.

- **Label Wizard** creates mailing labels for name and address data.

Unless you want to create charts or labels, the Report Wizard is the easiest and fastest way to create an Access report. If the wizard doesn't produce a report that looks just the way you want it to, you can then switch to Design view and format the report and report objects to meet your needs.

Microsoft
Exam
Objective

Create and format reports

Creating Reports Using the Report Wizard

In Exercise 30.1, you'll create a report using the Report Wizard. For this exercise and the rest of the exercises in this chapter, you should open the sample Northwind Traders database that comes with Access 2002. You can find this database by launching Access and choosing Help ➢ Sample Databases ➢ Northwind Sample Database. This is a fully functioning database that contains populated tables, forms, queries, and reports, in addition to data access pages, macros, and modules. To access the database window, click OK to open the Northwind Traders splash screen and click the Display Database Window button on the Northwind switchboard that appears. Before you display the database window, however, you may want to explore the database by clicking the buttons on the switchboard to view product and order information. You can return to this switchboard after closing it by choosing Main Switchboard from the Forms tab of the database window.

Creating a Report Using the Report Wizard

1. Select Reports from the Objects list in the database window of the Northwind Traders sample database (see "Creating Reports Using the Report Wizard" earlier in the chapter if you have not yet opened this database).

2. Click the New button on the database window to see the list of New Report options.

3. Choose Report Wizard and select Customers from the Choose The Table Or Query Where The Object's Data Comes From drop-down list. Click OK.

4. Select CompanyName from the list of Available Fields and click the Select button (right arrow) to add the field to the list of selected fields.

5. Select the Orders table from the Tables/Queries drop-down list. Select the OrderDate field and click the Select button to add it to the Selected Fields list.

6. Select the Products table from the Tables/Queries drop-down list. Select ProductName from the list and add it to the Selected Fields list.

7. Select the Order Details table (scroll up the list to find this table) and click the Select All button (double right arrow) to add all of the fields to the Selected Fields list.

8. Select OrderID from the Selected Fields list and click the left arrow to remove the field from the report. Use the same procedure to remove ProductID from the Selected Fields list.

9. Click Next to move to the second step of the wizard.

Access assumes you want to view your data by Customer and then by OrderDate. You could choose to produce a report that focused on Orders, Order Details, or Products instead. Each of these reports provides different information to its readers by changing how the same data is organized.

10. Click Next to move to the third step of the wizard. Here you could add additional grouping levels if you wanted to. For now, click Next.

11. Select ProductName from the first drop-down list to sort the data in each group by the ProductName field. Ascending order is the default, but you could click Ascending to toggle to Descending order. If you wanted, you could choose additional fields to sort by.

Note: Notice that the CompanyName and OrderDate fields are not available in the Sort drop-down list. Records are automatically sorted by the fields upon which they are grouped.

12. Click Next to move to the next step of the wizard.

13. Choose a layout for the report from the six choices. Click each one to see a preview of the layout. For this exercise, choose Stepped.

14. Select Landscape to choose the page orientation. Generally, you'll want to choose Landscape if you have more than five or six fields so you can fit as many on the page as possible.

Access automatically truncates field labels and data so they fit on one page width. Clear the Adjust the Field Width So All Fields Fit On A Page check box if you do not want Access to truncate fields. Leave this check box selected for now.

15. Click Next to move to the next step of the wizard.

16. Choose a style from the six available styles—click each one to see a preview. Choose Corporate for this exercise.

17. Click Next to move to the final step of the wizard.

18. Enter **Customer Orders** in the Title text box, and click Finish to create the report.

Note: The title you enter here is used as the database object name and also appears as the title in the report header. If your company uses a naming convention for database objects, you can apply the naming convention to the name you enter in the Title box (for example, rpt??) and then change the header in the report, or you can give it the name you want to appear in the report and then rename the report in the database window (right-click the report and choose Rename).

Access creates the report and displays it in Print Preview. See "Previewing and Printing Reports" later in this chapter for more about preparing a report for printing.

19. Click the Close button on the report window to close the report.

Note: If you click the button with the text label Close on the Print Preview window, Access switches you to the Design view of the report. Click the Close button in the top-right corner of the report window to actually close the report and return to the database window.

Formatting Reports and Report Objects in Design View

Whether or not you use the wizard to create a report, you always have the option to change the formatting of the report and of individual objects in the report. In Exercise 30.2, you format the report you created in the previous exercise by opening the report in Design view. Design view can be a bit overwhelming when you see it for the first time—there is a lot going on. In addition to the report window itself, the Toolbox toolbar may appear on the screen. The Toolbox toolbar contains a number of tools you can use to format and add controls to reports. You may also see the list of available fields from the tables in the report in case you want to add fields to the report that you didn't choose when you went through the wizard. Don't worry if neither of these objects appears on the screen or if they are there and you want to get them out of the way; you can open and close them as you need to. If they are open, click their Close button, and if you want to reopen them, click the corresponding button on the Report Design toolbar.

The objects that appear in the report are either text boxes or labels. Text boxes are placeholders for data fields, variables, or calculated fields. You cannot change what appears in a text box while in Design view or Access won't know where to find the data it represents. Labels, on the other hand, are not dependent on external data and so can be edited freely. Therefore, it is important to know the difference before you make changes to a report in Design view. You can find out if a control is a text box or a label by opening its properties sheet

EXERCISE 30.2

Formatting Report and Report Objects

1. On the Reports page of the database window, select the report you created in Exercise 30.1, Customer Orders, and click the Design button on the database window toolbar.

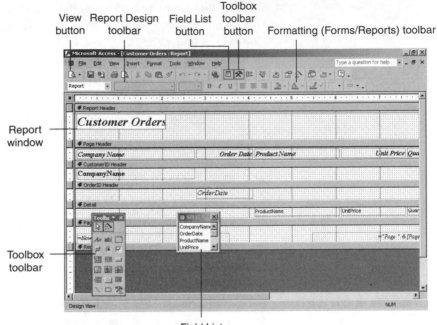

2. Close both the Toolbox toolbar and the Field List by clicking their close buttons, if necessary. Maximize the report window if it is not maximized.

As you are working on the report's design, you can switch back and forth between Design view and Print Preview by clicking the View button on the Report Design toolbar.

3. Click the View button to see the report in Print Preview and click it again to switch back to Design view.

A report typically consists of several sections. In this case, the Customer Orders report has a Report Header, which appears only on the first page of the report, and a Page Header and Page Footer, which appear on every page. The Report Footer section is visible but it is empty at the present time. The data from the selected fields appears in the CustomerID Header, the OrderID Header, and the Detail sections. Even though you chose CustomerName and OrderDate when you selected fields in the wizard, Access creates group headers based on the key fields in each of the corresponding tables.

EXERCISE 30.2 *(continued)*

4. Double-click Company Name in the Page Header section. When the property sheet opens, look in the title bar to see Label: CompanyName_Label. This clearly defines this object as a label. You can edit the text in this label without creating any problems for the report.

5. Click inside the Company Name label in the Page Header section of the report and delete Name from the label.

6. Without closing the properties sheet, click CompanyName in the CustomerID header to see an example of a text box. Notice that the title bar of the Properties dialog box says Text Box: CompanyName. Also notice that below Name on the All tab of the CustomerName properties sheet, the Control Source also says CompanyName. The Control Source tells Access where the data that should appear in this field comes from, in this case, the CompanyName field. Only text boxes have control sources. If you edit the text in this control, for example, by putting a space between Company and Name, Access will look to the control source and not find any matching data. As a result, the report will be unable to display it.

7. Click the Close button on the properties sheet to close it.

8. To resize controls on a report, click the control and drag one of the black handles in the direction you want to resize. Click Company in the Page Header and then hold Shift and click CompanyName in the CustomerID Header to select both controls. Drag the right-center handle to the left to the 2" mark on the ruler. Release the mouse button to finish the resizing.

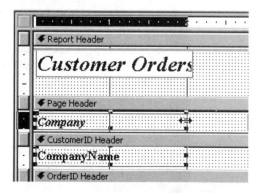

9. To move controls, select the control or controls you want to move and point to them. When the pointer changes to a full hand, drag in the direction you want to move. Select Order Date in the Page Header; hold down Shift, and select the remaining controls to the right of Order Date in the Page Header. Use the horizontal scroll bar to scroll to the controls you cannot see. While still holding Shift, select Order Date in the Order ID Header and then each of the controls in the Details section: ProductName, UnitPrice, Quantity, and Discount. Scroll back to the left and point to any one of the selected controls. With the full hand pointer, drag to the 1" mark on the ruler.

Note: If you accidentally move controls differently than you intend, click the Undo button on the Report Design toolbar.

10. Click the View button to see how the report has changed. Click View again to return to Design view.

11. Select all of the controls in the Page Header by moving the mouse pointer to the vertical ruler on the left of the report, and click when the pointer changes to a black right-pointing arrow. This selects all the controls in the path of the arrow.

12. Click the Font drop-down list on the Formatting toolbar and change the font to Arial.

With the font change, the text in the Quantity label is too large for the control. To fix this, you could change the font size or resize the control. But before you can resize the Quantity label, you first have to make room for it. Unit Price is larger than it needs to be, so that is a good place to gain the extra space you need. If you aren't sure, switch to Print Preview view and see for yourself.

13. Select the Unit Price label, hold Shift, and select the UnitPrice text box. Drag the right-center handle to the 5.5" mark on the ruler.

14. Select the Quantity label and the Quantity text box and drag the left-center handle to the left of the 5.5" mark on the ruler.

15. Click the View button to see the results of the changes, and then click View again to return to Design view.

16. Click the Save button on the Report Design toolbar to save the changes you made to the report.

17. Click the Close button to close the report and return to the database window.

In addition to the changes you made in the previous exercise, you can use any of the tools on the Formatting toolbar to change font size, font style, alignment, fill/back color, font color, line/border color, and line/border width. You can also add special effects such as Raised and Shadowed to objects. To prepare for the exam, practice with each of these options so you can easily change any formatting requested.

Adding Calculated Controls to Reports

A calculated control is used to calculate numbers in a database report. It contains an expression that includes a formula, such as =Sum([UnitPrice]). Rather than displaying the text of the expression in the report, Access adds the data in the UnitPrice field and displays the results. Expressions can be simple or complex and can include operations such as addition and subtraction and functions such as average and absolute value.

Microsoft ✔ *Exam Objective*	**Add calculated controls to reports**

Access helps you write calculated expressions through the use of the Expression Builder. You can build a formula by choosing from a variety of options, depending on what you want to calculate. Often, a calculated control appears in a section footer, so it clearly shows a summation based on the previous section. For example, a total of all the orders for a particular date may appear in the OrderDateID Footer or a particular customer may appear in the CustomerID Footer. A total of all orders may appear in the Report Footer. Before you can add controls to these sections, you must make them visible in the report. You can do this in the Sorting And Grouping properties sheet. In Exercise 30.3, you'll create a calculated control and then copy that control to other places on the report for different results.

EXERCISE 30.3

Adding Calculated Controls to Reports

1. Select the report you modified in Exercise 30.2, Customer Orders, on the Reports page of the database window, and click the Design button to open it in Design view.

2. Click the Sorting And Grouping button on the Report Design toolbar to open the Sorting And Grouping properties sheet.

3. To turn on the group footer for CustomerID, click CustomerID in the Field/Expression column and select Yes from the Group Footer drop-down list in the Group Properties section.

4. To turn on the group footer for OrderID, click OrderID in the Field/Expression column and select Yes from the Group Footer drop-down list in the Group Properties section.

5. Click the Close button to close the Sorting And Grouping properties sheet.

6. Click the Toolbox button on the Reports Design toolbar to open the Toolbox toolbar if it is not already visible.

7. Click the Text box button on the Toolbox toolbar.

Move the pointer to the OrderID Footer section and click in line with the UnitPrice text box in the Details section. This creates an Unbound text box and an associated label.

8. Reposition the Unbound text box so that it is lined up with the Unit-Price text box located in the Detail section. Because this is a numeric field, the text is right aligned, so it's best to align the right borders of the text boxes.

◆ Detail				
		ProductName	UnitPrice	Quantity
◆ OrderID Footer				
		Text24	Unbound	
◆ CustomerID Footer				

9. Double-click the Unbound text box to open the properties sheet for the new control.

10. In the Name property box, enter **UnitPriceTotal** as the name of the control.

11. Click the Control Source property box and click the Build button that appears to the right of the box. This launches the Expression Builder.

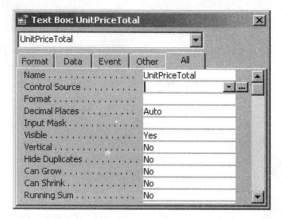

The Expression Builder displays the main categories of expression elements, i.e., database objects and functions, constants, operators, and common expressions, in the first column. Subcategories of expression elements appear in the second column. Expression elements based on the category and subcategory selected appear in the third column.

12. To create a sum expression using the SUM function, start by double-clicking the Functions folder in the first column to open it.

13. Click the Built-in Functions folder to access the built-in functions.

14. Scroll through the subcategories in the second column and click SQL Aggregate Functions. Although not an obvious choice, this is where you find the most commonly used functions such as SUM and AVG (Average).

15. Double-click Sum in the third column to add it to the expression you are building. It appears as Sum («expr») in the Expression Builder.

Note: («expr») is a placeholder that you replace with the field you want to Access to sum.

16. Click («expr») in the top pane of the Expression Builder to select it.

17. Scroll up the list of categories in the first column and click the Customer Orders folder at the top of the list. A list of all of the controls in the Customer Orders report appears in the second column.

18. Scroll down the second column and double-click UnitPrice when you find it. The expression is now complete.

Note: Be careful not to select UnitPrice_Label. Access would have a hard time adding up the labels.

19. Click OK to close the Expression Builder, and click the Close button to close the properties sheet.

20. Click the View button to see the newly calculated control.

As you can see in the report, a sum appears at the end of each order totaling the unit prices of each item in the order. However, the number is not formatted as currency and the label, Text#, is not very descriptive. You can fix both of these problems by returning to Design view.

21. Click the View button to switch back to Design view.

22. Double-click the Text24 label (the number of the label may be slightly different when you create the control) to open the properties sheet.

23. Enter **Order Total:** on the All tab in the Caption property box of the properties sheet. Press Enter.

24. With the control still selected, drag the left-center handle to make the control large enough to hold the new label.

25. Point to the handle in the top-left corner, and when the hand pointer changes to a hand with a pointing finger, drag the label closer to the UnitPriceTotal text box.

Note: If you attempt to move a text box or a label that appears in the same section of the report, you may find that they are connected—you can't move one without the other. By pointing to the top-left handle of the control you want to move, you can drag using the pointing finger and move only one of the two controls.

26. To change the format of the results to match the individual unit prices of currency format, double-click the UnitPriceTotal text box to open its properties sheet.

27. On the All tab or on the Format tab, select Currency from the Format Property drop-down list.

To create a total for each customer and a grand total for all orders, you can repeat steps 7–25 or you can simply copy the control to another section of the report. Access runs the expression based on the section in which the calculated control appears.

28. Right-click the UnitPriceTotal text box and choose Copy from the shortcut menu.

29. Click the CustomerID footer section. Right-click again and click Paste from the shortcut menu. Move the new controls into position in line with the other unit price controls.

30. Double-click the Order Total label in the CustomerID Footer section and change the Caption property on the All tab to **Customer Total:**. Press Enter.

31. To add a total for all orders, right-click the Report Footer section band and click Paste from the shortcut menu. Move the new controls into position in line with the other unit price controls.

32. Double-click the Order Total label in the Report Footer section and change the Caption property on the All tab to **Grand Total:**.

33. Click the Print Preview button to see the results of the changes you made.

34. Click the Close button to close the report and save the changes.

If you think about it for a minute, you'll realize that totaling unit prices, as we did in the last exercise, does not reflect the total cost of an order unless each customer purchased only one of each item they ordered and there were no discounted items. For the Customer Orders report to be really valuable, you need to calculate the unit price of each item times the quantity and subtract the discount amounts. The formula you might build in the Expression Builder for total cost of each item ordered is =[UnitPrice]*[Quantity]*(1-[Discount]). If you really want to become comfortable with formulas, give it a try. Insert a text box in the Detail section of the report and invoke the Expression Builder. That's why we moved the fields over in Exercise 30.2—so you'd have room to insert a TotalCost control to the right of Discount.

> In order to total the results of these calculations to get the total cost of an entire order, the total spent by a customer, and the grand total of sales, you would have to create the TotalCost expression in a query and then base the report on the query rather than the tables. Access can't calculate the results of another calculation in a report.

Previewing and Printing Reports

Print Preview is the default view for Access reports. Because you'll be switching back and forth between Design view and Print Preview pretty frequently to see the results of changes you make to reports, it's worthwhile to become very familiar with how to get around in Print Preview.

Microsoft
✓ *Exam*
Objective

Preview and print reports

In Exercise 30.4, you'll examine a report in Print Preview and then send it to the printer.

EXERCISE 30.4

Previewing and Printing a Report

1. Open the report you modified in Exercise 30.3, Customer Orders.

2. In Print Preview, the mouse pointer changes to a magnifying glass, and you can click anywhere in the report to increase the zoom to see the report more clearly. You can also adjust the zoom by clicking the drop-down arrow on the Zoom button and selecting a specific zoom percentage. The next time you click the report with the magnifying glass, the report will switch between Fit and the newly selected zoom percentage.

3. To view two pages side-by-side, click the Two Pages button. Click the Multiple Pages button and drag down and over to choose how many pages you would like to see at one time.

4. Click the navigation buttons at the bottom of the screen, near the horizontal scroll bar to move between specific pages. The single-arrow buttons move you forward one page or back one page at a time. The arrow and line buttons take you to the first page or the last page of the report. Move to the last page of the report to see the Grand Total you entered in Exercise 30.3. Use the Previous Page button to see to a Customer Total. Click the First Page button to take you back to the beginning of the report.

5. To adjust page margins, the page orientation, or the number of columns in a report, click the Setup button on the Print Preview toolbar. This opens the Page Setup dialog box, a trimmed down version of what you would find in Word and Excel. View each of the three tabs—Margins, Page, and Columns—to see the available options. Click OK to return to Print Preview.

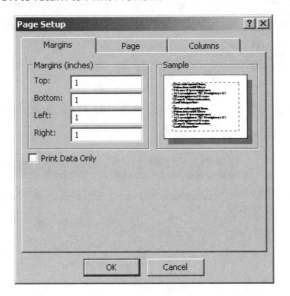

6. Rather than printing a report, you can use the OfficeLinks button to send it to Microsoft Word or Excel. Click the drop-down arrow on the OfficeLinks button to see the available options.

EXERCISE 30.4 *(continued)*

On the Print Preview toolbar, you can also find a button to return you to the database window and a New Object button to let you jump right into creating a new table, query, form, report, page, macro, module, or class module.

7. When you are satisfied with your report, click the Print button on the Print Preview toolbar to send the document directly to the default printer.

8. If you want to verify the print options before sending a lengthy report to the wrong printer, choose File ➤ Print to open the Print dialog box.

9. Select a printer from the Name drop-down list in the Print dialog box.

10. Select the print range by choosing All or entering the pages you want to print in the Pages text box.

11. Enter how many copies you want to print in the Number Of Copies text box. If you want the pages collated, i.e., 1,2,3 as opposed to 1,1, 2,2,3,3, select the Collate check box.

12. When you are ready to print, click the OK button to send the document to the printer. For this exercise, click Cancel—this report is quite long and you would waste a lot of paper printing it for no reason.

Now that you can create, format, and print reports, you are ready to turn your storehouses of raw data into a wealth of useable information. Add a few well-placed calculated controls, and you can garner vital answers that until now have remained hidden.

Integrating with Other Applications

If you have data in one place, you don't have to re-create it to use it in another. With the Access importing and exporting tools, you can move data between databases and even between applications. You can also share data with others through the use of data access pages and a web browser. In this section, we'll introduce you to the features used in getting data in and out of Access.

Importing Data from Other Applications

When you create a new database, it really pays to think about where the data you want already exhibits. If you can save yourself even an hour of creating and populating tables, it is worth it in the end.

**Microsoft
Exam
Objective**

Import data to Access

In Exercise 30.5, you'll import a table of U.S. states and their abbreviations. This is a handy table to have in any database where you want to create a lookup field so users can pick their state from a list rather than typing it.

EXERCISE 30.5

Importing Data to Access

1. Open the Northwind Traders database, if it is not already open (Help ➤ Sample Databases ➤ Northwind Sample Database). Click OK to close the splash screen and click the Display Database Window button on the switchboard.

2. Choose File ➤ Get External Data ➤ Import.

3. Click the Files Of Type drop-down list and choose Microsoft Excel (*.xls).

4. Navigate to the folder that contains the files you downloaded for this chapter.

5. Select States.xls and click Import. This launches the Import Spreadsheet Wizard. The purpose of the wizard is to analyze the data in the spreadsheet you want to import and resolve any questions about the data before it is imported into a table.

6. In the first step of the wizard, you can choose which data to import from the workbook by choosing the worksheet or named range. In this case, the first worksheet, States, is already selected. Click Next.

7. The first row contains column headings, so click to select that check box. The column headings are designated as the field names. Click Next.

8. In the third step of the wizard, select In A New Table as where you'd like to import the data. If you choose In An Existing Table, Access appends the data to an existing table. In order for Access to be able to successfully append the data, the field names and order of the fields must be identical. Click Next.

9. The next step of the wizard defines the type of data you are importing in each field. Change the name of the first field from Abbreviation to StateID by entering **StateID** in the Field Name text box. Choose Indexed (No Duplicates) from the Indexed drop-down list to add this field to the database's index for faster searching. No Duplicates assures that no one accidentally changes the StateID for Minnesota or Mississippi to MI.

10. To check the options for the State field, click State in the bottom portion of the wizard. Leave these options as they are and click Next.

Note: If you were importing data that contained a column of numbers or dates, you could assign a data type such as Date from the Data Type drop-down list.

11. In this step, you can choose if you want Access to assign an Auto-Number as the primary key, choose your own primary key, or assign no primary key. Select the option Choose My Own Primary Key. Because StateID is indexed with no duplicates, the wizard recommends this field, but you are able to choose another from the drop-down list. Click Next.

12. Enter a name for the new table. Enter **States Lookup** in the Import To Table text box.

If you were importing a large table with many fields, you would want to click the I Would Like A Wizard To Analyze My Table After Importing The Data check box. The Table Analyzer Wizard reviews the table and recommends how you might split the table into multiple related tables based on basic database normalization rules. If you agree, it also makes the tables and splits the data.

13. Click Finish to import the data.

EXERCISE 30.5 *(continued)*

14. Click OK to acknowledge that the data has been successfully imported.

15. From the list of tables in the database window, double-click to open States Lookup. Review the data to make sure it imported correctly (51 records with the District of Columbia). Click the View button and verify that StateID is set as the primary key. Close the table. The data is successfully imported.

If you would like to maintain a data table in another database or workbook but still have access to it in your database, you can import the data as a linked table. The only difference is that when you choose File ➢ Get External Data, you would choose Link Tables. If you are linking to an Excel worksheet, the Import Spreadsheet Wizard still starts but takes you through only the first two steps and the last step, selecting the correct data, assigning the first row as field names, and naming the table. The other options are inherent to the table in its primary source. While the imported table shows the standard Access table icon, the linked table shows a right-pointing arrow and the source of the table.

Exporting Data to Other Applications

If you want to use Access data in another database or use Excel tools to analyze it, you can also chose to export data from an Access table or query. You can, for example, export data to an Access database, a dBASE file, an Excel workbook, a Paradox file, or a simple text file.

Microsoft ✓ *Exam Objective*

Export data from Access

In Exercise 30.6, you'll export data from Access to an Excel workbook.

EXERCISE 30.6

Exporting Data from Access

1. Open the Northwind Traders database, if it is not already open (Help ➤ Sample Databases ➤ Northwind Sample Database). Click OK to close the splash screen and click the Display Database Window button on the switchboard.

2. Select Customers from the list of tables—you could also choose to export data from the list of queries.

3. Choose File ➤ Export.

4. Choose Microsoft Excel 97-2002 (*.xls) from the Save As Type drop-down list.

5. Navigate to the folder of files you downloaded at the start of the chapter.

6. Enter a filename in the File Name text box if you want to assign a different filename. Enter **Northwind Customers**.

7. Click Export to export the data.

8. To verify that the export was successful, launch Microsoft Excel and open `Northwind Customers.xls`. Close Excel when finished.

Exported data is not linked to the data in the database in any way. Any changes you make to the exported data are not changed in the Access database. This can be helpful if you want to work with the data and not risk injuring the primary data. However, it is also risky because you may forget about the primary data and make changes that you expect to see in future reports on the data and they will not be there. If you edit data in the Access database, be sure to re-export the data to have the current version available in the exported format.

Creating a Simple Data Access Page for the Web

Making data from an Access database available on the Web is another way to provide data to others who need to use it. A *data access page* is an HTML page that contains a direct link to the data in the database. Users can manipulate the data without impacting the primary data source. Figure 30.1 shows an example of data presented in a PivotTable format for data-analysis purposes.

FIGURE 30.1 This PivotTable data access page, viewed in Internet Explorer, is an example of the functionality you can incorporate into data access pages.

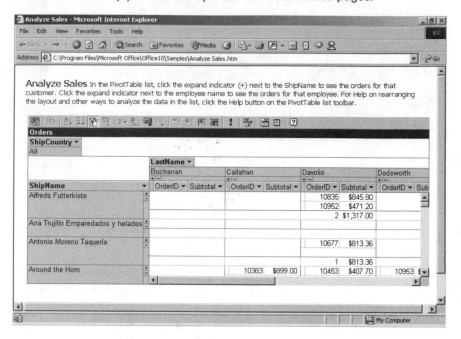

<table>
<thead>
<tr><th>Microsoft
✓ Exam
Objective</th><th>Create a simple data access page</th></tr>
</thead>
</table>

In Exercise 30.7, you'll create a data access page and view it in a browser.

EXERCISE 30.7

Creating a Data Access Page

1. Open the Northwind Traders database, if it is not already open (Help ➤ Sample Databases ➤ Northwind Sample Database). Click OK to close the splash screen and click the Display Database Window button on the switchboard.

2. Click Pages on the Objects bar of the database window and click New.

3. Choose Page Wizard from the New Data Access Page dialog box and click OK.

4. Select the table or query that you want to use as the basis for the data access page from the Tables/Queries drop-down list. Select Customers And Suppliers By City from the list of queries.

5. Click the Select All button to select all fields in the query for the report. Click Next.

6. Select City as a grouping level by double-clicking City. Click Next.

7. Sort the data by CompanyName. Click Next.

8. Enter a name for the page or accept the default. In this case, the default Customers And Suppliers By City is fine.

9. Select the Do You Want To Apply A Theme To Your Page check box if you want to apply a FrontPage theme to the page. Themes contain graphic backgrounds, fonts, colors, and other design elements. Leave the check box cleared at this time.

10. Click Finish to create the page and preview it in Design view.

11. Click where it says Click Here And Type Title Text and enter **Customers and Suppliers by City**.

12. Click the drop-down list on the View button on the Page Design toolbar and choose Web Page Preview to see the page as it would appear in a browser. Internet Explorer launches and displays the page. You must save the page outside of Access before you can preview it. Choose a location for the page and click Save to save with the default name.

You may receive a warning that data access pages are linked to an absolute path and may create problems if you don't have access to the page's location at all times, for example, if it is stored on a server that is available only during certain hours. Click OK to acknowledge the warning. You may also be presented with a dialog box asking if you would like to set the location of the file as the default for all data access pages. Click No at this time.

EXERCISE 30.7 *(continued)*

13. Click the Next button to move through the list of cities. When you find a city for which you want to see detail, click the Expand button in front of the city name.

14. If there is more than one record that matches the selected city, a second set of navigation links opens, and you can click the Next button on it to move through the customers and suppliers in that city.

15. Click the Close button to close the browser and click Close to close Access and the Northwind Traders database.

You can edit a data access page just like any other web page as long as you don't disturb the layout of the data access object. If you want to change the layout of the data access object, open the report in Design view in Access. You can add instructions to the page, you can incorporate analysis of the data the users are seeing, and you can reformat the page to fit your company's corporate image. Data access pages are a great way to make Access data available to others without giving them the keys to the kingdom—access to the database itself.

Summary

This chapter concludes the discussion of Access with an emphasis on ways to make Access data available to others through reports, exporting, and data access pages. In this chapter, we covered the following topics:

- Creating reports using the wizard

- Formatting reports using Design view

- Adding calculated controls to a report

- Previewing and printing reports

- Importing data from an outside source

- Exporting data to another database or application

- Creating a simple data access page

Microsoft Outlook 2002 Core Exam

Chapter

31

Composing and Viewing Messages with Outlook

MOUS OUTLOOK 2002 CORE EXAM OBJECTIVES COVERED IN THIS CHAPTER:

- ✓ Display and print messages
- ✓ Compose and send messages to corporate/workgroup and Internet addresses
- ✓ Insert signatures and attachments
- ✓ Customize views

I n this chapter, we will focus on the Inbox, the default mailbox where Outlook stores incoming messages. We will show you how to compose, send, open, and print messages. We will then explain how to customize your messages with signatures and add file attachments. You will also learn how to configure the application window with a customized view to suit your preferences.

The Outlook 2002 program window has several key elements that everyone should be aware of. Figure 31.1 shows the main features within the program window labeled.

FIGURE 31.1 Outlook 2002 window

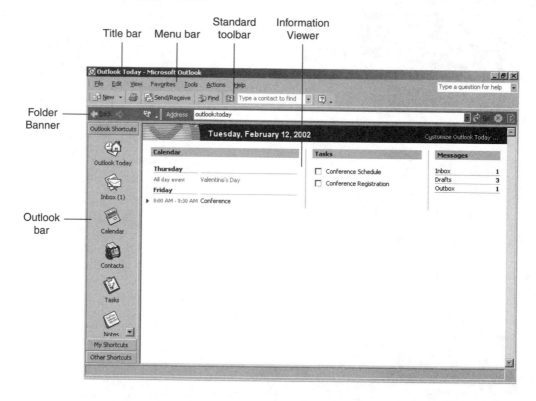

Before you begin this chapter, you should go to the Sybex website and download the file 4113Ch31.zip. This package contains the necessary files to complete some of the exercises in this chapter.

Opening and Printing E-mail Messages

When retrieving messages using Outlook 2002, it is imperative to know how to open your received messages. You may sometimes want a printed or hard copy of the message for your records as well. In this section, we will guide you through the appropriate steps for opening and printing messages.

Microsoft ✓ *Exam* *Objective*	**Display and print messages**

Displaying and printing messages requires that you master the following skills:

- Navigating to the appropriate folder using the Outlook bar, Folder List, or View menu
- Opening mail messages using the menu, mouse, or keyboard
- Printing messages using the toolbar or the menu bar

Navigating to Folders

Outlook 2002 has many different folders designed to manage individual features of the program. It is important to be able to move through the different folders with ease to ensure productivity in the workplace. As shown previously in Figure 31.1, the Outlook bar is one of your main navigational tools in Outlook (the Folder list is the other). The Outlook bar contains shortcuts to the main folders within the program. For example, to view the contents of the Inbox, simply click the Inbox icon, and the contents of the Inbox will be displayed in the details area.

The View menu also has the majority of the available folders listed on the Go To submenu. These are the two most popular methods of navigation within the folders, and they are the foundation for all of your work within Outlook.

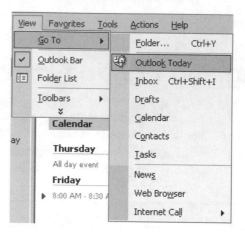

Opening Mail Messages

To open a new or previously viewed mail message, the procedure is the same: Simply double-click the message. Alternatively, you can select the message and choose File ➤ Open ➤ Selected Items. Notice that your Inbox will have some messages listed in bold and others in regular text. Messages shown in bold with the envelope icon closed are newly received messages that have not been read. Once a message has been read, it appears in regular text with the envelope icon open.

When you have new messages that have not been opened, you will see a number in brackets beside the Inbox icon. The number represents the number of unopened items in your Mail folder.

In Exercise 31.1, you will import some Outlook items into your Outlook folders from the files you downloaded from the Sybex website. You will use these items in the subsequent exercises in this chapter and the other Outlook chapters in this book.

EXERCISE 31.1

Importing Items into Outlook

The following guidelines explain how to import the Sample Outlook.pst file into Outlook.

1. Unzip the 4113Ch31.zip file onto the Desktop.

2. With Outlook open, select File ➤ Import And Export. The Import Export Wizard dialog box opens. If you have the Office Assistant open, click No, Don't Provide Help Now.

3. Select Import From Another Program Or File. Click the Next button. The Import A File window opens in the Import Export Wizard.

4. Scroll through the list and select Personal Folder File (*.pst) from the Select File Type To Import From list. Click the Next button. The Import Personal Folders window opens.

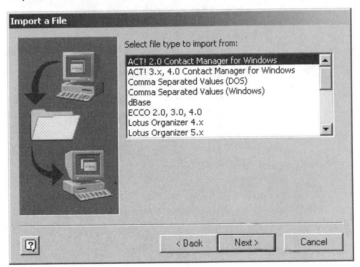

5. Click the Browse button. Navigate to the Desktop to select the Sample Outlook.pst file.

6. Accept the default selection, Replace Duplicates With Items Imported. Click the Next button.

EXERCISE 31.1 *(continued)*

7. Verify that the Include Subfolders checkbox is selected.

8. Select Import Items Into The Same Folder In [Your Folders Name].

9. Click the Finish button.

You have now imported all of the necessary items you will be asked to use throughout the Outlook section of this book.

In Exercise 31.2, you will learn how to open a new mail message. We have provided sample messages in the files that you imported in the previous exercise.

EXERCISE 31.2

Opening a Mail Message

1. Click the Inbox icon on the Outlook bar to navigate to the Inbox folder. You may have to click the My Shortcuts group button at the bottom of the Outlook bar to locate the Inbox icon.

2. Double-click Sales Meeting file or right-click the message and choose Open from the short-cut menu.

EXERCISE 31.2 *(continued)*

Alternatively, you can select the message and choose File ➤ Open ➤ Selected Items.

3. Keep this message open for the next exercise.

Printing Mail Messages

Printing e-mail messages will give you a hard copy for filing purposes or for reference at meetings. You can print using the Print button on the Standard toolbar or using the File menu. Using the Print button on the Standard toolbar is the most efficient method of printing, but you do not have the capability to customize your print job. Using the File menu, you have access to all available options in the Print dialog box, such as selecting the destination printer, print range, and number of copies. Exercise 31.3 guides you through printing a received message using both the toolbar and the menu bar.

EXERCISE 31.3

Printing Messages

1. Ensure that the Sales Meeting message is the active window on your screen. If you do not have the Sales Meeting message open, locate the message and double-click to open it.

2. To print the document to the default printer, click the Print button on the Standard toolbar or select File ➤ Print from the menu bar.

3. Close the Sales Meeting message.

You can preview most messages before you print using the Print dialog box. The Preview button is not available if the message is in HTML format. The Preview button allows you to see how your message will appear when printed.

Creating and Sending Messages

When you create and send messages in Outlook 2002, you are addressing mail to recipients and sending it to their electronic mail boxes. This is a two-step procedure: First you compose the message, and then you send it to the recipient.

Microsoft ✓ *Exam* *Objective*	**Compose and send messages to corporate workgroup and Internet addresses**

Composing and sending messages requires the following techniques:

- Composing new mail messages using multiple methods, for example, clicking buttons on the Standard toolbar, choosing options from the File menu, or using the details section of the Inbox

- Sending composed mail messages

- Sending all messages from your Outbox

Composing and Sending Messages

Composing is the first step in sending a message to a recipient. When you are satisfied with the content of the message, you then click the Send button to deliver it to the recipient's mailbox. When you send the message, it moves to your Outbox. The Outbox holds all outgoing messages until you are connected to the Internet. Once your connection is established, you can click the Send/Receive button on the Standard toolbar to deliver all outgoing messages. Exercise 31.4 guides you through composing and sending a message requesting company information.

> **EXERCISE 31.4**
>
> ### Composing and Sending a New Mail Message
>
> **1.** If necessary, navigate to the Inbox.
>
> **2.** Choose File ➤ New ➤ Mail Message, or click the New Mail Message Button on the Standard toolbar.
>
>

EXERCISE 31.4 *(continued)*

3. Enter the recipient's e-mail address in the To text box: **1charmichael@xyzincorporated.com**.

4. Type the following text in the Subject field: **Request for company information**.

5. Type the following message into the body of the message:
Good Afternoon,

I have recently visited your web site and I am interested in your products. Would you please send a printed brochure to my home address that I have included below.

Your Name
123 – 32 Broadway Blvd
Salinas, California 91045

Thank you for your assistance,

Your Name

6. To send the message, click the Send button on the Standard toolbar.

The e-mail addresses used throughout this chapter are fictitious. You will receive an undeliverable message in your Inbox when the messages are sent.

Forwarding and Replying to Messages

Frequently when messages are received, you need to respond to the original message. With the received message open, you can simply select the Reply button on the Standard toolbar, and a new message is automatically created, addressed to the original sender of the message. The message may include the original message that was sent along with your response. However, some messages need to be forwarded to other recipients. The forward message feature includes the original message but you must select the recipient. With the original message open, you click the Forward button on the Standard toolbar and enter a recipient's name and an appropriate message. When you are satisfied with the message, you click the Send button on the Standard toolbar. The Forward and Reply buttons on the Standard toolbar increase productivity when responding to or forwarding received messages. Periodically, you are not the only recipient of a message. When you need to reply to that message and would like all of the original receivers to get your message as well, you can use the Reply To All button on the Standard toolbar. Exercise 31.5 demonstrates how to reply to and forward received messages.

EXERCISE 31.5

Forwarding and Replying to Messages

1. Open the message Sales Meeting in your Inbox.

2. Click the Reply button on the Standard toolbar.

    A new message window appears with the original sender's address information automatically inserted into the To field.

3. Type the message **Thank you, Kim.**

4. Click the Send button. You will be returned to the original message.

Sometimes you may want to forward a message to a colleague or a friend. The next steps outline how to forward a message to a new recipient:

5. With the original message Sales Meeting open on the screen, click the Forward button on the Standard toolbar.

6. Enter **kcameron@xyzconsulting.com** in the To field.

7. Enter the following text in the body of the message:
    Please enter this date into your calendar.

    Thank you

8. Click the Send button on the Standard toolbar.

9. Close the original message, Sales Meeting.

Using Address Books

Address books are useful tools that store contact information, for example, people's names and e-mail addresses. Outlook 2002 has a default address book, called the Outlook Address Book, which many home users set up for their personal contacts. However, many offices set up a global list of contacts that is available to all staff members throughout the organization. The Global Address Book is set up by the systems administrator and is then made available to staff members. The Outlook Address Book is saved on your computer. You can easily access both the Global Address Book and the Outlook Address Book when creating new messages, thereby ensuring that the correct address is assigned to outgoing messages.

The Select Names dialog box is used for addressing mail to existing contacts. You can select the contact you would like to address the message to from the Name list box and then click the To, Cc, or Bcc button. The selected contact will move into the Message Recipients list.

The To field is the most common way to address mail to recipients, but on occasion you may want to send a courtesy copy to an additional recipient. To send a courtesy copy to a recipient or a list of recipients, you input their e-mail addresses in the Cc, or courtesy copy, field. Periodically, you might like to send a copy to another contact without the knowledge of the recipient in the To field. To do so, you would send a blind carbon copy to the individual using the Bcc field.

When addressing mail to multiple recipients, you can move several contacts into the To, Cc, or Bcc Message Recipients list.

Exercise 31.6 guides you through addressing a new message using the Outlook Address Book.

EXERCISE 31.6

Creating a New Message Using the Address Book

1. Click the New Mail Message button on the Standard toolbar.

2. Click the To button to open the Select Names dialog box.

EXERCISE 31.6 *(continued)*

3. Select James Richardson in the Name list box.

4. Click the To button.

5. Click OK to return to the message window.

6. Enter the following subject: **Confirmation of meeting**.

7. Type the following text into the body of the message:
   Good Afternoon, James,

   I would like to confirm our scheduled meeting to discuss the upcoming conference on March 9, 2002 at 2:00pm. Please let me know if this time is still convenient for you.

   Thank you,

   Your Name

8. Click Send on the Standard toolbar to forward the message to the recipient.

Please remember that the e-mail addresses that have been used throughout this chapter are not assigned. When you click the Send button to forward the message, you may receive an error message advising you that the message is undeliverable.

Inserting Signatures and Attachments

Creating automatic signatures is helpful when sending messages. A signature can be automatically added to each new mail message that is created. For example, if you always sign your message with your name, title, and contact information, you can have Outlook add these key pieces of information to all outgoing messages.

Exchanging files with branch offices, coworkers, family, and friends has become simple. You can insert files as attachments to outgoing messages. The following sections guide you through inserting both signatures and file attachments.

Microsoft ✓ *Exam Objective*

Insert signatures and attachments

Inserting signatures and attachments requires you to master the following:

- Creating signatures
- Attaching signatures to new mail messages
- Attaching files to mail messages

Creating and Using Signatures

Creating signatures can assist the sender to quickly sign every outgoing message. Multiple signatures may be created for different scenarios. For example, if you have Outlook configured for multiple e-mail accounts, you may want a different signature for each account. Exercise 31.7 explains the appropriate steps to create a signature for outgoing messages.

EXERCISE 31.7

Creating a Signature

1. Navigate to the Inbox.

2. Select Tools ➤ Options and then choose the Mail Format tab within the Options dialog box.

3. Click the Signatures button in the Options dialog box. A new dialog box appears called Create Signature.

4. Click the New button in the Create Signature dialog box.

5. The Create New Signature dialog box prompts you to name your signature and allows you to select whether you want to start with a blank signature or base it on a file. Type the name **Personal** in the Enter A Name For Your New Signature field. Accept the default to start with a blank signature.

EXERCISE 31.7 *(continued)*

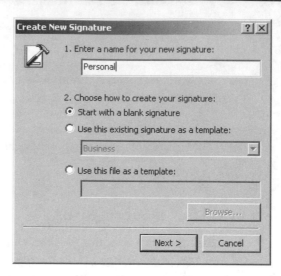

6. Click the Next button. The Edit Signature – [Personal] dialog box opens.

7. In the Edit Signature dialog box, type your name in the Signature Text field.

8. Click the Finish button to complete the signature. You will be returned to the Create Signature dialog box. Notice that the Personal signature has been added to the Signature list, and a preview is displayed of the selected signature.

9. Click OK to return to the Options dialog box. By default, if this is the first signature you have created, it will automatically be attached to all new messages. On the Mail Format tab of the Options dialog box, notice that Personal is currently selected in the Signature For New Messages drop-down list box.

10. Click OK to close the Options dialog box and accept the changes.

11. Create a new mail message. Your name is automatically inserted into the body of the message.

12. Close the new message without saving.

Inserting Attachments into Messages

E-mail has become an easy way to exchange files with coworkers or clients. Exercise 31.8 outlines how to attach a file to a message.

Adding a File Attachment to a Message

1. Navigate to the Inbox.

2. Click the New Mail Message button on the Standard toolbar.

3. From the Contacts folder, address the message to James Richardson in the Select Names dialog box.

4. Type the following text in the Subject field: **Conference Schedule**

5. Enter the following text as the body of the message:
Good morning James,
I have attached the file outlining the proposed schedule for the guest speakers at the upcoming conference. Please let me know if you think this is suitable.
Sincerely,

Remember that we previously set up the default signature to automatically insert your name in every new message you create. You should not have to type your name after typing Sincerely.

6. Select Insert ➢ File or click the Insert File button on the Standard toolbar.

7. Navigate to the folder where you saved the documents from the Sybex website, and select the Conference Schedule.doc file. Outlook attaches the document to the mail message.

Making Data Accessible with Outlook Views

O utlook 2002 comes equipped with many different views to assist you in various tasks. For example, the Inbox has a view where only messages you have received during the past seven days are displayed. This can help minimize scrolling through old messages to locate a recent message.

You may find that some views have everything you need except one detail. Outlook 2002 lets you customize the current view or design a view from scratch. In the following sections, we will guide you through switching among various predefined views, modifying existing views, as well as defining a custom view.

Microsoft ✓ *Exam* *Objective*	**Customize views**

Customizing views implies your knowledge in the following areas:

- Switching among views
- Modifying table views
- Customizing views to your preference

Switching among Predefined Views

Working in different views offers various advantages depending on the job at hand. You may find that you are looking for a message from a particular contact. By simply changing your view to By Sender, you can quickly locate all messages you have received from that contact. Exercise 31.9 guides you through the process of changing from your current view to several of the examples we have discussed so far.

EXERCISE 31.9

Switching Views in Outlook 2002

1. Navigate to the Inbox.

EXERCISE 31.9 *(continued)*

2. Select View ➢ Current View. The Current View submenu is displayed below.

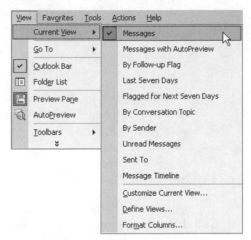

3. Choose By Sender in the Current View submenu. The messages in your Inbox are now grouped together by sender, as in the following graphic:

EXERCISE 31.9 *(continued)*

4. Select View ➤ Current View ➤ Last Seven Days. Notice that only messages that have been received during the past week are displayed.

5. Select View ➤ Current View ➤ Messages With AutoPreview. AutoPreview displays the first three lines of the body of the message below the sender's name and subject.

The Messages With AutoPreview view is typically the most common view in a mail folder. We will use the current view setting for the remainder of exercises in this chapter.

Modifying Table Views

Table views are designed with the most common fields shown. You may find that you require a different field in addition to the default fields, or perhaps you would prefer the column to be centered rather than its current alignment. It is a simple procedure to remove or add fields in a view, as well as to arrange the fields in a particular order. Exercise 31.10 explains how to add fields, remove fields, adjust column alignment, and rearrange fields in Table view.

EXERCISE 31.10

Modifying the Default Table View

1. Navigate to the Inbox if necessary.

2. Select View ➤ Current View ➤ Messages With AutoPreview if you have changed your view since the previous exercise.

3. Select View ➤ Current View ➤ Format Columns or right-click the field header and select Format Columns from the short-cut menu. The graphic below displays the short-cut menu when you right-click the field header.

4. Select the From field in the Available Fields list, and change the Width to Best Fit.

5. Select the Subject field, and change the Width to Best Fit.

6. Select the Size field, and change the Alignment to Center.

7. Click OK to accept the changes and return to the main program window where the Inbox will be displayed.

8. Open the Field Chooser dialog box by right-clicking one of the field headings and selecting Field Chooser. The Field Chooser dialog box appears on your screen.

9. Scroll through the Field Chooser dialog box to locate the Categories field. Click and drag the Categories field into the field header between the Subject and Received fields. Notice that when you drag the field into the headings, the mouse pointer changes to have two red arrows.

10. Adjust the column width for the Categories field to Best Fit by right-clicking the Categories field header and selecting Best Fit from the short-cut menu.

11. Remove the Size field by clicking the Size label and dragging down-ward. Notice that the field moves with your mouse and a large black X appears across the field.

12. Close the Field Chooser dialog box.

When adjusting the Table view, the changes you have made will automatically be remembered. To revert back to the original layout, open View ➤ Current View ➤ Define Views, select the view you have modified, and click the Reset button.

Customizing the Current View

Periodically, you may be working in a view and need to see additional information. Adding or removing fields is relatively simple using the drag-and-drop method. Customizing the current view follows steps similar to those we reviewed previously when we discussed customizing the Inbox in a Table view.

To modify the settings for the current view, open the View Summary dialog box by choosing View ➤ Current View ➤ Customize Current View.

The following customization options are available in the View Summary dialog box:

Fields   This button changes the fields that appear in the current view.

Group By   This button changes the groupings in the current view. For example, if you group your messages by date, you could quickly see all of the messages you have received by date.

Sort   This button changes the sort order of your messages in the current view.

Filter   This button specifies which items to display in the current view. The Filter button allows you to view only specific messages based on the criteria you have entered. Filters help narrow down your search when you are trying to locate a particular message.

Other Settings   This button specifies fonts and other miscellaneous items.

Automatic Formatting   This button sets the colors used in the background of appointments that meet conditions specified.

Exercise 31.11 guides you through the steps involved to customize the current view.

EXERCISE 31.11

Customizing Your Current View

1. Navigate to the Inbox if necessary.

2. Select View ➢ Current View ➢ Message Timeline. Notice that the field headers are no longer visible.

3. Select View ➢ Current View ➢ Customize Current View. The View Summary dialog box opens.

4. Click the Other Settings button to open the Format Timeline View dialog box.

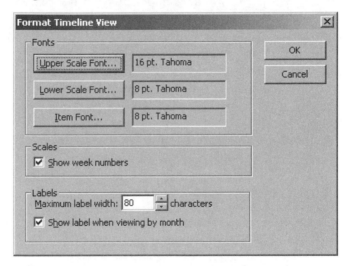

5. Place a check mark in the Show Week Numbers check box.

6. Click OK to return to the View Summary dialog box.

7. Click OK again. Notice that the week numbers have been inserted before the date.

Summary

In this chapter, you learned how to compose, read, and send messages. We covered the following topics:

- Opening and printing messages
- Composing messages using Outlook Address Book
- Adding signatures and file attachments to messages
- Sending messages
- Switching among predefined views
- Customizing views to suit your preferences

Chapter

32

Scheduling with Outlook's Calendar

MOUS OUTLOOK 2002 CORE EXAM OBJECTIVES COVERED IN THIS CHAPTER:

✓ Add appointments, meetings, and events to the Outlook calendar

✓ Apply conditional formats to the Outlook calendar

✓ Respond to meeting requests

✓ Use categories to manage appointments

✓ Print calendars

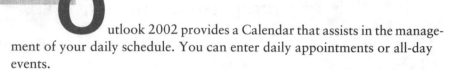

Outlook 2002 provides a Calendar that assists in the management of your daily schedule. You can enter daily appointments or all-day events.

In this chapter, we will discuss adding appointments and events, responding to meeting requests, and printing the Calendar. We will also explain how to use categories to manage appointments.

Before you begin this chapter, you must download the files for Chapter 31 from the Sybex website and import the Sample Outlook.pst file as described in Exercise 31.1 before you begin the exercises in this chapter.

Scheduling Using the Calendar

Entering time commitments into the Calendar folder in Outlook 2002 can help keep your daily schedule organized. Outlook's Calendar lets you enter appointments as well as events. Appointments are scheduled for a portion of the day, whereas events are scheduled for the whole day. For example, if you have a lunch meeting planned from 12:00 P.M. until 1:30 P.M., you would schedule an appointment. However, if there is an all-day conference planned for May 4, 2003 with no times associated with it, you would schedule an event.

The Calendar folder defaults to show the current day's appointments in Day/Week/Month view. Figure 32.1 displays May 2, 2003 with three appointments scheduled. Notice that the current date is highlighted in gray in the month area, called the Date Navigator.

FIGURE 32.1   The Calendar folder

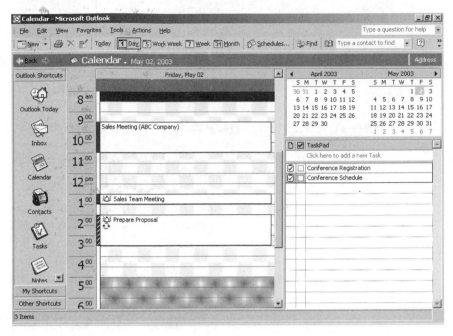

Figure 32.2 depicts the Standard toolbar when viewing the Calendar.

FIGURE 32.2   The Standard toolbar in Calendar

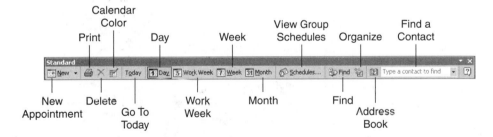

At times you may want to view your schedules a week at a glance. Outlook includes several built-in views to assist you when working with the Calendar, including Day, Work Week, Week, and Month.

Microsoft ✓ ***Exam Objective***   **Add appointments, meetings, and events to the Outlook calendar**

Adding appointments, meetings, and events into the Outlook Calendar requires you to be able to perform the following tasks:

- Create appointments and events in Day/Week/Month view
- Create appointments and events in the appointment form
- Invite others to meetings

Adding Appointments in Day/Week/Month View

Creating appointments can be as simple as selecting the correct date and time and starting to type. This method is the fastest for creating new appointments; however, important organizational options are not available unless you open the Appointment form. The Appointment form allows you to enter the location of the appointment, indicate whether it is an online meeting, set a reminder time, provide specific details about the appointment, as well as choose a contact and a category. In Exercise 32.1, you will create an appointment in Day/Week/Month view.

EXERCISE 32.1

Creating an Appointment in Day/Week/Month View

1. Click the Calendar icon on the Outlook bar or in the folder list to switch to the Calendar and click May 5, 2003 in the Date Navigator.

2. Select the timeframe 9:00 A.M. to 10:00 A.M. by clicking 9:00 am and dragging down to 10:00 am in the details area.

3. Type the following text: **Sales Meeting**

4. Press Enter.

When working with appointments and events, it is common to need to revise existing appointments. To open a scheduled appointment, navigate to the appointment and double-click it. The Appointment form opens on the screen, and you are able to revise any of the details as necessary.

Creating Appointments and Events in the Appointment Form

When creating appointments and events in the Calendar, you can customize your appointments if you use the Appointment form. Figure 32.3 displays a blank Appointment form.

FIGURE 32.3 Blank Appointment form

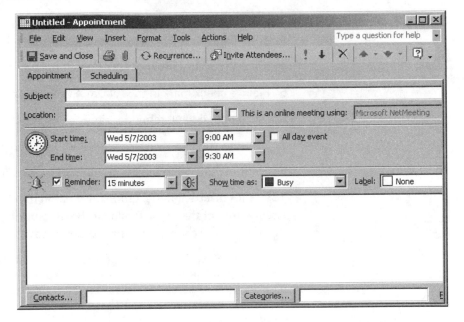

The Appointment form has its own Standard toolbar, customized to include buttons relevant to the form. Figure 32.4 shows the Standard toolbar for the Appointment form.

FIGURE 32.4 Standard toolbar in the Appointment form

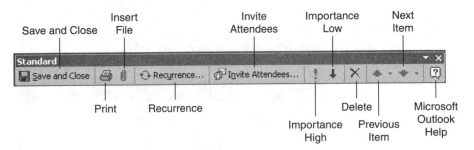

In Exercise 32.2, we will create an event using the Appointment form.

EXERCISE 32.2

Creating an Event Using the Appointment Form

1. Navigate to May 2003 in the Date Navigator. Click May 4, 2003.

2. Click the New Appointment button on the Standard toolbar.

3. Type **Sales Conference** in the Subject field.

4. Enter **Plaza Downtown** in the Location field.

5. Place a check mark in the All Day Event check box.

6. Accept the default reminder time.

7. Click the drop-down list for Show Time As, and select Out Of Office.

8. Enter the following details in the notes area of the form:

Topics for discussion are: Empowerment in the Workplace, Practical Accounting for the Small Business, Restructuring within the Small Business, and Technology? How to Embrace It.

9. Click the Save And Close button on the Standard toolbar, or choose File ➢ Save and then close the appointment.

Inviting Others to a Meeting

Scheduling meetings in Outlook where invitations need to be sent has been simplified with the Invite Attendees button on the Appointment form. The Invite Attendees button adds the To field to the form. The To field is the same field we used in the previous chapter to address messages to recipients. The Standard toolbar will also update: The Send button replaces the Save And Close button. In Exercise 32.3, we will invite attendees to the Sales Conference event that we created earlier.

EXERCISE 32.3

Inviting Others to Meetings

1. Open the Sales Conference event scheduled on May 7, 2003.

2. Click the Invite Attendees button on the Standard toolbar.

EXERCISE 32.3 *(continued)*

Notice that the window has updated to include the To field as well as the Send button on the Standard toolbar. Notice also that the navigation buttons on the Standard toolbar—Previous Item and Next Item—have been removed.

3. Type **lcarmicheal@xyzcorporation.com** in the To field.

4. Click the Send button on the toolbar.

Applying Conditional Formatting to Items on the Calendar

Outlook 2002 has included a new feature called Calendar Coloring that is used to apply a background fill color to your appointments and events. The colors are a visual cue to indicate the type of appointment or event.

The colors are visible only in the Day/Week/Month view or Day/Week/Month with AutoPreview view of the Calendar. You can either apply colors manually or set up rules to automatically apply color to items that meet certain conditions.

Microsoft
✓ *Exam*
Objective

Apply conditional formats to the Outlook calendar

Applying conditional formats to the Outlook calendar requires you to be able to perform the following tasks:

- Customize color labels
- Set up conditional formatting rules to apply calendar colors to appointments and events

Customizing Color Labels

Each color has a label that is associated with the color. The label can be customized to your preferences. For example, red is by default labeled Important; however, you may want red to indicate Personal items. The Edit Calendar Labels dialog box, shown in Figure 32.5, is used to modify the labels. In Exercise 32.4, you will modify Calendar's color labels.

FIGURE 32.5 Edit Calendar Labels dialog box

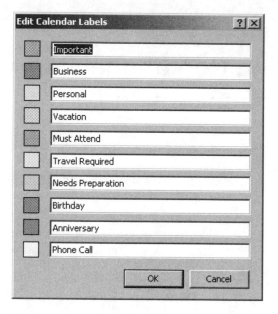

EXERCISE 32.4

Editing Calendar's Color Labels

1. Navigate to the Calendar if necessary.

2. Click the Calendar Coloring button on the Standard toolbar.

3. Select the Edit Labels option from the drop-down menu.

The Edit Calendar Labels dialog box is displayed.

4. Select the label Travel Required beside the turquoise color indicator.

EXERCISE 32.4 *(continued)*

5. Type the text **Sales Meeting**.

6. Click OK to close the Edit Calendar Labels dialog box.

Applying Color Labels Using Conditional Formatting

When using Calendar Coloring, you can apply colors manually or automatically with Automatic Formatting. To apply a color label manually, select an appointment or event and click the Calendar Coloring button on the Standard toolbar to select the appropriate label. In Exercise 32.5, you will set up conditional formatting rules for Outlook to apply colors automatically to appointments based on criteria you set.

EXERCISE 32.5

Applying Conditional Formats to the Calendar

1. Switch to Day/Week/Month view of the Calendar by choosing View ➢ current view ➢ Day/Week/Month.

2. Choose View ➢ Current View ➢ Customize Current View to open the View Summary dialog box.

3. Click the Automatic Formatting button.

4. Click Add to enter a name for the conditional formatting rule you are creating.

5. Type **Sales Meetings** as the name of the new conditional formatting rule.

6. Select Sales Meeting from the label drop-down list (the Sales Meeting label was created in Exercise 32.4. If you didn't complete that exercise, choose Travel Required).

7. Click the Condition button to open the Filter dialog box.

The Filter dialog box can be used when creating a new view or customizing an existing view to select only Outlook items that meet the criteria you define, for example, only e-mail messages from a certain sender, or only calendar appointments at a particular location. In this case, you are using the Filter dialog box to set the condition upon which Outlook will apply the Sales Meeting label.

EXERCISE 32.5 *(continued)*

8. In the Search for the Word text box, enter **Sales**. Leave the default in the Subject Field Only.

9. Click OK to close the Filter dialog box, OK again to close the Automatic Formatting dialog box, and OK a third time to close the View Summary dialog box.

10. View the Sales Conference you entered for May 4, 2003. It should reflect the turquoise color you assigned to sales meeting.

11. Enter a sales meeting in the calendar for April 3, 2003. Notice how it changes to turquoise immediately after entering it.

From this point forward any calendar item that contains the word *sales* in its subject will be assigned the Sales Meetings label.

If you decide you no longer want to use a conditional formatting rule, you can disable it or delete it. Choose View ➤ Current View ➤ Customize Current View. Click Automatic Formatting to reopen the dialog box. To disable it temporarily but keep the rule available, click the check box in front of the rule. All previously colored appointments will appear without a color label until you reactivate the rule. To delete the rule completely, select the rule and click the Delete button.

When using Calendar Coloring, any colors you manually apply take precedence over any automatic colors you have applied.

Responding to Meeting Requests from Others

Periodically, you may receive an e-mail message in your Inbox requesting your attendance at a meeting. While you have the message open, you can use the buttons on the Standard toolbar within the message to accept the invitation, mark the appointment as Tentative, decline the invitation, or propose a new time for the meeting. Figure 32.6 shows a sample meeting request.

FIGURE 32.6   Meeting request message

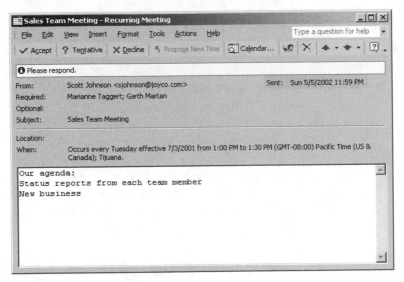

Microsoft ✓ Exam Objective   **Respond to meeting requests**

Responding to meeting requests requires you to be able to perform the following:

- Accept, mark as tentative, decline, or propose a new time for meetings

The Standard toolbar in the meeting request message contains toolbar buttons specific to meeting requests. Figure 32.7 shows the Standard toolbar in a meeting request message.

FIGURE 32.7   The Standard toolbar in the meeting request message

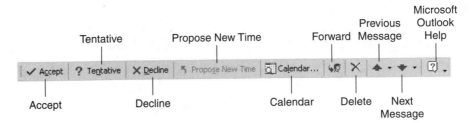

Responding to the Request

If you receive a meeting request that you would like to accept, click the Accept button on the Standard toolbar. A message box appears, explaining that the meeting will be entered into your Calendar and inquiring whether you would like to send a response. There are three options to choose from: Edit The Response Before Sending, Send The Response Now, or Don't Send A Response. If you select Edit The Response Before Sending, you can type a message to the sender before the acknowledgment is sent to them. The Edit The Response Before Sending option is useful if you want to include a message, such as *Who is bringing the cookies?* to the meeting organizer when you respond to the meeting request. If you accept the default, Send The Response Now, you will send a standard acceptance message to the recipient. When you accept a meeting, it is automatically added into your Calendar. In Exercise 32.6, you will accept a meeting request message.

EXERCISE 32.6

Accepting a Meeting Request

1. Open the Mountain Board Meeting message in your Inbox.

2. Click the Accept button on the Standard toolbar.

   A message box appears, inquiring whether you would like to send a response now.

3. Select Edit The Response Before Sending, and type the following message:

   **I look forward to receiving the agenda for the meeting.
   See you there,
   Your Name**

4. Click the Send button on the Standard toolbar.

Categorizing Outlook Appointments

Categories are keywords or phrases to assist you in locating common items. When categories are used, you will be able to quickly find, sort, or group items.

Microsoft *Exam* *Objective*

Use categories to manage appointments

Using categories to manage appointments requires you to be able to perform the following tasks:

- Apply a category to an appointment

- Create a new category

NOTE   Categories can be applied to any item in Outlook, including e-mail messages, appointments, events, contacts, tasks, and notes.

Assigning Appointments to Predefined Categories

When assigning categories to appointments, you can access the Categories dialog box from the Appointment form. Figure 32.8 displays the Categories dialog box.

FIGURE 32.8   The Categories dialog box

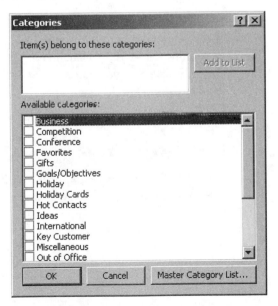

To assign categories to an item, place a check mark next to the categories you would like to associate with the item. In Exercise 32.7, we will apply a category to the Sales Conference event we created earlier in this chapter.

EXERCISE 32.7

Assigning Predefined Categories to an Event

1. Open the Sales Conference event scheduled for May 7, 2003.

2. Click the Categories button on the Appointment form to open the Categories dialog box.

3. Place a check mark next to the Business category.

4. Click OK to return to the Appointment form.

   Notice that the Category field has been updated to display the Business category.

5. Click the Save And Close button on the Standard toolbar.

Another method of assigning categories to an item is by selecting the item and right-clicking. A short-cut menu appears with several options, including Categories. Clicking the Categories option opens the same Categories dialog box we opened from the Appointment form. This is the fastest method of assigning categories to existing items. Alternatively, if the appointment or event is selected, you can access the Categories dialog box using the menu and choosing Edit ≻ Categories.

Creating New Categories

Outlook offers many categories to choose from, but you may decide to customize the Category list to suit your specific needs. You can add new categories to the Available Categories list in the Categories dialog box. Exercise 32.8 guides you through the required steps to add a new category.

EXERCISE 32.8

Creating a New Category

1. Locate the Sales Conference event scheduled for May 7, 2003.

2. Right-click the event and select Categories from the short-cut menu.

3. Remove the check mark from the Business category.

4. Type **Conference** in the Item(s) Belongs To These Categories text box.

5. Click the Add To List button.

When adding new categories to the Available Categories list, they will be applied automatically to the open item.

6. Click the Business category to place a check mark by that option.

7. Click OK to close the Categories dialog box.

8. Open the Sales Conference event.

Notice that the Category field has both Conference and Business listed.

9. Close the Sales Conference event and save the changes.

Printing Calendars

Once you have entered your appointments and events into the Calendar, you may occasionally need a hard copy. Outlook 2002 allows you to select several different formats for your printout, depending on your requirements.

Microsoft ✓ *Exam Objective*

Print calendars

Printing Calendars requires you to perform the following tasks:

- Select the print style of your Calendar

- Select the date range of the desired printout

Figure 32.9 displays the Print dialog box, where you can specify the print style as well as the date range you would like to print. In Exercise 32.9, you will print your Calendar in several different print styles as well as date ranges.

FIGURE 32.9 The Print dialog box

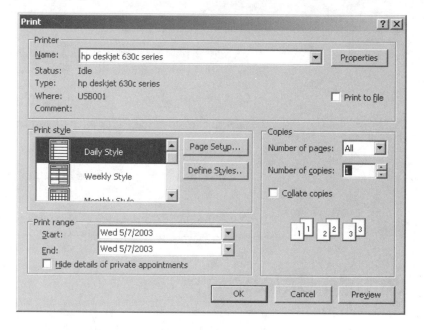

EXERCISE 32.9

Printing Your Calendar

1. Choose File ➤ Print to open the Print dialog box.

2. Select Weekly Style from the Print Style list box.

The Weekly Style displays the appointments without the details that have been entered into the Appointment form. This format is useful when you need a hard copy of your appointment times throughout the week.

3. Set the Print Range to Start **May 5, 2003** and End **May 11, 2003**.

EXERCISE 32.9 *(continued)*

4. Click OK to print the Weekly Calendar.

5. Choose File ➤ Print.

6. Select Calendar Details Style from the Print Style list box. The Calendar Details Style is useful when you need to see specific details that have been entered about your appointments.

7. Click the Preview button in the Print dialog box. Notice that you are able to view the layout of the printout before you actually print the schedule.

8. Click the Print button on the Standard toolbar.

9. Click OK to print the Weekly Calendar.

Summary

In this chapter, you have learned how to create and modify appointments and events, assign categories to help organize your meetings, invite others to meetings, as well as respond to meeting requests and print the Calendar. We covered the following topics:

- Using the Calendar to schedule appointments and events
- Adding appointments by selecting the date and time in Day/Week/ Month view
- Creating appointments and events in the Appointment form
- Inviting other attendees to meetings
- Applying conditional formatting to items on the Calendar
- Responding to meeting requests from others
- Applying categories to appointments and events
- Assigning appointments to predefined categories
- Creating new categories
- Printing the Calendar in various layouts

Chapter

33

Managing Messages and Contacts in Outlook

MOUS OUTLOOK 2002 CORE EXAM OBJECTIVES COVERED IN THIS CHAPTER:

- ✓ Move messages between folders
- ✓ Search for messages
- ✓ Save messages in alternate file formats
- ✓ Use categories to manage messages
- ✓ Set message options
- ✓ Create and edit contacts
- ✓ Organize and sort contacts
- ✓ Link contacts to activities and journal entries

In this chapter, we will discuss how to organize incoming and outgoing messages in folders, move messages between folders, search for messages, save messages in alternate formats, use categories to manage messages, and set message options. We will also review how to create and edit contacts, organize and sort contacts, and link contacts to activities and journal entries.

You must install the Sample Outlook.pst file from Chapter 31 before you begin the exercises in this chapter.

Managing Messages

When you work in Outlook, developing a method that organizes messages will help considerably when you need to retrieve them in the future. One method is to create custom folders in which to save important messages. For example, if you are corresponding with a potential client, you can save any received messages in a folder labeled with the new client's or the company's name. This will help you easily retrieve those messages in preparation for your next meeting.

Microsoft ✓ *Exam* *Objective*   **Move messages between folders**

Moving messages between folders requires you to be able to perform the following tasks:

- Drag messages between folders
- Create new folders

Viewing Outlook Folders

The standard Outlook folders are located as shortcuts on the Outlook bar. The Outlook bar has three default groups: Outlook Shortcuts, My Shortcuts, and Other Shortcuts. When navigating to different folders, you can simply click the folder on the Outlook bar you would like to view or use the Go To feature on the View menu. Figure 33.1 shows the Outlook bar with the available groups.

FIGURE 33.1 Outlook bar

Alternatively, you can use the Folder List to navigate to all folders in Outlook, including custom folders. The Folder List is accessible by clicking the Folder List button on the Outlook toolbar or choosing View ➢ Folder List. In Exercise 33.1, you will use all methods to navigate to multiple folders.

EXERCISE 33.1

Viewing Outlook Folders

1. Click the My Shortcuts banner on the Outlook bar. Notice the additional icons listed: Drafts, Outbox, Sent Items, Journal, and Outlook Update.

2. Click the Outbox icon. If you have any messages waiting to be sent, they will be listed here.

3. Select View ➤ Go To. A pop-up menu will appear displaying the available folders.

4. Select Outlook Today. Your program window updates to show the Outlook Today window.

5. Select View ➤ Folder List. The Folder List displays all available folders in Outlook.

6. Select Inbox. Notice that the program window displays your Inbox.

7. Close the Folder List. You can either click the X in the top-right corner of the Folder List or select View ➤ Folder List.

You can create new groups on the Outlook bar by right-clicking the Outlook bar. A shortcut menu appears with the Add New Group option. Once you have created the new group, you can add shortcuts to the custom folders you have created or the folders you use most often.

Creating New Folders

The Create New Folder dialog box, shown in Figure 33.2, is used to create new folders. In Exercise 33.2, you will practice creating new folders.

FIGURE 33.2 Create New Folder dialog box

EXERCISE 33.2

Creating New Folders

1. Click View ➢ Folder List or click the Folder button on the Outlook toolbar to open the Folder List.

Note: You may also click a folder name on the Outlook banner to open the Folder List. If you opened the Folder List by clicking the banner, click the thumbtack button to anchor the Folder List.

2. Right-click the Inbox and select New Folder. The Create New Folder dialog box opens.

3. Type **Urgent** in the Name text box.

4. Verify that Mail And Post Items is selected in the Folder Contains drop-down list.

5. Select the Inbox folder from the Select Where To Place The Folder list. By selecting the Inbox folder, you are creating a mail subfolder below your main Inbox.

EXERCISE 33.2 *(continued)*

```
Create New Folder                              ? X
Name:
┌──────────────────────────────────────────────┐
│ Urgent                                        │
└──────────────────────────────────────────────┘

Folder contains:
┌──────────────────────────────────────────┬───┐
│ Mail and Post Items                       │ ▼ │
└──────────────────────────────────────────┴───┘

Select where to place the folder:
┌──────────────────────────────────────────┬─┐
│ ⊟─ Personal Folders                     ▲ │
│    ─ Calendar                             │
│    ⊞─ Contacts                            │
│    ─ Deleted Items                        │
│    ─ Drafts                               │
│    ⊞─ Inbox                               │
│    ─ Journal                              │
│    ─ Notes                                │
│    ─ Outbox                               │
│    ─ Sent Items                         ▼ │
│    ─ Tasks                                │
└──────────────────────────────────────────┴─┘

                    ┌────────┐   ┌────────┐
                    │   OK   │   │ Cancel │
                    └────────┘   └────────┘
```

6. Click OK. A dialog box opens, inquiring whether you would like to add a shortcut to the Outlook bar.

7. Select Yes. The dialog box closes and the My Shortcuts group flashes, indicating that a new shortcut has been added.

8. Click the My Shortcuts group if it is not already active. Notice that a new shortcut for the folder Urgent has been added. Keep this folder open for the next exercise.

Moving Messages between Folders

After you have created the new folders, you can physically move your items from the default folder to the new folder. In Exercise 33.3, you will move mail messages from the Inbox to the new folder you created in Exercise 33.2.

EXERCISE 33.3

Moving Messages to New Folders

1. Navigate to the Inbox by clicking the Inbox folder.

2. Select any message in the Inbox and drag the message to the Urgent folder below the Inbox folder in the Folder List. If the Urgent folder is not visible, drag the message to the Inbox folder and, without releasing the mouse button, hover there until the Inbox folder expands to display the Urgent folder. When the Urgent Folder turns blue, drop the message on the Urgent folder.

3. Click the Urgent folder in the Folder List. You will see that the message has been moved to the Urgent folder.

Locating Mail Messages

When you work with Outlook for an extended period of time, the quantity of messages you receive may become overwhelming. Storing messages in custom folders will help you organize your messages. However, sometimes it still may be difficult to find a particular message. The Find feature will save you time and trouble by searching your folders for you. Figure 33.3 shows the Find bar active in the Inbox window.

FIGURE 33.3 Find bar

The Find feature was designed to help you quickly retrieve the items stored in your folders. In Exercise 33.4, you will locate several items using the Find feature.

Microsoft Exam Objective

Search for messages

EXERCISE 33.4

Locating Mail Messages

1. Navigate to the Inbox by clicking Inbox in the Folder List. If the Find bar is not visible above the Inbox Information viewer, click the Find button on the Standard toolbar.

2. Type **Away From Office** in the Look For field on the Find bar.

3. Type **Meeting** in the Look For field on the Find bar.

4. Click the Search In drop-down list and select Choose Folders. The Select Folder(s) dialog box opens.

5. Place a check mark next to Inbox if it is not already selected and also check Calendar and Drafts. If you would like to search subfolders, you can also place a check mark in the Search Subfolders option at the bottom of the window.

6. Click OK. You are returned to the main program window.

7. Click the Find Now button. Outlook searches through the folders selected and displays all messages and appointments that contain the word *Meeting*.

Saving Messages

Periodically, you may want to save a message in a different file format on your local drive. For instance, you may want to keep the message for future reference and want to be able to open it independently of your e-mail browser. When messages are saved on your local drive, you can also transport the information to other computers by copying them to a floppy disk or burning them to a CD.

Microsoft ✓ *Exam Objective*	**Save messages in alternate file formats**

Saving messages in alternate file formats requires you to perform the following tasks:

- Save incoming messages as text or message files
- Save outgoing messages in various file formats

Saving Incoming Messages As Text and Message Files

When you receive a message that you want to include in another document or if you have restrictions on the size of your Outlook mailbox, you might want to save a message outside of Outlook. You can save messages in a variety of different formats including Message format. A message saved in Message format retains all of its properties as an Outlook message so you can reopen it, forward it, and reply to it, but you can store it on your local or network drive separate from Outlook. You could also save a message in Text Only format (.txt) for opening in any word processing program, HTML format (.htm, .html) for use on the Web, and Outlook Template format for reuse within Outlook. Text Only format strips out all graphics and other images and displays only the text of the message. Message, HTML, and Outlook Template formats retain the original format of the message. In Exercise 33.5, you will open an existing message and save it first in Message format and then in Text Only format.

EXERCISE 33.5

Saving an Incoming Message As a Message

1. Navigate to the Urgent folder in the My Shortcuts group or click the Urgent folder below the Inbox in the Folder List.

2. Open any message in the Urgent folder.

3. Select File ➢ Save As. The Save As dialog box opens so you can select the location where you want to store the message as well as the file type you want to save it as.

4. Select Message Format in the Save As Type drop-down list.

5. Click the Save button. The message is saved in your default save folder with the Subject line used as the filename.

6. Click File ➢ Save As again and repeat steps 4 and 5, this time choosing Text Only from the Files of Type drop-down list.

7. Close the message in Outlook.

8. Switch to the Desktop by clicking the Show Desktop button on the Quick Launch toolbar on the Windows Taskbar and navigate to your default save location.

Note: To find your default save location, you may have to navigate through My Computer or just click the My Documents icon on the Desktop.

9. In your default save location, you should find two files with the same name. The Outlook Message format file has an envelope icon (and an .msg extension, if Windows is set up to display file extensions) and the Text Only format has a Notepad icon. Double-click the Message format file. The message opens and looks the same as if it had been opened within the mail browser. Close the message.

10. Double-click the Text Only message. When the message opens in Notepad (or whatever software is set up on your system to open text files), notice that all the formatting has been stripped from the message. Close the message.

11. Switch back to Outlook by clicking the Outlook button on the Windows Taskbar.

Organizing Messages with Categories

Categories are used to group together common items. Categories can be used to design your own personal system of organization in Outlook for easy retrieval, printing, and review.

Microsoft
✓ *Exam*
Objective

Use categories to manage messages

Using categories to manage messages requires you to master the following skills:

- Assign categories to messages

Assigning Categories to Messages

Categories were developed to assist you in organizing common items into groups. You can apply the same categories to several different items such as contacts, appointments, events, tasks, or messages and then conduct a search by category to locate all the related items. In Exercise 33.6, you will assign a category to a message and then search for messages organized by categories.

EXERCISE 33.6

Applying Categories to Messages

1. Open the Away From Office message in the Urgent folder.

2. Select View ➤ Options. The Message Options dialog box opens.

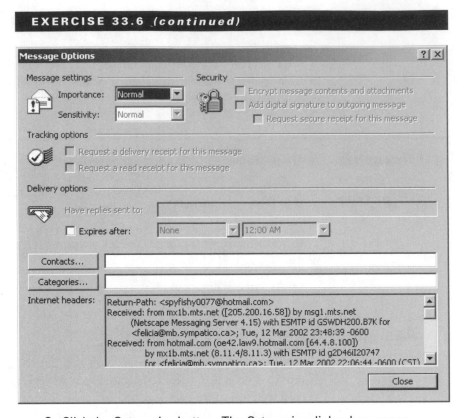

EXERCISE 33.6 *(continued)*

3. Click the Categories button. The Categories dialog box opens.

4. Select the Business category.

5. Click the OK button. You are returned to the Message Options dialog box.

6. Click the Close button.

Applying Message Options

When sending outgoing messages, you can set several options. You are able to set the importance and sensitivity of messages, and you can request delivery and read receipts. You can also set outgoing messages to not be delivered before a specified date. These options are available through the Message Options window, which is available by clicking the Options button on the Standard toolbar. Figure 33.4 displays the Message Options dialog box.

FIGURE 33.4 Message Options dialog box

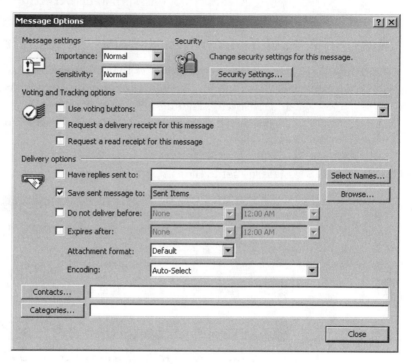

You can also set Voting options in the Message Options dialog box. With Voting options, you can add voting buttons to messages for your colleagues to respond to based on a question you have asked. Outlook automatically tallies the results of these polls. For more information about Voting options, see our book, *Mastering Microsoft Outlook 2002*, from Sybex.

Microsoft ✓ *Exam* *Objective*

Set message options

Setting message options requires you to use the following skills:

- Set priority and sensitivity to messages

- Request delivery and read receipts

- Set delivery options, such as delivery dates

Setting Message Importance and Sensitivity

Messages have two features that assist the receiver in determining whether they are of an urgent nature or contain sensitive information: importance and sensitivity. Figure 33.5 shows that a message of High importance has been received. In Exercise 33.7, you will create a message with High importance that is marked Confidential.

FIGURE 33.5 Message set to High importance

EXERCISE 33.7

Setting Message Importance and Sensitivity

1. Navigate to the Inbox.

2. Click the New Mail Message button on the Standard toolbar.

3. Click the Importance: High button on the Standard toolbar to set the outgoing message to High priority. Click the Importance: Low button on the Standard toolbar.

Notice that you are unable to set a message to be of both High and Low importance.

4. Click the Options button on the Standard toolbar. The Message Options windows appears with the Importance set to Low.

5. Click the drop-down list for Importance to display the three options: Low, Normal, and High.

6. Select High.

7. Click the drop-down list for Sensitivity to display its four options: Normal, Personal, Private, and Confidential.

8. Select Confidential from the list.

When a message is received with the sensitivity set, a banner will be displayed across the message indicating that the sensitivity that has been set to a specific level.

```
⚠ Please treat this as Confidential.
This message was sent with High importance.
```

9. Close the Options dialog box.

10. Close this message and save it in your Drafts folder.

11. Navigate to the Drafts folder in the Folder List or in the My Short-cuts group on the Outlook bar. Notice that the message you created is marked with a red exclamation point. When a message is received that has been marked as High importance, you will see the exclamation point indicating the High importance setting.

Requesting Delivery and Read Receipts

Outlook includes features to allow you to send messages that are time-sensitive in nature and require verification that they have been read. In Exercise 33.8, you will request delivery and read receipts for an outgoing message.

Delivery and read receipts may seem like a good idea, but be aware that not all e-mail servers process them and not all users allow them to be returned (yes, you have the option to say no). If you receive a delivery receipt, all you know is that the message has reached the recipient's mail server (not necessarily their own mail box). If you receive a read receipt, all you know is that the message has been marked as read. Anyone can do that by right-clicking a message in the Inbox and clicking Mark As Read without ever opening the message. We recommend using read and delivery receipts only after making a prior arrangement with the recipient about what the receipts mean and how they will be used.

EXERCISE 33.8

Requesting Delivery and Read Receipts

1. Navigate to the Inbox, if necessary.

2. Click the New Mail Message button on the Standard toolbar.

3. Click the Options button on the Standard toolbar. The Message Options window opens.

4. Click the Request A Delivery Receipt For This Message check box.

5. Click the Request A Read Receipt For This Message check box.

6. Close the Message Options dialog box.

7. Address the message to a friend or colleague of yours, include some text about what it is you are doing, and click Send to send the message. You should receive a message from the Systems Administrator when the message has been received (if the receiving mail system allows it) and a second message when your friend opens the message to read it.

Setting Delivery Options

Outlook includes several delivery options to ensure that your messages are sent on the correct dates. For example, you may have a message that is ready to send but is not required until a later date. You can set the delivery option to send the message on the date you specify. The message will be saved in the Outbox until the date you have set arrives. In Exercise 33.9, you will create a message that will be sent at a later date.

EXERCISE 33.9

Setting a Delivery Date on Outgoing Messages

1. Create a new mail message.

2. Click the Options button on the Standard toolbar.

3. Click the Do Not Deliver Before check box.

4. Select the date May 22, 2003 from the date drop-down list.

5. Select 9:00 AM from the time drop-down list.

6. Close the Message Options window.

7. Close the message without saving.

Creating and Managing Contacts

The Contacts folder is used to save all pertinent information about your clients, vendors, and other people you need to contact. The Contacts folder is displayed in Figure 33.6.

FIGURE 33.6   Contacts folder

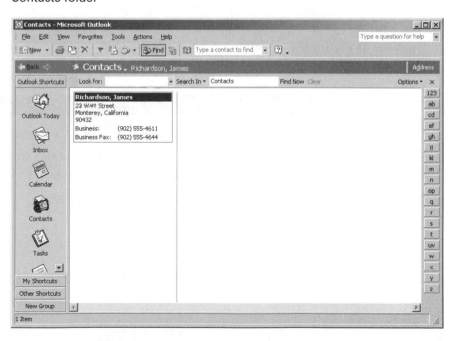

Figure 33.7 shows the Standard toolbar when the Contacts folder is active.

FIGURE 33.7 Standard toolbar in Contacts view

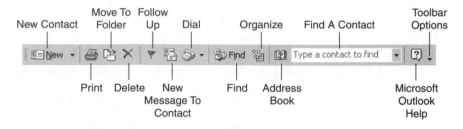

| Microsoft ✓ Exam Objective | **Create and edit contacts** |

Creating New Contacts

The Contact form has multiple tabs for entering new information about each person or company. The General tab is used to enter the person's name, company, address, phone numbers, e-mail address, and web page. The notes box, found at the bottom of the form, allows you to type notes or attach files to the contact itself. The Details tab is where you enter the department they work in, the office where they are located, as well as their profession, manager's name, assistant's name, nickname, and anniversaries. In Exercise 33.10, you will learn how to create a new contact.

EXERCISE 33.10

Creating New Contacts

1. Navigate to the Contacts folder by clicking Contacts in the Folder List or clicking Contacts on the Outlook bar.

2. Click the New Contact button on the Standard toolbar.

   A blank Contact form opens.

3. Enter your name in the Full Name field.

4. Enter your job title in the Job Title field.

5. Enter your company in the Company field.

6. Select Business from the drop-list of telephone number types and enter your work phone number.

7. Select Business Fax from the drop-list of telephone number types and enter your work fax number, if you have one.

8. Select Business from the drop-down list under Address and enter your work address in the Address field using this format:

   Street Address
   City, State Postal Code

9. Enter your company's web address if they have one in the Web Page Address field.

10. Click the Details tab to display the next page of the Contact window.

11. Enter your department in the Department field.

12. Click the Save And Close button on the Standard toolbar.

Editing Existing Contacts

After your contacts have been entered into the Contacts folder, it essential to keep their information current. As time passes, people may receive promotions or move to new companies. As the changes occur, you will need to modify their Contact information. In Exercise 33.11, you will modify the contact you created in the previous exercise.

Editing an Existing Contact

1. Open your contact in the Contacts folder.

2. Select an additional telephone number type from the third telephone number type drop-down list that you would like other professional contacts to have, such as a mobile phone or pager.

3. Click the Save And Close button on the Standard toolbar.

Organizing Contacts

When organizing contacts, you have three options to assist you: moving contacts into custom folders, applying categories to individual contacts, and changing views. The following section explains all three methods to help you determine which method will be appropriate for you. Figure 33.8 shows the Contacts window with the Organize pane active in the top portion.

FIGURE 33.8 Organize pane

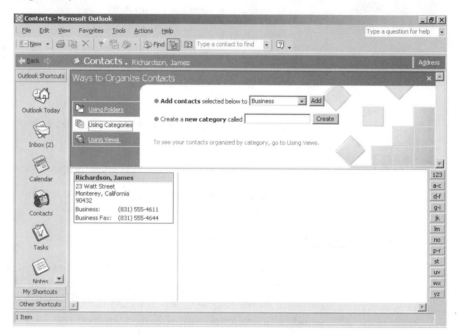

Microsoft
✓ *Exam*
Objective

Organize and sort contacts

Organizing and sorting contacts requires you to master the following skills:

- Organizing contacts using folders, categories, and views
- Sorting contacts in different views

Organizing with Folders, Categories, and Views

When you enter contacts in the Contacts folder and use the default Address Cards view, your contacts are organized alphabetically by last name. You can add additional organization to your contacts by moving them to different folders, assigning them to specific categories, and changing to views that allow you to sort the contacts by different fields. All of these options are available from the Organize pane that you can access by clicking the Organize button on the Standard toolbar. In Exercise 33.12, you will apply a category to an existing contact and apply different views to the Contacts folder.

EXERCISE 33.12

Applying a Category to a Contact

1. Navigate to the Contacts folder.

2. Click the Organize button on the Standard toolbar.

3. Select the contact you created for yourself in Exercise 33.10.

4. Click the Using Categories link and select the Business category from the Add Contacts Selected Below To drop-down list.

5. Click the Add button. The message "Done!" appears beside the Add Contacts Selected Below To drop-down list.

6. Double-click your contact to open it Notice that the Business category is listed in the Categories field at the bottom of the Contact form.

7. Close the Contact form.

8. Click the Using Views link in the Organize pane at the top of the Contacts window.

9. Select the Phone List option in the Change Your View list. The details section of the Contacts window is updated to appear in table format.

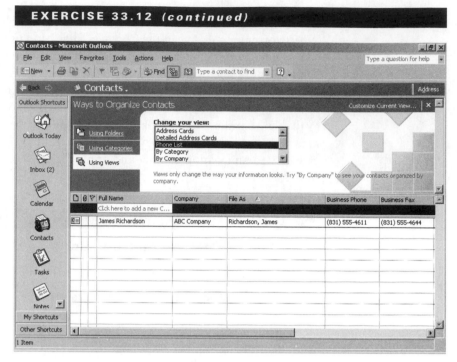

10. Select By Category in the Change Your View list. The Contacts list is reorganized into Category groups.

Note: The Category groups may appear collapsed, which means you can't see contacts in the groups. Click the Expand button (plus icon) next to the category to expand the group. If the group is already expanded, click the Collapse button (minus icon) to collapse it. You can set this preference by choosing Expand All or Collapse All on the View ➢ Expand/Collapse Groups menu.

11. Select the Address Cards option in the Change Your View list to return to the default view for the Contacts window.

12. Click the Organize button on the Standard toolbar to close the Organize pane.

Sorting Contacts in Table Views

When you use any of several table views for contacts, you can quickly sort by field names. When you click the field name, Outlook sorts the field in ascending order. If you click the field name a second time, it sorts the list in descending order. In Exercise 33.13, you will sort contacts in a table view.

Tracking Activities Related to Contacts   **899**

EXERCISE 33.13

Sorting Contacts

1. Navigate to the Contacts folder.

2. Select View ➢ Current View ➢ Phone List.

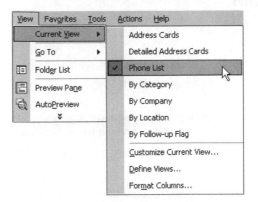

3. The Information viewer updates to display the contacts in table view.

4. Click the Company field header. An upward-pointing triangle is added beside the field name. This indicates that the field is now sorted in ascending order.

5. Click the Company field header again. The triangle is now pointing downward, indicating that the contacts are now sorted by company in descending order.

6. Click any other field header, except for Categories, to sort by that field.

7. Select View ➢ Current View ➢ Address Cards to return to the default Contacts view.

Tracking Activities Related to Contacts

The Activities tab of the Contact form shows all activities associated with a contact, including correspondence, appointments, tasks, or other contacts. Some items, such as e-mail sent to and received from a contact automatically appear on the Activities list. To associate other activities with a contact, such as appointments, tasks, and journal entries, you must manually assign them.

Microsoft ✓ *Exam* *Objective*   **Link contacts to activities and journal entries**

In Exercise 33.14, you will link an existing contact to various activities and journal entries.

EXERCISE 33.14

Linking Contacts to Activities and Journal Entries

In this exercise, you are going to link the contact you created for yourself to activities in Outlook. Normally you would be linking contacts other than yourself to activities that relate to them.

1. Click the Calendar icon on the Outlook bar.

2. Navigate to August 15, 2002.

3. Double-click to open the Mountain event.

4. Click the Contacts button at the bottom of the General tab and select your contact to associate it with this appointment. Click the OK button to assign the contact and close the Select Contacts dialog box.

5. Click the Save And Close button on the Standard toolbar to close the Calendar item and save the changes to the appointment.

6. Navigate to the Contacts folder and reopen your contact.

7. Choose Actions ➢ New Journal Entry For Contact to open a Journal Entry form related to the contact. Enter **Learning about Outlook Activities** in the Subject text box. Click the Save And Close button on the Standard toolbar to save the journal entry.

Note: Normally when creating a journal entry, you would select an entry type, date, and time and add comments in the notes box. We just kept it simple for our purposes here. For more about the Journal, see Chapter 34, "Tracking Tasks and Keeping Notes."

8. Click the Activities tab of the Contact form. Outlook searches the folders for any item associated with the contact. When it finds something, it displays it in the Activities list. In this case, it displays the Calendar and Journal items you associated with the contact in this exercise.

Note: Because you are the contact we are working with, you may see additional lists here. Any e-mail that you have sent or received using the e-mail address you included in the contact may also be listed here.

9. Click the Save And Close button on the Standard toolbar to close the Contact form.

Every time you click the Activities tab, Outlook generates a new list based on the current contents of your Outlook folders. If you have deleted an item, it will no longer appear in the Activities list.

Summary

In this chapter, you learned how to manage messages and contacts in Outlook. We covered the following topics:

- Managing messages by moving messages to custom folders
- Locating messages using the Find feature
- Saving incoming and outgoing messages as text and message files
- Applying categories to messages
- Setting message options such as importance, sensitivity, delivery time, and read receipts
- Creating and modifying contacts
- Organizing contacts using folders, categories, and views
- Sorting contacts
- Tracking activities using the Contacts folder
- Viewing journal entries associated with contacts

Chapter

34

Tracking Tasks and Keeping Notes

MOUS OUTLOOK 2002 CORE EXAM OBJECTIVES COVERED IN THIS CHAPTER:

- ✓ **Create and update tasks**
- ✓ **Modify task organization and Task view**
- ✓ **Accept, decline, or delegate tasks**
- ✓ **Create and modify notes**
- ✓ **Use categories to manage tasks and notes**

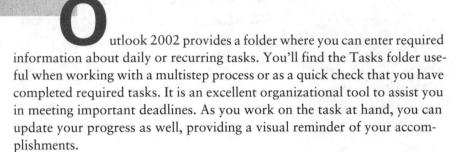

Outlook 2002 provides a folder where you can enter required information about daily or recurring tasks. You'll find the Tasks folder useful when working with a multistep process or as a quick check that you have completed required tasks. It is an excellent organizational tool to assist you in meeting important deadlines. As you work on the task at hand, you can update your progress as well, providing a visual reminder of your accomplishments.

The Tasks folder is also helpful if it becomes necessary to assign a task to another individual. You can enter all the required details and then assign the task to the designated person. The receiver can then either accept or decline the task. If the task is accepted, you can receive updates of their progress, which will help you monitor the status of the task.

Outlook 2002 has also included a folder where you can create "sticky notes" inside your computer. You can quickly enter a reminder note or a piece of vital information, and you can assign categories to these notes for organizational purposes.

In this chapter, we will discuss how to create, update, assign, accept, and decline tasks. We will then discuss how to create and modify notes. To assist in organizing your tasks and notes, we will show you how to assign categories to both.

Tracking Tasks

The Task list constitutes a to-do list. As you finish each task, you can review the notes section to ensure that you have met all the requirements.

Then you can mark the task as complete. Figure 34.1 shows the Tasks folder with two tasks visible.

FIGURE 34.1   Tasks folder

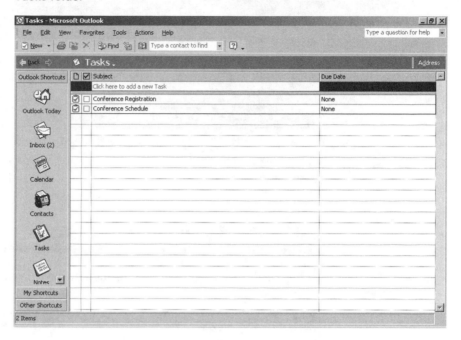

Microsoft
✓ *Exam*
Objective

Create and update tasks

Creating Tasks

Creating a task can be as simple as navigating to the Tasks folder and entering some text in the Subject field; however, important details will not be entered in this fashion. Using the Untitled - Task form is the most comprehensive way of creating a task. You can click the New Task button on the Standard toolbar or double-click in a blank area of the Tasks folder to open the Untitled - Task form, shown in Figure 34.2.

FIGURE 34.2 Untitled - Task form

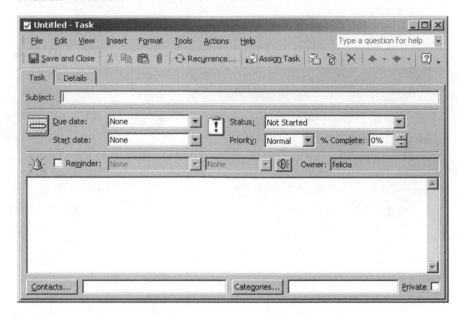

In Exercise 34.1, you will step through the process of creating a new task.

EXERCISE 34.1

Creating a New Task

1. Navigate to the Tasks folder.

2. Click the New Task button on the Standard toolbar.

3. Type **Schedule conference room for Staff Wellness Conference** in the Subject field of the Untitled - Task form.

4. Select April 30, 2003 in the Due Date field.

5. Select April 22, 2003 in the Start Date field.

6. Set the Reminder to April 28, 2003 at 2:00 PM.

EXERCISE 34.1 *(continued)*

7. Set the priority to High.

8. Enter the following message in the notes section of the task: **Schedule conference room at the Greenwood Inn for May 1, 2003.**

9. Click the Save And Close button on the Standard toolbar. The Tasks folder should now show the task you have created.

 To quickly enter a task with few details, you can click the Click Here To Add A New Task field in the Tasks folder and type in the subject of the task. You can then tab to the Due Date field and enter a date. To add details to the task, simply double-click the task and update the Task form.

Updating the Status of Tasks

When using tasks, you can update your progress as you complete portions of the task at hand. Doing so helps you manage your time and keep your coworkers informed as to the progress of your work. In Exercise 34.2, we will update the progress of the task we created previously.

EXERCISE 34.2

Updating the Status of a Task

1. Navigate to the Tasks folder if it is not already open.

2. Double-click the Schedule Conference Room For Staff Wellness Conference task to open it for editing.

3. Update the status to 75% complete by entering **75** in the % Complete field and pressing Enter. Notice how the Status automatically changes to In Progress.

4. Click Save And Close to close the Task form.

EXERCISE 34.2 *(continued)*

5. Switch to Simple List view by choosing View ➤ Current View ➤ Simple List if it is not already active. Click the Complete check box in the column to the immediate left of the task to mark the task as 100% complete. Notice that a strikethrough line is applied to the task, indicating that the task has been completed.

6. Click the Complete check box a second time to clear it—the task is now updated as an outstanding task and reset to 0% completion.

Organizing and Viewing Tasks

Creating a list of tasks does you little good if you can't organize the tasks in ways that make sense to you. With Outlook, you can sort tasks in any order, for example, by due date or by % complete. You can also assign categories to tasks, similar to the way you assigned categories to Calendar items and contacts in Chapter 33, "Managing Messages and Contacts in Outlook." Finally, you can switch between different Outlook views to display tasks grouped by category or by any other Task field.

In this section, we'll show you how to sort tasks and how to switch between views. Later in this chapter, we'll assign categories to tasks so you can display all the tasks from the same project together by switching to By Category view. You can also update your Tasks folder to display different views to help you locate grouped tasks.

Microsoft ✔ *Exam* *Objective*	**Modify task organization and Task view**

Modifying Task Organization

You may find it necessary to modify the organization of your tasks. You can either sort the tasks by any of the Task fields or manually arrange the default list of tasks.

In Exercise 34.3, you will learn how to reorder your current tasks.

EXERCISE 34.3

Rearranging the Task List

1. Navigate to Tasks folder if necessary.

2. Add the following tasks and their due dates to the Task list:

a.	**Confirm guest speakers**	**Sept 23, 2002**
b.	**Reserve hotel rooms at the Greenwood Inn for guest speakers**	**Jan 2, 2003**
c.	**Arrange car rentals for guest speakers**	**Feb 1, 2003**
d.	**Arrange Breakfast, Lunch, and Afternoon snack with the hotel**	**Feb 1, 2003**

3. Click the Due Date field label at the top of the Due Date column. When you click an individual field label, you sort the tasks in ascending order by that field. If you would like to view the task items in descending order, click the field label a second time to change the sort to descending order.

Changing Task View

While you are working with tasks, you can switch to different views to focus on particular tasks. For example, you can view only active tasks, that is, tasks that have not been completed or tasks due in the next seven days. In Exercise 34.4, you will practice changing the current view settings in the Tasks folder.

EXERCISE 34.4

Changing the Current Task View

1. Navigate to the Tasks folder if it is not already open. By default, the Tasks folder is in Simple List view.

Note: To always be able to see what view you are in and to be able to easily switch between views, turn on the Advanced toolbar by choosing View ➢ Toolbars ➢ Advanced. The Advanced toolbar, which you can keep visible in all Outlook folders, has a Current View drop-down list.

EXERCISE 34.4 *(continued)*

2. Select View ➢ Current View ➢ Detailed List. The Tasks window updates to include several important fields such as Priority, Attachment, Status, Due Date, % Complete, and Categories. With the addition of these fields, you will be able to track outstanding tasks more effectively.

Note: If a task's due date has passed, the task appears red in the list.

3. Select View ➢ Current View ➢ By Category. The Tasks window updates to group your tasks by Category. This view is excellent when tracking several tasks related to a single project. At a quick glance you will be able to see which tasks are outstanding for the project.

Note: Later in this chapter, you will learn how to assign categories to tasks.

4. Mark the task you entered in Exercise 34.1, Schedule Conference Room For Staff Wellness Conference, as complete by clicking the % Complete column, selecting 0%, and replacing it with **100**. The task is marked with a strikethrough. Now select View ➢ Current View ➢ Completed Tasks to see a filtered list of just the tasks that are marked 100% complete.

5. Switch back to your favorite view, such as Detailed List or Active Tasks, by choosing View ➢ Current View and then choosing the view you want as your default Tasks view.

Working with Tasks on a Team

When you work with a group of people, you may need to delegate tasks to other individuals. In this section, we will examine how to assign tasks to other individuals as well as how to accept or decline assigned tasks when they are received.

Microsoft ✔ *Exam Objective*

Accept, decline, or delegate tasks

Delegating Tasks to Others

When delegating a task to another individual, you send a message with the task as a file attachment. When the message is received, that person can either accept or decline your offer.

In Exercise 34.5, you will assign a task to another individual.

EXERCISE 34.5

Assigning a Task to Another Individual

1. Navigate to the Tasks folder.

2. Open the Confirm Guest Speakers task.

3. Click the Assign Task button on the Standard toolbar.

The To field is added to the Tasks window so that you can address the task to the desired contact. Two other options are also added to the window: Keep An Updated Copy Of This Task On My Task List and Send Me A Status Report When The Task Is Complete.

4. Click the To button and assign the task to James Richardson.

5. Accept the default settings for the check box options Keep An Updated Copy Of This Task On My Task List and Send Me A Status Report When The Task Is Complete.

6. Enter the following details in the message area of the task:
I would appreciate your help in finalizing some of the details for the Staff Wellness Conference. Please let me know by 5:00 pm today if you will be able to assist with the attached task.

7. Click the Send button on the toolbar.

The message has now been sent to the contact to whom you have delegated the task.

8. Click the Sent Items icon in the My Shortcuts group on the Outlook bar or in the File list. You will see that the message has been sent to the recipient.

Accepting and Declining Task Assignments

When you receive delegated tasks, you have two options: to accept or decline the task. When you accept a delegated task, the task is automatically added to your Tasks folder and a response is sent to acknowledge that you agree to complete the task. Figure 34.3 shows a message that assigns a task to another individual.

FIGURE 34.3 A message assigning a task to another individual

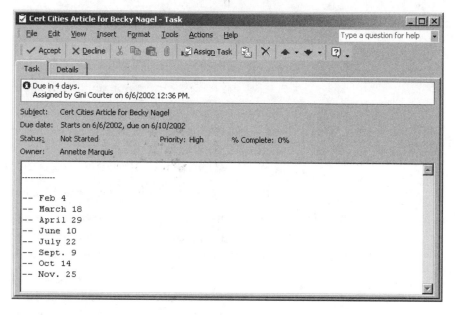

The Standard toolbar on a message that contains a task assignment includes Accept and Decline buttons. In Figure 34.4, you can see the Standard toolbar on a message that contains a task assignment.

FIGURE 34.4 Updated Standard toolbar

In Exercise 34.6, you will learn how to accept a task that has been assigned to you. In order to complete this exercise, ask a friend to assign two tasks to you as described in Exercise 34.5. You can then accept or decline the task as described below.

EXERCISE 34.6

Accepting or Declining a Task

1. Navigate to the Inbox in the Folder List.

2. Open the first Task Request sent from your friend.

3. Click the Accept button. A dialog box appears informing you that the task will be moved to your Tasks folder and asks if you would like to modify the outgoing message.

4. Accept the default option, Send The Response Now.

5. Navigate to the Tasks folder. The task has been added to your list of outstanding tasks.

6. Switch back to the Inbox and open the second Task Request sent from your friend. Click the Decline button to decline this task.

7. Select Edit The Response before sending it and write a message to your friend about why you are declining the task.

8. Click Send to send the response. The task does not appear on your Task list. It appears as a regular task on the sender's Task list.

Keeping Notes

When you work in an office, there are times when you need to write a short note that does not fall into the typical categories of Message, Appointment, Event, or Task. Outlook 2002 Notes allows you to record these details for later retrieval.

Figure 34.5 shows the Notes window with a couple of notes included.

FIGURE 34.5 Notes window

The Notes window has customized the Standard toolbar to include buttons you can use to manage your notes. Figure 34.6 shows the Standard toolbar with the new buttons labeled.

FIGURE 34.6 Notes Standard toolbar

Microsoft ✓ *Exam Objective* **Create and modify notes**

In Exercise 34.7, you will learn to create and modify notes. Figure 34.7 shows a blank Notes window.

FIGURE 34.7 New Notes window

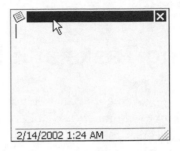

2/14/2002 1:24 AM

EXERCISE 34.7

Creating and Modifying Notes

1. Navigate to the Notes folder.

2. Click the New Note button on the Standard toolbar.

3. Type the following text:
   Conference Room Price Guide
   Greenwood Inn $350/day (including meals)
   Plaza $425/day (including meals)
   Delta $300/day (not including meals)

4. Close the note.

Tip: The first line of text becomes the note's subject, so enter a short subject and then double-space before typing the note.

5. Double-click the note to open it. Edit the "$425/day" to read **$450/day**.

6. Close the note. The note is automatically resaved.

Notes can be resized manually if you hover your mouse over the bottom-right-hand corner of the Notes window. The mouse will change to a double-headed arrow so you can click and drag the note to the required size.

Categorizing Tasks and Notes

Categories can be effective when organizing your tasks and notes. The same technique is used for organizing messages, appointments, and events in the other folders of Outlook 2002. (See Chapter 33 for information about how to assign categories to messages.)

Microsoft Exam Objective	**Use categories to manage tasks and notes**

In Exercise 34.8, you will learn how to assign categories to a task as well as a note.

EXERCISE 34.8

Assigning Categories to a Task and a Note

1. Navigate to the Tasks folder.

2. Click the Organize button on the Standard toolbar and select Using Categories.

3. Select all the tasks related to the Staff Wellness Conference.

4. Click the Add Tasks Selected Below To drop-down list and choose Conference from the list of categories.

Note: If Conference is not on the list, click the Add Tasks Selected Below To drop-down list button again and type **Conference** in the Create A New Category Called task box. Click Add, and then repeat step 4.

EXERCISE 34.8 *(continued)*

5. Navigate to the Notes folder.

6. Double-click the Conference Room Price Guide note to open it.

7. Click the Note icon in the top-left corner to display the menu:

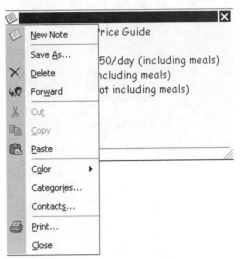

8. Select the Categories option from the Note menu.

9. Select the Conference category and click OK to close the Categories window.

10. Close the note.

11. Select View ➢ Current View ➢ By Category. You will see that the Notes window has been updated to group the notes by their assigned categories.

12. Click the plus signs to expand the categories and display the notes for each category.

Summary

In this chapter, we covered the following topics about tasks and notes:

- Creating and updating tasks
- Managing tasks by assigning categories to individual tasks and changing the Task view
- Assigning tasks to others
- Accepting and declining assigned tasks
- Creating and modifying notes
- Assigning categories to tasks and notes.

Index

Note to the Reader: Throughout this index **boldfaced** page numbers indicate primary discussions of a topic. *Italicized* page numbers indicate illustrations.

C

G

J

N

P

Q

X

Y

Z

The PC Problem-Solving Wonder!

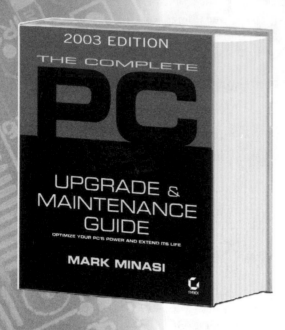

Using easy-to-follow language, this book shows you how to prevent disasters, fix the ones that occur, and maximize your PC's power and longevity. Based on author Mark Minasi's popular $800 seminars, it is an unbelievable value.

ISBN: 0-7821-4075-0
$59.99 US

Updated to Cover Recent PC Advances
Over 1.5 Million copies sold!

Major Coverage of the 2003 Edition includes:

- QuickSteps Section
- Distinct Troubleshooting Sections
- Exclusive Mark Minasi Video
- Visual Guides to Nine Essential Upgrades
- New Section on Scanners

- Building the Ultimate Computer
- Rejuvenating Your Old Computer
- Buyers Guide
- Notebook Computers
- Flash Memory Cards

www.sybex.com SYBEX®

The Sybex®
Office XP/2002 Library

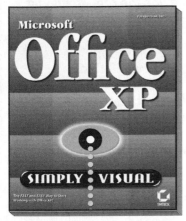

ISBN: 0-7821-4004-1 • $24.99 US

**ISBN: 0-7821-4000-9
$49.99 US**

Now that you

have Windows® XP,

get the most

out of your

Office software.

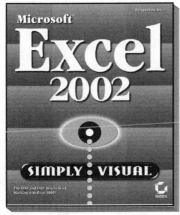

ISBN: 0-7821-4006-8 • $24.99 US

ISBN: 0-7821-4007-6 • $24.99 US

SYBEX®

www.sybex.com

JumpStart™ Your Career!

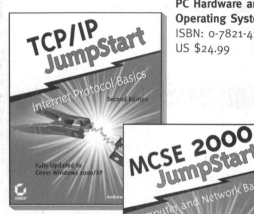

CCNA JumpStart:
Networking and
Internetworking Basics
ISBN: 0-7821-2592-1
US $19.99

A+ JumpStart:
PC Hardware and
Operating Systems Basics
ISBN: 0-7821-4126-9
US $24.99

TCP/IP JumpStart:
Internet Protocol
Basics
ISBN: 0-7821-4101-3
US $24.99

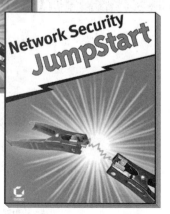

MCSE 2000 JumpStart:
Computer and
Network Basics
ISBN: 0-7821-2749-5
US $19.99

Network Security JumpStart
ISBN: 0-7821-4120-X • US $24.99

JumpStart books provide the firm grounding
you'll need to approach certification training
with confidence.

In each JumpStart book you'll find:

- **Clear and concise explanations of complex**
  computer and network topics

- **Review questions to help reinforce your**
  understanding

- **Real-world insights from expert trainers**

Once you've covered the basics, you'll be ready t
start down the road in pursuit of certifications
such as Microsoft's MCSE, Cisco's CCNA,
and others.

SYBEX®
www.sybex.com

From self-study guides to advanced computer-based training, simulated testing programs to last-minute review guides, Sybex has the most complete CompTIA training solution on the market.

Sybex Covers
CompTIA
CERTIFICATION PROGRAMS

Study Guides

Designed for optimal learning, Sybex Study Guides provide you with comprehensive coverage of all exam objectives. Hands-on exercises and review questions help reinforce your knowledge.

STUDY

- In-depth coverage of exam objectives
- Hands-on exercises
- CD includes: test engine, flashcards for PCs and Palm devices, PDF version of entire book

Virtual Trainers™
software

Based on the content of the Study Guides, Sybex Virtual Trainers offer you advanced computer-based training, complete with animations and customization features.

- Customizable study planning tools
- Narrated instructional animations
- Preliminary assessment tests
- Results reporting

Virtual Test Centers™
software

Powered by an advanced testing engine, Sybex's new line of Virtual Test Centers give you the opportunity to test your knowledge before sitting for the real exam.

PRACTICE

- Hundreds of challenging questions
- Computer adaptive testing
- Support for drag-and-drop and hot-spot formats
- Detailed explanations and cross-references

Exam Notes™

Organized according to the official exam objectives, Sybex Exam Notes help reinforce your knowledge of key exam topics and identify potential weak areas requiring further study.

REVIEW

- Excellent quick review before the exam
- Concise summaries of key exam topics
- Tips and insights from experienced instructors
- Definitions of key terms and concepts

Look to Sybex for exam prep materials on major CompTIA certifications, including A+®, Network+™, I-Net+™, Server+™, and Linux+™. For more information about CompTIA and Sybex products, visit www.sybex.com.

Sybex—The Leader in Certification

www.sybex.com

Take the Next Step with PMP!

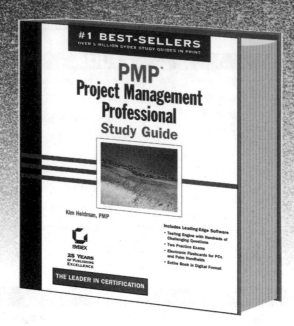

PMP®. Project Management Professional Study Guide
By Kim Heldman
ISBN: 0-7821-4106-4
Available May 2002
US $59.99

Project management skills are in high demand and Sybex can help you acquire them with the *PMP: Project Management Professional Study Guide*. Whether you're looking to advance your career as a project manager or simply strengthen your business skills foundation, the highly respected PMP certification from the Project Management Institute is the credential you need to succeed in today's competitive marketplace.

◆ More comprehensive than any other PMP exam prep package

◆ In-depth coverage of all official PMP exam objectives

◆ Project management case studies included to provide real-world insights

SYBEX®

www.sybex.com

TELL US WHAT YOU THINK!

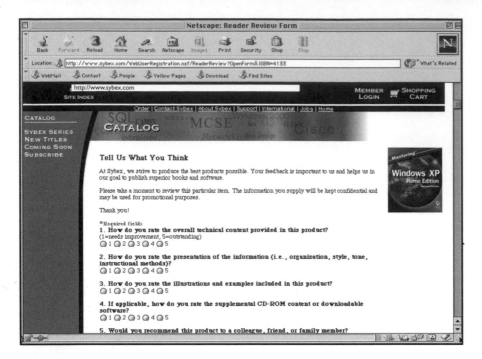

Your feedback is critical to our efforts to provide you with the best books and software on the market. Tell us what you think about the products you've purchased. It's simple:

1. Go to the Sybex website.
2. Find your book by typing the ISBN number or title into the Search field.
3. Click on the book title when it appears.
4. Click **Submit a Review.**
5. Fill out the questionnaire and comments.
6. Click **Submit.**

With your feedback, we can continue to publish the highest quality computer books and software products that today's busy IT professionals deserve.

www.sybex.com

SYBEX Inc. • 1151 Marina Village Parkway, Alameda, CA 94501 • 510-523-8233